**WORLD BANK LATIN AMERICAN
AND CARIBBEAN STUDIES**

Viewpoints

Managing the Regulatory Process: Design, Concepts, Issues, and the Latin America and Caribbean Story

*J. Luis Guasch
and Pablo Spiller*

*The World Bank
Washington, D.C.*

The complete backlist of publications from the World Bank is shown in the annual Index of Publications, which contains an alphabetical title list (with full ordering information) and indexes of subjects, authors, and countries and regions. The latest edition is available free of charge from the Distribution Unit, Office of the Publisher, The World Bank, 1818 H Street, N.W., Washington, D.C. 20433, U.S.A., or from Publications, The World Bank, 66, avenue d'Iena, 75116 Paris, France.

The painting on the cover, MORRO, by Emiliano Di Cavalcanti, was provided by Christie's Images. Permission to reproduce it was granted by Mr. Jorge Getulio Veiga Filho.

J. Luis Guasch is Lead Economist for Latin America and the Caribbean Region and the Development Economics and Chief Economist Office at the World Bank, and Professor of Economics, University of California, San Diego. Pablo T. Spiller is Professor of Economics and Public Utilities, University of California, Berkeley.

Library of Congress Cataloging-in-Publication Data

Guasch, J. Luis.
    Managing the regulatory process : design, concepts, issues, and the Latin America and Caribbean story / J. Luis Guasch and Pablo Spiller.
        p. cm. — (World Bank Latin American and Caribbean studies. Viewpoints)
    Includes bibliographical references.
    ISBN 0-8213-4497-8
    1. Trade regulation—Latin America. 2. Industrial policy—Latin America. 3. Deregulation—Latin America. I. Spiller, Pablo T. (Pablo Tomas), 1951– . II. Title. III. Series.
HD3616.L33G828 1999   99-38444
338.98—dc21   CIP

CONTENTS

5. CREATING THE DETAIL ENGINEERING OF REGULATION: PRICE-SETTING POLICIES

6. CREATING THE DETAIL ENGINEERING OF REGULATION: ACCESS TERMS AND PRICING IN NETWORK INDUSTRIES

7. DETAIL ENGINEERING EXPERIENCES IN LATIN AMERICA AND THE CARIBBEAN

8. FRANCHISES AND CONCESSIONS AS MODES OF PRIVATE SECTOR PARTICIPATION AND "ALTERNATIVES" TO REGULATION

9. THE DESIGN OF CONCESSION-TYPE ARRANGEMENTS: COMPETITIVE PROVISION OF GOODS AND SERVICES TO GOVERNMENT BY THE PRIVATE SECTOR IN DEVELOPING COUNTRIES

10. PRIVATIZATION RESTRUCTURING AND REGULATION: ACTIONS AND SECTOR RESTRUCTURING PRIOR TO PRIVATIZATION

11. REFORM AND REGULATION IN THE POWER SECTOR

12. NEW FRONTIERS IN REGULATION IN THE COMMUNICATIONS SECTOR: MANAGING AND REGULATING THE SPECTRUM

ACKNOWLEDGMENTS

J. Luis Guasch is Lead Economist for Latin America and the Caribbean Region and the Development Economics and Chief Economist Office at the World Bank, and Professor of Economics, University of California, San Diego. Pablo T. Spiller is Professor of Economics and Public Utilities, University of California, Berkeley. The findings, interpretations, and conclusions expressed in this paper are those of the authors and should not be attributed in any manner to the World Bank, to its affiliated organizations, to the members of its Board of Executive Directors or the countries they represent, or to the educational institutions with which the authors are affiliated. The authors are grateful to Antonio Estache, Michael Klein, Phil Gray, Robert Marshall, Joel Sobel, Joseph Stiglitz, Jean Jacques Laffont, Roberto Chama, Vincent Crawford, Jennifer Sobotka, and Lisa Taber for helpful comments and suggestions; to Jorge Serraino and Joy Troncoso for technical assistance; and to Diane Stamm for editorial support.

LIST OF ABBREVIATIONS

AAJ	Airports Authority of Jamaica
AMPS	American mobile phone standard
ASA	Aeropuertos y Servicios Auxiliares (Mexico)
AT&T	American Telephone & Telegraph
BAA	British Airport Authority
BANOBRAS	Mexican public works bank
BIA	Belfast International Airport
BOO	Build-own-operate
BOOT	Build-own-operate-transfer
BOT	Build-own-transfer
BR	British Railways
BT	British Telecommunications
CAA	Civil Aviation Authority
CADE	Competition Policies Commission (Brazil)
CAMMESA	Compañía Administradora del Mercado Mayorista Eléctrico Sociedad Anónima (Argentina)
CAPM	Capital Asset Pricing Model
CAPUFE	Caminos y Puentes Federales de Ingresso y Servicios Conexos (Mexico)
CfD	Contract for differences
CFE	Comisión Federal de Electricidad (Mexico)
CMET	Complejo Manufacturero de Equipos Telefónicos
CMRS	Commerical mobile radio service
CNT	Telefónica del Sur S.A.
COBEE	Compañía Boliviana de Energía Eléctrica
CORFO	The government development corporation of Chile
CPI	Consumer price index
CRTC	Canadian Radio, Television, and Telecommunications Commission
CTC	Compañía de Teléfonos de Chile
CTM	Compañía Telefónica Manquehue
DBS	Direct broadcast satellite
DOE	Department of the Environment for Northern Ireland
ECPR	Efficient component pricing rule
ELDC	Economic Load Dispatch Center
Endesa	The dominant electricity generator in Chile
ENERSIS	An investment group in Chile
ENOHSA	Ente Nacional de Obras Hídricas de Saneamiento (Argentina)
ENRE	Ente Nacional Regulatorio de Energio (Argentina)
Entel	Empresa Nacional de Telecomunicaciones (Chile)
Entel	National Telecommunications Company of Argentina
Entel	National Telecommunications Company of Bolivia
EPA	Environmental Protection Agency
ESMR	Enhanced specialized mobile radio

ESVAL	Empresa de Obras Sanitarias de Valparaiso	NAFTA	North America Free Trade Agreement
ETOSS	Ente Tripartito de Obras y Servicios Sanitarios (Argentina)	NEC	National Energy Commission
FBO	Fixed-base operator	NIAL	Northern Ireland Airports Limited
FCC	Federal Communications Commission	NTC	National Telecommunication Commission (Canada)
FIRE	Finance, insurance, and retail trades	OECD	Organization for Economic Cooperation and Development
FNM	Mexican National Railways	Oftel	Office of Telecommunications (United Kingdom)
GATT	General Agreement on Tariff and Trade	PAC	Procurement Assistance Commission
GDP	General Directorate for Competition and Pricing (Portugal)	PCS	Personal communications services
GDP	Gross domestic product	Pemex	Petróleos Mexicanos
GNP	Gross national product	PSTN	Public switched telephone network
GUATEL	National telecommunications company of Guatemala	PUC	Public Utilities Commission
IAC	Individual airport concession	REC	Regional electricity companies
ICP	Institute for Communications in Portugal	RIA	Regulatory impact analysis
		ROE	Rate of return on equity
INDECOPI	Institute for the Defense of Competition and Intellectual Property	ROR	Rate of return
		RPI	Retail price index
		SCT	Secretaria de Comunicaciones y Transportes (Mexico)
IPP	Independent power producer		
ISDN	Integrated services digital network	SEGBA	Servicios Electricos Gran Buenos Aires
ITS	Interconnected Transmission System	SIA	Sangster International Airport
		SMR	Specialized Mobile Radio
ITT	International Telephone and Telegraph	SNR	Signal-to-noise ratio
		Subtel	Subsecretary of Telecommunications (Chile)
JPUC	Jamaican Public Utility Commission		
		Telebras	The Brazilian telephone company
JTC	Jamaican Telephone Company	TELCOY	Compañía de Teléfonos de Coyhaique
LAC	Latin America and the Caribbean		
LAN	Local access network	TEU	Twenty-foot equivalent units
LATC	Lockheed Air Terminal of Canada, Inc.	TOJ	Telecommunications of Jamaica
		TRANSELEC	The Endesa transmission subsidiary (Chile)
LEC	Local exchange carrier		
LRMC	Long-run marginal cost	TTLP	Terminal Three Limited Partnership
MDS	Multipoint distribution service		
MEBO Co.	Management and employee buyout team	TUFs	Títulos de Uso de Frecuencias
		UIT	Unidad Imposition Total
MEM	Mercado Eléctrico Mayorista Argentina	UTRP	Unión Telefónica del RPo de la Plata
MGC	Montevideo Gas Company	WACC	Weighted average cost of capital
MMC	Monopolies and Mergers Commission (United Kingdom)	WTO	World Trade Organization

LIST OF TABLES

LIST OF FIGURES

LIST OF BOXES

1

THE COSTS AND BENEFITS OF REGULATION: THE CALL FOR REGULATORY REFORM

IN DEVELOPED COUNTRIES, the past two decades have witnessed an unparalleled rise in new regulations related to the environment, health, and safety. During this period, there also has been substantial economic deregulation of several industries in some countries, including airlines, trucking, railroads, financial markets, energy, and telecommunications. At the same time, developing countries, complementing their far-reaching privatization programs, are engaged in deregulating various sectors of their economies and devising new regulatory frameworks for others, particularly the utilities sectors.[1]

This trend toward economic regulatory reform is likely to continue as a result of the increased questioning of the need for regulation, the globalization of markets, and the ongoing privatization of the utilities sectors. Historically, regulatory interventions were often motivated by economic conditions no longer applicable, or by political considerations and interest group pressures to secure transfer of rents. Many sectors were viewed as either natural monopolies or as being of vital social or strategic interest, requiring significant regulation, if not direct public ownership. These rationales in many sectors are no longer considered valid. Changes in technology and experience, and the more organized voice of consumer groups, have called into question those arguments. Regulatory reform is also

driven by the recognition that many existing regulations have become obsolete and even harmful to economic growth. In addition, government failures may be as capable of creating inefficiencies as market failures. As such, the consequences of that type of regulation were an increase in the cost of goods and services and an overall significant welfare loss, as reported below. As economies become more open, pressures on countries to become more competitive drive the call for regulatory reform to reduce costs and foster increased productivity, competitiveness, and growth.[2]

As the political costs of regulating specific sectors of the economy increase, politicians will see deregulation as a cost-effective strategy for promoting growth. Other things being equal, those countries where the economic and political gains are likely to be greatest can be expected to proceed most rapidly. Those industries with a more complicated economic or politically linked structure can be expected to be deregulated more slowly.

Not all regulation is on the decline, however. Citizens in many countries express a desire for more regulation in several areas, such as utilities, environmental protection, and public health and safety standards. The increased interest in regulating these areas can be partly explained by the privatization trend and increases in income. The privatization trend in both developing and developed economies, particularly in the utilities sector, has brought a call for a companion and effective regulatory framework for the sector. In addition, as consumers become wealthier they demand more amenities, such as cleaner air and water and better sanitation. As these demands increase, politicians will supply more of these goods and services, but they will also explore ways of supplying them more efficiently.

Current political concerns about limiting tax increases in many countries are creating even more incentives to use certain kinds of regulation. When legislators constrain themselves in terms of spending and taxes, regulation can be a useful tool for achieving political objectives, such as transferring wealth to particular interest groups in exchange for political support. In this kind of political environment, legislators substitute regulatory requirements or mandates whose costs are not directly paid for by taxpayers with less visible, but nonetheless real, costs.[3] From the government's perspective, the effort appears to be relatively low cost. The federal budget is barely affected when a major change is mandated by regulation. Most of the costs of regulation show up in budgets outside that of the federal government. Regulated firms incur direct costs as they try to bring their operations into compliance. Moreover, they may contract the work out, move elsewhere, or cease to operate, destroying jobs and reducing the local tax base. The altered service or product may be less appealing to consumers than the old one. Productivity may decline in the short run as unit costs rise, and in the long run as regu-

lation-driven projects absorb funds that could otherwise be used to improve or expand the plant. The bill for all these costs is paid partly by the firms that are regulated and partly by the rest of society, depending on the ability of firms to raise prices in their product markets.

The impact of regulatory activity on country economies continues to be hotly debated. While few would deny that regulation can increase consumer welfare, this depends on how regulation is designed and implemented, and the specific problem it is attempting to solve. Moreover, regulation can add substantially to the costs of doing business, and those costs frequently are passed along to consumers in the form of higher prices, reducing welfare and decreasing the competitiveness of the economy.

This chapter has three objectives: (a) to provide an overview of the costs and benefits of regulation throughout the world, (b) to highlight the potential gains from the reform of regulation and deregulation in developed and developing countries, and (c) to glean some fundamental lessons from the experience with government regulation and make suggestions for improving regulation in developing countries. Given the scarcity of data on these subjects in developing countries, most of the data presented here comes from the United States and other developed countries.

Briefly, this chapter defines regulation and explains its justification and the root causes of its inefficiencies, reviews the literature on the aggregate costs and benefits of regulation,[4] provides some general estimates of the potential gains or realized gains from reform and a more detailed analysis of the potential for structural reform of specific industries in developed and developing countries, and presents the key findings and offers some policy recommendations.

REGULATION: DEFINITION, RATIONALE, AND PROBLEMS

There are many types of regulation. While some overlap is inescapable, a common classification scheme consists of three parts: economic, social, and process regulation. Economic regulation refers to restrictions on prices, quantity, and entrance and exit conditions for specific industries. Social regulation refers to regulations that affect a wide array of industries. Typically, environmental and public health and safety regulation are placed in this category. Finally, process regulation refers to government management of the operation of the public and private sectors, such as paperwork requirements and administrative costs incurred by both producers and consumers. These categories are not as neat and tidy as they might first appear. Paperwork requirements, for example, might be a significant component of some social regulation, such as environmental protection or worker safety. Moreover, some regulations, such as those affecting education and social services, do not fit neatly into any particular category here. Despite these deficiencies, this framework is a useful starting point for measuring many of the most important costs and benefits of regulation. Most of this book is concerned with economic regulation, particularly the regulation of utilities.

There are several economic arguments supporting regulation (MacAvoy 1992). The most common arguments are based on correcting for market failures, economies of scale, or equity considerations. In the case of social regulation, a primary rationale is that individual companies may not take into account the full social cost of their actions without government intervention. For example, a firm will tend to pollute excessively unless it incurs some implicit or explicit cost for polluting. In the case of workplace safety, workers may not have adequate information on hazards to make fully informed choices. Direct regulation represents one approach to the problem of obtaining such information. In the case of economic regulation, the primary economic rationale has to do with the potential for improving production efficiency. If there are economies of scale or scope, a single firm may, in theory, be able to produce more efficiently than several competing firms, but then its monopolistic power may need to be restrained through regulation. In addition, there may be additional value to consumers as more consumers use a network, such as telephones.[5] While it is possible to provide some

economic rationales for regulation for a wide range of economic activity, such rationales are often not persuasive in practice. Just as there is potential for many kinds of "market failure," there is also potential for "government failure."

There are two reasons for inefficient regulation; one is economic and the other is political. The economic reason is that it is difficult for a government authority to regulate companies because it lacks the necessary information. For example, a business might have a good idea of its cost and demand structure, but a regulator typically does not have access to such information. The firm usually is better informed than the regulator; moreover, it rarely has an incentive to tell the regulator all it knows. Such "information asymmetries" imply that economic regulation will rarely achieve a "first-best" or efficient outcome. In addition, uncertainty or the lack of accurate estimates of the byproduct or external effects of agents' actions or new products can induce inefficient regulation. This is very common when considering social regulation. The regulator imposing social regulation must frequently base decisions on very limited information (Lewis 1996). For example, in setting the overall emission limitation for acid rain, the U.S. government had some crude estimates of the costs and benefits. After the program was implemented, however, the costs of achieving the emission standard were lower than expected. The lower costs resulted, in part, because of the flexibility inherent in the market-based regulatory approach that was adopted. At the same time, unforeseen changes in energy and transportation markets also played an important role. This does not mean regulation is not a useful approach for increasing economic efficiency when an industry is subject to increasing returns to scale, or when there are network externalities or significant coordination costs. It does mean, however, that the effectiveness of regulation is limited and that it has some serious structural defects. These defects need to be kept in mind when comparing this approach with viable alternatives.

Political considerations concerning regulation also lead to inefficient economic results. Since regulation redistributes resources and rents, politicians often use it to secure political gains rather than to correct market failures. An array of regulatory instruments, such as quotas, licenses, and subsidies, are used to transfer significant amounts of wealth from consumers to small groups of producers. The result is often that regulation is inefficient. Some classic examples arise in the area of agriculture, including peanuts (see box 1.1), sugar, wheat, and dairy products. Moreover, the wealth transfers also arise in social regulation. Environmental and energy regulations that involve mandates frequently carry a heavy price tag. For example, Anderson and others (1995) estimated the savings from the use of market incentives in environmental regulation at US$8 billion (1986 dollars) in 1992, and projected that potential savings in 2000 could be as high as US$38 billion, or 26 percent of estimated compliance costs. When transfers are that large, beneficiaries will be willing to expend considerable resources on lobbying and other activities that

enhance their earnings and protect these transfers, even when there are huge efficiency costs to the economy as a whole. Since often the cost of regulation to each individual in the economy is relatively small, there is little incentive for individuals to expend much effort and voice opposing the regulation.

Regulation can potentially have large intended or unintended welfare consequences. Because regulation, by design, interferes with firm-level pricing and investment decisions and often constrains entry, it restricts competition in one form or another. This is particularly true for economic regulation. When properly designed it can add to welfare; otherwise it will induce welfare losses. The hypothesis is that excessive or improper regulation can increase transaction costs and reduce competition, adversely affecting productivity growth, efficiency, capital formation, and technological innovation, and often leading to higher user prices. Because firms in regulated sectors are able to pass higher costs and inefficiencies on to the final user in the form of higher prices, they have little incentive to lower costs or to achieve productive efficiency. This can translate into overinvestment of capital, employing excess labor, or inefficient organization of production. Lack of regulation-induced competition can result in excess rents going to producers, labor, or both, and thus prices, profits, and wages are higher than they would be under competitive conditions. In addition, lack of competition tends to provide little incentive for firms to engage in technological innovation in production or in creating new products or services, and makes firms less eager to adapt the quality mix of goods and services delivered to address changing consumer needs. Regulations can impose high compliance costs on government, firms, and consumers. When the social gains from regulation are large, the costs are worth bearing. If the gains are small, the costs are punitive and perverse. For this reason, positive gains are often associated with deregulation, such as the delivery of better products or the use of lower-cost technologies. Ample evidence exists of the costs associated with excessive or misguided regulation, as reported below.

Box 1.1 The U.S. Peanut Market

An example of a small group benefiting from regulation at the cost of a large group is the peanut-quota system. Since 1949 the federal government has run a program that limits the number of farmers who can sell peanuts in the United States. Imports are also severely restricted. On top of these restrictions, price supports are used to guarantee that farmers with peanut quotas can cover their production costs each year. This generally results in the minimum selling price being about 50 percent higher than the world price. For 1982–87 it was estimated that the average annual consumer-to-producer transfer was $225 million (in 1987 dollars), with an associated deadweight loss of $34 million (Rucker and Thurman 1990). In 1982 there were 23,046 peanut farmers, which means that on average each received a net transfer of $11,000. In contrast, the cost to the average consumer of this program was only $1.23. Few consumers would be willing to spend their own time and money to dismantle the peanut program when they would gain only $1.23. However, the program is worth $11,000 to the average peanut farmer, and that would certainly make it worth one's while to see that the program continues.

Source: Viscusi, Vernon, and Harrington 1995.

Unlike the situation with social regulation, with some clear exceptions it is, arguably, difficult to find substantial benefits for economic regulation. Generally, whatever benefits accrue from the regulations are so swamped by their costs that economists typically focus on the efficiency costs or deadweight losses. These are simply wasted resources, losses imposed on one part of society that are not offset by equal gains to another. For example, by 1984 "voluntary" restrictions on automobile imports that the United States and Japan had negotiated were creating annual efficiency losses of $5 billion to the United States, reflecting $14 billion in higher prices that consumers paid for cars that were only partially offset by $9 billion in higher U.S. auto profits.

Of course, if regulation becomes very inefficient and visible, there may be pressure for change. Firms with new technologies may lobby for reduced regulation. In addition, consumers and businesses may find ways to buy products and services at lower prices by opting out of the regulated markets. For regulation in tradable goods markets, the pressures to deregulate will come from declining market shares of domestic producers who are vulnerable to less regulated imports. In addition, tradable goods producers that rely on heavily regulated nontradable goods sectors will have an interest in facilitating deregulation of these sectors to lower their overall productions costs.

Another source of pressure for regulatory reform comes from scholarship that documents the costs of regulation. As noted above, as technology evolves, we find that there are fewer industries in which classic economic regulation can be justified on efficiency grounds. In addition, economists have also documented a wide array of cases in which more flexible regulation, such as performance standards and market-based approaches, can achieve better results at a lower cost (Anderson and others 1995; Hahn 1996).

THE COSTS AND BENEFITS OF REGULATION

Most systematic economic studies of regulation have focused on federal regulation in the United States (Weidenbaum and DeFina 1978; Litan and Nordhaus 1983; Hahn and Hird 1991; Hopkins 1992; Winston 1993). The first study to synthesize data on the costs and benefits of regulation was done by Hahn and Hird (1991). Tables 1.1 and 1.2 provide estimates for the costs of economic regulation and the costs and benefits of social regulation. Hahn and Hird demonstrate four key ideas. First, it is possible to systematically explore the costs and benefits of regulatory activity using standard economic analysis. Second, the efficiency costs of economic regulation appear to be much smaller than the costs associated with transfers (for example, between producers and consumers). Third, such information can be useful in gaining a better understanding of the economic impacts of regulation. Fourth, there is a great deal of uncertainty in the data, and these uncertainties should be conveyed as clearly as possible to policymakers.

Focusing on the cost side of regulation, Hopkins (1992) has extended the work of Hahn and Hird. Hopkins' principal insight is that the costs of process regulation are substantial. Table 1.3 provides estimates of the cost of social, economic, and process regulation as of 1991and for selected years from 1977 to 2000. The total cost of regulation in 1991 is estimated at US$542 billion (1991 dollars), or about 9.5 percent of gross domestic product (GDP).[6] The largest component of those regulatory costs was process regulation, or US$189 billion in annual expenditures related to government paperwork requirements, primarily for tax compliance. The tax compliance costs do not necessarily represent efficiency costs, however, since one must consider all aspects of a tax system in evaluating its impact on efficiency. Nonetheless, the shear magnitude of the process costs suggests that paperwork could be reduced dramatically while improving efficiency.

To place the numbers in context, each American household would be billed US$5,683 (1991 dollars) annually in addition to its current taxes if this regulatory compliance cost were shared equally and collected directly and not imposed on business instead. Those regulatory costs amount to 9.6 percent of the gross domestic product (GDP) and constitute $189 billion in

Table 1.1 Annual Costs of Economic Regulation in the United States in 1988
(in billions of 1988 dollars)

Regulated Sector	Efficiency Costs	Transfers	Sources[b]
International Trade	17.3	85.6–110.6	Hufbauer, Berliner, and Elliot 1986
Telecommunications	< 14.1	< 42.3[a]	Wenders 1987
Agricultural Price Supports	6.7	18.4	Gardner 1987
Airline	3.8	7.7	Morrison & Winston 1986, 1989
Rail	2.3	6.8[a]	Winston 1985
Postal Rates	n.a.	4–12	President's Commission on Privatization 1988
Milk Marketing Orders/Price Supports	0.4–0.9	0.9–3.5	Ippolito & Masson; Buxton & Hammond (*reported in* MacAvoy 1977)
Natural Gas[c]	0.2–0.4	5.0	Loury 1983
Barge	0.2–0.3	0.6–0.9[a]	Litan & Nordhaus 1983
Davis-Bacon Act	0.2[a]	0.5	Thieblot 1975 (updated)
Credit	0.05–0.5	0.15–1.6[a]	Litan & Nordhaus 1983
Ocean	0.05–0.08	0.15–0.22[a]	Jantscher 1975
Trucking	0[d]	0	
Oil Price Controls	0	0	
Cable TV	0	0	
Total	**$45.3–46.5**	**$172.1–209.5**	

n.a. = Not available.

a. Figures estimated using 3:1 ratio of transfers to efficiency costs.

b. Indicates primary source of estimate.

c. Cost of natural gas regulation expected to approach zero as all price controls are lifted.

d. If estimate is zero, federal regulation is assumed to be negligible.

Source: Hahn and Hird 1991.

annual expenditures related to government paperwork alone. From another perspective, total federal spending in 1991 was about US$1,200 billion, or approximately twice the total cost of regulation. This 2 to 1 ratio between government spending and regulatory costs certainly does not correspond to the relative emphasis each receives in either the government's statistics or its decisionmaking.

There are no aggregate estimates of the benefits and costs of regulation outside of the United States. In Australia, the total cost of regulation was

Table 1.2 Annual Costs and Benefits of Social Regulation in the United States in 1988
(in billions of 1988 dollars)

Regulated Sector	Costs	Benefits	Sources[b]
International Trade	17.3	85.6–110.6	Hufbauer, Berliner, and Elliot 1986
Environment	55.4–77.6	16.5–135.8 (58.4)[a]	Hazilla & Kopp 1990; Freeman 1990; Portney 1990
Highway Safety	6.4–9.0	25.4–45.7	Crandall 1986
Occupational Safety and Health (OSHA)	8.5–9.0	negligible	Crandall 1988; Denison 1979; Viscusi 1983
Nuclear Power	5.3–7.6	n.a.	DOE policy study 1979 (*reported in* Litan & Nordhaus 1983)
Drugs	< 1.5–3.0	n.a.	Peltzman 1973
Equal Employment Opportunity (EEO)	0.9	n.a.	Weidenbaum & DeFina 1978; Litan & Nordhaus 1983
Consumer Product Safety	> .034	n.a.	U.S. Federal Budget, FY 1990 (administrative costs only)
Total	**$78.0–107.1**	**$41.9–181.5**	

n.a. = Not available.

a. Point estimate is in parentheses.

b. Indicates primary source of estimates.

Source: Hahn and Hird 1991.

Table 1.3 Annual Costs of Federal Regulation in the United States
(in billions of 1991 dollars)

Regulations	1977	1988	1991	2000
Environmental Regulation	42	87	115	178
Other Social Regulation	29	30	36	61
Economic Regulation Efficiency	120	73	73	73
Process Regulation	122	153	189	221
Subtotal of Costs	*313*	*343*	*413*	*533*
Economic Regulation Transfers	228	130	130	130
Total Costs	**$540**	**$473**	**$542**	**$662**

Source: Hopkins 1992.

estimated to be between 9 to 19 percent of GDP in 1986 (OECD 1996a). Mihlar (1996) provides a preliminary estimate for the costs of regulation in Canada of 12 percent of GDP. Based on an assumed ratio between private compliance costs and regulatory program spending, he extrapolated national regulatory costs from federal and provincial administrative budgets. While the calculation is crude, it provides a rough estimate of the size of the regulatory burden.

Three points are worth noting about these regulatory cost estimates, since they are often cited without careful analysis. First, the figures are highly uncertain and often incomplete. Yet, estimates as reported in the press and even scholarly papers sometimes fail to reflect this uncertainty. Second, the figures developed using this approach to cost estimation are likely to understate the total impact of regulatory costs because they do not include the adverse impact that regulation typically has on innovation. Third, as shown in tables 1.4 and 1.5, the cost of regulation as a fraction of GDP is fairly significant for countries where such estimates are readily avail-

Table 1.4 Costs of Regulation and Gains from Deregulation
(as a percentage of GDP)

Country	Cost of Regulation[a]	Projected Benefits of Economic Deregulation[a]	Source
United States	7.2–9.5%	0.3%	Hopkins 1992;[b] Winston 1993[c]
Australia	9–19%	5.5%	OECD 1996a[d]
Canada	11.8%		Mihlar 1996[e]
Japan		2.3–18.7%	OECD 1996b[f]
European Union		3–7%	OECD 1996b[g]
Germany		0.3%	OECD 1996b[h]
Netherlands		0.5–1.1%	OECD 1996b[i]

a. These numbers are underestimates of the effects of deregulation since the studies do not include all sectors where deregulation can be beneficial.

b. The cost estimates, as of 1991, include process costs. The range reflects the inclusion of economic transfers.

c. Winston estimated the gains of deregulation in the United States at 0.7 to 0.8 percent of GDP in 1990. The 0.3 percent estimate represents the potential gains if the industries could achieve optimality.

d. The costs of regulation, as of 1986, are derived from Commonwealth (1986). The projected benefits from deregulation are based on both the Hilmer and related reforms (Industry Commission 1995). These reforms essentially cover legislative and regulatory changes in order to provide a national competition policy framework and to broaden the coverage of competition policy instruments. They also cover moves to foster competition in national infrastructure areas such as electricity, gas, water, and road transport.

e. The cost estimates were calculated in 1993–94.

f. Projections of savings from deregulation are based on reducing the price and productivity gap with the United States. See Shimpo and Nishizake (1997) for an overview of the studies.

g. Citing Emerson 1988. Projections of savings from deregulation are based on dismantling technical trade barriers and custom formalities, enhanced economies of scale, and lower profit margins from enhanced competition.

h. Citing Lipschitz and others 1989. Projections of savings from deregulation are based on more market-oriented pricing in agriculture and mining, the dismantling of tariff and nontariff barriers in selected industries, and reforms in product and labor markets.

i. Citing Van Bergeijk and Haffner 1995. Projections of savings from deregulation are based on the reduction of product market rigidities in twenty major sectors of the Dutch economy.

Table 1.5 The Economywide Effects of Regulatory Reform

	United States	Japan	Germany	France	United Kingdom	Netherlands	Spain	Sweden
Partial effects[a]								
Labor productivity	0.5	2.6	3.5	2.3	2.0	1.3	3.1	1.7
Capital productivity	0.5	4.3	1.3	3.3	1.4	2.9	3.1	1.3
Factor productivity	0.5	3.0	2.8	2.7	1.8	1.8	3.1	1.5
Business sector employment	0.0	0.0	–1.0	–0.4	–0.5	0.6	–0.7	0.6
Wages	0.0	–0.1	–0.4	0.0	0.0	–0.2	–0.1	0.0
GDP price level	–0.3	–2.1	–1.3	–1.4	–1.2	n.a.	n.a.	n.a.
Economywide effects[b]								
GDP	0.9	5.6	4.9	4.8	3.5	3.5	5.6	3.1
Unemployment	0.0	0.0	0.0	0.0	0.0	0.0	0.0	0.0
Employment	0.1	0.0	0.0	0.0	0.0	0.0	0.0	0.0
Real wages	0.8	3.4	4.1	3.9	2.5	2.8	4.2	2.1

n.a. = Not available.

a. These effects are based on an aggregation of estimated sector-specific effects. They cover the business sector only.

b. The effects include long-term and dynamic interactions in the economy as a whole and are based on simulations with a simplified macroeconomic model (see "Assessing the Gains from Regulatory Reform," below). The simulations for the Netherlands, Spain, and Sweden are preliminary, but the estimates nevertheless include some dynamic effects, and thus go beyond those reported in the individual Country Notes tables. For Spain, the estimates are based on 1990 cost structures, and subsequent reforms may have affected them to some degree.

Source: OECD 1997a.

---

able, ranging from 7 to 19 percent. The impact of deregulation on a number of economic indicators such as labor, capital, and factor productivity and price level as shown in table 1.5 is also quite significant. Further evidence of the significant benefits to deregulation is described below.[7]

Many studies have attempted to estimate the adverse impact of regulation using measures other than economic cost. For example, Christainsen and Haveman (1981) examined the effect of regulation on labor productivity in the U.S. economy during the 1960s and 1970s, when productivity growth (output per person-hour) declined considerably and government regulations accelerated, using three measures of aggregate regulation: the cumulative number of major pieces of regulatory legislation in effect, the amount of federal expenditures on regulatory activities, and the number of full-time federal personnel engaged in regulatory activity. The authors estimated that between 12 and 21 percent of the slowdown in the growth of labor productivity in U.S. manufacturing during 1973–77, as compared with 1958–65, was due to the expansion of federal regulation. MacAvoy (1992) examined the long-term growth effects of regulation on eight industries from 1973 to 1987. He found economywide

losses of 1.5 to 2.0 percent of U.S. gross national product (GNP). Studies examining environmental, health, and safety regulation have yielded qualitatively similar impacts. For example, Jorgenson and Wilcoxen (1990) found the cost of pollution control was associated with a reduction of over 2.5 percent of U.S. GNP between 1974 and 1985. In an examination of the impact of environmental and occupational health and safety regulation on the manufacturing sector, Robinson (1995) concluded that the cumulative effect was to reduce multifactor productivity by more than 10 percent over a twelve-year period.[8]

Other studies describe the relationship between regulation and output growth. For example, Friedman (1995) argues that the growth in regulation is at least, in part, responsible for the slowdown in U.S. economic growth in the decade whose midpoint was 1969. The number of pages in the *Federal Register* more than doubled during the Nixon administration, rising from roughly 20,000 in 1969 to 45,000 in 1974, when he resigned, and to 60,000 the year after. The all-time peak, reached in 1980, was 87,000. The number of pages declined sharply during the Reagan administration, then rose again under presidents Bush and Clinton. Many federal programs were initiated during the Nixon administration. In addition, affirmative action and wage and price controls were introduced. During the high-growth period between 1946 and 1969, the number of pages in the *Federal Register* was low; during the low-growth period after 1969, the number of pages was high. Clearly many other factors affected the rates of growth during the postwar period, yet as Friedman points out, dismantling the regulatory state would allow the United States to grow at roughly 4 percent a year.

In a study of eleven Organization for Economic Cooperation and Development (OECD) countries, Koedijk and Kremers (1996) tested the relationship between market regulation and output growth, shown in figure 1.1. They constructed an index of regulatory intensity in the countries, and showed a sharp negative correlation between regulatory intensity and output growth. The countries with the least regulation enjoyed the highest growth in output per person. The measures the authors construct are admittedly crude, but they probably serve as a proxy for the degree to which markets are regulated in different countries.

The economic impact of different labor regulations on employment growth can be seen in table 1.6. The table suggests that countries with less onerous labor market restrictions (at the top of the table) enjoyed robust employment growth, while countries with more severe restrictions (at the bottom of the table) suffered declining employment growth. While many other factors can affect employment growth, there are strong reasons to believe that flexible labor market policies are likely to increase employment (Guasch 1997).

The preceding tables and figures present the overall trends in regulatory costs and impacts, but they fall short of providing a basis for ultimate judgments about specific regulations. Such judgments require information on the benefits of regulation as well as costs. More important still, judgments require analysis of incremental rather than total effects. Only then is it possible to assess whether the economic benefits of a particular proposal outweigh its costs.

ASSESSING THE GAINS FROM REGULATORY REFORM

While information on the economic impact of regulation is limited, there is a fairly comprehensive database in the United States and in some

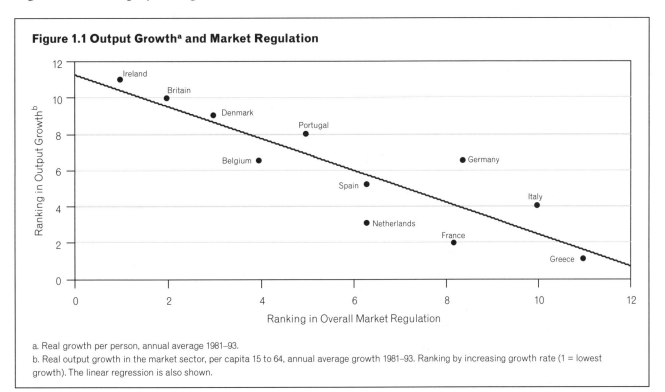

Figure 1.1 Output Growth[a] and Market Regulation

a. Real growth per person, annual average 1981–93.

b. Real output growth in the market sector, per capita 15 to 64, annual average growth 1981–93. Ranking by increasing growth rate (1 = lowest growth). The linear regression is also shown.

Table 1.6 Labor Regulations

Country	Payroll Taxes[a] (percent)	Severance Payments[b]	Collective Bargaining	Unemployment Rate (1996)	Employment Growth (1992–1995)[c]
Australia	27.8	Low	Centralized	9.0	1.0
Chile	20.9	Low	Firm Level	6.3	2.3
Japan	22.9	None	Firm Level	2.5	0.6
Malaysia	24.3	Low	Firm Level	2.8	3.3
New Zealand	11.5	None	Firm Level	8.0	1.4
United States	20.1	None	Firm Level	5.5	1.8
Argentina	50.0[d]	High	Centralized	17.2	−0.7
France	54.7	High	Centralized	11.6	−0.4
Italy	52.8	High	Centralized	10.2	−1.7
Spain	38.2	High	Centralized	22.4	−1.6

a. Payroll taxes are firm donations plus obligatory personal contributions. The values for France, Italy, Japan, and Spain correspond to 1994, those for Malaysia to 1995, and those for Argentina and Chile to 1996.
b. Severance payments based on OECD indexes.
c. Employment growth is measured as annual average percentage growth.
d. Argentina amended its labor laws in 1996, and payroll taxes now average 41.0 percent.
Source: Guasch 1997.

other countries that provides a good indication of the scope for regulatory reform. Moreover, several countries are in the process of developing useful information that would help streamline the regulatory process (see box 1.2). Here, we first examine the potential for improving social regulation and then examine the potential gains from reforming economic regulation.

Social Regulation

In the area of social regulation, it is essential to examine the likely impact of individual regulations. Hahn (1996) has compiled the most comprehensive analysis of the benefits and costs of recent regulation based on studies by government agencies. He surveyed over ninety Regulatory Impact Analyses (RIAs) for environmental, health, and safety rules from 1990 to mid-1995 and found that there is considerable variation in the type and quality of analysis agencies perform for individual rules. Benefit analyses were often incomplete, and in less than 20 percent of the rules did agencies show that quantified monetary benefits would exceed quantified costs.

To make the analysis consistent across different programs and regulations, Hahn converted dollar estimates to 1994 dollars, and introduced a common discount rate and a consistent set of

Box 1.2 Regulatory Reform in Mexico

The government of Mexico is now implementing a far-reaching program to carefully examine the country's regulatory structure at the federal, state, and local levels. The aims of the Agreement for the Deregulation of Business Activity include streamlining federal regulation, reducing corruption by codifying regulation, and helping to promote more efficient and effective regulation. The program, while new, has enjoyed some early successes. Recent legislation simplifies administrative procedures, requires a quicker administrative response time, and reduces paperwork for foreign investors. In addition, a series of legal reforms aims to simplify court proceedings and reduce the costs of commercial lending. As a result of these reforms, Mexico City's Superior Court reports that the number of civil suits filed decreased by 24 percent from 1995 to 1996. Agency-by-agency rule simplification and elimination is also proceeding swiftly. For example, the approval time for a business requiring health, safety, and environmental controls to begin operation has been reduced from an average of over 200 working days to a maximum of 21 working days. Finally, a complete inventory of federal rules in effect is available on the Internet. Making such information more easily accessible should help reduce corruption and compliance costs.

Source: Secretaria De Comercio y Fomento Industrial 1996.

values for reducing health risks. The results are summarized in figure 1.2, which provides an overview of the distribution of net benefits of fifty-four final regulations. The left side of the figure shows the number of rules with net costs that fall in various categories. The right side of the figure shows the number of rules with net benefits that fall in various categories. The figure illustrates that the average benefit for a rule with net benefits exceeds the average cost for a rule with net costs.

Several conclusions emerge from this analysis. First, using government agency data, it would appear that there is a present value of about US$280 billion (1994 dollars) in net benefits to government regulation in those areas since 1990. Yet over half the final rules would not pass a benefit-cost test, even when we use government agencies' numbers. Aggregate net benefits are positive because many of the rules that do pass have substantial benefits. Eliminating final rules that would not pass a benefit-cost test could increase the present value of net benefits by more than US$115 billion.

There are reasons, however, *not* to take the agency numbers at face value. Both theory and empirical evidence suggest that agencies are likely to overstate substantially the aggregate

numbers for net benefits. Agencies with a single objective (for example, protecting the environment or improving safety in the workplace) have an incentive to overstate the benefits of their program relative to the costs so that they can better meet the demands of interest groups.

Another measure of the impact of regulations is how many lives a regulation is likely to save. Interestingly, a review of several final and proposed regulations reveals the amount spent for each premature death that would be avoided because of the existence of the regulation varies over eight orders of magnitude—from roughly US$100,000 to over US$5 trillion (1990 dollars) (Morrall 1986)! This suggests that regulations could be developed that would prevent many more premature deaths while still saving consumers money. Recent studies have attempted to quantify potential gains in both the United States and abroad. Reallocating the current U.S. investment in 185 life-saving interventions could avert an additional 60,000 deaths, or twice those at present (Tengs and Graham 1996). In addition, reallocating recent domestic regulatory expenditures of about US$8 billion (1994 dollars) could save more than 100 million additional life-years in developing countries (Hahn 1996).

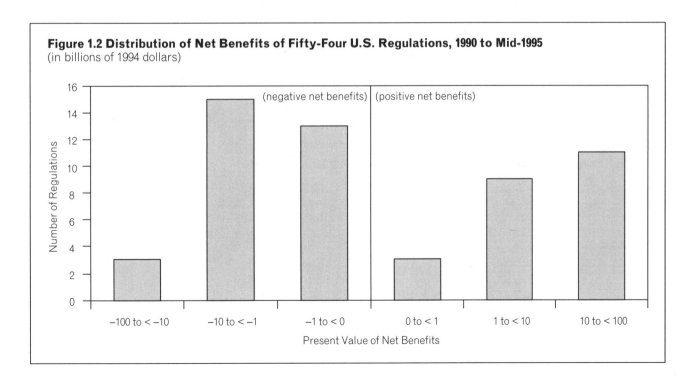

Figure 1.2 Distribution of Net Benefits of Fifty-Four U.S. Regulations, 1990 to Mid-1995
(in billions of 1994 dollars)

Economic Regulation

There was much economic deregulation in developed countries in the late 1970s and early 1980s, particularly in transportation and energy. Since the early 1980s, however, economic regulation has not advanced very rapidly, even though there is ample room for further deregulation in areas such as telecommunications, electricity, and the financial services (Noll 1997). Developing countries have been late entrants in the move toward deregulation, but are quickly catching up. Indeed, some countries, such as Chile, have progressed even further than most developed countries. And some countries in the Latin America and Caribbean region, such as Argentina, El Salvador, Peru, and Mexico, are undertaking major economic deregulation initiatives.

In this section we review additional evidence on the potential benefits of economic deregulation. We will first consider the developed countries with a focus on the U.S. experience and on the experience of other OECD countries, and then examine the record of the developing countries.

Developed Countries

The overall welfare gains from deregulation across sectors in the United States have been substantial. The focus was eliminating entry and exit restrictions and freeing prices to their market levels. Table 1.7, taken from Winston (1993), shows more recent estimates of the benefits of deregulation and the potential gains from further

reform. Aggregate welfare gains amounted to US$35 to US$46 billion (1990 dollars) per year. Consumers had annual gains of US$32 to US$43 billion per year from lower prices and better services. Producers gained about US$3 billion per year from increased efficiency and lower costs. Winston estimates that additional gains from remaining distortions could be in excess of US$20-plus billion per year.

However, there is evidence that the gains from deregulation that economists have estimated are likely to be significantly understated. In a 1996 paper, Winston argues that the time it takes for industry to adjust to the newly deregulated environment is substantial. Winston notes that although industry may adjust prices to reflect marginal costs quickly after deregulation, it takes time to optimize production. He argues that policymakers and the public tend to notice only the short-term effects and, therefore, undervalue the benefits of deregulation. Frequently, the positive impact that deregulation has on innovation is overlooked. Innovations in technologies and operations sparked by deregulation increased productivity and reduced operating costs by 24 percent to over 50 percent in different industries.

Sectoral studies examining the effect of regulation yield similar results on the adverse consequences of economic regulation. Caves, Christensen, and Swanson (1981) undertook a cross-country study to compare total productivity growth for U.S. railroads from 1956 to 1974 to growth achieved by Canadian railroads over the same period. Both industries had access to the same technology, but Canadian railroads were sub-

Table 1.7 Welfare Gains from Deregulation in the United States in 1990
(in billions of 1990 dollars)

Industry	Consumers	Producers	Total	Further Potential Gains
Airlines	8.8–14.8	4.9	13.7–19.7	4.9
Railways	7.2–9.7	3.2	10.4–12.9	0.4
Road Freight	15.4	(4.8)	10.6	0
Telecommunications	0.7–1.6	—	0.7–1.6	11.8
Cable Television	0.4–1.3	—	0.4–1.3	0.4–0.8
Brokerage	0.1	(0.1)	0	0
Natural Gas	—	—	—	4.1
Total	**$32.6–43.0**	**$3.2**	**$35.8–46.2**	**$21.6–22.0**

Source: Winston 1993.

ject to less regulation than U.S. railroads. The authors argue that regulation substantially reduced productivity growth. Average total productivity growth was 3.3 percent a year for Canadian railroads and only 0.5 percent for U.S. railroads, and the authors estimate that, if the United States had experienced the same productivity growth as Canada, the cost of providing rail services in 1974 would have been US$13.8 billion (1985 dollars) lower. After railroad deregulation in the United States, Willig and Baumol (1987) estimated that between 1980 and 1985, annual operating expenses dropped 26 percent while traffic volume remained virtually unchanged. Deregulation of the rail sector also led to increases in investment (the capital formation effect). Following very little investment during the 1970s, during 1981–85 the United States invested $27 billion in railroad structures, roadways, and maintenance, and invested $30 billion in rail cars, locomotives, and other equipment (Willig and Baumol 1987).[9]

Deregulation of the trucking sector led to major improvements in efficiency. Average unit costs dropped dramatically after deregulation— from $0.343 in 1977 (before deregulation) to $0.100 in 1983 (after deregulation); a large number of firms had the lowest unit costs while facing more competition after deregulation; and many of the inefficient firms were forced to leave the industry, leaving behind those firms with low unit costs (McMullen and Stanley 1988). The annual welfare loss due to allocative inefficiency resulting from regulation of rail and motor carrier rates has been estimated to be US$1 billion to US$4 billion (1977 dollars) (Braeutigam and Noll, 1984; Winston and others 1990). Similarly, deregulation of the gas industry led to significant improvements in productivity and cost reduction, as illustrated in figures 1.3 through 1.6.

A comparison of the pre- and postderegulated U.S. airline industry also provides striking evidence of regulation's impact on productivity and production costs. Cost per unit of service was reduced by approximately 25 percent— within a year of deregulation—and was accompanied by sharp work-force reductions,[10] with little effect on output in the first few years following deregulation (Caves and others 1987).[11]

In addition, excess capacity decreased and productivity increased. Morrison and Winston (1995) estimate the net annual gains to travelers from airline deregulation at US$18.4 billion (1993 dollars).[12]

Similar postderegulation effects have been observed in other sectors, such as stock exchanges and banking, where deregulation has improved productivity and lowered unit costs. For example, when stock brokerage fees were deregulated, rates dropped by 25 percent.[13] Employment dropped from 260,000 in 1987 to 190,000 in 1990, and the overall consolidation and cost reduction was 30 percent in the sector (Jarrell 1984). While firms may have changed the services offered, a number of studies have shown that even after accounting for changes in service, cost reductions were significant.

The productivity gains secured by U.S. banks following partial deregulation of the banking and savings and loan sectors have also been significant. Jobs decreased more than 20 percent in the sector during 1984–93, and productivity (as measured by revenue per employee) increased by more than 300 percent throughout the same period (Guasch and Spiller 1997). At the same time, there was a serious problem with the monitoring of financial institutions during this period, which resulted in some major financial losses (White 1991). The large losses stemmed in part from regulators not taking appropriate actions.

Likewise, the breakup of AT&T and (partial) deregulation of the telecommunications sector in the U.S. during the 1980s, led to significant productivity gains and price decreases and an overall increase in efficiency, as shown on figures 1.9 and 1.10.

REGULATION AS AN INSTRUMENT DELAYING THE INTRODUCTION OF NEW PRODUCTS

Another adverse effect of regulation can be in explicitly delaying the introduction of new technologically available services. The welfare cost of those delays can be considerable. For example, in a number of countries, such as the United States, Canada, and some Latin American countries, very

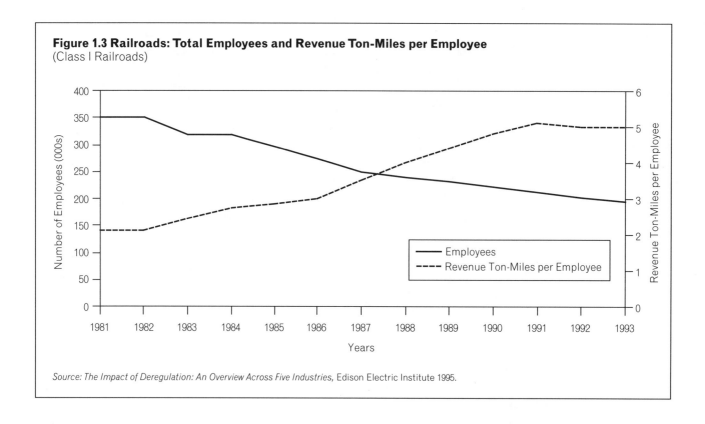

Figure 1.3 Railroads: Total Employees and Revenue Ton-Miles per Employee
(Class I Railroads)

Source: The Impact of Deregulation: An Overview Across Five Industries, Edison Electric Institute 1995.

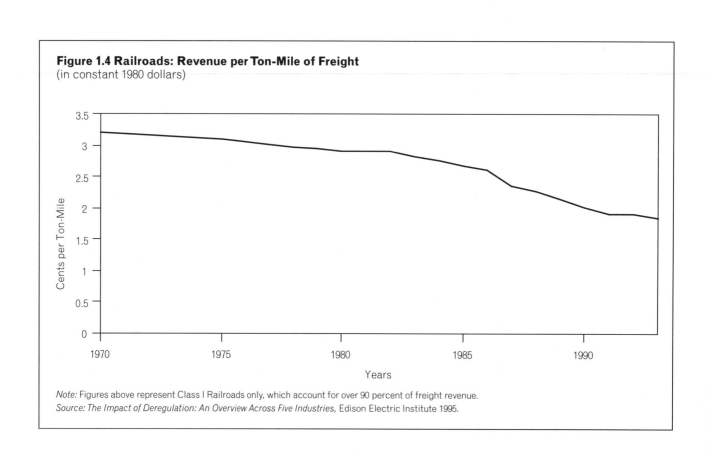

Figure 1.4 Railroads: Revenue per Ton-Mile of Freight
(in constant 1980 dollars)

Note: Figures above represent Class I Railroads only, which account for over 90 percent of freight revenue.
Source: The Impact of Deregulation: An Overview Across Five Industries, Edison Electric Institute 1995.

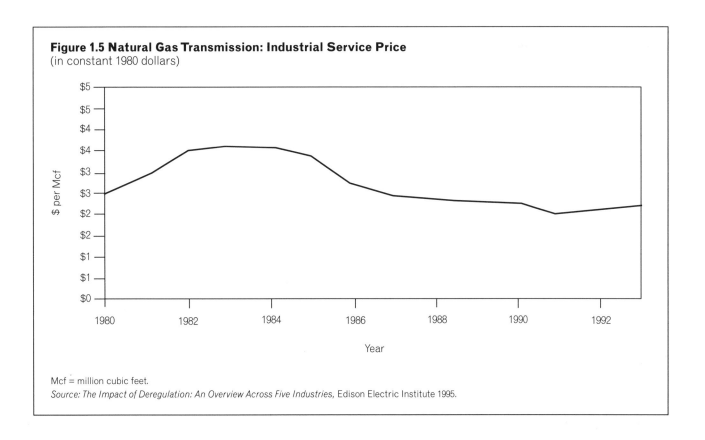

Figure 1.5 Natural Gas Transmission: Industrial Service Price
(in constant 1980 dollars)

Mcf = million cubic feet.
Source: The Impact of Deregulation: An Overview Across Five Industries, Edison Electric Institute 1995.

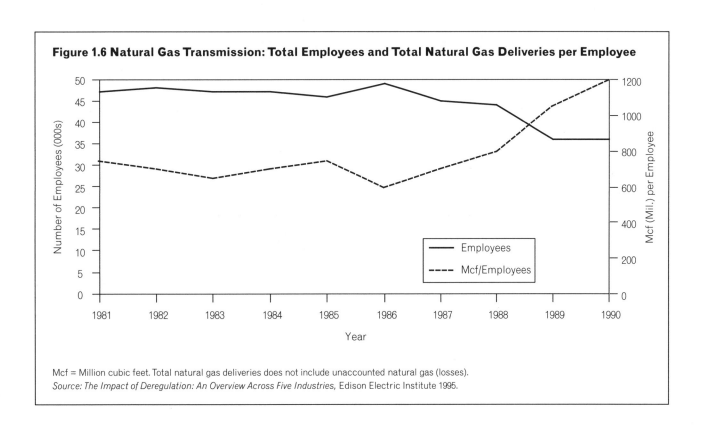

Figure 1.6 Natural Gas Transmission: Total Employees and Total Natural Gas Deliveries per Employee

Mcf = Million cubic feet. Total natural gas deliveries does not include unaccounted natural gas (losses).
Source: The Impact of Deregulation: An Overview Across Five Industries, Edison Electric Institute 1995.

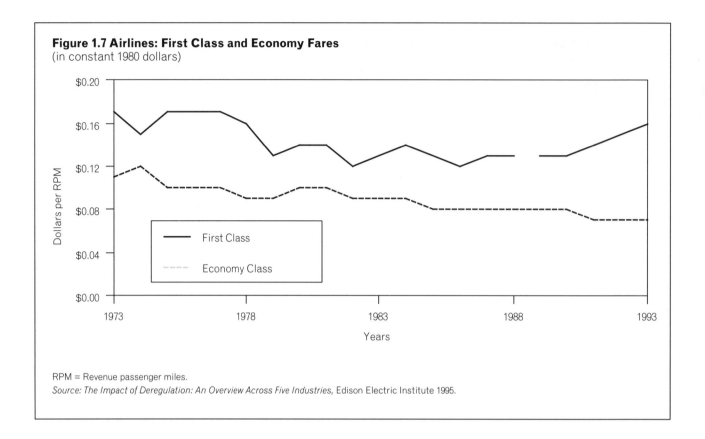

Figure 1.7 Airlines: First Class and Economy Fares
(in constant 1980 dollars)

RPM = Revenue passenger miles.
Source: The Impact of Deregulation: An Overview Across Five Industries, Edison Electric Institute 1995.

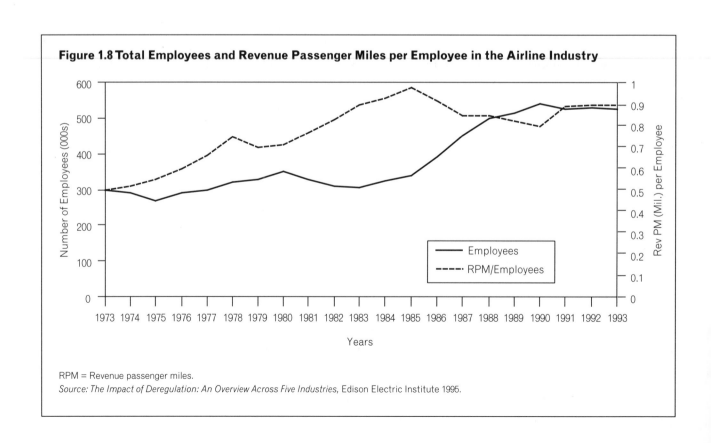

Figure 1.8 Total Employees and Revenue Passenger Miles per Employee in the Airline Industry

RPM = Revenue passenger miles.
Source: The Impact of Deregulation: An Overview Across Five Industries, Edison Electric Institute 1995.

Figure 1.9 Long-Distance Telecommunication: Total Employees and Interstate Switched Access
(minutes per employees)

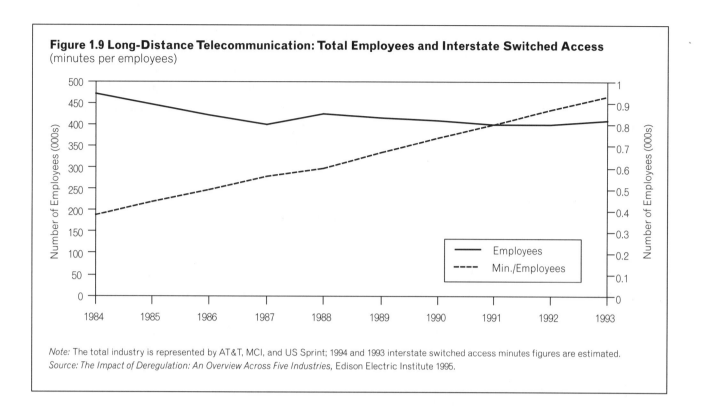

Note: The total industry is represented by AT&T, MCI, and US Sprint; 1994 and 1993 interstate switched access minutes figures are estimated.
Source: The Impact of Deregulation: An Overview Across Five Industries, Edison Electric Institute 1995.

Figure 1.10 Long-Distance Telecommunication: Interstate Toll Charges
(in constant 1980 dollars)

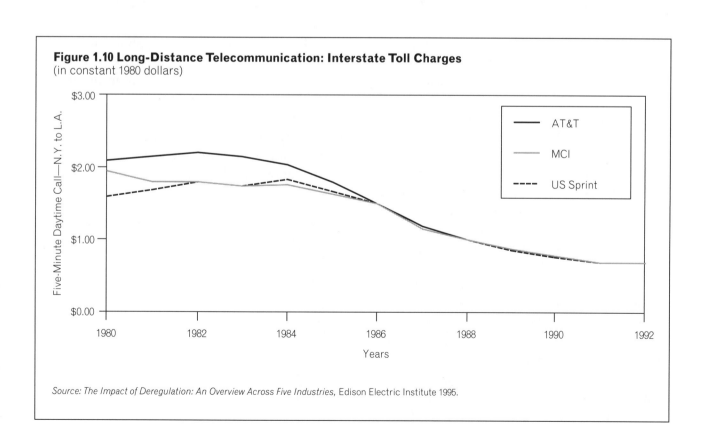

Source: The Impact of Deregulation: An Overview Across Five Industries, Edison Electric Institute 1995.

strict regulation has limited the ability of companies to compete freely in telecommunications. The impact of that often misguided regulation can be quite significant. In the telecommunications sector in the United States, long-distance telephone rates as of 1998 have decreased by more than 80 percent since the divestiture of AT&T in 1984 and deregulation of the sector (Taylor and Taylor 1993; *Wall Street Journal* 1991). The examples of cellular telephony and voice messaging in the United States illustrate how regulation can also slow the introduction of new products and discourage innovation, and cost the consumers hundreds of millions of dollars. While the cellular telephony concept was discussed in the late 1940s and was clearly available in 1973, it was only in 1983 that the Federal Communications Commission (FCC) began to issue licenses using a nonmarket mechanism. That delay in licensing cellular telecommunications cost the U.S. economy more than US$25 billion per year (1983 dollars) (Rohlfs, Jackson, and Kelly 1991).[14] Those losses were about 2 percent of GDP in 1983, when cellular service began. Similarly, the delay in introducing voice messaging services cost more than US$1.3 billion (1994 dollars) per year (Hausman and Tardiff 1996). Even if those two services had been offered at monopoly prices the consumer welfare lost remains significantly high.[15]

More broadly, deregulation facilitates new entry and decreases costs significantly. As a result, products or services which previously were not financially or legally feasible to produce can now be provided either by existing firms or by new entrants. For example, as transport costs and delivery times fall as a result of deregulation of the sector, time- and transport-sensitive products, such as cut flowers and other agricultural products, can be produced and/or exported. The welfare impact as described can be quite significant.

This is particularly relevant for developing countries. Delays in privatization of state utility companies induced de facto delays in the introduction of new products and in penetration of existing products, inducing in turn significant welfare losses. Among the best welfare estimates of privatization of utilities are Galal and others (1994). Current legislation/regulation in many

developing countries hampers the development and competition of new products, particularly in the telecommunications sector.

While the database outside the United States is less extensive, there is reason to believe that the gains from deregulation of many industries elsewhere could be substantial (see table 1.4). For example, lifting price and entry restrictions on air travel in Europe could lead to substantial gains for consumers. Table 1.8 provides some price information for trips of similar length and demand characteristics. The table suggests that fares for trips are roughly twice as expensive in Europe as in the United States. And despite the higher fares, the profitability of many of the European companies is far below that of the U.S. carriers. Indeed, the European high-cost carriers, such as Iberia and Air France (both state owned), have survived until now only with government aid. Good, Röller, and Sickles (1993) argue that liberalization would lead to competition among international carriers and a convergence of cost structures. They estimate that, in 1986, if the European airline industry were as efficient as the U.S. airline industry they would have achieved cost savings of approximately US$4 billion (1986 dollars).

There are also significant opportunities for gains in deregulating electricity markets. Table 1.9 shows electricity prices in Europe and the United States. To the extent these prices reflect incremental costs, there are likely to be significant gains from reducing entry barriers into different markets. For example, strict regulations in Germany require domestic companies to pur-

Table 1.8 Fare Comparison of Similar U.S. and European Routes

Route	Miles	Fare
Boston to New York	187	$153
London to Paris	211	$263
Washington to New York	216	$153
Houston to New Orleans	302	$89
Copenhagen to Oslo	311	$315
Dallas to Minneapolis	853	$435
Frankfurt to Madrid	887	$720

Source: Airfare Management Unit 1995, 1996; and Consulting Services Group 1995, 1996.

Table 1.9 Costs of Energy in the European Community, 1995
(cents per kilowatt-hour)

Country	Cost
Germany, Rep. of	11.88
Italy	10.00
Portugal	9.65
Belgium	9.12
Spain	8.50
United Kingdom	8.09
Luxembourg	7.62
Ireland	7.40
France	7.39
Netherlands	7.27
United States	7.01
Greece	6.87
Denmark	5.89
Finland	5.72
Norway	4.72
Sweden	4.22

Source: Electricity Association, London 1995.

chase electricity from regional producers, even though lower-cost power is often available nearby. The extent of the potential gains for consumers is difficult to estimate, but in the United Kingdom, energy deregulation resulted in a 70 percent increase in productivity and an 18 to 21 percent reduction in franchise contract prices, and a 33 percent reduction in generation costs (implying annual savings of 2,300 million pounds). Users have benefited by seeing their average domestic bills fall nearly 10 percent. The savings for domestic customers in England and Wales is worth £580 million per year and in excess of £650 million for industrial and commercial customers (OECD 1997b).[16] The absence of similar deregulation in other European Union countries has led to firms paying over 50 percent more for their electricity than do their American counterparts. Moreover, the impact of higher energy prices on the overall economy can be quite significant (Navarro 1996).[17]

Overregulation has clearly had negative effects in the United States and in other industrial countries, particularly Japan and Germany.[18] As an example, the largest retail chain in Japan, Mr Max Corp., spent two years persuading more than twenty farmers to sell their land in the city of Saga on the island of Kyushu and petitioning the government to rezone it for commercial use.

This was followed by at least eighteen more months of haggling with local merchants who were demanding concessions when the new stores opened nearby. Mr Max expected to open its new outlets by early 1998, but the stores were probably at least 20 percent smaller than planned and had to pay inflated membership fees to a local trade association. To placate smaller local retailers further, Mr Max has to close stores twice a month by taking twenty-four days of "holiday" a year. In Japan, laws designed to protect consumers from "confusion" prohibit discount coupons, and fire laws are designed for cramped, multistory buildings. As a result, Mr Max must install fire shutters that lower automatically to prevent fires from spreading to other floors, even though the company builds only large, single-story buildings. In all, Mr Max calculates that the requirements add 30 percent to construction costs.

Germany also has a daunting list of regulations, some dating to the Kaiser's era. Laws that limit store hours and competition give store clerks regular hours and help smaller stores, but do a great disservice to customers. Allkauf stores (a large retail chain) can be open only 68.5 hours a week and must close at 6:30 p.m. on weekdays and 2 p.m. on Saturdays. Sunday shopping is forbidden. Meanwhile, under a Hitler-era "rebate law," German stores can hold full-scale sales only twice a year, usually in January and late July. Even then, they cannot discount food. Germany's regulatory system is designed to keep peace between labor and management, but at high cost to consumers.

German companies must buy electricity from regional providers, whose rates are inflated, rather than from international providers, whose rates are cheaper. This problem is not unique to Germany. Energy prices all over Europe are substantially higher than in the United States, primarily because European states exercise a monopoly over the power sector. Supporters of deregulation would like to open the market to competition from all countries. This move would provide an opportunity for companies in the United States and elsewhere to develop a natural gas market in Europe but, more important, it would support local businesses, boosting profits by reducing costs and creating jobs. The United Kingdom deregulated its energy market in 1990, realizing a 4 percent decrease in real prices for residential consumers—a benefit that the rest of Europe would like to copy. In the current environment, electricity-intensive industries are unlikely to open new plants in countries with unusually high rates (see table 1.9). And the impact of higher energy prices in the overall economy can be significant. For example, a 30 percent increase in electricity prices raises the price of goods such as paper and pulp, metals, chemicals, and glass by roughly 2.5 percent, and the price of plastics, telecommunications, and textiles by 1 to 2 percent (Navarro 1996).

A variety of process regulations also creates costly burdens. In 1990, paperwork requirements alone consumed more than 5 billion hours of the private sector's time, mostly to comply with tax laws. This deprives the private sector of an important productive resource: time. Available research on valuing time translates this burden into $110 billion annually. Furthermore, many federal spending programs have reporting and paperwork requirements that fall on state and local governments and on the private sector. One example is reimbursement for the cost of health care. These paperwork requirements cost about $25 billion annually. There, are of course, unquantified benefits associated with these requirements, such as a lower incidence of tax fraud, but whether these benefits could be achieved at lower cost is an open question.

Although regulations exist in theory to address market failure, they sometimes enable a weak sector to maintain stable and adequate levels of profitability or allow influential interest groups to capture rents. The regulation of trucking occurred in response to the competitive pressures felt by the railroads, and the Interstate Commerce Commission played the role of a cartel setter. Obviously, this was not an appropriate reason for regulation, and the positive effects of deregulation seen in the airline, gas, freight, and brokerage sectors prove false the concerns raised in support of regulation. Regulated sectors are often correlated with enormous sectoral inertia

and low productivity growth, and regulatory activity also leads to enormous inertia. The United States provides a striking example. As of 1994, U.S. regulations totaled 202 volumes numbering 131,803 pages; of these volumes, sixteen contained environmental regulations, nineteen contained agricultural regulations, and two contained employment regulations. In 1994 the total was fourteen times greater than it was in 1950, and nearly four times greater than in 1965.

The impact of economic deregulation on the price level is also considerable, and table 1.10 provides estimates of significant price reduction secured after deregulation of road transport, airlines, electricity, financial services, professional services, and telecommunications for a number of OECD countries. As shown, the percentage of price reductions ranges from 5 to 66 percent.

DEVELOPING COUNTRIES

The evidence of the adverse impact of economic regulation on productivity and efficiency can serve as a lesson for developing countries. Lower productivity in regulated industries translates into higher costs for products and inputs produced domestically, thus reducing a country's ability to pursue a successful export-led growth strategy. The precise impact of regulation on developing country economies is difficult to estimate in many cases. Yet, data from the developed world and a few studies in developing countries suggest that the potential welfare gains from regulatory reform could be quite significant.

For countries that have deregulated, the efficiency gains have been quite significant. For example, deregulation of entry into the long-distance telephone market in Chile has cut rates by over 50 percent, making them close to U.S. rates (Guasch and Spiller 1997). Allowing for private sector participation in the telecommunications sector has cut waiting time for installation of new lines from a minimum of two years to a matter of weeks in those Latin American countries that have privatized the sector. Privatization and deregulation of the Argentine railroads has produced real gains in performance, a turnaround in traffic trends, a quadrupling of labor

Table 1.10 Price Reductions After Elimination of Economic Regulation
(price reduction may be in part attributable to factors other than regulatory reform)

Sector	Country	Price Reductions in Real Terms (percent)
Road transport	Germany	30
	Mexico	25
	France	20
	United States	19
Airlines	United Kingdom	33
	United States	33
	Spain	30[1]
	Australia	20
Electricity	Norway (spot market)	18–26[2]
	United Kingdom	9–15[3]
	Japan	5
Financial services	United Kingdom	70[4]
	United States	30–62[4]
Professional services	United Kingdom	33
Telecommunications	Finland	66[5]
	United Kingdom	63[6]
	Japan	41[6]
	Mexico	21[5]
	Korea	10–30[7]

1. Refers to discount fares on the highest-density route. Larger drops have been registered on other routes.

2. The former figure refers to reductions for industrial customers who renegotiated contracts with their traditional suppliers, the latter refers to industrial customers shifting to new suppliers.

3. The former figure refers to electricity rates for households, the latter for industrial customers.

4. Refers to stock exchange commissions. In the U.S. case, the former figure refers to rates for small transactions, the latter to rates for large transactions.

5. Prices of long-distance calls.

6. Average prices of telephone services.

7. The former figure refers to domestic long-distance calls, the latter to international calls.

Source: OECD 1997a.

productivity, improvements in service quality, reductions in price, and a reduction in the public deficit of about US$600 million a year (equal to 0.5 percent of GDP) (Thompson and Karim-Jacques Budin 1997). Similarly, in the port sector, the opening of the port terminals in Buenos Aires to competition has led to an 80 percent reduction of the fees. In addition, the opening of stevedore operations to multiple parties in the port of Montevideo has increased productivity by 300 percent.[19] All these results were achieved within a year of deregulation (Guasch 1996).

A study of Argentina, summarized in table 1.11, assesses the welfare cost of regulations and other government interventions in the 1980s (Fundacion de Investigaciones Economicas Latinoamericanas 1991). The total costs of regulation and state intervention amount to over US$4 billion per year (1990 dollars), and this is only for

the selective listed interventions. While the measure of costs for different activities differs somewhat (for example, efficiency costs, additional cost to consumers, and subsidy cost), the overall total suggests that the cost of government intervention is significant. The values given are likely to underestimate the total costs, since they usually do not account for the additional impact on economic activity.

It would be useful to assemble data on regulatory costs in other developing countries that is comparable to that assembled for Argentina. Yet, there is no shortage of specific cases where economic regulation has had adverse consequences. For example, Uruguayan firms and consumers are paying an implicit tax of at least 30 percent for water, phone, and electricity. This implicit tax exceeds that of other countries in Mercosur, thus hindering the competitiveness of Uruguayan

Table 1.11 Examples of the Costs of Regulation in Argentina
(in millions of 1991 U.S. dollars)

	Period	Average Annual Cost
Financial System		
$ High reserve requirements and subsidized credit by the central bank	1987	1,000
$ Inflation taxes on checking accounts	1983–1987	670
Fuel price controls	1977–1987	350
Health Services		
$ Extra costs from double affiliation	1986	150
$ Idle capacity in public hospitals	1987	172
Fishing export subsidies	1986–1987	12
Efficiency costs from domestic consumption restrictions in cattle markets	1984	104
Efficiency costs of the special fund for tobacco	1987	30
Air transport regulations	1988	75
Restrictions on rail transport of cement, wine, and grain	1987	95
Truck transport		
$ Costs of road deterioration	1987	100
$ Costs of provincial regulations in the transport of grains	1987	30
Port restrictions on price and entry	1987	90
Regulations imposed on business	1965–1987	1,200
Regulations on employment in the public sector	1987	120

Note: The costs of regulation presented in this table measure different concepts, such as efficiency losses in the economy, cost premiums to consumers, tax reductions, and subsidies. Thus, it might not be technically correct to total them.
Source: Fundacion de Investigaciones Economicas Latinoamericanas 1991.

products vis-à-vis those of other Mercosur countries.[20] In Brazil, economic regulation has also reduced efficiency. For example, although trucking costs are almost three times as high as rail costs, rail transport has only a 12 percent share of relatively short trips and a negligible 3 percent share in the longer-haul interregional market. The absence of an inverse relationship between cost and market share is to a large extent attributable to inefficient regulation.

One of the few and particularly nice studies of the impact of privatization/deregulation of the utilities sector in Argentina on economic activity is that of Chisari, Estache, and Romero (1997a). Using a computable general equilibrium model, they estimate the efficiency gains of the privatization/deregulation of the energy, gas, telecommunications, and water sectors and their impact on labor productivity, investment, and average tariffs (tables 1.12 and 1.13). On all accounts the gains were significant. Even more interesting and novel is their estimation of the impact of good,

effective regulation, as show in tables 1.14 and 1.15. Effective regulation is modeled as with endogenous tariffs to dissipate any supranormal rents to operators, while ineffective regulation is modeled as fixed tariffs. Chisari, Estache, and Romero find that when the regulators are effective, the annual gains from the private operation of utilities are about US$3.3 billion, or 1.25 percent of GDP, and equally important, all income classes benefit. Ineffective regulation cuts the gains from the reform by US$1 billion, or 0.35

Table 1.12 Impact of Effective Regulation in Argentina

Annual Gains for Private Operation of Utilities		
US$ (billion)	GDP (%)	Implicit Tax to Users (%)
Effective Regulation 3.3	1.25	
Ineffective Regulation 2.3	0.90	16

Source: Chisari, Estache, and Romero 1997a.

Table 1.13 Changes in Performance Between 1993 and 1995

	Electricity Generation	Electricity Distribution	Gas Distribution	Water Distribution	Telecoms.
First year of private operation	1992	1992	1992	1993	1990
Efficiency gains (measured as reduction in intermediate inputs purchases as a share of total sales value)	19.51%	6.26%	8.84%	4.86%	11.28%
Labor productivity gains (measured as GWh/staff for electricity, 000m³/staff for gas, population served/staff for water, lines in service/staff for phones)	23.1%	17.59%	4.79%	−27.58%	21.25%
Increases in investment (as in concession contracts for gas and actual investments for the other sectors)	8.65%	n.a.	4.56%	75.97%	28.1%
Improvements in quality (measured as reductions in losses [net of consumption by transmission]/production for electricity and gas, water unaccounted for/production for water, lines in repair/lines in service for phones)	n.a.	10%	27.8%	6.12%.	4.56%
Changes in real average tariffs (defined as total sales value by a physical indicator of production)	n.a.	−9.5%	-0.5%	5.5%	−4.9%

n.a. = Not applicable.
Note: The table reflects the changes achieved under private management of the services. Indeed, 1993 data reflects the first year in which all sectors had benefited from some initial adjustment by the private operator. The last year for which data was available at the time of this writing was 1995.
Source: Chisari, Estache, and Romero 1997a.

percent of GDP. This cut in gains represents an implicit tax of 16 percent on the average consumers paid directly to the owner of the utility rather than to the government. For the poorest income class, this implicit tax is about 20 percent, meaning that good regulation is in the interest of the poor. The implications are that good regulation matters significantly and that all income groups benefit.

Similarly, Mexico has secured significant efficiency gains through its extensive deregulation program in most transport sectors—aviation, ports, railroads, and trucking. Tandon (1995) analyzes the impact of airline deregulation in Mex-

Table 1.14 Gains from Private Operation of Public Utilities

Income Class	Saving from Operational Gains (A) (in millions of 1993 US$)	Saving from Effective Regulation (B) (in millions of 1993 US$)
1 (poorest)	197	138
2	259	142
3	373	121
4	403	214
5 (richest)	1,047	302
Total	**2,279**	**915**

Note: These figures represent annual gains. (A) is the equivalent variation computed in terms of the dollar revenue of each income class. It is calculated by applying the total gains in the fixed-price simulation to the income in the base year. (B) is computed by applying the differences in gains between the fixed price and the flexible price simulations. In net present value and over a period of ten years, the (A) gains represent a total varying between US$8.2 billion and US$14.4 billion, with discount rates varying between 12 and 18 percent, and amortization rates varying between 0 and 10 percent. The gains from efficient regulation under similar assumptions vary between US$3.3 billion and US$5.8 billion.
Source: Chisari, Estache, and Romero 1997a.

Table 1.15 Sector-Specific Macroeconomic Effects of Private Management of the Sector
(measured in changes over base year 1993)

	Electricity Generation		Electricity Distribution		Gas		Water		Telecoms		Total	
	p fixed	p flex	p fixed	p flex	p fixed	p flex	p fixed	p flex	p fixed	p flex	p fixed	p flex
GDP	0.05	0.10	0.17	0.21	0.36	0.31	0.02	0	0.07	0.19	0.70	0.79
Industrial production	−0.01	0.09	0.21	0.29	−0.07	0.20	−0.01	0	0.04	0.10	0.16	0.66
Unemployment	0	−2.47	−1.08	1.17	−1.93	−6.76	−3.22	−2.36	6.75	3.21	2.35	−4.50
Prices of tradable/Price of non-tradable	−0.12	0.18	0.77	0.78	−0.33	0.64	−0.05	−0.02	0.22	0.88	0.49	2.48
Exports/Imports	0.09	0.67	−0.25	0.67	−2.95	0.42	−0.31	0.02	0.75	0.77	−2.47	2.52
Industrial exports	0.41	1.41	0.36	2.15	−6.84	−2.11	0.50	0.07	1.40	1.59	−4.91	2.72
GDP/Employment	0.09	−0.13	0.09	0.39	0.19	−0.42	−0.29	−0.22	0.88	0.60	1.01	0.32

n.s. = Not significant.

Source: Chisari, Estache, and Romero 1997a.

ico. While the two state-owned Mexican airline companies were sold in 1988 and 1989, as a practical matter full sector deregulation did not take place until 1991. The reform was far reaching. Entry of a new airline is free from regulation. Airlines can freely add new routes and new flights on existing routes, and fares are practically free from regulation. On routes served by more than one airline or on regional routes where intermodal competition is strong, fares are totally free from regulation. On trunk routes served by only one airline, fares continue to be regulated; however carriers must simply notify the Secretary of Transport of their intention to raise prices. The Secretary must then decide whether to object; otherwise the fare increases go through. Table 1.16 shows some of the cumulative impact after three years of deregulation. It led to a rapid expansion of capacity, new entry, increased productivity, lower prices, and increased demand. However, as of 1995 the two privatized Mexican airlines, Aeromexico and Mexicana, experienced serious financial difficulties and the government took them over. As a result, the sector performance appears to have deteriorated,

with claims of cross subsidies and other anticompetitive behavior by those two airlines.

The extensive deregulation of port operations in Mexico and institutional changes in 1993 have had significant effects. Relative to 1993 and as of 1997, productivity increased by over 100 percent in most ports, capacity usage increased from 41 to 57 percent, tariff fees and levies declined by over 60 percent, ship waiting time was cut in half, and total tonnage moved increased by over 20 percent—all at an annual rate twice as high as that of the years prior to deregulation. The 1991 deregulation of federal trucking also led to significant improvements. Effective fees dropped by 50 percent, delivery

Table 1.16 Impact of Airline Deregulation in Mexico

	1992–1994 Percentage Change
Real Yields (Prices)	−29
Available Seat/Km	70
Traffic Revenue/Km	73

Source: Tandon 1995.

time was cut by over 30 percent, volume increased by a rate twice as high as before, and the fleet of trucks was almost fully renewed. Yet the gains have not been as great as they could have been because Mexican states, which have jurisdiction over interstate trucking, have not followed with similar deregulation efforts. Preliminary evidence of the 1997 railroad privatization/deregulation already indicates significant gains. These include a 30 percent reduction in delivery time, a 60 percent decrease in thefts, and an over 10 percent increase in volume.

The costs of various kinds of process regulations can also be substantial in developing countries due to inefficient bureaucracies and high levels of corruption. For example, customs administration in many countries tends to be plagued by inefficiency and corruption, imposing a high cost to traded goods.[21] Surveys in a number of developing countries indicate that managers spend between 10 and 30 percent of their time managing process regulation, and that imputed costs on produced goods or services due to process regulation are in the 5 to 15 percent range (World Bank 1997).

The available evidence underscores the significant gains developing countries can secure by further deregulating their economies and reducing the costs of process regulation. Estimates of those gains vary from country to country, but are at least a few percentage points of GDP (Chisari, Estache, and Romero 1997a; Guasch and Spiller 1997).

Additional anecdotal evidence of regulation and of its impact in developing countries is quite ample, as shown in boxes 1.3 and 1.4.

SUMMARY

The lesson here is not that regulation is bad, but that it is often grossly abused for political rather than for economic—welfare—objectives, and that it transfers surplus from consumers to producers. Even when political considerations are not a factor, regulation is a second-best solution, and one loaded with informational problems. The tradeoffs of regulation should be evaluated before regulation is set in place, and caution is

Box 1.3 Montevideo Taxicab Market

Entry restrictions in the taxicab market in Montevideo induced a market price of a taxicab license in 1990 of some US$60,000 (in 1990 dollars). While lower than the US$125,000 price in New York, lower Uruguayan per capita income means that the market value of the license as a proportion of per capita income is more than four times higher in Montevideo than in New York City. The regulation of the taxicab market has led to a scarcity of taxicabs, reflected in difficulty in hailing taxicabs in the downtown area and in long waits when requested by telephone, in high costs borne by consumers, and in capture and wasteful rent-seeking activity by the taxi-owners association.

Source: Guasch and Spiller 1997.

needed about the possible consequences of partial deregulation, a policy that is often considered. Partial deregulation tends to encourage firms to enter only the more profitable markets and to leave the less profitable ones to regulated firms.

The review of the literature on the costs and benefits of regulation demonstrates that it is possible to systematically explore the costs and benefits of regulatory activity using standard economic analysis. For a description of the analytical framework for cost-benefit analysis see figure 1.11. Moreover, this analysis can serve as a useful aid to policymakers (Arrow and others 1996). It also shows that regulation can have a significant adverse impact on economic growth and welfare. Specifically, regulation aimed at controlling prices and entry into markets that would otherwise be

Box 1.4 Municipal Regulation in Peru

In one municipality, companies are required by law to fumigate their factories once every year. The municipality has licensed only one firm as the official fumigator. While its prices are double that of other fumigation companies and its service is very poor, it is the only fumigator that can issue a certificate of compliance with the regulations.

Source: Guasch and Spiller 1997.

Figure 1.11 Cost-Benefit Analysis Framework for Regulation

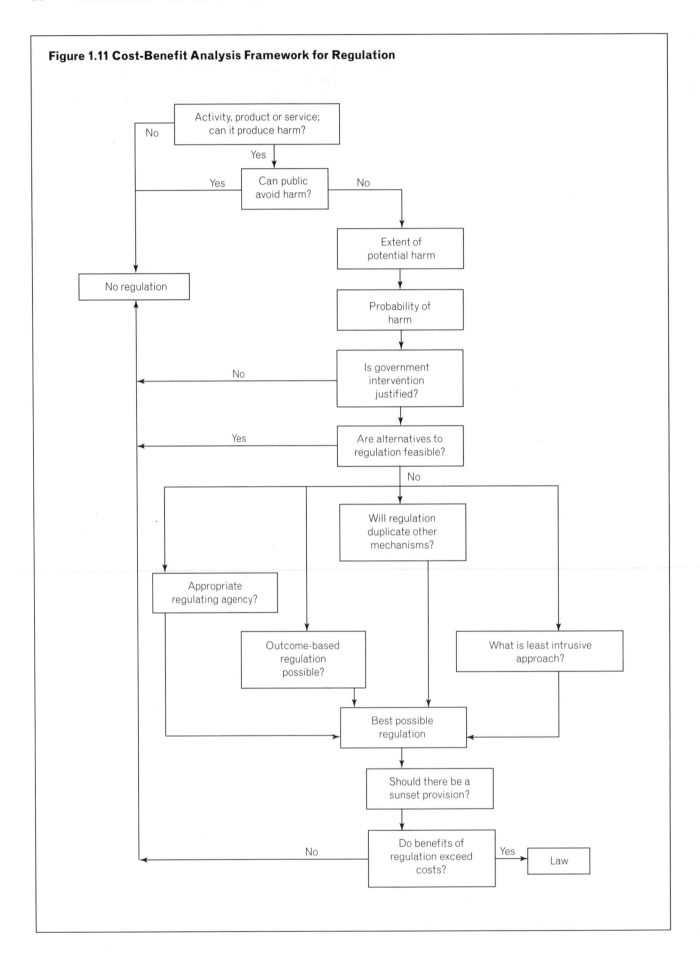

workably competitive is likely to reduce the average standard of living. In addition, process regulation that is unnecessary can impose a significant cost on the economy. Nonetheless, social regulations may have significant net benefits for the average consumer. At the same time, these regulations may not meet goals in an effective manner and in some cases may result in a net decline in living standards. This underscores the importance of doing economic analysis that will enhance the quality of regulations.

While this chapter has focused on the economic impact of regulations on the average individual and the entire economy, it is important to recognize that regulations may be needed in some cases to achieve other social goals. Indeed, some regulations may be desirable from a social point of view, even if they have an adverse impact on economic growth. For example, providing medical assistance and food for society's poor may not increase economic growth, but may be the correct policy for social and moral reasons. Similarly, helping to reduce discrimination may or may not increase economic growth, but it is a correct policy in principle. Even when such policies are justified for other reasons, their economic impact should be assessed so they can be implemented in the most effective manner.

Compared with budgets, regulations receive relatively little scrutiny. This is partly because politicians wish to hide the cost of regulation from citizens, and partly because it is more difficult to estimate the costs and benefits of regulation. Information on the economic impact of different approaches to regulation needs to be improved to enhance public decisionmaking. Fortunately, several countries are beginning to place more emphasis on developing a better information base on the costs and benefits of regulation (OECD 1995).[22]

There are several policies developing countries might consider adopting to improve their general approach to regulation. The recommendations here are purposely general. In that spirit, the first important point to recognize is that effective policies will differ across countries. The appropriate regulatory tool and framework will depend on several factors, including bureaucratic expertise, availability of resources, political constraints, and economic impact.

There is a general need, however, to enhance the capability to evaluate regulation at the local and national levels. This need is illustrated by the absence of even rudimentary data in several developed and developing countries on the impact of regulation. Even rough calculations of regulatory costs, such as the one completed for Canada, can be quite beneficial in developing a reform strategy. Countries should attempt to develop a "regulatory budget" that would show the economic impact of regulations. This budget could be published along with the government's fiscal budget. Such a capability will take time to develop.

Several jurisdictions, including some in developing countries, are putting procedures in place that would require a cost-benefit analysis for significant regulations. We believe this will have a constructive impact on public policy by providing better information and holding government officials and political leaders more accountable. In the short term, it is important for agencies charged with administering regulations to begin assembling crude cost and benefit data. For example, an agency could specify the rationale for a proposed regulation, the likely direct and indirect costs, a qualitative description of benefits, an assessment of other alternatives, including the status quo, and an explanation of why other alternatives were not selected if they are likely to be better for the average citizen.

Such analyses should not be overly burdensome. For "small" regulations, no analysis may be necessary. For regulations having potentially "large" economic impact, more resources should be devoted to evaluation. Ideally, such analyses should be both prospective and retrospective, so that analysts can learn how to improve their impact assessments. To get the process started, however, the emphasis should be on developing an information management system that is low cost and implementable. It is extremely important to get front-line agencies involved in the process so that they become more sensitive to the economywide impact of their proposals.

As administrative capabilities evolve, large regulations and regulatory reforms should be subjected to more thorough cost-benefit analyses. These analyses should be an important factor in decisionmaking. In the case of economic regulation, the burden of proof should be on those who wish to maintain it, since the case for most economic regulation is weak in terms of economic efficiency. In the case of social regulation, flexibility should be encouraged so that consumers and producers are able to innovate in response to regulations. Thus, for example, performance standards for meeting a pollution goal are generally preferred to standards that dictate the use of a particular technology. Of course, the amount of flexibility in a regulatory policy should be based, in part, on the ability of the administrative agency to effectively implement the policy (Hartman and Wheeler 1995).

While economic analysis can be helpful, its limitations need to be recognized. As noted earlier, the costs and benefits of regulatory policies are often quite uncertain. This uncertainty stems, in part, from a lack of analysis of specific policies. An important part, however, stems from a fundamental inability to predict how regulations will actually affect behavior. Regulations often have unexpected and perverse consequences (Ackerman and Hassler 1981). Thus, when regulating, one should proceed with extreme care and err on the side of less regulation, particularly when considering economic regulation.

Where there is no clear economic rationale for a regulatory policy, these policies should be removed. There are many policies involving licensing and price or quota intervention in developed and developing countries that do not serve the public interest (Huber and Thorne 1997; Guasch and Spiller 1997). Examples include applications for licenses and license renewals where the government's primary function is to transfer political favors to their preferred constituencies. Removal of such barriers may not be simple in many cases, and may involve making resource transfers to politically powerful constituencies.

A great deal more thought needs to be given to the design of regulatory frameworks. In some instances, even where deregulation is justified, partial deregulation may not lead to an improvement over the status quo. For example, removing price restrictions but retaining entry barriers could lead to inefficient pricing. Full deregulation can lead to problems with monopoly, unless great care is successfully taken in managing the transition to a deregulated environment. The point here is that the strategy for regulatory reform is critical to the effectiveness of the reform.

Another serious design issue relates to the bureaucratic problem of "tunnel vision," or the tendency of a single mission agency, such as health, education, or the environment to consider only its mandate. If an agency considers only its mandate, it will naturally tend to overstate the benefits of its program and understate the costs. As noted above, one way to address this problem is to require the agency to develop more data on the costs of specific regulatory proposals. A second way is to limit the agency's mandate. Other ways include sunset requirements that would limit an agency's authority to a fixed time period, unless renewed by a legislature; and having a central agency review and approve or disapprove proposed regulations. Such an agency should be designed so that it has some independence, and so that it is primarily concerned with the economywide impacts of regulations.

Finally, there is a natural tendency for regulators to write regulations that are unduly complicated. This complexity allows bureaucrats and lawyers to have more power. It also makes it difficult for average people to understand the implications of regulations. It is important to make regulations more transparent because greater transparency is likely to reduce corruption. Moreover, careful scrutiny of regulation, content, and constant benefits would diminish the likelihood of political capture by interest groups. Greater transparency is likely to increase the perceived legitimacy of the system. The move toward greater transparency will occur only as people begin to appreciate some of the hidden costs of regulation.

A few developing countries have begun to realize the benefits of reforming economic regulation, and clearly there is great potential for reform in many other developed and developing countries. Still, much remains to be done in the areas of utilities and social regulation. However, regulation is beginning to appear on policy agendas of developing countries due to both domestic pressure and pressure from interest groups. Thus, as developing countries begin to address these issues, and given their resource constraints, they need to think carefully about designing effective and efficient regulatory approaches.

The overall lesson is not that regulation is generally undesirable, but that it often has undesirable economic consequences, and that when desirable, its design, structure, and enforcement significantly matter. Moreover, these impacts result partly from political forces that lead to certain kinds of wealth redistribution (Stigler 1971a). While not denying such forces, we believe they can be mitigated by more sharply evaluating the consequences and tradeoffs involved in regulating before a regulatory policy is set in stone, and by carefully crafting its design, using economic principles and experience.

NOTES

1. This chapter draws extensively on Guasch and Hahn 1997.

2. In addition, regulators are becoming more constrained by the increased mobility of capital and labor (Lee and McKenzie 1991). If they choose to keep prices substantially above the costs of production, firms will consider moving to a more hospitable economic environment or find a way to bypass the system. One example is the state-sanctioned telephone monopoly in some countries. Increasingly, consumers and businesses are finding ways around these monopolies by making use of Internet services and services that provide long-distance calls more cheaply. This natural tendency to control for monopoly prices leads to increased pressure for deregulation and privatization.

3. For example, in 1993 U.S. cities incurred a cost of more than $3.6 billion to comply with the unfunded mandates of the Clean Water Act.

4. All estimates presented in this paper are expressed in the year dollars of the original study.

5. For example, e-mail will be more useful to a user if more people have e-mail addresses. On the subject of the economics of networks, see Klein 1996; Katz and Shapiro 1991; Liebowitz and Margolis 1994; and White 1997.

6. Hopkins' estimate for the total cost of regulation includes transfer costs. Total costs without transfer costs are $412 billion.

7. The OECD (1996a) also estimated that regulatory reform programs could increase GDP in the long run by as much as 3.5 percent in the United Kingdom and by as much as 6 percent in Japan, Germany, and France.

8. The incremental impact of regulation grew from a 1.1 percent annual reduction in multifactor productivity in 1974–75 to a 2.5 percent annual reduction in 1985–86.

9. In their assessment of the effects of regulations governing the transport of surface freight, Willig and Baumol (1987, p. 31) state that, "Various studies estimated, for example, that between 1950 and 1980, more than a billion dollars a year was wasted in transporting freight by truck rather than by rail. Another billion dollars a year was wasted in transporting freight on rail routes that were too long or were utilized with too little traffic density. Another $1.5 billion a year or more (in 1977 dollars) was wasted on unnecessary mileage traversed by empty cars, unnecessary demurrage time between car unloadings and loadings, and circuitous loaded routings."

10. For example, work-force reductions at American Airlines and United Airlines were 17 and 24 percent, respectively.

11. Under regulation, the 3.0 percent annual decline in unit costs for U.S. airlines was far below the 4.5 percent decline of non-U.S. airlines from 1970 to 1975. Following deregulation, from 1978 to 1983, costs of U.S. airlines fell by 3.3 percent, compared to 2.8 percent for non-U.S. airlines.

12. The authors estimate that consumers are gaining US$12.4 billion annually from lower fares under deregulation and US$10.3 billion from greater flight frequency. While increases in travel restrictions, travel time, load factors, and the number of connections have reduced consumer welfare, the annual gains to travelers are substantial.

13. For orders in excess of 10,000 shares, rates fell in excess of 50 percent.

14. In addition, the expenditures to obtain those licenses cost society between US$500 million and US$1 billion.

15. The delay in provision of cellular telephones was caused by regulatory indecision and the subsequent licensing procedure used by the FCC, which was in charge of cellular spectrum. The FCC could not decide whether to allow AT&T to provide cellular service alone or to allow non-AT&T companies to provide cellular services alone or to allow competition between the two groups. AT&T had invented cellular and argued, not surprisingly, because of significant economies of scale in spectrum usage, that only one cellular provider should be present in each service area. Potential entrants into cellular argued, not surprisingly, that cellular could provide competition to AT&T's landline local monopoly at some time in the future so that

AT&T should be barred from cellular. The FCC made decisions and subsequently reversed itself. Finally, in the early 1980s the FCC decided to allow two cellular providers in each service area. Cellular service began in Chicago and Los Angeles in 1983–84 and reached most other major U.S. cities by 1985 (Hausman and Tardiff 1996).

16. Franchise contract prices from generators to distributing companies have fallen by 21 percent in real terms, and those to direct industrial and commercial consumers have fallen by 18 percent in real terms.

17. For example, a 30 percent increase in electricity prices tends to raise the price of goods such as paper and pulp, metals, chemicals, and glass by roughly 2.5 percent.

18. This paragraph draws heavily on a 1995 *Wall Street Journal* article, "For Retailers, Red Tape Is Worse Abroad."

19. Comparable measures in the port of Guayaquil, Ecuador have decreased costs by 60 percent and increased productivity by 55 percent.

20. Mercosur is a free-trade area comprised of Argentina, Bolivia, Brazil, Chile, Paraguay, and Uruguay.

21. According to the Nigeria Manufacturers Association, permission to clear goods in that country has to go through twenty-seven stages and the process takes five to eight weeks (Nigeria Manufacturers Association 1996). These numbers are not uncommon in other developing countries.

22. Analyses, such as those contained in OECD (1995), can be helpful in assessing the strengths and weaknesses of different administrative approaches to regulation.

2 THE REGULATION OF UTILITIES

SINCE THE LATE 1980s developing countries have been massively privatizing or concessioning the provision of public services (utilities) for two reasons. The first reason is fiscal, since the urgent need for massive investment in those sectors to bring them up to modern standards of service and coverage cannot be fulfilled by the public sector. Macroeconomic stabilization objectives and the need to invest in the social sector restrict government ability to provide the needed funds in those sectors. The second reason is economic, induced by a better understanding of the role of the public and private sectors in utilities. It is now well under-

stood that the private sector can and is more than willing to effectively operate and invest in utilities. In addition, governments have come to terms with what the new role of the public sector should be: one of broad policy formulation and regulatory oversight, and not of ownership. It is also now well understood that not only does regulation matter, but that there is good regulation and bad regulation. That is, its design is critical to inducing efficient second-best sector performance.

Designing effective regulatory frameworks and enforcing them is not easy. The issue is highly complex and requires highly trained workers and a well-designed incentive structure. Most of this book is concerned with the design and enforcement of regulatory frameworks for

the utilities and transport sectors. This is complemented with an empirical evaluation of how existing regulation has fared, mostly in the Latin American and Caribbean region. That region has been in many senses a pioneer, and has taken the lead in privatization and regulation efforts.

THE CASE FOR THE REGULATION OF UTILITIES

Utilities generally have three distinctive features. First, they require technologies that are commonly considered to be specific, sunk investments; second, they display aspects of natural monopoly (economies of scale and scope in the physical provision of basic services, economies of scale in planning and managing the network,

network externalities, and advantages in raising capital, which are being gradually eroded by technological innovations); and third, their products are massively consumed, usually by captive customers with fairly inelastic demand. For example, an electricity company's assets have very little value in an alternative use, its network externalities and economies of density mean that multiple wires cannot be deployed economically on the same street, and its customers (a large proportion of the urban population) have an inelastic demand for electricity.

Other industries might exhibit some, but not all, of these characteristics. The steel industry, for example, has large sunk investments and little value in alternative uses, but the economies of scale and scope are trivial compared with the size of the market.[1] Furthermore, although everyone indirectly consumes steel products, few individuals pay attention to the price of steel. Consider, too, the newspaper industry, for which large economies of scale and scope clearly exist in urban areas. Increases in the speed of communication and the use of computer design have drastically amplified the newspaper industry's economies of scale, resulting in fewer newspapers per city but relatively stable readership. Although readers usually constitute a large portion of the population (at least of the voting population), newspapers are not utilities: despite the substantial amount of sector-specific human capital (for example, reporters whose principal contacts are with local politicians), the technology is increasingly generic and investments are transferable. Shutting down a newspaper and moving the printing presses, desks, computers, and so forth elsewhere has become more and more common. These features distinguish the newspaper from the electricity sector, whose features more closely resemble those of most utility subsectors (see box 2.1).

The abovementioned three features also distinguish the utility sector from the rest of the economy and are at the core of the contractual problems that have traditionally raised the need for governmental regulation of utilities (Goldberg 1976; Williamson 1988; Barzel 1989; North 1990; Baysan and Guasch 1993; Levy and Spiller

---

Box 2.1 Economic Features of the Electricity Sector

The following characteristics are relevant to the design of a new institutional environment for the electricity supply industry:
- Electricity is essential to most productive processes and is an element in final demand.
- Electricity cannot be stored.
- The electricity network has strong externalities.
- Investment in electricity cannot be divided and is specific.
- Close coordination is needed because supply and demand need to be balanced continually throughout the system.
- Economies of scale and scope are present.
- The network takes a long time to build.
- Both demand and supply fluctuate randomly (demand fluctuates by day and season and with variations in the weather, and power outages cannot be predicted).
- User electricity demand is highly inelastic to changes in price.
- To a large extent, it is a captive market.

Because electricity is essential and cannot be stored, power outages are costly, which encourages overinvestment in order to secure ample reserves. To ensure these reserves, high-voltage networks are constructed that provide the service economically and in fixed quality. Interconnection is possible only if the network is closely coordinated among the different generating plants, because actions by any one actor strongly affect the whole system.

The traditional response to these technological characteristics has been vertical and horizontal integration under state control (through ownership and regulation). Technological changes that took place during the 1980s allowed the introduction of a market approach to power supply. For instance, reduction in the optimal size of generation plants, together with the increase in the size of the market, have undermined the natural monopoly characteristic of this industry and allowed the introduction of competition and the unbundling of the sector.

1993; and Guasch and Marshall 1993). In the utility sector three types of contractual problems are particularly important: (a) problems between firms and the government, which distort the investment incentives of utility companies; (b) problems between firms and their customers, which result in the utility's exercise of market power; and (c) problems between governments and interest groups, which prompt governments to distort utility pricing for purposes of income distribution (cross-subsidization). Moreover, along with the standard distortionary and distributive effects of monopoly pricing, contractual problems affect the competitiveness of the overall economy. In today's global economies, competition and competitive prices are essential, particularly for the success of the export-led strategies pursued by most developing countries. The production of goods and services relies heavily on utility products as inputs. If their pricing is high or inefficient, the country is unnecessarily vulnerable to off-shore competition, which adversely affects overall growth and welfare. In an attempt to correct these problems, appropriate regulation provides the incentives for firms to invest at efficient levels, induces firms to price their services at second-best levels, creates the framework for productive efficiency, minimizes opportunities for cross-subsidization or for interest groups to lobby for inefficient policies, and significantly reduces the nation's vulnerability to off-shore competition.[2]

Finally, regulation is an issue not of decision theory but rather of game theory.[3] The regulatory outcome is obtained by the regulated company's strategic response to the regulatory structure. The regulations set the incentive structure and elicit a strategic response and behavior from the regulated company. The strategic component, or the interaction between the regulator and the regulated company (and other affected third parties), is what makes the regulatory process a game theory issue rather than a decision theory problem.

REGULATION AND COMMITMENT: CONTRACTUAL PROBLEMS BETWEEN FIRMS AND THE GOVERNMENT

Because a utility's assets are largely sunk and its customers constitute a large proportion of the population and are mostly captive and vocal, governments might have an incentive to expropriate the utility's quasi-rents.[4] This does not mean that the government takes over the operation of the company, but rather that it sets maximum prices for a utility's products that just compensate for its operating costs and the return on its nonspecific assets. These prices provide sufficient ex post incentives for the firm to operate, but not to invest at efficient levels.[5] Indeed, the expropriation of quasi-rents is more prevalent in Latin America than the direct takeover or expropriation of utilities without compensation.[6]

The expropriation of quasi-rents may be profitable for a government if the direct costs (loss of reputation vis-à-vis other utilities and lack of future investments by utilities) are lower than the short-term benefits (such as achieving reelection by reducing the price of utilities or by attacking the utility as a monopoly), and if the indirect institutional costs (such as disregarding the judiciary or bypassing traditional administrative procedures) are not too large. Thus, incentives for the expropriation of quasi-rents are expected to be largest in countries where (a) indirect institutional costs are low (for example, formal or informal governmental procedures or checks and balances are not required to make regulatory decisions, regulatory policy is centralized in the administration, or the judiciary does not have a tradition of reviewing or power to review administrative decisions); (b) direct costs are also small; and, perhaps more important, (c) the government's horizon is relatively short (for example, key constituencies must be satisfied before an election). When private utilities anticipate expropriation they will not undertake investment in the first place, and government direct intervention may then become the default mode of operation.

If the government wants to motivate private investment, it has to design an institutional arrangement that limits its own ability to behave opportunistically once a private utility has embarked on an investment program. Such an arrangement is a regulatory framework that stipulates price-setting procedures, impartial conflict resolution (arbitration or judicial review), investment policies, and so forth. Unless such a regulatory framework is credible, however, investments will not be undertaken or, if undertaken, will not be efficient.[7]

Credible regulation solves a key contractual problem between the government and the utilities because it restrains the government's opportunistic expropriation of a utility's quasi-rents. As such, it is needed for investment to be undertaken (even publicly owned companies will not invest if their quasi-rents can be taken over by the government; see Goldberg 1976 for one of the first treatments of this problem; see also Williamson 1976). This does not mean that the utility will necessarily receive assurances of some specific rate of return or that it will receive exclusive licenses.[8] In some countries, however, such guarantees may be the only way to limit the government's discretionary power and to reassure private investors.

REGULATION AND MARKET POWER: CONTRACTUAL PROBLEMS BETWEEN FIRMS AND CUSTOMERS

Contractual problems between firms and their customers, or the asymmetric bargaining power between the sole firm supplying the service and its customers, provide what is usually called the "market failure" rationale for regulation. For example, if an electricity distribution company is unable to enter efficient long-term contracts with residential customers, social losses (of either real or deadweight resources) occur as a result of the exercise of market power or inefficient investment policies (which encourage duplicate investment or discourage investment). Regulations could at least partially alleviate these problems.

Contracting between firms and customers may fail either because the sector is not contestable, which results in the exercise of market power, or because the sector is contestable but not "sustainable," which implies inefficient investment policies (see Baumol, Panzar, and Willig 1982 in general, and chapter 16 in particular, for an insider view of the policy implications of this literature).[9] Because solving this contractual problem would benefit both consumers and the firm, a demand for regulation arises.

REGULATION AND CROSS-SUBSIDIES: CONTRACTUAL PROBLEMS BETWEEN INTEREST GROUPS AND THE GOVERNMENT

Contractual problems between interest groups and the government are behind the regulations that govern the creation or extraction of rents. Consider a politically powerful interest group that is demanding a cash transfer from the government. The contractual problem can be solved if the government is able to ensure that cash transfers are restricted to members of that interest group. In most circumstances, however, efficient cash transfers are politically difficult to implement, and the government introduces distortive regulations in order to transfer rents to a particular interest group (Stigler 1971a).

An interest group that can convince the state to use the power of coercion to the group's benefit can improve its own well-being. The state can benefit, as well, because the policy can increase the political support of the well-organized group that benefits. Individual producers, which are typically few and well organized, stand to gain a great deal from regulation, whereas consumers, who number in the millions and are poorly organized, stand to lose. However, each individual consumer stands to lose only a small amount, which explains the relatively weak incentive for them to voice complaints and organize. Regulation can create harm that, although large in the aggregate, is small for each individual consumer.

Regulation can be an effective tool for redistributing wealth among population groups. For example, textile import restrictions limit U.S. consumer access to inexpensive clothing while allowing domestic producers to charge higher prices. Without these import quotas, consumers would pay at least $1 billion less for the same apparel. When transfers are that large, beneficiaries will be willing to expend considerable resources on lobbying and other activities that enhance their earnings and protect these transfers. This was extensively illustrated in the previous chapter. Other examples are the California energy bill described in box 2.2, and the licens-

Box 2.2 California's Energy Bill

In April 1994 California decided to let large companies pick their own electricity suppliers, breaking up an eighty-two-year monopoly. All other customers, even individual households, were to be allowed the same choice by 2002. About two dozen states in the United States started down the same path. But just thirteen months later, California regulators disavowed their decision, bowing to a torrent of criticism that their pro-competitive ruling could wreck the state's three largest utilities, shift costs to small power users, and harm the environment. The much-heralded revolution in the California power business died.

Meanwhile, California is still paying electricity rates that are twice as high as Oregon's and 50 percent higher than the national average. At issue are the "stranded costs" incurred by the utilities in the late 1960s and early 1970s, when California's utilities built big nuclear plants that at the time appeared to be economical. In the 1980s a federal law aimed at creating an alternative-energy industry forced many utilities into long-term power supply contracts with nonutility generating companies.

Both initiatives turned into financial disasters. Industrywide, the cost of these commitments over and above market prices for power—the utilities' "stranded costs"—may total $135 billion according to a Moody's Investor Service report. In this round, the utilities shareholders won at the expense of the ratepayers, who will have to continue paying for those stranded costs.

Soon after the initial decision, the utility companies launched a massive lobbying campaign to attack the free market plan and alternative-energy contracts, and some pushed for a power pool scheme. One company alone spent $440,000 in three months to lobby regulators and lawmakers. As expected, the alternative being considered, the "English model," is not necessarily a panacea for the ratepayers. It requires the companies to pool their electricity, then dispatch it under a coordinated, highly regulated system. However, the efficiency and welfare effects of that system are questionable, as the British experience indicates. The pool system raised British electricity bills. The price of power coming from the pool shot up 46 percent between March 1990, when the pool was launched, and January 1994. The reason: With few large suppliers in England and Wales, market prices are highly subject to manipulation and collusion. The same would appear to be true in California.

Source: Wall Street Journal, November 12, 1995.

ing of taxicabs. The restrictions on entry raised the value of a taxicab license in the secondary market to more than $200,000 in New York City as of 1993, and to $32,000 in Boston as of the mid-1980s (all dollars are U.S. dollars). In cities that have relaxed the restrictions on entry, the price of a license is considerably lower. In Portland, San Diego, and Seattle a license costs between $1,000 and $5,000 (Frankema and Pautler 1984; Viscusi, Vernon, and Harrington 1995, table 10.4).

Although the extraction of rents is sometimes the only reason for regulating a particular sector, governments are sometimes motivated by more than efficiency. Thus, some regulatory institutions arise in response to conflicts over distribution among private interest groups, while others arise in response to contractual problems between private enterprises and government agencies. In either case, a regulatory institution created to respond to one kind of problem can, over time, serve an entirely different purpose.

Regulations that solve contractual failures may take many forms, depending on the nature of the sector and the country's legal, political, and institutional history. To be credible, however, the regulatory mechanism must take into account the potential for regulatory shortcomings.

The nature of the demand for regulation and the institutional characteristics of a country naturally affect the type of regulatory framework that is implemented. Mismatches between the two will produce "unintended" effects,[10] such as regulatory failure, inefficiencies, and reduced productivity growth.

Regulatory Failure

Regulations are implemented not by omniscient machines but by government entities subject to informational, political, and institutional constraints. The same information and enforcement problems that cause private contractual failures may also hamper the implementation of regulatory policies, causing regulatory failure.

Modern regulation theory suggests that regulatory bodies have less information about technology, costs, and, to some extent, demand, than the firms they regulate (see Baron 1988 for a survey of the modern agency theory approach to regulation). Efficient regulatory systems (that is, second-best efficiency given the regulatory objectives) must design policies that overcome these informational disadvantages. Such policies require substantial regulatory discretion and substantial administrative capabilities and sophistication. But regulatory discretion can exacerbate the contractual problems, such as a government's opportunistic behavior, that were at the core of the initial demand for regulation. Thus, if a country's institutions do not limit administrative discretion, designing a regulatory system that grants substantial discretion to the regulator as a means of overcoming informational disadvantages may be self-defeating because this same discretion may be used opportunistically to extract a company's quasi-rents. (This seems to have been the case with Jamaica's Public Utility Commission from 1967 to 1975 [Spiller and Sampson 1993].)

If an industry is characterized by substantial price and cost volatility, a second-best regulatory framework will also require sophisticated administrative capabilities. If the country lacks such capabilities, implementing a sophisticated regulatory framework may fail either because the utility manipulates the process or because regulators do not follow the specified process and methods.[11]

Regulatory failure reflects a mismatch between regulatory institutions and a country's institutional characteristics. Avoiding regulatory failure, then, may require introducing substantial rigidities in decisionmaking. If the regulatory framework engenders regulatory failure, then public ownership may become the default institutional arrangement, because private firms will be unlikely to invest. The resulting inefficiencies can be significant. (For discussions of how the U.S. Administrative Procedures Act produces rigidities and delays in the process that seeks to

control the regulatory agency, see McCubbins, Noll, and Weingast 1987 and 1990; for analyses of the role of judicial review in controlling agency discretion, see Spiller 1990).

Interest Group Politics

A second unintended regulatory effect results from the prevalence of interest group politics. Consider a country where traditional checks on an administration's decisionmaking are weak, either because the executive is responsible for interpreting legislation (as in Argentina, Bolivia, and Uruguay) or because electoral laws and legislative institutions grant a single party control over both the executive and the legislature (as in Mexico, or in Jamaica, which has a parliamentary system with single-party voting districts). In such cases, granting the administration substantive discretion over regulatory outcomes could allow interest group politics to overtake the regulatory process. Interest groups seek not only to obtain cross-subsidization but also to block the entrance of new producers or products, adversely affecting overall welfare.

The capture hypothesis argues that a vote-maximizing government has an interest in allowing regulatory programs to reflect the will of powerful interest groups. A particular concern is that groups in a regulated industry will influence the regulatory environment, hence "capturing" the process. One way to test whether a regulatory package has been captured is to compare the stock market returns (or earnings if the company is not listed on the stock exchange) for a regulated company with the returns for a comparable sample of firms not affected by the regulation. Abnormally high returns could indicate regulatory capture if they can be statistically associated with changes in the regulatory environment.

For example, data is available for British Telecom (BT) for the period 1984–94. After privatization, BT's average daily returns were not significantly higher than the market index. This does not mean that BT did not attempt to capture the regulatory process—simply that it did not do so. The regulating body (Oftel) set low interconnection charges for BT's competitor, and this ruling showed up as a robust negative. Furthermore, investors appear to have gained some confidence from negotiations between Oftel and BT in which Oftel agreed not to ask the Monopolies and Mergers Commission to investigate BT. Overall, BT appears to have had normal market returns, indicating that it did not capture the regulatory process. A detailed review of events revealed no clear pattern favoring or opposing's commercial interests. Moreover, because BT was not pushed below a normal return, there is also no evidence that consumer interests captured the regulatory process. Oftel seems to have carried out its regulatory function effectively. Similar conclusions cannot be drawn from many Latin American utilities because after their participation their rates of return appear, at first glance, to be abnormally high. Finally, the "unintended" effect of regulation on productivity growth has already been extensively discussed in the previous chapter.

Institutions and Regulatory Discretion

In trying to understand the ability of different countries to commit themselves to particular regulatory processes and institutions, it is useful to look at regulation as an "engineering" problem. Regulatory design has two levels: basic engineering and detail engineering. Basic engineering comprises the mechanisms through which societies place substantive or procedural constraints on regulatory discretion and resolve conflicts that arise in relation to these constraints. (Such constraints on regulatory decisionmaking have been called "contractual governance institutions"; see Williamson 1985, p. 35; and Levy and Spiller 1993). Detail engineering comprises the rules governing utility pricing, direct or cross-subsidies, entry, interconnection, and so forth. While basic and detail engineering are endogenous policy variables, the sets of choices are constrained. Basic engineering choices are constrained by the nature of the contractual problems discussed above and by the institutional characteristics of a particular country. Similarly, detail engineering choices are constrained both by a country's institutional characteristics and by

its basic engineering choices. Although most policy work on regulation has focused on detail rather than on basic engineering, regulatory impact, whether positive or negative, comes to the forefront only when basic engineering has been designed properly.[12]

Institutional and Administrative Endowment and Basic Regulatory Engineering

Following North and others, we define the institutional endowment of a nation as comprised of at least five elements:

1. The country's legislative and executive institutions, which include the formal mechanisms for appointing legislators and decisionmakers, for creating laws and regulations (apart from judicial decisionmaking), for implementing these laws, and for determining the relations between the legislature and the executive.
2. The country's judicial institutions, which are the formal mechanisms for appointing judges and determining the internal structure of the judiciary and for impartially resolving disputes among private parties or between private parties and the state.
3. Informal but broadly accepted norms that tacitly constrain the action of individuals or government.
4. The administrative capabilities of the nation.
5. The character of society's contending social interests and the balance between them, including the role of ideology (Levy and Spiller 1993; North 1990).

The extent and characteristics of a country's institutional and administrative endowments limit the choice of regulatory instruments and institutions. To be effective, regulation has to match the sector's and the country's endowments and institutional characteristics. Although economists have devoted much effort to sector-specific issues (as witnessed by the features described in box 2.1), country-specific issues traditionally have received much less attention. Two features of many developing countries are the discretionary power of the executive and centralized decision-making.[13] Thus, to promote private sector participation in the utility sector, for example, developing-country governments may have to design regulatory processes that restrain their discretionary power so investors can be confident that the rules of the game will remain stable and not subject to arbitrary or opportunistic changes by the government.

The main challenge is to design regulatory processes that, while limiting discretion, are compatible with the country's institutional structure of government and with the legal and administrative traditions of the country. For example, the antitrust laws in Colombia, Mexico, and Peru use independent courts (in Colombia) and specialized courts (in Peru) to enforce innovative checks and balances of a nature not observed before. (See Baysan and Guasch 1993 for a discussion of antitrust enforcement in Colombia and Peru, respectively; see Guasch 1994 for an overview of Latin American enforcement policies). Similarly, Chile's approach to regulating telecommunications and electricity, and enforcing antitrust legislation, is based on checks and balances (the result of very specific legislation) that require sophisticated use of the court system, including multiple decisionmakers. (For a discussion of electricity regulation, see Spiller 1993; for a discussion of telecommunications regulation and antitrust, see Galal 1994.) In Jamaica the telecommunications regulatory framework limits discretion through contract law rather than administrative law, using the courts to protect contracts and property (Spiller and Sampson 1993).

These innovations were all designed with the nature of each country's political institutions in mind. They are intended to restrain the government rather than to grant it wide regulatory powers. When making regulatory decisions, governments should consider and extract lessons from the experience gained in diverse countries with the ways in which distinct forms of regulation—and regulation in general—affect productivity.

In most scenarios, regulatory instruments may have to be relatively inflexible to provide regulatory credibility. Moreover, the menu of commitment instruments is larger in countries where the decisionmaking process is highly decentralized than in countries where it is highly centralized. The following discussion highlights the relation between a country's institutions and the development of a credible regulatory system.

Credible regulatory structures are easier to implement in countries where decisionmaking is naturally decentralized. In countries where decisionmaking is heavily centralized, achieving regulatory credibility is possible only if structures are relatively rigid. To show the difficulties in building commitment, consider the case of the United States, where decisionmaking is naturally decentralized in a presidential system, with a legislature composed of two chambers elected under different rules and at different times and with electoral rules that tie legislators to their local constituencies and limit, but do not eliminate, the power of political parties. Finally, the U.S. judiciary is reasonably well respected by the population, and its decisions are widely accepted and even implemented. In such a system, regulatory commitment can be introduced in different forms: It can be achieved, for example, by writing a specific piece of legislation and delegating its implementation to a regulatory agency, whose decisions, on both substance and process, can be reviewed by the judiciary. Alternatively, regulatory credibility can be achieved by hardwiring the decisionmaking process to safeguard the interests of the regulated companies against administrative expropriation (see McCubbins, Noll, and Weingast 1987; on hardwiring, see also Hamilton and Schroeder 1994; and Macey 1992). Here again, the courts may review the agency's decisions, both on substance and on procedure. Finally, regulatory credibility can be achieved by granting the utility a license specifying the regulatory process through which its prices will be determined. Deviations from the license can be challenged relatively easily through the courts. These three regulatory instruments have different implications for both regulatory credibility and for flexibility, and they are the subject of chapters 3 and 4.

The design and effective operation of a regulatory framework and enforcing agency are rather complex, and although some aspects are clear-cut, others involve tradeoffs. Box 2.3 provides a checklist of the main issues to be considered in that design, and discussion is provided in the ensuing chapters.

NOTES

1. This may not be so in developing countries where the production of steel is protected, because only a few steel mills are producing for a relatively small local market.

2. A constraint that prevents the attainment of at least one optimal condition also makes other optimal conditions undesirable; a second-best solution then becomes the preferred choice.

3. Game theory can be described as interactive decision theory. In game theory the behavior of each decisionmaker affects the choices of others. In decision theory decisionmakers make choices in isolation.

4. Quasi-rents are the portion of operating returns that exceed what a company could obtain if it devoted its capital to alternative uses. Because the assets of utilities are largely sunk, quasi-rents may equal the return on capital.

5. The company will be willing to continue operating because its return from operating will exceed its return

from shutting down and deploying its assets elsewhere. However, the firm will have very little incentive to invest in new capital because it will not be able to obtain a return. Although it is feasible to conceive of loan financing for new investments, failure to repay would bring the company to bankruptcy and eventual liquidation. Note that bankruptcy does not mean that the company shuts down. Because the assets are specific, bankruptcy implies a change of ownership from stockholders to creditors. Creditors would have the same incentives to operate as does the firm, and they would be willing to operate even if quasi-rents were expropriated. Loan financing would not be feasible here either.

6. Consider, for example, the case of the Montevideo Gas Company (MGC). Throughout the 1950s and 1960s MGC, which was owned and operated by a British company, was not allowed to raise prices. During a period of rapid inflation in the 1960s, it went bankrupt and was taken over by the government. Compare this example with the Perón administration's takeover of International Telephone and Telegraph's (ITT's) majority holdings in the Unión Telefónica del RPo de la Plata (UTRP). (UTRP was the main provider of telephones in the Buenos Aires region.) In 1946 the Argentine government paid $95 million for ITT's holdings ($623 million in 1992 prices). Given UTRP's 457,800 lines, this translates into $1,360 per line (in 1992 prices, capital equipment producer prices deflator). Because the marginal cost of a line in a large city today is approximately $650, the price paid by the Perón adminis-

---

Box 2.3 The Twenty-One Basic Regulatory Design Questions

1. What is the true extent of natural monopoly elements in the sector?
2. Is vertical or geographical unbundling a desirable policy for the sector?
3. What is the best way to signal a credible commitment to a regulatory regime?
4. Should there be a single regulator or a commission?
5. Should the regulatory entity be "independent" of government?
6. How much discretion should be granted to the regulator?
7. How should regulators be chosen and how should their service period be staggered?
8. How should responsibility be divided among the regulatory entity and other government authorities?
9. What should be the interplay between the regulatory and antitrust agency to oversee the functions and operations of the sector?
10. Should exclusivity rights be granted, and if so for how long?
11. Which kind of guarantees should be offered, if any?
12. What activities or parameters should be regulated?
13. What are the control mechanisms for price and quality?
14. How should the initial values be chosen for the prices or parameters to be regulated, and what should be the criteria for access (to the network) prices?
15. How are regulatory rules created and enforced?
16. How should concessions and the transfer process be designed?
17. What is the best way to dissuade frivolous renegotiation and what should be the conditions for renegotiation?
18. How should conflicts be resolved?
19. How can transparency be built into the regulatory process?
20. What information is needed to best assist the regulator and how should it be acquired?
21. Who "regulates the regulator"?

tration does not seem unusually low (Hill and Abdalla 1993).

7. In this sense it is not surprising that private telecommunications operators have rushed to develop cellular rather than fixed-link networks in Eastern European countries. Although cellular networks have higher long-run costs than do fixed-link networks and are sometimes of inferior quality, the magnitude of investment in specific assets is much smaller than it is in fixed-link networks. Furthermore, many of the specific investments in cellular telephony are undertaken by the customers themselves (who purchase the handset).

8. Indeed, Colombian regulation of value-added networks specifically stipulates that the government cannot set prices; neither does it allow exclusivity provisions. Regulation here means total *lack* of government discretion.

9. A contestable market is one in which *potential* entrants, as well as actual rivals, compete with existing firms. The primary requirement for contestability is free entry to and exit from the market. The irretrievable sunk costs common in utility companies frequently impede entry.

10. We use quotation marks because it is uncertain whether the persons who set up a regulatory framework were naïve in not foreseeing the potential effects, or whether the unintended effects were at the core of the demand for regulation.

11. The regulatory processes for Chile's electricity and telecommunications sectors are some of the most sophisticated in the developing countries. Every five years regulators must develop a price scheme that provides a standardized company with a "fair" return and sets maximum regulated prices close to long-run marginal costs. The implementation of such a regulatory process in a country with very few administrators and lawyers versed in economics could result in wildly different outcomes, depending on the nature of the country's institutions. On the one hand, regulators could decide not to follow the regulatory procedures and instead design their own. On the other hand, regulators could follow the regulatory process, which is being completely manipulated by the utility.

12. Commenting on the interaction between technology (institutions), governance (basic engineering), and price (detail engineering), Williamson (1985, p. 36) says that, "In as much as price and governance are linked, parties to a contract should not expect to have their cake (low price) and eat it too (no safeguard)."

13. Indeed, Weingast (1992, p. 1) claims that such discretionary powers and centralized decisionmaking lie behind the lack of economic development of many countries. He states, "Thriving markets require not only the appropriate system of property rights and a law of contracts, but a secure political foundation that places strong limits on the ability of the state to confiscate wealth."

3

CREATING THE
BASIC ENGINEERING
OF REGULATION

THREE COMPLEMENTARY MECHANISMS must be in place for basic

engineering to provide regulatory stability and credibility. First, substantive restraints on regu-

latory discretion must be embedded in the regulatory framework; second, formal or informal

constraints must limit the ability of the executive branch to change the regulatory framework

itself; and third, institutions must enforce those substantive or procedural constraints.

Assume, for example, that the regulation is institutionalized through passage of a general

piece of legislation, like Jamaica's Public Utilities Act of 1966, which set up a public utility

commission similar to that of the United States. The legislation does not specify procedures that the regulator has to follow or the criteria that the regulation must satisfy to be "legal." In this case, the basic engineering fails to satisfy the first criterion of stability because it is not embedded in the regulatory framework. Another instance might be a country whose legislative institutions and fragmented political parties make it difficult to pass new legislation, as is the case in Bolivia, Chile, Colombia, or Uruguay. Basic engineering under such circumstances would satisfy the second criterion of regulatory stability because the executive branch has limited ability to change the regulatory framework. In yet another situation, the country's judiciary is an independent entity, able to enforce limits on administrative

discretion and able to determine that presidential decrees violate the law or the constitution and are therefore illegal, as in Colombia. Basic engineering in this case would satisfy the third test of regulatory stability, as well. However, the choice of basic engineering could still be flawed if the administration exercises almost total discretion over regulatory policy. Further, the presence of institutions that make new legislation difficult to enact, (such as a multiplicity of parties, none of which has a clear majority in congress), also implies that regulatory policy could be altered concurrent with changes in government. Under such circumstances, basic regulatory engineering would fail to provide regulatory stability and would provide poor investment incentives to utilities.

THE CHOICE OF BASIC REGULATORY INSTRUMENTS

The four types of basic regulatory instruments are specific legislation, presidential decrees, contracts, and administrative procedures. Clearly there is also a fifth choice—a composite or mixture of some of the four types—and indeed some countries have chosen the composite. The choice and level of commitment depend on the country's institutional endowments. Each instrument represents a different level of credibility and signals a different level of commitment to the regulatory structure.

Specific Legislation

Consider, first, the use of specific legislation as a way to restrain regulatory discretion. Several countries have enacted specific pieces of legislation to provide basic engineering. Compare two pieces of U.S. legislation: the 1935 Federal Communications Act and the 1990 amendments to the Clean Air Act. The 1935 Federal Communications Act, which is still in effect, was developed to regulate monopolies, although the Federal Communications Commission (FCC) currently regulates competitive industries. The act did not guide the FCC's regulatory actions, but rather mandated that the FCC should undertake actions to improve the welfare of U.S. citizens. It granted the FCC total discretion in this mandate, imposed only the limits of administrative law, and provided for continual congressional supervision of the agency. The 1990 amendments to the Clean Air Act specified precise actions that the Environmental Protection Agency (EPA) had to undertake. In particular, the amendments ordered the EPA to institutionalize a market for pollution permits and determine how many pollution permits each electrical utility in the nation could have, based on a generic determination (with 1985 levels as the baseline) and a long list of exemptions. Further, failure of the EPA to implement the market for permits could be contested in court as failure to comply with the law.

More specifically, consider the conditions for achieving regulatory credibility through the

different instruments. Let us start with a U.S.-style presidential system. To simplify the analysis we make drastic assumptions about the organization of such a system. These assumptions imply that we can represent the preferences of both chambers of Congress and of the president through multidimensional ideal points, as in figure 3.1. (Although this is a simplified version of the U.S. system, a more complex framework is not needed to understand the main issue.) Figure 3.1 assumes that there are three veto players: the House (H), the Senate (S), and the president (P).

Very specific legislation is equivalent to Congress and the president agreeing on a particular policy, call it x_0, and writing such policy into law. To be an equilibrium, this policy has to be inside the contract set of H, P, and S. Call this set $W(H, S, P)$. The agency's latitude in implementing the policy is minimal, but it may nevertheless deviate from x_0. Such deviations may or may not be checked by the courts. Even if we abstain from the courts' preferences on outcomes, the courts may not uphold x_0 under all circumstances. Assume, as in figure 3.1, that x_0 is initially inside $W(H, S, P)$ but, because of electoral changes, becomes outside the new contract set depicted as $W(H', S', P')$. Now x_0 is no longer an equilibrium. Indeed, if the agency implements x_1, a court knowing that x_1 could come out of the legislative process may not reverse the agency. Furthermore, reversing the agency will trigger new legislation, because by being outside $W(.)$, x_0 is no longer an equilibrium.

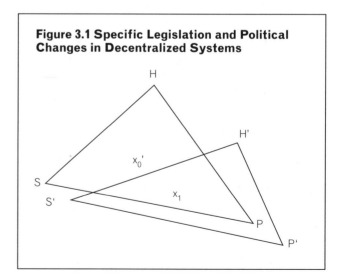

Figure 3.1 Specific Legislation and Political Changes in Decentralized Systems

Thus, specific legislation may provide commitment insofar as the electoral system is expected to return to Congress and to the presidency politicians who are so divided in their preferences that changes in membership should not drastically affect the probability that the initial legislation will remain inside the new $W(.)$. In other words, specific legislation can provide regulatory commitment if the set $W(.)$ is large. Consider, for example, figure 3.2, which depicts two $W(.)$ sets, one linking ideal points H, S, and P—$W(H, S, P)$—and another, wider set, linking ideal points H_w, S_w, and P_w—$W(H_w, S_w, P_w)$. The initial status quo, x_0, is in both sets. Assume, now, that a given change in public preferences implies a shift of a given magnitude in all three main veto players. Now the relevant $W(.)$ sets are $W(H', S', P')$ and $W(H'_w, S'_w, P'_w)$. Assume also that the change in political preference moves all politicians in the same general direction, so that the change does not affect the size of each of the $W(.)$ sets. With a larger $W(.)$ set, a given change in preference has a smaller probability that the initial status quo will be left outside the new $W(.)$ set.

This discussion implies that analytical emphasis should be placed on the set of conditions that, for a given preference structure, magnifies the set $W(.)$. Consider, first, electoral rules for the different houses of the legislature. Often, as in the state assemblies in the United States, both chambers are elected with essentially the same electoral rules. In such cases, S and H will

be close to one another in the policy space. This type of electoral rule creates a legislature that can be described as "false" bicameral. Figure 3.3 shows that such closeness in policy space reduces the set $W(.)$ and that an electoral change has a higher probability of bringing x_0 outside the new $W(.)$ set, eliminating the credibility of the regulatory structure. (For an interesting public choice perspective on bicameralism, see Levmore 1992.)

Consider, now, parliamentary systems, even those with two houses. Usually the government requires support only from a single chamber. (For an excellent comparative discussion of the virtues of different presidential and parliamentary systems, see Shugart and Carey 1992.) It is reasonable to assume that the executive is located close to the lower house. In figure 3.4, E represents the executive and is assumed to reflect the preferences of the house. $W(.)$ now resembles a contract curve between the executive and the senate. If, as is the case in most bicameral parliamentary systems, the upper house has restricted legislative powers, then the outcome of a bargaining process between E and S will be very close to E and H. As a consequence, even minor changes in political preferences will imply that the initial status quo x_0 is untenable.

This discussion has important implications for the use of specific legislation to provide regulatory commitment. Indeed, specific legislation will not provide regulatory credibility in traditional parliamentary systems and should not be

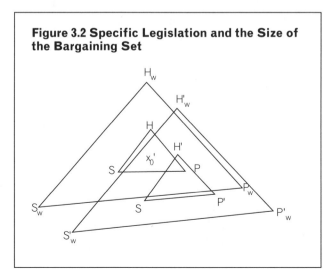

Figure 3.2 Specific Legislation and the Size of the Bargaining Set

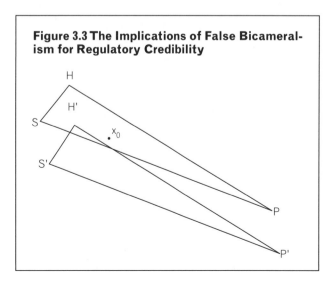

Figure 3.3 The Implications of False Bicameralism for Regulatory Credibility

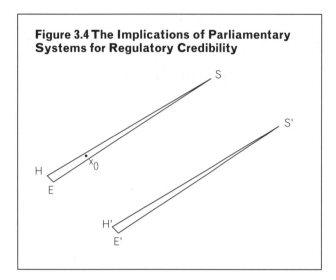

Figure 3.4 The Implications of Parliamentary Systems for Regulatory Credibility

used in those instances. Instead, specific legislation can be used to provide credibility only in systems with substantial division of powers. This raises a major question of implementability: Because legislative specificity is hard to implement in a legislature with substantial division of powers—after all, the status quo may well be inside the set $W(.)$, preventing legislative action—under what conditions can legislative specificity be implemented in a divided polity? One possibility involves transitory unified governments. Unified governments sensing that future elections will bring about a wider $W(.)$ may legislate extremely specific policies that will, most probably, bind future governments. Indeed, this was the case in both Argentina and Chile.

Specific legislation as a basic engineering choice satisfies the first requirement for regulatory stability (that substantive restraints on regulatory discretion be embedded in the regulatory framework). Whether it also satisfies the second and third requirements depends, however, on the nature of the country's institutional endowments. If the legislative institutions make it easy to pass new laws, then the second requirement for regulatory stability, (that formal or informal constraints limit the executive's ability to alter an established regulatory framework), may fail, because the executive could always upset the regulatory understanding by passing new legislation.[1] Thus, unless widely accepted norms prohibit opportunistic changes in the law, specific legislation does not satisfy the second require-

ment for regulatory stability. A second instance where specific legislation may not be a sound basic engineering choice is where the judiciary is not truly independent, and therefore is not capable of restraining the executive. In this case, the executive could deviate from the direct instructions of the law, without triggering a legal challenge. Specific legislation in this case will not satisfy the third requirement for regulatory stability (that institutions be capable of enforcing substantive constraints). To strengthen the power of specific legislation as a basic engineering choice, the important elements of regulation may be incorporated into the constitution, giving them greater stability even where it is otherwise easy to overturn legislation not covered in the constitution. That perhaps is the greatest signal of commitment.

To summarize, specific legislation may serve as a basic engineering choice in countries where legislative action is costly and where the judiciary is relatively independent from the executive. In such countries, however, passing the initial legislation will require an unusual level of legislative consensus, because legislation with a high degree of specificity will be more difficult to pass than a general piece of legislation.[2]

Presidential Decrees

A particularly popular regulatory tool in Latin America is the presidential decree. There are two basic types of presidential decrees. The most common is simply an administrative determination. Latin American countries in general have yet to develop a tradition of a "fourth" administrative branch, as in the United States. Thus, administrative determinations are usually ministerial decisions that take the form of a presidential decree. Such decrees are commonly modified or replaced by other decrees as time passes. For example, Bolivia's electricity code, which stipulates how tariffs are to be set for all electric utilities, is based on a 1968 presidential decree (*decreto supremo*). This decree can be modified, in turn, by another *decreto supremo* (as was done in Argentina's telecommunications regulatory framework).

The second most common type of presidential decree exists in the "regulation" or "instrumentation" of legislation. Most legislation in Latin American countries is relatively general, and implemented by a "regulatory" presidential decree. In effect, the regulatory agency is left to interpret a particular law. Courts seldom contest these decrees, except when the decree clearly violates a direct stipulation of the law. "Regulatory" decrees, however, cannot easily be replaced by another presidential decree, but they may be reinterpreted or further "regulated" (totally replacing them may require new legislation). The potential for further regulation opens the door for future administrations to distort or amend the initial understanding. Regulatory frameworks introduced through presidential decrees may, therefore, fail the second requirement for regulatory stability (that formal or informal constraints limit the ability of the executive branch to change the regulatory framework).

Contracts

Because the basic contractual problem in utilities is related to the inability of governments to commit themselves to a regulatory framework once it has been put in place, several countries have embedded the regulatory framework in formal contracts. These contracts take the form of operating licenses that specify the regulatory framework in which the firms operate. The license stipulates the regulatory process to be applied, and if the government deviates from that process, the courts step in. In parliamentary systems the use of contracts to regulate is innovative because courts uphold contracts but do not restrain regulators in administrative decisions.

Consider the example of British utilities. British utilities are, in general, regulated by different sorts of price caps. These price caps are embedded in each company's license rather than in an agency decision or piece of legislation (indeed, the enabling laws in the United Kingdom are silent about pricing schemes). The advantage of regulatory frameworks instituted through licenses is that, because licenses usually have the power of contracts between governments and firms, any amendment to the license will usually require the agreement of the company.[3] This feature provides credibility at the cost of inflexibility. The disadvantage of licenses is that they give the operator substantial bargaining power if there is a need to amend the license, which limits the flexibility of the regulatory framework. For example, if a technological breakthrough eliminates economies of scale in a segment of the market, the regulator may have to "bribe" the company into relinquishing its exclusive legal rights over that segment. In a more flexible basic engineering choice, such a decision could be made administratively.

For contracts to satisfy the first criterion for regulatory stability, then, they must be very specific and clearly limit what the regulator can do. A license that does not specify the regulatory mechanism in detail, but rather leaves the administration free to make all regulatory decisions, will fail the first criterion for regulatory stability. (Comparing the licenses issued in Jamaica under the Jamaican Public Utilities Act of 1966 to those issued prior to 1966 or after the privatization of 1988 shows the total failure of licenses to restrain the regulators; see Spiller and Sampson 1993). Operating licenses in the United States, for example, do not serve as a basic engineering mechanism, because they deal mostly with issues related to eminent domain and franchises. Whether specific licenses will satisfy the second requirement for regulatory stability depends on whether the courts see licenses as binding contracts. In particular, courts must be willing to uphold contracts against the wish of the administration. If courts do not treat licenses as contracts, or if they grant the administration substantial leeway in interpreting those contracts, license-based regulatory contracts will fail the second and third criteria for regulatory stability. Observe, then, that contracts can be implemented in nations with very strong or very weak executives and either parliamentary or presidential systems. Indeed, a basic requirement is that the judiciary must be independent *and* see licenses as contracts.

Contract-based regulations, however, are particularly appealing to systems whose set $W(.)$

is very narrow or small. In such cases, as in figure 3.4, changes in political preferences would bring about either the creation of a new piece of legislation, if the current regulatory regime is based on specific legislation, or a modification of the agency's interpretation of the statute, if the current regulatory regime is based on general administrative procedures. In contrast, if x_0 was initially hardwired through a license, then the fact that x_0 no longer belongs to $W(.)$ is irrelevant. Changes in x_0 require the acquiescence of the company. Thus, introducing the regulatory process in the license introduces an additional veto point, namely the company itself. The relevant set of parties required to change the status quo x_0 now includes the company as well, and, in figure 3.5, the set $W(.)$ is now the contract set given by the ideal points (H, S, E, C), where C represents the company's ideal point. The figure shows how regulatory credibility is enhanced even in a situation where electoral changes move against the company. (For a model of regulatory decisionmaking in the United Kingdom, see Spiller and Vogelsang 1993a). It is not surprising that countries like Jamaica, the United Kingdom, and many of the other Caribbean countries have adopted license-based regulatory systems. It would be interesting to see whether other parliamentary systems in Europe move toward such systems when and if they fully privatize their utility sectors.

Finally, informal norms may also provide some regulatory stability even if licenses can be unilaterally amended by the government. For example, the United Kingdom has been granting operating licenses since at least 1609 (Spiller and Vogelsang 1993a). Although licenses initially were granted by the king, eventually Parliament took over this role.[4] Because licenses were granted by acts of Parliament, Parliament could, in principle, change the conditions under which future licenses were to be granted. Parliament could, furthermore, unilaterally change the operating rights of current license holders. Such parliamentary power, however, made licenses a fragile instrument. Over the years, however, Parliament has developed an informal (constitutional) norm of not revoking licenses without compensation. Indeed licenses have been revoked only once—during the massive restructuring of the electricity sector in 1926. In that case, however, license holders received very favorable transitory rights that compensated them for whatever losses might arise from the compulsory shutdown (Spiller and Vogelsang 1993a).

To summarize, the use of licenses as a regulatory instrument requires the existence of a judiciary that firmly respects contract agreements or the existence of widely accepted norms that inhibit the opportunistic revocation of licenses. Countries that are only now starting to regulate utilities have not yet developed these types of norms, and thus the key ingredient is the existence of an independent judiciary that considers licenses to be contracts.

Administrative Procedures

Administrative procedures may serve as the choice of basic engineering.[5] The regulation of utilities in the United States is based on a well-specified body of administrative procedures, at both the federal and state levels. These procedures determine how agencies make decisions and specify the independent appeals process. U.S. regulatory agencies are required to announce their intentions to hold hearings well ahead of time, to hold open hearings, to substantiate their decisions, and to make public all communications among interested parties (that is, ex parte communication rules do not allow commissioners to

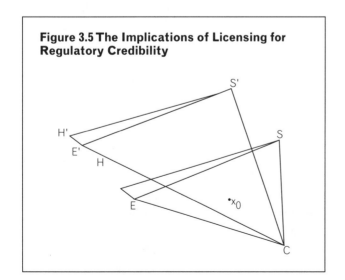

Figure 3.5 The Implications of Licensing for Regulatory Credibility

communicate with their staff or with individuals from regulated companies on issues under consideration). Freedom of information limits the ability of agencies to keep information from the public. These rules evolved in the United States over a period of more than fifty years and are based on the constitutional provision of due process. Furthermore, each piece of enabling legislation complements these general administrative procedures with specific stipulations regarding who is allowed to participate in hearings, what type of rule-making powers an agency has, and so forth. However, administrative procedures slow down the regulatory process, providing a way for interested parties to bargain over the issues and providing procedural grounds on which to appeal. (Administrative procedures have been used in the United States to keep regulatory outcomes from deviating from the initial regulatory bargain; see McCubbins, Noll, and Weingast 1987.)

The use of administrative procedures as a generic way to enforce regulatory bargains requires not only a previously developed body of law but also a judiciary that is accustomed to challenging administrations on procedural grounds. Although it may be possible to pass legislation requiring regulators to follow particular procedures in their decisionmaking, and even if such legislation is difficult to change (thus satisfying the first and second requirements for regulatory stability), this body of law will only provide regulatory stability if the courts can be expected to challenge the administration on procedural grounds. Indeed, in most Latin American countries, administrative law has not been developed extensively, except in relation to government procurement. (Bolivia's SAFCO law establishes substantial procedures in procurement but is totally silent on regulatory decisionmaking). Thus, in most but not all Latin American countries, regulatory frameworks based on general procedural requirements may fail to satisfy the third requirement for regulatory stability, because institutions are not in place to enforce procedural constraints.

The use of administrative procedures as a generic way to enforce regulatory bargains also requires a set of institutions that guarantees that the set $W(.)$ is sufficiently wide. Indeed, if because

of electoral rules the set $W(.)$ is narrow, as is the case in two-party parliamentary systems, agency decisions will have to move with the set $W(.)$, limiting the credibility of the initial bargain. If, however, the outcome of the regulatory process as specified in the law is outside the set $W(.)$, then there will be incentives to adjust procedures to reflect more closely the preferences of the legislators and of the executive. Thus, as in legislative specificity, a necessary condition for administrative procedures to provide regulatory credibility is that the set $W(.)$ be wide. Hardwired administrative procedures are easier to implement than specific legislation. At the same time, because administrative procedures do not strictly limit how the agency or the courts may interpret the statute, they provide a measure of regulatory flexibility that limits the agency's own commitment. As with specific legislation, administrative procedures may not serve as a mechanism of commitment in traditional parliamentary systems.

In summary, three institutional characteristics are key to understanding the constraints that limit a country's basic engineering options: the existence of an independent judiciary that enforces regulatory constraints, the role of legislative and executive institutions, and the existence of widely accepted informal norms that limit opportunistic behavior.

First, a judiciary with a strongly held tradition of administrative law facilitates the use of administrative procedures. Such a judiciary can provide assurances that the government will not deviate from specific legislative or constitutional commitments that underpin the regulatory system. A judiciary that respects contracts and property rights also makes contracts (licenses) a feasible choice of basic engineering. Second, legislative and executive institutions that grant the executive substantial control over legislative agendas and outcomes do not favor the basic engineering option of specific legislation because turnover in the executive may have a more important implication for regulation than it does in other countries. If legislative powers alternate between political parties with substantially different interests, specific legislation does not provide a safeguard against administrative discretion, because a new administration could modify the laws. Third, informal norms may substitute for legislative flexibility. In particular, nations that have a strong set of norms that determine acceptable legislative behavior may consider specific legislation as a feasible basic engineering option. (For an analysis of informal norms as equilibrium behavior, see Calvert 1992.)

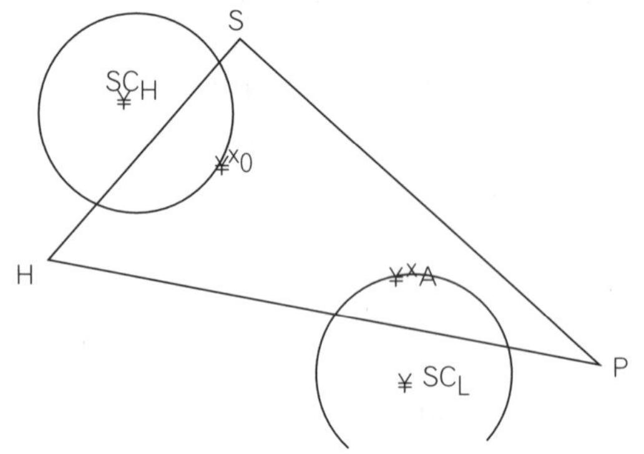

INSTITUTIONAL STRUCTURES AND JUDICIAL CONTROL OVER THE EXECUTIVE

The previous sections assumed that the courts will review administrative or regulatory decisions according to the precepts stipulated in the law. First we assumed that the courts are sympathetic to regulatory deviations from the specific stipulations in the law. Then we assumed that the courts are sympathetic to complaints about procedural deviations. Finally, we assumed that the courts agree to hear complaints about contractual deviations. Courts, however, do not operate in a vacuum. The norms that govern judicial decisions and procedures evolve over time. Judicial norms will develop differently under different legislative and executive organizations. In particular, in a decentralized decisionmaking environment, courts can more easily challenge administrative and regulatory decisions on both procedures and substance. Such interventions, in most cases, may not trigger a legislative response, leaving standing the court's decision. (On congressional reversals of Supreme Court decisions, see Eskridge 1991.) In contrast, in very centralized systems, attempts by the courts to reverse an administrative decision may trigger a legislative or executive response that overrides the court.

Consider, for example, figure 3.6 in which the court faces the three-veto structure characteristic of a bicameral presidential system with a fragmented legislature. Assume that the legislation is vague and that, as a consequence, the agency attempts to implement a particular point in the set $W(H, S, P)$, x_A, which differs from the status quo x_0. The parties may challenge the agency's decision on procedural grounds. Assume, now, that the court has preferences with regard

Figure 3.6 Judicial Discretion in Bicameral Presidential Systems

to policy outcome. Say that there are two types of courts, SC_H and SC_L. In the figure, SC_H prefers the original status quo, while SC_L prefers the agency's choice. The court, then, may or may not reverse the agency's decision. (For a rational choice model of Supreme Court statutory interpretation, see Spiller and Gely 1990.) In any case, the Court's decision will not be reversed, because either decision is in $W(H, S, P)$.

In two-party parliamentary systems, though, where the number of veto points is substantially reduced, the court cannot reverse administrative decisions without facing a challenge. In figure 3.7, for example, a political move has made the initial status quo untenable. An agency's decision has moved the policy to x_A. Attempts by the court to reverse the agency's decision (SC prefers x_0 to x_A) will directly trigger a cabinet response, reversing the court and bringing the policy back to x_A. (For a fascinating discussion of cabinet control of the judiciary in Japan, see Ramseyer 1994; for a similar analysis in the United Kingdom, see Salzberg 1991.) This, however, may not be the case in multiparty parliamentary systems, in which governments are formed from multiparty coalitions and the potential for the coalition to break up is substantially greater.

This discussion suggests that the norms of judicial supervision over an agency's decisions may vary substantially across countries. In countries where decisionmaking is traditionally decentralized, regulatory deviations may not be restrained if the court's preferences are aligned with those of the agency. Thus, purely administrative procedures may not provide as much regulatory credibility as they would if the courts behaved in a more mechanical fashion. Within a decentralized political structure, a judicial norm that pressures the executive to respect very specific legislation can develop and thrive, because such judicial decisions, in general, can stand up under legislative scrutiny.[6] Such norms may not develop in a political system similar to that presented in figure 3.7. In those cases, judicial activism will only trigger a legislative reversal and political recrimination. In centralized political systems of the type being discussed here, contracts between companies and the government may be the only instrument that provides regulatory credibility. Courts, in this case, must have developed a norm of treating contracts between governments and the private sector in the manner ruled by contract law. Furthermore, it is reasonable to expect that such a norm will develop over time because it will reduce the government's costs of procurement and of capital. (For a discussion of the evolution of political institutions in the United Kingdom as a way to limit the government's own cost of capital, see North and Weingast 1989.)

To summarize, because administrative procedures provide vague standards for judicial review, they may not provide substantial regulatory credibility in countries with multiple veto points. Furthermore, in countries with unified governments, such procedures will provide no regulatory credibility because courts will, in any case, not be able to enforce the status quo in the event of electoral changes. Legislative specificity can provide regulatory credibility in the first type of political system, but not in the latter. Regulatory contracts, then, seem to be the main conduit for providing regulatory credibility in political systems that boast a unified government.

A "MODEL" OF EFFECTIVE AUTONOMOUS REGULATORY INSTITUTIONS

Whatever the basic regulatory instrument chosen, the conduit and oversight of regulation are delegated to a regulatory institution. Regulation is an ongoing task of fine-tuning and adapting decisions as foreseen and unforeseen events unfold. This argues, on efficiency grounds, that the regulatory agency be accorded a fair amount of flexibility and that the principles that will be followed in adjusting decisions be clear and publicly known so that other parties (particularly the operator) can assess the economic impact on their operations and plan and act accordingly. In practice, two problems often arise with that framework. One is that the commitment to stick to these principles is not credible and is often violated, with the changes affecting the economic returns of the operator. The other is that the high level of discretion embedded in that framework is vulnerable to influence and to capture by interest groups.

To minimize these problems five conditions are essential for regulatory institutions to be effective: (a) managerial freedom, (b) political autonomy (freedom from political and interest group influence), (c) accountability (the duty of an agent or employee to respond to and fulfill his or her responsibilities to his or her principal or employer), (d) checks and balances (to limit the power of single individuals within the institution), and (e) incentives (to reward good performance and to punish arbitrary or inadequate performance).

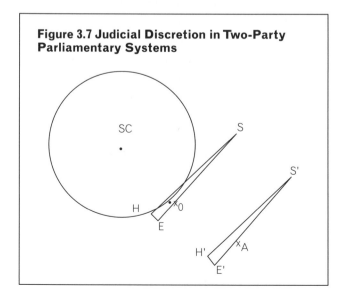

Figure 3.7 Judicial Discretion in Two-Party Parliamentary Systems

Managerial Freedom

The agency has to enjoy managerial freedom in obtaining given objectives. This freedom, including the freedom to set the conditions of employment, is intended to create the incentive for administrative efficiency and technical capability. This is essential to good performance. The regulatory agency needs to retain a permanent cadre of technically proficient and highly motivated professionals. To do this, it may need to create a professional career structure, such as that enjoyed by many central banks. This will require, among other things, paying higher salaries. In turn, higher salaries will require more resources.

Political Autonomy

The agency has to enjoy political autonomy. That is, somewhat like the judiciary, the agency must be insulated from the pressures exerted by other parts of government and by interest groups. Political autonomy, combined with the technical capability that results from managerial freedom, leads to well-informed and fair decisions. This means a good quality of "output." In reality, political autonomy cannot simply be legislated. Autonomy grows as the public perceives the high technical quality of the agency's work and the effectiveness of its results. The regulatory agency needs to establish its reputation, with successes in large cases of market abuse or flagrant violations of regulatory or contract norms, so that the public can see how the agency's interventions improve the quality of their lives. The appearance of a conflict of interest will, of course, compromise the agency's autonomy, and its management must keep this in mind.

Accountability

The agency must be accountable, fulfill defined objectives, and submit substantive financial reports to the government (elected officials). The institution performs as a servant of the government (and thereby of the people who elected it) through the close oversight of the executive or legislative branches or, as in the more recent

experiments of New Zealand and the United Kingdom, through the contract-like system of an ex ante agreement followed by ex post controls on implementation of that agreement. This is the incentive for an "output" that is not only good quality, but also desired.

Accountability is often the most difficult problem a regulatory agency faces. At present most accountability is informal and ill-defined. The regulatory agency is accountable to the executive, but in a way that is personalized, which means it is based on relations between the president or minister and the head of the agency, and on the character of the top people in the agency. In other words, the accountability is not institutionalized, which means incorporated in formal procedures. If accountability is not institutionalized in one way or another, the agency will be at risk. The experience of most countries in Latin America and the Caribbean suggests an "iron law" of bureaucracy: If bureaucracies are not controlled enough, they take on a life of their own, they seek extra resources, and they justify their holding of these resources by using their monopoly of specialized knowledge to invent new tasks. There are two broad paths to greater accountability, and governments and regulatory agencies must consider both:

• First, government oversight can be strengthened. Better oversight could be achieved through a stronger executive. The executive could impose better reporting requirements and even consider moving in the direction of New Zealand's contractual model. The legislature could also play a stronger role in oversight. Perhaps a super-regulatory body could be created with a semi-independent constitutional standing similar to that of the central bank, the national election board, or the judicial council. The choices are many.

• Second, the agency can seek to improve its direct accountability to the public. Public accountability is particularly important when the branches of government are weak and when most of the services (conflict resolution between two parties and registration of individual rights) are provided directly and individually to the public.

To achieve legitimacy and credibility, the regulatory process has to be made as transparent as possible. Transparency means openness, specifying the rules, opening up the process, and explaining the decisions, preferably in writing (so they can be appealed). Thus, the agency should improve its transparency by publishing as many of its decisions, deliberations, and views as possible. It should also improve its "listening" techniques and public access to its services by, for instance, decentralizing its operation or strengthening its procedures for hearing complaints.

Checks and Balances

The agency has to have internal checks and balances that limit the power of single individuals. Checks and balances are often the easiest condition to design, although they are often ignored. They complement accountability and make arbitrary decisions, bribery, and corruption more difficult. They have to do with how regulators are appointed and with how and who makes the decisions. Examples include making decisions by committees (rather than by an individual), staggering decisionmaking as a function of the impact of the decision, using consultative groups, and instituting quarantine periods in which various parties have the opportunity to object before a decision goes into effect. Both Chile and Peru have relatively well-built checks and balances.

Incentives

The agency has to have the right set of incentives, financial and otherwise, to reward and punish performance (Shepperd 1995). Regulators ought to be financially rewarded according to private sector salary scales, and the conditions for career advancement should be clearly delineated. Promotion ladders can be the greatest tool for providing incentives and motivation, and they are needed to attract highly capable personnel and to minimize the possibility of influence. The most common obstacle in most developing countries is the prevalence of quasi-uniform pay scales for public servants. However, countries can make exceptions, as we often see in the compensation

paid to tax collectors. The same arguments should apply to regulators. Likewise, dismissal for improper behavior is also in order. Clearly, dismissal can only be effective if salaries are high enough and career promotions are available and genuine so that dismissals constitute a significant loss to the public servant. In addition, bonus payments, linked to the performance of both the regulator and the sector, should enhance the likelihood of inducing a good "output," as should rewarding top-performing workers with external educational, management, and training programs. Compensation contracts should take four factors into account: (a) the regulator's aversion to risk, (b) the regulator's aversion to effort, (c) the marginal contribution of effort, and (d) the precision of the measure of performance or behavior.

THE STRUCTURE OF A REGULATORY INSTITUTION

Conventional wisdom and incentive theory suggest that, to be efficient, regulation requires an independent, self-financed regulatory agency. Such emphasis, although correct, may be misplaced because the primary focus ought to be on reducing the opportunities for undue influence. And independence and self-finance often are taken as proxies or as necessary conditions for an absence of opportunities to exercise undue influence. The difficulties in designing a regulatory agency that can be trusted to deliver bona fide performance and is strong enough to withstand political or economic forces lead to the second-best (or third-best) solution to limiting its discretionary powers.

Consider first the size and budget of a regulatory agency. A regulatory agency's size must be commensurate with its tasks. A large agency managing few regulatory tasks is likely to deviate from the initial understanding by increasing bureaucratic barriers to justify its existence. Consider the idea that regulatory agencies ought to be independent entities. Much debate has focused on whether agencies should form part of a ministry or have separate identities. The discussion above suggests that an independent regulatory process is best achieved, tautologically, by limiting a regulator's discretion. Only when regulators are granted substantial discretion is the location of the agency of importance, because it would not be reasonable to allow a regulatory authority to be totally independent. The separation of jurisdictions between the ministry and the regulator should be clear and not arbitrary.

Box 3.1 illustrates the appropriate normative functions of the two entities, respectively, in telecommunications. Accountability is important, and checks and balances such as budgetary reviews and political oversight provide ways to control regulators. Discretion can only be granted when the right incentive and accountability structure is set in place, generating the likelihood that the regulatory agency will behave appropriately. The example of Colombia, shown in box 3.2, illustrates the difficulty that governments have in letting go of regulatory institutions and the political arguments often used to defend their continued meddling in regulatory matters.

At issue in the process of designing regulatory institutions is whether there should be a single regulator or a commission. Each design has its strengths and weakness. There are tradeoffs that need to be evaluated in individual contexts. Individual decisionmaker's designs are superior in terms of speed of decisionmaking, accountability of decisions, minimizing resource demands and costs, and predictability of results. Moreover, in fragmented multiparty political systems (often leading to government coalitions), there is a tendency to allocate commission slots to the different parties, increasing the chance that the appointments will be political rather than technical/professional. On the other hand, commissions are superior in terms of resistance to individual agendas, resistance to improper influences, potential to reflect multiple perspectives, and potential to stagger terms to enhance stability and weaken links with particular governments. The optimal choice will depend in large part on the tasks entrusted to the regulatory entity, the country or sector context, and the broader implementation environment. And performance is ultimately determined by the quality of the persons appointed to the positions. Examples can be found of individual decisionmakers performing

Box 3.1 Public Utility Regulatory Commissions in Colombia: Autonomous Experts or Politicians?

As a response to the regulatory demands that arose as the private sector increased its participation in the utilities sector, the Colombian government abolished the National Tariff Board and created three modern regulatory commissions: one for telecommunications, one for water supply and sanitation, and one for electricity and gas. These commissions were created to foster competition and to prevent monopolistic practices. More precisely, they were charged with setting rate formulas, fees, conditions for auctions, and technical and commercial conditions for developing a competitive market. While promoting competition, the commissions were also charged with establishing general rules, investigating complaints against unfair practices, and ordering the vertical disintegration and suspension of, for example, output restraints and market segmentation (overlapping with the Antitrust Commission). These commissions were comprised of government officials and independent experts.

The government's initial proposal was to establish fully independent commissions—independent from both the government and private carriers—somewhat akin to U.S. regulatory commissions. But some ministers and members of congress insisted on, and eventually propelled, the creation of more public and thus less autonomous entities. Some ministers argued, for example, that setting tariffs could have a strong political impact and that responsibility should not be left in the hands of technical experts, because the government ultimately would be blamed for poor decisions. Likewise, some members of congress feared that regulations crafted solely by experts would be excessively technocratic and would suffer from the absence of regional and consumer input. As a compromise, congress approved three semi-independent regulatory commissions.

Source: Montenegro 1995.

very well and commissions performing poorly, and vice versa. On balance, the choice of commission should be made on the basis of resistance to capture by improper influences, since that is the factor most affecting the regulatory outcome. That would slightly favor commissions over individual decisionmakers. But even that has to be weighted in the local context.

Box 3.2 Responsibilities of the Minister and the Regulator

Minister of telecommunications:

- Translates general government policy into sector policy
- Translates sector policy into regulatory framework and unbundling choices
- Approves major capital expenditures (while state owned)
- Determines subsidies to customers and regions
- Oversees regulatory performance
- Establishes controls in the presence of real national security concerns.

Telecommunications regulator:

- Issues and enforces licenses and concessions
- Sets prices and access terms in the absence of competition and monitors compliance
- Monitors financial viability of operators
- Sets quality of service standards and monitors compliance
- Resets prices and access terms at the end of the review period
- Arbitrates disputes between operators
- Arbitrates disputes between operators and consumers
- Collects information on the costs and earnings of regulated sector companies
- Provides information and advice to the ministry and information to the general public.

Another issue is the extent to which regulatory agencies should be sector specific. Conventional wisdom suggests that regulatory agencies would be more professional if they were specialized, but in many countries administrative capabilities are weak, thus limiting the pool of available manpower. When the concern with government capacity to regulate is deeply rooted in a long history of government failure, often due to political interference, the best organizational approach is likely to be simple and transparent. An effective yet simple way to improve a country's or a province's capacity to regulate is to create a single (covering all sectors) and independent regulatory agency staffed with competent professionals. If administrative capabilities are vulnerable, then the regulatory framework should be extremely simple and should limit regulatory discretion. Regulatory agencies could then be

relatively small, eliminating the need for a large, well-qualified technocracy. In some cases, provinces or states have initially considered separate regulatory bodies for each subsector. But the experience of large decentralized countries suggests that at some point the subnational authorities end up with at least two or three of their infrastructure and utilities sectors controlled by a single agency. In environments with a shortage of qualified individuals and in small countries, it is desirable to integrate regulatory jurisdiction across sectors into a single agency. Conceptually the arguments are strong for the integration. Most of the problems and issues to be addressed are similar, and the synergies are strong. Furthermore, economies of scale would lower the administrative costs of regulation. For instance, the legal departments would not need to hire specialized staff for each subsector, because many of the legal issues are similar across subsectors. This does not preclude each subsector from having a small, technically specialized cluster of professionals with competencies only in that subsector.

A single agency has further advantages, including the ability to resist manipulation by a specific industry (Estache 1995). It eases the cross-sectoral coordination and improves the likelihood that policy will be consistent across subsectors. Also by design, a multisector agency has a larger constituency than a sector-specific agency. Increasing and broadening the constituency reduces the influence that any one industry can exert on regulators. The standard organizational structure of an integrated regulatory agency should include an administrative department and a legal department common to all subsectors. It should also include specialized departments, one for each subsector. However, the technical departments for each subsector, such as engineering, price and access regulation, and industry research and analysis should be quasi-integrated, because many of the issues, concepts, and modes of analysis cut across subsectors. (For a detailed analysis of the structure of an integrated regulatory agency, see Estache 1995.) A partial example of a single agency is Bolivia's National Regulatory Commission (see box 3.3).

Box 3.3 The National Regulatory Commission in Bolivia

The Bolivian government created the National Regulatory Commission to regulate the communications, electricity, hydrocarbon, and transport industries. The commission has three core functions: It assists in administering and enforcing concessionary arrangements, administers price regulation agreements, and enforces antitrust norms. The agency contains four sector-specific national superintendents overseen by a commissioner. The superintendents are responsible for day-to-day decisionmaking, performing tasks such as regulating prices and supervising compliance. They are appointed for staggered five-year terms and are protected from arbitrary removal. The commissioner oversees the superintendents and hears appeals regarding their decisions. The cross-sectoral focus is intended to promote policy consistency and to protect the agency from improper government or industry influence. The commissioner is named by decree and also serves a five-year term protected from arbitrary removal. The supreme court is the ultimate appellate body for decisions by the commissioner.

Box 3.4 Funding Colorado's Public Utilities Commission

Colorado's Public Utilities Commission (PUC) was established in 1913. It has responsibility for electricity, gas, telecommunications, water, intrastate aviation, and some motor carriers in a state with a population of around 3.5 million.

The PUC has three commissioners and a staff of around 95. Its expenditures in the fiscal year ending June 1993 totaled $6.1 million, all of which was obtained from levies on regulated firms. The PUC's annual funding process includes the following features:

- The PUC's total expenditures for the present year are determined by the state legislature, and are subject to a maximum based on a levy of 0.2 percent of firms' gross operating revenues from intrastate business in the previous year.
- Assessments are calculated by the Department of Revenue to meet the income approved by the legislature. The percentage contribution is uniform across regulated sectors.
- Firms pay the levy to the treasurer in quarterly installments.
- Levies received by the treasurer are placed in a dedicated fund. Surplus income at the end of the year is used to reduce levies in the next period.

The most appropriate option for funding the operation of the regulatory agency is to let the agency generate its own revenues rather than to have allocations from the general budget, which is the other obvious alternative. First, it detaches the agency from political interference; second, the users who benefit from its existence finance the costs of its operations. Revenues could be obtained by means of an access fee levied on users of the service or an industry levy assessed on operators (see box 3.4 as an example). In any event, the cost is likely to be passed on to consumers. In the case of an industry levy (such as license fees in the United Kingdom and regulatory assessments in the United States), the cost could be expressed as a percentage of the industry output or as a fixed amount. (In many countries, these levies tend to be the agency's main source of revenue, often exceeding 70 percent of total financing.) A second potential source of financing is a usage or service fee for a specific service requested. For example, a filing fee could be charged when the operator or a consumer files a complaint (with the fee for the

operator being larger than the fee for the consumer). The fee could have two components, particularly for complaints or requests by the operator: a smaller, nonrefundable part and a larger part refundable in the event of merit or a positive ruling on the complaint. The latter feature is particularly attractive because it would deter frivolous complaints, which often tie up many of the resources of the regulatory agency. All the fees and bases for them should be set by law or a similar instrument, and they should not be easily amended or revoked by the government. The levies should be set to cover operating costs. If surpluses or deficits persist, the rates could be adjusted. A reassessment every three to five years might be appropriate, subject to legislative approval. (For other views on the funding of regulatory agencies, see Smith 1994).

The regulatory agency's terms of reference should include the gathering of information and the dissemination of sector-specific performance indicators. Such information would allow the assessment of the evolution of the sector and the creation of incentives for transparency, compliance, self-monitoring, and efficient performance. Box 3.5 describes one method of appointing regulators.

To summarize, the available evidence and theory suggest that the issue of the independence of regulatory agencies, though correct in principle, is poorly focused. In the absence of the three pillars of regulatory institutional design, and particularly of credible accountability, the goal of regulatory engineering is to design flexible and efficient rules and to incorporate them into a system that restrains arbitrary administrative

action and therefore does not impede private investment. A single, integrated regulatory agency generating its own financing is preferable to a proliferation of sector-specific agencies with funds from the general budget. Finally, regulators should do what their legislated statute enables them to do; no more, no less. They should not be free to determine their own mandate. An initial period, say five years, of inflexible regulatory rules and very limited discretion, while all interested parties are learning, is warranted for most developing countries without a tradition of regulatory practice. Subsequently, additional flexibility can be considered.

Box 3.5 Appointing Regulators

Appointing regulatory commissions (with between three and five members) is more common than appointing a single regulator (and there is evidence that this is the right way to go). In this case, selecting the members is the first severe political challenge that provincial authorities have to face. Experience shows that elections are not appropriate because they reinforce short-term political perspectives when longer-term perspectives are required.

Best practice includes the following steps:
• Prescribe professional qualifications for appointees.
• Involve both the executive and the legislative branches in the appointment process.
• Provide regulators with secure tenure, subject to removal only in case of proven misbehavior.
• Exempt agencies from civil service rules that limit salaries to levels below those needed to recruit qualified staff.

• Provide agencies with funding from industry levies and user fees to reduce their reliance on politically directed budgetary allocations.

Measures that insulate regulators from the political process have to be reconciled with the need to ensure that regulators are accountable for their actions. Although the means of striking the appropriate balance between autonomy and accountability will vary from context to context, common measures include:
• Permitting the removal of regulators in cases of proven misbehavior.
• Prescribing particular duties and obligations as clearly as possible in law and providing an effective appeals process, whether involving the courts or another forum.
• Mandating high standards of transparency in regulatory proceedings.

Source: Estache 1995.

Appendix
Regulatory Agencies—Selected OECD and Latin American Countries

Agency	Staff	Budget	Funding Source
I — SELECTED OECD COUNTRIES			
Canada			
Federal			
NEB (electricity & gas)	343 (1992)	$37.1m (1992)	General taxation
RTC (telecommunications, cable, radio, & broadcasting)	423 (1992)	$35.6m (1992)	Levies on regulated firms
Provinces			
Alberta PUB (electricity, gas, & telecommunications)	31 (1993)	$3.1m (1993)	33% general taxation, 66% levies on regulated firms
Nova Scotia URB (electricity, telecommunications, & water)	31 (1993)	$1.3m (1992)	64% general taxation, 36% levies on regulated firms
Quebec TB (telecommunications)	30 (1991)	$1.7m (1992)	Levies on regulated firms
United Kingdom			
OFGASS (electricity)	228 (1993)	$16.0m (1994)	Levies on regulated firms
OFGASS (gas)	31 (1993)	$6.7m	Levies on regulated firms
Oftel (telecommunications)	151 (1993)	$12.7m (1994)	Levies on regulated firms
OFWAT (water)	138 (1993)	$13.1m (1994)	Levies on regulated firms
United States			
Federal			
FERC (electricity and gas)	1,472 (1993)	$140m (1992)	General taxation; some fees recovered to the budget
FCC (telecommunications, cable, radio, satellite, and broadcasting	1,783 (1993)	$126.3m (1992)	General taxation; some fees recovered to the budget
States			
California PUC (electricity, gas, telecommunications, transport, water, and wastewater)	1,029 (1992)	$83.9m (1992)	92% from levies on regulated firms, 4% from general taxation, and 4% from specific transaction and investigation fees
Colorado PUC (electricity, gas, telecom, transport and water)	95 (1993)	$6.1m (1993)	100% from levies of up to 0.2% of industry gross revenues
Florida PSC (electricity, gas, telecommunications, water, and wastewater)	391 (1992)	$20.5m (1992)	100% from levies on industry gross revenues Electricity: Up to 0.5% (0.375% actual) Gas: Up to 0.125% (0.0833% actual) Telecom: Up to 0.25% (0.15% actual) Water/wastewater: Up to 4.5% (4.5% actual)
New York PSC (electricity, gas, telecommunications, and water)	686 (1992)	$55.9m (1992)	99% from levies on regulated firms
II — SELECTED LATIN AMERICAN COUNTRIES			
Argentina	85	$15.6m	Levies on regulated firms
ENRE (electricity)	86	$22.6m	Levies on regulated firms
ENERGAS (gas)	74	$9.4m	Portion of concession fees paid by regulated firms
CNTF (rail)	400	$22.1m	0.5% on industry revenues, plus radiospectrum fee
CNT (telecommunications)	72	$15.7m	2.67% consumers' water-sewage bills
ETOSS (water in B.A.)			
Colombia	35	$3.9m	Up to 1% of industry's functioning expenses, excluding operating expenses and energy purchases
CREG (electricity & gas)			
Peru	65	$6.0m	0.5% of industry gross revenues
OSIPTEL (telecommunications)	45	$2.5m	Up to 2% of industry gross revenues
SNSS (water)			
Venezuela	80 (1993)	$2.9m (1992)	0.5% of regulated firms' revenues
CONATEL (telecommunications)			

Note: All figures for 1995 unless otherwise specified.

NOTES

1. Such would be the case in parliamentary systems with electoral rules that promote a two-party system, or in a presidential system with electoral laws that foster a single-party system, where that party almost always wins the elections for both the legislature and the executive.

2. See Schwartz, Spiller, and Urbiztondo 1994 for a model of endogenous determination of legislative specificity that takes into account the costs of writing specific legislation. Their main result—that, for legislative specificity to be an equilibrium in a signaling model, "congress" must care a lot about the issue and must expect the costs of reversing the decisions of an agency or court to be low—is consistent with the result that legislative consensus is needed to implement specific legislation.

3. British law stipulates that if the company does not agree to a license amendment proposed by the regulator, the regulator may use a process involving the Monopolies and Mergers Commission to amend the license against the will of the company. See Spiller and Vogelsang 1993a.

4. Licenses were granted in many different forms. Until 1919, prospective utilities commonly applied to Parliament for a particular license. A select committee heard the case and either recommended a license or rejected the application. The select committee's recommendation was then presented to Parliament for approval, a step referred to as "private bills" and considered a formality. A license could also be granted by an order in council, whereby the Privy Council would grant a license recommended by a minister and the cabinet. Licenses were also granted by general acts of Parliament. For example, the Public Health Act of 1875 granted municipalities the right to establish water and gas services in districts where no one else had undertaken the task. Provisional orders were also common, granted by a minister following a request for a license. The minister's order would then be formalized by an act of Parliament. Finally, the 1919 Electricity (Supply) Act created an electricity commission that issued licenses through special orders, which had to be approved by the minister of transport but did not require formal parliamentary approval. Parliament, however, did retain the right to reconsider those licenses. See Spiller and Vogelsang 1993a.

5. Administrative law controls the administrative operations of government. It sets forth the powers that may be exercised by administrative agencies, lays down the principles governing the exercise of those powers, and provides legal remedies to the parties aggrieved by administrative action. This definition divides administrative law into three parts: the powers vested in administrative agencies, the requirements imposed by law on the exercise of those powers, and the remedies against unlawful administrative action (Schwartz 1984). Many developing countries are deficient in the first and second parts.

6. An argument could be made that such a norm is against the court's own interest because it prevents the court from achieving its own desirable policy outcome. Although appropriate, this argument fails to take into account a basic difference between implementing the court's more desirable policy when the legislation is vague and when it is very specific. When the legislation is specific, the court is trading off policy outcomes against legitimacy. Such a tradeoff is nonexistent when the legislation is vague.

4 BASIC ENGINEERING EXPERIENCES IN LATIN AMERICA

THE CHOICES OF BASIC engineering design vary greatly across Latin America. They include the successful use of contracts in Jamaica (prior to 1966 and after 1988), Brazil, Mexico, Peru, and Venezuela; the disastrous use of presidential decrees in Argentina to regulate telecommunications; the unfortunate choice of administrative procedures in Jamaica from 1966 to 1975; the successful application of specific legislation in Chile to regulate electricity and telecommunications and in Argentina to regulate electricity; and the use of licenses in Bolivia to regulate the private electricity company. As a result of the issues and tradeoffs

described in chapter 3, the salient choice for most Latin American countries in the 1990s appears to be contracts. A brief summary of examples of the various choices of basic engineering in LAC is presented in table 4.1

THE USE OF CONTRACTS IN JAMAICA, BOLIVIA, CHILE, PERU, AND MEXICO

Jamaica has had very successful experience with regulation by contract. (For an in-depth discussion, see Spiller and Sampson 1993.) Jamaica instituted regulation by contract early in the twentieth century to regulate development of the telecommunications and electricity sectors. Indeed, contract regulation was the norm in

Jamaica until the Jamaican Public Utility Commission (JPUC) was created in 1967. Until 1967 Jamaica's telecommunications and electricity licenses stipulated the process by which prices were to be set (rate of return on assets), the minimum real rate of return (8 to 10 percent), the operations of the regulatory body (through ad hoc rate review boards), and the process by which disputes between parties were to be resolved (appeal to the courts, all the way up to the Privy Council in London). These licenses provided the local telecommunications company with substantial guarantees against opportunistic government behavior. In fact, in several instances the company went to court to request rate increases above those granted by the government, and won. With the creation of Telecom-

Table 4.1 Examples of Basic Engineering in LAC: Instruments Embodying Regulatory Norms

Constitution	The Constitution of *Colombia* provides for proper indemnification for the expropriation of private property (Art. 58). It also specifically gives the state control of the electromagnetic spectrum and the mandate of combating monopolistic practices in the use of the spectrum (Art. 75).
Parliamentary Laws	In *Chile* the 1982 Mining, Electric Power Services Law (DFL-1) provides the basis for the regulation of electricity generation, transmission, and distribution, and sets out the provisions for rate setting.
Decree-Laws	In *Peru* the 1992 Decree-Law of Electric Concessions (Decree-Law 25.844) was adopted by the government (president and cabinet members), acting under emergency powers, and replaced previous electricity laws.
Presidential Decree	In *Argentina* the creation of the Comisión Nacional de Telecommunicaciónes, the telecommunications regulator, came in a presidential decree (Decreto 1185/90). In addition to the structure of the agency, it described procedures for the award of licenses, control of prices, and interconnection rules.
Ministerial Decree	In some cases a decree may be issued by a sector ministry, such as *Costa Rica's* decree by the Ministry of Natural Resources, Energy and Mines in 1989 (Decree No. 18.947), which established parameters for private investor participation in some power projects.
Licenses	In *Jamaica* the license for the national telecommunications operator includes provisions fixing the rate of return to be earned by the company.
Contractual Arrangements	A concession contract for the operation and maintenance of the water and wastewater systems in Cancún, *Mexico* sets out service efficiency standards and the tariff regime.
Decisions by Regulatory Agencies	In *Colombia* the Comisión de Regulación de Energia y Gas, a specialized regulatory agency, plays an active role in implementing competition regulation in the sector. The Comisión imposed a system of free access to the electricity network and issued decisions requiring the state oil company to divest its gas transportation assets.

munications of Jamaica (TOJ) in 1987, licenses again became the regulatory norm in Jamaica (see box 4.1 for the components of TOJ's license). The licenses designate the price–setting process, specify the company's responsibilities and the regulator's limits, and define the procedures for

Box 4.1 Main Components of the 1988 Legislation Granting a License to Telecommunications of Jamaica

1. The Jamaican Telephone Company (JTC) is granted a monopoly over all domestic (both local and toll) telephone services, while Jamintel is granted a monopoly over all international communications. Both are fully owned subsidiaries of TOJ.
2. Both licenses are for twenty-five years, with a renewal period of twenty-five years.
3. Both companies are regulated on a rate-of-return basis; net after-tax (and special dividend) profits must be not less than 17.5 percent nor more than 20 percent of (accounting) shareholders' equity, where assets are revalued annually.
4. Rates are set as follows: (a) If the company wants to adjust its tariffs, it proposes a new tariff to the minister of public utilities and transport; (b) if the ministry accepts, then that tariff goes into effect; (c) if the ministry does not accept, and the minister's offer is not accepted by the company, there is

a relatively simple arbitration procedure, with the arbitrator having to set rates that satisfy point 3 above.
5. TOJ is not required to obtain permission to undertake investments, nor can the government disallow investments undertaken by the company.
6. The government may supervise the quality of service.
7. If for any reason the government decides to cancel one of the two companies' licenses, it has to cancel the other's, as well.
8. If the government cancels a license it may be required to buy the assets of the company at fair market value, should the company fail to obtain an alternative investor.
9. TOJ may appeal to Jamaica's supreme court the government's violation of the license.

Source: Spiller and Sampson 1993.

arbitration. Although they allow the government to cancel a license, they also specify how the government must pay for the assets.

These licenses substantially limit the discretion granted to Jamaica's regulators. Although the present regulatory framework could be improved, it offers the provider sufficient guarantees of stability. Moreover, the level of investment and the quality and availability of service have risen dramatically, while real prices have fallen. The question here is not whether the Jamaican government could have designed a better regulatory framework, but rather what the rationale was for limiting discretion through the use of specific licenses.[1] The reason for using licenses rather than administrative procedures or specific legislation can be found in the nature of Jamaica's electoral rules and its constitutional division of powers. Jamaica's parliamentary system was designed to accommodate two strong parties. Indeed, since the 1959 election (the last election prior to independence), independent candidates have won less than 1 percent of the popular vote. Consequently, the governing party usually has a strong majority in parliament, and members of parliament cannot extract rents from the leadership. The Jamaican parliament serves mostly as a forum for discussion, while policy decisions result from the interplay of the prime minister, different ministries, and their respective bureaucracies.

In these circumstances, regulatory stability cannot be achieved through specific legislation. Electoral changes would alter the constituencies in power and might translate into drastic regulatory changes implemented through new legislation. Jamaica's two-party system resulted, as in the United Kingdom, in a judiciary system that has no leverage in administrative matters, but has substantial influence on constitutional issues. Thus, Jamaica's judiciary has kept the administration from expropriating assets without paying compensation, but has never blocked an administrative decision on other than constitutional grounds. To block an administrative decision the court would have to claim that the decision is against the law. And because the government controls parliament, it can always amend the law to clarify its meaning and support its decision.

On the one hand, therefore, Jamaica has a weak body of administrative law, particularly regarding legal restrictions on the exercise of powers and remedies against unlawful administrative action. On the other hand, Jamaica's judiciary has a long tradition of upholding private property and contracts, and so its judiciary and legislative institutions substantially limit the set of basic engineering choices. Although legislation-based regulatory frameworks or administrative procedures would not satisfy the second and third requirements for regulatory stability, using contracts as a regulatory instrument would.

Bolivia is one of the few countries in Latin America that has had a private, profitable electricity company since the beginning of the century. The Compañía Boliviana de Energía Eléctrica (COBEE) started operations in 1912 and serves the cities of La Paz and Oruro.[2] Its regulatory framework is stipulated in its license, and, although the regulatory setup is not ideal, it is important to understand the reasons why Bolivia chose to use licenses rather than administrative procedures or specific legislation.[3]

Bolivia has a presidential system with electoral laws that facilitate a multiplicity of parties in congress. Consequently, a presidential candidate is seldom able to win a majority of the popular vote. In most cases, the incoming congress has to determine who will be president, and it is not required to select the plurality winner. The result is a coalition government. This coalition, however, does not translate into control over congress, because electoral rules grant legislators substantial independence from the central party. Bolivia's political situation makes it very difficult to pass new legislation, so that using specific legislation as basic engineering would seem to be suitable, because once passed such legislation is difficult to amend. But because the executive branch seldom controls the legislature, it bases most of its actions on presidential decree, such as the Electricity Code of 1968. Because these decrees can be amended by the next administration, COBEE's decree was inserted into its license. That way, an amendment to the electricity code will not necessarily affect COBEE's regulatory framework, which is based on a license contract.

Chile used contracts in the late 1980s and early 1990s to insulate the private sector from changes in legislation regarding foreign investment regimes. In Chile, foreign investors signed foreign investment contracts with the Central Bank that guaranteed them access to the formal foreign exchange market (and the same rate of exchange as the domestic banks) for payment of dividends, interest, and eventual repatriation of capital. Since the obligations of the Central Bank were contained in a contract, they could not be altered by subsequent legislation. The constitutionality of these contracts was supported by "reasoned" legal opinions from the Central Bank and the private sector.

Mexico's monolithic party system, with a congress controlled by the executive branch, makes legislation easy to enact and weakens the credibility of regulation (see box 4.2). The possibility is always high that new legislation will amend an existing law. As a result, contracts have been used because they are deemed to represent a more credible commitment.[4]

Peru has used a mixture of presidential decrees and contracts. This choice reflects the transition from a conflictive and fragmented political party structure to a system—following President Fujimori's dissolution of congress and the subsequent out-of-term elections—in which congress is controlled by the executive branch. In that changing environment, contracts are a more credible instrument of commitment than legislation.

THE USE OF SPECIFIC LEGISLATION IN CHILE, ARGENTINA, AND BOLIVIA

In 1980 Chile began to restructure its system of regulation by restructuring the electricity sector. These same reforms were also implemented in the telecommunications sector and use very specific legislation to restrain administrative discretion. (For a discussion of Chile's electricity regulatory reforms, see Spiller and Viana 1992; for a discussion of Chile's telecommunications regulation, see Galal 1994.) The level of detail is such that the law even stipulates the type of regression to be used in estimating a fair rate of return to

Box 4.2 Regulatory Void Slows Mexican Development

Although Mexico's lumbering deregulation process progressed somewhat in 1995 due to the economic crisis, the government still needed to address certain pricing and competition issues if it hoped for more visible improvements. The liquidity crisis that nearly caused the country to default on government bonds underlined the importance of the receipts expected in return for power generation or gas distribution concessions. In April 1995 the government enacted legal reforms authorizing private contractors to construct and operate natural gas pipelines in an attempt to encourage private sector participation in the industry. Unfortunately, substantial deterrents to private investment in gas remained.

Legislation governing private participation was anticipated by October 1995, and, until then, there were few indications of what the electricity pricing policy might be. That made it unlikely that the private sector would enter the field. The heart of the problem was the fact that the basic institutional structure of the Mexican power industry would not change, essentially for political rather than economic reasons. Petróleos Mexicanos (Pemex) controlled all aspects of the oil industry in the country, while the Comisión Federal de Electricidad (CFE) was the only body allowed to distribute and supply electricity. Prices were decided by a committee of officials at the CFE, while the National Hydrocarbons Commission helped set the tariffs for gas, oil, and other hydrocarbons. These calculations took into account only changes in the inflation rate and purchasing power, ignoring the return to equity. As a result, prices could be set so as to recover about 12 percent of the investment made by the power company.

Mexico must remove these obstacles if the country is to comply with the targets set for 1998 by the 1994 Clean Air Act, and generating capacity should increase at least 2 percent a year for the next ten years to keep pace with the demand from a growing population and industrial base. Neither of these goals can be accomplished if the regulatory difficulties are not resolved. The central dilemma of gas distribution remains ensuring that a private distributor will not be squeezed between Pemex, the provider of the gas, and CFE, which either consumes the gas directly or is responsible for setting electricity prices.

Source: Financial Times 1995, p. 23.

the "efficient" firm. Initially introduced in 1982, it was amended in 1985 to make some aspects more specific, and was further amended in 1987 prior to privatization of both operating companies. Box 4.3 presents the main highlights of the price-setting procedures in Chile's telecommunications law. The Chilean experience shows how difficult it is to write such a comprehensive law in a sector characterized by technological change. Indeed, the telecommunications law was changed several times prior to privatization and prior to the advent of democracy. (Electricity

regulation was easier to prepare and implement than telecommunications regulation; see Spiller and Sampson 1993 and 1994.) The Argentine congress has passed a similarly precise regulatory law for its electricity sector, making Chile and Argentina the only two countries where very specific regulatory laws are in effect. (The Argentine law was passed prior to privatization, in December 1992, of the company that distributes electricity to Buenos Aires.) At the same time, these are the only two Latin American countries where the private sector is investing massively in all segments of the electricity sector. (Mexico allows private sector investments only in activities that generate electricity.)

What is remarkable about the regulatory framework in Chile and Argentina is that both countries have electoral systems that promote party fragmentation, regionalization, and legislative independence.[5] In both countries the number of parties in the legislature has traditionally exceeded three, so enacting laws with the degree of specificity presented in box 4.3 is a great political achievement. It is not surprising, however, that such legislative action was undertaken in both countries during periods of unified government. During the Pinochet regime the president exercised control over legislation, making a de facto unified government. In Argentina President Menem's Peronist party held a majority in both houses of congress. The implications of political fragmentation were underscored in Uruguay when congress failed to pass a referendum privatizing the country's telecommunications company in 1992. These cases show that although using specific legislation as basic engineering is an option for countries with fragmented legislatures, it is less plausible in cases where writing specific bills is difficult in general.

Bolivia has one of the worst telecommunications sectors in Latin America. In response, the government sought to achieve wide-ranging reform of the regulation and management of both local and long-distance companies by bundling the two services together to attract more private investment capital. More important, perhaps, the government committed itself to establishing a new legal and regulatory frame-

---

Box 4.3 Procedures for Setting Prices in Chile's Telecommunications Law

Demand is first estimated for each bundle of service, zone, and firm. The efficient firm is defined as one that starts from scratch and uses only the assets necessary to provide the service. For each service, the incremental cost of development is calculated, which is the long-run marginal cost, provided no investment plans are considered. The law stipulates that regulated companies must have investment plans of a minimum of five years. These plans are prepared by the companies and are presented to Subtel on the basis of a detailed outline defined in Law 18,168 (article 301) under the heading "Technical and Economic Basis." Revenue for each service is estimated such that the net present value of providing the service is equal to zero. This revenue is the incremental cost of development. Moving from the incremental cost of development to the long-run average cost, full coverage of cost is attained by increasing efficient tariffs in a least distorting fashion. The fair rate of return is defined as the sum of the rate of return on the risk-free assets and the risk premium of the activity, weighted by the systematic risk of the industry. That is, $R_i = R_f + b_i (R_p - R_f)$, where R_i is the rate of return on revalued capital for firm i, R_f is the rate of return on risk-free assets, b_i is firm i's systematic risk, and R_p is the rate of return on a diversified portfolio. Because tariffs are calculated every five years, the law allows firms to adjust tariffs every two months, using the inflation index of each service and the Divisia index. Disputes between the companies and regulators are settled by a committee of three experts, one nominated by each party and a third by mutual agreement.

Source: Galal 1994.

work for the sector, which it secured in 1996. To capitalize the sector, the national telecommunications company (Entel) became a mixed corporation, comprised of the government's shares and the shares purchased by Entel workers. All telephone cooperatives were then invited to join this corporation, and the new group was capitalized by shares issued to private investors through a public bidding process. The strategic partner, an Italian company, was given control of management through a management contract. The government's shares have been transferred to all adult Bolivians and are being held in trust until pension funds are established to manage them.

The contract between the government and the newly created Entel SA grants Entel (a) the exclusive right to provide all long-distance and international basic voice service in Bolivia for five years, (b) the exclusive right to provide local service for five years in those areas where former local cooperatives joined Entel, and (c) the right to compete for local services even in those areas where the local group did not join Entel. This last provision was designed to improve efficiency by increasing competition. In return, Entel must provide services to rural areas, including areas now being served by Entel and another company. The coverage, maintenance, quality of service, and areas of operation will be specified individually in the various agreements. Finally, the government presented a telecommunications law to congress that delineated the specific responsibilities of the Superintendency of Telecommunications, defined new tariff structures and interconnection charges, and facilitated immediate entry by the private sector into such areas as leased lines, cellular phones, and data transmission. The law specifies that where there is no competition, the superintendency will regulate tariffs using an automatic adjustment formula based on a price cap.

THE USE OF PRESIDENTIAL DECREES IN ARGENTINA, ECUADOR, AND VENEZUELA

Although using specific legislation to regulate electricity seems to match Argentina's institu-

tional characteristics, using presidential decrees to regulate telecommunications does not. Telecommunications regulation was introduced in a series of presidential decrees, each one superseding the previous one (see box 4.4). These continual adjustments had less and less relation to the original regulatory scheme, and the resulting regime could not provide potential investors with any protection from administrative discretion. Moreover, when Argentina decided to privatize, no regulatory agency was in place, and regulated prices had not been determined, so many qualified bidders chose not to participate. Prices were negotiated between firms and the government once firms won their respective bids, but before 40 percent of outstanding shares had been paid.[6] Ownership and management were transferred in

---

Box 4.4 Evolution of Argentina's Telecommunications Privatization and Regulatory Scheme

- *September 1989:* Initial privatization plan under the Menem administration, with three regional monopolies, one for the metropolitan area and one each for the north and south.
- *January 1990:* Basic two-company plan, one for the north and one for the south.
- *March 1990:* Price increase of 300 percent.
- *April 1990:* Change in the terms of reference, including several service requirements and a three-period regulatory plan consisting of (a) a two-year transition with a 16 percent rate of return, (b) a five-year exclusivity with a current price index of 2 percent, and (c) a three-year renewal with a current price index of 4 percent.
- *October 1990:* Agreement on price indexation for the transition period consisting of 60 percent domestic inflation and 40 percent devaluation, and setting of the initial pulse price at $0.038 per pulse, including elimination of 31.5 percent tax with no change in the final price and a price increase of 42 percent.
- *November 1990:* Transfer of ownership.
- *April 1991:* Price freeze following convertibility law and a price reduction of 5 percent.
- *November 1991:* Dollarization of rates for the remainder of the transition period, with rates indexed to U.S. inflation.

Source: Spiller 1993.

November 1991 without a solid regulatory framework, but rather with a series of decrees that granted operating licenses and specified price-setting procedures and operators' responsibilities. Prices were subsequently frozen, then reduced, and eventually dollarized and indexed. The regulatory regime was eventually defined in a series of presidential decrees that did not provide investors with any type of assurances against administrative discretion. As a result, when the time came to privatize the industry, many potential investors were daunted, and offers were low because the risk was high. In fact, only two of the twelve enterprises that expressed interest at the onset of the process ended up submitting bids, and they were state-owned companies— one from Spain and the other from France and Italy.

The prices paid by the initial investors reflected the lack of assurance against administrative discretion coupled with the absence of informal norms against opportunism (McCubbins 1995), and investments were financed primarily through cash flow and debt. Even though prices were partially frozen less than six months after the start of operations, both firms operated quite profitably during that period. At the time of the public offering, Telefónica reported an after-tax gross operating profit of $384 million, while Telecom reported gross after-tax profits of $314 million.[7] If one considers that the private investors paid approximately $1.25 billion for 60 percent of the two companies, Telefónica's and Telecom's cash flows seem quite profitable given their initial investment.[8] In fact, they amortized their investment in less than six years.

The fragmented and conflictive structure of Ecuador's, and to some extent Venezuela's, political parties complicates the enactment of comprehensive legislation. Unsuccessful attempts to enact legislation in congress have led Ecuador and Venezuela to use presidential decrees to privatize and regulate utilities. The presidential decree establishes the regulatory framework, authorizing long-term leases with private corporations that are structured to approximate ownership and to ensure that the lessee will maximize long-term returns rather than short-term gains. The under-

standing for investors is that the government will continue its effort to pass appropriate legislation. The effect on private investors in Ecuadorian utilities is still unclear because this approach was adopted only in late 1994. However, some parties in congress are strongly opposed to legislation, and this should reduce investor confidence in the stability of the regime because presidential decrees can easily be reinterpreted.

THE USE OF ADMINISTRATIVE PROCEDURES IN JAMAICA

Upon independence in 1962, the Jamaican government began a process of regulatory reform in the utility sector, with the intention of moving away from U.K.-style license regulation and toward more modern regulation based on the U.S. Public Utility Commission.[9] The Jamaican Public Utility Commission (JPUC) was created in 1966, with traditional U.S. regulatory powers. However, by 1975 the Jamaican Telephone Company (JTC) was requesting that the government purchase it, and, given the socialist tendencies of then–Prime Minister Michael Manley, the purchase was carried out. This takeover reflected a mismatch between the public utility commission system and Jamaica's political institutions more than it reflected the ideology of the Jamaican government.

Negotiations to renew JTC's license began in October 1963 (its license was to expire in 1966), which postponed JTC's requests for rate increases.[10] In 1962 the company froze its investment plans until an exclusive all-island license was granted that contained a specific pricing policy. From 1962 to 1967 the number of main lines remained stagnant, and the estimated demand for telephones increased to three times the size of the network (Spiller and Sampson 1993; World Bank 1974, p. 52).

The license renewed in 1966 included several new features: a public utilities commission-style regulatory system, a twenty-five-year term renewable for another ten years, and a clause stating that Jamaicans should hold a large proportion of the company's shares, with no shareholder holding more than 20 percent of the company.[11] Unlike the 1945 license, the 1966 license did not provide for a minimum rate of return on the base rate, but rather provided for a "fair" return, with the base rate to be determined by the JPUC.[12] Upon receiving the new license, JTC's major shareholder decided to sell its holdings. In mid-1967 the Continental Telephone Company (a Canadian-based holding company with local telephone operations in Canada, the United States, and the Caribbean) bought the majority shareholder's stake in JTC. As a condition for the transfer of shares and of the license, Continental Telephone agreed to undertake several financial and developmental obligations, with specific goals for the provision of new service and the expansion of existing service.

The JTC's regulatory environment had completely changed by the time Continental Telephone purchased stock. The company now faced a traditional rate-of-return system, but one without implicit or explicit juridically protected minimum rates of return or a defined conflict resolution process. Indeed, despite a doubling of prices and requests to increase rates, no increase was granted between 1960 and 1971. (In its August 1972 report, the JPUC stated that its policy was to make prices contingent on the quality of service provided). A series of conflicts involved definition of the base rate (whether the investments undertaken were actually proper),[13] accounting procedures (whether depreciation should be computed at the beginning of the period or at the beginning of each month), the company's cost of capital,[14] and reasonable costs. These issues elicited substantial hostility. The price of JTC's stock fell to J$0.28 by March 1972, well below Spiller and Sampson's (1993) estimate of a book value of J$1.3 for December 1971 and the J$1.13 per share paid by Continental Telephone.

Two other major changes occurred in the regulatory environment. The first was that third parties were allowed to participate in the rate hearings. As a result the Jamaican Tax and Ratepayers Association and the Jamaican Hotel and Tourist Association presented evidence against the JTC during rate hearings. (The Tax and Ratepayers Association even asked the supreme court to review JPUC's decision to grant the JTC a rate increase.) A second change was that the courts had a smaller role in the regulatory process. Prior to creation of the JPUC, the supreme court reversed decisions of the rate board that did not allow the company to recoup past profit deficiencies. Following passage of the JPUC Act, the court refused to hear JPUC cases. Two aspects of the new regulatory environment may have affected the court's implicit approach to JPUC decisions. First, the 1966 license was less forthcoming in providing minimum rates of return. Second, while the rate boards were ad hoc commissions, the JPUC was a fully staffed, semijudicial organization. More important, because the JPUC was directed by political appointees, its decisions were thought to reflect the will of parliament. Thus, unless the JPUC violated a procedural formality or a license stipulation, the court did not find it proper to intervene. Consequently, the JPUC Act provided no coherent process for resolving conflicts between the JPUC and JTC, essentially granting full discretion to the JPUC and dooming the JTC to continual financial difficulties.

The JTC's lack of incentives and poor performance during the first half of the 1970s are best understood in light of two factors: first, the initial conditions under which Continental Telephone agreed to buy a majority shareholder's stake in JTC, and second, the passage and implementation of the JPUC act. The former implied that JTC would have to undertake a substantial development program, which to a large extent was supposed to be underwritten by Continental Telephone itself. The JPUC's workings, however, dampened Continental Telephone's desire to increase its exposure in the JTC, leaving the JTC reliant on cash flow or international loans to finance its expansion. Both these options were restrained by JPUC policies. By late 1975 the JTC's financial situation was so precarious that Continental Telephone agreed to sell the government its holdings in the JTC. Another example of the problems of commitment that is not credible is presented in box 4.5, concerning toll roads in Thailand.

Box 4.5 The Problem of Commitment

The Economist of June 12, 1993, printed the following description of problems with the development of road infrastructure in Bangkok:

If proof were needed that Bangkok's traffic is the worst in the world, then it has arrived in the shape of the "Comfort 100," a red plastic bottle which is being sold as a portable urinal.... Thai motorists are not alone in finding the Comfort 100 symbolic of governmental inaction on traffic. Foreign construction companies, which had been salivating at the thought of some $20 billion of promised infrastructural spending, are now having second thoughts. Three mooted mass-transit systems have got no further than the drawing board. And the one new highway that is almost complete—Bangkok's second-stage expressway—has now become the subject of a bitter dispute.

The road is a 20 kilometer (12 mile) six-lane tollway, built by a Japanese-led consortium and financed by a $200 million loan, in which 31 foreign banks have an interest. The consortium has built the expressway on a "build, operate and transfer" basis. Its profits were supposed to come from levying a 30 baht ($1.20) toll. At the last moment, the government balked, unilaterally setting a new price of 20 baht. In theory, the missing 10 baht will come out of the state's share of the toll-money. The government now wants the consortium to open the expressway in the next few weeks. The road itself is still only partly completed, with four of its 18 ramps "ski-jumps" which end in midair. In the meantime, competi-tors to the Comfort 100 are already appearing on the market. A Taiwanese device called "Easi Pee" is advertised as ideal for children. And from Japan comes a more unwieldy piece of equipment, the ominously titled "Thunderbox."

The Economist of September 4, 1993, printed the following continuation of the Bangkok road infrastructure saga:

On August 31st the government took legal action to force an international consortium to open a new motorway in Bangkok.... Initially, the government balked at levying the 30 baht ($1.20) toll specified in the contract, though it later agreed to it. But when the company said that other matters remained unsettled, the government lost patience and obtained a court order. Agreeing to open the road, the presiding judge said that the government had law on its side, but added, "The people's suffering is the highest law."

...On September 2nd, Chuann Leekpai, the Thai prime minister, gave the go-ahead for a ribbon-cutting ceremony at the disputed expressway. His action angered international bankers connected with the motorway consortium.... They argue that under the original contract they are already owed 2 billion baht in tolls from a stretch of motorway controlled by the government. Bankers close to the Bangkok Expressway Company say that it is under threat of bankruptcy. The government responds that the priority is to get the road opened and that all investors will be paid, once negotiations resume.

NOTES

1. Spiller and Sampson (1993) claim that although the government could have designed a better regulatory framework (in particular, one where competition was allowed in value-added and other services), attempting to liberalize the international market would have required such a large increase in domestic utility rates that the reform program would have been blocked entirely.

2. COBEE is a Canadian-based private company whose major shareholder is a U.S. company (Leucadia National Corporation). COBEE has distribution and generation licenses for the La Paz and Oruro regions. All generation is hydroelectric and of relatively low investment costs because it uses water in very steep and long areas.

3. The license specifies that regulation of the company will be based on the electricity code as detailed by the presidential decree of 1968. Thus, changing the electricity code would not affect COBEE because its regulatory framework cannot be amended unless its operating license is amended, and COBEE must agree to such an amendment.

4. However, given the considerable discretion accorded to regulatory agencies, regulatory influence may lead to noncompliance. Indeed, in a suit filed against Telmex at the Federal Competition Commission, Iusacell claimed that Telmex did not comply either with its own license or with the law (*The News*, November 8, 1995, p. 28).

5. Consider, for example, Argentina's electoral rules. Deputies (members of the lower house) are elected from provincial party lists, which are put together by regional party leaders. Senators are elected in the provincial legislatures, requiring only a plurality of votes. Two senators represent each province, and two represent the capital. Deputies serve four years, while senators serve nine. Half of the deputies are elected every two years. A third of the senators are elected every six years. The president is elected every six years (concurrent with congressional elections) and is not eligible for reelection. Thus, the staggering of

elections for the lower and the upper houses and for the presidency, and the regionalization of parties, make the probability of having a unified government relatively low (McCubbins 1995, pp. 11–12).

6. Two bidders had appropriate financing: Telefónica de España, and the Stet and France Telecom consortium. Telefónica was granted a license to operate only in the south, while the consortium led by Stet and France Telecom received an operating license for the north. Telefónica's group paid $114 million in cash plus $2.7 billion in notes for Argentina's foreign debt instruments, which were bought at an 80 percent discount. The Telecom group paid $100 million in cash plus $2.2 billion in Argentine debt. The government agreed to assume more than $2 billion of Entel's debt, two-thirds of which had accrued during the year before privatization.

7. This value is the net operating profit plus depreciation minus taxes. Interest was not deducted from profits. The net after-tax profit reported for eleven months ending November 30, 1992 was $115 million (Telefónica de Argentina 1991).

8. Previous reports in the Argentine press estimated higher profits. For example, *La Nación* (June 26, 1991) reported expected profits for the two companies combined to be more than $1.8 billion, of which 40 percent ($748 million) belonged to the government. Thus, firms were expected to receive $1.1 billion, which was approximately the value of their combined payments for the two companies.

9. Jamaica has two main political parties, the Jamaican Labor Party and the People's National Party, which have dominated the political scene since the early 1940s, alternating power every other election. The two parties were quite similar in their politics until the late 1960s and early 1970s; the middle and upper classes represented the swing voters, while the poor composed both core constituencies. Consequently, until the mid-1970s and again beginning in the mid-1980s, both parties have had very similar policies, although they have differed in their rhetoric.

10. In 1962 the company requested a substantial rate increase to compensate for previous revenue deficiencies (as allowed by its current license and a 1956 supreme court decision). A rate board was established in June 1963. The rate board, however, did not allow any important rate increase during its tenure, and the next rate increase came only in 1971, five years after the creation of JPUC.

11. Telephone and General Trust was the majority shareholder at the time, with 50.2 percent of the outstanding stock. It was given six years to dispose of its 30.2 percent excess holding.

12. The Public Utilities Commission Act determined that the JPUC should set rates that would provide the utilities *not more* than 2.5 percent above the redemption yield of government long-term bonds issued in the United Kingdom, instead of requiring a minimum rate of return. The Telephone Act, however, provided for an 8 percent return on the base rate. The JPUC interpreted this provision to mean "permitted" rather than "entitled to."

13. The JPUC's main complaint was that the number of new lines was expanding more slowly than was the base rate. Essentially, the company seemed to be replacing technically and physically obsolete equipment without expanding its network at the same rate.

14. The license was amended in early 1974 to specify both how depreciation was to be measured, and the minimum allowed rate of return.

5 CREATING THE DETAIL ENGINEERING OF REGULATION: PRICE-SETTING POLICIES

THE STANDARD ELEMENTS that are often subject to regulation vary from country to country and from sector to sector. The general principle of detail engineering is to regulate (economic regulation) those segments of the market that display natural monopoly characteristics to curtail abuses of monopoly power. The three main instruments of regulation, or decision variables, are price(s), quantity, and the number of firms. Other less common instruments include product quality, service timeliness, and investment. Often, the failure to use a potentially powerful instrument of regulation, such as quality, has to do with the

existence of severe informational problems and the high cost of monitoring and enforcement. More specifically, regulation commonly encompasses the following activities:

- Licensing carriers or operators
- Setting operator prices or tariffs for services
- Setting technical standards
- Monitoring the quality of service provided by operators and initiating corrective action if necessary
- Approving operators' programs for construction and capital investments
- Setting the financial, administrative, and technical terms for interconnecting the networks of different operators, including access pricing

- Controlling the type and approval of equipment on the customer's premises and its connection to the public network
- Considering complaints from telecommunications users and taking corrective action if necessary
- Collecting market or cost information and requiring operators to provide technical information on their operations
- Acting as a binding arbitrator in the event of conflicts between service providers and network operators.

Not all of these elements must be regulated. The regulatory functions and the regulated elements depend by and large on the country's regulatory philosophy, endowments, and characteristics; the sector's characteristics; and the extent of competition allowed. For example, New Zealand has virtually no regulatory control of the prices charged to end users, Hong Kong has no control of equipment on the customer's premises, and the FCC in the United States often chooses not to impose technical standards. As mentioned, there are tradeoffs in regulatory design, and a country should evaluate them carefully when choosing how much regulation to impose.

THE RELATION BETWEEN DETAIL AND BASIC ENGINEERING

Theories of regulation presume that the choice of detail engineering can be properly computed and undertaken in any political or institutional environment. These theories fail to recognize that, in the absence of a reasonable match between detail engineering and the basic engineering on which it rests, achieving the desired outcome will be difficult. Normative theories of natural monopoly as applied to comparative regulation presume that second-best detail engineering is readily transferable across countries. For example, if appropriate basic engineering translates into specific regulatory rules that limit opportunism, then flexible pricing schemes requiring regulatory judgments are not feasible. Thus, second-best pricing is not attainable, and attempting to create a regulatory system with substantial flexibility is not credible. However, if the appropriate basic engineering allows for a flexible regulatory framework, then discretionary regulatory schemes might be credible.

Regulatory management is crucial to both the economic and the political success of privatization programs. Privatization has the potential to bring credibility to the government and to provide revenue that can alleviate short-term fiscal problems. Utilities are particularly sensitive because their operations affect voters directly. It is not uncommon for economically successful privatization programs to arouse a fair amount of political opposition, which can damage not only the utility in question but also the entire privatization program. There are two basic approaches to regulating utilities: structural and conduct. In many countries, especially in Western Europe,

policymakers have attempted to alter the *structure* of public utilities before privatizing in order to increase competition afterward. One aspect of the structural method is that it separates the activities in the industry, such as transportation from provision. The United States and the United Kingdom regulate the *conduct* of the utility. The United States favors the rate-of-return approach to regulation, while the United Kingdom leans toward price caps and performance standards.

In the United States the public utilities commission of each state determines the prices that the monopoly franchise can charge. The criterion used to determine these prices is that the firm cannot earn more than a "fair and reasonable" rate of return on its capital stock. The U.S. approach keeps the utility from earning monopoly profits, but not from investing heavily in its capital stock. However, attempts to tackle this problem have led to legal battles with firms over whether new investments can be justified because they are needed to meet demand. Litigation has made regulating the cost of capital very expensive.

Detail Engineering and Country Endowments

A country's legal and administrative endowments can limit its potential for undertaking a complex regulatory framework, thereby restricting its choice of basic and detail engineering. Consider implementing flexible price systems in a nation whose institutional characteristics call for inflexible detail engineering. Jamaica, with its two-party parliamentary system, substantial government turnover, and lack of informal norms limiting administrative discretion, offers an example.

Jamaica could not implement rate-of-return regulation of public utilities because this approach would give the Public Utility Commission too much discretion in setting the rate base and the appropriate level of return on capital. If implemented, this type of regulation would have to restrict the extent to which the regulator could determine rates of return, capital levels, and costs. The implementation of a price cap would have similar implications, because price caps have to be reset every few years to avoid profit over- or undershooting, and leaving such a decision to the regulator might grant too much discretion. Again, the system of revising the price cap would have to limit regulatory discretion and discourage opportunistic behavior on the part of the regulator.

The Tradeoff Between Commitment and Flexibility

Countries differ in the extent to which efforts to limit opportunistic administrative behavior require that the regulatory framework be specified in great detail. Some countries can afford more flexibility in their regulatory design than others. In particular, countries with informal norms restraining arbitrary administrative decisions, or with institutionalized decisionmaking requiring a consensus, can limit administrative expropriation without specifying in great detail the regulatory framework for doing so.[1] In contrast, countries whose exogenous endowments have neither feature may have to settle for more rigid detail engineering. In those countries the tradeoff between flexibility and commitment is the most visible. In the extreme, some countries may lack the basic institutional features needed to design workable and credible regulatory systems, and public ownership of utilities may become the default mode of ownership. The tradeoff between commitment and flexibility is seen in three types of policies in particular: price-setting policy, competition policy, and competition boundary policy. This chapter focuses on price-setting policies.

PRICE-SETTING POLICIES

Optimal second-best prices are flexible. They must adjust to technological changes and to movements in demand and costs. The main thrust of the optimality conditions are that (a) firms should benefit when showing lower than expected costs and should be penalized when showing higher than expected costs;[2] (b) firms should neither benefit nor suffer too much as a result of changes in demand and exogenous changes in technology;[3] and (c) attempting to extract all the rents from a firm may trigger inefficient regulatory regimes. However, flexibility

requires that a regulatory commission be granted extensive discretion, but such discretion can invite wasteful rent-seeking activities. Traditional and novel types of detail regulation take some subset of the optimality principles into account. A discussion of the salient mechanisms of detail regulation—methods of setting prices—follows.

Rate-of-return regulation

The principle behind rate-of-return regulation, which is common in Canada, Japan, and the United States, is to constrain prices so that the regulated firm earns only a fair rate of return on its capital investment. This regulation has three components: the rate base, the rate level, and the rate structure. The rate base refers to the investments that are allowed to earn a rate of return, the rate level refers to the relation of overall revenues to costs, and the rate structure determines how individual prices are set for different services or customers. These components can be seen in the following accounting relation: Sum $(i = 1 \ldots n)$ $p_i q_i$ = costs and expenses + $r(RB)$, where p_i is the price of service i, q_i is the quantity of service, n is the number of services, r is the fair rate of return, and RB is the rate base, a measure of the value of the regulated firm's investment. The usual components of the rate base are plant minus depreciation and working capital, while the rate level is based on the fair rate of return, and the rate structure is based on the price of service. (See box 5.1 on how to estimate the cost of capital or rate level.) A commission generally ensures that prices charged by the regulated firm are fair and that there is no undue discrimination. The procedure is to set prices that cannot be changed until the next case or hearing. The essence of this form of regulation is deciding what type of investments will be included in the rate base and selecting the rate of return. Then the prices are a sort of residual and should satisfy the above accounting relation. In assessing the value of the rate base, the salient method is to determine the original cost; that is, the amount the company originally paid for the plant and equipment minus depreciation, with some adjustment for inflation.

Box 5.1 How to Compute the Cost of Capital

The standard approach adopted by regulatory agencies and governments to compute the cost of capital is to use the weighted average cost of capital (WACC). Formally, WACC can be estimated as follows:

$$WACC = [(1-g) \times r_e] + [g \times r_d],$$

where g is the level of gearing/leverage in a company, that is, the proportion of debt in the total capital structure (debt + equity); and r_d is the cost of debt finance. This is simply measured as a risk-free rate, r_f plus a debt premium over this rate, p_d. The premium is measured either directly from the yield of a company's bond or through comparable information, (yields on new bonds are listed in the *Financial Times* at the date of issue and are available from commercial information sources on a daily basis), and r_e is the cost of equity finance. The estimation of the cost of equity finance raises bigger problems, and yet for privatized infrastructure monopolies, it is quite important since access to debt finance can be quite restricted for the privatization projects of many developing countries.

One of the common approaches adopted to measure the cost of equity is the Capital Asset Pricing Model (CAPM). This estimates the cost of equity as follows:

$$r_e = r_f + \beta_e(r_m - r_f),$$

where r_e is the cost of equity finance; r_f is the risk-free return; β_e is the equity beta which measures the relative risk of the company's equity (and sometimes the sector's risk) compared to the market as a whole (its value depends on the type of regulation used); r_m is the level of market return; and $r_m - r_f$ is the market risk premium.

Establishing the values for each of these items is relatively straightforward when developed capital markets exist and companies are quoted on a stock exchange. Approximations have to be used in most less-developed countries. The average asset beta in infrastructure (which accounts for the leverage in the capital structure of the projects) is around 0.7 for high-powered incentive regimes and around 0.3 for low-powered incentive regimes.

Source: Alexander and Estache 1997; Alexander, Mayer, and Weeds 1996.

Utilities often provide a variety of services and products to various types of customers. In addition, utility facilities are commonly used by all types of customers for all types of services. Examples are power plants, transmission lines and pipelines, telephone switching centers, scheduling centers, and rail beds. The issue is how to allocate common costs among customers and services. With utilities, the production of all products is often subadditive, which means that total fixed costs for all products produced together are lower than if each product is produced separately. Under cost subadditivity, efficiency for most utilities requires joint production and allocation of fixed costs among all products, without cross-subsidization (accounting for externalities whenever present).

Common costs are often allocated on the basis of some common measure of use or in proportion to costs that can be assigned directly to the various services or products. Any regulatory pricing scheme should pass two subsidy-free tests. The test of stand-alone average cost, which

requires the price for product x to cover average cost and to exceed what would be charged if product x were produced separately, passes the subsidy-free test in that it does not produce incentives for customers to break away and produce x alone. The average incremental cost test, which requires each product to contribute to total revenue an amount that at least covers any extra costs that its production adds to the production of the other products, passes the subsidy-free test in that the price of the product equals or exceeds the product's average incremental costs. The two tests are practically equivalent, and their violation implies cross-subsidization.

Rate-of-return regulation suffers from three essential problems. First, it provides little incentive for productive efficiency, because firms can pass production costs on to the final users in the form of higher prices. Second, it leads to excessive investment and capital use because the firm is guaranteed a return on its investments. And finally, it grants the commission a high degree of discretion and induces incentives for rent seeking by the regulated firm. These undesirable effects have led to the development of alternatives to the standard rate-of-return regulation, including a sliding scale plan, Ramsey pricing, the Loeb-Magat proposal, and price caps and performance standards.

Sliding-Scale Plan

Proposed by Joskow and Schmalensee (1986), this mechanism allows risks and rewards to be shared between the owners and consumers. It falls between cost-plus regulation and fixed-price regulation. It works as follows: let $r*$ be the desired fair rate of return and let r_i be the actual rate of return at current period i prices. The sliding scale would adjust prices so that the actual rate of return (r_a) at the new prices would be $r_a = r_i + h(r* - r_i)$, where h is a constant such that $1 < h < 0$. If h is 1, we have cost-plus regulation, with a constant $r*$ rate of return and no incentives for efficient operations. Alternatively, if h is 0, we have fixed-price regulation. All gains from efficiency accrue to the firm, as do any cost increases. At an h of 0.5, unexpected costs and benefits would be shared equally.

Ramsey Pricing

Ramsey, or "value-of-service" pricing involves varying the ratio of price to long-run incremental cost in inverse proportion to the elasticity of demand. This pricing scheme is applicable to a natural monopoly that handles multiple products. Because linear marginal cost pricing would generate losses for a natural monopolist, Ramsey (1927) devised an alternative second-best pricing scheme. Ramsey prices are linear prices (one for each product) that satisfy the total revenue equals total cost constraint and minimize deadweight welfare losses. In other words, this pricing method results in the smallest deadweight loss triangles of all possible outcomes that yield revenues equal to costs. This result is achieved by setting prices, or the markup over marginal cost, in inverse proportion to demand elasticities, as in $(p_i - MC_i) / p_i = k / e_i$, where k is a constant. This is value-of-service pricing and results in a

second-best solution. An alternative and more general way to describe Ramsey pricing (which also applies to interdependent demands) is to evaluate outputs where price equals marginal cost. This allocation generates losses in natural monopolies. To eliminate losses in an efficient way, the output of all goods can be cut by the same proportion until total revenue just equals total cost. The resulting prices are Ramsey prices and tend to be subsidy free.[4] Once there is competition, the elasticity of demand facing a firm may be difficult to define, because it will depend on the impact of the price change on the other firms(s) and on their reaction to it.

Loeb-Magat Proposal

A drawback of Ramsey pricing is that it requires the regulator to know the firm's cost function, which is usually very difficult to evaluate. Loeb and Magat (1969) proposed an alternative method that does not require the regulator to have knowledge of the firm's cost function. The method presumes knowledge only of the demand function, which is easier to evaluate. This scheme allows the monopolist to set its own price and the regulatory agency to subsidize the firm by an amount equal to the consumer surplus at the selected price. This leads to marginal cost pricing, because the objective of the monopolist is to maximize total surplus, which leads to efficiency. Objections to this form of pricing are based on distributional grounds, because the monopolist appropriates the entire economic surplus. However, this can be corrected by tying the scheme to a franchise bidding scheme in which the right to operate the monopoly franchise is auctioned. Overall, informational problems about the demand curve and the existence of a subsidy lessen the appeal of this approach to regulation, making it unlikely to be the best solution to (pricing) regulation.

Price Caps and Performance Standards

Price caps and performance standards are the most common form of regulation in Europe for privatized gas, telephone, electricity, and water, and they have been used by the FCC in some states in the United States in lieu of rate-of-return regulation. They have also been the choice for regulation in Australia, Puerto Rico, Singapore, and particularly Latin America. Under this regulatory scheme the firm is free to raise its prices between review periods, at the rate of inflation (RPI) minus some amount (x) chosen to reflect expected increases in productivity (mostly technology driven). At the end of the review period the regulator can choose a new x. The process to guide the new price adjustment at the review period is described in figure 5.1. This method provides the regulated firm with an incentive to operate efficiently (productive efficiency). Like sliding-scale regulation, owners and users share the risks and rewards. This system provides incentives for cutting costs and raising efficiency. The firm may keep any cost savings at least until the end of the review period. For the next review period, the initial price and the new x will reflect the new cost constellation, thereby enabling consumers to benefit from the greater efficiency. This system avoids the pitfalls of rate-of-return regulation, in which inefficiencies may be rewarded through higher rates and utilities have few incentives to cut costs, which are likely to result quickly in mandatory price reductions.

Revenue Caps

A variation of price-cap regulation is revenue caps, where the constraint is that revenues, defined as actual outputs times price weights set by the regulator, cannot exceed a given value. As with price caps, revenue caps provide incentives for cost reductions, since they are fully captured by the operator, and the output measures required for implementation are relatively easy to obtain (as opposed to cost information). The disadvantage is that revenue caps induce limited incentives to expand output (coverage). For an assessment and comparison of price caps, revenue caps, and rate-of-return regulation, see tables 5.1 and 5.2.

However, some general difficulties are also involved in setting up an $RPI - x$ regulatory system. They include:

- *Regulatory capture.* To guarantee that the privatization program as a whole is successful, the government wants shareholders to receive a good return. This pressures the regulator to ensure that dividends are satisfactory for at least the first few years. However, regulators face considerable criticism from consumers for what is perceived to be excessive generosity toward the utilities when determining the level of x, as the U.K. experience shows. The regulatory authorities also face a barrage of criticism from the utilities, which resent interference.
- *Regulatory risk.* Price controls based on $RPI - x$ can distort investment incentives. Given the political nature of the regulatory process, investors must take account of the fact that public policy toward the utilities is likely to remain high on the political agenda.
- *Cost calculations.* Limited information is available to regulators. In setting prices, regulators ideally want to know the lowest feasible unit costs of the firm. A key task for public policy is thus to increase the information available to regulators. However, feasible unit costs often cannot be calculated, even with cooperation from regulated firms.
- *Cross-subsidization.* In network industries, the costs of supply are significantly influenced by the location and density of consumers, yet consumers dislike paying different prices in different areas for what appears to be the same service. This causes considerable public pressure for cross-subsidization between geographical markets, while the utilities would like prices to reflect costs fully.
- *Pricing network access.* Providing a network of services entails large fixed costs. Marginal cost pricing fails to reflect fully these fixed costs and penalizes the network provider.
- *Regulatory lag.* The cost reductions that can be gained from privatizing a utility tend to be large at first but to diminish over time. As a result, there is a danger that the regulator will overestimate the potential profit of the utility in the review following privatization and will set targets too high. If the review period is longer than the lag, it can

Figure 5.1 Flow Chart for a Price Control Review Process

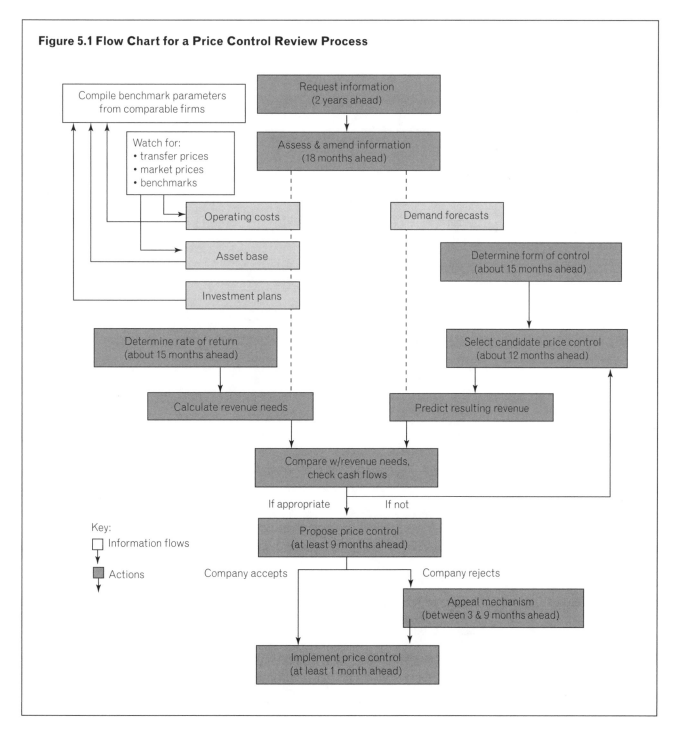

lock regulators and companies into a framework that quickly becomes inappropriate and is difficult to adjust. If reviews are too frequent they can increase regulatory risk and deter investment.

• *Income risk of investment*. With rate-of-return regulation the operator is guaranteed the rate of return on new investments; however, that is not necessarily the case with income risk of investment. Rate of return should be

taken into account, but needs a good argument. This hints that for sectors requiring massive investments, a preferable approach would be rate-of-return regulation with proper monitoring of investments.

The price-cap system has several variations. The following description of the U.K. price-cap system across different sectors—telecommunications, water, airports, gas, and electricity—illustrates how price caps are determined in practice,

Table 5.1 Formulas for Price-Basket, Revenue, and Rate-of-Return Caps

Method	Formula	
Price-basket cap	Prices x quantity weights (set by regulator)	< cap
Revenue cap	Revenues	< actual output x price weights (set by regulator)
Rate-of-return cap	Proposed tariff x predicted output	< predicted costs + fair profit

Source: Green 1997a.

Table 5.2 Key Features of Price-Basket, Revenue, and Rate-of-Return Caps

Feature	Price-Basket Cap	Revenue Cap	Rate-of-Return Cap
Constraint set by cap	Weighted average of prices cannot exceed cap	Revenues cannot exceed limit (related to output set by cap)	Tariff cannot predict a rate of return above regulated level
Coverage	Specified prices (line rentals, domestic calls)	Specified types of sales (such as to captive small consumers)	Regulated business's predicted revenues
Implementation requirement	A list of prices	Output measures	Tariffs that give revenue predictions
Weights on quantities	Set by regulator	Actual quantities	Predicted quantities
Price weights in cap	None explicit	Set by regulator	From tariff
Constraint on cross-subsidy	Subsidiary cap required	Separate constraint required	Regulator could disallow tariff
Opportunity for manipulation	Very small	Some (likely to be small in practice)	Some (likely to be small in practice)
Cost pass-through terms	Might be included in cap (difficult)	Simple to include in cap	Tariff might contain escalation clause
Correction factor	Not required	Required	Not required
Advantage	Simple to define and monitor	Allows constraint to respond to actual output and pass-through costs	Investors face lower risk, reducing cost of capital
Limitation	Needs a full list of prices	Needs homogeneous output measures (revenues must be < output x weight)	Needs predictions of revenues and costs for each new set of tariffs
Example	British Telecom	British Gas	U.S. utilities

Source: Green 1997a.

and presents some of the variations. This mode of regulation is being extensively introduced in Latin America and the Caribbean.

The United Kingdom Price-Cap System

In 1984 the U.K. government privatized British Telecommunications (BT), thus converting it from a statutory monopoly of network services to a virtual monopoly with a sole fledgling competitor, Mercury Communications Limited. Recognizing that BT would long remain the virtually monopolistic, or at least a strongly dominant, supplier of network services, the government set up a regulatory system, to be administered by the Office of Telecommunications (Oftel), which is headed by a director general of telecommunications who controls BT's prices in market segments where BT enjoys significant market power.

As the fundamental instrument for controlling the large bulk of BT's prices, the government applies the price-cap formula $RPI - x$ to a basket of services. The formula dictates that in each year between regulatory reviews BT may raise the average nominal price of services within the basket by a percentage determined by the composite effect of the past year's percentage increase in the official retail price index (RPI) minus a temporarily fixed parameter (x), which is intended to estimate the average annual rate at which BT can improve its total factor productivity. If, for instance, the retail price index increased by 10 percent in the past year and if x was set at 5 percent, then BT could increase the average basket price by no more than 5 percent. If in any year BT took less than full advantage of the price ceiling, it could carry over the unused allowance for up to two years. Restated, the price for the basket of services must fall, in real terms, by at least x percent each year. Although this rule sets a ceiling on BT's year-on-year price movements, it sets no floor.

The value of x is normally reset at the time of regulatory reviews, which have taken place at intervals of four or five years, although a number of mid-term adjustments were made in 1991. Originally, in 1984, x for the main cap was set at 3 percent. Since then it has been increased successively to 4.5 percent (1989–91), 6.25 percent (1991–93), and 7.5 percent (1993–97). See figure 5.2 for a comparison of the x-factor across industries. In considering the level at which x should be set, for either the main cap or any of the special caps, the director general has repeatedly relied on BT's rate of return on capital employed (both overall and on particular services), and on the relation between BT's price for a particular service or for a bundle of services and the costs incurred by BT in supplying those services.

Figure 5.2 also provides information on the annual real price increases for Britain's regulated industries: electricity distribution, electricity transmission, gas, telecommunications, and water from the time of privatization, which is when $RPI - x$ was first instituted, to 1997.

- Since privatization, water and sewage companies have been granted positive x values, meaning that prices have risen each period. Even in this sector, however, the amount by which prices can rise decreased from 4 percent to approximately 1 percent in 1995, where it is expected to remain until 2005.
- Similarly, electricity distribution companies benefited from a negative x value for the first five-year evaluation period, but that value dropped to 2 percent for 1995 onward, indicating real price reductions.
- Electricity transmission companies used an x value of 0 from 1990 to 1993, and then decreased prices by about 3 percent. A new assessment was made in 1996.
- Gas and telecommunications companies have never received positive x values and, therefore, have reduced prices since privatization. British Gas was granted a slight reversal in prices in 1994 when the x value was revised from 5 to 4 percent. Telecommunications companies were forced to adjust prices downward three times to the current level of 7.5 percent from the initial value of 3 percent.

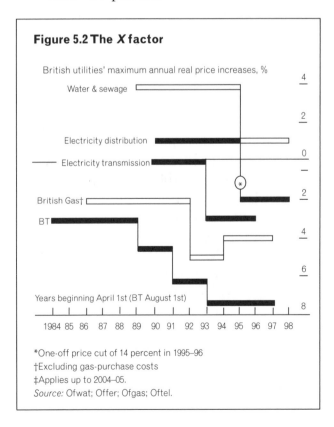

Figure 5.2 The *X* factor

British utilities' maximum annual real price increases, %

Water & sewage

Electricity distribution

Electricity transmission

British Gas†

BT

Years beginning April 1st (BT August 1st)

1984 85 86 87 88 89 90 91 92 93 94 95 96 97 98

*One-off price cut of 14 percent in 1995–96
†Excluding gas-purchase costs
‡Applies up to 2004–05.
Source: Ofwat; Offer; Ofgas; Oftel.

The contents of the so-called main basket, governed by the "main cap" of $RPI - x$, are also subject to change. The main basket (1984–89) originally included only exchange-line rentals and direct-dialed inland calls. In 1991 it was substantially extended to include international calls and directory service (for which BT began to charge separately) and tariff packages (and other optional charging arrangements for heavy-usage customers). From 1993 to 1997, the main basket was extended to cover connection charges, but tariff packages and other quantity discounts were excluded.

The private-circuit basket, when first subjected to price controls in 1989, included only inland circuits. For 1991–93 the basket was extended to cover international circuits as well. The single basket for 1993–97 was partitioned into three baskets covering inland analog circuits, inland digital circuits, and international circuits, each subject to a separate price cap.

The standing-charge basket (1984–89) originally included only residential exchange-line rentals, which, though within the main basket, were controlled by a separate price cap. This special basket was extended in 1989–91 to cover exchange-line rentals of business and residential customers, both of which were inside the main basket, and connection charges, which until 1993 remained outside the main basket. In 1991 this basket was divided into three smaller baskets, each subject to a separate price cap: exchange-line rentals, single-line residential use, and business use; exchange-line rentals, multiline use, and wholesale use; and connection charges. For 1993–97, exchange-line rentals of all sorts were regrouped in a single basket, and connection charges placed in another, although all figure in the main basket as well.

Annual changes in the price of the main basket are calculated by a weighted average. The change in the price of each individual service within the basket is weighted by a fraction measuring the relation between BT's turnover from that service and BT's total turnover from the entire basket of services. This weighted average is the figure that cannot rise annually by more than $RPI - x$. Similar weighted averages establish the price of baskets other than the main basket.

A successful program for regulating privatized industries should embrace the following principles:

- Seek to prevent the abuse of monopoly power
- Ensure that economic regulation does not distort business decisions
- Limit the costs of regulation to what is essential
- Have regulation of a monopoly replicate the behavior of a competitive market as far as possible.

The $RPI - x$ system of price control follows these basic principles. Experience, primarily in the United Kingdom, has shown the mechanisms to be broadly workable and coherent. Six governments have recently privatized their telecommunications systems (Alberta, Canada; Argentina; Australia; Japan; Puerto Rico; and Singapore); only Japan and Alberta have chosen rate-of-return systems rather than $RPI - x$. Moreover, the United States—the largest economy to embrace rate-of-return mechanisms—is in the process of switching from rate of return to $RPI - x$. Nevertheless, $RPI - x$ can fail in two ways. It can become either unnecessarily intrusive or too detailed. The former tendency goes against the second principle listed above, while the latter ignores the third.

Practical Experience with Price Caps in the United Kingdom

Different price-cap formulas have been used for the industries that have been privatized in the United Kingdom. This section presents those formulas and discusses their potential dangers and the overall success of this particular method of regulation.

British Telecommunications. Littlechild (1983) provides a framework for the privatization of BT and argues that direct price regulation should be used until sufficient competition develops. (This section is adapted from Glynn 1992). Littlechild's proposal links prices to a general index of inflation, which would allow BT a period without price changes (about five years) that is long enough to produce incentives for improved efficiency. That is, price reductions would not instantly remove the profits from increased profitability. A second feature of Littlechild's proposal is that the controls should apply to a basket of tariffs in which management is free—with some constraints—to alter relative prices. This means that BT could incorporate new information about costs or markets without involving the regulator. In this case the regulator would be Oftel, which has the responsibility to prevent undue discrimination in tariffs.

A "pure tariff basket" control limits the prices charged, not the revenue per customer or per call:

$$(5.1) \qquad W_t = RPI_{t-1} - x + Z_t$$

where W is the weighted average increase in charges for a basket of services, RPI is the percentage change in the retail price index, x is 4.5, and Z is unused allowance from the previous year. The left-hand side of the inequality is the weighted average increase in charges in year t for the basket of regulated services. This calculation is straightforward: Weights are given by each tariff item in the previous year, and the price increase proposed for each is multiplied by that weight. On the right-hand side, RPI_{t-1} refers to the increase in the retail price index during the previous year; x was originally set at 3 and was increased to 4.5 for the following four years. A 1991 review further increased x to 6.25 percent and included international telephone calls in the basket. The final item, Z_t, is unrecovered entitlement (if any) from the previous year.

British Gas. The British Gas formula differs from that of BT:

$$(5.2) \qquad M_t = RPI_{t-1} - x + GPI_t - Z_t + E_t + K_t$$

where M is the maximum revenue per therm, RPI is the percentage change in the retail price index, x is 5, GPI is the gas price index, Z is the efficiency factor, E is the cost incurred in promoting energy efficiency, and K is the correction factor. The left-hand side is the maximum average revenue or price per therm in the relevant year. The price constraint is set in relation to the

gas price index, which reflects escalation arrangements in the purchase contracts of British Gas. To allow customers to share directly in this benefit, the formula includes two efficiency factors. One variable relates directly to the purchase contracts, while the other represents costs incurred by British Gas in promoting efficiency. A major difference in the formulas for gas and telecommunications is that, in the formula for telecommunications, the controlled prices are guaranteed to be reduced in real terms, whereas in the formula for gas, prices depend on changes in the cost of gas to British Gas.

British Airport Authority. The controls applied to British Airport Authority introduce further features:

$$(5.3) \qquad MG_t = RPI_t - x + SG_t - KG_t$$

where MG_t is the increase in maximum revenue per passenger, RPI is the percentage change in the retail price index, x is 1, SG is the allowable security cost per passenger, and KG is the correction factor. As is the case with British Gas, the control applies to the forecast revenue yield. To protect the airport authority from excessive losses if it becomes necessary substantially to increase security expenditures, the formula allows 75 percent of these costs to be recovered. British Airport Authority is subject to an additional $RPI - x$ control on total revenue earned. This price control covers airport charges such as landing fees for planes and parking fees for passengers. Attempts to rebalance charges within the overall limit led to complaints from airlines, and the authority eventually agreed to restrict the extent of rebalancing if it had greater effect on a particular airline. This is an example of the "creeping extensions" of regulation.

Water companies. The price cap for water companies is similar but not identical to the previous ones:

$$(5.4) \qquad W_t = RPI_{t-1} + K_t + Z_t$$

where W is the weighted average increase in charges for a basket of services, RPI is the percentage change in the retail price index, K is a variable correction factor, and Z is the unused allowance from the previous two years. The water industry needs price increases to finance steeply increasing investment. This investment, in general, does not increase supplies for which a charge can be made, but it does improve the environmental effects and raise the quality standards of existing supplies. The peculiar importance of quality in this industry, the very long lives of the assets involved, and the difficulty in knowing the condition of assets have led asset management plans to become part of the regulatory contract. Companies can recover the costs of changed standards through price increases. Another novel feature of the water price cap is that it is a hybrid of revenue yield and tariff basket methods. This is because the weighted average increase in charges (W) is a combination of the increased charges for metered supplies, which are calculated on tariff basket principles (that is, as the increase in pure price), and for unmeasured supplies, which are calculated as the increase in the average bill per chargeable supply. This hybrid protects the company's revenues from losses if customers switch from an unmetered to a metered supply.

Electricity companies. In all of the cases considered here, there is a tradeoff between competition and regulation. This tradeoff means that countries privatizing a monopoly power industry must decide whether to restructure or to break up an integrated business to create the conditions for competition. The restructuring of the electrical sector in England and Wales has made it possible for the regulator *not* to set prices for companies that generate electricity, although their initial contracts will have to be approved by the government for at least the first three years following privatization. Even under this reformed structure, however, many parts of the industry retain monopoly power and will be subject, accordingly, to *RPI - x* price caps:

- Distribution minus use of the regional electricity company's lines: $M = RPI - x$, where M is maximum change in the average charge per kilowatt-hour, and x is between 0 and 2.5, according to regional circumstances.

- Regional electric company's supply minus the price charged by the company for electricity: $M = (RPI - x) + p + Y$, where M is maximum change in average charge per kilowatt-hour, x is 0, p is the price for services provided by companies other than Y, and Y is the cost of transmission, distribution, and the fossil fuel levy.

- Charges for the regional electric company's small customers (less than 1 megawatt): $M = RPI$, where M is the maximum change in average charge per kilowatt-hour.

- Transmission minus use of the grid: $M = RPI - x$, where M is the maximum change in the average charge per kilowatt-hour, and x is 0.

Each of the twelve regional electricity companies is subject to three price caps. The first one sets a limit on the amount that companies can charge for use of their distribution lines. The second one prevents them from charging more than the average amount they paid (plus outside or separately regulated costs and increases in their profit margins). The final cap controls the price that regional companies can charge to customers that consume less that 1 megawatt of electricity. As joint owners of the National Grid Company, regional electric companies also face limits on price increases for use of their high-transmission wires. As a wholly owned subsidiary of the regional electric companies, the grid company need not be too concerned with differences between income and investment, so x is set at 0 in this formula.

These arrangements allow the following to occur:

- Where there is a monopoly, the owners use the asset available at a nondiscriminatory price.

- The caps on profit and minor expenses protect customers and give companies added incentives to increase efficiency.

- Costs that are outside the control of the companies can be passed on in full.

- Smaller customers are guaranteed that prices will not increase more than the retail price index.

- A fully competitive retail market develops in which any buyer that consumes more than 1 megawatt of power each year can purchase power from any producer in England and Wales.

In the United Kingdom the privatization of electric utilities has enjoyed economic success:

- Output per employee has increased 70 percent.
- Nonfuel costs per unit of output have decreased 25 percent.
- Investment in new technologies has been large and successful.
- Contract prices have dropped, in real terms, 21 percent for distribution companies and 18 percent for direct industrial and commercial consumers.
- The United Kingdom is the only country in the European Union that has had falling real electricity prices.
- Competition has increased, with the market share of the largest firm projected to decline from 33 percent in 1989 to 22 percent in 1997.

Despite this apparent success, political pressure has slowed the drive to privatize utilities in the United Kingdom. The electricity regulator reneged on a promise to maintain prices at a certain level because of the public outcry against "abnormal" profits. New electricity price caps were announced on schedule in August 1994 and were due to take effect in April 1995 and to last for five years. In early March, however, the electricity regulator expressed concern over "evidence of previously unsuspected financial strength" on the part of the generating companies. Accordingly, the agreed prices were reviewed, resulting in lower caps (the electricity regulator's announcement was made the day after the government sold its remaining shares in the two major generating companies at a high premium). The significance of and potential damage resulting from this incident should not be underestimated. The key feature of the British system, which distinguishes it from rate-of-return capping, is the credibility of the interval between reviews, which is crucial to companies undertaking long-term investments or other actions designed to cut costs.

The political pressure arose for a number of reasons. First, more could have been done to increase competition by splitting up the capacity into a larger number of smaller units at the time of privatization. After privatization took place, the regulator asked the two major generating companies to divide themselves into smaller enterprises, but they failed to do so. The regulator then threatened action from the Monopolies and Mergers Commission. Second, the shares of the generating companies were seriously underpriced at the time of privatization. Indeed, large profits were made in a short time from increases in the stock market value of these shares. Third, after the electricity regulator announced the new price caps in August 1994, one of the major generating companies successfully countered an attractive takeover offer from a major conglomerate. Fourth, a significant amount of political heat has been generated in the United Kingdom about the high salaries of chief executive officers and other senior managers of the privatized utilities.

Countries should consider several approaches to privatizing utilities. First, competition is always preferable to regulation. The extent to which competition can be introduced is growing all the time thanks to technological developments. To put it another way, natural monopolies are becoming less natural with every year that passes. To ease the burden on regulators, the competitive framework should be put in place *before* privatization. In the United Kingdom, the task of regulation was made more onerous because inadequate restructuring took place before privatization, which forced regulators to introduce competition ex post. Second, where the industry is not a candidate for perfect competition, it is important to identify the causes of market failure in advance and to gear the powers of the regulator accordingly. Finally, the relationship between the regulator and the regulated industry is best thought of in contractual terms. Like all contracts, it should be clearly specified and should minimize the ability of either party to resort to discretionary or arbitrary tactics. This includes a cheap, rapid, and fair means of resolving disputes, whether they are between the regulator and the regulated firm or within a regulated industry. In the United Kingdom, the Monopolies and Mergers Commission is the only arbiter of disagreements, and appeals are time consuming and the commission's decisions are not universally regarded as impartial.

If these conditions are not in place or are inadequate, the regulatory system is susceptible to political interference. When that happens, the regulator is more likely to succumb to outside pressures, and governments are more likely to interfere, to the detriment of both the regulator and the utility companies, as seems to be the case in the United Kingdom (see box 5.2). Many of these problems could be avoided if the government ensured that the utilities had the right structure before privatization. In the United Kingdom, only in electricity were the parts liable to market failure separated from the rest of the industry. Short-term politics are to blame because the British government wanted to make

soon-to-be-privatized firms attractive to potential buyers, and increasing competition would not have served this purpose. Despite these defects, British regulation is a big step forward. The process of setting price caps is transparent, debate is formalized, and regulated firms can appeal if they do not like a decision. Additionally, regulation is cheaper in the United Kingdom than in the United States, where regulatory disputes provide huge dividends to lawyers. Furthermore, British utility bosses have by and large been given the right incentives to keep prices and costs low.

ANALYSIS OF RATE-OF-RETURN AND PRICE-CAP REGULATION

The rate of return used in the United States and the price caps applied in the United Kingdom

Box 5.2 Renegotiation of the U.K. Electricity Distribution Tariff

One of the most controversial events in the United Kingdom's utility regulation was the regulator's decision to revisit the price controls placed on electricity distributors nine months after they were initially agreed on. Paradoxically, this decision was made after the imposition of tough price controls that resulted in an initial drop in prices of 11 to 17 percent in one year, followed by an *x* factor of 2 percent thereafter, despite there being a positive *x* factor (that is, real price increases) in the initial five-year period. Critics have seized on this renegotiation as the "end of price-cap regulation," and indeed the United Kingdom is engaged in a vigorous debate about moving away from price caps toward forms of sharing rules, partly as a result of this debacle.

The history of the revision began with the privatization of electricity distributors on the basis of a regulatory regime featuring positive *x* price caps that allowed the distribution price to increase in real terms, an action taken by government to ensure a successful privatization and urged on it by the companies, which cited the sector's substantial investment needs. This regime allowed companies to increase dividends substantially in the first few years and to buy back shares; as investors realized that the regulatory regime was much less risky than envisaged, market values increased substantially. In fact, beginning with an initial share price of £240 in 1990, market values rose to an

average of £710 by April 1994, a threefold increase in four years.

The mounting cash pile of the distribution companies—the result of a generous initial settlement—exerted pressure on the regulator to get tough in the forthcoming price review, which was to set prices from 1995 to 2000. In April 1994, midway through the price review process, a letter from the regulator to the companies was leaked that suggested an initial price drop of between 20 and 30 percent in the first year, followed by an *x* factor of 4 percent in the following four years. The market values of the companies fell sharply following this announcement, and shareholders became increasingly concerned about the severity of the potential settlement. Institutional shareholders wrote open letters demanding that the companies stand firm against the depredations of the regulator.

The outcome of the review process was announced in 1994. Although tough relative to price reviews in other utilities, the 11 to 17 percent initial drop in prices and 2 percent *x* factor were seen as lax relative to the proposals made in the April letter. The market value of the companies rose sharply and continued to rise in the next few months. One investment briefing carried the headline "Companies 2—Regulators 0," which reflected what was seen as the lenient outcome in the price reviews of both the water and electricity industries.

are the two most commonly used schemes. The U.S.-style rate-of-return regulation, if strictly implemented, will eventually isolate the firm's profitability from its cost performance and hence imply highly inefficient outcomes. However, as implemented in the United States, rate-of-return regulation has provided the firm with "excess" profits when costs are falling and with below-normal profits when costs are increasing.[5] U.K.-style price-cap regulation has a similar feature as long as the cap is held constant for a relatively long period of time. Price-cap regulation with profit sharing, as implemented in the United States in some states and at the federal level in the regulation of American Telephone and Telegraph (AT&T), would also limit the correlation between demand and a firm's profits. (For a discussion of state price-cap innovations, see Face 1988.)

Both price-cap regulation and rate-of-return regulation are relatively flexible regulatory designs. Their flexibility arises from various sources. Consider rate-of-return regulation as implemented by state public utility commissions. First, lags, arising from the endogeneity of rate reviews, provide some cost incentives to the firms. Second, regulators have strong incentives not to accept all costs and investments at face value, which restrains, to some extent, incentives to invest excessively, if they ever existed. (For a discussion of investment disallowances see Lyon 1992.) Finally, because there is no such thing as an exogenously given required rate of return, regulators could penalize the firm for unusually high costs.[6] Price-cap systems, whether similar to the system of the United Kingdom or of the United States, provide cost incentives as long as price caps are adjusted every four or five years.

Box 5.2 continued...

As the market values of the companies continued to rise throughout autumn 1994, the regulator was pressured to revise the formula. In the winter of 1995 a complicating factor came to light: the imminent expiry of the government's golden share in the distribution companies, which was due to be retired in April 1995. The golden share had effectively prevented hostile takeovers of the companies until that point.

On December 19, Trafalgar House, a conglomerate, announced a bid for Northern Electric, one of the regional electricity companies, valuing it at £1.2 billion or £10.77 a share. Subsequently, Northern's defense, which included a £5 per share one-off dividend twice the value of the initial purchase of shares, notionally triggered the intervention of the regulator.

In February the regulator declared that he was going to review the distribution prices again. Despite the poor precedent caused by this action, the regulator felt that action now would prevent worse pressures later on. He cited the "new information" contained in the Northern Electric defense document as one reason for the intervention.

This decision created a huge political controversy, not only because it reopened what was seen as a closed five-year deal, but also because the announcement was made on the day after flotation of the government's remaining 40 percent shareholding in the generation companies. Although these companies are in a separate part of the market and are regulated on a completely different basis, the market impact was immediate and dramatic. Prices of the generation shares fell, and a number of investors, particularly those that had planned to "stag" the issue—that is, sell them quickly for a profit—threatened to sue both the government and the regulator.

In the end, the second review resulted in an additional one-off reduction in prices of between 10 and 13 percent and an increase in the ongoing x charge to 3 percent. None of the companies, which had pronounced the original price review tough but fair, disputed the details of the outcome.

In any case, the concerns of the sector had moved on as a series of intended takeovers in the sector were announced. By April 1996 eight of the original twelve distributors were the subject of takeover bids.

What are the lessons here? Some commentators have argued that this was the end of price caps in their conventional form and that the information requirements and political difficulties associated with setting a stable price for five years are too great. However, price caps have been used successfully in many other countries and sectors. Perhaps what this illustrates more vividly is the difficulty that any regulatory regime will have in changing the status quo in one direction or another, and the intrinsically political nature of utility regulation.

Because the price cap may not be adjusted because of unusually high or low profitability, higher-than-expected cost reductions benefit the firm, while lower-than-expected cost reductions penalize the firm. However, U.S.-style price caps with profit sharing limit the extent of rents that companies can capture, increasing consumer or taxpayer surplus (Laffont and Tirole 1993). Furthermore, under any price-cap system, the company's price flexibility allows it to adjust its price structure to new technologies and competition.

Where comparison is possible, as it is between different states in the United States, the evidence indicates that price-cap regulation leads to lower prices than does rate-of-return regulation. For example, Face (1988) has reviewed the experience of Michigan Bell's contract and estimated that the change from rate-of-return to price-cap regulation saved about $40 million (1982 dollars) in costs over what would have been incurred if rate-of-return regulation had continued. Similar results were obtained in an Oftel report (1988). Mathios and Rogers (1987) estimated that the rates of AT&T's Message Telecommunications Service are on average between 7 and 10 percent lower in states that have a price-cap approach than in states that use rate-of-return regulation. Moreover, cost-reduction investments are higher under an optimal price-cap regime. In addition, Braeutigam and Panzar (1989) report that more than twenty states in the United States have moved from rate-of-return regulation to a combination of sliding-scale and price-cap regulation for telephone companies. For example, a telephone company is allowed to retain all earnings under price-cap rates as long as the rate of return is less than a specified amount, typically in the neighborhood of 13 percent. The limited U.S. evidence available seems to support the view that price-cap regulation is an effective means of controlling the prices of dominant firms when their profits are controlled by the competitive marketplace. Thus, as has been observed many times, price-cap regulation is probably most effective as a transitory step on the path toward total deregulation and full competition.

However, a caveat on the difference between these two modes of regulation is in order. Actions by U.K. regulators illustrate that, in practice, the two systems have a tendency to converge. Regulators announced new electricity price caps on schedule in August 1994 that were due to begin in April 1995. In early March, however, the regulator professed concern over "evidence of previously unsuspected financial strength" on the part of the generating companies. Accordingly, the prices agreed to in August were "reviewed," and lower caps were set.[7] Legally the regulator was acting within his powers—the new caps were not yet in place, and the period of consultation was still in force. This behavior has tended to reduce the incentives for utility companies to reduce costs and improve efficiency, because the gains from these improvements will be captured only throughout the remainder of the review period. Come next review period, companies will be penalized by being assigned higher x values. Similar tendencies have begun to surface in Latin American countries, again as the result of the significant earnings that a number of regulated companies appear to be enjoying. This argues in favor of fairly long intervals between reviews. If the period is too short, the regulated company has an incentive to influence the regulator's use of its discretion rather than to operate efficiently within a clear framework. The shorter the period, the closer the system is to the rate-of-return regulation system.

Consider, now, implementing a flexible price system in nations whose institutional characteristics call for inflexible detail engineering. In Jamaica, which has a two-party parliamentary system with a substantial amount of government turnover and no informal norms limiting administrative discretion, a rate-of-return system could not be implemented, because the Public Utility Commission would have too much discretion in setting the rate base and determining the appropriate level of return on capital and the nature of allowable costs. Consequently, rate-of-return regulation would have to restrict the extent to which the regulator could determine capital level, rates of return, and costs. (This is precisely the type of regulation that was designed for the newly privatized Telecommunications of Jamaica.) Another variation is the implementation of either a U.K.- or U.S.-style price cap. Because price caps have to be reset every few years to avoid profit over- or undershooting, leaving such a decision to the regulator might grant the regulator too much discretion. Hence, if price-cap regulation were to be implemented, the price-cap revisions would have to be determined so as to limit regulatory discretion. The United Kingdom designed such a system by allowing price caps to be adjusted in two ways: (a) by obtaining the agreement of the company, and (b) by having the regulator request a decision from the Monopolies and Mergers Commission on whether such an adjustment is in the "public interest." Given the nature of the Monopolies and Mergers Commission, such an arrangement limits opportunistic behavior by the regulator.

A U.K.-style arrangement could in principle be implemented in political systems like Jamaica's that have a tradition of independent agencies. Otherwise, independent arbitrators would have to resolve disagreements between the company and the regulator. The following arrangement could be the basis for a price-cap system in countries like Jamaica. First, the initial price cap would be set in the company's license. Second, the price cap would be set for an indefinite period of time. Third, the license would stipulate that, after a minimum number of years (such as four), the regulator might ask for an amendment to the price-cap provision of the license. If the company agrees, then the license would be amended. If the government and the company do not agree, an ad hoc board of arbitrators would be formed by agreement between the parties, and its decision on a new provision would be binding. The board of arbitrators would be required to bring forward a price cap that assures a minimum rate of return to the company, with that minimum set in the license.[8] Although the design of this detail engineering would be compatible with the choice of basic engineering, it might not fit Jamaica's legal and administrative capabilities. For example, the regulator would have to develop a model showing how the company would perform under alternative price-cap scenarios. If no model were developed, then the board of arbitrators would use information provided by the company, which might lead to excess rents. If the development and maintenance of such models are beyond the administrative capabilities of Jamaica's bureaucracy, this choice of detail engineering would not be feasible.[9]

Finally, whichever price-setting policy is adopted, the rules of the game must be clear. Uncertainty about prices or the criteria used to determine them deters investment in the sector. For example, in Mexico, the Comisión Federal de Electricidad (the Mexican parastatal electricity company) has refused to set and commit itself to a purchase price for electricity from private, independent operators, and this refusal dissuades domestic and foreign firms from investing in the sector. Failure to establish transparent regulatory procedures increases the risks for private sector participants and adversely affects the development and competitiveness of the sector.

Summary

Despite the apparent differences in regulation across industries, several common themes appear in all $RPI - x$ regulation. Predominant among these themes is the long interval between periodic reviews. If the interval is too short, the regulated company will try to influence the regulator's decisions rather than to increase efficiency, because the framework is unclear. Although the detail and emphasis on quality will vary considerably, another common feature is that some control will always be necessary to avoid creating an incentive to produce a cheaper basket of products. Another important feature is that when price controls are set, they reflect forecasts of the rate of return and other financial ratios rather than actual levels. This calculation should not cause difficulties if the company keeps its costs under control. The inclusion of the rate of return in some of the formulas can lead one to believe that there is not much difference between rate-of-return and price-cap systems. That is not the case. For example, when prices are reset following a periodic review, companies that have achieved exceptional profits should expect tighter x factors so that, over a period, they are likely to return to normal rates of profit. Thus, the x factor preserves incentives and mimics the way in which a competitive market would work.

There are occasions for regulators to extend or curtail their control. Although the BT regulatory system was supposed to be reduced as competition increased, in practice the controls have become more detailed and intrusive. Overall, there is a danger of the $RPI - x$ system becoming excessively detailed and intrusive. How far does the practical experience in the United Kingdom meet the objectives listed at the beginning of this section? The price limits have always been effective, so that the system has clearly prevented the abuse of monopoly power (except to the extent that x factors may have been set too generously). There has been controversy over the limits on management's freedom to rebalance tariffs in telecommunications and to adjust prices of gas. However, there has been no serious suggestion that investment decisions are being distorted in major ways. More research is needed before it is possible to determine whether the cost of administering this form of regulation is excessive. One obvious fact is that as more regulators intervene, the system becomes more costly.

ALTERNATIVE DESIGNS

Several less common types of basic (price setting) regulatory design also exist, and they are discussed next.

Incentive Regulations

Incentive regulations, which are variants of price-cap regulation, involve more complex rules or additional incentive clauses. Incentive regulatory mechanisms include automatic rate adjustments, optional tariff menus, and profit sharing. In the United States incentive schemes linked to performance standards are becoming more common for electric power plants. A specific standard of plant performance is established. If performance is above the standard, rewards are granted

to the firm, but if performance is below the standard, penalties are levied against the firm. Joskow and Schmalensee (1986) report the case of the scheme imposed by the Arizona Public Service Company on its Palo Verde 1 nuclear plant. The target is the plant's capacity factor—the actual amount of electricity generated by the plant divided by the amount it could generate if it ran continuously throughout the year. Ideally, because of the low costs of running a nuclear plant, the capacity factor should be high. The incentive scheme is as follows. No penalty or reward is given if the capacity factor is between 60 and 75 percent. If the capacity factor is between 75 and 85 percent, the company is rewarded by 50 percent of the fuel cost saved by running the plant more. If the capacity factor is between 50 and 60 percent, however, the company is penalized by 50 percent of the fuel cost incurred by running more costly plants (Viscusi, Vernon, and Harrington 1995). Other incentive regulations in the United States allow telephone companies to retain a share of the earnings in excess of a given rate of return.

Yardstick or Benchmark Regulation

Yardstick regulation seeks to introduce competition in single-firm market environments to induce efficient behavior. Market discipline is introduced by comparing the performance of similar firms in different markets to the performance of an efficient prototype and basing the allowed profits on the regulated firm's relative performance. The advantage of this type of regulation is that it introduces competition that fosters incentives for efficient behavior and eliminates the adverse effects of common risks (relative performance standards).[10]

Regulation by Threat

An alternative form of regulation is the absence of any form of direct intervention in setting the parameters that constrain the behavior of a firm, but with the proviso that the regulatory body reserves the right to intervene if it decides that the actions or prices chosen by the utility are creating significant distortions or welfare losses, according to specified criteria. The principle behind this form of regulation is that the threat of intervention will create incentives to comply with general efficiency principles. In the game theory lexicon, this is a "tit-for-tat" regulatory strategy between the commission and the firm.[11]

No Explicit Regulation

At the end of the spectrum, no explicit regulation is always an option. Historically, this was the standard mode of regulation in Latin America when the utility services were provided by state or nationalized firms. A current example is French municipalities, where no separate regulatory agency exists. As in the case of nationalized or state firms, consumers can exercise their rights by complaining and by voting in mayoral or national elections. Perhaps the most interesting example of no explicit regulation is the New Zealand case, where none of the utilities, whether privately or state owned, is subject to direct regulation. Utilities are, though, subject to several basic constraints. First, there are no exclusive licenses, so that entry into all markets is guaranteed by law. Second, utilities are subject to reporting requirements. Third, utilities are also subject to the Commerce Act, which limits anticompetitive behavior. Indeed, claims against utilities may be heard by the Commerce Commission if they involve violations of New Zealand's Commerce Act. In that sense, the Commerce Commission may play the role of a super-regulator, albeit without specialized staff or knowledge. Fourth, customers can file suits against utilities for antitrust violations. Indeed, interconnection problems between Clear Communications and New Zealand Telecom have been litigated, and only partially resolved, through the court system.[12]

Other Regulatory Issues Affecting Price Setting

Rebalancing of Tariffs

The use of competition in non-natural monopoly segments obviously requires substantial price rebalancing, particularly in the telecommunications sector. Indeed, in telecommunications the non-natural monopoly segment is the most used by businesses and, consequently, has the most distorted pricing. Likewise, the prices of local calls are usually heavily subsidized at the expense of interurban and international calls. Similarly, before privatization, the prices for water and electricity are often regressive and do not reflect marginal costs. Introducing competition ought to reduce prices, substantially rebalancing prices and, particularly in the telecommunications sector, increasing local exchange prices. Rebalancing yields significant economic welfare benefits and removes a big impediment to the development of local competition. The issue is how fast rebalancing should occur, because it has important economic and political impacts. In the United States such rebalancing was partially accomplished through a gradual reduction in access charges and a gradual increase in monthly subscriber access charges. In 1984 the FCC wanted to move quickly toward competitive pricing by setting subscribers' monthly charges much higher and access charges for interexchange carriers much lower. The FCC backed down and followed a more gradual process only because of congressional threats (Ferejohn and Sipan 1990).

The transition toward competitive prices has become a key ingredient in the reform of telecommunications regulation. In the United Kingdom free entry into long-distance service was not allowed for seven years following privatization of BT, thus guaranteeing a cozy duopoly for BT and the other provider, Mercury. In Argentina long-distance competition was also prohibited for a ten-year period. In Chile long-distance and local service rebalancing was based on a formula that reduced cross-subsidization over a five-year period (from 1987 to 1992). Similar approaches have been used in Peru and Venezuela.

In some countries, however, cross-subsidization prior to privatization may be so extensive that lessening it sharply might not be politically feasible, at least in a relatively short period of time. Consider Jamaica, where prior to privatization in 1987, international revenues were 60 percent of total telecommunications revenues, while fixed assets fully dedicated to the international segment comprised less than 15 percent of local (and inland toll) fixed assets. Thus, liberalizing international operations would have reduced international prices substantially, affecting the viability of the local operating company.[13] To compensate for the loss in international revenues, real local prices would have had to increase substantially, a feat that few governments would attempt in a highly contested electoral environment.[14]

In principle, however, access charges could be set to maintain international calls at their initial levels and then be reduced gradually so that at the end of, for example, a decade, they would approximate the long-run costs of access. On the one hand, if such a transition had been designed, competition in international calls could have been implemented. On the other hand, the need to restrain administrative discretion in Jamaica may have required specifying the evolution of the access charges ahead of time. Such a transition would have been very difficult to design, and the process would have required substantial modification during the period, increasing the potential for opportunistic behavior. With the exception of Mexico, where prices were adjusted significantly prior to privatization, most of the telecommunications sale contracts in Latin America included a time schedule for rebalancing tariffs gradually. The window of opportunity presented at the time of privatization ought to be used to make significant price adjustments. The faster full rebalancing is achieved, the faster competition will develop. As long as some prices differ from marginal costs, protection and exclusivity rights have to be provided at the expense of competition and the benefits it can produce. Likewise, as competition develops, the operator ought to have the discretion to adjust prices (downward) to respond to competitive pressures. This is often an issue in the distribution segment of the electricity sector, where the trunk costs are distributed across the users. As major users are offered better prices from independent generators, their exodus from the market of the main distributor (if not allowed to match prices) implies higher charges to small users, because the

same fixed costs now have to be distributed among fewer users, producing an inefficient outcome.

Granting of Exclusivity Rights

Further to that point and in consequence, extreme care should be exercised when granting exclusivity rights. They obviously deter competition, and their induced benefits are unlikely to enhance welfare or private sector participation. There is little conceptual support for granting exclusivity rights. If the activity does possess natural monopoly characteristics, it has de facto exclusive rights, and granting exclusivity rights de jure is not necessary. If the activity does not possess natural monopoly characteristics, there is no justification for granting a legal monopoly through exclusivity rights. Exclusivity rights should only be contemplated in situations with significant coordination problems or transaction costs (or significant risks), such as central dispatches or logistics. Exclusivity rights are sometimes justified because of (universal) service obligations, with implicit or explicit subsidies to certain groups or areas. Again this is a weak argument. Institutionalizing cross-subsidies is better handled either with transfers specifically to the operating company, or preferably with transfers directly to the targeted consumers through vouchers or income tax credits. This ought to eliminate the need for cross-subsidization.

Although potential investors prefer exclusivity rights, the absence of exclusivity does not deter their participation. The examples are multiple. New Zealand Telecom was successfully privatized in a policy environment of open entry in all market segments. The same was true in Chile, as illustrated in box 5.3. In the Philippines foreign investors such as Nynex, Cable & Wireless, and Telstra have entered the market as competitors or as partners of competitors. In Mexico a large domestic cellular operator with support from Bell Atlantic has proposed installing a fixed wireless network to serve 1.5 million customers. In southern India, U.S. West has proposed a telecommunications build-own-operate scheme and has not asked for an exclusive franchise.

Box 5.3 Chile's Open Telecommunications Market

In 1989, on privatizing Entel, the local monopoly, Chile immediately introduced competition in long-distance and international traffic from Telex, and in 1994 it opened the market completely. A scheme allowing customers to select their carrier by simply dialing a three- or four-digit company code and then the number required (made possible by an almost 100 percent digital network) every time they make a call has attracted two Baby Bells and five Chilean operating companies and produced significant price competition, driving down international tariffs to the lowest level in Latin America. As a result, in 1995 a three-minute call to the United States during peak hours cost $1.65, compared with $5 in Mexico and $6 in Argentina, and by 1997 it had dropped to nearly $1.

Investors have accepted competition in telecommunications in Australia, Malaysia, Sweden, the United Kingdom, and the United States, and in the cellular market in almost every country.

Complexity and Administrative Capabilities

An additional criterion for distinguishing among alternative regulatory schemes is the intensity of the administrative demands they impose on regulators. Administrative intensity is a slippery notion, with two relevant dimensions: (a) how cumbersome, time-consuming, and controversial the tasks imposed are on a regulatory agency; and (b) how difficult to understand, and thus to implement properly, is the regulatory scheme. A country's ability to handle both dimensions of administrative intensity is likely to depend on the quality and technical skills of its human capital.

Complex detail engineering solutions may require a level of administrative capability not available in the country in question. For example, Chile's bureaucracy and judiciary have a level of sophisticated regulatory training that is unlikely to exist in many other developing countries. Such training is crucial for understanding the nature of a regulatory system and for determining whether computed prices approximate those of an efficient firm. Further, because dis-

putes will naturally arise, individuals involved in resolving them must understand and evaluate competing proposals. Although Chile and many Latin American and Asian countries have a large number of well-trained professionals who can perform those tasks appropriately, this may not be the case in all countries. Accordingly, sophisticated detail engineering like Chile's may exacerbate contractual costs between the government and the firm, further reducing the incentives for private sector investment.

By either dimension of administrative intensity, $RPI - x$ emerges as a simple regulatory scheme. Its underlying logic is straightforward, and it imposes only limited tasks on the regulators. Viewed solely from an administrative perspective, it is the hands-down winner. By contrast, both traditional and benchmark rate-of-return regulatory schemes can be administratively cumbersome and technically demanding. Benchmark regulation requires regulators to simulate the costs of the best-practice firm; to adapt this simulation periodically to changes in best-practice technology; to estimate the allowable, risk-adjusted competitive rate of return; and to calculate a detailed set of prices. Chilean regulators have apparently struggled to implement this system adequately, relying on international consultants to prepare the necessary technical material. But the complex technical work of benchmark regulation needs to be undertaken only infrequently (every five years in Chile). By contrast, a traditional rate-of-return approach requires regulators to monitor the utility's revenues, costs, and capital stock annually to ensure that the utility remains within the imposed rate-of-return ceiling. Inevitably, traditional rate-of-return regulation gets bogged down in controversies about what should be included in the capital base against which a utility's rate of return is computed. This problem is bypassed by benchmark regulation, which simulates the prices charged by a theoretically efficient firm.

Benchmark regulation falls short, however, in the second dimension of administrative capability, because it requires sophisticated regulatory training to understand and judge whether the prices calculated according to its rules are indeed reasonable approximations of the behavior of an efficient firm. In Chile an explicit process is laid out for resolving price disputes between the regulator and the utility. The success of this process, however, depends on the ability of the major actors to evaluate competing proposals on their empirical merits. Chile and a number of other Latin American and East Asian countries are well endowed with professionals capable of performing such evaluations.

Where that is not the case, the risk of wildly unstable regulatory outcomes is likely to be high. In those environments, price-cap regulation, $RPI - x$, is a reasonable choice of detail engineering, regarding the criteria of administrative requirements. Rate-of-return regulation is the least desirable because of both incentive effects and administrative capacity (measurement and monitoring problems). In any event, it should be applied only to the natural monopoly stages (that is, the local fixed-link network), allowing competition in the remaining sectors. Clearly preferable overall would be a simplified form of benchmark regulation that avoids the inefficiencies of traditional regulation but that could be evaluated in a relatively straightforward way.

The Administrative Cost of Detail Regulation

A consideration in designing detail regulation is that decisions are made in a quasi-judicial environment in which consumer groups, industry representatives, and other interested parties are allowed to present arguments. Because the potential gains from a favorable action can be substantial, rational interest groups might devote substantial resources to lobbying activities.

Crew and Kleindorfer (1985) describe one of the few attempts to measure actual administrative costs of regulation for New Jersey water companies. They found that administrative costs averaged 0.87 percent of total revenue for large water companies, 5.25 percent of revenue for small companies, and 0.92 percent of revenue overall. Similarly, unpublished research suggests that regulatory costs typically amount to 1 to 2 percent of turnover for large regulated companies and even more for smaller ones. There

appear to be substantial economies of scale due to the regulatory process itself. The indirect costs of regulation are much more difficult to quantify. Experience with telecommunications suggests that once market entry becomes technically feasible, both the regulated firms and the potential entrants may be prepared to expend considerable resources to intervene in the regulatory process.

Resolution of Conflicts

Concessions or operational contracts in the utilities sector often span ten years or more and routinely include clauses allowing the parties to renegotiate in the event of unforeseen circumstances. These clauses simply state that under certain conditions either party may request a renegotiation of the price or terms, with no criteria given as to how the new level or terms should be set. They foster rent-seeking behavior and exploitation of regulatory capture. Incentives to dissuade frivolous and rent-seeking renegotiations should be built into the contract, so that the firm is financially penalized if the renegotiation attempt is deemed inappropriate. In addition, to reduce the concessionaire's leverage and thus its incentive to renegotiate the contract for rent-seeking purposes, overlapping and split concessions should be favored whenever they are technologically feasible (Guasch and Marshall 1993). A further advantage of multiple concessions is that they enrich the information set, foster competition, and base rewards on performance.

Agreements on how to resolve conflicts or impasses during renegotiation should be established. In environments where the independence or expertise of the court system is questionable, international arbitration should signal the government's commitment and increase the confidence of potential investors. Although arbitration should not be the first choice for resolving disputes, any contract that is a complex concessionary agreement must have a mechanism for settling disputes. Two essential elements of this mechanism are a forum selection clause and a choice of law provision. The forum selection clause will govern where the dispute will be resolved. The choice of law provision will specify which law the forum will use. Care should be taken to secure proper legal counseling to preempt potential arguments. For example, some legal regimes might not permit a simple contract arbitration to achieve a conclusive and binding decision. The apparent legal basis for the argument is that infrastructure tariffs are a matter of fundamental interest rather than of the parties' rights under the contract, and hence cannot be decided in a court of law. Arbitration is likely to be on its firmest legal footing when it is addressed in the statute that sets up the overall regulatory framework. Constitutional and other legal challenges are more apt to arise where the regulatory authority itself decides to submit disputes to commercial or other types of arbitration regimes. It is also essential that there be confidence that tariffs will be paid and governments will support policies to induce compliance. Laws such as those in Mexico that prohibit cutting off service to delinquent accounts signal a questionable commitment to sustaining cost-linked tariffs, and are a barrier to private sector participation and to efficient levels of investment.

A second source of conflict is the terms by which new entrants have access to networks and the quality of service provided by transmission-network operators. This is an issue because of economies of scale; often no more than one network is sustainable, and the operator is often a competitor in the market served by the entrants. Access rules that are clearly enunciated in the contract with network operators can reduce the number of complaints, yet discrepancies in interpretation are likely to arise. Transparency, accountability, and consistency must characterize the procedures and decisions of the regulatory agencies. In some cases the administrative procedures for handling consumer complaints and for resolving disputes between operators and new entrants will have to be modified to meet these criteria. In the event of technical rather than legal discrepancies, with consequences exceeding a significant income threshold, binding arbitration by a technical committee or a specialized court should be preferred to a decision by the

mainstream judiciary system. This would improve the speed and predictability of decisions and would deter frivolous complaints.

A particularly interesting example is Mexico's 1995 telecommunications law, which stipulates that interconnection is to be determined by negotiation between the parties. If the parties fail to reach an agreement in sixty days, any party may request that the regulator make a determination. The regulator has, in turn, sixty days to make a final determination. Although the law provides for expedient resolution of a key issue for competition, it may be difficult to apply. First, the law does not specify the terms under which the regulator will settle the dispute. Indeed, there is no practical way for the parties to challenge the regulator's decision, unless it is grossly arbitrary. Second, the time constraint on the regulator is not binding. Indeed, Mexico's institutional weakness turns what seems to be a reasonably good law into an ineffective law. The law should have stipulated how the regulator is to arbitrate those disputes and the pricing schemes that would limit regulatory discretion.[15] The law could have taken the regulator out of the picture altogether by requiring conflicts to be solved by binding private arbitration. Instead, it granted the regulator undue discretionary powers in an environment where the executive is subject to minimal checks and balances. Given the nature of Mexico's political hegemony, a preferable approach would have been to insert these regulatory requirements in Telmex's initial license. The reform of telecommunications legislation would have been a useful time to limit regulatory discretion and potential capture.

A third source of conflict is the granting of exclusivity rights, particularly in sectors, such as telecommunications, where technological innovation is difficult to predict. The conflict tends to arise when innovations used by third parties affect the activities and revenues of the providers (such as call-back services, bypass options, and so forth), and when exclusivity rights are interpreted. This obviously is one more argument, although not the essential one, for disposing of exclusivity rights in concessions and privatizations.

Appendix
The Full Formulation of *RPI* – *x* Controls for the United Kingdom

This appendix is based on Glynn 1992.

British Telecommunications

(5A.1) $W_t \leq RPI_{t-1} - X + Z_t$

The *RPI* – *x* formula for BT upon privatization is detailed in condition 24 of BT's license. This sets a limit for price increases for its main inland services that was to apply for five years beginning August 1, 1984. Price increases for business and residential rentals, local calls, and trunk calls weighted according to their proportion of revenue, W_t, had to be at least 3 percent (the *x* factor) less than the retail price index (as calculated over the twelve months preceding the previous June 30). If the actual increase was less than this figure, BT was allowed to carry this credit forward for two years, the correction factor Z_t. Rental charges for the first telephones connected to exchange lines were excluded beginning on December 31, 1984, when BT's monopoly of such telephones ended.

In 1989 Oftel amended BT's license, increasing *x* to 4.5 percent. The carry forward of price increases is allowed within the new control period (1989–93), but not from the previous period. A 1991 review increased *x* to 6.25 percent and included international calls in the basket.

In addition, BT and Oftel have agreed to an *RPI* + *2* formula to limit exchange-line rentals and correction charges. This formula has never been incorporated into BT's license. BT has indicated that it would prefer to be released from this agreement, but both Oftel and the government believe it should be retained.

British Gas

The price limits of gas charges to tariff customers are set out in condition 3 of British Gas's authorization. The tariff market for gas is for customers using less than 25,000 therms a year and does not apply to larger consumers (the contract market), which are now charged according to an unregulated price schedule set by British Gas. Average price per therm beginning on April 1, 1987 is determined according to the formula:

(5A.2) $M_t = \left[1 + \dfrac{RPI_t - 2}{100}\right] P_{t-1} + Y_t - K_t$

where M_t is maximum average price per therm in relevant year t; RPI_t is the percentage change in the retail price index with respect to the index published in October in relevant year t and the index determined with respect to the preceding October.

P_{t-1} is given by the following formula:

(5A.3) $P_{t-1} = P_{t-2}\left[1 + \dfrac{RPI_{t-1} - 2}{100}\right]$

but in relation to the first relevant year, P_{t-1} and P_{t-2} have a value equal to the average price per therm in the financial year beginning April 1, 1986, minus the allowable gas cost per therm in that year.

Where Y_t is the allowable gas cost per therm in relevant year t; K_y is the correction per therm derived from the formula:

(5A.4) $K_t = \dfrac{T_{t-1} - (Q_{t-1} M_{t-1})}{Q_t} \bullet \left(1 + \dfrac{I_t}{100}\right)$

where T_{t-1} equals tariff revenue from tariff quantity in year $t-1$; Q_{t-1} equals tariff quantity in relevant year $t-1$; Q_t equals tariff quantity in relevant year t; M_{t-1} equals maximum average price per therm in relevant year $t-1$; I_t equals the percentage interest rate in the relevant year t, which, where $K_t > 0$, is equal to the average specified rate plus 3, or where $K_t < 0$, is equal to the average specified rate.

Cost pass-through in terms of allowable gas cost, Y_t, is an aggregate of the amount paid by British Gas to gas suppliers, subject to certain undertakings that to the best of its knowledge represent "no more than the market value."

In addition, condition 4 sets a price limit for an increase of standing charges or the "imposition of charges having a similar effect on a tariff consumer to a standing charge" to not more than the retail price index in the twelve months preceding December of the relevant year.

British Airport Authority

Airport charges are subject to price limits in accordance with airport licenses. This sets limits for five years beginning April 1, 1987. In the case of, for example, Gatwick Airport, it limits the average revenue yield per passenger using Gatwick Airport from airport charges to an amount not exceeding the maximum average revenue yield per passenger calculated according to the formula:

(5A.5) $MG_t = \left[1 + \dfrac{RPI_t - XG}{100}\right] YG_{t-1} - KG_t$

Appendix continued...

where MG_t equals the maximum average revenue yield per passenger using Gatwick Airport in relevant year t, RPI_t equals the percentage change in the retail price index over the preceding twelve months from September of the relevant year, G equals 1, YG_{t-1} equals the specified average revenue yield per passenger determined by the formula:

$$(5A.6) \qquad YG_{t-1} = YG_{t-2}\left[1 + \frac{RPI_{t-1} - XG}{100}\right] + SG_{t-2}$$

where SG_{t-2} is the allowable security cost per passenger to be applied, and KG_t is the correction per passenger determined by the formula:

$$(5A.7) \qquad KG_t = \left[\frac{TG_{t-2} - QG_{t-2}\,MG_{t-2}}{QG_{t-2}}\right]\left(1 + \frac{I}{100}\right)^2$$

where TG_{t-2} is total revenue from airport charges levied at Gatwick Airport; QG_{t-2} is the number of passengers using Gatwick Airport; I is the appropriate interest rate, which is calculated the same as the rate applying to British Gas.

Allowable security costs mean 75 percent of the annual equivalent of the increase or decrease in security costs at the airport (or airports) in question in relevant year $t-2$, which results from directives certified by the Civil Aviation Authority, divided by the total number of passengers using the airport in that year.

In addition, the total revenue from such charges at Gatwick Airport, when aggregated with total revenue from such charges at Heathrow and Stanstead, divided by the total number of passengers, does not exceed the maximum revenue yield per passenger calculated in accordance with the formula:

$$(5A.8) \qquad M_t = \left[1 + \frac{RPI_t - X}{100}\right]Y_{t-1} - K_t$$

where the variables have the same meaning as before but are applied to the three airports, as opposed to just Gatwick (and hence the letter "G" is omitted from the title of each variable).

Water

The price limits set for the water industry are contained in the instruments of appointments under condition B. This limits increases in standard charges to the sum of movement in the retail price index and an adjustment factor, K, plus an allowance, Z, for the unused allowance from the previous two years.

$$(5A.9) \qquad W_t \le RPI_{t-1} + K_t + Z_t$$

W_t, the basket of items, is determined by

$$(5A.10) \qquad W_t = \sum_i^1\left(\frac{A_t(i)}{A_{t-1}(i)} \bullet r(i)\right) + \sum_i^1\left(\frac{B_t(j)}{B_{t-1}(j)} \bullet r(j)\right) - 1$$

where i identifies unmeasured water and sewerage services, and j identifies measured water and sewerage services.

Unmeasured supplies, $A(i)$, are calculated by reference to changes in average revenue per chargeable supply, where the number of chargeable supplies is, in each case, as of December 1 in the year before the charges applied or will apply; whereas measured or metered supplies, $B(j)$, are calculated by reference to actual consumption in a single weighted year. Each is weighted in proportion to its share of total revenue (r).

The adjustment factor, K, allows for projected real price increases and varies between companies. K is set for ten years, although it can, subject to certain conditions, be reviewed at five-year intervals.

Electricity in England and Wales

Price caps for the regional electricity companies are set out in their respective public electricity supply licenses. These are set out in condition 3. There are two basic charge restrictions, the basic formulas of which are:

1. *Initial restriction of distribution charges (condition 3A):*

$$(5A.11) \qquad M_{dt} = \left[1 + \frac{RPI_t - X_d}{100}\right]P_{dt-1} \bullet A_t - K_{dt}$$

where M_{dt} is the maximum average charge per unit distributed in relevant year t; RPI_t is the percentage change in the retail price index; X_d equals various charges, for each regional electricity company, between 0 and 2.5; P_{dt-1} is the amount per unit distributed; A_t is a factor in respect of distribution losses; and K_{dt} is a correction factor.

2. *Initial restriction of supply charges (condition 3B):*

$$(5A.12) \qquad M_{st} = \left[1 + \frac{RPI_t - X_s}{100}\right]P_{st-1} + Y_t - K_{st}$$

Appendix continued...

where M_{st} is the maximum average charge per unit supplied in year t; X_s equals 0; RPI_t is the percentage change in the retail price index; P_{st-1} is the allowed amount of supply unit category; Y_t is the allowed costs of electricity, which include the fossil fuel levy and transmission and distribution costs; and K_{st} is a correction factor.

In addition, condition 3C places supplementary restrictions on supply charges to regulated customers (those receiving 1 megawatt or less). This states that for the first three years the licensee must ensure that the average charge per regulated unit shall not exceed the maximum average charge, M_{pt}, in accordance with the formula:

$$(5A.13) \qquad M_{pt} = \left[1 + \frac{RPI_t}{100}\right] P_{pt\text{-}1} + F_{pt}$$

where RPI_t is the percentage change in the retail price index, P_{pt-1} is the amount per unit supplied to regulated customers in the previous year, and F_{pt} is the fossil fuel levy per unit supplied to regulated customers.

3. *Initial restriction of transmission charges (condition 4A).*

The regional energy companies are joint owners of the National Grid Company, which also faces price caps in its transmission license. The charge restrictions are set out in condition 4 of the license and are determined according to the basic formula:

$$(5A.14) \qquad M_t = \left[1 + \frac{RPI_t - X_g}{100}\right] P_{t\text{-}1} \bullet G_t - K_t$$

where M_t is the maximum average charge per kilowatt, P_{t-1} is the price in the previous period, G_t is a weighting factor of system maximum ACS demand, K_t is an adjustment factor, and X_g equals 0.

G_t is calculated in accordance with

$$(5A.15) \qquad G_t = \frac{AQ_t}{Q_t}$$

where AQ_t is the average system maximum ACS demand over the five-year period, $t-4$ is equal to t, and Q_t is equal to the system maximum ACS demand in the relevant year.

NOTES

1. The United States provides the obvious example of such a process. However, even in the United States the credibility of the regulatory system rests ultimately on the demonstrated commitment of the judicial system to ensuring that utilities receive a "fair" (admittedly ill-defined) rate of return.

2. For example, in mechanism design models, both the price/marginal cost markup and the lump-sum payment are negatively correlated with the level of reported marginal costs.

3. This is based not so much on the existence of risk aversion as on the fact that distortionary taxation implies that rents left to the firm pose a nontrivial cost to the government. (See Laffont and Tirole 1993.)

4. Dependent on the sustainability of a natural monopoly; prices will not be subsidy free when a natural monopoly is not sustainable. In such cases, least-cost pricing requires a single firm, but no price can keep all monopoly products invulnerable to entry.

5. Strict implementation of rate of return would make rate reviews mandatory at short intervals, for example, one year. In the United States, rate reviews are open to being called by either the firm or the state public utility commission. The firm will call a rate review when it expects to get a higher price (for example, when its costs have gone up sufficiently to make the expense, and the risk, of the rate review worth taking). The public utility commission will call a rate review when the observable profitability, or cash flow, of the firm is too high. (See Joskow 1974.)

6. Indeed, the reluctance of public utility commissions to grant rate increases in the early 1970s could have been a response to surprising cost increases arising from the inflationary environment. Once it became clear that much of those cost increases were indeed inflationary, automatic adjustment clauses were introduced. (See Joskow 1974.) In the meantime, however, electric utilities experienced their lowest level of returns.

7. The timing of the regulator's announcement was also significant. Just the day before, the government had sold its remaining shares in the two major generating companies at a high premium. Share prices of these companies and of the twelve privatized distribution enterprises fell sharply.

8. To ensure its reliability and impartiality, the board of arbitrators might have to be formed by foreign academics. Unless a minimum rate of return is specified, the arbitrators would have no way of anchoring their discussions, and a wide range of outcomes could arise from the arbitration.

9. Although it would certainly be feasible to contract out the creation of the initial model, its continuous updating and maintenance would have to be done in-house. Given the complexity of sectors like telecommunications and electricity, spending the resources necessary to maintain high-quality professionals in that job may not be politically feasible. In the United Kingdom it takes three full-time economists to maintain Oftel's model of BT. Similarly, it took three full-time senior engineers from Chile's National Commission of Energy two years to develop a model of Chile's electricity sector.

10. For an analysis of relative performance mechanisms, see Bhattacharya and Guasch 1988. This type of regulation is being used in Chile and Spain. Similarly, in France the performance of water companies across the country is compared in order to establish rewards and thus regulation, while in the state of Mississippi the allowed rate of return for power companies depends on their performance relative to comparable utilities.

11. This type of regulation is being used extensively in New Zealand, with reasonable success to date. Another example is the telecommunications sector in the state of Nebraska, where utility firms are not allowed to raise the price of basic local service by more than 10 percent in any year, or the state of Kansas, where telephone companies are allowed to increase rates by 4 percent and to decrease them by 7 percent without the need for a rate case. Beyond this restriction, the operation and performance of the firm are not controlled by the state utility commission unless 2 percent of the firm's customers complain to the commission about the firm's activities. This scheme grants substantial discretion to the agency in determining what sorts of actions or results would trigger its intervention. Decreed guidelines can reduce but not completely eliminate this discretion.

12. The fact that the conflict between Clear Communications and New Zealand Telecom was not resolved through the courts has triggered a reconsideration of the idea of no direct regulation. (See New Zealand Ministry of Commerce 1995.)

13. At that time, users on a monthly flat rate paid only $9 for local calls, plus toll calls. Calls from Jamaica to the United States are priced more than double the cost of calls from the United States to Jamaica under discount plans. Since international calls are based on accounting rates negotiated among the international providers, reducing those rates would be necessary to promote competition in international calls.

14. If the demand for international calls has no price elasticity, then liberalizing international calls should reduce prices 50 percent. A 50 percent loss in international revenue would have to be compensated for by an 80 percent increase in domestic rates. Yet Spiller and Sampson (1993) find that the demand for international calls is relatively elastic, suggesting that a reduction in international calls could well bring about an increase in total international revenues.

Whether a 50 percent reduction in price would still increase total revenues, however, cannot be precisely predicted.

15. Although the 1995 telecommunications law requires incumbent operators to implement interconnec-tion tariffs by September 1, 1995, according to rules set by the Mexican regulator, by mid-November 1995 the regula-tor still had not published the rules under which operators are to do so.

6 CREATING THE DETAIL ENGINEERING OF REGULATION: ACCESS TERMS AND PRICING IN NETWORK INDUSTRIES

ALONG WITH THE PRESSURE to rebalance and renegotiate tariffs, organizing and pricing access to networks, such as electricity transmission, local telephone exchanges, and railroad rolling beds, continue to be the key emerging regulatory issues in Latin America, the Caribbean, and elsewhere. Technological innovations have brought into question the economies of scale associated with some components of utility production. Significant economies of scale are related to the transmission, but not the generation, of electricity. In communications, economies of scale exist in local exchange service, but not in long-distance service. This

understanding has fostered the push toward facilitating competition in the non-natural monopoly segments of the production of utilities services. Because the network component of the production line has (for the time being) natural monopoly characteristics, it needs oversight and regulation. Otherwise incumbents or network operators might deny new entrants access at fair terms and conditions, resulting in market foreclosures, bottlenecks, and rents in key monopoly essentials facilities.

The natural monopoly argument does not imply that complete systems of infrastructure need to be owned and managed by a single firm. Complete systems, for example, a telephone system, may be composed of several small interconnected systems that are each the sole provider in

a particular geographical area. Examples are telephone franchises in Finland and Hungary (fifty-six small systems), gas transmissions in Germany, railways in the United States, and road systems managed by different regional government entities. Issues such as interconnection and terms for access to networks and vertical integration options are critical to fostering competition and reducing market dominance. Network operating companies are dominant players in the local loop, which is an input into the provision of their own interexchange services and those of their competitors. Similar structure exists in the transmission segment of the electricity sector. Regulation should ensure that access charges promote an efficient structure of production, use, and consumption; allow network operators to make a sufficient return; and promote efficiency on the part of the network operators, while avoiding unnecessary construction of duplicate networks.

The impact of these terms on the final cost to users, and thus on social welfare, can be quite significant. In the telecommunications sector, 45 percent of a long-distance company's operating cost in the United States is for access to telephone lines—access to the network—that is paid to the local phone companies that control the network. Similarly in the United Kingdom, 51 percent of Mercury's total costs are interconnection fees and settlement rates that are paid to other operators and networks. Aside from providing the quality of connecting calls (which is an issue in itself because the network provider and external users of the network often compete in the same market), interconnection fees are often contentious, because the regulatory framework is frequently vague on the subject of interconnection fees, which companies typically justify on the basis of reasonable costs. Those costs can be calculated in several ways—should they include marginal cost, full cost, replacement cost, or opportunity cost?—and disputes often take months, if not years, to resolve. Indeed, there are complexities in apportioning costs into line-sensitive and traffic-sensitive areas; peak and off-peak hours; central business district, metropolitan, provincial, and rural areas; and different areas of the network hierarchy. Yet, there are methods for approaching the problems and securing second-best solutions.

One of the key issues of interconnection or access policy is the set of rules under which interconnection is negotiated. For example, when interconnection involves a collocation agreement, what power does the government have to impose conditions on a regulated firm? What is the proper role of antitrust legislation in providing a framework for negotiating interconnections? The court fight between New Zealand Telecom and Clear Communications illustrates a fundamental problem with interconnection that is not mandated by the regulator. Likewise, the introduction in Chile of a multicarrier long-distance telecommunications service, offering a range of services second only to those in the United States, has not proceeded without problems. The country has experienced total shutdown of the network, occasional blockage of competitors' dialing codes by the main basic carrier, and long delays in connecting dialed calls. In Mexico, as the Telmex monopoly in the provision of long-distance service withers (it expired in 1996), the terms for interconnection to the local exchange are being hotly contested. Regulators from the Communications and Transportation Ministry rejected, quite appropriately, the Telmex plan for establishing ten interconnection points. Instead, the regulators approved a plan for establishing 200 such points to be available by the year 2000. The key issue is to define the terms under which the privatized Telmex will face competition. As of 1997 two new firms, Alestr-AT&T and Avantrel-MCI, both joint Mexican-U. S. consortiums, have entered the long-distance service market, and prices are beginning to fall from their current US$0.30 a minute for border calls. The reluctance of incumbent operators to open the network to external users is not surprising because significantly lower revenues are expected to accompany such a move. For example, in the telecommunications sector, the estimated loss of revenue induced by an equal access policy—an incremental loss of 5 percent of traffic due to the ease in switching providers—is around 20 percent; a low interconnection rate that causes a 15 to 25 percent loss in international traffic can decrease revenues more than 50 percent (Beardsley and Patsalos-Fox 1995).

Setting standards for interconnection is essential to fostering parity and effective competition. Chile's telecommunications market is an example. Chile's multicarrier system in the long-distance and international telecommunication market allows users to access any carrier at any time by simply dialing a code before the desired number. This framework enabled one of the new service providers to claim 16 percent of the Chilean international service market after only seven months of operation. The absence of direct or indirect costs associated with switching operators makes the price of service the major factor guiding customer choice of operator, and enhances competitive behavior. With free entry and an almost 100 percent digital network that allows for clear standards, seven new firms have entered the long-distance market, bringing the price of long-distance calls to by far the lowest levels in Latin America. Otherwise, the carrier operating the network has incentives to engage in unfair competition by unnecessarily delaying connections and interfering with the quality of those connections. Imposing standards such as minimum average differentials in connecting time, and quality between the connections of the main carrier and those of other carriers, is critical. Likewise, issues such as collocation, divestiture strategies (for example, proposals made by companies such as Rochester Telephone and Ameritech to trade greater access for greater regulatory freedom) ought to be considered as well.

At the other end of the spectrum, the access charges that were imposed by the FCC when the Bell System was divested in the United States illustrate the problems with solutions that are unilaterally mandated by the regulator without proper attention to market conditions and alternative delivery technologies. Pricing interconnection as an intermediate service or "bottleneck" facility should ensure that neither the incumbent nor the entrant is disadvantaged by the pricing structure. Moreover, in the context of alternative delivery systems, such as the alliance between AT&T and McCaw Communications, or the bypass of the exchange carriers by companies such as the subsidiaries of TeleCommunications Inc., the correct access prices become vital to ensure efficiency of the total system.

The worldwide trend toward privatization and deregulation of public carriers raises these issues in a broader context. An example is the communications sector in the United States since the breakup of AT&T. While in 1984 only 3 percent of U.S. telephones had the ability to access, under "equal access conditions," more than one long-distance carrier, by 1991, 90 percent of telephone lines had such ability (Mitchell and Vogelsang 1991). Interstate access rates have been falling in the United States, from an average of $0.173 per minute in 1984 to $0.072 in 1991

(Mitchell and Vogelsang 1991). Access rates for intrastate calls are regulated by the state public utility commissions, and today they average $0.105 per minute. At the same time, telephone users pay monthly flat access fees that increased from $1.00 in 1984 to $3.50 in 1991 (Mitchell and Vogelsang 1991). These access charges constitute a large percentage of the retail price of long-distance telephone calls and are vital to the financial viability of local operators. Approximately 27 percent of local loop costs are recovered from monthly and interexchange access charges.[1] For example, since AT&T's current price for an 800-mile one-minute call is $0.023, the access charge of $0.072 constitutes approximately one-third of the total cost.

Appropriate pricing and terms of access are key to the development of a competitive market (see box 6.1). Similar issues appear in other network industries such as power, gas, and railroad. Issues such as pricing and tolls, timeliness in connections, service quality, and the rights of independent users ought to be clearly spelled out for both network operators and independent producers in the concessionary contract, as should a process in the event of disagreements.[2] The failure of contracts to provide clear rules for the terms and pricing pertaining to access has been and will be one of the most common and critical problems affecting Latin American regulatory regimes. At best, policies prohibiting vertical integration across monopolistic and competitive segments of the production cycle have been established to facilitate competitive access terms and to eliminate conflicts of interest. The threat of market foreclosure to upstream competitors has led to a policy of unbundling, or separating, the stages of utility production in some countries. For example, U.S. local telephone service providers are not allowed to enter the long-distance market unless they have opened their local markets to competition. This is not the case in the United Kingdom or in Latin America. Most Latin American countries allow exclusive provision of a full range of services for a limited number of years. Granting long-distance service monopoly rents was, arguably, essential to the privatization of telephone companies and has

---

Box 6.1 Interconnection in Independent Networks

Network access for independent producers is key to fostering competition. Users of infrastructure systems, such as telephone or electricity transmission lines, gas pipelines, or time slots on rail tracks, are interdependent in the sense that they influence each other's marginal costs of access. This creates a complex problem of pricing user access to a system. Such pricing is particularly important where infrastructure systems are being unbundled to allow users more options.

Importance of interconnection in networks
- Increases supply of network services by extending the geographic area of coverage and increasing resources (capital, expertise) in the network sector.
- Improves the performance of the sector by introducing and intensifying competition, resulting in lower-cost services, a broader range of services better matched to market tastes, and innovation in service supply.
- Increases the value and productivity of the network infrastructure, resulting in a positive consumption externality and increasing network traffic (utilization).

Key analytical concepts
- Interconnection is an essential input to production that is often a bottleneck input that the competing

firm cannot easily produce itself, such as access to telephone subscribers or electricity users in different geographical areas.
- Interconnection requires a degree of continuing operation between the two operators that is unusual in ordinary purchaser-supplier relationships.
- The network suppliers are often unequal in the size and value of their markets and in the extent to which they integrate network components and services.

Policy options
- Do nothing: laissez-faire.
- Establish a right to interconnect, with terms left to negotiations; pass antitrust (competition) laws to limit abusive behavior.
- Publish the terms of negotiated agreements; impose terms by regulatory action if parties fail to agree.
- Have the regulator or legislature establish terms and conditions by tariff, and set the quality of service delivered by the network operator to other carriers comparable to its own.
- Establish public service obligations for interconnecting firms.

Source: Adapted from World Bank 1994.

---

been used to secure investment commitments and subsidization (which will eventually be phased out) of local exchange service. In Argentina, Peru, Bolivia, and the United Kingdom electricity transmission companies cannot enter and compete in the electricity-generation market, while in Chile they can. Yet, prohibiting vertical integration, without providing clear terms for access, is not sufficient even in the most advanced and capable environments.

CREATING COMPETITION THROUGH INTERCONNECTION: PRICING OF ACCESS

Technological improvements have led to a new set of issues in the area of public utility regulation. Some utilities no longer qualify under the natural monopoly rubric and, as such, should face different constraints from in the past. In the telecommunications industry, for example, interconnection charges will clearly play a greater

role as competition develops in local segments and networks proliferate. Policymakers have taken one of two approaches in responding to these developments. The radical approach has been to break up the vertically integrated dominant firm and to prohibit the essential facility spin-off from reentering the competitive market. This is the salient approach in the power sector, where both generating and distributing companies are forbidden to participate in the transmission segment of the cycle, precisely to prevent market foreclosure to competitors, or inferior quality of service. The divestiture approach, while helpful and often quite appropriate, is often criticized as ignoring economies of scope or as being cumbersome. A more common policy consists of preserving the vertically integrated firm as a monopoly, while regulating either final prices to consumers or access prices to competitors (or both) to promote competition. The best conceptual analysis is provided by Laffont and Tirole (1994), who give a simple account of the theoretical recommendations, draw policy implications, and analyze current practice and policy proposals in this light. The following analysis is adapted from their work.

In recent years a broad array of recommendations and practices has been suggested to increase competition. Entrants typically argue for a cost-based access charge, such as a long-run incremental cost of access. Although this approach was adopted in Australia for telecommunications, it is widely accepted that marginal cost pricing of access keeps the dominant telephone operator from recovering the fixed costs of the network or the deficit stemming from the universal price constraints. Many regulators and economists have suggested using, instead, long-run incremental cost plus a markup to allow recovery of the access deficit.

There are really two main questions: What is the theoretically correct benchmark, and how can theory be translated into a workable policy? Although cost-based rules are advocated as more practical, most economists consider use-based arguments more theoretically legitimate. For example, both Baumol and Willig advocate the efficient component pricing rule (ECPR) as the logical implication of their theory of contestable markets. Laffont and Tirole support the idea that use-based rules are the proper theoretical benchmark and discuss the practical difficulties in implementing such rules. They develop a theoretical framework in which to assess cost- and use-based rules and offer a new and simple policy for interconnection. This policy's main attraction is that it follows the theoretical precepts. And, although it imposes some informational demands, it requires no more information than existing schemes. The policy consists of regulating the owner of the essential facility according to a global price cap, which includes both access charges and final goods prices. By decentralizing price decisions, including those relative to access, a global price cap implements the optimal Ramsey price structure conditional on the firm's knowledge of its demand and cost structures. It does not require the regulator to measure marginal costs or to estimate demand elasticities. The key insight provided by Laffont and Tirole (1994) is that the inclusion of access prices in the price cap—making it a global price cap—reestablishes the symmetry between access goods and final goods, and partly reconciles the firm with the existence of competition. There are two versions of the global price cap: the plain version; and an enriched version, in which the ECPR defines a ceiling on access prices. The structure of the global price cap for a telecommunications firm is shown below, and is based on Laffont and Tirole (1994).

Set-Up

Assume that a monopolistic telephone operator fully controls the local network and faces competition from at least one competitor in the long-distance market. Let q_1 and q_2 represent the quantity of local calls required for the long-distance calls of the monopolist and the competitor, respectively; q_0 represents the quantity of purely local calls; and Q represents the sum of these three quantities or the total amount of local call units required for all calls. If all long-distance activities exhibit constant returns to scale, then the total costs will be the marginal cost times the quantity. Using a fixed cost, k_0, in the local network, the cost equations would be as follows:

(6.1) $C_0 = c_0 Q + k_0$ for the local network of the monopolist
$C_1 = c_1 q_1$ for the long-distance network of the monopolist
$C_2 = c_2 q_2$ for the long-distance network of the competitor.

Prices to consumers are p_0 for local calls, p_1 for long-distance calls carried by the monopolist, and p_2 for long-distance calls carried by the competitor. To use the local network, the competitor must pay the monopolist an access charge of a. Because the competitors have no market power, they will charge their marginal price of $p_2 = a + c_2$.

Three Common Pricing Rules

The most common approach is the *fully distributed costs* method under which costs are allocated according to some mechanical accounting rule. For example, one might divide the fixed cost by the total usage and add that quantity to the price that the monopolist can charge for local and long-distance calls and to the access fee. In this model the benefits earned by the monopolist from providing local service, long-distance service, and the access charge to the competitor exactly equal the fixed costs for the monopolist of maintaining the local network. One can also use price (or marginal cost) proportional markups instead of the quantity proportional ones used above. This method is known as the Allais rule. Fully distributed cost pricing has met with its share of opposition from economists. It does not encourage cost minimization because it is cost based and, therefore, subsidizes less elastic demands at the expense of more elastic demands. Nor does it grant sufficient flexibility so that firms can make efficient allocations regarding large customers. Finally, it encourages inefficient entry in the competitive sector. Box 6.2 provides a more technical description.

To avoid these problems, some regulators have opted for a use-based rule, which forces entrants to internalize the opportunity cost of the monopolist—that is the forgone profit from allowing others access to a particular segment of the network. The British Office of Telecommu-nications (Oftel) designed one of these use-based schemes. Under this rule, competitors pay a tax or access deficit contribution to the monopolist in proportion to the profit that the monopolist (BT) would have earned. The determination of the access deficit contribution can only be based on historical data or on forecasts, not on actual usage at the time. Of course, this applies to all the rules, whether they are cost or use based. This rule also allows the regulator to define different access charges depending on the product supplied. For example, Oftel sets different prices for national and international calls, with the latter being more costly (see box 6.3).

This is not a price-setting system for final consumption, but simply for access (to allow and yet to regulate competition). Consumer prices are set using a partial price-capping system that will be discussed in the section on global caps. The system is a partial cap because the basket of goods that it regulates includes only the final goods, while the price of the intermediate access good is determined by the formulas in box 6.3. As a final note: When the monopolist's budget is balanced, the access prices exactly equal the opportunity cost, so the external and internal costs are the same. This means that, under a balanced budget, the Oftel rule is the same as an efficient component pricing rule (see box 6.4).

Box 6.2 Fully Distributed Cost Pricing

Variables defined in the text.

Prices
$p_0 = c_0 + k_0/Q$
$p_1 = (c_0 + k_0/Q) + c_1$
$p_2 = a + c_2$
$a = c_0 + k_0/Q$

Benefits or Variable Profits
$B_0 = (p_0 - c_0) q_0$ Local calls
$B_1 = (p_1 - c_0 - c_1) q_1$ Monopolist's long distance
$B_2 = (a - c_0) q_2$ Competitor's long distance

In this case the total benefit equals total cost so that the monopolist's budget is balanced:
$B_0 + B_1 + B_2 = (k_0/Q) * (q_0 + q_1 + q_2) = k_0$

The Allais Rule
$p_0 = c_0 + \delta c_0$
$p_1 = (c_0 + c_1) + \delta (c_0 + c_1)$
$a = c_0 + \delta c_0$

For this rule the coefficient of proportionality, δ, is chosen to satisfy the following budget constraint:
$(1 + \delta) [c_0 (q_0 + q_1 + q_2) + c_1 q_1] = k_0 + c_0 (q_0 + q_1 + q_2) + c_1 q_1$

Note that under this marginal cost-proportional markup, inefficient firms can enter because they will make profits even if $c_2 > c_1$, as long as:
$a + c_2 = c_0 (1+\delta) + c_2 = p_1 - [(1 + \delta) c_1 - c_2 < p_1.$

Box 6.3 Use-Based Pricing (the Oftel Method)

The access charge under the Oftel rule is:

$a = c_0 + ADC$ (access deficit contribution),
where $ADC = (k_0 / q_1) [B_1 / (B_0 + B_1 + B_2)]$.

This formula can be generalized for multiple competitive segments, with different access prices for each segment. Oftel, for example, currently requires the competitor, Mercury, to pay separate access rates for national and international calls:

$$a_1 = c_0 + (k_0 / q_1) [B_1 / (B_0 + B_1 + B_2 + B_3 + B_4)]a$$
$$a_3 = c_0 + (k_0 / q_3) [B_3 / (B_0 + B_1 + B_2 + B_3 + B_4)].$$

$B_3 = (p_3 - c_0 - c_3) / q_3$ is BT's profit on its own international calls, B_4 is profit on the competitor's calls, p_3 is the markup charge on the calls, c_3 is the nonlocal marginal cost, and q_3 is the international output.

The inclusion of BT's profitability means that access for international calls is higher than access for national ones ($a_3 > a_1$) because the benefits from Mercury's access charges become $B_2 = (a_1 - c_0) / q_2$ for domestic calls and $B_3 = (a_3 - c_0) / q_4$ for international calls, where q_4 is Mercury's international output.

Assuming that the monopolist's budget is balanced: $B_0 + B_1 + B_2 + B_3 + B_4 = k_0$, and the formulas for the access charges simplify to:

$$a_1 = (c_0 + B_1) / q_1 = p_1 - c_1$$
$$a_3 = (c_0 + B_3) / q_3 = p_3 - c_3.$$

Box 6.4 The Efficient Component Pricing Rule (ECPR)

The ECPR equates the access price to the difference between the monopolist's price and the marginal cost on the competitive segment, or the difference between the net benefit and marginal cost of providing access:

$$a = p_1 - c_1 = c_0 + [p_1 - (c_0 + c_1)].$$

The more general form would be:

$$a = c'_0 + [p_1 - (c_0 + c_1)] = p_1 - c_1 + (c'_0 - c_0)]$$

where the cost of providing access to the competitor, c'_0, is not the same as the cost for the monopolist, c_0.

The ECPR sets the access price equal to the net benefit earned by society when that service is provided competitively. Baumol and Willig, among others, have repeatedly stressed that the proper yardstick for defining access prices is that of the perfectly contestable market, and that the supplier must be permitted to charge enough for the good to receive compensation for the sacrifice caused by supplying another firm. The ECPR defines in effect an upper limit for access prices, because it still allows the incumbent vertically integrated operator to make excessive profits. A lower bound is set by the marginal cost of granting access to the network. The marginal cost may, however, fail to compensate the network operator for the fixed costs of maintaining the network. Such costs should also be incorporated in the access price possible in the form of a two-part tariff, with a fixed charge covering network set-up costs, including the cost of capital, and a variable cost covering the short-run cost of access. Then such an access price would be equivalent to the ECPR without compensating the incumbent for loss of excessive profit. One of the expected social benefits of charging the opportunity cost is that the rule sends the right signal to entrants. Unlike in a cost-based system, companies can only enter the market profitably if they are more efficient than the current telephone (or other utility) operator at providing the service in question. Another benefit is that entry will be revenue neutral to the monopolist and, therefore, will not interfere with the cross-subsidization of the monopoly and the competitive segment. In other words, it will not be possible for firms to enter the profitable segment and siphon off profits from other segments so that the monopolist can no longer afford to provide less profitable services. This protection, in turn, screens the regulator from the political pressure of politicians who are trying to protect their local subsidies. Revenue neutrality also reduces the monopolist's incentive to skimp on the quality of access in order to destroy the level playing field. An example of how to compute the access price under the ECPR is presented in box 6.5.

Unfortunately, not all is perfectly settled in the world of the ECPR. The ECPR assumes that all

Box 6.5 An Example of the Efficient Component Pricing Rule

	Route AB Town A		Town B	Route BC Town C	
	Marginal Cost (AB)	Marginal Cost (BC)	Joint Cost	Access Price	Price (Average Cost over AC)
Incumbent	5	5	10		20
Efficient Entrant		4		15	19
Inefficient Entrant		6		15	21

This is a simple example of the Efficient Component Pricing Rule (ECPR) developed by Baumol as a principle for setting access prices. In this example, provided by Baumol, a vertically integrated incumbent offers a rail service between towns A, B, and C. An entrant wants to develop a rival rail service between towns A and C but has to pay for access to the vertically integrated incumbent for its bottleneck service between towns A and B (route AB), and will provide the service itself between towns B and C (route BC).

The costs of the service are as follows: There is a marginal cost (assumed constant) of service of 5 for each leg of the route AB and BC. In addition, there is a joint cost of service of 10 (an average fixed cost incurred by the incumbent for operation of the entire rail network) so that the average cost of the service AC is the sum of the marginal costs and the joint cost; that is, 20. The incumbent charges the average cost of the service (20), and the entrant charges a price equal to its marginal cost over BC and the access price to AB.

As illustrated in the table above, the ECPR states that the correct access price to charge the entrant for the bottleneck service (route AB) is the sum of the mar-

ginal cost of access to the bottleneck AB which equals 5, and the joint costs of service 10 (the opportunity cost of entry to the incumbent). The efficient access price is therefore 15.

This example is illustrated by two entrants. The first, the efficient entrant, has marginal costs of 4 over the route BC. It therefore can profitably enter at the ECPR access price of 15 and undercut the incumbent with an average cost of 19, which is less than the incumbent's average cost of 20. If an inefficient entrant has marginal costs of 6 for the route BC, then it will have an average cost of 21, that is, more than the incumbent, and hence will not enter. In other words, the correct access price induces efficient entry. An access price less than the ECPR (in this simple example) will induce inefficient entry.

Access Price (under ECPR) = $MC(BC) + JC$
Average Cost (to incumbent) = $MC(AB) + MC(BC) + JC$
Average Cost (to entrant) = $MC(BC) + AP$.

Source: Klein 1996.

firms face identical cost structures (that they are equally efficient) and that they provide perfectly substitutable goods. It also abstracts from incentives so that there is no reason to have more than one firm in the competitive segment. Therefore, entrants must be *more* efficient than the monopolist or they would never choose to enter the market. In that case, however, the monopolist would cease providing long-distance service at all because it would earn higher profits by selling those rights without incurring any costs. This rule is very stark in its predictions. Its main advantage is that, when it works, it avoids inefficient entry. But it does so at the expense of

maintaining the incumbent's monopoly power over the final good. Economides and White (1995) show that with reasonable assumptions about demand elasticities and cost disadvantages, the loss in consumer welfare from maintaining the monopoly would overcome the loss from productive inefficiencies arising from inefficient entry. Furthermore, maintaining the monopoly limits the development of dynamic efficiencies arising from competition. (For a discussion of the advantages and disadvantages of the ECPR, see Armstrong and Doyle 1995; Economides and White 1995; Kahn and Taylor 1994; and Baumol and Sidak 1994.) One could, however, build on its insights and on those of its critics and develop a model with actual competition in the competitive segment. To do so one must allow for cost and demand asymmetries between the monopolist and the competitors and introduce product differentiation to allow for several competitors. This normative framework will help answer the two key questions about the ECPR: (a) What is the proper price reference, p_1, for computing the access price, and (b) is the ECPR optimal?

The Optimal Price in Theory

In a "first-best" world—one without constraints—a necessary condition for optimality would be that the competitors internalize the marginal cost of operating the local network or "bottleneck." In that situation, the regulator would set the access price equal to the marginal cost of operating, c_0, and the rates for final goods would also obey marginal cost pricing. Assuming, on the one hand, that the monopolist also must have a balanced budget, one can calculate the optimal prices for p_0, p_1, and a. If the monopolist and its rivals are equally efficient on the competitive segment and the demand is the same for both firms' long-distance service (no product differentiation), then the access price will be the same as the ECPR, so $a = p_1 - c_1$. Consider, on the other hand, either of the following two scenarios in which prices differ for the two providers. If there is some kind of product differentiation (brand loyalty, name recognition, or switching costs), then the monopolist will have a certain number of captive customers who will always choose its service if the price difference is small. This advantage will allow the monopolist to charge $p_1 > p_2$, because not all customers will switch when faced with a higher price. At the same time the access price charged to the competitor will be lower than under the ECPR, because p_1 reflects the opportunity cost of a relatively more inelastic demand. Another cause of unequal prices would be if the demand functions are the same but the monopolist has lower costs. In this situation, the monopolist should be able to charge the public less on the competitive segment than its competitor due to

a cost advantage. However, the access charge will be less than that of the ECPR due to the absorption of costs. See box 6.5 for a more complete analysis.

The conclusion that access prices should be based on use has been challenged by both regulators and economists who have argued correctly that these rules are difficult to implement. This is true for two reasons. First, it can be very difficult to calculate the correct prices. Box 6.5 demonstrates some of the calculations that would be necessary to set optimal rates. This argument is most accurate if one is discussing a rapidly changing industry such as telecommunications, rather than a more steady industry such as electricity, in which the calculations would not have to be redone after each technological improvement. At least as important a point, however, is that any complication in setting prices increases the probability of regulatory capture. The more discretion the regulator has, the more effort (and money) the industry will devote to influencing the outcome. The result may be an inefficient rate structure and a waste of resources in the lobbying effort. For an industry like telecommunications, the only promising way to base a rate structure on demand considerations while avoiding these problems is to allow the monopolist to set prices under a price cap. One can obtain the same results as in the ECPR by imposing a global price on the monopolist provided that (a) the intermediate good (access to the local network) is treated as a final good and included when computing the cap (this is, in fact, the difference between a partial and a global price cap); and (b) the weights used to determine the cap are proportional to the predicted quantities of the relative goods.

In other words, a price cap will induce the firm to use the proper Ramsey prices as long as all the goods are included in the determination of the cap and the weights are fixed *exogenously* at the level of output expected. This result holds for any structure and allows for substitution between access goods and final goods without requiring the regulator to estimate any demand functions. The global price cap, despite its apparent advantages, is at odds with standard practice.

Box 6.6 Is the Efficient Component Pricing Rule Optimal?

Assuming no government subsidies (a balanced budget constraint for the monopolist), the optimal prices can be represented by standard Ramsey-Boiteaux ratios (for further details see Laffont and Tirole 1994):

6.1 $\quad (p_0 - c_0)/p_0 = [\lambda/(1 + \lambda)](1/\eta_0)$
6.2 $\quad (p_1 - c_1 - c_0)/p_1 = [\lambda/(1 + \lambda)](1/\eta_1)$
6.3 $\quad (p_2 - c_2 - c_0)/p_2 = [\lambda/(1 + \lambda)](1/\eta_2)$

where λ is the shadow price of the budget constraint and the η_is are "superelasticities." That is, if the demand for the calls is independent, then the cross-elasticities will be the same as normal elasticities.

More specifically, if ε_i is regular elasticities and e_{ij} is cross-price elasticities then:

$$\eta_0 = \varepsilon_0$$
$$\eta_1 = \varepsilon_1 \left[(\varepsilon_1 \varepsilon_2 - \varepsilon_{12} \varepsilon_{21}) / (\varepsilon_1 \varepsilon_2 + \varepsilon_1 \varepsilon_{12})\right] < \varepsilon_1$$
$$\eta_2 = \varepsilon_2 \left[(\varepsilon_1 \varepsilon_2 - \varepsilon_{12} \varepsilon_{21}) / (\varepsilon_1 \varepsilon_2 + \varepsilon_2 \varepsilon_{21})\right] < \varepsilon_2.$$

From the above formulas one can calculate the access charge as:

$$a = c_0 + [\lambda/(1 + \lambda)](p_2/\eta_2).$$

The question remains whether ECPR will obtain these optimal prices as solutions. Consider the following:

Case 1. Assume the demand and cost functions of the monopolist are identical to those of the competitor. Then $\eta_1 = \eta_2$ and from equations 6.2 and 6.3 we get $(p_1 - c_1 - c_0)/p_1 = [\lambda/(1 + \lambda)](1/\eta) = (p_2 - c_2 - c_0)/p_2$ or $a = p_1 - c_1 = p_2 - c_2$. Under these assumptions, ECPR is the optimal price.

Case 2. Assume the monopolist has $a_1 - a_2 > 0$ captive customers. In this case the quantities demanded will be: $q_1 = a_1 - bp_1 + dp_2$ for the monopolist and $q_2 = a_2 - bp_2 + dp_1$ for the competitor; $b > d$ to reflect the captive customer effect, which leads to $p_1 > p_2$ and $a < p_1 - c_1$. In this case the ECPR prices are not optimal and the efficient access price is lower than that predicted by ECPR.

Case 3. Assume that demand is again symmetric but that the monopolist has lower costs on the competitive segment so that $c_1 < c_2$. This inequality implies that $p_1 < p_2$ and that the access price $a < p_1 - c_1$. In this case the ECPR access price again overestimates the efficient level. If the inequalities reversed, the relatively inefficient monopolist would undercharge using ECPR.

For example, BT's cap does not include intermediate products. In fact, the very debate over access pricing rules results from the general opinion that intermediate and final goods should be treated differently. It is important, therefore, to confirm the logic of a *global* price cap. Adopting a partial cap and the ECPR would bear much resemblance to the policy of the United Kingdom. The monopolist would maximize profit subject to this cap and use approximations for anticipated output. If the expectations are accurate, the price of local calls will be lower than the Ramsey price, while the price of long-distance calls and access charges will be higher. Because the access charge is not included in the cap, the bottleneck segment is subsidized at the expense of the competitive segment. A global price cap, in contrast, will result in Ramsey prices, provided that the weights used to determine the individual prices are proportional to actual output.

Global Price Cap with the ECPR

Adding the ECPR to a global price cap would yield a *partial* price cap, but the weights on the prices would be different from those under a general partial cap. Box 6.7 provides a full description. Under a pure ECPR, an increase in the final price p_1 also raises the access price. From the point of view of profit, the price increase effects the *total* demand on the competitive segment. Under a price cap, the increase only changes the demand for the monopolist's product on the competitive segment. A partial price cap, therefore, tends to cause higher prices on the competitive segment, while the global cap results in proper pricing incentives. There are two reasons to combine the ECPR and a global price cap: to facilitate weight setting and to avoid predation. Weights must be proportional to forecast outputs, but a precise forecast may require information that regulators do not have. In prac-

Box 6.7 A Partial Price Cap

Using a *partial* price cap for external prices, combined with the ECPR price setting for internal rates, a monopolist would face the following problem:

$$\text{Max } \pi = (p_0 - c_0)q_0 + (a - c_0)q_2 + (p_1 - c_0 - c_1)q_1 - k_0$$
$$= (p_0 - c_0)q_0 + (p_1 - c_0 - c_1)(q_1 + q_2) - k_0$$

subject to $w_0 p_0 + w_1 p_1 \leq P$, where P is the price cap and the w_is are weights to determine the relative importance of local and long-distance calls in determining the cap. Even if one chooses weights equal to the expected outputs so that the constraint becomes $q_0 p_0 + q_1 p_1 \leq P$, the prices will not be efficient because the value of the access charge is not included.

To achieve Ramsey prices, the monopolist's constraint should read $q_0 p_0 + q_1 p_1 + q_2 a \leq P$, where the q_is are *actual* quantities of outputs for the different types of services. This particular setup represents a *global* price cap because both intermediate and final goods are included.

A *global* price cap with an ECPR-derived access charge $a = p_1 - c_1$ looks very much like a partial cap, but the weights will differ from the standard ones: $q_0 p_0 + (q_1 + q_2)p_1 \leq P$.

tice, weights are frequently based on recent outputs or revenues. BT's weights, for example, are the previous year's revenue shares. To limit the pricing distortions induced by endogenous weights and to accelerate the convergence toward Ramsey prices, regulators operating under a partial price cap must come up with a reasonable forecast of the total demand on the competitive segment and of the market share of the monopolist.

Regulators and policy advisers are generally concerned about the possibility that incumbents will prey on entrants. It is very easy for an incumbent to do so under a simple global price cap by raising the access charge while lowering p_1. This practice allows the monopolist to undercut the price of its competitors without losing undue profits. The increased access charge raises the rivals' costs, making it that much more difficult to meet the monopolist's lower price. Without substantial financial resources, rival firms are forced to exit the market. A more relevant question is how much the incumbent would actually benefit from this sort of predatory behavior under a global price cap. If the potential entrants are financially weak, the predation should prove to be relatively successful. Competitors will be forced out, and the incumbent will earn long-run monopoly rents. One way to protect entrants is to make predation less profitable. The ECPR can accomplish that to a certain degree by making it impossible to separate access prices from final goods prices. In that situation, the only option available to the monopolist is to increase both the access charge and the final goods price. By charging a very high price for long distance while requiring the competition to do the same by raising costs, the monopolist may succeed in lowering demand to a point where no firms will enter the competitive market. The difficulty with this strategy is that it will likely prove too expensive for the monopolist to maintain.

The final assessment of an ECPR policy under a global price cap would have to be mixed. A disadvantage of the ECPR is that it may introduce some distortions in the case of asymmetric demand or cost functions. From a policy point of view, it can be quite costly to implement, because regulators must verify compliance. Furthermore, the ECPR requires measuring the incumbent's marginal cost on the competitive segment, which regulators may not be able to do. However, the ECPR can provide a certain amount of protection against anticompetitive behavior and allows for a more efficient choice of the weights used in the price cap. From a purely practical perspective, the ECPR can be used as an upper bound when real threats of predation exist due to asymmetric industrial structure. If this danger is not present and competition exists between at least two or three strong networks, the additional constraints created by the ECPR may result in substantial distortions, costing the industry and the consumer more than it benefits them. The simplicity of the global price cap may be more illusory than real. Introducing a global price cap has substantial informational requirements. Regulators have to set prices, or at least price caps and weights, on all products produced by the incumbent. This provides for continuous regulatory effort and facilitates manipulation of the regulatory process. Finally, in sectors where the setting of global price caps is not feasible as a result of vertical integration restrictions, the best solution would be to implement the ECPR.

TIMETABLING—ESTABLISHING OPTIMAL DELIVERY SCHEDULES

In the case of power or natural gas it does not matter whether a customer receives electrons or molecules produced by the supplier with whom he or she has contracted for delivery, because the product shipped is sufficiently homogeneous. A different issue arises in transport ventures like airlines, railways, or telecommunications, where freight, passengers, or callers need to reach a particular customer or point in the network. This imposes a more complex set of constraints on the network optimization problem than the requirement that total inflows match total outflows (including storage).

For example, if one were to define rights to use the rail tracks and allocated them to multiple parties, secondary trading should yield the optimal set of paths given the valuations by producers and consumers for the service in question, that is, person or good x delivered to point y at time z. The optimal set of paths forms the optimal delivery schedule or timetable. The problem is whether an optimal timetable can be generated through decentralized bargaining or whether a market is needed that simultaneously generates the optimal set of paths through the network and the prices for all the paths contained therein. Because the value of each right to use a piece of track at a particular time is dependent on what happens with all adjacent pieces of track, one may need a single optimizing market. A further issue is whether short-run adjustments to the optimal schedule due, for example, to mechanical breakdowns or other emergencies, can be made in a timely manner by the dispatch center, or whether the loss of vertical integration translates simply into higher transaction costs.

Timetables need not be preannounced. Ideally, transport and congestion prices could be determined through segments of the transport network competing to provide the service. Through demand and supply conditions, prices on individual segments could be set independently and competitively. How might this work in practice? Optimal use would be obtained if users of the system faced prices that forced them to use the system optimally. For pricing in a phone system one might imagine the following system. The caller would dial. The system would then determine the optimal path at the desired time and quote a price that would appear on the phone. The customer could then "conclude" the contract by pressing a yes button or abort the call attempt. This would yield a system of spot prices on the basis of which longer-term contracts could be established, enabling callers to have assured call rights at given prices at certain times.

Similar access issues exist in the power sector, (and in the railway and gas sectors), which also displays network characteristics through the transmission grid. The issues will become even more pressing in the years ahead, because between 50 gigawatts and 85 gigawatts of new capacity will be added in Latin America in the coming decade. Most of these additions will be generated from the private sector, which will require access to the transmission network. Several Latin American countries have legislated power sector reforms to improve operating performance, reduce sector financial dependence on public resources, and enable private participation. The structure of the sector and the policy environment for various Latin American countries are shown in chapter 11, where power sector reforms are discussed. Approaches to reform differ depending on the structure of each country's industry and regulatory framework. Some countries, including Argentina, Colombia, Norway, Peru, and the United Kingdom, have opted for a sector with mostly separate generation, transmission, and distribution, allowing private ownership of these functions. They seek to establish a highly competitive power-generating subsector by using contracts between generators and consumers or distributors to establish market prices for electricity at the bulk level. Price regulation is reserved for open access transmission and distribution grids and for retail tariffs for "captive" consumers. Other countries, like Costa Rica, Jamaica, and the United States, have so far opted for limited competition in power generation. Independent power producers supply bulk power to a monopoly grid owner through a competitive bidding or contract process.

In Mexico legislators passed a new energy law in 1992 providing for third-party ownership and operation of power projects, with electricity sales to the Comisión Federal de Electricidad (CFE), the national electricity company. Under Mexican law, independent power generation is to be allowed using three vehicles: self-generation, in which facilities are owned by industrial users; third-party cogeneration; and stand-alone independent power producers. Electricity is to be sold to CFE at negotiated rates, subject to CFE 's competitive-bidding obligations. Access issues and terms are still to be stipulated. Similarly, in the telecommunications sector the regulatory framework remains quite vague with respect to implementation of "essential facilities." The mandatory rules, which were released in 1997, when the monopoly of Telmex in the long-distance market expired, remain biased in favor of the incumbent and subject to quality-of-service manipulation. Such unwarranted delays do not inspire confidence or allow for long-term planning by potential investors and entrants, or even Telmex, due to the uncertainty of the final terms. In Latin America and the Caribbean, perhaps with the exception of Chile, the terms for interconnection to the grid have been left fairly vague, and this is and will be a permanent source of conflict and loss of welfare. In Argentina, Chile, Norway, Peru, and the United Kingdom the power-generating subsector is or will be self-regulating, with basic concessions and operating standards the main requirements for generators. Regulation in these countries focuses on transmission and distribution operations, which are commonly considered to be natural monopolies. Regulation in these subsectors aims at providing substitutes for market-based competition through the use of efficiency models, pricing and access policies for power transport, and competition for the larger consumer market. In Norway and the United Kingdom, commercialization activities require a license, but pricing for the end consumer relies on market forces. In other countries retail distribution tariffs are still regulated. An option is to forego regulation if society were willing to accept monopoly rents, which would always be limited to some degree by competition from substitute products. This is often politically unacceptable; however, we do observe a number of sectors that are not or are only partially subject to economic regulation. Such is the case when substitute product markets exist and society accepts possible remaining monopoly rents, as in the examples of railways vs. trucks (United States, Argentina), or natural gas vs. petroleum (Germany, Finland, and Hong Kong).

At present, interconnection contracts in most Latin American countries, which allow private sector participation in some stages of the production process, are negotiated between the network provider and the value-added service providers and generating companies. Conflicts have already begun to appear among the involved parties. In general, the current regulatory agencies in Latin America are poorly prepared to handle disputes between network providers and new entrants, particularly on issues such as whether network costs are allocated properly in establishing access prices, and the quality of service provided to network users. These disputes will certainly increase as the economies expand and new entrants seek access to the network's bottleneck facilities, illustrating the importance of clear access and service rules.

In the electricity sector in Guatemala prices are to be negotiated freely for output generated by the independent power producers (IPPs) and sold to the transmission network operator. In the event of an impasse in those negotiations the regulators can dictate the final price. There are no clear guidelines on how to set that price. While in principle such a system has some attractive features, it is highly vulnerable to capture on two fronts. First, since the transmission firm remains a state firm, its incentives are questionable, and in principle its managers can be swayed to offer a sweet deal to the IPPs in exchange for pecuniary or nonpecuniary benefit, (a recent contract paid US$0.10 per kilowatt to IPPs for output). That firm can always pass the costs to the final users or pass the losses to the state. In addition, the broad discretion of the regulator in dictating the final price makes him vulnerable to influence by either party.

NOTES

1. Because this access charge compensates the local exchange carrier for what essentially is a fixed cost, the access charge creates a distortion by reducing long-distance volume and promoting bypassing of the local loop. (See Mitchell and Vogelsang 1991.)

2. For example, one of those rights in the United States is equal access. Telephone users who are served by a dominant local network operator can access any long-distance carrier (interexchange carrier) by dialing the same number of digits, through the same technical arrangements and with the same quality of service. In the United Kingdom, a carrier other than BT, say a cellular operator, may be unable to agree with BT on technical or financial arrangements for interconnection to BT's network. If so, they may apply to the regulator, Oftel, for a binding decision fixing the terms for interconnection.

7
DETAIL ENGINEERING
EXPERIENCES IN LATIN AMERICA
AND THE CARIBBEAN

THIS CHAPTER EXAMINES how several Latin American and Caribbean countries are undertaking regulatory reforms in their utility sectors, taking into consideration the requirements across sectors. Some countries, such as Argentina and Chile, are well advanced in their reform process, while others, such as Bolivia, Colombia, El Salvador, Jamaica, Mexico, and Peru, have made and continue to make important inroads. The bulk of this chapter provides examples of detail engineering choices, mostly in telecommunications, such as Jamaica's rate of return, Chile's benchmark competition, Mexico's and Venezuela's price caps, and Argentina's

price indexation. Table 7.1 illustrates the basic components of price regulation in the telecommunications sector.

RATE OF RETURN IN JAMAICA

Jamaica's rate-of-return regulation is a transparent system that provides regulated companies with a 17.5 to 20 percent rate of return on equity, which is not unusually high for international telecommunications operators (British Telephone's rate of return is in that range). The regulator may neither disallow investments nor attempt to change the rate of return, and any disagreement between the company and the regulator goes to binding arbitration (as would be the case if the government disallowed some costs).

Finally, firms have exclusive licenses to operate in the domestic and international markets for a relatively long period of time.

The choice of detail engineering seems, in principle, to fit Jamaica's institutional characteristics; there is very little regulatory discretion, the extent of administrative complexity is limited, and the maintenance of the cross-subsidy toward local operations is assured, which facilitates privatization. The system, however, could be improved by limiting rate-of-return regulation to the local network and instituting a more competitive framework for long-distance regulation.

Although inefficiencies are associated with Jamaica's approach to rate-of-return regulation, the system does accommodate an environment characterized by lack of administrative capabili-

Table 7.1 Price Regulation in Telecommunications in Sample Countries

	Pricing Formula	Frequency of Tariff Review	Inflation Adjustment	Productivity Parameter/ Rate of Return
Argentina	PC	Semiannual	Indexed to U.S. CPI	Partial
Chile	BM	Every five years	Indexed to CPI	Full
Jamaica	ROR	Company request	Indexed to CPI	None
Malaysia	PC	Company request	Indexed to CPI	None
Mexico	PC	Every four years after 1998	Indexed to CPI	Partial
Philippines	ROR	Company request	None	Partial
Venezuela	PC	Quarterly	Fully indexed to WPI until 1996. Partial indexation for 1997–2000	Partial

PC: price caps; BM: benchmark; ROR: rate of return; CPI: consumer price index; WPI: wholesale price index.

ties *and* institutional characteristics. This situation requires very specific procedures to provide regulatory stability. In such circumstances, the choice of rate-of-return detail engineering may be close to the only option available.

REFORM OF CHILE'S TELECOMMUNICATIONS SECTOR

The performance of Chile's telecommunications sector has been quite extraordinary. Since 1987, the year before the government privatized the main local phone company, the number of telephone lines rose dramatically—from 581,000 in 1987 to almost 3,700,000 in 1997—reflecting a penetration rate of about 30 percent, the highest in Latin America. Outgoing international traffic amounted to approximately 21 million minutes in 1987 and exceeded 175 million minutes in 1996, while the mobile telephone system, which started operations in 1988, could claim more than 340,000 subscribers by the end of 1996. The local phone network, which was 37 percent digital in 1987, has been fully digital since 1993. The privatization of telecommunication firms also led to substantial improvements in their internal efficiency, as exemplified by the number of phone lines per worker, which rose from 74 to 235 between 1987 and 1995. In addition, the cost of long-distance calls is by far the lowest in the Latin American and Caribbean region, due mostly to the competitive opening of the segment. More generally, it is quite impressive that over 70 percent of the required investments in

electricity and telecommunications have been made by private operators.

The keys to success. The commitment by privately owned utilities to make significant investments can be explained by many of the macroeconomic reforms, including the relaxation of the financial constraints faced by public enterprises; the isolation of public services from political pressures; and rapid economic growth—averaging about 7 percent between 1986 and 1997—to which privatization itself has contributed. But a key factor in explaining the static and dynamic efficiency gains observed was probably the introduction of an explicit regulatory framework embedded in a law that encourages such efficiencies. The embodiment of the regulatory framework in a law provides for the credible commitment and stability of the regime, an essential ingredient to secure investor confidence and, thus, optimal levels of investment. Chile's new regulatory system includes detailed regulations, with explicit mechanisms for settling disputes between the regulators and utilities, with the judiciary as final arbiter. These regulations were innovative in their use of very specific legal provisions restraining administrative discretion.[1] The level of detail in the law is such that, in the case of telecommunications, it even stipulates the type of regression to be used in estimating a fair rate of return to the "efficient" firm (see box 7.1). This experience also shows how difficult it is to write a comprehensive law in a sector characterized by technological change. Indeed, the telecommunications law was changed several

Box 7.1 Price-Setting Procedures in Chile's Telecommunications Law

1. Demand is first estimated for each service/zone/firm bundle.
2. The efficient firm is defined as one that starts from scratch and uses only the assets necessary to provide that service.
3. For each service, the incremental cost of development is calculated, which is the long-run marginal cost (LRMC), provided no investment plans are considered. The law stipulates that regulated companies must have investment plans of a minimum of five years. These plans are prepared by the companies and presented to Subtel on the basis of a detailed outline defined in Law No. 18, 168 (Article 301) under the heading "Technical and Economic Basis."
4. Revenue for each service is estimated such that the net present value of providing the service is equal to zero. This revenue is the incremental cost of development.
5. Moving from the incremental cost of development to the long-run average cost, full coverage of cost is attained by increasing efficient tariffs in a least distorting fashion.
6. The fair rate of return (ROR) is defined as the sum of the rate of return on the risk-free assets and the risk premium of the activity, weighted by the systematic risk of the industry. That is, $R_i = R_f + b_i (R_p - R_f)$, where R_i is the ROR on revalued capital for firm i, R_f is the ROR on risk-free assets, b_i is the firm i's systematic risk, and R_p is the ROR on a diversified portfolio.
7. Since tariffs are calculated every five years, the law allows firms to adjust tariffs every two months, using the inflation index of each service and the Divisia index.
8. Disputes between companies and regulators are settled by a committee of three experts, one nominated by each party, and the third by mutual agreement.

Source: Galal 1994.

times prior to privatization, and prior to the advent of democracy.

At the beginning of the 1970s Chile's telecommunications sector was dominated by three publicly owned companies: Compañía de Teléfonos de Chile (CTC), providing local telephony throughout most of the country; Empresa Nacional de Telecomunicaciones (Entel), providing some domestic and all international long-dis-

tance services; and Correos and Telégrafos, providing domestic and telegram services, sharing the international market with ITT and Transradio. All of these companies lacked the resources needed to expand and adopt new technologies. Cross-subsidies between local and long-distance services were the norm within price controls often adjusted below inflation. Regulation, operation, and to some extent policymaking were all in the hands of these public companies. These were the conditions at the time the government decided to deregulate and reregulate the Chilean telecommunications sector once more before the actual privatization of the sector through a regulatory law introduced in 1982. The law was amended again in 1987 and in 1993 to allow for competition in long-distance telephone services.

The reform of Chile's telecommunications sector was undertaken at the same time as that of the electricity sector. Indeed, the philosophical foundations of the regulation of both sectors is the same: freedom of entry into all areas of the sector, licenses required only for the taking of public or private property (and in the case of telecommunications, for the use of the spectrum), very minimal obligation to serve, and minimal government intervention in the sector. There were, however, two main differences in the implementation. First, the belief that telecommunications was an inherently competitive sector led the drafters of the 1982 law to not introduce any stipulation concerning the regulation of prices. Although interconnection was required, the legislation left the terms of interconnection to be decided by the parties. Second, unlike in the electricity sector, the government did not attempt to change the initial market structure, and hence did not restructure the two main telephone companies. Thus, competition started with two monopoly companies, one a local service (CTC), and the other a domestic and international long-distance provider (Entel).[2]

The Long and Winding Road to Sector Restructuring

In 1982, Chile was the first country to introduce open competition in all sectors of telecommunications, with minimal governmental regulation and with no restructuring of the sector.[3] Such path-breaking status, however, did not last long, because in 1987 a major revision of the telecommunications law introduced a tariff-setting process.[4] Following a determination by the Antitrust Commission that neither local service nor long-distance service were competitive,[5] Subtel started the price-setting process which culminated a year later, in September 1989, with the first regulated telecommunications tariffs. Thus, purely from a "free-market perspective," the 1987 reforms seem to be a backward movement toward price regulation.

A closer examination, however, suggests otherwise. Although since 1982 CTC and Entel, the main telecommunications operators,[6] were allowed to set prices freely, in fact they set their prices following informal consultations with Subtel and the Ministry of Economics (Galal 1994). Furthermore, competition in both local and long-distance service did not develop rapidly. Although since the opening of the telecommunications markets five local companies were created, they tended to locate in areas where CTC did not have a license,[7] or where it provided relatively bad service.[8] The latter companies, however, faced growing difficulties, and by 1994 they had gained only 2 percent of the market. Some of these difficulties could be related to normal market conditions, but others were related to the fact that interconnection

agreements were not easy to develop.[9] Indeed, all three companies obtained their interconnection agreements only after the Antitrust Commission ordered the agreements be made.[10]

Thus, by 1987 it was clear that competition had not come to the telecommunications sector. Furthermore, from passage of the 1982 Act until 1987, the network was growing only slightly faster (6.5 percent in terms of numbers of lines) than prior to passage of the Act (3 percent). From 1987 on, though, the sector has been growing very fast (at more than 20 percent per year). Indeed, by 1991, only three years after its privatization, CTC doubled its number of lines. More specifically, since privatization the number of lines in service has increased from less than 600,000 in 1987 to over 2 million in 1996, and phone density has increased from 4.65 per 100 people in 1987 to 14.3 in 1996 (see table 7.2).

The free-market approach to telecommunications regulation, then, did not help develop the sector prior to 1987. The difference could not be explained by the different spread of privatization. The main generating companies (Chilgener and Endesa) were privatized at roughly the same time as CTC and Entel. Nevertheless, there was competition in and network growth of wholesale electricity from the beginning. Macroeconomic circumstances also do not seem to be behind the differential performance because electricity generation capacity grew rapidly even during the early 1980s,[11] a period characterized by slow

Table 7.2 Lines in Service, Density, and Waiting List; Chile (1987–95)

Year	Lines in Service (thousands)	Density (lines/100 people)	Waiting List (thousands)
1987	581	4.65	232
1988	631	4.93	236
1989	689	5.40	284
1990	864	6.56	308
1991	1.956	8.02	241
1992	1.279	9.56	314
1993	1.516	11.10	198
1994	1.657	11.97	117
1995	1.894	13.42	52
1996	2.+	14.30	30

*CTC figures.
Source: Subtel Annual Report.

economic growth.[12] Although other reasons could be offered to explain the lack of dynamism of the telecommunications sector, one feature seems important: The regulatory framework based on pricing freedom was not credible, particularly when the government also owned the two main telecommunications entities. The 1987 reforms, by formalizing the price-setting process, reduced government discretion in the determination of telecommunications prices, providing a more credible framework in which to invest. CTC aggressively responded to those incentives.[13]

Although the 1987 reforms had an important impact on both CTC's and Entel's incentives to invest, the reforms do not seem to have drastically affected the companies' ex post performance. The profitability of both companies improved following passage of the 1982 law, although it seems that the main beneficiary was Entel, because its return on net worth reached almost 40 percent by 1986. The 1987 reforms also benefited Entel; its profitability exceeded 40 percent in 1988 and 1989. CTC's profitability also increased a bit, but remained below 20 percent. In fact, the companies' ex post performance started to improve not in 1987 but in 1982 (Galal 1994).

The Regulatory Institutions

Since 1977 the telecommunications regulatory body in Chile has been the Subsecretary for Telecommunications (Subtel) at the Ministry of Transportation and Telecommunications. Subtel shares responsibilities for rate setting with the Ministry of Economics. Its other main duties are to present proposals for national policies in the area, develop and update technical standards, ensure compliance with regulation and legislation, administer and control the use of the radiomagnetic spectrum, process franchise applications, and administer the rate-setting procedures. Its decisions are also subject to the rulings of the Antitrust Commission. Subtel is a public sector agency subject to public sector salary scales. These scales are not very competitive and many of Subtel's most able staff end up working for the regulated firms.

The 1982 telecommunications law established total separation between the regulatory function and the operation of services. The services that are subject to price setting are determined by the Resolutive Commission, according to a broad legal criterion regarding services provided under insufficiently competitive conditions. This regulation has two clear goals: (a) providing the incentive for firms to minimize long-term marginal costs, as identified through hypothetical efficient firms; and (b) ensuring that the efficiency gains are passed on as benefits to consumers. All telecommunications services are, however, subject to some degree of regulation either through the granting of licenses used to regulate entry, or through the technical standards, including those covering the obligation to establish and accept interconnections or through the rate-setting mechanisms to which the monopoly services are subject.

Price Regulation

The price-setting process designed for the telecommunications sector is almost identical to that of the electricity sector. There are, however, two important exceptions: (a) the use of the capital asset pricing model to compute the cost of capital of the efficient telecommunications firm, and (b) disputes among the companies and the regulator are settled through binding arbitration rather than through a fixed formula, as in the electricity sector. Thus, again in 1987, the reformers chose to limit regulation at the expense of regulatory flexibility. Prices are based on long-run marginal costs of putatively efficient firms. Currently, only the local telephone service and access to long-distance service are subject to price regulation. Price reviews are supposed to take place every five years, with indexation in the interim years. The resulting prices are supposed to ensure that the firms earn a fair rate of return on revalued assets. The procedure involves estimating demand for each service, zone, and firm bundle, the incremental cost based on a benchmark efficient firm and a fair return for the firm. Rules are spelled out quite specifically. Disputes are resolved through a three-member arbitration commission.

The specific pricing rules for local telephony are discussed next to illustrate some of the outstanding regulatory problems.

Local telephony rate setting. Local phone rates are set so that the net present value of expansion projects equals zero, when discounted at a rate reflecting sectoral risk. The local service is metered, and the billing has two components: a fixed monthly charge for connection, and a variable charge per minute. There are two per-minute rates, corresponding to peak and off-peak hours. Rates are adjusted every five years on the basis of cost studies prepared by the phone companies in accordance with government guidelines. Once a study is completed, regulators have 120 days to object and draw up counterproposals. Differences are brought before a panel of experts. Although the final decision rests with the regulators, it is unlikely that they will not follow the panel's advice, in view of the fact that companies can take them to court.

Despite big efficiency gains in the sector, local phone charges have not fallen since privatization; on the contrary, they have increased. According to Chile's National Institute of Statistics, in April 1989 a family's average bill was Ch$2,825 (US$11.21), increasing to Ch$3,814 (US$15.13) by May 1996 at constant prices[14] (see table 7.3, and table 7.4 for an evolution of all tariffs). Some of the increase is explained by the partial abolition of the subsidy paid by long-dis-

tance carriers to local phone firms and by the abolition of the surcharge on phone line installation. However, the main explanation is that CTC has not passed efficiency gains on to its clients. Indeed, CTC's rate of return on equity, which was 14.8 percent in 1990, climbed to 22.5 percent by 1993. In 1995 it dropped back to 16.9 percent, due to strong competition in the long-distance market, rebounding to 18.4 percent in 1996.

The last rate-setting process made explicit the problem of information asymmetry in the telecommunications sector. The existence of one dominant provider prevented benchmarking and, moreover, regulators had serious difficulties gathering precise traffic data and other information from the companies. Even regulation of efficient firms requires actual data from the firms, because costs depend on, among other things, customer density and traffic per line. It is therefore difficult for regulators to build a credible counterproposal when they do not have full access to the regulated firm's data (there is no specific sanction for withholding information). However, there is a single regulatory change that could reduce this problem, whereby the regulatory agency prepares the rate study. In that case the regulated firm would have to provide verifiable information if it wished to challenge the ruling. This proposal would shift the burden of proof from those who have little information to those who have full information.

Access Rules

Concessions are required for operation and use of local public phones, national and international long-distance services, and radio broadcasting. These concessions are granted by Subtel and are free (except for rights to use the radio electrical spectrum), granted for an indefinite term on a first-come, first-served basis (although more than one concession can be granted for each area), and spell out service obligations. What they imply for long-distance calls and mobile telephony is discussed next.

Long-Distance Calls

Following privatization of the long-distance monopoly, regulatory ambiguities generated legal

Table 7.3 Monthly Local Residential Rates
(fixed charge plus variable rate with tax, in Ch$ as of April 1989)

Date	Tariff
April 1989	2,825
July 1991	3,278
December 1991	3,197
June 1992	3,349
December 1992	3,341
June 1993	3,718
December 1993	3,623
June 1994	3,921
December 1994	3,885
June 1995	3,773
December 1995	3,834
May 1996	3,814

Note: The exchange rate was 252 pesos/US$.
Source: National Institute of Statistics, Chile. Price levels.

Table 7. 4 Evolution of Domestic Local and Long-Distance Tariffs

1985 Ch$ per line			Local Service Flat Rate			Domestic Long Distance — Without taxes, in June 88 Ch$					
				80 KM Operator	DDD		400KM Operator	DDD		3250KM Operator	DDD
RESID	COMM	3 min	1 min	1 min	3 min	1 min	1 min	3 min	1 min	1 min	
1970	1243.9	3342.2	175.03			557.04			1799.71		
1971	971.7	2610.8	175.03			557.04			1799.71		
1972	778.7	2092.5	175.03			557.04			1799.71		
1973	360.9	1575.6	174.41			555.25			971.77		
1974	906.4	3063.3	191.32			620.89			984.20		
1975	842.6	2848.0	163.37			530.82			841.67		
1976	576.0	1942.7	131.76			429.43			679.14		
1977	694.1	2346.1	144.94			445.79			691.35		
1978	848.6	2868.0			80.15			246.44			382.20
1979	785.0	2653.2			86.21			265.09			411.23
1980	830.3	2806.3			80.11			180.90			243.66
1981	788.0	2663.3			83.14			177.32			209.00
1982	870.9	2945.1			83.14			177.32			209.00
1983	1034.5	2413.9			83.14			184.03			216.89
1984	983.1	1994.7			56.60			125.29			147.68
1985	1390.7	2387.1			49.65			109.92			129.56
1986	1384.2	2048.2			40.17			85.17			93.20
1987	1498.1	2433.7			35.97			76.49			79.39
1988	1486.1	2511.3			32.00			68.27			70.77
1989	1653.5	2576.7			24.12*			44.72*			84.52*
1990	1845.0	2700.6			19.74			32.65			67.53
1991	2079.0	2892.6			18.54			29.2			62.76
1992	2305.8	3079.7			16.69			23.89			55.2

*In 1989 there were changes in the distance bands.
DDD: Domestic direct dial. RESI: Residential tariff. COMM: Commercial tariff.
Source: Galal 1994.

entry barriers to the industry, which combined with inappropriate rate-setting schemes to keep prices significantly above marginal costs for several years. In practice, the long-distance company achieved average rates of return on capital above 30 percent. Legislation passed in 1993 eliminated legal barriers to competition in long-distance services, paving the way for a multicarrier system launched in October 1994, in which long-distance callers choose their carrier for each phone call by dialing two digits. The new legislation also facilitates competition by allowing long-distance carriers to have access to end users directly through private circuits.

Until the beginning of the 1990s, telecommunications services were dominated by two firms in Chile: CTC and Entel. CTC had a virtual monopoly on fixed telephony throughout the country, while Entel monopolized long-distance services. The antitrust agency's decision in 1992 directing Telefónica, which owned Entel, to divest its 20 percent share in Entel, was essential for the emergence of competition, because this would have been impossible if both CTC and Entel had been controlled by Telefónica. Currently, eight firms are competing in the long-distance market. The opening of the sector to competition eliminated the need to fix rates, and these are now market determined. On the other hand, given that a carrier needs access to and from local networks in order to provide long-distance services, regulation of this aspect has become crucial. The law obliges all local telephone franchise holders to give access to carriers on a nondiscriminatory basis, and the cost of interconnection between the public network and long-distance carriers is set by the regulator. This access toll approximately reflects costs (two-thirds of a local call, for each origin–destination end point). However, the access toll for incoming international calls clearly exceeds the cost of providing this service (it is fourteen times the local peak rate).

The 1987 reforms and the subsequent privatization had all the predicted effects. The network expanded and prices for long-distance services fell more rapidly, while those for local service increased more rapidly, thus tending to eliminate the extent of cross-subsidization from long-distance to local service. Furthermore, the profitability of the long-distance market provided a strong signal for potential competitors, and in 1989 CTC and other local exchange providers attempted to enter the long-distance market by requesting from Subtel licenses to build and operate long-distance facilities (see table 7.5 and figure 7.1).

Here is where Chile's institutional framework starts to have an impact on the sector's development in an unexpected way. Opposing the entry of the local-exchange companies into the long-distance market, Subtel requested in 1989 that the Central Preemptive Commission consider whether entry of local-exchange companies into long distance was in the public interest.[15] Although the Central Preemptive Commission sided with the government, it was rapidly reversed on appeal by the Resolutive Commission, which

Table 7.5 Return on Net Worth
(in percentages)

	CTC	ENTEL
1960	7.9	—
1965	14.1	—
1970	10.7	—
1975	-8.6	—
1979	1.68	12.31
1980	4.45	12.14
1981	2.61	11.23
1982	−15.14	11.53
1983	11.89	13.05
1984	9.17	16.79
1985	−15.29	19.97
1986	21.02	35.37
1987	10.91	38.98
1988	12.31	45.54
1989	17.22	45.63
1990	13.46	38.76
1991	15.17	38.93

— = Not available.
Source: Galal 1994.

ordered that there be no segmentation of local and long-distance services, and requested the introduction of a multicarrier system whereby customers can choose their long-distance provider. Thus, by 1989 Chile could have moved directly to long-distance competition.

Entel, however, appealed to the supreme court which, in 1990, requested from the Reso-

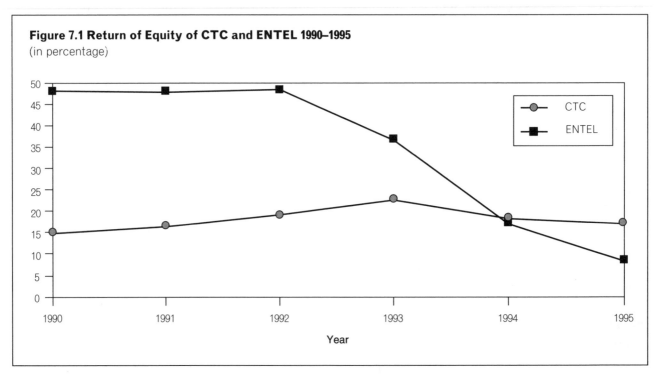

Figure 7.1 Return of Equity of CTC and ENTEL 1990–1995
(in percentage)

lutive Commission a more in-depth study of the technical conditions that would allow for fair playing conditions, including the supervision of interconnection quality. The Resolutive Commission took three years to study this issue anew. In 1993 it upheld its prior decision[16] and ordered the government to implement the multicarrier system in less than eighteen months. The system was introduced in late August 1994 outside Santiago, and a month later in Santiago. Prior to its introduction, and to some extent reflecting the strong pressure exercised by Entel,[17] congress amended the General Telecommunications Act limiting for the next five years each operator's market share in the domestic and international long-distance market. Those carriers affiliated with local exchange companies (mostly CTC) were subject to stronger restrictions. Table 7.6 shows the nature of the bargain: CTC was initially limited to 35 percent of the long-distance market, while Entel was required to initially relinquish at least 30 percent of the market. But the market share restrictions also provided CTC with some protection from competition from Entel. If Entel decided to enter into local service during 1995, it had to relinquish 80 percent of its current long-distance market share, or 50 percent more than if it stayed out of the local-service market. Thus, table 7.6 reflects a particular bargain struck in Law 3-A among the companies that allowed implementation of the Resolutive Commission's ruling. Although Entel lost in the Resolutive Commission, litigation provided a delay of five years.

Table 7.6 Market Share Restrictions in the Long-Distance Markets, Chile

| | Domestic Long Distance | | International Long Distance | |
Year	Affiliated (%)	Non-Affiliated (%)	Affiliated (%)	Non-Affiliated (%)
1995	35	80	20	70
1996	45	70	30	65
1997	55	60	40	60
1998	60	60	—	—

— = Not available.
Source: Law 3-A, Chile.

Relationship Between Regulation and Sector Performance

The combination of this regulatory environment and state-owned-enterprise privatization has led to a remarkable expansion in the quality and diversity of services provided. Currently, multiple telecommunications services are provided by many firms, of which the most important are CTC, Entel, VTR, Telex Chile, and Bell South. The largest of these, CTC, owns about 95 percent of all telephone lines, controls the largest cellular phone company, has a long-distance subsidiary with the second-largest market share, and controls the company providing cable TV to almost half of all subscribers. Foreign investors participate in the ownership of most telecommunications companies: Telefónica de España controls CTC; the Italian company STET, and Samsung respectively own 19.5 percent and 12.5 percent of Entel; Southwestern Bell owns 49 percent of VTR.

In spite of good progress in telephone density, universality of service is for the moment a distant goal, although it is realistic to consider universal access, for which reason a decision has been made to subsidize public and community telephone service solutions in remote areas, financed out of the Telecommunications Development Fund. Subtel prepares a needs list and draws up the corresponding projects, which are put out to tender among interested firms and awarded to those seeking the lowest subsidy.

So far, deregulation, and thus the ensuing competition for long distance, has had the expected results. First, twelve firms requested long-distance licenses, and by 1997 eight firms had entered the market and three more have been approved by Subtel to provide the service[18] (see table 7.7). Following a hectic advertising campaign by all the long-distance providers, prices of long-distance services fell by more than half of Entel's prices prior to September 1994 (see table 7.8). Take, for example, the prices carriers charge on calls to the U.S. At the beginning of 1997 the normal rate was about US$0.90 per minute, with one carrier charging less than US$0.40 (carriers charge their large customers even lower rates). By

Table 7.7 Telecommunication Companies and Services Offered

Firm	Associated Foreign Operations	Local Service	Long Distance (national & international)	Business & Value-Added Services	Mobile Services	Equipment & Terminals	Cable TV	Internet Access
			Services Offered					
CTC	Telefónica	x	x	x	x	x	x	x
Entel	STET-Italia	x	x	x	x	x		x
Telex-Chile		x	x	x		x		x
VTR	SBC-EE.UU.	x	x	x	x	x	x	
Bell South	Bell South		x		x			x
CIA. Telef. Manquehue		x						
CMET		x						x
Iusatel	Iusacell-Mexico		x					x
Transam			x					

Table 7.8 Average Monthly Advertised Rates of Long-Distance Telephone Calls in Chile, 1994–95
(U.S. dollars per minute)

Rate	September 1994[a]	October 1994	November 1994	December 1994	January 1995
National long-distance, daytime	0.047	0.028	0.040	0.083	—
National long-distance, nighttime	0.017	0.026	0.016	0.059	—
International long-distance, United States	1.602	0.407	0.390	0.328	0.428
International long-distance, other countries	2.676	0.497	0.607	0.461	1.285

a. Entel tariffs, prior to introduction of the multicarrier system.
— Not available.
Source: Survey of advertising in *El Mercurio*.

the latter part of 1997 that charge had dropped to US$0.34. By way of comparison, AT&T in the U.S. charges US$0.15 per minute under its One-Rate Plan (see table 7.9).

These prices can be contrasted with the pre-multicarrier regulated rates: If the rate-setting scheme in force from 1988 onward had been maintained, a call to the U.S. today would cost US$2.40 per minute. The drop in prices led to a substantial increase in traffic: International calls per month rose from about 6 million minutes before the multicarrier system in September 1994 to around 19 million minutes by March 1997. Entel's market share more than halved overnight. Even without including public telephones, its market share had not reached 50 percent by December 1994.[19] And the rates of return in the

regulated segment (CTC) fixed-link contrast sharply with those in the non-regulated segment (Entel), the long-distance market, pre- and post-competition (see table 7.10 and figure 7.1).

Table 7.9 The Impact of Competition in Chile's Long-Distance Service
(price per minute [US$] CTC /Entel, 1997)

Domestic	0.17
To U.S.	0.34
From U.S.	0.51

These prices represent the basic rate for a typical domestic long-distance call and an international call to the U.S., expressed in US$ at the 1997 exchange rate.

Source: Spiller and Cardilli 1997.

Table 7.10 Rates of Return on Equity for Chilean Firms
(1995—latest comparable data available)

Electricity Distribution (regulated) 30%	Electricity Generation (competitive) 15%
Basic Telephony (regulated) 16.9%	Long Distance (competitive) 8.4%

So far, the fear that CTC would capture a large percentage of the market has not materialized; CTC is still the third-largest long-distance carrier, with less than 30 percent of the market. The introduction of the multicarrier system, then, completed the first round of reforms that started in 1987 with the Resolutive Commission determination that both local and long-distance services were not competitive. While the multicarrier system improves upon the degree of competition in the long-distance market, it does not affect the extent of competition in local services. That is the next battlefront in the Chilean telecommunications war.

As with the introduction of long-distance competition, competition at the local exchange will require further refinements in the regulatory framework, which, given the constraints involved in the regulatory scheme, will have to await the results of litigation now before the antitrust authorities and the courts. Yet, competitors are currently positioning to compete in that market through the construction of facilities, since Chile does not require unbundling or resale. Already there are six local exchange providers within the Greater Santiago area, including CTC and Entel; two original competitive local exchange carriers in Santiago, Complejo Manufacturero de Equipos Telefónicos (CMET) and Manquehue; VTR, a large cable TV provider (which subsequently merged with CTC); and Telefónica Andina, a new entrant. As a result, in a number of areas in Santiago, consumers already have a choice of local providers. This strategy to integrate is a consequence of the level of competition induced in the sector.

The counterpart of the consumers' gain is a reduction in the industry's profits: In 1993 Entel made profits of about US$80 million, whereas the total profits of all carriers in the new system in 1995 amounted to US$31 million. These meager results are explained by three factors: (a) the dissipation of monopoly rents aggravated by a price war during the first quarter of 1995, (b) high but transitory restructuring costs to cope with a competitive environment, and (c) a narrowing of the imbalance between incoming and outgoing traffic. International carriers settle their traffic imbalances at so-called accounting rates, which are a multiple of the actual cost of providing the service. A carrier handling more incoming than outgoing traffic receives significant revenue from foreign carriers. In 1993 international traffic coming into Chile was approximately 1.3 times outgoing traffic. Estimates put incoming traffic at 160 million minutes during 1996, 15 million minutes less than the outgoing traffic in the same year.

Mobile telephony. In setting up the mobile phone system, the government defined two franchise zones for cellular phones, with two companies operating in each. Prices are freely determined by the firms. At the beginning of 1996 two cellular phone companies with disjoint concession areas jointly set up a new enterprise—Startel—serving the whole country. CTC owns 55 percent of Startel; the other 45 percent belongs to VTR. In 1996 there were about 340,000 cellular phone subscribers, of which 190,000 were clients of Startel, 109,000 were clients of Bell South, and the rest were with Entel.

Mobil telephony prices (Ch$120 per minute in peak periods) are higher than fixed telephony prices (Ch$13 per minute), reflecting higher operating costs. The biggest part of the cost of communicating from or to a mobile phone is always paid by the mobile service subscriber, although mobile phone companies argue that the party initiating the call should pay for this. CTC has opposed such a change, arguing that fixed telephony subscribers should not have to pay for the development costs of cellular telephony. What probably explains CTC's opposition is that the change would make mobile telephony a closer substitute to fixed telephony.

In November 1996 Subtel auctioned three nationwide franchises for personal communications services (PCS), with geographical coverage as the auction variable. Franchises were awarded in March 1997 and the service came into operation a few months later. Two franchises were awarded to Entel and the third to Chilesat. However, with the aim of increasing competition, in 1995 the Preventive Commission recommended that no company should possess more than one mobile phone franchise in the same geographic area. It argued that competition among potential competitors is an important factor in market discipline. It is not yet known what position Subtel will adopt in response to the two franchises awarded to Entel.

REGULATORY PITFALLS: INTERCONNECTION, ACCESS, VERTICAL INTEGRATION, AND COMPETITION

The discussion so far should have made clear that, in spite of many good features, the Chilean regulatory framework had a number of deficiencies. First, access issues. The right to and terms of interconnection to the fixed link were completely neglected, with serious adverse consequences, such as unnecessary lengthy delays in competition, with the associated welfare losses to telephone users; and years on interconnection-related lawsuits, highly costly to entrants. The deadlock was eventually broken through legislation and intervention by the Chilean supreme court. Similarly, the legislation did not specify equal access (to the network), leading to the expected delays and restraints by the provider and to lengthy litigation and delays in receiving the benefits of competition. The pattern was that CTC would contract for wholesale long distance and would assign outbound calls randomly to long-distance carriers in proportion to the size of that carrier's contract. Again, the deadlock was eventually broken by a supreme court decision to let customers choose their own long-distance carrier and place all carriers on an equal basis, by allowing the customer to dial the carrier's unique access code. Likewise, the legislation is mute regarding unbundling (the requirement by the incumbent to provide entrants basic network ele-

ments and services individually, such as lines, switching, and transport).

Second, the rigidity of the regulatory framework with its embedded checks and balances proved, not unexpectedly, to have costs. The introduction of the multicarrier system is an excellent example of how the original design of a system of checks and balances in utility regulation limits the ability of the government to tightly control the evolution of the industry. Indeed, the participation of the antitrust authorities reversed an original position of the regulator against vertical integration. The participation of the supreme court,[20] another part of Chile's complex system of checks and balances, delayed the de facto deregulation of long distance by four years.[21] This seems to be another example of the reformers choosing credibility over flexibility. This time, as may often be the case, credibility came at a cost.

It would seem that the path chosen by the authority is one of competition among firms providing a multiplicity of services, to take advantage of economies of scale and scope. Moreover, for the users, the concept of one-stop shopping is highly attractive, and this has led firms in competitive segments (such as long distance) to realize that it is essential for them to integrate services, and have direct access to the client, for which purpose they need to be local-access providers or local providers. As mentioned, in late 1997 five providers started providing local phone service through subsidiaries in areas overlapping the CTC area.[22] Thus, competition, which had been opened up in other areas, is now promoting competition in local service.

However, achieving competition among providers of multiple services confronts Subtel with a real challenge when a single company holds about 90 percent of all local telephone subscribers, and when its own resources are limited. Is there any chance of achieving real competition in basic phone service? In certain areas there have been overlapping franchises in local telephony since the early 1980s. These arose mainly as a result of the inability of CTC —at that time in state hands—to satisfy demand. However, these franchises never represented real competition for CTC. Weaknesses in the legislation, especially as regards interconnection norms, inhibited true competition. The situation was resolved when the 1993 law was passed introducing regulated access tolls, a change which facilitated competition in fixed telephony.

PCS may provide cost-effective alternatives in the future, but joint provision of cable TV and basic phone services is nowadays a more realistic possibility. VTR, which controls a company holding about a 50 percent participation in the cable TV market, is experimenting with the joint provision of local phone and cable TV services. Unfortunately, the parent companies of VTR and CTC are considering merging the two firms, and if that happens the possibility of competing through joint operation with cable TV would disappear. In the meantime, the Preventive Commission has stated that any merger between CTC and VTR would have to obtain its prior approval. Thus, competition in basic phone services still seems a remote possibility. It remains to be seen whether CTC's dominance of basic services will allow for competition in other telecommunications services.

One example of the risks involved in vertical integration is illustrated by a special joint-service offer made by CTC and its subsidiary, CTC Celular (before it merged with VTR Celular), in which their clients were offered a so-called "super-phone." Callers trying to reach the owner of a super-phone would call the subscriber's basic phone number. If nobody answered, the call would automatically be transferred to the subscriber's mobile phone. Bell South complained to the Resolutive Commission about this type of bundling and also about subsidies made by CTC, a regulated company, to CTC Celular, an unregulated company. The Commission not only sanctioned CTC with a fine of 2,500 UTM (equivalent to US$142,500), but it also asked the government to introduce legislation requiring subsidiaries of basic phone companies providing other communication services to be organized as common stock companies supervised by the Securities Commission, as was required in the case of long-distance carriers which were subsidiaries of basic phone companies.

The current law allows local phone companies to enter the long-distance market through subsidiaries. But while competition consolidates, the law has set limits on the main firms' market share during the first three years. In addition, local telephone companies are obliged to supply any relevant information on long-distance traffic to all carriers, because discrimination in favor of an affiliated long-distance carrier is always a possibility while the local phone service remains a natural monopoly. So far, the long-distance market has worked comparatively well; it remains to be seen whether these conditions will be maintained in the future.

More worrisome is CTC's expansion policy. To start with, through acquisition and merger it has gained control of a cable TV company providing services to half the nation's 700,000 TV cable subscribers. Then, the merger of CTC's and VTR's cellular operations created the largest mobile phone company in the country. Any future merger between CTC and VTR will challenge Entel's dominance in long-distance services, so it remains to be seen how the regulatory agencies will react to CTC's merger drive.

Comparing with Argentina and the U.K.

Prior to privatization in 1990, Entel, the Argentine telecommunications company, was broken up into four companies, two of which provide basic domestic services in disjoint areas, and two which provide value-added and long-distance services. Ownership of the latter two companies was divided equally between the two basic service providers. These four companies now monopolize most telecommunications services in Argentina, having been awarded a ten-year (seven initially, plus an extension of three) guarantee of exclusivity in basic, value-added, and long-distance services.

The charges for basic services were negotiated after the companies had submitted their bids and the franchises had been awarded, but before the companies signed the license agreements in November 1990. Between December 1989 and September 1990 the price of a pulse went up from US$0.0058 to US$0.0332, and it was established that the rate would remain constant in real terms for two years, then decline by 2 percent per year over the following three years. In November 1991 the tariff-setting scheme was modified: Prices were fixed in U.S. dollars after an initial increase of 1.3 percent. In 1994 the rate per call unit stood at US$0.0413. Argentine telecommunications price regulation now adheres to an *RPI - X* scheme, where the efficiency factor (*X*) is set at 2 percent until 1997, and 4 percent between 1998 and 2000.

According to Petrazzini (1995), the explanation for such favorable treatment of private investors is that privatizations were largely a financing instrument for stabilization policies. The economic and political instability in Argentina would have prevented achieving liberalization and the sale of the companies at the floor price set by the government. Investors would not consider purchasing Entel (the first utility privatization in Argentina), unless the market was protected for an extended period. The Argentine government had initially planned a sweeping liberalization of the telecommunications sector.

In the U.K., until 1981 the post office held a virtual monopoly on licenses to operate telecommunications services. Only when the post office was unable to provide a service was another operator allowed to do so. In 1981, post office telecommunications services were hived off to a new company, British Telecommunications (BT), which was privatized in 1984. In 1981, the firm Cable & Wireless (C&W), which provided telecommunications services in the former colonies, was privatized, and a new company, Mercury, was formed which from 1982 became a competitor to BT. BT's license includes price controls and an obligation to provide interconnection facilities at predetermined prices and service quality. A regulatory agency (Oftel) was also set up. Oftel regulates prices using an *RPI - X* formula for a basket of services. Initially a productivity increase factor of 3 percent was considered, but this was raised to 7.5 percent in 1993.

In 1991, it was concluded that this duopoly had not been successful in terms of reducing concentration in the sector because Mercury's participation was marginal, and consequently the restriction on telecommunications licensing was lifted. Moreover, BT was prohibited from entering mobile telephony and cable TV, and it was also ruled that BT and Mercury had to provide circuits to other operators. Following the ending of the duopoly, new companies were born. The main competitors to BT at the local level are cable companies offering television and telecommunications services, and Energesis, owned by the National Grid Group, has built a digital network using power transmission lines (Boulding 1997).

In 1995, fourteen years after the introduction of deregulation, BT was invoicing 87 percent of the basic telephony market (local and long distance), with the rest mainly in the hands of Mercury. All vestiges of competition would disappear if a merger between BT and C&W—owner of Mercury—occurred, and currently the only real threat to BT comes from cable TV companies. BT's license includes price controls on calls and exchange-line services, an obligation to offer standard interconnection facilities at predetermined prices, and service quality.

In general, the market structure in Chile is more competitive than in Argentina and the United Kingdom, for the following reasons. First, franchises have not been awarded on an exclusive basis since before the privatization process. Second, at the time of privatization there were two large companies, one in basic telephony and the other in long distance, which the antitrust agencies prevented from falling into the hands of a single owner. Third, competition was facilitated by the way the multicarrier system was implemented.

Upcoming Regulatory Challenges

To sum up, the main regulatory challenges to be addressed by the Chilean system can be divided into two areas (with some inevitable overlap). The first area is improving equity. This entails improving the design and incentive structure to ensure that (allocative and technological innovation-induced) efficiency gains are passed on to users and are not captured as additional rents, establishing incentive-based, nondistortionary universal system obligations. A salient choice for the latter is the use of competitive bidding of the minimum subsidy to provide the service. The alternative, a direct, targeted subsidy to the appropriate income groups, is often administratively too costly. The second area of regulatory challenge is improving efficiency. The main issues here are revisiting access pricing and terms of that service to ensure alignment of (efficient) costs and prices and equal treatment of service quality; facilitating or not foreclosing viable alternatives to the fixed-link network; and better, more effective implementation and enforcement of the antitrust legislation in the sector.

A key issue in addressing the efficiency consideration is the need to define the proper role of antitrust legislation in the framework for interconnection negotiations. The introduction in Chile of a multicarrier long-distance telecommunications service, second only to that in the United States in the choices offered, has not proceeded without problems. The country has experienced total network shutdowns; occasional blockage of competitors' dialing codes by the main basic carrier, CTC; and longer delays in dialed calls getting through. In Mexico, as the Telmex monopoly in the provision of long-distance service withers, the issue of the terms for interconnection to the local exchange is being hotly contested. Regulators from the Communications and Transportation Ministry rejected, quite appropriately, the Telmex plan for ten interconnection points. Instead, the regulators approved a plan for 200 such points, to be available by the year 2000. The key issue is to define the terms under which the privatized Telmex faces competition. The reluctance of incumbent operators to open the network to external users on equal terms is not surprising, given their expected significant decreases in revenues associated with such a move. For example, in the telecommunications sector, estimates of the loss in revenue induced by an equal access policy—an incremental loss of 5 percent in traffic due to ease in switching operators—are around 20 percent; or a low interconnection rate causing a 15 to 25 percent loss in international traffic can induce over a 50 percent decreases in revenues

(Beardsley and Patsalos-Fox 1995). The setting of standards for interconnection is essential to foster parity and effective competition, and to reap its benefits.

In summary, the main lessons from the Chilean experience derive from the institutional design and the impact of opening the sector to competition. Regarding the latter, note that drastic price reductions have only occurred in cases where competition has emerged. Regulated local phone rates have risen by about 35 percent since privatization, whereas deregulated prices of long-distance phone calls have fallen by over 50 percent. In 1996 the price of one minute for a national long-distance call in Chile was even lower than in the U.K. Electricity distribution prices, for their part, do not reflect the enormous reduction in distribution losses that has been achieved since privatization. The price of electricity for residential customers increased from US$0.805 per kilowatt hour in 1988 to US$0.1313 per kilowatt hour in 1995.

Overall, this situation has led to significant increases in the profits of regulated firms in electricity distribution and local telephone services, with regulated segments reporting much higher rates of return on equity (ROE) than unregulated segments in the same industry (see tables 7.10 and 7.11). This difference is even more striking when one considers that there are fewer risks in the regulated segments because they are natural monopolies. In the electricity sector, the average ROE among regulated distribution companies was 30 percent in 1995, whereas for (largely) unregulated generating companies the figure was 15 percent. In the same year the ROE in the largest basic phone service company was 16.9 percent,

Table 7.11 User Prices	
Average Household Telephone Bill (in constant Ch$ prices)	
1989	1996
2,825	3,814
Electricity Price Distribution	
1988	1995
8.05 KWh	13.13 KWh

while for the largest long-distance carrier it was 8.4 percent. To see why all this is happening, it is necessary to understand how regulation was designed, introduced, and implemented in each sector. These factors are discussed next.

Benchmark Regulation in Chile

The main characteristics of Chile's regulatory framework are (a) prices are set independently of current costs and are related instead to the costs of a putatively "efficient" firm; (b) prices adjust automatically during the year, with major revisions every five years; (c) no company has an exclusive license; and (d) the arbitration procedure is well specified. Because the regulatory system is supposed to compensate an "efficient" firm for its cost of capital, this system can be called benchmark regulation.

Chile's regulatory framework, then, is relatively flexible. While price indexation holds during the interim period, flexibility is achieved by adjusting prices every five years according to specified formulas. Flexibility is further enhanced because the set of prices to be regulated is not specified ahead of time, but rather the regulator asks the Antitrust Commission to determine the segments to be regulated.[23] Consequently, Chilean regulators have limited ability to change the composition of the regulated sector because they must first convince a very independent body.

Chile's benchmark regulatory system is sophisticated and requires intensive administrative capabilities. It would be well suited to an environment in which institutional characteristics require specific regulatory procedures to provide regulatory stability. Thus, it would naturally suit a country like Mexico, where the executive has few checks and balances, but where a large cadre of well-trained professionals exists, or countries like Argentina, Brazil, Colombia, and Uruguay, which have strong administrative capabilities.

Price Caps in Mexico

Telmex, the state-owned telecommunications enterprise, was privatized in 1990 when the government sold a controlling block of shares ($1.76 billion) to a consortium comprised of Southwestern Bell; France Telecom; and Grupo Carso, a Mexican holding company. The consortium was granted a monopoly on long-distance service until the end of 1996 and a monopoly on local service until 2026. The regulatory scheme was price-cap regulation, applied to an overall weighted average price of Telmex's services, rather than a specific price cap for each service.

Prior to privatization of Telmex, all telephone taxes (in practice) except the general value-added taxes were abolished, and all prices (except for international long distance) were sharply increased so that on average consumers paid much higher tax-inclusive prices.[24] For example, the tax-inclusive price of measured local calls increased from Mex$16 (around US$0.005) per minute to Mex$115 per minute (about US$0.037). The price-cum-tax reform in 1990 was aimed at making the company more attractive to potential buyers. The privatized Telmex monopoly was subject to price-cap regulation whereby the average price of a basket of services could not increase by more than the retail price index (*RPI*) minus an index of technological progress in the telecommunications industry (*X*). For the period 1991–96, *X* was set at 0, and for 1997–98 it was set at 3 percent. After 1998, rates would be regulated to yield a fair return on capital. This pricing formula, incorporated in the license contract, was much more generous than the BT formula after which it was modeled (see box 7.2 for the *X* factor in the U.K.).[25] Services were not regulated where competition was present or permitted, such as cellular telephony, yellow pages, and private networks. The license agreement permitted Telmex to diversify into related businesses as long as those activities were carried out through separate subsidiaries. Telmex was free to compete in value-added services, yellow pages, equipment manufacturing, installation and maintenance services, and private branch exchanges. The only exclusion was television services. Telmex was also granted the only national license for cellular telephone service with the condition that it could not enter any region until another competitor had already entered that market.

Box 7.2 The *X* Factor in the U.K.

Since privatization, the water and sewage companies have been granted positive *X*s, meaning that prices have risen each period. Even in this sector, however, the amount by which the prices can rise, the *X* factor, decreased from 4 percent to approximately 1 percent in 1995, where it is expected to remain until 2005.
- Similarly, electricity distribution benefited from a positive *X* value for the first five-year evaluation period, but the *X* dropped to -2 percent for 1995 onward, indicating real price reductions.
- Electricity transmission used an *X* of zero from 1990–93, and then had to decrease prices by about 3 percent. A new assessment will be made in 1996.
- British Gas and British Telecommunications have never received positive *X* values and, therefore, have reduced prices since privatization. British Gas was granted a slight reversal in prices in 1994 when the *X* value was revised upward from -5 to -4 percent.
- The telecommunications industry, on the other hand, has been forced to adjust prices downward three times to the current level of -8 percent, since the initial value of *X* was set at 3 percent.

Box 7.3 Expansion Targets Proposed for Privatized Telmex

- The number of lines in service are to be expanded at a minimum rate of 12 percent a year until 1994. By 2000, telephone density should be 10 per 100 population, compared with 5 per 100 population in 1989.
- All towns with a population of 500 or more should have telephone service by the end of 1994.
- The number of public telephones is to be increased from 0.8 per 1,000 persons to 2 per 1,000 in 1994 and 5 per 1,000 in 1998.
- In towns with automatic exchanges, waiting time for a new connection must be no more than six months by 1995 and one month by 2000.
- The quality of service must be improved as stipulated in the concessionary contract.

The government chose not to divide Telmex into regional companies (as in Argentina) or along types of services (long-distance versus basic local service, as in Chile).[26] The long-distance market opened to competition after August 1996. Telmex was required to expand the number of lines at least 12 percent a year until 1994, and to increase the number of public telephones from 0.8 per 1,000 persons in 1990 to 5 per 1,000 persons in 1998 (see box 7.3). As shown in table 7.12, by 1993 most of the targets had been met. Regulatory jurisdiction was given to the Ministry of Communications and Transport until an autonomous entity was created. The fact that Mexico decided not to establish an autonomous regulatory body could be interpreted as a favorable signal for potential buyers, because it demonstrated that the government was disposed to renegotiate the terms of the contract in the event of a financial downturn for the privatized firm. This could have been more difficult with an autonomous regulatory agency. Mexico's mono-

lithic political system (in which historically a single party has dominated congress, although recent political events have weakened this dominance) favors regulatory commitment by contracts over legislation, because legislation is easily passed and the court system is relatively independent. On the other hand, the lack of an autonomous regulatory body increases uncertainty over possible actions. The absence of predictability can lead to lower interest and participation of potential providers, to lower prices, to less than efficient investment levels, and to wasteful rent-seeking activities.

In 1988 Mexico underwent a process of price reform, almost doubling (in real terms) domestic tariffs on rentals and measured service, increasing installation charges by four to five times their price, and increasing domestic long-distance charges by 45 percent. Less drastic increases followed in 1989. Even by 1988 tariff revisions more than offset the real declines in telephone charges over the 1981–87 period. Consequently, prior to divestiture total real fiscal flows (the sum of taxes and dividends paid to the government) approximately doubled to around $900 million by 1989. Thus, the tariff level in 1989 was already reasonable enough to sustain a substantial expansion program, financed in large measure from profits. This obviously made Telmex more attractive to potential buyers and

Table 7.12 Telmex's Performance with Respect to Quality of Service in Mexico, 1990–93
(percentages)

Performance measure	1990 Base[a]	1991 Actual	Target	1992 Actual	Target	1993 Target
Service continuity index						
Lines with failure	10.0	9.43	8.00	9.12	7.00	6.00
Same-day line repair	45.00	52.94	48.00	68.81	50.00	50.00
Three-day line repair	82.00	90.96	86.00	93.23	90.00	91.00
Service quality index						
Local calls, first try	92.00	93.45	92.00	96.35	94.00	94.00
Long-distance calls, first try	90.00	92.46	92.00	96.02	92.00	92.00
Dial tone in 4 seconds	97.00	98.46	97.00	99.50	97.00	98.00
Special operators answering in less than 10 seconds	90.00	83.11	90.00	83.62	91.00	91.00

a. Benchmark before privatization.
Source: Ministry of Communications and Transport, and Telmex concessionary contract of August 1990.

demonstrated the government's commitment to supporting regulation linked to prices related to market costs. The rebalancing process continued through 1994, as indicated in table 7.13, with increases in real domestic tariffs and decreases in real international tariffs.

The process of ending the long-distance monopoly started in 1993, with Telmex submitting a general proposal, as government regulations required. Appropriately, no limit has been set on the number of competing companies that can enter the long-distance market. Already more

than a dozen companies, including AT&T, Bell Atlantic, MCI, and Motorola, have formed joint ventures with Mexican banks and telecommunications companies.[27] The handling of their access to the Telmex network will be a test of the effectiveness of regulation in Mexico. Preliminary evidence is mixed. On the one hand, Telmex planned to provide for ten interconnection points through which all long-distance calls would have to pass no matter which company handled them. The regulators rejected the plan and approved one that provided for 200 such

Table 7.13 Telmex's Tariffs by Service in Mexico, 1989–93
(constant 1992 Mexican pesos)[a]

Type of service	1989	1990	Percentage Change 1989–90	1991	Percentage Change 1990–91	1992	Percentage Change 1991–92	1993	Percentage Change 1992–93
Installation (thousands)									
Residential	2,463	1,944	-21.0	1,343	-30.9	1,500	11.7	1,541	2.7
Commercial	3,658	2,888	-21.0	2,306	-20.2	2,600	12.8	2,671	2.7
Basic rent (monthly)									
Residential	7,573	10,045	32.7	14,661	46.0	14,851	1.3	19,533	31.5
Commercial	21,839	31,141	42.6	41,517	33.3	42,053	1.3	46,822	11.3
Measured service (per minute)									
Residential	39	425	990.1	387	-9.0	392	1.3	402	2.5
Commercial	58	300	413.6	387	28.8	392	1.3	402	2.5
Long-distance									
Domestic	2,230	3,940	76.7	4,332	9.9	4,389	1.3	4,486	2.2
International	16,163	11,263	-30.3	11,162	−0.9	10,437	−6.5	10,355	−0.8
World	39,861	25,280	-36.6	21,890	−13.4	20,467	−6.5	20,336	−0.6

ª Adjusted by the domestic retail price index. A 7 percent increase is assumed for 1993.
Source: World Bank 1993.

points to be available by 2000. Long-distance competitors would have to pay fees, based on time and distance, for the use of local telephone lines to the interconnection points. Because there are 200 points, long-distance callers will spend far less time on Telmex's local network, lowering total fees and Telmex rents and improving the speed of service. On the other hand, the regulators' approach to granting long-distance licenses is very slow and fraught with bureaucratic uncertainties. Furthermore, regulators have neither specified the approach to solving interconnection disputes nor provided guidance on how to price interconnection. Although some of these delays can be blamed on administrative capabilities, they also reflect the workings of administrative discretion under political constraints.

PRICE CAPS IN VENEZUELA

The model adopted in the privatization of telecommunications in Venezuela resembles that of Mexico and Argentina. The companies were sold with a monopoly on "basic service" for a fixed exclusivity period, but with requirements to expand and improve basic service. These obligations, along with a tariff structure and adjustment mechanism, were defined in the concessionary contract. Other key conditions of the Venezuelan concession included (a) the new operator, CANTV, was granted a nine-year monopoly on basic wire-line service,[28] which included local, national, and international long-distance telephone service (all other services were open to competition, including cellular, private lines, value-added services, and terminal equipment); and (b) CANTV was required to carry out an aggressive expansion program (3 million new lines plus 6 million replacement lines over nine years, or 400,000 lines annually), and to meet a number of annual service performance targets. The concession was submitted to and approved by congress and published in the *Gaceta Oficial*, number 34820, dated October 15, 1991. The local exchange concession is effective for thirty-five years beginning in November 1991, and may be extended for an additional twenty years.

The telecommunications law and the telecommunications regulations provide the general legal framework for telecommunications regulation in Venezuela. Under this framework, any provider of public telecommunications services must operate under concessions granted by the Ministry of Transportation and Communications and approved by the Venezuelan congress. Concessions provide a price-cap rate regime for services, promote operating efficiencies, and allow progressive rate rebalancing to match the price of services with costs. The price cap varies directly with the producer price index published by the Central Bank of Venezuela, allowing a company to raise rates in accordance with wholesale inflation, although there is usually a three- to five-month lag in the implementation of rate changes.

The concession allows quarterly price increases for telephone services, according to a price-cap mechanism. The increases must be approved by the Regulatory Commission and the Ministry of Communications. Rates were grouped into three baskets, with full indexing until the end of 1996, followed by partial indexing for the remainder of the exclusivity period, the end of 2000. Phased rebalancing of local and international rates was to begin in 1994.

The company is required to pay the government annually a total of 5.5 percent of billings for all services. Concession expenses amounted to approximately Bs3,323,544,000 and Bs5,256,684,000 during 1992 and 1993, respectively.

Conatel, the agency principally responsible for regulating telecommunications services in Venezuela, was created by a presidential decree issued in September 1991. Conatel is not an autonomous agency and depends on the Ministry of Transportation and Communications. The decree gives Conatel the authority to supervise telecommunications services; to grant concessions, licenses, and administrative authorizations; and to promote investment and technological innovation in telecommunications. Its dual role as regulator and granter of concessions is troublesome.

A price adjustment and rebalancing schedule was initiated prior to privatization. Rates were increased in mid-1991 and again on January 1, 1992 (the anticipated takeover date for the new operator). As a result, average revenue per service line was expected to increase from $275 in 1990 to $500 in 1992. Rates were grouped into three baskets and fully indexed to inflation through 1996, with partial indexing through the remainder of the exclusivity period ending in 2000. Phased rebalancing of local and international rates was to commence in 1994, when a new telecommunications law was introduced in congress. This law set the legal and regulatory framework for the development and operation of the sector; provided for Conatel's autonomy; and, consistent with international practice, reduced taxes on CANTV from 5 percent of gross revenues to 1 percent. The legislation stalled in congress because of television and broadcasting issues, rather than because of the telecommunications provisions. To provide legal authority to enforce the regulatory features of the proposed privatization in the absence of a new telecommunications law, the government enacted a series of decrees establishing a partially autonomous Conatel and defining service regulations. The regulatory regime for competitive services was specified in CANTV's concessionary contract.

CANTV and Conatel have generally been satisfied with the price-cap system. Every quarter Conatel establishes a maximum weighted tariff increase for each of CANTV's three price baskets. Although CANTV and Conatel like the flexibility and ease of the price-cap system, both agree that quarterly rate filings are burdensome. Average annual revenue per line (including both residential and commercial) more than doubled from 1990 to 1992 ($275 and $563, respectively, per subscriber), and by 1993 had reached $623 per line. Despite rate adjustments prior to and following privatization, rates and revenue per subscriber remain below those of other countries in the region. Residential rates include the installation charge, the basic monthly rental, and a usage charge. The basic monthly rental remains very low for residential clients—$3.25 in January 1994—and residential service continues to be cross-subsidized by commercial service and by long-distance and international calls. Under the

concessionary contract, rebalancing was scheduled to start in 1994 and will be phased in through the remainder of the exclusivity period.

Sustained rate adjustments are essential if full competition is to occur by the end of the exclusivity period. Quarterly rate increases must be approved by the Ministry of Transportation and Communications on the recommendation of Conatel. A draft law that would establish Conatel as a fully autonomous regulatory agency with final authority on tariff matters was presented to congress in early 1993. This legislation stalled with the departure of the Perez government and has not been reintroduced.

In addition to the expansion of CANTV's basic network, there has been a major expansion in competitive services provided by independent operators. By mid-1993 Conatel had granted twenty-six concessions to independent operators for a range of services, including cellular telephony (two), private networks (ten), value-added services (five), trunking (eight), and data transmission (two). In 1992 these companies invested $350 million, and together with CANTV's expansion program, investment in the telecommunications sector accounted for 1.65 percent of gross domestic product (compared with 0.25 percent from 1981 to 1990), making telecommunications the fastest-growing segment of the economy.

Cellular service is also expanding rapidly. The first concession was awarded through competitive bidding in 1991 (before CANTV was privatized) to Telcel, a consortium led by Bell South. Telcel started operating in November 1991, and by mid-1993 had 65,000 subscribers. This is the fastest growth ever reported by a cellular company. Telcel invested $130 million in 1992, in addition to the $106 million paid to the government for the license. CANTV operates the other cellular band through a wholly owned subsidiary (Movilnet) and had 35,000 subscribers by mid-1993. Both Telcel and Movilnet pay CANTV an access charge.

Although CANTV has exclusive rights under the concession to provide basic switched telephone services in Venezuela, it believes that some concessions that have been granted by Conatel to third parties may infringe on these rights. In

1993 government delays in the approval of contractual tariff increases resulted in revenue losses of approximately Bs1.7 billion. CANTV continued to experience delayed tariff increases in early 1994.

PRICE CAPS IN ARGENTINA

Argentina's current telecommunications regulatory framework indexes prices to the U.S. consumer price index, (although when the convertibility plan was enacted in 1991 and indexation was disallowed, action as of 1996 was still converted), allowing for some rebalancing. This regime, however, has no semblance to the one that existed when the bid was presented, which jeopardizes its credibility. The regulatory structure granted each licensee a maximum exclusivity period of ten years. These ten years were divided into three basic periods, during each of which the firms would be allowed to set prices so as to achieve some stated pretax return on assets.

This three-period regulatory system was extremely murky for several reasons. First, it was unclear whether, during the transition period, the regulators had the power to block price increases if the rate of return on assets did not reach the determined 16 percent.[29] Second, the licenses provided the regulators with substantial discretion in determining the rate base and allowable expenses. Third, the licenses specified a long list of minimum service requirements that had to be achieved at different points in time.[30] The requirements, coupled with the fact that the regulatory agency could exclude investments and costs from the rate-of-return computation, implied that the regulator would have substantial discretion in setting tariffs and fines at renewal time.

The scheme never worked as intended. The terms were changed again, as were the price adjustment mechanism and profitability assurances. Instead of a rate of return for the transition period, the licenses stipulated a monthly price adjustment mechanism. This mechanism consisted of a monthly price increase based on the previous month's inflation rate (a 60 percent weight) and on movements in the exchange rate

(a 40 percent weight). Although prices would be indexed monthly, the companies could, in principle, bring about real price increases every six months during the twenty-four-month period. Consequently, the initial price level became crucial, and discussions between the companies and the government centered on the price per pulse, which was eventually set at $0.038 per pulse. This price was achieved by eliminating a 31.5 percent tax on telephone services without changing the retail price, and then by increasing the price by more than 42 percent just prior to the transfer (*La Nación,* October 29, 1990; and Telefónica de Argentina 1991). The companies were allowed to rebalance their rates, and the resulting price level was quite high. The rebalancing implied a local rate increase of approximately 10 percent and a long-distance and international rate decrease of about 20 percent. Rates for domestic calls vary according to distance and time of day. A call between Buenos Aires and La Plata (a city just 50 kilometers from downtown Buenos Aires), for example, costs six pulses per minute, or just above $0.23 per minute. A call to the city of Córdoba, located approximately 400 kilometers from Buenos Aires, costs more than $1.00 per minute.[31] When Argentina implemented the 1991 Convertibility Plan (setting by law a one-to-one exchange rate to the U.S. dollar) the government unilaterally reneged on the indexation clause stated in the contract scale. This remains an issue of contention between the provider and the government.

Neither Argentina's detail engineering nor its basic engineering matches the institutional features of the country. Although the regulation framework has some positive features, such as regulatory flexibility, this flexibility is lost in an atmosphere where the executive is essentially not constrained in the interpretation of its own decrees. Argentina's framework could be better implemented in a country where administrative decisions are subject to more substantive checks and balances. Finally, table 7.14 shows the structure and regulatory framework in the telecommunications sector for selected OECD countries, and Appendix tables 7A.1 to 7A.4 present a summary of the ownership, market structure, and

Table 7.14 Telecommunications Sector: Tariff Regulation in Organization for Economic Cooperation and Development Countries

	Regulatory Body	Coverage	Action/Method
Australia	Austel	Overall Telephone Basket Some sub-baskets: – A group of connections, rentals, and local calls – A group of all trunk calls – A group of all international calls	Price-cap regulation 1989–1992: CPI -4% 1992–1998: CPI -5.5% CPI -2% CPI -5.5% CPI -5.5%
Austria	N/A	N/A	N/A
Belgium	Ministry of Communications and Public Corporations	Service with exclusive concession	Price-cap regulation
Canada	Canadian Radio, Television, and Telecommunications Commission (CRTC)	All services except from the services CRTC decides not to regulate	Approval
Czech Rep.	Ministry of Finance Ministry of Economy	Domestic tariff International tariff	From 1977, price-cap regulation
Denmark	National Telecom Agency	Tele Denmark's tariffs for basic telephony and leased lines (national and international); mobile communications under "special rights" services	From 1995 to 1997, price-cap regulation (Net Price Index -3%) Principle of maximum tariff regulation
Finland	Operators can freely set	Tariffs without approval	
France	Direction General des Postes et Telecommunications	Monopoly services Other services	Individual approval Price-cap regulation by "contrat de plan" (from 1995–1998, CPI -5.25%)
Germany	Ministry of Posts and Telecommunications	Telecommunication services Digital Cellular Mobile Radio	Approval based on a basket approach using prescribed benchmarks Price-cap regulation From 1993. CPI -4%
Greece	National Telecommunication Commission (NTC)	Tariff of new service enters into force after months from announcement if there is no opposition from NTC. Telecommunication services included in the basket for the price-cap regulation	Price-cap regulation 1995: CPI 0% 1996: CPI +2% 1997: CPI +3%
Hungary	Ministry of Transport, Telecommunications and Water management	Telecommunication services with three subtariff classes	Price-cap regulation
Iceland	N/A	N/A	N/A
Ireland	N/A	N/A	N/A
Italy	Ministry of Posts and Telecommunications	Monopoly services	Set by Ministry
Japan	Ministry of Posts and Telecommunications	Services which have substantial influence on the everyday life of citizens and national economy	Rate-of-return regulation (approval)
Luxembourg	N/A	N/A	N/A

Table 7.14 continued...

	Regulatory Body	*Coverage*	*Action/Method*
Mexico	Secretaria de Comunicaciones y Tranportes (SCT)	Services with monopoly or dominant provision	SCT must approve tariffs using a basket and price cap Price caps used from 1997
Netherlands	Ministry of Transport, Public Works and Water Management	The Overall Package The Small User's Package	Price-cap regulation 1994–1998 CPI
New Zealand	Ministry of Commerce (via the Kiwi Share)	Residential services	The price of residential service must not increase ahead of CPI (unless it would unreasonably impair the PTO's profits) Residential lines must be priced on a uniform basis
Norway	Ministry of Transports and Communications Norwegian Telecommunications Regulatory Authority	Reserved service	Cost-oriented price PTOs set tariffs but the structure of tariffs is considered a matter for the Ministry
Portugal	General Directorate for Competition and Pricing (GDP) Institution for Communications in Portugal (ICP)	Monopoly services –Coverage of telephony, telegraph, telex, and leased lines –Leased lines	Price-cap regulation for telephony in 1995: CPI -3% (nominal terms) 1996, 1997: CPI -2% (real terms) (There are also individual price caps) Price-cap inflation rate (no increase in real terms)
Spain	N/A	N/A	N/A
Sweden	National Post Telecom Agency	Basic services of Telia AB	Price-cap regulation: Net Price Index -%
Switzerland	Federal Department of Transports, Communications and Energy (OFCOM)	National tariffs are proposed by PTT	Approval
Turkey	N/A	N/A	N/A
U.K.	Oftel	BT's main retail tariff (includes international, from 1993) Leased line	Price-cap regulation 1984–1989: RPI –3% 1989–1991: RPI –4.5% 1991–1993: RPI –6.25% 1993–1997: RPI –7.5.% RPI: 0
U.S. (2)	FCC FCC Public Utility Commissions	For AT&T services Basket 1: Residential Basket 2: 800 Basket 3: Commercial For LECS	Price-cap regulation from 1989 Price-cap regulation from 1991

regulatory framework for the telecommunications sector for selected LAC countries.

PRICE-SETTING REGULATION IN ARGENTINA'S ELECTRICAL POWER SECTOR

The Argentine electrical power sector has adopted a very different method for pricing its services because, among other reasons, the sector does not exhibit increasing returns to scale in all areas. As can be seen from the descriptions below, the choice of pricing system depends on the perceived degree of competition.

In pricing electricity generation, the price p^m of the distribution companies' supplier is unique, set by the market, and computed at local prices. It is equal to the system's marginal cost of generation, which is determined by the marginal cost of the most expensive thermal power plant running to meet demand at any given hour. It is established by Compañía Administradora del Mercado Mayorista Eléctrico Sociedad Anónima (CAMMESA) for each generator on the basis of its fuel cost and thermal efficiency. This method ensures that the price of the last megawatt bought is equal to the cost of supplying it. It also signals to the power users the proper value of their electricity use and allows distribution companies to make informed decisions on this component of their costs. Although not a serious problem, this signal is somewhat biased. There are indeed other components to short-run marginal cost that deserve some attention in view of the vast differences in technologies across generators.

In practice, a price p^n is set at each node to remunerate the generator supplying electricity to node n and is paid by users located at the exit node. It is determined by p^m and a nodal factor. This nodal factor is a measure of the established transmission losses between the entry or exit point and the load center of the Ministry of Energy and Mines. It varies according to the season and time of day and depends on whether the nodal point is importing or exporting power. CAMMESA dispatches power from generating plants by order of merit, which means by order of increasing short-run marginal costs of production. The market-clearing price is generally set by the most expensive generator needed to meet demand. Any generator with a lower cost makes a profit. The existence of this profit pushes generators to cut their costs as much as possible to improve their standing.

Transmission pricing uses an $RPI - x$ rule, with x initially set at 0. The real key to the transmission regulation, however, is open access to the network. Because the main carrier, Transener, enjoys exclusive rights for the provision of high-voltage transmission (500 kilovolts) on the existing network, it has to be regulated. Its regulation is based on prices and quality standards. A penalty for failing to comply with obligations, and a prohibition on buying and selling electricity, protect distributors and generators from abuses. The objectives of Transener's price regulation are to transmit accurate signals of costs from producers and carriers to distributors and large users and to give the operator strong incentives to develop transmission infrastructure. The short-run marginal costs of the transmission of electricity are mainly the physical losses of the line and the congestion costs when the line cannot absorb all the power injected by generators. To relate positively the transmission company's profits to the power losses on the lines is clearly not a very good incentive for the company to improve the quality of its equipment. Therefore, Argentina's regulations impose quality objectives on the transmission company. Three types of fixed transmission charges are regulated by Ente Nacional Regulatorio de Energio (ENRE)—connection, capacity, and energy.

- *Connection charges* cover the cost of maintaining the equipment needed to connect the user and are levied by CAMMESA.
- *Capacity charges* distribute among all users the total costs of operating and maintaining the existing transmission equipment.
- *Energy charges* reflect the difference between the value of the energy received at a receiving node and the value of energy at a sending node.

The connection and capacity charges are fixed for the first five years, after which ENRE can reduce them yearly to improve efficiency. This decrease cannot be larger than 1 percent a year with a maximum cumulative effect of 5 percent in each ten-year management period. To reduce the volatility of revenue from the energy charge, due to its dependence on the market value of electricity, this charge is always fixed for a five-year period. When justified, transmission companies can apply to ENRE for tariff adjustments. Similarly, users can complain to ENRE if the tariffs are too high. In that case, public hearings are organized, which means that many of the provincial private operators are likely to have regular interaction with ENRE.

ENRE calculates the tariffs used in distribution pricing. The tariffs include a complete pass-through of the Ministry of Energy and Mine's seasonal prices allowing for technical losses (11 percent) plus a distribution cost defined in the concessionary contract. The prices that were fixed before the monopoly positions were conceded are used in price caps. This means that the price regulation system is of the *RPI - x + y* type. In other words, prices are allowed to increase at a rate equal to the retail price index, less some productivity gain *x*, plus the increase *y* in the price of inputs over which the firm has no control (essentially the costs of energy in the wholesale market). The prices are automatically adjusted every six months on the basis of the current price index and the producer price index of the United States for set *x* and *y* values. This pricing mechanism is a good incentive to promote cost-reducing activities, but it can result in a decline in quality. The other problem with this type of regulation is that it promotes a strategic behavior of less-than-expected effort when the managers know that the present cost will be used to determine next

period's *x* value. Prices applied by distribution concessionaires are based on five specific elements:

1. Energy charges that are based on seasonal electricity costs of the Ministry of Energy and Mines and on electricity bought under long-term contract with Central Puerto and Central Costa Zera
2. Loss charges corresponding to technical and nontechnical losses that are equivalent to about 11 percent of the distributor's losses
3. Connection and transmission costs
4. Costs of capacity of the Ministry of Energy and Mines
5. Distribution charges that are fixed for small users or are based on a charge per unit of maximum demand for medium and large users.

The loss charge corresponds to a recognized allowance for technical losses. The 11 percent allowed may not cover actual losses but is a reasonable benchmark. It is intended to give an incentive to distributors to achieve a level of losses acceptable to consumers and regulators. Obligating distributors to grant access to the network to all interested parties is a key ingredient of the system, but it has a cost. That is why distributors can charge a toll for that use. The toll essentially corresponds to the connection and transmission component of the standard tariff, and also includes a loss charge.

Finally, figures 7.2, 7.3, and 7.4 present comparative prices in the telecommunications sector for a selected group of LAC countries, and table 7.15 presents the comparative sector performance and best practices also for selected LAC countries.

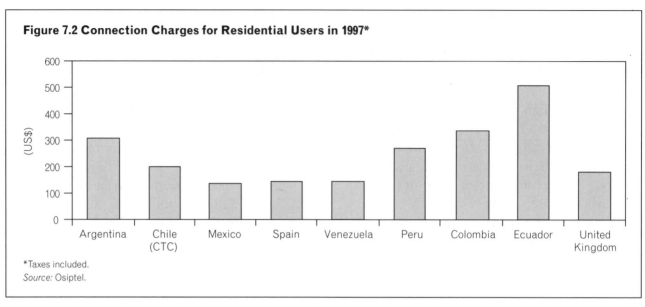

Figure 7.2 Connection Charges for Residential Users in 1997*

*Taxes included.
Source: Osiptel.

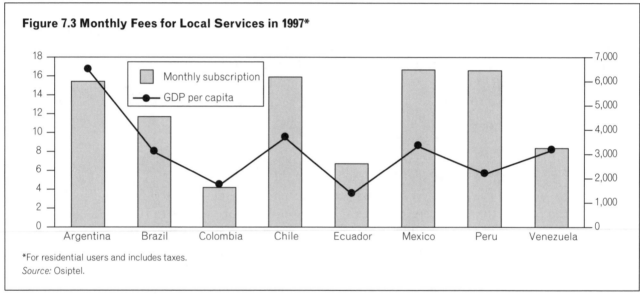

Figure 7.3 Monthly Fees for Local Services in 1997*

*For residential users and includes taxes.
Source: Osiptel.

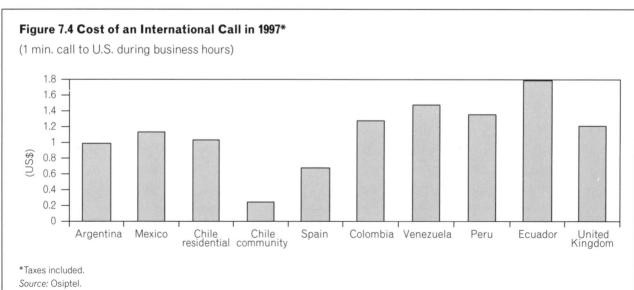

Figure 7.4 Cost of an International Call in 1997*

(1 min. call to U.S. during business hours)

*Taxes included.
Source: Osiptel.

Table 7.15 Comparative Performance Indicators
(best practice in each country)

Service	Uruguay	Argentina	Brazil	Mexico	Chile	"Best Performance" (and reasonable benchmark)
Degree of Coverage						
Telecoms (Teledensity in large cities in 1994 = number of lines per 100 inhabitants)	32.6	21.2	11.8	11.6	15.4	65.1 (U.S.)
Electricity (% of population connected in 1992)	92%	95%	87%	92%	95%	100%
Water (% of population served)	83%	64%	92%	83%	87%	89% (upper-middle income)
Tariff						
Telecoms (monthly fee for business in 1994 in US$)	19.3	29.3	6.2	18	21.8	N/A
Electricity (residential in cts/kwh in 1995 except U.S. and OECD)	14.53	11.85	9.5	3.09	13.66	N/A
Water and Sanitation (residential cts/cubic meter)	150	28	73	99.2	114.2	N/A
Reliability						
Telecoms (faults/100 main lines/years in 1994)	12	29.3	43.2	N/A	8	1.7 (Spain)
Electricity (losses in % in 1992)	19	20	15	15	14	8 (U.S.)
Water (% of unaccounted for water)	46.8	40	39	50	41	9 (Singapore)
Labor Productivity						
Telecoms (main lines per employee)	88	155	121	174	153	294 (Korea)
Electricity (customer per employee)	102 (in 1995)	280	177	208	285	285 (Chile)
Water and Sanitation (employees/ 1000 connection)	8	3	5.2	4	2.1	1.8 (Malaysia)

N/A = not available.
Source: World Bank 1997.

Appendix

Table 7A.1 Private Ownership, Regulation, and Performance of Telecommunications Utilities in Selected Countries

Country	Ownership	Private Regulatory History	Private Performance
Argentina	Nationalized in 1946, privatized in 1990	Repeated changes in regulation, 1989–92	Highly profitable, but too soon to determine the impact on service quality and national welfare
Chile	1930–58, controlled by multinational, ITT	Regulatory law quite open-ended; no independent regulator	Initially rapid expansion of the network, followed by a slowdown
	1958 to late 1960s, controlled by ITT, partial government takeover in 1967, government intervention in 1971, and nationalization in 1974	Regulatory subagreements in 1958 and 1967 that eliminated some vagueness; superseded by nationalization	Acceleration of network expansion to levels existing before the slowdown prior to intervention and nationalization
	Privatized during 1988–90	Highly detailed benchmark regulation supervised by regulatory agency with explicit arbitration process	Unprecedented high rates of investment and network expansion subsequent to privatization; substantial increase in national welfare
Jamaica	1925–66, privately owned, with separate domestic and international companies	Rate of return stipulated in license agreement; ad hoc temporary rate boards responsible for rate reviews	Sustained network expansion in 1950–62, followed by stagnation; steady moderate rate of return
	1966–75, privately owned until nationalization of international company in 1971 and domestic company in 1975	Regulation by permanent, independent commission; license specifying only maximum rate of return	Initial network expansion, then slowdown; low profitability after 1970
	Merger of domestic and international companies in 1985 and subsequent privatization	Rate of return specified in license agreement; no independent regulator	Major investment in domestic network and increased national welfare, high profitability
Mexico	Privatized in 1990	Price-cap regulation corrected by increased productivity on the weighted average price; initial large price correction; regulatory body within the ministry	Major investment in domestic network, exceeding concessionary commitments; all service improvement targets met
Peru	Privatized in 1994	Price-cap regulation, quarterly adjustment; rebalancing of tariffs over a five-year period; formulas contained in the license agreement; autonomous regulatory agency established to regulate tariffs according to the contract and to monitor compliance	Too soon to evaluate
United Kingdom	Publicly owned from 1912 until privatization in 1984	Price-cap regulation and complex mechanisms of conflict resolution specified by license	Takeoff of investment in 1983, with large gains in national welfare
Venezuela	Privatized in 1991	Price-cap and regulation and rebalancing of tariffs over a nine-year period; any tariff change requires approval by the regulatory agency and the Ministry of Communications; any structural change in the price-cap formula needs congressional approval	Major investment in domestic network, by far exceeding concessionary commitments; all service improvement targets met

Table 7A.2 Restraints on Regulatory Arbitrariness in the Telecommunications Sector in Selected Countries

Country	Substantive Restraints within System	Restraints on System Changes	Enforcement of Restraints
Chile 1940s–1973	Limited, strengthened somewhat in 1958, stipulated in legislation	Separation of powers and divided legislature (especially pre-1958)	Strong judiciary
1987–present	Very explicit, precise price regulation based on rate of return of efficient firm plus explicit process for defining noncompetitive activities subject to price regulation; both stipulated in law	Separation of powers and divided legislature	Explicit conflict resolution with strong judiciary as final arbiter
Jamaica Pre-1962 and post-1987	Monopoly rights plus precise rate of return for long period written into license	Consent of company needed to alter license	Strong judiciary
1966–75	"Fair" rate of return	None, given generality of license	Strong judiciary
Mexico	Main regulatory issues, including RPI - x, with a specific x written into license contract	Consent of company needed to alter license; company allowed to appeal to the executive to secure changes	Medium judiciary
Peru	Explicit price-cap regulation with price adjustments and rebalancing of the tariff formula in the concessionary contract	License altered only by mutual agreement	Medium judiciary
United Kingdom, 1984–present	Main regulatory issues, including RPI - x, with a specific x written into license	License changed only with consent of company or through a precise process requiring the approval of three separate bodies; informal restraints on abuse of power by sovereign	Strong judiciary, plus custom
Argentina	Explicit price adjustment formula	Appeal to executive	No judicial appeal
Venezuela	Explicit price adjustment and rebalancing of the tariff formula in the concessionary contract	License altered only by mutual agreement; any conflict or disagreement between parties resolved by arbitration; appeal to executive for changes	Medium judiciary

Table 7A.3 Current Regulation of Telecommunications Competition in Selected Countries

Country	Restrictive Licensing Practices	Rules Governing Interconnection
Argentina	Two companies given exclusive licenses to supply basic services in separate regions for up to ten years; plus one exclusive license for international and long-distance services for a limited period	Operators required to provide; regulatory agency has right to intervene
Chile	No exclusive licenses; price regulation in "noncompet-itive" sectors	Obligatory interconnection according to prespecified terms; enforcement adjudicated by regulator, antitrust commissions, and courts
Jamaica	Single, exclusive monopoly over all telecommunica-tions services for twenty-five years	None
Mexico	Single, exclusive monopoly over basic telecommunica-tions services for six years	Operators required to provide extensive service and access; regulatory agency has right to intervene
Peru	Single, exclusive monopoly over all telecommunica-tions services for five years	After monopoly period expires, operators required to provide extensive service and access to potential entrants; terms will be provided at a later date; regula-tory agency has right to intervene
Venezuela	Single, exclusive monopoly over all telecommunica-tions services for nine years	After monopoly period expires, operators required to provide extensive service and access to potential entrants; terms will be provided at a later date; regula-tory agency has right to intervene
United Kingdom	Entry into fixed-link services restricted to duopoly, 1983–90; subsequently opened, but all licenses pro-vided at discretion of regulator and department of trade and industry (on parliamentary authority)	Obligatory interconnection, subject to payment to fixed link provided this is negotiated by parties with regulator as arbiter

Table 7A.4 Regulatory and Competitive Environment in Telecommunications

Environment	United States	Argentina	Brazil	Chile	Colombia	Mexico	Peru	Venezuela
Regulation	Independent, government-regulated monopoly prior to 1984; open competition for long-distance services since 1984; regional monopolies for local service	Privatized in 1990; government regulatory entity is CNT; monopoly for seven (plus three) years	Government-owned monopoly since 1972; twenty-eight state-run companies (eight regional companies in future), four private companies. All privatized in 1998	Gradual privatization, 1985–89; regulatory entity is National Controllers Office	Government-owned international carrier, twenty-six local companies; since 1992 operates under private law, international now open for competition	Privatized in 1990; government regulatory entity is SCT; monopoly until 1996	Privatized in 1994; autonomous regulatory entity is Osiptel; monopoly until 1999	Privatized in 1992; government regulatory entity is Conatel; monopoly until 2000
Competition								
Local	One local monopoly in all locations; some competition in urban areas in data services	Monopoly with two carriers: Telefónica de Argentina (Spain) and Telecom Argentina (France-Italy); 30 percent traded on stock exchange since 1992	Three geographically segmented firms and one more licensee per area granted	Entel had de facto monopoly in international long distance until 1995; many providers after that. Competition in domestic long distance: Entel, CTC, VTR, and Telex-Chile	Telecom plus twenty-six regional companies	Monopoly Telmex (Southwestern Bell, France Telecom, AT&T, others)	Single monopoly of CPT local (Lima), Entel local (rest of Peru), and Entel long distance (separate subsidiary: Telefónica and local group)	Monopoly CANT (GTE, Telefónica de España, and local groups)
Long distance	Three major carriers and several hundred minor carriers and resellers	One firm with exclusive rights until 1998	One operating firm; a second license granted, and open competition in 2002	Open entry; more than four firms	One state-owned monopoly	Open entry	One firm with exclusive rights until 1998	One firm with exclusive rights until 1999

Table 7A.4 continued...

Environment	United States	Argentina	Brazil	Chile	Colombia	Mexico	Peru	Venezuela
International data	Many competitors	Open competition, but only one operator (owned by Telefónica and Telecom)	At least two operators	Local geographical monopolies: CTC, CMET (Providencia and fifth region), CTM (Las Condes), CNT (tenth region), and TCC (eleventh region)	Telecom, open competition	Telecom, Telmex		
Mobile	Two carriers in each metropolitan area	Two carriers in Buenos Aires (one independent and one owned by Telefónica and Telecom)	Two carriers in each of eight geographical areas (the privatized company and an additional licensee)	Data: open competition, Telex-Chile, VTR, ITT, ECOM, Entel, and Chile PAC; open competition, CTC-cellular, CIDCCOM, VTR, and Telecom	Open competition (projected)	Telmex and at least one other carrier	Two carriers	Two carriers
Private network	Open competition	Open competition	Open competition	Open competition			Open competition	Open competition

Notes

1. See Spiller and Viana (1992) for a discussion of Chile's electricity regulatory reforms, and Galal (1994) for a discussion of Chile's telecommunications regulation.

2. A third government company was Telex Chile, which was formed in 1982 and which took over the telex activities of the post office. Several other private companies were formed during the late 1970s and early 1980s, but they held less than 5 percent of the overall revenue.

3. This is the same policy implemented by New Zealand.

4. Cellular and other services were specifically exempted from price regulation.

5. The telecommunications law specified that if a sector is determined by the Resolutive Commission to be noncompetitive, Subtel can regulate its prices according to a particular process determined in the law.

6. Until their privatization, the two companies' shares were held by CORFO, the government's development corporation. CORFO implemented a policy of segmentation of the two companies' activities, moving CTC mostly to local service and Entel to long-distance services.

7. Compañía de Teléfonos de Coyhaique (TELCOY) and Telefónica del Sur S.A. (CNT) operate in areas where CTC has no operating license.

8. These companies are Complejo Manufacturero de Equipos Telefónicos (CMET), which operates in parts of the metropolitan region and in other regions; Compañía Telefónica Manquehue (CTM), which operates only in parts of the metropolitan region; and SERTEL. CTM, CMET, CTC, TELEDUCTOS, and others also provide fiberoptic services around the metropolitan region.

9. The law provided for interconnection agreements to be negotiated by the parties.

10. Each time, though, the Antitrust Commission castigated CTC for undertaking "activities that have tended to limit free competition in the telecommunications market and tended to limit entry...." (See Resolution 151 of July 18, 1983.)

11. Electricity projects require large investments and have a relatively long amortization period. On the other hand, the deregulation of electricity generation has drastically reduced the gestation life of new projects.

12. Chile suffered one of the worst recessions in 1982/1983.

13. A particularly compelling alternative explanation is that, at the time, the government required a 100 percent dividend payout from all public companies, including CTC. This, however, cannot be a full explanation for the slow performance of the sector. First, by 1987 CTC's debt equity ratio was a mere 65 percent. It could have, even under public ownership, doubled its debt by increasing its debt

equity ratio to 125 percent, a ratio that it had in the past without much problem. Such an increase in debt would have allowed the company a rapid increase in assets (Galal 1994, p. 269). Second, even if CTC could not invest, if the pre-1987 regulatory framework provided was so credible, then such investment could have been undertaken by the private sector. The fact that the private sector did not invest much prior to 1987 suggests that the pre-1987 regulatory framework did not provide adequate investment incentive. Our reasoning is as follows: CTC doubled its size from 1988 to 1991. Essentially it created another CTC. Assuming that the 100 percent dividend payout was the main limit to CTC's investments and that the free pricing regime provided strong ex-ante investment incentives, why is it that the private sector did not create a separate CTC prior to 1987? Instead, the private sector built just 5 percent of the total number of lines. If the free pricing regime gave strong incentives, and macroeconomic conditions were not blocking development, then it has to be that CTC's presence preempted the competing companies from investing. In other words, was it the fear of predatory investment by CTC that preempted the privately owned companies from expanding prior to 1987? But since CTC could not expand rapidly because of the 100 percent dividend payout policy, how could CTC be predatory? Indeed, the 100 percent dividend payout should have facilitated private sector entry by limiting CTC's response. Thus, the private sector had to face other constraints on its expansion. As discussed in the text, the vagueness of the regulatory framework as it relates to interconnection was one important factor, but another factor, the uncertainty about the future evolution of prices, may have provided a strong disincentive for private sector development.

14. The exchange rate was then 252 pesos/US$.

15. Subtel's opposition to the integration of local exchange companies into long distance was based on the potential anticompetitive impact that CTC could have on the long-distance market. (See Resolutive Commission's Resolution No. 389 of April 16, 1993.)

16. Note that by then the composition of the Resolutive Commission had changed.

17. See, for example, El Mercurio, January 10, 1994, p. B1, "New Competition in the Market for Telecommunications."

18. Apart from CTC and Entel, Chilesat (the owner of Chile Telex) and VTR (the owner of CNT and of TELCOY) were already providing long-distance telecommunications services. New entrants include Bell South and Iusatel. CNT also started providing long-distance services.

19. El Mercurio (January 13, 1995, p. B20) estimates that without counting public phones (where CTC has the majority of the outgoing calls) and private lines, Entel has 46.2 percent of the market, Chilesat 30.6 percent, CTC-Mundo 11 percent, VTR 7.4 percent, Bell South 2.4 percent, and CNT-Carrier 2.4 percent.

20. Recall that the law explicitly granted the right to appeal to the supreme court decisions of the Resolutive Commission (Antitrust) in a few specific cases involving, among other issues, changes in the statutes of companies, as seems to have been the case here.

21. Indeed, CTC complained bitterly about what seemed to have been the manipulation of the system by Entel. (See Ramajo 1992.)

22. These long-distance companies with small local phone operations see participation in the PCS market as a chance to gain direct access to final users.

23. The Antitrust Resolution Commission's composition is not fixed, but rather is made up of three ad hoc members randomly selected: one from a list of law school deans, another from a list of economics department heads, and another from members of Chile's supreme court.

24. A 29 percent telephone tax was imposed, but 65 percent of it could be offset against investment, making it an investment subsidy. This tax was applied only on selected revenues.

25. From the beginning BT was required to raise prices by inflation minus 3 percent because of the anticipated economies of scale in telephone service operations. The BT formula was changed to allow increases in 1989 of *RPI* - 4.5 percent, in 1991 of RPI - 6.25 percent, and in 1993 of *RPI* - 7.5 percent (Gillick 1992, p. 730).

26. The alleged arguments were that divisions of Telmex would create unequally attractive parts and would create legal, administrative, and accounting nightmares that could delay privatization for years.

27. In November 1994, AT&T, which already handled 60 percent of long-distance service, announced a joint venture with Mexican Grupo Industrial Alfa S.A. to provide long-distance telephone service in Mexico beginning in 1997. While its stock fell 8 percent with the news of this forthcoming competition, Telmex reacted to the news by reaffirming its plans to expand in Mexico and to meet all competition head-on.

28. Mexico allowed a six-year monopoly on basic service. The government of Argentina created two separate local service concession areas, with the two operators sharing long-distance operations. The monopoly period was seven years, extensible to ten if performance targets were met.

29. Again, it was unclear whether the 16 percent rate of return was a floor or a ceiling. The director of Entel, Ing. María Julia Alsogaray, claimed that the rate was a ceiling (*La Nación,* international edition, March 19, 1990). The fact that prices were increased in March 1990 by 300 percent provided, according to the companies, reasonable real prices. Later the companies bargained hard to have real prices remain at the March 1990 level (*La Nación,* international edition, October 29, 1990.)

30. The licenses, however, did not specify minimum investment requirements in monetary terms. Instead the companies were allowed to determine how to satisfy their service requirements.

31. A call to La Plata is similar to a call from San Francisco to a city across the bay in Contra Costa County, like Concord. A call from San Francisco to Los Angeles would cost $1.33 per minute in Argentina. Comparable AT&T rates in 1991 were $0.1975 and $0.2160 per peak time minute for 50- and 400-kilometer calls, respectively (Mitchell and Vogelsang 1995). Long-distance prices in Argentina are therefore 125 to 600 percent higher than comparable calls made in the United States.

8

FRANCHISES AND CONCESSIONS AS MODES OF PRIVATE SECTOR PARTICIPATION AND "ALTERNATIVES" TO REGULATION

FRANCHISES AND CONCESSIONS are related to the price-setting regulation mechanisms described in previous chapters. They are viewed as alternatives to regulation in natural monopoly settings and are often used to compete for the market, to transfer operating rights (and use of assets) to the private sector, and to set the initial price of services (and subsequent adjustment mechanisms). Franchises or concessions are usually granted or issued for a specified length of time to the firm that proposes to offer the service for the lowest cost (price or tariff) while meeting certain criteria concerning quality and investment. They

substitute competition for price regulation at the bidding stage. As long as there is sufficient competition at the bidding stage, and governments can credibly commit to no opportunistic or inefficient renegotiation, franchises can result in average cost pricing and operation of the most efficient firm. In principle no regulatory agency needs to be created. The regulatory structure is superimposed by establishing how, subsequently, that initial price or tariff is allowed to vary. For example, it may follow a price-cap rule or any of the other described mechanisms. Their advantage over regulation is that they impose no informational requirements on a government agency. The competitive bidding process (for the market) can implicitly elicit efficient (second-best) pricing, and dissipates monopoly rents. Under regulation,

to achieve average cost pricing, the regulatory agency needs information on costs and demand. Franchises and concessions are also the salient scheme for introducing private sector participation in situations or sectors where the state cannot or does not want to transfer ownership of assets to the private sector.

FRANCHISES

Franchising involves the granting of a right or a license to operate a defined service and to receive associated revenues, usually following some form of competitive bidding process. Under franchise regulation, potential franchisees determine the level of the regulated economic variable (a maximum price to users or a rate of return to the operator) through a bidding process. The concession is assigned to the firm bidding the best value (the lowest price or rate of return). The principle is that competitive bidding for the natural monopoly dissipates all the monopoly rents. This is termed "competition for the market," which is distinct from the more usual competitive process that takes place continuously between rival suppliers within a given market ("competition in the market"). Competitive bidding requires establishment of an independent franchise authority and franchising of the natural monopoly. Franchising has been proposed as a substitute for regulation in natural monopoly situations. However, because a franchise arrangement is essentially contractual, franchising requires the continual involvement of the regulator in monitoring compliance, in reconciling interpretations, and in renegotiating terms in light of experience. The role of the state then becomes one of setting the rules for competition at the bidding stage and enforcing the terms of the agreement.

A typical franchise or concession has the following features:

- The relationship between the concession-granting authority and the private concessionaire is of a contractual nature.
- The concession is awarded for a limited, and potentially renewable, period.
- The concessionaire enjoys the right to use the existing facilities and equipment necessary to provide the service, without assuming their ownership.
- The concessionaire designs, finances, and is responsible for developing all new facilities and investments, and retains only temporary ownership until they are handed over, usually at no charge, to the concession-granting authority when the contract expires.
- The concessionaire ensures, at its own risk, the full extent of public service provision, so that all installations and customer service activities operate and are maintained in good working order; its contractual obligations are obligations of performance, not of means.
- The concessionaire is remunerated according to a contractually established tariff collected directly from users.

The franchising of natural monopolies has multiple benefits. First, it reduces opportunities for regulatory capture and lessens the scope for political interference in management because in most cases there is no need for ad hoc government intervention. Regulatory interference occurs only in response to issues not covered in the contract. Second, franchising encourages cost efficiency, because franchise contracts specify maximum prices for set qualities of goods or services and promote productive efficiency, and because such contracts permit cost savings to accrue to the franchisee during the life of the contract. Third, franchising fosters productive efficiency, because the competitive nature of contract bidding assures that prices are as low as possible while still allowing the franchisee to cover costs, including a normal return on investment. Finally, franchising can achieve optimal pricing even when sunk costs rule out contestability, because competition occurs before firms commit themselves to investment programs.

The disadvantages include the need for complex design and monitoring systems when there are multiple bidding targets, inability to cover every conceivable circumstance, difficulty in enforcing contracts (incentives to renegotiate), poor service quality and lack of investment incentives due to the fixed-term nature of contracts, and inability to commit to a path of price adjustments over the life of the concession. The inability to make a credible commitment creates opportunities to use and abuse renegotiation opportunities, rendering the initial price bid, on which the concession is awarded, almost meaningless. The issue of incentives for the franchisee to maintain the transferred assets properly can be addressed to some extent by compensating the current franchisee at the end of the concession period, with an amount linked to the winning franchise bid for the new period. Overall, franchise bidding is superior only if abuses after the franchise is awarded are contained, and repeated bidding is practical.

The successful franchising of local cable television networks in the United States and historical attempts at municipal franchising are well documented (Schmalensee 1979). The Boston, New York, and Paris underground railway systems were originally leased in this way. As predicted by the theory, the main problems with these franchises were the lack of price-revision formulas, difficulties enforcing contracts, the need for continued oversight, and a lack of long-term investment incentives due to the fixed-term nature of contracts and the failure initially to transfer ownership of assets.[1]

The sectors that seem most fitted for franchise-bidding regulation are water and sanitation; other municipality-provided services such as solid waste collection and urban transportation, rail, airport, and subway services; toll roads; and cable and television. These sectors have significant externalities that are not captured by the operator, and thus justify indirect subsidies. From both an economic and a social perspective, (and the political ramifications related to their provision and perhaps their monopolistic characteristics), these sectors have all tended to discourage transferring ownership of facilities to the private sector. In addition, the magnitude of required new investments favors franchise concessions rather than straight privatization, which requires the private operator to mobilize large amounts of capital to purchase facilities. Everything being equal, these funds become unavailable for financing further improvements and expansion of service. Moreover, the transfer at no charge can be thought of as an implicit subsidy: The concession usually entails a temporary transfer of state assets to the concessionaire at a zero price. This implicit subsidy can be partially dissipated through competitive bidding for the concession. In the 1990s in Latin America, franchise-bidding regulation has been used to assign concession operating rights, mostly in the water sectors in Brazil, Uruguay (Maldonado), Argentina (Buenos Aires, Corrientes, Córdoba, Santa Fe, and Tucuman), and Colombia (Cartagena and Barranquilla); toll roads in Argentina, Chile, and Mexico; construction rights for airport terminals in Argentina, Bolivia, and Chile; airport runways in Colombia; and railways in Argentina and Brazil. The criteria for the assignment of concessions in those sectors ranged from a minimum

average price for water usage in Argentina, minimum concession periods for toll roads in Mexico, minimum present value of revenues for toll roads in Chile, and minimum passenger fees for the airport terminal in Chile.[2]

THE SPECIFIC CASE OF RAILWAY FRANCHISES

Franchises have also been used recently in rail services in Boston, Los Angeles, Buenos Aires, Manchester (United Kingdom), Argentina (freight and intercity), and Sweden.[3] The specific case of railway franchises illustrates the dimensions and complexities that often involve franchising schemes. The type of franchise agreement will vary greatly across industries. The following economic and technological features of railways determine the type of franchising contract best suited to that industry.

Asset Longevity

Railway rolling stock and infrastructure are long lived. British Railways (BR) currently depreciates rolling stock over periods varying between fifteen and twenty-five years. In fact, the economic life of many types of equipment appears to be thirty years or more. Track and signaling assets, especially on the less heavily used parts of the network, can last up to thirty years, while certain types of structures, such as railway bridges, stations, and tunnels, last indefinitely.

Asset Specificity

Most railway capital equipment is highly specific in the sense that it has few or no alternative uses. Although passenger rolling stock is less location specific than infrastructure assets, the number of alternative routes or services on which the equipment can be used may be quite small. Railway equipment, therefore, is very different from other long-lived transport equipment such as airplanes or buses, which have a wide range of uses outside the market they serve. The flexibility of buses and aircraft has encouraged the development of active second-hand markets for these assets. That is unlikely to occur with railway assets.

Interdependencies

There is a high degree of interdependency in railway operation both between different trains and between trains and tracks. *Train-to-train* externalities mean that a delay affecting one train causes delays affecting all trains following on that same route. If all of the services operating over a section of the track are supplied by the same franchise, the costs of these sorts of breakdowns are internalized. If several franchisees share the use of the tracks, however, the delay to one operator's service can affect the costs and revenues of other operators as well. If the contract does not address this problem, total expenditure could be below the socially efficient level. Similar problems can occur from *track-to-train* externalities if different companies are responsible for infrastructure and actual train service.

How will these interdependencies affect the decisions made by the government and the bidders for the railway franchise? The two parties have to agree on the following issues:

- How long a time period the contract should cover
- Who will be responsible for investment costs
- When the service suppliers should retain the service revenues
- Whether the franchise should be vertically integrated.

Franchise Length and Financing

The combination of long-lived assets and a high degree of specificity has particularly important consequences for the length of the franchise contract. If the residual value of an asset at the end of a franchise period is highly uncertain, franchisees will tend to write off any assets acquired during the franchise over the remaining term. Therefore, if this term is short and franchisees have to fund investment in those long-lived assets, they might demand substantial subsidies in exchange for the guarantee of a given level of service. The effect of a shorter contract can be mitigated if assets are

acquired at less than the replacement cost (that is, used assets) and if the franchiser promises to repurchase them at a fair-market value should the franchise be lost to the investor. Nevertheless, this does not mean that short-term franchising is not viable or even that it is less attractive than long-term franchising.

In fact, each approach has advantages and disadvantages. Short-term franchising allows more frequent competition, and therefore maximizes the incentive to increase efficiency. An example of short concessions is the distribution and transmission in the power sector in Argentina. The regulatory agency fixes the tariffs for five years. At the end of this period, an international bid is called for the sale of the control package of the concessionaire. The incumbent puts its "reserve price" into a sealed envelope. Bids are accepted from all interested parties. If the incumbent is the higher bidder it keeps the concession with no payment. If the incumbent is outbid it is paid the amount of the highest bid (net of any debt to the state) and the bidder gets the concession. Shorter-term franchise contracts coupled with competitive rollovers at the end of a contract can be a powerful efficiency-inducing device, as long as the firm is compensated for incurred investments. Long-term franchising not only minimizes some of this incentive but also fosters a relationship that is more akin to that of regulator and regulated than to a true business contact. Long-term franchising, however, also maximizes the opportunities for shifting responsibility to the private sector. It encourages more innovation and cost efficiency than a short-term contract. Which of these factors will weigh more heavily with policymakers will depend on the specific local circumstances. For example, on a network where the assets have been recently renewed, the attraction of frequent competition might outweigh the benefits of long-term franchising. In parts of the network where track and rolling stock are in urgent need of renewal, a long franchise period might be attractive.

Revenue

Another important characteristic is whether the franchisee retains the service revenues. If so, franchise bids will be based on the expected value of the revenue stream from the franchise minus the expected costs of providing the service. If service revenues accrue to the franchiser, then the bids will reflect only the costs. Revenue-risk contracts are more attractive to the franchiser than cost-only contracts. They offer greater incentive to the franchisee to maintain and develop service quality, and they eliminate the need to monitor its efforts to protect revenue. However, revenue risk contracts are, in some respects, less attractive for the franchisee, which is now exposed to uncertain costs *and* revenues, particularly because revenues are generally believed to be less predictable than costs. All else remaining the same, the increased risk of a "with revenue" contract tends to depress franchise bids, especially when franchising is first introduced and experience of the market is limited. To counteract this effect, franchisees may request the additional security of a longer-term franchise or a contract for interim reviews and possibly renegotiation if external circumstances change.

Vertical Integration

Until quite recently it was widely assumed that track-to-train externalities and complementarities between railway infrastructure and vehicles meant that railways had to be run as vertically integrated businesses. Thus, the high degree of coordination required in day-to-day operations and investment planning could be achieved within a command structure that maximizes corporate benefit. Supporters of the vertical *separation* of infrastructure from operation argue that track-to-train externalities, which could encourage the infrastructure operator to offer a suboptimal level of service to the provider of train services, can be internalized through contracts. Assuming that the terms of the contract properly reflect the costs imposed on the train operator, the existence of such contracts would offer appropriate incentives to ensure that the socially optimal quality of service is provided. In practice, unfortunately, the tasks of writing, monitoring, and enforcing contracts covering all possible contingencies are prohibitively costly. There is also a risk that substituting contractual for

informal command relationships could introduce rigidities that actually reduce the system's capacity.

Another important issue is whether on-rail competition is truly compatible with train service franchising in conditions where services are generally unprofitable. Franchising agreements usually require that the franchisee receive the *exclusive* right to use a brand name or to provide a branded service in a specific market area. Allowing several franchisees to operate simultaneously in the same market introduces a free-rider problem. Each company tends to leave the marketing and promotion to others so that the total effort, from the franchiser's point of view, is suboptimal. A policy of dividing franchised services along a route therefore tends to depress the value of bids for the franchise and to increase the subsidy required to maintain any given level of output. In itself, this offers a strong inducement to the franchising agency not to do so.

CONCESSIONS

Another policy option that is similar to franchising is the granting of concessions. The differences are minimal, and one could even say semantic. If there are any differences, they tend to be that concessions often involve more detailed follow-up supervision, and more future obligations of the operator are built into the contract. Moreover, franchises do not necessarily involve state physical assets, as in the case of cable or television franchises, while concessions almost universally transfer the right to use state assets. Concessions also include build-own-operate (BOO) and build-operate-transfer (BOT) schemes. Franchises tend to be a one-shot deal, but many of the optimal design features of franchises also apply to concessions. Concession arrangements are well suited to sectors with monopoly characteristics. Under this approach, the government delegates the right to provide a particular service but maintains some control over the sector by dictating the rights and obligations of the provider. The service must be provided under the conditions specified in the contract or license. The private sector takes over operational responsibility and some of the commercial risk of provision. Generally, the concessionaire must achieve specified targets, but can choose how to meet them.

The least involved of the concession methods is the lease-and-operate contract, under which the private contractor provides the service, including operating and maintaining the infrastructure. In this case the concessionaire receives a fee. In more complex agreements, the concessionaire is also responsible for building and financing new investments. At the end of the concession term these assets revert to the state, and for that reason these schemes are known as build-operate-transfer. The final type is similar, but the assets remain with the private sector owner; hence the name build-own-operate. In both of these cases, the private sector company is responsible for financing and carrying out the investments specified in the contract, but under

BOO agreements, the ownership of existing assets and the responsibility for their future expansion and maintenance are transferred to the private sector. For a sample of government responsibilities for concession, see box 8.1.

The legal status of assets built and financed by the private operator may also vary. Under certain concessions, for example, the state owns the assets from the moment they are built, but the private operator maintains control until the end of the concession period. In many BOT schemes legal ownership remains entirely private until the end of the contract term. Under BOO contracts the assets remain private, which may protect investors and make these assets available as collateral.

The duration of the contract tends to (and should) reflect the number of years that investors need to recoup their investment, although

---

Box 8.1 A Sample of Government Responsibilities for Concessions

Framework
- Adopting legal provisions to enable the granting of concessions
- Establishing or identifying regulatory authorities
- Managing government support of infrastructure projects
- Managing public relations and information.

Project identification and analysis
- Identifying projects amenable to concessions (including in-house and unsolicited proposals)
- Prioritizing projects amenable to concessions
- Hiring advisers
- Performing a preliminary review of the costs and benefits of the project (without duplicating the analysis to be performed by the private sector), especially in cases where the government will be assuming part of the market risk
- Reviewing legal and regulatory issues
- Determining preliminary selection criteria
- Granting permission for the project to go ahead (for example, for the opening of the bidding process)
- Setting a timetable for the project.

Enabling and supporting measures for specific projects
- Granting permits and other necessary authorizations (such as environmental permits, rights of way)
- Determining the form of government support for the project.

Design of the concession arrangements
- Choosing legal instruments
- Allocating responsibilities
- Choosing and designing pricing rules and performance targets
- Determining bonuses and penalties
- Determining duration and termination
- Designing adaptation mechanisms to new or unforeseen circumstances
- Choosing and designing a dispute settlement mechanism.

Concession award
- Choosing the method of award
- Making decisions regarding prequalification and shortlisting
- Determining bid structure and evaluation method
- Determining bidding rules and procedures
- Proceeding with the bidding
- Negotiating.

Exercising regulatory function
- Implementing regulatory function
- Supervising and monitoring
- Enforcing rules (for example, imposing penalties).

Source: Kerf and others 1998.

matching the time to secure full amortization is not essential. First, the government generally reserves (under certain conditions and with compensation, if appropriate) the right to terminate the contract before its stated end date. Second, infrastructure services require continuous investment that cannot be predicted decades in advance. Investments almost always have to be made toward the end of the contract that cannot be amortized before its expiration. Moreover, the true value of the business includes the value of the incumbent's unamortized assets and such intangibles as know-how and reputation. Therefore, schemes should be designed to give proper incentives to maintain all the facilities related to service provision. For example, the state could pay the private operator according to the evaluation of an independent expert. Or the concessions could be rebid periodically, as Argentina has done in the power sector. Although the Argentine concessions are for a period of ninety-five years, they are rebid after the first fifteen years, and then every ten years. If the incumbent can outbid its opponents, it retains control. In monopolistic sectors, even the BOO schemes do not imply permanence. Although the private company owns the assets indefinitely, in order to provide the service it needs an operating license, which the government can revoke at any time.

Concession arrangements embody a regulatory framework and in practice should be viewed as an integral part of regulation rather than as a substitute for it. The terms of the contract need to be monitored, enforced, and occasionally revised. Concessions, therefore, may provide the regulator with a certain amount of discretion, while still providing the concessionaire with some recourse in the event of unacceptable requirements. Whatever the approach, all concessions contain some form of regulatory mechanism. Self-regulation may also play an important role because concessionaires should be extremely concerned about their reputation.

Because concessions can be made as specific as required, they are well suited to situations in which more general and vaguely defined approaches would deter investors. Additionally, they can be tailored to allocate risks in a variety of ways

that provide investors with their desired comfort level. They are flexible, which is clearly a strength, but that flexibility makes them more complex. The objectives and the means required to achieve these objectives must be clearly defined. Experience in one country or sector will not provide much guidance to a different country or sector. For the moment each concession is likely to remain a special case with unique features.

Unfortunately, the number of cases are quite frequent where privatizations/concessions have gone sour and the contract renegotiated, impacting the credibility and reputation of the process and the country. The incidence of renegotiation of concessions is excessively high and should be a source of concern. Over 60 percent of concessions appear to be renegotiated within three years of the award. While some of them are indeed efficient renegotiations, many others are opportunistic, and those should be deferred. The common problems are poor concession design, unclear concession/regulatory rules, ex post changes of the rules of the process, and inappropriate bending to requests to renegotiate deals. A few examples follow.

Regulatory Surprises in Ukraine Lead Motorola to Pull a $500 Million Investment

In 1997 the Ukrainian government decided to award by tender two frequencies to launch cellular phone networks. The winners of the hotly disputed tender were a Motorola-led consortium and a Deutsche TeleKom AG-led consortium. Both had pledged to invest more than US$500 million. After the winners were announced, the government changed the rules of the tender by demanding an annual US$65 million frequency fee from the winners (not a trivial amount considering that the total 1996 revenue from the country's largest mobile phone operator—albeit using an outdated analog system—was less than US$50 million), after having assured the potential buyers that no such fee would be imposed; by, without notice, awarding a third frequency to a domestic company, Kievstar, with no known sources of financing or operational experience in telecommunications; and by putting the frequency allocations on hold for five months, presumably to allow the domestic company to catch up. As a result Motorola decided to pull out of the investment.

Philippines Faulty Harvest of Concessions/ Privatizations

GEC-Marconi, U.K. won a US$133 million radar contract, but the government says it is no longer bound by it as a result of unresolved turf battles among government agencies. This is an example of unclear jurisdiction and, thus, opportunities for capture.

CEPA Ltd., Hong Kong submitted the lowest bid to build a 1,200-megawatt power plant, but lost the contract because of controversy over use of technology previously banned in the Philippines. This is an example of mis-specifications in the concession contract.

Hopewell Holdings Ltd., Hong Kong won a $450 million highway contract, but the agreement was canceled after a dispute over terms and interpretation of the contract. This is an example of the consequences of vague concession contracts.

Renong Bhd., Malaysia submitted the top bid to buy the Manila Hotel, but the deal was locked in court after the losing bidder sued, claiming Philippine companies should have preference in privatization, even though there was no such provision in the terms of the sale. This is a classic example of renegotiation over unspecified rules.

Aramco Co., Saudi Arabia's, purchase of 40 percent of the Petron Corporation has been delayed for over two years after Malaysian senators sued to stop the sale, claiming national security concerns. This is an example of capture and political economy.

Poor Concession Design and a Hurried Pace Lead to Financial Disaster and Renegotiation in the Mexican Highway Program

In 1997 the Mexican government announced outlays of US$3.3 billion over the next thirty years to restructure the financing of fifty-two highways built under private concessions of toll roads in the early 1990s. This renegotiation and bailout of the private operators followed a program riddled with design problems. The first problem was that concessions were awarded to the operator submitting the shortest time to operate the concession. This criterion is highly inappropriate by any economic principle. The second problem was that the government provided traffic volume guarantees (terribly optimistic, based on a period of months rather than the standard 1.5-year process, and on the most traveled stretches of highway and at the busiest times of day), implicit insurance for construction overruns, and a friendly state-run banking sector that facilitated project loans. Finally, the hurried pace of the program led to incomplete design and specifications for road construction, and rushed engineering studies and hasty cost projections created ample opportunity for padding the budgets. All this led to bids of ridiculously small concession periods of six to twelve years, (there was even one bid of eighteen months!), to significant cost overruns, and to high tolls to support the short concession periods, low usage ratios and, as should have been anticipated, to overall economic and financial disaster, with the government having to assume a number of the concessions. In addition, there have been claims questioning the transparency of the process (Foote 1997). The overall cost to Mexico was estimated to be US$6 billion.

Renegotiation of Mexican Railway Privatization

In December 1996 the Mexican government auctioned the Northeast Railway line as part of its previously announced plan to privatize Mexican National Railways (FNM). The winning bidder (a consortium of Kansas City Southern and Transportes Maritimos Mexicanas-KCS|TMM) offered three times more (US$1.5 billion vs. US$500 million) than the next highest bidder for the 80 percent stake in the line that was being auctioned. This lead to speculation that the winners had bid too much ("the winner's curse"), and their respective share prices dropped. Shortly thereafter their financial backers pulled out, and the consortium was forced to recognize that they could not finance the deal. The consortium then sought to renegotiate their bid. The government accepted this proposition after first assuring itself of the legality of such an action. The renegotiated deal was that KCS | TMM would purchase a 55 percent share for US$700 million, FNM would retain a 25 percent share, and the Secretaria de Comunicaciones y Transportes (SCT) would retain, as originally planned, the remaining 20 percent. This renegotiation was done after the award to KCS | TMM, without reopening the bidding process and in absolute secrecy from other bidders. This is an example of complying with inappropriate renegotiation requests.

Renegotiation of the Buenos Aires Water Concession

In 1993 the operation of water and sanitation services in Buenos Aires was concessioned through competitive tenders to the private sector. Aguas de Argentina, a consortium of both domestic and foreign firms, won with a bid that would reduce average user tariffs by 27 percent (the second bid was for a reduction of 26 percent). About a year later, the tariff was renegotiated, granting the operator a 13.5 percent increase in tariffs. Justification for this change was partly that the government wanted to step up the scheduled timing of investments (particularly in sanitation) and to replace nitrate-contaminated wells in the next few years, and partly a recognition of higher labor costs beyond the inflation formula included in the contract. Yet as of 1997 the contracted investment commitments did not take place, and an implicit agreement (renegotiation) was reached in which a fee for infrastructure investments the operator was allowed to charge was eliminated in exchange for modifying (accepting) the operator investment program. Still the tariff increase remained.

These last two examples show the problems with renegotiation. The consequences are obvious. The precedents set are worrisome and the message is "bid very high and then renegotiate better terms." The end result is not only loss of credibility, but that the awards are likely to go not to the most efficient operators, as desired, but to the most talented in the art of renegotiation and capture.

All these cases illustrate the importance of clear rules, unambiguous terms, and binding contracts. The precedents set can have ominous consequences for future initiatives, affecting credibility and reputation, and ultimately revenues, investment, and private sector participation, with adverse effects on efficiency and welfare.

FRANCHISE-CONCESSION BIDDING IN ARGENTINA

In Argentina, responsibility for water and sewerage services was decentralized to the provinces in 1980, but the central government retained control over services in the capital city. In 1993, the operation of water and sanitation services in Buenos Aires was concessioned, through franchise bidding, to the private sector. Tables 8.1 and 8.2 shows the Buenos Aires concession. The main objective of arranging a private concession for water services in Buenos Aires was to expand water and sewerage services to the unserved population in the absence of adequate public financial resources (in a city of 9 million, half lacked access to one or both services). Selection of a concessionaire followed a two-phase process. First, five firms were prequalified to bid on the basis of their technical, administrative, and financial capacity. A price competition followed, in which a baseline tariff was specified and the contenders submitted a price bid as a percentage above or below the reference tariff. They submitted one envelope with detailed technical offers and one with financial and economic offers. Aguas Argentinas (a consortium of both domestic and foreign entities) won the price competition with a bid that would reduce average user tariffs by 27 percent.[4] The Argentine government ultimately decided to forgo compensation for the rights to use existing facilities, either in the form of a lump-sum payment or a rent. The value of these use rights was not trivial: The water company was operating with positive cash flows and earning a positive rate of return on its assets. The expectation was that the competitive bidding process would transfer that rent to water users and that the subsidy could be justified because of externalities in the provision of water and sanitation services.

Table 8.1 Contract Structure and Regulation of Aguas Argentinas for the Greater Buenos Aires Area

Bidding Procedure	Term	Contract Requirement	Rate Regulation	Quality Requirements	Investment
• Technical pre-qualification by Obras de Sanitación Nacional and the privatization commission • Two envelopes: Envelope one includes detailed technical offers (such as legal aspects of the bidders, mission statement, operational plans, regulation for users); envelope two includes the financial and economic offers (including the coefficient of adjustment)	• Thirty years	• Obligation to provide the public service of water and sanitation in a way that ensures the continuity, regularity, quality, and generality to users and the protection of the environment • Obligation to extend, maintain, and renew as needed the external network and connect them to all inhabited buildings in the concession zone	• Cost plus • Initial tariff level set in the privatization process • Trigger rule for changes based on an agreed cost structure	• Spelled out water quality levels • No quality norms with respect to service cuts or water pressure levels	• Improvement and expansion plans included as part of the contract • Investments required to be bid out • Timing requirement for the investment program, but subject to renegotiation

In May 1993 the federal government awarded a thirty-year concession contract to the consortium. While the contract did not specify required investment levels, it set gradual performance targets for such parameters as water and sewerage coverage (percentage of population served), percentage of wastewater to receive primary and secondary treatment, percentage of water and sewerage network to be renovated, and a maximum percentage of unaccounted-for water. Additionally, it spelled out general water levels and required that all investments be bid out. The set targets for the first fifteen years of the concession imply the connection of approximately 1 million inhabitants every five years to both the water supply and sewerage system. The investment necessary to comply with these performance targets is an estimated $100 million per year. What is not clear in the concession contract are the consequences of failing to comply with the performance targets. This will weaken compliance unless the consortium finds the targets to be profitable. The operator was required to put up a $150 million performance bond as security

for the first five-year period. Aside from default, however, it is unclear what level of underperformance would trigger loss of the bond. For example, in 1996 the government regulatory agency pressured the operator to return revenues linked with contractually allowed price increases, since it claimed the operator had not complied with contractually agreed investment targets. Not surprisingly the operator contested the claim and decision.

Under the concession terms, Aguas Argentinas assumed full responsibility for the entire water supply and sewerage system, including commercial and technical operations and maintenance of all components. It must also finance and execute the investments necessary to achieve service targets as specified in the contract. Aguas Argentinas also assumed all financial risk and can disconnect users who do not pay their bills. As is the case with franchise bidding, additional regulation was kept to a minimum. (See box 8.2 for a description of Argentina's water regulatory agencies.) Under the contract provisions, the rates use a cost-plus system and water rates would be

Table 8.2 Contract Structure and Regulation of Electricity Distribution for the Greater Buenos Aires Area

Bidding Procedure	Term	Contract Requirement	Rate Regulation	Quality Requirements	Investment
• Two envelopes: Envelope 1 specifies the technical requirements and determines the prequalified bidders; it contains the share of actions to be subscribed by each cobidder, shows a single unified local residence, proof of legal existence; $10 million guarantee for offer; proposed action plan for contractual obligations • Envelope 2 has the economic offer with amount in cash and public bonds; bidders had to have assets of at least $300 million and proven net wealth of no less than $200 million which did not decline by more than 5 to 10 percent over the previous year • All bids must identify at least one but no more than two experiences • The winner would have to pay the consulting fees for the lawyers ($1.5 million each for the transmission and distribution deals) and the financial consultants (paid only if there was a deal and equal to 1 percent of the value of the deal)	• Concession for ninety-five years for exclusivity in a specific zone after which new bidding will have to be made; proceeds of bid go to the incumbent who is also allowed to bid • The term can be extended for a period up to ten years to be determined by the regulatory entity, which can also modify or suppress the zonal exclusivity • The term of the concession is divided into management periods of ten years (except for the first, lasting for fifteen years) • At the end of each management period, the regulatory entity organizes an international bidding to sell majority bundles of stock and will set the tariff regime to be applied for the following five periods • The new majority owner, an independent inspector nominated by the regulatory entity will ensure one year before the end of the management period and the first year of the new management period, the proper functioning of the company (including disclosure of information)	• Distribute as a public service in the concession zone • Commit to specific quality levels • Respect the rights of users as specified in the "reglamento de suministro" • Satisfy the total demand for service, including demand for new services • Provide energy for public lighting • Provide electricity at 3X380/220 V, 13 kV, 2 kV, 33 kV, 132 kV, 220 kV, or any other as agreed with the regulatory agency • Make the investment and maintenance required to achieve established quality requirements	• $RPI - X + Y$ • Maximum price with total pass-through of the costs of energy in the wholesale market (Y) and indexation to U.S. price index (RPI) • The index used is 67 percent producer price index and 33 percent current price index • Initially X was set to 0 • The RPI is applied to a specific tariff structure • Tariffs are set in U.S. dollars	• Minimum quality standards covering: (a) product (tension), (b) technical service (duration and frequency of outages), and (c) commercial service (complaints by clients, time to get connection, bill estimates) • For measurement, two steps were defined with different goals: (a) during the first thirty-six months, measurement of medium tension, and (b) as of the thirty-seventh month, measurement of every user • Failures to meet quality standards are penalized through a detailed fine system; the proceeds go to the users victim of the gaps	• No control of investment by the public sector, although investments over $2 million need the regulatory entity's approval and a public hearing

---

Box 8.2 Regulatory Agencies in Argentina's Water and Sanitation Sector

Unlike in the energy sector, no one agency is in charge of formulating broad policy or providing incentives and financing. Of the dozen or more public agencies involved in the water and sanitation sector, the following are the most important:

- The Public Works Secretariat, which has prepared and implemented the national water resources policy and coordinated related projects since 1994.
- The Subsecretariat of Water Resources, which has the actual responsibility for accomplishing the tasks of the Public Works Secretariat and for promoting general policies.
- The Ente Nacional de Obras Hídricas de Saneamiento (ENHOSA) may replace the Consejo Federal de Agua Potable y Saneamiento. Its main role will be to mobilize and channel financial (mostly international) resources to the provincial sanitation companies of local communities in exchange for sector reforms.
- The Secretariat of Natural Resources and Human Environment, whose mandate since 1991 has been to coordinate environmental issues among federal agencies.
- The provincial public works ministries and secretariats and the provincial environmental secretariats,

which have direct responsibility for environmental protection in their areas.

Another important regulatory agency is the Ente Tripartito de Obras y Servicios Sanitarios (ETOSS) for the greater Buenos Aires area. In terms of purely economic regulation, this is an independent agency. ETOSS represents the interests of the national government, the municipality, and the province of Buenos Aires. It maintains and develops equipment, supervises the quality and continuity of service delivery, protects health, water resources, and the environment, and ensures that the specifications of the contract are met. It is financed by revenues from the three governments involved and by a tax levied on all consumers. It is ruled by a directorate whose members are appointed by the administration for a six-year term, renewable for one additional term.

National actors include the interior ministry, which monitors interprovincial rivers; the health ministry, which sets norms for drinking water, assesses the environmental impact of infrastructure projects, and manages the registry of polluting sources; and the economic planning secretariat and the social development secretariat, which finance projects and provide technical assistance to the provinces.

---

reassessed every five years, based on the next five-year updated investment plan and updated estimates of expenditures. An inflation index formula specified in the contract enables the regulatory institution, the Ente Tripartito de Obras y Servicios Sanitarios (ETOSS), to monitor cost increases. (ETOSS is a tripartite entity with equal representation among the municipality of Buenos Aires, the province of Buenos Aires, and the federal government.) The contract stipulates that the rates can be revised only if cost increases due to inflation are above 7 percent.

In July 1994, a little more than a year after the concession was granted, the tariff was renegotiated, and ETOSS was granted an increase of 13.5 percent. Apparently this increase was granted partly because the government wanted to step up the scheduled timing of investments (particularly in sanitation) and to replace nitrate-contaminated wells in the next few years, and partly because labor costs were increasing faster than the inflation formula included in the con-

tract. This illustrates one of the shortcomings of franchise bidding. When the incentives for renegotiation are not properly addressed, the original bidding—the strong point of franchise bidding regulation—can be rendered almost meaningless. In other words, it becomes a matter not of potential efficiency but rather of competence and expected renegotiations. See tables 8.3 and 8.4 for a detailed comparison of the concession contracts in four provinces.

Argentina also concessioned freight and metropolitan transport operations, in packages that were financially viable. Box 8.3 describes the concession.

FRANCHISE BIDDING IN MEXICO

Private sector participation in Mexico City's water supply services had two objectives: to reduce physical leakage and to improve cost recovery. The arrangement in Mexico City has some unique features. Private operators are

Table 8.3 Structure of Water Concessions in Argentina's Provinces

Characteristic	Corrientes	Tucuman	Santa Fe	Córdoba
Type of contract	Concession	Concession with equity of 25 percent required and three years experience in providing services to at least 1 million people	Concession	Concession
Duration	Thirty years	Thirty years	Thirty years	Thirty years
Bids	Two stages: stage 1, technical and financial prequalification; stage 2, a proposal on tariffs (as a percentage of the current tariff)	Two stages: stage 1, technical and financial prequalification; stage 2, a proposal on tariffs for successive years of the concession (as a percentage of the current tariff)	Two stages: stage 1, technical and financial prequalification including requirement of a guarantee of financing of credit institutions for $100 million to be disbursed in five years; stage 2, a proposal on tariffs per cubic meter, debt service coverage of at least 1, and debt to revenue ratio of 1.5	Two stages: stage 1, technical and financial prequalification (such as an investment plan, quality, and local involvement); stage 2, a proposal on tariff (as a percentage of current), price of concession labor cost commitments
Investment needed	$75 million	$320 million	$100 million in first five years	Not available
Customer base	500,000 inhabitants in ten cities for water and sewerage	700,000 inhabitants in 120 urban communities for water and 327,000 people in ten communities for sewerage	Not available	City of Córdoba
Responsibilities of private operator	Operation and maintenance as well as investments	Operation and maintenance as well as 100 percent water coverage after sixth year and 100 percent sewerage services after eleventh year plus emergency work in first two years	Operation and maintenance with minimum target and objectives set in the contract and a maximum time frame for each goal (expansion, quality, pressure rehabilitation, and treatment)	Operation and maintenance as well as investment

Table 8.4 Regulation of Water and Sanitation in Argentina

Characteristic	Buenos Aires	Córdoba	Santa Fe
Broad sector reforms			
Reorganization	• At the national level, no major sectoral reforms yet • Several proposals still under discussion for reform		
Main objective	• At the metropolitan area level (under federal responsibility), to privatize the Obras Sanitarias de la Nación, the public enterprise serving about 1.1 million connections for a population of 5.9 million in water and 4.75 million in sewerage • To create a privatization commission • To create a regulatory entity • To reduce overall staff in the sector	• At the provincial level, to get the private sector more involved and to improve cost recovery	• At the provincial level, to get the private sector more involved and to improve cost recovery
Legal support	• Law 23696 (reform of the state), Decree 9999/92 for regulatory framework		
Objectives of regulatory framework	• To guarantee the water and sanitation services and promote their expansion		
Regulatory entity	• Ente Triparito de Obras y Servicios Sanitarios (ETOSS)		
Concession			
Bidding	• Technical prequalification by Obras Sanitarias de la Nación and the privatization commission • Two envelopes after that; envelope 1 includes detailed technical offers (including legal aspects of the bidders, mission statement, operational plans, regulation for users); envelope 2 includes the financial and economic offers (including the coefficient of adjustment to the current tariff to be expressed in value; this is the coefficient by which the current tariff will be multiplied to obtain the new tariff, financial commitment, aptitude, and all the information explaining how the bidder would achieve the adjustment coefficient • Bid awarded to operator with the lowest adjustment coefficient		
Terms	• Thirty-year concession		
Causes of termination	• End of term • Decision of concessionaire • Bankruptcy of concessionaire • End of the service		
Contract requirements	• To provide the public service of water and sanitation in a way that ensures the continuity, regularity, quality, and generality to users and the protection of the environment • To extend, maintain, and renew as needed the external network and connect them to all inhabited buildings in the concession zone		

Table 8.4 continued...

Characteristic	Buenos Aires	Córdoba	Santa Fe
Regulation Tariffs principles	• Tariffs have to be designed to ensure a rational and efficient use of the services provided and of the resources needed for their delivery • Tariffs have to guarantee an equilibrium between demand and supply • Tariffs have to address the sanitation and social objectives linked directly to the delivery of the services assigned through the contracts • The prices and tariffs have to reflect the economic costs of the services, including the profit margin of the concessionaire and the costs due to the approved expansion plans • Tariffs have to allow cross-subsidies		
Type of regulation	• Cost plus • Initial tariff level set in the privatization process • Trigger rule for changes based on a known cost structure		
Quality requirements	• Spelled-out water quality levels • No quality norms with respect to service cuts or water pressure levels		
Investment requirements	• Improvement and expansion plans included as part of the contract • Investments have to be bidded out • Timing requirement for the investment program, but subject to renegotiation		
Functions and obligations of the regulatory entity	• Enforce the contract and the regulatory framework • Approve the user regulation (specifying the regulatory norms for the dealings with and complaints by users) to be proposed by the concessionaire • Request from concessionaire the data required to conduct its supervision and ensure the confidentiality of the information provided • Publicize the expansion plans, service improvement plans, and the tariffs • Monitor compliance of the concessionaire with the various plans • Record the complaints by users on service and tariff problems • Make decisions on complaints and other conflicts based on careful examination of facts • Assess and endorse or reject the request for revised tariffs • Enforce commitments and obligations by concessionaire on investment and maintenance • Intervene in decisions on renegotiation of contract • Apply sanctions on concessionaire as specified in the contract and return the revenue from penalties to users as additional investment or tariff reductions to be specified in bills • Request the assistance of executive power when the actions of the concessionaire threaten the health of the population.		

Source: Prepared by Estache, Helou, and Rodriguez-Pardina 1995.

Box 8.3 Comparison of Award of Freight and Metropolitan Concessions

Aspect	Freight Concessions	Metropolitan Concessions
Timing of awards	1991–93	End 1993
Duration	30 years (with possibility of 10-year extension)	10 years (with possibility of multiple 10-year extensions)
Scope of concession	Vertically integrated	Vertically integrated
Allocation of commercial risk	To concessionaire	To concessionaire
Nature of bidders	Mainly domestic; freight users were well represented	International bidding; local bus companies were well represented
Number of bidders	0–2	3–7
Number of packages offered	Six groups of lines	Seven groups of lines (no single bidder to take more than six)
Selection mechanism	Double envelope, with multiple bid criteria	Triple envelope, with single (lowest subsidy) bid criterion

involved in distribution and commercial activities, but not in production. Further, the city is divided into four zones, and contracts are awarded to a different contractor for each zone. The arrangement is structured in three phases, so that the private companies gradually assume more responsibility. During the first two phases, the contractors are compensated on a fee-for-service basis. They begin to assume commercial risk only in the third phase. However, the operator is not allowed to discontinue service to users who fail to pay.

In March 1993 the Federal District Water Commission awarded general contracts for an extendible ten-year period. Several firms were prequalified, and six submitted bids. The number of attractive bids made it possible to award contracts to four groups. Each contractor signed a general contract with the commission under which it has the right to negotiate specific contracts to conduct the work planned for the three phases in one zone of the city. The city retains ownership of all facilities. Under phase 1 (scheduled to last about two years) contractors will map the distribution system, determine its condition, identify repairs to prevent water losses, and install meters for all users. In phase 2, contractors will develop and implement a billing and collection system. Investments in the first two phases

are underwritten by BANOBRAS, the Mexican public works bank. Depending on consumer response to phase 2's rigorous billing and collection, the commission may go forward with or delay phase 3, under which the contractors will purchase bulk water from the city and take on full responsibility for distribution and commercial activities. Ultimately, the Mexican law on water services will have to be amended to make it possible for private providers to take a commercial position as envisioned in phase 3.

FRANCHISE BIDDING IN CHILE

Between 1988 and 1989, new legislation decentralized responsibility for publicly owned water and sewerage services in Chile by creating autonomous regional service companies. The national government owns the majority of shares in these companies through its Development Corporation. A national regulatory agency, the Superintendency of Sanitary Services, was created to regulate both public and private water and sewerage services. Under Chilean law, all water service companies, whether public or private, are structured as stock corporations and operate by virtue of concessions granted by the Ministry of Public Works. Concessions are granted for an indefinite period of time and are transferable only with authorization of the Superintendency of Sanitary Services and approval of the Ministry of Public Works. However, water companies may contract with third parties for the execution of any of the functions that fall within their concessions (meter reading and construction or operation of a specific component) without approval, and are encouraged to do so to improve service efficiency.

In June 1993 the Empresa de Obras Sanitarias de Valparaiso (ESVAL) entered into a thirty-five-year contract for the operation and maintenance of water and sewerage services, and for the financing of an agreed investment program in an area that forms part of its jurisdiction. After bidding, Aguas Quinta Region was awarded a contract to operate the ESVAL facility under which it retains 95.6 percent of the tariff revenues. ESVAL remains the concessionaire for the services, and the Superintendency of Sanitary Services continues to regulate ESVAL but cannot override the conditions of its contract with Aguas Quinta Region.

PROBLEMS IN USING FRANCHISE BIDDING TO ALLOCATE THE SPECTRUM: THE CASE OF GUATEMALA

Guatemala has a monopoly fixed-link supplier, GUATEL, a state-owned company. GUATEL's operations are dismal. According to the Centro de Investigación Económica Nacional (CIEN), a think tank in Guatemala City, GUATEL has a penetration rate of less than 2 percent, with penetration in Guatemala City of about 7 percent and in rural areas of less than 0.5 percent).[5] Guatemala is a country with 10 million people, and at last count there were only 2,100 public telephones. There are no good statistics on the time it takes to get a phone, but according to the CIEN, it varies from two to twenty years. GUATEL is extremely inefficient. It has twenty-three employees per 1,000 lines. By comparison, phone service providers in Japan and Spain have from two to three employees per 10,000 lines. Nevertheless, GUATEL is highly profitable. According to CIEN, GUATEL's return on equity reached 80 percent in 1992. The solution to the puzzle of

low quality and high profits is that GUATEL is a monopoly with extremely high prices. Indeed, GUATEL's international calls are the source of its profitability. A ten-minute call to the United States costs approximately US$25, a similar call to a South American country costs approximately US$45, and to a European country approximately US$62.[6] These are, by all considerations, extremely high prices. These prices cross-subsidize, to some extent, local service. But because local service is not profitable by itself, except as a conduit for an international call, GUATEL has no incentive to develop its local network except in high-income areas.

GUATEL's monopoly is not seriously challenged by other technologies and providers. Guatemala has, so far, a single cellular licensee, COMCEL, a private operator, in what is called the B band. COMCEL's service is not particularly popular, reaching only 12,000 clients after six years of operation (Crónica, June 25, 1995, p. 37). Because the American Mobile Phone Standard (AMPS) technology allows for two operators in the 800 megahertz band,[7] the government decided in mid-1994 to promote competition in telecommunications by opening a second cellular supplier. GUATEL, as the regulatory entity, had the responsibility of adjudicating the license. A year after announcing its intention to grant a second cellular license, in June 1995 GUATEL provided the actual bases for the bidding. The bid was going to be adjudicated by the Receiving, Qualifying, and Adjudicating Commission (Comisión Receptora, Califocadora y Adjudicadora). The commission was composed of GUATEL employees, including trade union representatives.[8] Eleven firms showed interest in the bidding, and seven actually presented bids. On August 18, 1995, the commission adjudicated the auction, granting the license to Mastec. Box 8.4 shows the bases for determining the winning bid. As can be seen, the bases were murky. Promised technology, coverage, service, and nature of payments were all considered by the commission.

Table 8.5 shows the points that the commission gave to each company in the first and second rounds of the bidding. After the commission announced its determination, GUATEL's

---

Box 8.4 Receiving, Qualifying, and Adjudicating Commission Report, 18 August 1995

Technical Justifications

1. The design of the interconnection network and base stations is well defined, according to the bases required by GUATEL.
2. The design of the interconnection network includes circuits to all base stations.
3. The telecommunications infrastructure to achieve interconnection with the fixed-link network is independent of GUATEL's network, achieving the necessary network autonomy.
4. Its network is of medium capacity, assuring the transport of the traffic generated by cellular users.
5. They consider power coverage levels between -75 dBm and -105 dBm, making the service useful for urban and rural areas.
6. They offer a dual (AMPS/TDMA) system, allowing digital or analog access, providing customers with more and better services.
7. The design includes a detail of spectrum use.
8. The design satisfies the requested level of service, thus assuring quality of service.
9. Interconnection: They consider redundant circuits for signaling and synchronization.
10. They plan to cover the highway from the capital, Guatemala City, to Puerto Barrios in the inauguration.
11. They plan good coverage (including more localities than required) for the inauguration.
12. They accept various providers of terminal equipment, and detail percentage utilization of some of the more important ones.

13. They plan higher than required reliability, complementing the quality of service.
14. They offer a shorter execution plan than required in the bases.
15. They consider a relatively high average coverage per year (41,005).

Economic-Financial Considerations

Mastec's marketing plan includes publicity campaigns utilizing mass communications (radio/newspapers,)... equipment distribution will be undertaken by third parties, ... like Radio Shack....It also proposes that GUATEL be a distributor, providing it with commissions.

Apart from that, Mastec... provides the best economic and financial conditions, being the first one of highest weight because they are linked to the economic and social activity of the state, given that the tariffs that the company offers to charge are the most favorable for the user....Furthermore, it must be mentioned that Mastec is the one that offers the best payment to GUATEL....It should be mentioned that this was not the point that most influenced the evaluation, but the previously mentioned [the tariffs]. In terms of the financial analysis,...it is the one that presents the best indicators, thus we conclude, taking in consideration the points for the areas Technical and Economic-Financial that Mastec de Guatemala Sociedad Anónima must be the licensee.

Source: Report of the Commission, as appeared in newspaper advertising paid by Mastec de Guatemala. Translated and edited by the authors.

---

board invalidated it, claiming, among other things, that the winning company was not legally incorporated.[9] The board then instructed the commission to reconsider its determination. The board did so and came back with a different evaluation for each of the bidders. It now qualified two of the previously disqualified bidders, and gave GUACEL, a company that had a very poor showing in the first round, the highest value, exceeding the previous number two by less than one point.

There are, then, three winners in this franchise bidding process: number one in the first round, number two in the first round, and number one in the second round. All three claimed publicly that they indeed were the winners. The losers filed for legal recourse, and following sub-

stantial discussion in the press and elsewhere, GUATEL canceled the licensing procedure altogether. Following the cancellation, the winner in the second round also filed for legal recourse, requesting it be given what it legally deserved.

As a consequence of the process, no license has been granted, and most probably none will be until all three legal challenges find their way through the court system. In the meantime, GUATEL does not collect its licensing fees, and the commencement of competition with COMCEL and GUATEL will have to await other developments. Indeed, it could be the case that PCS licenses would be granted prior to the granting of a second cellular license.

The commission's reasons for changing the values of each of the bids are not clear. Although

Table 8.5 Points Granted to Each of the Bidding Consortia

Bidder	First Round	Second Round
MASTEC	88.75	disqualified
GUACEL	69.01	85.46
LONDRINA	84.90	84.49
COM. ELECTRICAS	51.42	56.10
UNICOM	disqualified	33.37
SEMELEC	disqualified	32.20
BSC	disqualified	disqualified

Source: *Crónica*, September 29, 1995, page 19.

there may be good reasons for such changes, the subsequent evolution of the licensing process shows the problems associated with granting licenses not based on objective criteria.

The discretion associated with the bases provided by GUATEL would in most circumstances raise questions about undue influence. These problems may be even more extreme in countries with little or no experience in administrative procedures and administrative law. Thus, in those countries it is imperative that spectrum allocations not be based on administrative-intensive procedures, but rather on auctions requiring little or no administrative capabilities. Auctioning to the highest bidder is one such system.[10]

CONCESSIONS IN CHILE

The Chilean government has used concession granting as a main tool for promoting competition. Laws regulating the electric and telecommunications sectors in Chile guarantee all firms applying for a concession the right to receive it, unless increasing the number of firms is not technically feasible. Therefore, the law requires that the government grant concessions even when, theoretically at least, rejecting them is relatively more efficient. In essence it favors the market test over the textbook prescription. Concessions have been provided to any private sector agent desiring one, even in industries or stages that are natural monopolies. The rationale behind this law is that the regulator, by increasing the number of producers, favors consumers by creating the conditions for more competition, but the result is that concessions frequently overlap.

A single-tariff concession zone may generate a subsidy for subzones that have the largest access costs and a tax to subzones that have the lowest access costs. This cross-subsidization is largely efficient, given the greater cost that society would incur if the regulator were to set tariffs equal to each district's marginal costs. Setting rates in this manner can be detrimental when concessions overlap because when new firms enter the subsidized zones the incumbent's return could fall. Further, an incumbent that anticipates the entrance of new firms, and thus a fall in its own rate of return, would not apply marginal cost rates.

Other costs are associated with regulation that attempts to induce competition at a level where it is not convenient. The first is excessive investment as a defensive strategy to impede entry by firms that compete within the overlapping area. Investments are commonly undertaken even though they waste resources based on capacity levels and on the estimated demand a firm faces. The second cost associated with overlapping concessions is the loss of the economies of scale that normally occur when production increases and average costs are reduced. Overlapping concessions would increase average costs without reducing rates because excessive concessions decrease the size of the market that each firm serves, and concessions that redefine service areas frequently wipe out cross-subsidy effects in zones, further increasing costs. Obviously, social welfare losses are associated with such cost increases. The concession area should be coherent with the tariff charged.[11]

Following privatization in the electricity sector in Argentina, public companies such as Entel and Endesa were, inappropriately, left with regulatory capacity mostly because they had the infrastructure and human resource capacity. This leftover regulatory capacity gives them an abnormal advantage over potential competitors and provides them with undesirable market power. Both Entel and Endesa, for example, still authorize concessions, giving them a degree of monopoly power and an informational advantage, because they receive strategic information about the plans of their competitors.

NOTES

1. Other competitive tendering experiences include the assignment of local authority services, such as catering, maintenance, and refuse collection. The bidding has often been in terms of the lowest price at which the service will be offered, with contracts specifying level of service and containing provisions for cost-related price changes, enforced through financial penalties. The results show cost reductions in excess of 20 percent when competitive tendering has been used (Dornberger, Meadowcroft, and Thompson 1986). For a more extensive analysis of franchise regulation, see Dnes 1991, from which some of the material in this section has been adapted.

2. Although the two criteria used in Argentina and Chile were appropriate, the one used for toll roads in Mexico was not. Not surprisingly, it led to excessively high tolls, minimum use of toll roads, ample renegotiations, rethinking of the program, and change of the bidding criteria to minimum tolls (Guasch 1995).

3. This section is adapted from Kessides and Willig 1995.

4. The share distribution is 50 percent foreign, of which Lyonnaise des Eaux-Dumez holds 25 percent, and 50 percent domestic. For further details on the concession process, see Idelovitch 1994. The second- and third-highest bids offered rates of 26 and 12 percent lower than the water rate at the time of bidding. Prior to the call for bids, the government had increased water rates by 8 percent. The rates were $0.66 per cubic meter for households with both water and sewerage connections and $0.33 per cubic meter for households with water connections only.

5. We measure penetration as lines per inhabitants. Although popularly used throughout the world, this measure may not be completely appropriate when comparing countries with different family sizes. Guatemala, however, is the country with the second-lowest penetration ratio in Central America, after Honduras.

6. These high prices have promoted the use of call-back services, whereby a Guatemalan caller first calls a number in the United States whose call back provides a U.S. dial tone. Using these services, calls to similar places would cost no more than US$2 per minute.

7. Recall that other providers could enter using alternative technologies in other bands.

8. Unionists played an important role in the process from its very beginning. By the end of the process, recrimination between the two main unions about their participation in the process was quite strong. In particular, there were claims that the union with representation in the commission received money from GUATEL. (See "Otra Mano Peluda," *Crónica,* September 29, 1995.)

9. There seem to be many other reasons for the decision of GUATEL's board, including uncertainty about the company's ability to deliver the promised service. (See "Hubo Mano de Mono," *Crónica*, September 29, 1995, for a description of the licensing process.)

10. In the Guatemalan experience, Mastec was also the company that claimed to have submitted the highest bid. According to GUATEL, Mastec's offer was for a total of US$57.3 million, of which US$22 million would be in cash and the rest in kind, including a closed digital cellular network for exclusive use of the government (valued by Mastec at US$29.5 million) and a national radio communication network, and 2,000 handsets for exclusive use of the police (valued by Mastec at US$5.9 million). This was another reason for disqualifying Mastec, because GUATEL's terms of reference did not specify any in-kind payments and, furthermore, the offer was not directed to GUATEL. This information was contained in the August 25, 1995 resolution of GUATEL's board, which Mastec paid to have printed in newspaper advertisements.

11. An incumbent utility providing electricity services to different zones in Santiago sets a tariff that reflects the average long-run marginal cost considering different zones (high and low population density). The tariff implies a cross-subsidy in that zones with the largest access costs receive a subsidy, while zones with the lowest access costs are taxed. This rate setting is inconsistent with overlapping concessions because companies granted a concession will try to enter the subsidized zones, resulting in a fall in the incumbent's returns. The authority will therefore permit a larger tariff to compensate for this expected fall; thus overlapping concessions will initially increase tariffs.

THE DESIGN OF CONCESSION-TYPE ARRANGEMENTS: COMPETITIVE PROVISION OF GOODS AND SERVICES TO GOVERNMENT BY THE PRIVATE SECTOR IN DEVELOPING COUNTRIES

IN ADDITION TO THE TRANSFER or sale to the private sector of productive activities previously undertaken by the government, every government in the world procures goods and services from the private sector and transfers rights to the private sector.[1] This has become ever more relevant following the massive privatization programs being implemented in most developing countries. Whereas the state enterprise used to produce the goods or services, private firms are now producing them. The issue is how the government should transfer or sell productive activities to, and procure goods and services from, the private sector.

The problem of transfers and procurement can, at first glance, seem elementary: determine what to sell or buy (or what service to procure or what rights to transfer), solicit bids and announce how they will be evaluated, rank the bids accordingly, specify a recipient, and take delivery of the commodity. Why are procurements often wrought with arbitrariness, corruption, and waste? Why do governments often end up with underpriced sales, arbitrary winners, poor-quality merchandise or suboptimal services for which they have paid too much, and future unwarranted financial liabilities? Why are the regulations of government procurement so voluminous in industrial countries? Clearly, there are special nontrivial problems regarding government procurement and concession design.

Historically, government transfers of enterprises and procurements often have been characterized by waste, arbitrariness, and inefficient allocations. These difficulties stem from an underlying principal/agent problem, nontransparency of design, and opportunities for discretion and corruption. The government officials running the transfer and procurement typically have different objectives from those of the government. It is difficult for an outsider to assess whether the discretionary actions of officials are consistent with the objectives of government. Discretion is often abused through the scoring of bids. At a single-price auction bids are scored quite simply: monetary offers alone determine the winner and the price paid. In procurement, bids are scored by more than just cost, because the commodities offered by different vendors are often distinct. The typical constraints of civil service compensation make it impractical to implement high-powered incentive schemes for these officials.

Given that renegotiation of complex and often long-term franchises frequently occurs, features that enhance the stability of basic contract provisions may enhance the meaningfulness of the initial award procedure. At the same time, there are trade-offs involved in choosing relatively renegotiation-proof contractual provisions, particularly implications for efficiency incentives. For example, the contract may include investment obligations that will be undesirable ex post when demand shifts. Clearly there are solutions to these types of problems, such as pricing formulas that adjust to benchmark indexes or risk-sharing arrangements between consumers, taxpayers, and investors, but they carry their own burden in terms of transaction costs and institutional knowledge if they are to be carried out correctly.

Another problem area is designing the process the government will use to assign the concession, and then evaluating the bids. Many of the case studies presented in this book used a two-stage process where technical characteristics were scored first followed by a price bid, but another option is to simply weigh price against all other attributes. When there are several different factors being considered in choosing a winner, the committees frequently combine all the parameters into a single value. Although this does simplify one aspect, it also requires a weighting system. Additionally, even after the bids are evaluated it is possible that the initial bid will not be a good predictor of eventual performance in a long-term franchise. In certain cases it can be extremely difficult to evaluate the credibility of a franchisee. This is especially true if past performance does not provide adequate information about future behavior.

The ideal auction design will assign rights and obligations to the party or parties best able to perform, while minimizing the possibility for collusion and reducing the likelihood of ex post renegotiation. A bewildering array of mechanisms is available to achieve this end. For example, public bids will reduce the incentive to renege, but sealed bids will limit the opportunity to collude. Risk-averse bidders may prefer bidding on a stream of payments rather than a lump sum, but is that the preferred type of bidder? Descending (dutch) and ascending (english) auctions provide different types of knowledge about valuations, and the optimal design depends greatly on the concession. Finally, if the cost of preparing the bid itself is very high, the costs could be reimbursed to some extent to enhance the ferocity of competition, but the savings from more competition may be lower than the expenditures.

Even after the auction, the consigning entity may have to exercise a substantial amount of discretion to determine a winner. The issue is how to manage that discretion so that the process remains credible to investors and legitimate to the public. The government could use independent procurement bodies, staffed by people without conflicts of interest in the process, or the whole process could be contracted out to professional procurement agencies, which have their reputation on the line for future business. A difficulty with those options is that regulatory agencies will in any case be responsible for any recontracting issues arising under the franchise after the award, so perhaps they should be involved in the initial choice. Ideally the process should be transparent, and the results of making the evaluations public can be seen in the Guatel example in Guatemala. Against these advantages one must weigh the firm's need to safeguard legitimately confidential information.

If the government finds the competitive bidding process unwieldy it can opt instead for a negotiated agreement, but there is no guarantee that such an agreement will bring about a more efficient or more equitable result. Negotiated deals require large amounts of institutional knowledge, technical experience, and lots of available human capital. The institution must be equipped to check abuse through appropriate institutional arrangements and use of benchmark information. Moreover, although it may not make sense to negotiate with a single bidder without another challenger, it may be even less efficient and sensible to carry on simultaneous negotiations with a series of bidders. Many countries do not have these negotiating capabilities, and even if they do, simultaneous negotiations may not differ enough from the competitive evaluation process, with minimum specifications in the request for proposals, to make the choice worthwhile. The questions that must be answered before deciding between competition and negotiation include

- Are the rules clear and credible?
- How likely is it that discretion will be abused?
- Will bid costs render competition infeasible?
- Is the outcome of a competition meaningful given problems of scoring?
- How will the credibility of a bidder be established?

This chapter focuses primarily on "standard" procurements—that is, procurements that are not repetitive in nature. However, we also discuss some of the issues associated with "nonstandard" procurements, such as procurements where development occurs prior to production or, alternatively, where the contract extends over several periods and where the initial commodity specification is likely to change through time. Along with all the problems of standard procurements, additional problems arise with nonstandard procurements because incumbents make procurement-specific investments and seek informational rents during the progression of the contract.

We provide a simple conceptual framework within which to analyze standard procurement issues, and offer specific policy recommendations for procurement in developing countries followed by a discussion of the special issues related to nonstandard procurements.[2]

PROCUREMENT: SOLE SOURCE AND COMPETITIVE

Many procurements rely on the solicitation of competitive bids. Others involve negotiations with a single supplier. Sometimes a government is forced to conduct a sole-source procurement, because the commodity it wishes to obtain is produced by a monopolist. In the absence of a monopolistic supplier, sole sourcing might still be justifiable. For example, if the government has made a large investment in customizing some procedure to the products of a particular firm, converting to the products of another vendor might be too costly.

The process of procuring from a sole source is very different from the process of competitive procurement. Sole sourcing involves bilateral negotiation. One might think that a sole source is just the limiting case of a competitive procurement. That would be true if the government made a take-it-or-leave-it offer that the sole source, in turn, accepted or rejected. But in practice sole sourcing involves much more negotiation than that.

There is very little negotiation in a competitive procurement. Instead, competitive procurements are much like auctions. Offers by vendors are considered simultaneously. Simple procedural rules identify the probability of winning for each bidder and the payments that the government will make to bidders. The significant differences between procurements and auctions will be discussed later in this chapter.

This analysis focuses on competitive procurements, although sole sourcing is mentioned periodically. In general, sole-source procurements should be avoided whenever possible. The main reason is that a government official is typically at a gross informational disadvantage relative to a vendor in the private sector regarding the performance of a commodity. The vendor will, of course, attempt to maximize the informational rents earned in the sole-source procurement. Noncooperative competition between vendors greatly reduces informational rents. Simply put, with a competitive procurement a government official can get away with being relatively uninformed: Noncooperative competition will tell him what he needs to know.

In addition, and probably more important, sole sourcing induces wasteful rent-seeking behavior and may encourage bribery. If the government official must keep the solicitation of bribes confidential, then not all the rents for the sole-source vendor will be transferred through bribes to the government official. In other words, both parties will gain from the bribery. However, such an activity is obviously inefficient, and thus detrimental to social welfare.

A Simple Framework for Thinking about Standard Procurement: The Government's Objective

What is the objective of a government that is conducting a competitive procurement? For this chapter, we make a simple but encompassing assumption: The government wants to maximize its surplus from the acquisition.[3] What is meant by surplus? In a competitive procurement, each firm submits a bid that consists of two distinct components. First, each firm specifies exactly what it will produce for the government. We denote the gross benefit that the government derives from the acquisition of firm i's commodity, expressed in monetary units as Q_i. The function that maps the multidimensional commodity characteristics of firm i's bid into a single number, Q_i, is called the scoring function. Second, each firm specifies how much it must be paid to provide the government with the proposed commodity. We denote the acquisition cost for the government as X_i. Then, the surplus offered to the government by firm i is $Q_i - X_i$.

The scoring function is critical to many of the issues associated with procurement. More generally, each firm submits an X_i and a vector of function or product characteristics: $Z, Z, \ldots Z$; then $Q_i{}^o Q_i(Z, Z, \ldots Z)$. This scoring function, Q_i, maps the multidimensional characteristics of a procurement bid into R_1 for each firm i. Then, surpluses can be calculated for each firm and ranked, and a winner determined.

Surplus maximization may seem to be an overly simplistic goal. After all, many governments make "skewed" procurement awards. For example, fledgling companies that are viewed as vital to the national interest may receive awards as a form of government subsidy. How does this fit in with surplus maximization?

The key to answering this question, and to understanding many of the central issues with procurement, is to understand the scoring func-

tion, Q_i, and its origins. The cost component of a procurement bid has a transparent meaning. In trivial procurements, Q_i is not problematic either. For example, if a government wants to buy high-density 3.5-inch diskettes that meet certain quality standards, then Q_i is the same for all firms that can meet those specifications (presuming that no bidder receives credit for surpassing the specifications). Surplus maximization in this case is equivalent to cost minimization. However, for most procurements the commodities being offered by different firms are very different. A computer network offered by International Business Machines (IBM) is very different from a computer network offered by Apple. Forklifts offered by firm A have characteristics different from forklifts offered by firm B. Government officials, either explicitly or implicitly, will evaluate these very different commodities in such a way as to be able to compare them. The forklifts offered by firm A, with its maintenance costs and functional abilities, are mapped into another number, Q_1, while the forklifts offered by firm B are mapped into a number, Q_2.[4] Then, the X_i from each bid can be used to determine surplus. Support of fledgling companies can be reflected in how they are scored (that is, in their Q_i).

U.S. federal procurements are classified into two categories vis-à-vis the scoring function. With an invitation for bid, the scoring function is remarkably simple—all vendors that meet minimum standards are scored identically. An example might be the procurement of the 3.5-inch high-density diskettes mentioned above. With an invitation for bid, all compliant bidders are ranked by their cost bids, and the low-cost bidder is the winner. Other procurements are called requests for proposals. These are more complicated procurements in which bids specify heterogeneous commodities, such as the computer network and forklift procurements mentioned above. Suppose a U.S. federal agency wants to install a computer network for electronic access to manuals or other documentation. IBM's proposal may be very different from Digital Equipment Corporation's proposal, which might be very different from any other vendor's proposal. The scoring function provides a way to evaluate and rank these very different bids. A bid solicitation often will specify precise credits for upgraded equipment. For example, the bid solicitation might explicitly say that the personal computers on the network should not be technologically lower than 486/25, with 8 megabytes of random access memory, and 120-megabyte disk drives with access speeds of not more than 28 milliseconds. The solicitation may continue to say that a 486/50 will increase the score by $150 per machine, each megabyte of memory per personal computer above 8 will increase the score by $35, each megabyte of disk space above 120 but less than 250 will increase the score per personal computer by $2, while any unit increment above 250 will increase the score by $1. Alternatively, the solicitation may specify a functional scoring system. For example, secretaries will be asked to use demonstration models and will be surveyed immediately thereafter. The survey results (indicating, for example, user friendliness and compatibility with existing software) will be translated directly into a dollar value for the score.[5]

But what is the origin of the Q_is? The basic motivation for a procurement by a government agency is an underlying demand for some good or service. This underlying demand is then mapped into a scoring function, which in turn accomplishes the mapping described above.

The Procurement Mechanism

What mechanism should a government use for procurement and concession transfers? In this setting a mechanism is an allocation device whereby eligible bidders submit reports to the government agent running the procurement. Based on these reports, a winner is determined. The winning vendor then tenders the commodities bid in exchange for payments by the government. No attempt is made to establish a general allocation mechanism. We presume that the government solicits sealed bids simultaneously from bidders, ranks the bids by surplus, awards the contract to the bidder offering the highest surplus, and pays that bidder its bid price, X_i, to supply the commodity (or receives X_i if it is a concession). No other bidders receive anything from

the government. We call this a "first-surplus" procurement mechanism. Although an infinity of alternative mechanisms are available, much recommends the use of this first-surplus procurement. One primary recommendation is its robustness to collusion by the bidders (a not uncommon feature of procurement). If firms are bidding to supply a homogeneous product to the government, then the firm offering the lowest procurement cost wins and supplies the commodity for that price. We simply note here that first-surplus procurement is used throughout much of the world, and its procedural rules are quite simple.[6]

The Central Problem of Government Procurement

Government procurements are run by state employees. To the best of our knowledge, state employees are never compensated with high-powered incentive schemes that encourage them to maximize surplus.

As a point of comparison, consider auctions in the private sector. Auctioneers typically receive commissions from owners of the items being sold that are equal to, say, 10 percent of revenues generated. Consequently, auctioneers want to generate as much revenue as possible, a goal shared by owners of the items being sold. But the auctioneer's and the owner's interests are not directly aligned. There are actions that an auctioneer will not take when earning a 10 percent commission that he will take if he is the sole owner of the item for sale. However, in an auction setting, shirking by the auctioneer is, in many circumstances, easy to detect. For example, it is easy to determine how extensively the sale was advertised and whether the reserve price agreed with the consignor was enforced. In the vernacular of economics, even though the principal/agent problem could arise in an auction context, it typically does not because the actions of the auctioneer are verifiable (shirking can be established in court as a breach of contract between the auctioneer and the consignor).

With government procurement, we are not aware of a single case where a procurement official has received compensation directly tied to the surplus generated from the procurement.[7] Typically, the official is a government employee and is compensated according to civil service rules. Without close monitoring, it is natural to expect that a procurement officer would shirk his duty, at least relative to the desires of the citizenry of his country.[8] It might seem strange that the agency of government buying the commodity does not closely monitor the behavior of the procurement officer so that surplus is maximized. But the incentives of chief administrators are often distorted as well. For example, it is not uncommon for the central government to reduce or revoke budgetary allocations for an agency in future years if current spending falls below expectations. Consequently, an unnecessary urgency to procure arises. This pressure falls on the shoulders of the procurement officer. Measures that the officer will take to expedite a procurement are very similar to what he would do as an unpressured shirker. An officer who sees the outcome of the procurement affecting his career path typically confronts the distorted measuring sticks placed before him by his superiors, rather than looking to maximize government surplus. In other words, a "bad" procurement may occur because the procurement officer is dishonest or a shameless shirker, but it may also occur because the officer is honest and diligent but a victim of a hierarchical agency problem.

A typical manifestation of the principal/ agent problem is firm-specific favoritism. A single firm, or some small subset of firms, is clearly favored. This avoids the disutility of effort associated with full and open competition. The favored firms may be those that the procurement officer feels confident can at least provide a commodity that satisfies the demands of the government agency (but this may be quite far from the outcome of a surplus-maximizing procurement), or they may simply be a group of firms that are offering the officer direct personal enrichment. Once the officer begins the procurement process, it is extremely difficult for an outside observer to discern whether his discretionary judgment was exercised in a manner consistent with taxpayers' objectives.

The Decision to Include or Exclude, and Biased Scoring

Which firms can participate in the procurement? It might seem obvious that if a firm wants to submit a bid, it should be allowed to do so. However, in many procurements, the bids that describe the capability and function of the product are several hundred pages long. These bids are difficult to score. Doing so takes a great deal of time and expertise. Consequently, from the viewpoint of the social planner, who sees the costs of preparing such bids, it is reasonable to allow only a subset of bidders (presumably those with the highest ex ante probability of winning) to participate in the procurement. But who should be allowed to participate and who should not is largely dependent on what the government wants to buy. The exact commodity or functional demands of the government are typically specified by the procurement officer in a bid solicitation. Construction of the solicitation often requires a great deal of discretionary decision-making. Although the solicitation will not typically contain explicit declarations of who can and cannot bid at the auction, the specification of what the government agency wants to buy often makes it very clear to vendors that only a few bidders have any possibility of winning. Rather than being exclusionary, sometimes the scoring function in the bid solicitation will simply reflect the procurement officer's bias in favor of a subset of firms. Because the officer is not compensated for the disutility of effort involved in evaluating numerous bids, he has an incentive to abuse his discretion and to restrict unjustly the firms for inclusion or to dissuade many firms from bidding through the statement of his bias in the scoring function. In the extreme, the procurement officer will run a sole-source procurement. His superiors might be quite pleased with this: The procurement is conducted quickly and within a specific budgetary period.

Best and Final Offers

With relatively complicated procurements, bidders are often given an opportunity to revise their bids in a way that provides the agency with greater surplus. This revision process often involves communication between the procurement officer and vendors. At this juncture, there is obviously room for abuse of discretion. For example, the procurement officer can inform an unjustly favored firm of the contents of other bids, thereby providing the unjustly favored firm with the informational advantage needed to secure victory. Of course, if all firms know the contents of each other's bids, some other firm could emerge victorious.

Product Evaluations

After submission of the best and final offers, the products of firms are typically evaluated to ascertain whether they indeed have the functional characteristics asserted by the firms in their bids. As one can imagine, if a procurement officer unjustly favors a particular firm, then that firm could easily outperform all others in the evaluation. Again, the officer is given the opportunity to exert massive discretionary judgment behind closed doors.

Discretion of the Procurement Officer

The exercise of discretionary judgment is at the crux of the procurement problem. Unlike an auctioneer, a procurement officer chooses a scoring function and then implements it. The scoring process, both the ex ante declaration of it in the bid solicitation and the implementation of it in the product testing, involves the procurement officer's discretionary judgment. Misuse of this discretion is very difficult to detect. So, if we strip the officer of any ability to exercise discretion in the procurement process, does this solve the problem? We are now at the critical point in understanding the central problem of procurement. If the officer is a good agent of taxpayers, he should have maximum discretion with which to maximize surplus. However, if he is a bad agent of taxpayers, he should not have the ability to make discretionary decisions. Without knowing whether the procurement officer is a bad agent or a good agent, and with-

out having access to incentive schemes, what can be done?

In what follows, we discuss potential solutions to this principal/agent problem. Keep in mind that the theoretical literature in economics provides little guidance on this issue, because the compensation scheme of government employees is a given in any practical approach to this problem.

SOLUTIONS TO THE PROCUREMENT PROBLEM

The following discussion assumes that competition is good. Of course, arguably, limiting competition can be beneficial at times: Allowing a vendor to secure extranormal profits encourages asset-specific investments, and explicitly banning potential bidders that have little chance of winning avoids incurring the costs of formulating and evaluating their bids. Despite these exceptions, competition is good. More competition means more surplus for the government. More competition makes it easier for the procurement officer to become informed about commodities in the private sector.

As a corollary, the members of the community of firms are better informed about anticompetitive procurement abuses than any central enforcement agency would be. A vendor excluded from a procurement knows whether it can provide a commodity that satisfies the demands of the government agency. A firm knows better than anyone else if a product evaluation test was conducted with a bias toward a given firm. The result of such abuses is that excluded firms, disfavored firms, and procurement losers are forgoing expected profits.

The recommendations proposed here rely on the creation of an independent commission to work closely with developing-country agencies that are responsible for procurement while also overseeing the procurement process. We will refer to this commission as the procurement assistance commission, or PAC. The PAC will have the potential to be involved in all phases of the procurement process.

The Procurement Assistance Commission

The directives of the PAC should be
- To assist government agencies in procuring goods and services in order to facilitate the process of development
- To provide accurate information and expert assessments to international lending institutions regarding the status of procurement practices in specific developing countries
- To provide a protest forum for aggrieved bidders and governments and to conduct random audits of procurements.

The first point has already been discussed. The information and critical assessment aspect of the PAC's job involves both short-run and long-run evaluations of procurements. For example, a procurement may appear to have been completed successfully, but if, after one year, the commodity purchased is inoperable or the service has deteriorated significantly, there may have been a significant flaw in the procurement contract. Or suppose a procurement is successful but within-country personnel are no better informed about how to run a procurement in the future. Such phenomena need to be monitored and recommendations made to the international lending institutions to help the country improve its procurement process.

A primary role of the PAC is to provide mechanisms for oversight of procurements. Providing assistance ex ante does not preclude the possibility that something will go wrong with the procurement; inappropriate discretion can be exercised at many stages in the process. The oversight might be discovered through random audits. The PAC rarely conducts an audit itself; the general practice is to hire a firm from the private sector. The PAC would provide a protest forum. Aggrieved bidders and governments could bring their grievances to the PAC, in a strictly confidential manner, and the PAC would then determine if there were grounds for proceeding with an investigation. The PAC would keep a record of complaints and note which bidders or governments were bringing legitimate problems to their attention. A fee would be charged to any vendor or government that protests a procurement to the PAC. The fee would be refunded to prevailing protesters.

The PAC must maintain a reputation for fairness and integrity. Consequently, its initial construction is critical. Only general principles should be established for the process of procurement. Under no circumstances should voluminous regulations emerge from the PAC that all developing countries must follow. This should be part of its charter.

As with any administrative organization, PAC managers may envision that their prestige and power will grow with the size of the PAC's budget. If every procurement in a developing country must pass through a lumbering bureaucracy, the commission's role will be counterproductive. The PAC should be a clearinghouse to procure information, coordinate procurements, and hire procurement services.

A Worst-Case Scenario

Suppose that a culture of arbitrariness and corruption permeates government and that the private sector has little recourse but to cooperate. Government employees view their jobs as nothing more then rent-seeking opportunities. The judicial system is corrupt. The reputation of any government employee or firm that complains of procurement abuses suffers adverse effects or worse. No internal controls or enforceable regulations guide the procurement process. What should be done under these circumstances?

For each country, the PAC should maintain lists of two different types of firms: firms that can run procurements and firms that can provide specific kinds of commodities. The PAC will directly assist the government in selecting a firm to run the procurement and to educate in-country personnel about surplus-maximizing procurement procedures. Any procurement run by one of these firms should have the following characteristics and components:
- The demands of the government agency should be identified and mapped into a bid solicitation. The bid solicitation should be publicly advertised. All relevant vendors on the PAC's second list should be notified of

forthcoming procurements. Any firms that choose not to bid should be required to provide the PAC with a statement explaining their decision not to participate. The PAC retains the right to remove a vendor from its list at any time. (Certain procurements should be run where only firms on the list can participate. This artificial barrier to entry will encourage firms to take actions to preserve their status on the list.)

- Bids should be ranked as stated in the solicitation, best and final offers should be received, products should be evaluated, and an awardee should be determined.

- Any potential bidder that is aggrieved by any part of the process should be entitled to file a confidential grievance with the PAC, which would either investigate the grievance or hire an external investigator. In addition, any government grievance about the procurement should be filed with the PAC. The potential for grievances to be filed from both vendors and the government provides the best possible safeguard for assuring that the procurement maximizes surplus. Firms that run procurements that maximize surplus will be in good standing on the first list and will continue to be viable to run future procurements.[9]

- The PAC should have the right to audit any procurement at any point in the process to make certain that surplus-maximizing procedures are being followed and that surplus-maximizing outcomes are being attained. This threat of audit will deter the development of collusive relationships between in-country personnel or firms and the firm running the procurement.

An obvious question is, How does the PAC, with government assistance, procure the service of running a procurement? The answer is simple: It solicits bids and selects the firm offering the biggest surplus. The scoring function depends on the nature of the commodity being procured, the country in which the procurement is taking place, the amount of procurement-related instruction for in-country personnel that is required, and other relevant factors. Payment could consist of two parts:

an immediate payment for running the current procurement and a bonus if future procurements within the country are conducted in a manner that is consistent with surplus maximization. With both vendors and the home government overseeing the procurement through their access to the grievance process, the firm running the procurement will be largely deterred from abusing its position. Additional safeguards will also be required.

No firm that runs a procurement should be allowed to bid on that procurement. A careful record should be kept of firms that are running procurements and of firms that are awarded those procurements. If firm A runs a procurement that firm B wins in country X, while firm B runs a procurement that firm A wins in country Y, then the PAC should investigate the possibility of collusion. In fact, if firm A runs a procurement that firm B wins, then all business dealings between firm A and firm B should be disclosed to the PAC. If the PAC feels that a business relation exists that could have led to an outcome contrary to surplus maximization for the country, then the procurement should be put aside and a new procurement started.

By relying on an outside vendor to run the procurement, the PAC and the country buying the commodity avoid dealing with the typical disincentives for surplus maximization inherent in civil service employment contracts.

An Intermediate Scenario

A less extreme case might be the procurement culture in environments where the judicial system may not be corrupt, but where litigating a procurement abuse would damage the reputation of a bidder before the procuring agency.

In that case, procurements should be placed in one of three categories: (a) procurements that are very simple and can be run as an invitation for bids; (b) procurements that are more complicated but that can be broken into several smaller procurements, each of which can be run as an invitation for bids; and (c) very complicated procurements that must be run as a request for proposal. For a request for proposal, it is still advisable to use the procedures described earlier.

However, a simple invitation-for-bid procurement should be run by the country, but the PAC's protest forum should remain available to any aggrieved bidder. When a complicated procurement can be broken into several invitation-for-bid procurements, that should be done, and the country should run each of the procurements on its own. Before running any procurement, however, the government should be required to provide written documentation to the PAC of how the separate procurements will, together, accomplish its objectives.

The Best-Case Scenario

Suppose there is a relatively high level of confidence in the procurement procedures of a developing country. The courts have fairly high integrity. In that case the government should conduct all procurements on its own. The role of the PAC is only oversight. The protest forum provided by the PAC should still be available to any bidder who wants to take advantage of it. In addition, the PAC should randomly audit select request-for-proposal procurements to determine whether surplus-maximizing procedures were employed.

Finally, the PAC should watch out for rent-seeking activities. While sealed-bid and single-tendering criteria to assign concessions or sales are the most effective and resilient to manipulation, they are by no means corruption proof. Aggressive companies and entrepreneurial government officials can come up with creative techniques to extract rents or capture and manipulate the tendering process. Among some of these techniques are sitting on the dossier of a winning bid until the bidders "grease the wheel" or pay speed money; threatening to impose new conditions after the bids have been submitted; threatening to disqualify the winners on some technicality and tie up the process in courts; and accepting bribes from losing bidders to reject all tenders as inadequate, and then reopening the bidding process for a new round. (There has been speculation that some of these techniques were used in a 1996 tender of $25 billion worth of telecom licenses for cellular and basic services in India [*The Economist*, August 24, 1996]).

NONSTANDARD PROCUREMENTS

Consider a developing country with a port. To enhance trade, the country wants to enhance the capacity of the port to onload and offload commodities.

- *Procurement 1.* Suppose the country wants to purchase 100 forklifts. The dock is already well equipped with maintenance equipment and trained personnel. This would fall within the standard procurement framework.

- *Procurement 2.* This is the same as procurement 1, except that the country wants to purchase 100 forklifts per year for the next five years. Over time, the procurer may request modifications in the forklifts. The repeated nature of the procurement moves it out of the standard case.

- *Procurement 3.* This is the same as procurement 2, except that the forklifts must be highly specialized to the climate of the country: They must have specially designed coolant systems to withstand heat, and special air filtration systems to withstand highly abrasive airborne particles.

How should procurements 2 and 3 be conducted? What is the role of the PAC in these procurements? In procurement 3, investments are required by firms before the commodity can be produced and delivered. In both procurements 2 and 3, there is a temporal aspect to the procurement that was absent from our discussions in previous sections. A number of issues arise with multiperiod procurements. The government will want to use competition whenever possible. This implies that development contracts will be awarded separately from production contracts. But will the winner of a development contract underinvest because of the threat of not winning the production contract? In another vein, changes in an initial order will invariably result in rent-seeking efforts by a producing firm which has less information than the procurer. How can these moral hazard problems be controlled? Specifically, what mechanisms and incentive schemes should be employed to allocate procurement?

A simple starting point is to allow for the possibility of "split awards" when awarding a production contract. A "split award" is one in which two or more producers each manufacture some fraction of total output (Laffont and Tirole 1993, ch. 7). Consider procurement 2. The moral hazard threat in this case comes from the possibility of "change orders" during the course of the contract. For example, the dock authority realizes that the initial 100 forklifts are underpowered and wants the next 400 to have more lifting capacity. With a single producer the dock authority has no ability to challenge the assertion that the upgrade will be extremely expensive. However, if the dock authority had initially made a split award, it would be able to ask each firm to submit revised prices and "resplit" the contract based on these new bids. Why is this different from running a new procurement? First, a new procurement may be very costly to run because of delays, the need to test the products of new entrants, and so forth. Second, split awards provide firms with the incentive to make procurement-specific investments, because competition among the participating firms is naturally less vigorous (fewer firms are involved) than it would be with open procurement. Overall, split awards serve as a low-cost mechanism for curbing the delay that is inevitable when an order is changed.

If the firm is to make significant investments prior to production, it may be desirable to conduct two separate procurements. The first procurement would be for development, and the second would be for production. A critical issue in this respect is whether the investments from the development phase are observable and transferable. Difficulties with capital transfers arise when they are in the form of human capital and, more generally, when investments are difficult to measure. The latter may occur when the capital for a specific procurement is integrated into an existing production process (integration may be a time-consuming task that is very difficult to quantify). As a practical matter, we presume here that the investments at the development stage are not observable and are only partially transferable (Laffont and Tirole 1993, ch. 8, in particular, proposition 8.2). The production procurement

should be biased to favor the firm that won the development procurement. In addition, the incumbent should have a low-powered incentive scheme in the development stage and a higher-powered one in the production stage. At an extreme, the development contract should be a cost-plus contract, while the production contract should be a fixed-price contract. The intuition underlying this recommendation is simple. The incumbent must be given strong incentives to invest in the development stage. When the investments are only partially transferable (as one would expect in practice), the incumbent will naturally have a disincentive to invest, because it may not be able to capture the full benefits from the investment (for example, if the entrant wins the production procurement). The disincentive to invest can be overcome by two measures: favoring the incumbent in the production procurement, and compensating the incumbent to a great extent for cost overruns in the development phase. The latter measure lowers the incumbent's perceived cost of investment.

We can apply these principles to procurements 2 and 3. Procurement 2 should be run as a split-award contract. Procurement 3 should be run as a sequential procurement in which the winner of the development phase faces a low-powered incentive scheme and is favored in the production procurement. The production procurement should involve the possibility of dual sourcing (but still favor the incumbent). The role of the PAC in these procurements is exactly as described earlier. However, involving the PAC in assisting in the design of a procurement and incentive scheme takes on greater importance for the nonstandard case in light of the moral hazard issues.

The Issue of Collusion

Earlier, we assumed the use of a first-surplus procurement mechanism. (A first-surplus procurement is one in which the bidder offering the highest surplus is the winner. That firm provides the commodity described for the amount of the bid. In a first-surplus procurement, all bidders supply exactly the same commodity. Consequently, only cost is relevant in determining a winner. The bidder submitting the lowest cost wins and is paid the amount specified in its bid.) As a practical matter, it is difficult to envision how an alternative, such as a second-surplus allocation mechanism, might operate with a request for proposal where bidders can offer very heterogeneous products or services in response to the bid solicitation. (In a second-surplus procurement, all bidders offer the same commodity. The bidder offering the commodity at the lowest cost would win, but would be paid the amount of the second-lowest bid.) With a second-surplus allocation mechanism, the bidder offering the highest surplus wins. But what would that bidder provide and what would it be paid for providing it? Researchers have modeled such allocation mechanisms, but they are almost entirely of conceptual interest rather than practical importance. However, in the case of an invitation for bid, where the low-cost bidder is the winner, a second-surplus auction clearly means that the winner receives the amount proposed by the second lowest bidder (as opposed to receiving the amount that it proposed, as occurs with a first-surplus invitation-for-bid procurement).

For an invitation for bids, why should a first-surplus allocation mechanism be used instead of a second-surplus allocation mechanism? Assuming noncooperative behavior, some factors recommend the first-surplus allocation mechanism (ex ante bidder heterogeneity and risk aversion), while others favor the second-surplus allocation mechanism (affiliation). Understanding how each factor works to the relative advantage of a given allocation mechanism is beyond the scope of this chapter.[10]

For developing countries, it seems reasonable to be most concerned about collusion among the bidders. Relative to other potential factors, collusion has the greatest potential for having a negative impact on surplus. Given that fact, which allocation mechanisms are most resistant to collusion?[11] For simple procurements, where all vendors offer the same commodity, surplus is determined by cost. In that context a first-surplus procurement is a first-cost procurement. It seems reasonable to assume that a bidder's cost of production or cost of providing a service is pri-

vately known. Knowledge of another bidder's production or provision cost might alter the strategic behavior of a given bidder, but it would not alter the bidder's own cost. With that in mind, it is easy to demonstrate that a second-surplus procurement is far more susceptible to bidder collusion than a first-surplus procurement.

Consider the case where a fixed quantity of some commodity or service is being procured once by a government. In a second-surplus auction design all bidders report their production costs truthfully, assuming noncooperative behavior. How would collusion benefit bidders? If a coalition does not contain the two vendors with the lowest and second-lowest costs, there will be no advantage to the collusion. If the coalition contains the two bidders, then collusion will be profitable. All coalition members except the ones with low cost will bid either very high amounts or not at all. The coalition member with the lowest cost will bid its true cost, just as it would have done when acting noncooperatively. Again, presuming that the coalition is composed of the two bidders with the lowest cost overall, the coalition will win the procurement and pay the amount of the lowest-cost bid by firms that are not participating in the coalition. But, by assumption, this is more than the second-lowest cost. No member of the coalition has an incentive to cheat on this agreement, because decreasing the bid could only result in the coalition paying more to produce the item or, alternatively, winning the procurement themselves, but thereby earning negative surplus. The fact that members of the coalition have no incentive to cheat, and that the coalition's bid never leads to ex post regret, makes collusion easy to generate and very stable at a second-cost procurement. (The bid of the low-cost bidder is the same for collusion or for noncooperation, so if the coalition's bid loses, no one will regret having acted cooperatively.)

The first-cost procurement is much less susceptible to collusion. First, we need to understand noncooperative behavior. Because a winning bidder will receive the amount of its bid for supplying the commodity, every bidder will have an incentive to bid in excess of its true production cost. We will refer to the equilibrium phenomena of bidding in excess of one's cost as "puffing." How much a bidder puffs depends on the number of competitors and the information it has about the source of other bidders' costs.

Collusion at a first-cost procurement would be similar to that at a second-cost procurement. All colluding bidders except the one with the lowest cost either would not bid or would submit very high-cost bids. However, there is a critical difference. For the coalition to realize a gain, the bidder with the lowest cost would need to puff its bid beyond what it would have submitted if acting noncooperatively. This additional puffing may result in the coalition losing a procurement when the low-cost bidder would have won acting noncooperatively. In addition, members of the coalition may see opportunities for profitable deviations from the collusive agreement. By bidding slightly below the coalition's low-cost bidder, they might be able to win the contract and secure more profit for themselves than by complying with the collusive agreement. That possibility is absent at the second-cost procurement, where the low-cost bidder in the coalition acts no differently from if it were bidding noncooperatively.

There is one additional problem for a coalition at a first-cost procurement. This discussion has presumed that the coalition possesses some kind of mechanism for eliciting true information on production costs from members and for making side payments to share the collusive gain. Revealing information within a coalition at a second-cost procurement is somewhat complicated, but it can be done. The critical feature of the collusive mechanism that makes this possible is that the member that reports the lowest cost will bid just as it would have if acting noncooperatively. In other words, misrepresentation by a coalition member will not alter the strategic behavior of the bidder that has reported the low cost. However, at a first-cost procurement, information about the costs of others will affect a firm's bid. As a corollary, misrepresenting the true cost of a firm within the coalition may affect the low-cost bidder's collusive bid in a beneficial way.

The above analysis concerns single-shot procurements for a fixed quantity. In practice, the same bidders will often confront each other repeatedly. It is well known that repetition will allow collusion to be sustained when it could not be sustained in a single-shot play. In fact, many cases of bid rigging involve first-cost or first-surplus procurements. Some classic examples from U.S. law are the electrical contractors' conspiracy (known as the "phases of the moon conspiracy" because bidders took turns winning according to the phases of the moon), *U.S. v. Addyston Pipe* (in which steel pipe manufacturers divided territories and specified explicit side payment schemes among members of the coalition), and *U.S. v. Koppers* (in which one firm won all contracts in the western half of Connecticut, the other firm won all contracts in the eastern half). In U.S. federal procurement, Operation Ill Wind is the most notable case. In addition, the Justice Department has successfully fought bidder collusion by foreign firms that have bid to provide the U.S. military with supplies and construction services at foreign bases (an example is the case at the U.S. naval base at Sasebo, Japan). In other words, simply choosing a resistant allocation mechanism does not prevent collusion from occurring.

An unfortunate rule in the U.S. judicial system inhibits the detection of coalitions. Specifically, bidders that are not members of the coalition cannot bring a private antitrust action against the coalition. The argument is that a bidder outside the coalition can only benefit from the collusive activity since prices agreed to by the coalition are higher than under a competitive framework, and the outside bidder, presumably by underbidding the coalition price (guessing right), can secure the contract at better terms than if there had been no coalition. Because no damage is incurred, the bidder has no basis for bringing the case. However, it seems sensible to permit bidders to protest to PAC suspected collusion by others. After all, other vendors are certain to have better information about collusion among their competitors than anyone else could possibly possess. That kind of decentralized oversight could be encouraged by providing bounty to the reporting firm if collusion is proved.

CONCLUSIONS

The procurement or tender process should have clear and transparent rules of competition, selection criteria, and scoring function; an adequate prequalification process; and unequivocal project definition. It should also pay particular attention to construction programs. Otherwise, the inefficiencies loom larger. Bidders will concentrate on lobbying and salesmanship efforts; there will be few incentives for equity investment; the probability of litigation risks will grow; the credibility and interest of high-quality (foreign) potential bidders will be lost; proposals will not be comparable, will be difficult to evaluate, and will induce further rent-seeking activities; the high risks of cost overruns and renegotiation will be high; and contractors may siphon off equity.

In a worst-case scenario, an independent commission should assist the developing-country government in obtaining from the private sector the service of running a procurement. Part of the task of the firm running the procurement should be to train procurement personnel within the country. For intermediate cases, the government should conduct any procurement that can be structured so that the low-cost bidder is awarded the contract, under the oversight of an independent and autonomous commission. For all cases, if potential bidders or the government of the developing country are aggrieved by any part of the procurement process, they should have the right to file a confidential protest with the independent commission which, in turn, would conduct an investigation and levy sanctions. To inhibit the potential for collusion among bidders, all procurements should be sealed-bid and multiple-sequential auctions, when appropriate, where the winner supplies the commodity for the cost specified in its bid.

To prevent informational disadvantages that can lead to delays, the procurement should be structured to maximize competition. Where feasible, split awards should be made so that the winning firms can monitor one another as changes occur in the initial project. Further, if the project has an initial development stage followed by a production stage, separate procurements should be conducted for each in a way that encourages appropriate investment at the development stage.

NOTES

1. This chapter is adapted from Guasch and Marshall 1994.

2. Much of the procurement literature has been surveyed and beautifully exposited in a book by Laffont and Tirole (1993), on which we heavily rely. Specific references are contained at the end of chapters in their book.

3. We are assuming for now that the government is not a player in the game. Specifically, the government is not setting a strategic reserve policy, imposing an entry fee, or using any other device to take advantage of its monopsony power. Why are we concerned with surplus maximization rather than efficiency? If a fixed quantity is being purchased, surplus maximization generally produces efficient outcomes when the government is passive in the procurement. (This depends on the procurement mechanism used and the underlying characteristics of the bidders.)

4. Firm A's forklift may have higher maintenance costs, a tighter turning radius, and lower lift capabilities than firm B's forklift. Clearly, different functional demands would produce different scores for the two forklifts.

5. We advocate scoring based on functional capabilities rather than on product characteristics. The former is better understood by the procurer, while the latter is often used as a device to restrict competition unjustly.

6. Hansen (1988) analyzes a competitive procurement in which multiple homogeneous objects are being procured and the purchaser has a publicly known demand curve. The purchaser demonstrates that a first-surplus procurement provides the buyer with greater surplus than a second-surplus procurement and that the first-surplus procurement is preferred by buyers and is more efficient. This constitutes a very strong explanation for the prevalence of first-surplus mechanisms in the arena of procurement.

7. In practice, two or more kinds of government officials often run a procurement (technical officers, contracting officers, and others). For simplicity, we lump them into a single individual whom we refer to as the procurement official.

8. One of the most extreme forms of shirking is the acceptance of direct personal enrichment from a vendor (bribes or future employment) in exchange for determining the outcome of a procurement.

9. In a series of articles, Marshall, Meurer, and Richard (1990, 1991, 1992) have described and analyzed bidder protests in U.S. federal procurement. The authors identify beneficial aspects (such as deterrence) and detrimental unintended consequences (such as cash or subcon-

tract settlements). They propose specific policies for enhancing the former while limiting the latter.

10. A superb exposition of these tradeoffs for first-price versus second-price auctions can be found in Hirshleifer and Riley 1992, ch. 10. See also the survey by McAfee and McMillan (1987).

11. Graham and Marshall (1987) and Graham, Marshall, and Richard (1990) analyze bidder collusion at second-price and english auctions. Their coalitions use reporting and payment rules such that no member of the coalition wants to chisel on the collusive agreement. Mailath and Zemsky (1991) propose an ex post balanced budget mechanism for collusive behavior. McAfee and McMillan (1990) analyze collusion at a first-price auction under the presumption that the coalition is all inclusive. Hendricks and Porter (1988) provide empirical support for collusive behavior by bidders where the object being sold has a common underlying, but unknown, value. For a general assessment of the impact of auction design on collusive practices, see Guasch and Glaessner (1993).

10

PRIVATIZATION RESTRUCTURING AND REGULATION: ACTIONS AND SECTOR RESTRUCTURING PRIOR TO PRIVATIZATION

THE GOVERNMENTS OF MANY developing and industrial countries throughout the world are aggressively promoting the participation of the private sector in infrastructure sectors through privatization, concessions, or management contracts. There have been varying degrees of success.[1] The degree of success in attracting private sector investments in infrastructure may be related to the compatibility between the design of basic and detail engineering and a nation's institutional characteristics. Most importantly, actions taken prior to privatization can reduce the regulatory burden and induce more efficient outcomes. In

particular, restructuring—that is, breakup—of the enterprise prior to privatization ought to be an essential component of the process. Clearly the extent of the breakup will depend on the sector and on technological considerations. This chapter presents a conceptual analysis of optimal sector and firm restructuring, considering unbundling sequencing and minimum investment policies as part of that process, and evaluates the desirability and extent of restructuring prior to privatization.

Privatization involves more than transferring ownership of a utility's assets. It also has fiscal consequences because it relieves the government of a financial burden while relieving the company of the financial constraints imposed by the government's budgetary requirements. The fiscal consequences of privatization, however, often enter

into conflict with the second- or third-best optimal design of regulatory frameworks. For example, if prices are brought closer to long-run costs prior to privatization, the proceeds from privatization will be lower than if prices are left at higher levels, providing governments with an incentive to leave regulated prices relatively high.[2] A similar fiscal effect appears when opening a market for competition. Thus, fiscal considerations often argue for privatizing first, keeping the vertical and horizontal integration of the sector intact, and adjusting prices and competition only later, and even then, perhaps slowly. But that should not be the overriding concern. Rather, the efficient performance of the sector, should be the priority, and that often requires the restructuring and break-up of the sector prior to privatization.

An argument can also be made for restructuring prices and industry structure prior to privatization, because that would increase the sustainability of privatization, facilitate competition, and ease regulatory needs. If a privatized company remains a tight monopoly with very large profits following privatization (as can happen in countries where the regulatory framework is difficult to modify or ineffective), there is the potential for a political backlash against the regulated company and the efficiency losses. Structure and regulation are related. Restructuring can facilitate competition, reduce the need for explicit regulation, and increase efficiency.

Fiscal and revenue considerations should not be the main motive for privatization and regulatory reform. Increased efficiency and sector competitiveness should be. In that case, long-run efficiency considerations call for some form of sector and firm restructuring prior to privatization. In Argentina, Bolivia, Brazil, Chile, Peru, and the United Kingdom, some restructuring of the utilities industry was undertaken before privatization, although prices in the U.K. were usually left at levels set prior to the decision to privatize. Price-cap regulation and a rebalancing schedule were then used to bring prices slowly toward costs.

CONCEPTUAL ISSUES OF OPTIMAL RESTRUCTURING PRIOR TO PRIVATIZATION

The purpose of restructuring before privatization is to break up the firm to enhance the efficiency and competitiveness of the firm and sector. For that purpose it is necessary to set guidelines for how to determine an appropriate breakup of the state firm or state monopoly so that the ex post organization-cum-privatization better fosters economic efficiency. Organizational restructuring means breaking large enterprises into smaller units that can then be sold, and eliminating barriers to entry in most segments of the industry. The presumed advantages of smaller units stem from decentralizing information and control, changing management incentives, establishing divisional efficiency through direct and indirect

competition across units, and assessing (if necessary) relative performance, on which to base compensation of different units within the sector. While the analysis presented here is geared toward privatization, which is the desired course of action for state enterprises, it is also applicable, as a distant second-best option, to state firms that are not yet ready for privatization. The suggested breakup ought to induce efficiency gains while the firm continues to operate as a state firm, and clearly to continue to do so after privatization (Guasch and Blitzer 1993).

Prior to privatization, state enterprises have statutory monopoly over most or all stages of production, and therefore are fairly extensively integrated, both vertically and horizontally. For example, state oil companies are integrated companies whose activities include exploration, production, refining, distribution, foreign trade, and marketing of oil and natural gas and often petrochemicals. Similarly, state-owned electricity-holding companies usually monopolize all stages from generation to local distribution. Although it is often difficult to separate the effects of state ownership from the effects of lack of competition on the performance of state-owned monopolies, promoting effective competition, corporate governance, and financial discipline can significantly improve their performance.

Traditionally, most of the thinking on this issue has focused on the option of vertical break up and separation of ownership. That means creating different firms for each of the main types of activities within the monopolized sector. For example, Mexico is considering restructuring Pemex so that each of the main divisions (refining, exploration, production, and so forth) has greater autonomy and receives instruction on how to maximize the division's profits. A system of transfer prices (presumably either determined or regulated centrally) or bilateral bargaining would be introduced to measure each unit's or firm's profits. Major drawbacks of this approach (in the absence of privatization) are that appropriate transfer prices are difficult to determine (in part because "central" planning is necessary and numerous conceptual and informational problems exist), and no direct competition is introduced because each unit remains a monopoly within its subarea. The principle of vertical separation is to unbundle if the gains from competition (productive and allocative efficiency) are larger than the increases in transaction costs and losses from vertical separation. That is why full privatization remains the preferable option.

An alternative, albeit complementary, direction for organizational restructuring is horizontal breakup or separation. By this we mean creating and selling several firms, within a particular subarea in a government-owned sector, that directly compete with each other. For example, a state-owned railway system might be divided into several subsidiaries that compete (before and after privatization) in the market for freight traffic while sharing a common road bed system. Or a state-owned oil company might be divided into two or more vertically integrated, but smaller, companies that compete at all levels from leasing of acreage for exploration to refining and marketing. This approach has the obvious advantage of allowing direct competition, but in some cases may lack economies of scale and scope. In addition, the extent of restructuring, particularly horizontal (in the absence of privatization), depends on government-imposed constraints on private sector access or participation in certain segments of the operation, because private sector participation can provide competition and market discipline. This course of action clearly lessens the need to regulate the sector. For the restructuring or unbundling to be effective, it might require restrictions on reintegration, such as limits on cross-ownership, limits on ownership of several business units within one activity (that would also make yardstick competition possible), or requiring accounting separation (to facilitate regulation). For example, in the power sector, limits on cross-ownership of transmission generation avoids monopoly abuse, while limits on distribution-transmission avoids monopsony abuse.

In practice, a mix of horizontal and vertical separation, a sort of *karate* economics, will be called for in most cases. The literature on industrial organization and principal/agent problems has dealt extensively with issues of vertical and horizontal integration, decentralization, and

incentives.[3] However, the insights of that research have not been applied to the case of state monopolies being considered for privatization.

METHODOLOGY

When considering horizontal and vertical restructuring of state-owned monopolies before privatization, the following steps should be followed and relevant information gathered:

* Identify the stages of productive and service activities of the enterprises; for each stage, characterize the technology or cost structure and assess the existent stock of capital and labor and their degree of substitutability.
* Assess economies of scope and scale across different stages of the operation; characterize the most efficient scale for each activity on its own and in conjunction with others.
* Identify the activities or stages in production where the enterprise operates as a monopoly or has substantial market power (sheltered from domestic or foreign competition); distinguish natural monopoly conditions from other conditions; likewise, assess the extent of potential or existing intermodal competition for each stage, identify the stages of production where the enterprise operates in a relatively competitive market and the stages where there are second-sourcing alternatives from external parties.
* Identify possible fracture lines, horizontal and vertical.
* Identify productive or service activities that could be privatized, subcontracted, concessioned, leased, or open to external (private) parties; privatize concession as much as politically feasible.
* Identify observable variables related to performance or labor and managerial input for the different units or stages of production; identify costs of the risk and uncertainty factors for each stage of production; evaluate the options for the government/overseer (principal) to obtain information relevant to monitoring or overseeing the firms or units (agent), such as information about demand, own costs, and other firms in similar activi-

ties; carry this approach over to multilayered structures, where there are intermediaries.

- Establish performance measures (relative and absolute) for each stage of production, based on observable variables for those segments that remain in government hands.
- Identify and evaluate the institutional and contractual arrangements among the different units of the enterprise for those segments that remain in government hands.
- Design incentive schemes linking (relative) performance with compensation and allocating residual rights for those segments that remain in government hands.
- Consider building institutions within the enterprise to facilitate market-type transactions within the units for those segments that remain in government hands.
- Identify strategies the government can follow to ensure that each unit is subject to hard budget constraints; short of that, impose tight financial controls on each of the units and on the whole enterprise.
- Assess market demand, trends, and elasticities.
- Evaluate the tradeoffs among different modes of structure; assess the impact of restructuring reforms on prices, outputs, investments, and rates of returns by computing equilibrium levels for each viable configuration.
- Impose limits on cross-ownership, that is, on ownership of several business units within one activity, to avoid reintegration.
- Establish a regulatory entity with jurisdiction over enforcement and the resolution of disputes, and over any segment of the enterprise that is not subject to competition.

The concept and principles of restructuring prior to privatization have been used sparingly in Latin America and the Caribbean. Most of the cases have involved vertical breakups. Horizontal breakups are rare, and when they have occurred, they have been more like geographical partitions, which in principle do not generate head-to-head competition. Competition has been induced selectively, usually by opening the market to interested third parties. In the power sector, a number of countries have separated generation and distribution from transmission prior to privatization, and have opened the generation subsector to the private sector. In telecommunications, Chile separated the local exchange and long-distance services, Argentina created two regional monopolies, and Brazil partitioned geographically and by function (twelve companies) the state enterprise prior to privatization (see box 10.1).

In the railroad sector, Argentina separated the national network outside the capital into six regional freight companies and awarded them as vertically integrated concessions, combining operation of the service with maintenance and rehabilitation of the track. The metropolitan service was separated into seven groups of lines that were awarded as concessions to the private sector. The intercity passenger service that shared the same track with freight services was removed from the freight concession packages owing to its loss-making character. Only the profitable Buenos Aires–Mar del Plata service was awarded as a concession. All other passenger services outside the metropolitan area were earmarked to be discontinued, unless the corresponding provincial

---

Box 10.1 The Breakup of Telebras Prior to Privatization

The Brazilian telephone company, Telebras, was broken into twelve entities, each sold separately:

- Telsp, the land-line company in São Paulo state, the world's third-largest metropolitan area
- Tele Norte-Leste, the land-line phone company from Rio de Janeiro north
- Tele Centro-Sul, the land-line phone company for central and southern Brazil
- Embratel, the Brazilian long-distance telephone company
- Eight cellular phone companies located in various regions in Brazil; the largest is Telesp Cellular in São Paulo state.

In addition, to induce competition, the government also designed a system to build competition into the telecommunications system by selling "mirror licenses" granting twelve more companies the right to offer long-distance, land-line, and cellular services, paralleling the twelve entities described above.

governments were prepared to take on the associated financial burden. Five provinces elected to continue to provide intercity passenger services, paying track-access charges to the freight concessionaires. A similar breakup of the state railroad enterprise is being considered in Bolivia and Brazil. In Mexico, three geographically distinct parts of the company—Northeast, Northwest, and Southeast railways—were sold separately to the private sector.[4] In the ports sector, the approach has been, in multiple-terminal ports, to break the monopoly and award each terminal to a different concessionaire and open stevedoring operations. This has been the case in Argentina (Buenos Aires), Chile, Colombia, Ecuador, and Mexico. The power sector is being vertically and horizontally disintegrated in most countries, such

as Argentina, Bolivia, Guatemala, and Peru. The Argentine example is shown in table 10.1, and other examples are shown in table 10.2.

HORIZONTAL VERSUS VERTICAL RESTRUCTURING

The essential element of any restructuring process is to rethink the appropriate organizational structure to achieve the sector's most efficient performance (constrained efficiency). Often, the status quo of state-owned enterprises is a highly centralized structure with a small or weak incentive structure. When considering variations from the status quo, it is important to question whether a common, centralized, and single management or control system is necessary

Table 10.1 Structure of the Power Sector Industry in Argentina

	Preprivatization	Postprivatization
Horizontal structure		
Generation	Duopoly	Four companies
Transmission	Monopoly	Monopoly
Distribution	Several companies	Three companies
Ownership	Mainly state-owned, with one private integrated utility	Private (including transmission)
Competition	No competition	Competition in generation
Vertical integration	Vertically integrated	Vertically disintegrated

Table 10.2 Examples of Market Structure Reform

Sector	Reform	Country Examples
Power	Separating generation from transmission and creating competition in generation	Argentina, Australia, Colombia, New Zealand, United Kingdom
	Permitting free entry in generation	The countries above plus the United States
Gas	Separating production and supply from transmission and distribution	Argentina, Colombia, Mexico
	Permitting free entry in gas transmission	Chile, Germany, New Zealand
Telecommunications	Separating local from long-distance service	Argentina, Hong Kong, United States Australia, Chile, New Zealand, United Kingdom
	Permitting free entry in basic services	
Rail	Separating infrastructure (track) from rolling stock	Sweden, United Kingdom
	Separating railway lines by geographical region	Argentina, Mexico

Source: Kerf and others 1988.

to provide the output efficiently and, by implication, whether several firms with autonomous management and control or separate ownership can provide services as efficiently as, or more efficiently than, the original firm.

A useful point of reference to begin thinking about desired or "optimal" restructuring is the potential outcome in the privatized sector. Privatization entails selling the enterprise as a whole or in parts. A well-thought-out privatization policy would consider all the options, not only maximizing revenue from the sale but, more important, also creating a market structure conducive to competitive behavior, taking account of the technological characteristics of the sector, informational constraints, transaction costs, and degree of substitutability of the product. Such consideration is needed to identify the optimal fracture lines of the state enterprise.

Having identified that reference point, the organizational restructuring, for sale purposes, is achieved by breaking up or decomposing the enterprise, vertically and horizontally, into a number of smaller units or firms and eliminating barriers to entry. If the enterprise is to remain for a period of time in state hands, then appropriate incentive or compensation schemes should be based on relative performance among similar units, with each unit operating as a separate profit center with discretion in production, financing, pricing, product quality and range, choice of technique, innovation, and internal compensation. Each unit would be financially independent in the sense of having the ability to seek separate financing and to bid for the rights to use or have access to physical capital and financial assets, with the obligations being backed solely by the unit.[5]

The difficult practical questions involve deciding on the degree of disintegration and determining which subunits of an enterprise should be offered to the private sector as a group, accounting for constitutional and political constraints. This requires estimating the potential gains from greater or lesser disintegration, and attempting to balance them against any costs due to losses in economies of scale and scope, and losses due to transaction costs incurred not only in the breakup of the enterprise, but also in the routine interactions across the fragmented units.

The determinants of (dis)integration (either vertical or horizontal) include technological economies, transactional economies, and market imperfections. Incentives for integration are variable proportions, price discrimination, rent extraction and barriers to entry, elimination of successive markups, and internalization of the choice of product diversity and of service externalities. Integrations tend to occur when externalities or interdependencies are difficult to capture contractually.

The neoclassical approach to integration is based on the existence of market power at either side of the input or intermediate product market. That market power induces a divergence between marginal value and marginal cost. Integration eliminates that divergence and increases profits (when long-term contracting is not feasible or allowed; otherwise the problem is moot). More broadly, vertical integration arises from the interplay between production technology (economies of scale and scope) and the process of exchange (the need for coordination, incentives, and transaction costs). Other arguments for integration are uncertainty in the supply of the upstream product, the shifting of risk in the presence of stochastic availability of the input, tax evasion and price controls, the effort to foreclose entry or to avoid foreclosure, and the need to acquire information when markets for information are incomplete.

A departure from neoclassical thought is the "specific assets" approach. The argument is applicable when a vertical relation requires either party to invest in specific assets. Then the possibility of opportunistic behavior arises. In that case there will be a reluctance (less than optimal) to invest in specific assets unless protective governance structures, such as joint ownership or integration, occur. Outside contracting, allowing for the investment of some amount of specific assets, may become inefficient if demand, technology, or information change suddenly. Contractual problems are particularly severe when informational asymmetries are large.

The market test for the existence of many of the conditions listed above is obviously not applicable to public enterprises, which by law are usually restricted in their options. The fact that they are or are not integrated need not be consistent with economic principles. To evaluate the validity of any particular vertical or horizontal integration in a state-owned sector requires an analysis of the specific enterprise and of the environment in which it operates. Specific factors that need to be considered include the nature and strength of the economies of scale and scope, availability of substitute products and services, existing capital stocks, level and rules of employment, pricing and other forms of regulation, and the structure of financial liabilities.

Limits to Integration

The benefits to be gained from integration are limited by coordination, monitoring, and incentive problems associated with joint control, which increase with the size of the enterprise, and by potential market foreclosures to competitors that are not vertically integrated. The problems often outweigh the benefits and are reflected in shortages and surpluses, idleness and bottlenecks, and failure to provide the desirable quality and variety of services. Usually they result in budget deficits and economic losses. Aside from possible gains through economies of scale and scope, the strongest arguments in favor of integration are often stated within the context of the transaction cost paradigm. This paradigm argues that because it is difficult to negotiate reliably for inputs or services across autonomous agents, to achieve efficiency, direct control must be exercised over the production of goods or services. However, the transaction cost paradigm often fails to account for incentive problems, and presumes that selfish humans will become selfless. Moreover, the transaction cost paradigm can be bypassed by using transfer prices for resources exchanged across units, mimicking a market system, and by strengthening the incentives, such as assigning a share of residual (profit) rights to unit managers.

In addition, the organizational diseconomies of scale are well documented (see, for example,

Arrow 1974 on the effects of size on efficiency; Geanakoplos and Milgrom 1985 on the limits to the ability of individuals to process information; Quian 1990 on the costs of monitoring subordinates and the resulting inadequate effort levels; and McAfee and McMillan 1990 on the costs of hierarchies). Those diseconomies and competitive pressures have induced firms in modern market economies to become less hierarchical. For example, in the United States firms have been selling off some of their activities, and work once done in-house is often subcontracted. Companies are being reorganized, reducing the layers of management and moving decisionmaking down the hierarchy. Likewise, in Japan firms have reduced the number of levels of middle management.[6]

Moreover, in the absence of competition, firms or managers are not easily induced to pursue economic welfare. Aside from efficiency losses due to monopoly, when firms (or managers) do not have residual rights, they have little incentive to produce goods or services efficiently. Those two factors—competition and claims to residual rights (incentives)—are essential for the proper functioning of any enterprise and, by aggregation, any market. Both factors need to be present to reap efficiency gains. Competition without incentives accomplishes little, because no benefits accrue to the individual units. And incentives without competition likely lead to inefficient monopoly rents. Often both factors are absent, particularly competition, because the enterprises are state-owned monopolies. Successful restructuring should ensure the presence of both factors. Moreover, the resulting units are forced to rely on prices to make decisions about allocation. Then market and transfer prices and self-interest can allow the system to be well coordinated without centralized planning.

The presence of fixed and sunk costs often limit the degree of effective competition in a sector. Fixed costs are present because infrastructure, such as tracks, lines, networks and pipelines, must be in place before the service can be provided. Because it is often inefficient to duplicate the network infrastructure, or because coordination costs are too high, natural monopoly cost conditions exist. Therefore, the use and pricing of those elements need to be regulated. However, effective competition can be induced in other segments or activities without losing economies of scale, and those opportunities ought to be considered in any restructuring program.

Care should be exercised to prevent market foreclosure, which is a commercial practice that reduces the buyer's access to a supplier (upstream foreclosure), or limits the supplier's access to a buyer (downstream foreclosure). The exclusion of trading partners or the reduction of competition among these partners may serve to exploit monopoly power. For example, marginal cost in a network industry is typically well below average cost, so that the price needed to extract full rents will appear (to customers, vertically linked firms, and antitrust authorities) to be very high and an overt abuse of monopoly power. Foreclosure can achieve the desired goal much more subtly (Carlton 1983). Horizontal breakups might limit the chance of market foreclosures. The University of Chicago leverage theory on foreclosure, which argues that the presence of a monopoly in one link of the vertical chain renders competition in other parts of the chain irrelevant and thus creates no incentive to foreclose, has been challenged both conceptually and empirically (Posner 1976; Salinger 1988; Hart and Tirole 1990; Ordover, Saloner, and Salop 1990; Kleit 1989; and Grimm, Winston, and Evans 1992).

Breaking appropriate segments of the enterprise into several similar units engaged in equivalent activities can also provide information that would otherwise not be available for evaluating performance. It provides a basis for assessing competence and for setting incentives, based on relative performance, across those units. An important efficiency component is imbedded in that form of incentive setting, which dissipates the ill effects of risk factors common to all similar units.

Finally, the horizontal breakup of an enterprise can provide for an effective and less costly alternative to direct regulation. If competition is induced, the need to regulate dissipates. Not coincidentally, competition is often labeled the great regulator. Because the resulting (multiple) units have more than one alternative for transactions,

purchases, or sales, a market and competition can develop and the units can be forced to rely on prices to make decisions concerning allocation.

When considering whether to partition the enterprise into a number of separate firms, a key element to bear in mind is that the relationship between the units selling and producing services and the units actually producing necessary inputs for those services must be as transparent as they would be if the units were two different companies operating in a market setting. This entails allowing the business units ample management and decisionmaking autonomy and at the same time making them financially accountable. A unit or profit center should be thought of as a small firm managed by an entrepreneur.

The positive evidence on the use of profit units is overwhelming. According to a study by the U.S.-based Financial Executives Foundation (1991),

> Nearly all major U.S. corporations have segmented their enterprises into business units in order to hold a subordinate manager accountable for the performance of each line of business. They have extensively used rewards to "turn on" their profit center managers, motivating them to initiate actions that will result in high performance both for the profit centers and for the firm as a whole. Just as ownership of assets is a primary source of power in a society built on the concept of private property, so physical custody of resources is a primary source of authority in a centralized firm; ...for nearly two-thirds of profits managers, the size of their annual bonus is determined by a defined formula rather than by reliance on a potentially subjective judgment by their superiors. More surprisingly, for nearly half of those managers, their bonuses were determined solely by the financial performance of their profits centers.

Moreover, the pseudo market induced by the operations of the business units can usually provide coordination more efficiently than the pure centralized structure can. When properly designed, profit centers—combined with meaningful compensation schemes and autonomy to control pricing and costs—are a powerful mechanism to induce rational economic behavior.[7]

An example of appropriate horizontal/vertical disintegration is the power and hydrocarbons sectors. In principle, no economic argument clearly dictates either state ownership or a monolithic structure for the sector. However, in developing countries a single, integrated, state-owned enterprise often runs the sector. The stated reasons, when articulated, tend to be of a sociopolitical nature. With rare exceptions, the size of those companies often exhausts two or three times whatever economies of scale are evident in the activities at each stage, such as exploration, production, refining, distribution, foreign trade, and marketing of oil and natural gas. The efficiency gains in breaking up a monopoly enterprise into a number of smaller firms can be significant. The classical example is the breakup of Standard Oil in the United States in the early twentieth century. Contrary to claims of the parent company, negligible economies of scale were lost in the breakup, while the efficiency gained from increased competition was significant. Perhaps in the near future there will be another case to draw lessons from, because Pemex may be restructured into a number of smaller autonomous companies, albeit state-owned and with a monopoly in some segments. Additional evidence, in a different sector, is provided by the positive experience of the breakup of AT&T, which increased both producer and consumer surplus and improved overall welfare.

Accordingly, the restructuring process should (a) identify the various business units according to production or market segment; (b) assess the extent of the economies of scale existing at each stage of the production or service process to identify where effective competition is feasible; (c) restructure the company into a set of profit units that are clearly delimited and whose financial results can be measured; (d) assess the potential for market foreclosures and economic consequences; (e) decentralize management so that responsibility is clearly limited and not diffused; (f) implement an incentive scheme based on those financial results, on a per-unit basis, and allow each firm to claim residual rights; and (g) allow for new (private) entrants to have access to existing services and infrastructure. Each of those units produces specific goods or services that can be sold or assigned either to other parties inside and outside the company, applying market prices where available or feasible, or to other profit centers or business units within the company, applying prices agreed to by contractual negotiation or transfer prices. Transfer prices are usually determined through negotiations between profit center managers, just as they would be negotiated between an independent buyer and a seller. However, that process is not entirely free of problems because, as reported in the study by the Financial Executives Foundation, interdivisional squabbles over transfer prices are frequent and sometimes bitter.

TRANSFER PRICING

Transfer prices are the prices that different units within an enterprise charge other units, and are required in order to determine profitability across units. This is particularly relevant when vertical separation leaves some units with monopoly power over some intermediate products. In the case of railroads, an example would be the price charged for use of the road bed if a single unit "owned" and maintained the bed and leased access to other units "owning" rolling stock. It should not include costs plus normal profit because that would provide the firm with no reason to economize on costs. Here, pricing is complex because of economies of scale and lack of competition. In other cases, such as the price that refineries are charged for crude oil, opportunity cost measures are readily available. In other cases, transfer prices have to be decided through negotiations among the profit center managers. So an element of the transaction cost paradigm needs to be resolved. The transfer pricing problem has to be defined in terms of strategy, which is an agency problem, rather than in terms of profit maximization.[8]

A by-product of the multiple unit approach may help to resolve the conceptual puzzle of transfer prices, because multiple "using" units that buy and sell can create a de facto market for the intermediate goods. Moreover, the restructuring options and private sector access, prescribed to promote competition, are distinctly less onerous than common maximum-rate regulation, which mandates burdensome and unwieldy evidence on "stand-alone costs" over large portions of rail systems to determine whether rates are reasonable. Where competition is not feasible, a Ramsey-pricing approach, where prices are linked to demand elasticities, is appropriate. Moreover, Ramsey prices under optimal reimbursement rules can be computed from publicly available data and require no knowledge of the firm's cost function.[9]

INCENTIVES

Incentives, of course, are at the core of achieving any potential gains from organizational restructuring, because the critical issue is to induce financial discipline, competition, and productivity gains for the individual units and for the sector as a whole. Breaking down the enterprise into profit centers and separate units provides an infrastructure for competitive behavior, but incentives based on residual rights or a share of profits need to be assigned to the units. That is an issue of concern because in many countries employees of state enterprises are subject to fairly rigid and uniform salary scales. Principal-agent theory is one means of addressing this issue.

The theory of agency is concerned with the incentive problem in enterprises where the decisionmakers do not bear a major share of the income effects of their decisions, which is the standard case in state-owned enterprises. Theory suggests that the agency costs resulting from that separation of ownership and management can be limited by the existence of three markets: the capital market, the market for corporate control, and the managerial labor market. In the absence of those markets, agency costs increase. That is generally the case for state-owned firms where the absence of a market for corporate control and the existence of weak capital markets undercut the managerial incentive system. Therefore,

setting incentive schemes that link performance with compensation is crucial for the success of any restructuring.[10]

The process of restructuring, while not resolving that issue, can generate a richer set of information with which to implement better incentive schemes. It can also facilitate the undertaking of monitoring and financial controls. A number of compensation schemes and contractual forms effectively address the issue of incentives in principal-agent relations (see, for example, Lazear and Rosen 1981; Nalebuff and Stigiltz 1983; Bhattacharya and Guasch 1988; Tirole 1986; and Holmstrom and Tirole 1987). First, there is absolute performance-based compensation. Although attractive in principle, such compensation tends to induce little (below optimal) risk taking. Second, there is relative performance-based compensation. If there is enough information, relative performance-based compensation is likely to dominate absolute performance-based compensation, because it automatically controls for risks that are common to all participants. Third, there is the contract plan system, which retains public ownership and management but institutes tighter financial controls. Assets are leased, giving residual claims of the proceeds to the individuals involved in the productive activity. However, this approach is subject to possible distortions regarding long-term investment.

Finally, there is leasing to private agents part of the activities of the enterprise (such as secondary, marginal, or service activities) through private management contracts. This form of compensation could be practical and operational as a start. By leasing productive units, residual claims on the performance of the enterprise are retained by the productive agents, thus generating the right set of incentives, although ownership is retained by the state. Then, if desirable at some later time, outright sale of the productive unit could be considered. In that case, favorable terms for the purchase should be provided to the lessee, to avoid decapitalization or to induce efficient levels of investment. Insofar as doubts exist regarding the length of the contractual relationship and ownership of the added capital stock, efficient levels of investment are not attained in this scheme. Three connected issues need to be considered under this scheme: how to determine the value of the lease, how to distribute the residual profit, and how to handle claims of unfairness when employees of highly profitable units benefit more than employees of marginally profitable ones. Generally, open bidding for the right to carry out those activities and for residual rights can efficiently address these concerns. The resulting differences in lease contracts across activities would equilibrate the expected structural differences in profitability.

Although the case for organizational restructuring is substantial, there are limits to what it can achieve. The evidence on the performance of state-owned enterprises is quite clear. Although a small number perform rather well, the vast majority do not perform as well as most private enterprises, when the comparison is made using a number of efficiency measures. An issue in those comparisons is how to separate the effects of ownership from the effects of competition. In principle, breaking the enterprise into a number of units or profit centers—some similar, and some different—will quite likely foster competition within units of the government-monopolized sector. But even then, the efficiency gains relative to those to be secured through privatization are likely to be smaller. That structure is akin to management contracts, and their experience has often been quite disappointing (World Bank 1985). Moreover, if financial discipline cannot be induced, if severe penalties cannot be credibly imposed or enforced, or if performance is not properly remunerated, the distribution of payoffs facing the units is truncated at the lower level, but not at the upper level, creating strong incentives for excessive risk-taking strategies that increase the upper end of the range of profits.

PRIVATE SECTOR ACCESS

To the extent constitutionally feasible, participation of the private sector should be favored in corporate governance, and in the creation of incentives and competition. Private sector participation wholly or in segments of the operation can be effected through the direct competitive

sale of assets, the provision of outright access, free entry, competitive concessions, or more involved contractual arrangements, according to the nature of the activity. When the activity is such that the private operators have to depend on or compete with the state-owned enterprise for access to a service, inputs, or placement of output, activities incompatible with efficiency can arise, such as favoritism and opportunistic behavior by the state-owned enterprise. This possibility can be reduced by horizontal restructuring (if more than one unit of the state-owned enterprise provides the service), or by regulation. Likewise, private sector firms that have exclusive rights to a segment of the operations ought to be subject to regulatory oversight. Private sector participation is attractive because most state-owned enterprises are undercapitalized. Often the enterprise does not have the financial resources to update capital equipment or to fund needed expansion, nor does the government have the resources to provide the financing needed for such tasks. That is often the case in most developing countries in state sectors, such as railways, airlines, electricity, telecommunications, roads, water, and hydrocarbons.

The extent of private sector participation in both the number and segment of operations open to the private sector will affect the design of an effective horizontal/vertical restructuring of the state-owned enterprise. With private sector participation, there is an extensive and competitive interaction between any residual state firm and private firms, with the state firm having leverage or monopoly power in some transactions or rights. That conflict of interest might undermine efficiency. Thus, a regulatory agency should be established that is independent of the state-owned enterprise and has jurisdiction over prices for noncompetitive segments and access fees, the granting of licenses, concessions, and new investments, and the resolution of conflicts (prior to entering the court system). The issue is whether the quasi-monopolist should be free to negotiate transfer or access prices to be paid by customers and competitors, or whether the regulatory agency should prevent market foreclosures and, more generally, regulate a "fair transfer and access price." The answer clearly depends on the degree of contestability of the operation. In the absence of contestability there is a need for regulation.

SEQUENCING

Privatization shifts the government's role from being a direct operator and provider of infrastructure services to being a regulator of private utilities. However, few agencies in Latin America have completed this transition. Often privatization has preceded the creation of regulatory agencies and the development of a regulatory agenda. And when regulatory agencies have been created, they have often been staffed with former employees of the state-owned companies or ministries, who were ill-prepared to handle their new responsibilities and were oriented toward control. Many of the agencies have not clearly defined what their role should and should not be, or developed the core expertise to handle the new issues. Chile's approach to privatization of electricity and telecommunications was to restructure the industries first and to privatize later. The restructuring process included price adjustment, and was more successful in the electricity sector than in the telecommunications sector. Reform of the electricity sector started in 1978 and was implemented in a 1982 law. Privatization followed gradually throughout the 1980s. While in 1978 there were only two integrated companies, today there are twenty-one distribution companies and eleven generating companies in addition to the two integrated companies. By the time the system was finally privatized, the technical staffs of the operating companies were well acquainted with the regulatory system's workings, and the system had a financial history. Gradual privatization assured private investors that Chile's rather complex regulatory framework was indeed reliable.

During privatization of the electricity sector in Argentina everything was done simultaneously. The creation of Servicios Electricos Gran Buenos Aires (SEGBA) coincided with passage of an electricity law that restructured the sector's regulatory framework. In telecommunications, privatization was clearly the first step, while design of a regulatory framework came afterward. Although prices were adjusted prior to privatization, this adjustment was done exclusively to satisfy investors' profitability requirements rather than to bring prices closer to long-run costs or to reduce cross-subsidization.

In Jamaica, regulatory reform was introduced a year before the telecommunications sector was privatized. Regulatory reform started with the creation of Telecommunications of Jamaica (TOJ), a joint venture between Cable and Wireless (the minority shareholder, with 49 percent of Jamintel, the international operator) and the government (the majority shareholder of JTC, the local operator). Each partner contributed its holdings in Jamintel and JTC to the venture. When the joint venture was created, the partners designed a shareholders' agreement specifying the nature of the future regulatory regime. This agreement was similar to the regulatory regime that was stipulated in the licenses given to TOJ. While the regulatory regime was clearly negotiated ahead of time with the understanding of the operating companies, the cross-subsidies in the tariff structure were left untouched.

MINIMUM INVESTMENT POLICIES

Because privatization creates a naturally adversarial relationship between the government and the firm, a utility cannot be counted on to blindly follow the government's wishes. Instead, incentives are needed to encourage investment and cost savings, and to improve quality. In particular, when prices (including initial connection charges) are high and no competitive threats are introduced, the price can be close to the monopoly level. In such a case, the privatized firm may not have strong incentives to invest unless demand is growing rapidly. This is the rationale for the minimum investment levels observed in several privatization cases.

Minimum investment levels have several implications. First, private investors take these minimum investment levels into account at bidding time and adjust their payments accordingly. Second, and more important, if minimum investment levels are too high, the incentives for administrative expropriation increase, requiring even further restraints on administrative discretion. In other words, binding minimum investment levels require further safeguards, which are naturally costly, particularly in terms of regulatory flexibility and price-setting options. Unless minimum investment levels have no effect on the incentives for administrative opportunism, there will be a tradeoff between regulatory flexibility and minimum investments. Third, minimum investment levels can be considered an implicit subsidy ex post privatization, and may violate antidumping provisions. Often, firms being privatized are assigned to competitive bidders under criteria based not only on the highest price, but also as a function of the investment program the firm promises to carry out. Bidders will offer to buy the firm at prices that allow them to expect a competitive rate of return on equity. There is no reason to assume that they will earn excess profits ex ante. This is independent of the type of competitive sale used, whether stock flotation or a trade sale to a strategic investor. As a result, the buyer has no unfair advantage.

However, whenever the investment commitment is enforceable and higher than the investment level that would otherwise have been chosen, the firm is expected to have a higher share of the relevant market than it otherwise would have. In that sense, there is "unfair" competition, because other firms elsewhere cannot sell as much as they otherwise would have been able to sell. In that case, the purchase price paid to government is lower than it would have been if there had been no investment commitment. Such a low purchase price is equivalent to a subsidy. The "new" antidumping rules account for and can penalize such actions.[11] Likewise, the new rules also target subsidies provided prior to privatization. The issue is whether a government subsidy paid prior to privatization, but not through the choice of criteria for the sale or afterward, leads to unfair competition. If the subsidy paid prior to privatization resulted in the construction of production capacity that would not have been economical in the absence of such a subsidy, there would be unfair competition, as in the previous case. Again the buyer of the company would not have an excessive level of profit, because such profit would be eliminated under a competitive sale. It may be difficult to demonstrate that a previous subsidy resulted in "excess" capacity. For example, if the firm previously suffered from negative effective protection (excluding the subsidy), the subsidy would not have led to excessive investment. Or if the firm was inefficient, it might not have constructed excessively. If there was an "unjustified" subsidy, then given the "new" antidumping ruling, the buyers of the company would expect the imposition of countervailing duties following privatization. In the sales price they would discount such expected duties and thus offset their impact. Only an order to close the excess capacity would undo the subsidy effects. Ideally, subsidies should be granted directly to users. That often requires significant administrative capacity; thus a transfer to the provider is a second best. See table 10.3 for structure in Chile and Colombia.

Further, in private markets, troubled companies may receive new capital or obtain write-offs from lenders, sometimes as a result of bankruptcy protection. Would this also constitute an "unfair subsidy"? If we assume that it does not, then one would need to show that the previous government subsidy was different from similar cash infusions into private companies. To argue this, one would presumably need to apply a "prudence" standard similar in spirit to that in utility rate reviews. To make the case for countervailing duties, one would have to argue that a prudent private owner would not have obtained a similar capital infusion or debt relief from the parent company or its lenders. Private company bailouts may ultimately be supported by the government, if the government rescues the lenders involved in the company bailout. In that sense, many forms of explicit or implicit deposit insurance may be grounds for imposing countervailing duties. Equivalently, sales of companies that had benefited from debt write-offs or refinancing, such as those granted by Continental Illinois prior to its bailout, should be punished with countervailing duties. The question also arises of how far back one should go in arguing that subsidies were granted at some time in history.

Table 10.3 Comparison of Public Service Subsidy Schemes in Chile and Colombia

	Chile (water)	Colombia (electricity)
Type	Direct subsidy to operator	85% cross-subsidies 15% direct subsidies
Level	Covers 40%–85% of low consumption Aim to keep bills below 5% of income Total cost of scheme is $12 million	50% on average to residential users (65% on average to low-income users) Total value of subsidies $640 million
Eligibility	Multiple criteria: Regional income, wealth, family size, price Triennial reviews of eligibility	Zone of residence (classified by socioeconomic class)
Experience	All eligible urban households covered Successful replacement of cross-subsidies	Recent legislation aims to reduce levels (maximum 20% for high-income users) Problematic

Latin American countries have had mixed experience with minimum investment policies. Minimum investment requirements have either appeared nonbinding (in Mexico and Venezuela) or have been the source of extreme regulatory conflicts. Consider the case of telecommunications privatization in Argentina. Table 10.4 shows that the two operating companies fell just short of minimum investment plans in 1991, while in 1992 and 1993 they exceeded investment requirements by 100 percent. Telecommunications enterprises in Chile, Mexico, and Venezuela also have significantly exceeded minimum investment requirements. In those cases, minimum investment levels had no implications for regulatory design. That, however, was not the experience of the water sector in Buenos Aires,

Argentina, or in Jamaica during the JPUC period. In Argentina the failure of the privatized water company in Buenos Aires to comply with the investment commitments is inducing a major regulatory/contractual crisis. The minimum investment levels stipulated in Jamaica in the late 1960s and early 1970s were at the core of the conflict between the utility company and the JPUC.[12]

The JPUC began operations at the same time that JTC's new majority shareholder, the Continental Telephone Company, took over the company's management. As mentioned previously, the government imposed several financial and developmental obligations on the transfer of shares from T&GT to Continental Telephone, among them (a) the refinancing of a fifteen-year, $11.5 million World Bank loan to a twenty-five-year

Table 10.4 Investment Levels of Telefónica and Telecom in Argentina, 1991–93

Company and type of investment	1991	1992	1993
Telefónica			
Network investment (millions of U.S. dollars)	$208.6	$615.2	$549.2[a]
Lines in service added (fiscal year ending September 30, unaudited)	66,176	276,364	—
Lines in service to be added per calendar year			
Seven-year exclusivity	70,000	105,000	154,000
Ten-year exclusivity	91,000	137,000	200,000
Telecom			
Network investment (millions of U.S. dollars)	$132.0	$609.0	$771.4[a]
Lines in service added (fiscal year ending September 30, unaudited)	50,809		221,941
Lines in service to be added per calendar year			
Seven-year exclusivity	60,000	90,000	135,000
Ten-year exclusivity	79,000	117,000	175,000

a. Company estimates.
— Not available.
Source: Hill and Abdalla 1993, table 9.

loan at rates not to exceed the New York prime rate by 0.5 percent; (b) a $5 million government loan to JTC made under similar conditions (the loan was to be redeemed by selling JTC shares to the public); (c) reduction of Continental Telephone's ownership share in JTC to 20 percent by January 1971; and most important, (d) expeditious completion of JTC's J$13 million development plan within three to three-and-a-half years. The development plan had specific quantitative goals for the expansion of service.

In 1968, under Continental Telephone's ownership, JTC began to change its forecasted investment and revenue needs.[13] As table 10.5 shows, by 1970 JTC had already fulfilled its investment expenditure obligations. The JPUC, however, questioned the actual extent of JTC's investments. Although the number of main lines grew slowly, this growth was accompanied by increases in fixed assets (JTC claimed that it was investing to replace obsolete and poorly maintained facilities, rather than to increase nominal capacity; see *The Gleaner*, June 9, 1971). In the wake of its disagreements with the JPUC, JTC halted its investment program in July 1971. A series of conflicts with the JPUC over rate increases and capacity additions ended with the government takeover of the company in 1975.

The Jamaican case illustrates how minimum investment mandates can increase contracting costs if the basic regulatory engineering is relatively weak. Compare the performance of JTC under the JPUC with the performance after privatization in 1988. The 1988 privatization arrangement included no minimum investment requirements. Nevertheless, TOJ invested rapidly, doubling the value of its fixed assets in four years

while increasing the number of main lines in service by 38 percent during the same period. Minimum investment requirements did not expand the network in the 1970s, and were irrelevant to the improvements of the late 1980s.

In summary, the restructuring and unbundling of a sector prior to privatization ought to be seen as a major part of having an impact on, and a golden opportunity to impact, the performance and efficiency of the sector, through changes in market structure. This applies to most sectors—telecommunications, electricity, rail, ports, etc. The potential gains often outweigh the associated losses on transaction costs, and on economies of scope and scale. Increased competition, decreased opportunities and incentives for market foreclosures, and increased welfare are the payoffs of a well-designed restructuring program. Technological innovations are making the arguments for vertical and horizontal "karate" disintegration even more convincing. Such opportunities to shape market structure rarely occur. While there are mechanisms to influence structure, after privatization they are often costlier and time consuming. The evidence to date from countries that have restructured and unbundled sectors prior to privatization confirms the desirability of doing so.

NOTES

1. In Latin America, privatization of infrastructure accounted for more than 40 percent of total proceeds from privatization between 1988 and 1992, and telecommunications was the most active sector. Foreign investment in the privatization of infrastructure accounted for 56 percent of the total. However, outside Latin America and Asia, privatization of infrastructure has so far had a limited impact (World Bank 1994).

Table 10.5 Jamaica Telephone Company's Investments, 1970–91

Type of investment	1970	1971	1972	1973	1974	1975	1987	1988	1989	1990	1991
Investment (thousands of current Jamaican dollars)	21,191	3,255	5,889	15,678	12,348	13,294	—	—	—	—	—
Additions to main lines	558	373	1,496	888	4,490	4,405	3,574	5,032	3,469	4,779	16,223
Real fixed assets (millions of 1991 Jamaican dollars)	777.5	772.0	805.0	939.4	1,000.0	1,045.8	1,483	1,600	1,512	2,090	2,858

— Not available.
Source: Spiller and Sampson 1993.

2. Although if the demand is elastic, value-added revenues may increase substantially if prices are reduced. This seems to have been the case in Jamaica and the United Kingdom.

3. For a review of (dis)integration issues, see Katz 1989; Jacquemin and Slade 1986; Tirole 1988; and Williamson 1979, 1981. Regarding agency theory, see Grossman and Hart 1983, 1986; Holmstrom and Tirole 1989; Milgrom 1986; and Fama 1980. For relative performance assessment issues, see Lazear and Rosen 1980; Nalebuff and Stiglitz 1983; and Bhattacharya and Guasch 1988.

4. In the U.K. vertical separation of the rail sector has focused on three activities—tracks, signals, and service.

5. One of the issues to address is the degree of financial autonomy granted each unit within the monopolized, government-owned sector. A holding company arrangement, for example, may be used to regulate aggregate investment and constrain financial options, but also may provide financing at lower cost. In that regard, it is often claimed that one of the adverse effects of divestiture or restructuring is that it might raise the cost of capital for the divested or individually restructured units as a result of tighter financial controls. This may be a likely outcome, but it probably should be seen as a benefit or efficiency gain because the ex post capital costs would more closely reflect opportunity costs.

6. See, for example, *Business Week*, March 27, 1989; *The Economist,* October 14, 1989; *Far Eastern Economic Review*, August 17, 1989; and *New York Times*, September 24, 1989. McAfee and McMillan (1990) report that average output per firm in the United States fell 14 percent from 1980 to 1987, and that the number of persons employed in Fortune 500 industrial companies fell between the mid-1970s and the mid-1980s, both absolutely and relative to total manufacturing employment.

7. Among recent railway restructuring programs, profit centers have been used extensively, for example by railways in France, New Zealand, Spain, Sweden, and the United Kingdom. A more radical approach has been taken in Germany, Japan, and the United States, where restructuring has involved the institutional separation of the various enterprises among freight, intercity passengers, and suburban passengers.

8. The positive evidence on transfer pricing indicates that almost one-third of companies use only a full-cost basis for transfer prices, inducing perverse incentives in production, while the rest add a profit markup, for which there is no theoretical justification other than simplicity, that induces distortions in the downstream input mix.

9. This contrasts with Ramsey prices obtained in the conventional cost-of-service regulation model. Moreover, the cost-of-service regulation framework imposes a somewhat ad hoc budget constraint on the regulated firm.

10. A good incentive system has to account for the objectives of the agent. For example, regulated firms often avoid (efficient) peak-load pricing to justify higher investments in capacity, which presumably brings them higher rents. In addition, uniform pricing reduces the stakes that consumer groups have in regulatory decisions, and thus reduces the extent of their lobbying and the risk of regulatory capture. That knowledge ought to be used in setting and shaping the regulatory and compensation constraints. Other distortions can appear whenever there are multiple jurisdictions and conflicting objectives among principals. That is often the case when the enterprise is under both state and federal jurisdictions.

11. We are grateful to Michael Klein for pointing out this implication.

12. The JPUC determined that JTC was reneging on its investment plan and refused to grant a rate increase. The JTC meanwhile claimed that due to deterioration of the outside plant, its investment needs were much higher than expected at the time of ownership transfer. (See chapter 3.)

13. Immediately after taking over JTC, Continental Telephone revised its expansion plan upward to J$25 million. In 1969 the plan was increased further to J$42.2 million because of the poor quality of the outside plant.

11

REFORM AND REGULATION
IN THE POWER SECTOR

SINCE THE EARLY 1990S most developing and developed countries have restructured their energy sectors. The major motivation for restructuring has been to improve sector performance and to compensate for the lack of public sources of financing for much-needed physical investment. However, in the late 1970s and 1980s, the expansion programs of the power sector in many countries began to lose steam. First, tariff policies caused a reduction in funds available for investment in the sector. Second, both government and sector finances deteriorated as fuel prices escalated, economic growth fell dramatically or stagnated, inflation levels peaked, and local currency depreciation and rising interest rates increased the cost of external borrowing and imports.

Sector financing relied increasingly on government contributions; the financial resources of governments were strained, especially by heavy foreign debt burdens, high or hyperinflation, unstable currencies and, ultimately, in many cases, by the loss of international creditworthiness and restrictions on additional borrowing from external sources.

Since the 1980s, growing economies have fueled dramatic increases in energy demand, and electric power sector expansion needs have become very great. For example, new power supply requirements for six Asian countries—China, India, Indonesia, Malaysia, the Philippines, and Thailand—are estimated to be between 25 gigawatts and 30 gigawatts per year. For ten other Asian countries, estimated new (generation-transmission-distribution) capacity between 1994 and 2004 is estimated to be 290 gigawatts, requiring investments of about US$35 billion per year. And in Latin America, 40 gigawatts of new generating capacity will be needed during 1995–2000, requiring investments of about US$15 billion per year.

The need to improve operations and financial performance while making massive new investments in the power sector is the result of the accumulated effect of inadequate tariff levels and ineffective investment strategies (which are now being corrected). Efforts to allocate resources to meet these needs, however, are handicapped by the pressures faced by the financially-strapped governments to fund basic socioeconomic programs and obtain financing for critical nonpower infrastructure projects. Thus, significant private capital investment will be required by power sectors in developing countries.

Performance of the sector under the traditional, fully integrated state firm has been disappointing. In addition, the common fiscal austerity measures implemented to secure economic stability have reduced the state's ability to finance investment requirements, and increased the need to shift investment responsibilities for sector expansion and development away from the government to free resources for socioeconomic programs considered less attractive to private investors. Part of the blame for the disappointing performance (financial, quality, and coverage) of the sector has been the inherently weak and vulnerable incentive structure of state enterprises, lack of competitive forces, distorted pricing, and extensive subsidies. Recognition that the structure was not sustainable—that it hampered the growth of economic activity and impacted the competitiveness of domestically produced products, essential for success in the new export-led development strategy—has been the driving force behind the reforms in most developing countries.

Reform has taken place at three levels: ownership, structure, and regulation. Ownership reform has taken place through (a) privatization or concession to the private sector of former state enterprises (fully or in parts) in the areas of generation, transmission, and distribution; and (b) elimination of entry restrictions on private sector operators participating in the various segments of the energy sector, particularly generation. As a result, significant new private sector entry has taken place, mostly in generation activities. Structure reform has focused on shaping the energy market, both horizontal and vertical. The principle has been that the traditional, integrated firm is not efficient and, most importantly, that full integration is no longer justified by economic principles. Therefore, the reform drive has focused on isolating the components in the pro-

ductive process that embody significant economies of scale, or natural monopoly, and opening the rest of them to entry and market competition. In the electricity sector, supply, billing, customer service, and bulk purchase of electricity are potentially competitive, as is generation. The "wires" businesses—high-voltage transmission and low-voltage distribution—are natural monopolies. Pooling (operation of the market) and dispatch are also considered natural monopolies, although some believe that these two are potentially competitive through decentralized contract trading. That often involved (a) the breakup of the integrated firm not only along the three stages of production, but breaking (and privatizing) the generation component into separate firms; the thinking has been that vertical integration does not compensate for the benefits arising from competition; (b) the transmission component should be kept in government hands or should be concessioned to private sector operators, since it displays significant economies of scale; (c) there should be competitive concessioning or privatizing of the (segmented) distribution to private sector operators; and (d) cross-ownership restrictions should be established horizontally across generator operators and vertically across the three components of the production cycle.

For example, in Chile, the two main companies, Chilectra and ENDESA, were broken up—Chilectra into a generation and two distribution companies, and ENDESA into a generation and a transmission company, several regional distribution companies, and several companies for the new generation of projects. In Argentina the three main companies were broken up as follows: SEGBA into three distribution companies and several generation companies, Hidronor into several hydro companies, and AyE into transmission companies and generation companies. In Bolivia, for generation companies, there is a limit of 35 percent of market share; for distribution companies, generation cannot exceed 15 percent of peak demand of the distribution company; and transmission companies cannot operate in generation and distribution. This appears to be the sector structure pattern in LAC countries.

That is, to avoid abuses of dominant positions, generating companies have a limit on their market share, and to avoid market foreclosure, generating companies are prevented from participating in transmission and distribution operations. This process is what has been labeled the deregulation of the energy sector.

Regulatory reform has focused mostly on restrictions on prices, quality of service, and other actions by operators of the transmission and distribution segments of the cycle. The principle has been that in those segments where entry is not economically feasible as a result of significant economies of scale, restrictions on pricing and quality of service have to be imposed to deter monopolistic behavior and market foreclosure. Those segments are transmission, distribution, and system operator. Segments that need neither regulation nor separation are generation, energy supply (direct or by means of wholesalers), invoicing, and metering. Consequently, by and large, the pricing in the generating segment, spot markets, and bulk power markets, where there are no significant economies of scale, has been left to market forces and free entry, with perhaps some rules on the functioning of pools and bilateral contracts with large end-users. The trend in pricing regulation in the other two segments appears to be competition for the market through competitive concessioning bidding, and average cost pricing for transmission and price-cap regulation in the distribution segment, but with the principle, in the latter, of working toward end-consumer deregulation. Finally, two segments of the sector where the need for regulation is arguable are spot market operator and forward or futures market operator. As a result of the ongoing transformation of institutional arrangements in the power sector, various new structures have appeared, with a notable number featuring unbundled or separated generation, transmission (central dispatch), and/or distribution activities. In some cases, and in a period of transition, vertically integrated utilities may continue to operate, often alongside independent generators and distribution-only companies, for example, but with separate accounts required for each area of business activity.

Reforms and Private Participation

Several Latin American countries have legislated power sector reforms to improve operating performance, to reduce the financial burden imposed on government resources by the need to expand the sector, and to enable private participation. Latin America's regional reform movement has gained momentum because the Chilean and Argentine experiences with power sector reform have validated the expectation that operational efficiency can improve, and adequate levels of operating and investment resources can be raised, if the appropriate legal framework and financing mechanisms are developed to permit private participation.

As of 1996, fifteen LAC countries in addition to Argentina and Chile have made or initiated changes in the way in which business is done in the power sector. These countries are Belize, Bolivia, Colombia, Costa Rica, the Dominican Republic, Ecuador, El Salvador, Guatemala, Jamaica, Mexico, Panama, Peru, Trinidad and Tobago, Uruguay, and Venezuela. Most of these countries have sought to implement or approve legislation that changes the power sector's structure, ownership, regulatory, and pricing bases. Brazil, Honduras, and Nicaragua are grappling with major reform issues as well, but the policy direction in these countries has not yet been articulated, and efforts are too preliminary to be able to clearly identify possible outcomes.[1]

Approaches to reform differ depending on each country's industry structure and regulatory framework. Some countries, including Argentina, Chile, Colombia, El Salvador, Norway, Peru, and the United Kingdom have opted to separate and allow private ownership or concessioning of generation, transmission, and distribution functions. They have sought to establish a highly competitive generating subsector by using contracts between generators and consumers or distributors to establish market prices for electricity at the bulk level. Price regulation is reserved for open access transmission and distribution grids and for retail tariffs for "captive" consumers. Some countries, such as the U.K., still reserve residual regulation in generation along the lines of a global price cap. Other countries, such as Costa Rica, Jamaica, and the United States, have so far opted for limited competition in generation. Independent power producers supply the operator of the monopoly grid with bulk power by means of competitive bidding or contract, or through a pool arrangement.

Several steps have commonly facilitated the restructuring process in Latin America and the Caribbean:

1. *Cultivating the support of utility management, staff, and unions* is a major consideration in implementing power sector reform policies. This support has been sought through inducements such as employee stock options; improved career and salary tracks based on job performance; and training, retirement, and compensation programs.

2. *Corporatizing*, or allowing management to run an enterprise on a profit-oriented basis rather than attempting to achieve socioeconomic policy objectives, can be an effective means (if privatization is not politically feasible) of removing the political agenda from decisionmaking in state-owned enterprises. While privatization should be the salient choice, corporatization prepares government-owned companies to compete in the marketplace and facilitates the transition to private ownership. Furthermore, corporatizing before privatization can demonstrate a company's competitiveness and provide a better basis for evaluating its sales value.

3. Restructuring the power sector's existing utility monopoly by *functionally and geographically breaking down integrated power companies* into separate generating, transmission, and distribution entities is a means to ensure competition in power generation, to allocate costs for each level of service provided, and to make each function more responsive to its customers' requirements.

4. Countries that have undertaken utility restructuring have determined that a transparent, commercially-oriented *regulatory regime for the sector must be codified in law* to attract private investors. Electricity reform laws generally indicate authorities or agencies responsible for policymaking, rulemaking, tariff setting, quality control, planning and data col-lection, issuance of concessions, and technical operating guidelines.

5. *Establishing a regulatory authority with functional and budgetary independence* is necessary in order to implement, oversee, and enforce a reformed sector. Functional independence is achieved through the selection process for regulators, support by high-level professional staff, adequate compensation, and autonomous budget authority, all of which insulate the regulatory body from political pressures exerted by the central government or regulated industries.

6. *New pricing systems* should be introduced that aim to encourage efficiency in plant investment and operations by relying on competitive market forces for pricing electricity at the generation level, and on regulation for setting prices for the electricity transmission and distribution of electricity and for access to the grid terms. These pricing schemes vary depending on the degree of vertical and horizontal disintegration of the power sector structure and on the price-setting tradition in each country.

7. Although countries aspire to recover the costs of electricity through economic-based pricing, *subsidization* of low-income consumers is still accepted as necessary for equity and income distribution goals. Remaining subsidies, however, must be transparent and directly measurable (cross-subsidies have, for the most part, been removed with the breakdown of vertically integrated utility structures).

Post-Reform and Privatization Evaluation

The outcome of power sector reform efforts to date can be evaluated using the following criteria:

1. *Competition.* Most countries have increased or are expected to increase the number of entities participating in the electricity sector. The exception is Norway, where mergers to achieve more competitive positions in the sector have reduced the overall number of participants. In Argentina, Bolivia, Chile, Colombia, Peru, and the U.K. considerable deconcentration of the sector has occurred as the number of generators and distribution utilities has increased significantly. The trend is to induce competition in generation

by allowing its pricing by market forces. Competition in transmission and distribution is to be secured by competing for the market through competitive bidding for the concession.

2. *Private Sector Ownership.* Privatization of electricity generation capacity transmission and distribution assets increased considerably in Argentina, Chile, Bolivia, Peru, and the U.K. In Norway a small portion of commercialization functions are privately owned. Colombia, El Salvador, Guatemala, and Jamaica are still in the initial planning and implementation stages, so it is too soon to evaluate the degree of private sector ownership or involvement in the electricity sector.

3. *Degree of Deregulation.* In Argentina, Bolivia, Chile, Norway, Peru, and the U.K. the generating subsector is or will be self-regulating, with basic concessions and operating standards the main requirements that generators must meet. Regulation in these countries focuses on transmission and distribution operations, which are commonly considered natural monopolies. Regulation of these subsectors aims at providing substitutes for market-based competition through the use of efficiency models, pricing, and access policies for power transport, and competition for the larger consumer market. In Norway and the U.K., commercialization activities require a license, but pricing for the end-consumer is determined by market forces. In other countries, retail distribution tariffs remain regulated, but the overall tariff structure varies substantially in some cases. Regarding the pricing of large users, the trend is to allow bilateral contracts to coexist with pool structures. In Argentina, contracts between individual generators and distributors or large users use a market-based pricing system, as does Peru in those areas where competition exists. Chile, Colombia, Norway, the U.K., and the U.S. also allow large-scale customers to negotiate with utilities, while Costa Rica and Jamaica primarily use formulas. Table 11.1 provides detailed descriptions of these systems.

4. *Autonomy of Regulatory Entity.* It remains to be seen how efforts to set up independent regulatory authorities will succeed. Although structurally separate, regulatory entities are frequently supported through government budgets, rely on ministerial support for policy proposals, and lack sufficient in-house technical and staffing capability to fulfill their mandates. This threatens their political independence.

5. *Antitrust Regimes and Arbitration Mechanisms.* To safeguard the power sectors' newfound ability to compete, countries that have already implemented sector reforms rely on their regulatory entity or a previously established antimonopoly commission to handle disputes between buyers and sellers over price and quality of service or charges of anticompetitive behavior. Antitrust enforcement is critical for behavior control to deter agreements, abuses of dominant position, and market foreclosures to potential competitors. Despite judicial reforms, doubts about the integrity of judicial systems persist, and a modern antitrust regime is lacking in many countries. Although the industrialized countries generally have well-established antitrust laws and oversight authorities to deal with anticompetitive and monopoly issues, the legal basis related to power sector issues has often had to be modified or extended.

6. *Impact on Electricity Rates and Service Quality.* As private sector participation in the power sector grows, the impact on ratepayers will become measurable as trends in retail and wholesale tariffs and in service quality (reliability of the power supply system, coverage, etc.) become observable after an initial adjustment period. Downward pressure on rates is expected in all the countries that have undertaken reform. Privatization is also expected to result in higher levels of electric service coverage (in Colombia, Jamaica, and Peru) and enhanced service quality for customers. In the U.K. there has been a slight decline in prices, and large profits for the private operators. A longer track record of qualitative variables is needed to assess performance and establish trends.

7. *Projected New Investment.* Governments that are encouraging private participation in the power sector are concerned that investment will not be undertaken as needed to build new capacity to cover growing consumer demand. Some governments (Chile, Colombia, and Costa Rica) plan to remain involved in the planning and development of the sector due to concerns

Table 11.1 Basic Elements of Power Pricing System Reforms

Chile

Consumers requiring 2 MW or more can negotiate supply terms for bulk electricity with individual generators. Transfers with generators are priced according to the short-term marginal cost of energy plus a capacity charge and the cost of transmission losses to the delivery point. Bulk power prices to distribution entities include the system's 48-month, long-run marginal cost of generation, a peaking capacity charge, and transmission costs. Transmission tolls and tariffs include an access charge and entry and exit fees for the transfer of power between specific nodes. Retail rates are based on the price of power and energy taken at the node plus the value-added of the distribution service.

Argentina

Market-based pricing for firm power contracts between individual generators and distributors or large users; wholesale system spot prices for distributors or large users set by CAMESSA. Transmission tolls charged based on value of the service from entry to exit node, including a system access charge and an energy charge for amount of power transferred. Retail rates based on a federal formula based on node price for electricity taken by retailer, plus added value of distribution. Provincial utility tariffs determined by provincial regulators.

Peru

MgC-based prices for sales to distribution companies are set biannually for each busbar by CTE, based on 48-month forecasted demand, factoring in fuel costs, hydrology, etc. Retail rates based on busbar electricity price and aggregate value of distribution. Transmission tolls include a tariff for power transfers and a connection fee to cover total cost of transmission.

Colombia

Existing decrees permit IPPs to sell bulk power to large consumers and vertically integrated power utilities at negotiated prices; proposed legislation targets the introduction of deregulated bulk power prices between all generators and power purchasing distribution, commercialization, and nonregulated (2 MW or more) consumers. As a proxy for competition, the price to final consumers is the sum of the price paid for the electricity by the distribution company—including generation and distribution costs—plus the benchmark-based value added of distribution for an efficient enterprise model. The value added of distribution is calculated every four years; in the interim distribution companies can automatically adjust tariffs using approved formulas.

Costa Rica

ICE—the integrated power utility—proposes a purchase price to the IPPs (who then sell to the grid) using formulas established by the regulatory entity. The purchase price uses a basic price for energy and a capacity payment reflecting various technical and operating cost criteria for the entire system. The price for power sales considers the cost of providing power to the delivery point, plus a negotiated rate-of-return on investment costs and a risk factor.

Jamaica

Build-own-operate-type generators negotiate prices with the monopoly utility company. If the sector is restructured as currently proposed, it will become a regulated transmission-distribution company. Jamaica intends to compose retail prices by adding the costs of transmission and distribution services—including investment costs and a rate-of-return on capital—to generation prices.

Norway

Prices of firm bulk electricity delivered by the generators at a given point of the high voltage grid are freely negotiated between the generators and the distribution companies. The price for the latter is the sum of the negotiated purchase price plus the regulated transmission toll to be paid to the transmission company for wheeling the electricity from the generator delivery point to the distribution receiving point. Prices of bulk power transfers among and between generators and a power pool are driven by the marginal costs of power and energy on a spot-market basis. IPPs may sell to the grid or negotiate supply contracts with large consumers, commercialization entities, and retail customers. Retail prices for captive consumers are set through formulas, but technically all consumers can purchase electricity from any generator or supplier at negotiated prices. The information and metering systems needed for small end-users to take advantage of the deregulated supply market—normally through electricity brokers or traders—are being provided through local electricity suppliers.

United Kingdom

The prices of firm bulk electricity delivered by generators are negotiated as in Norway. Retail tariffs are subject to cap regulation that pegs prices to the "retail price index minus X" formula, where X is a factor intended to capture efficiency gains in the distribution side after considering demand growth and the supplier's capital investment requirements. Costs beyond the supplier's control (i.e., generating supply costs) are incorporated into a Y factor, which is simply passed on to ratepayers. Future U.K. reform will allow final consumers to obtain electricity and negotiate prices directly with generators through electricity traders and brokers who also arrange the electricity delivery.

United States

IPPs negotiate bulk power supply prices/contracts with vertically integrated utilities, or provide bulk power supplies to utilities through a competitive solicitation process. IPPs or utilities also supply distant bulk power markets under negotiated prices, wheeling the power through the transmission system of other utilities and paying negotiated tolls for the wheeling service. At the retail level, the U.S. employs rate-of-return regulation for electric power utilities, with about 210 investor-owned utilities providing between 75 and 80% of the generating capacity and end-customer service.

Source: Estache, Helou, and Rodriguez-Pardina 1995.

about the private sector's capacity or market-based motivation to back capacity-building projects. Other governments have declared they will not finance new projects (Argentina and Peru). Incentives to expand capacity through market pricing policy mechanisms are expected to be sufficient to promote expansion of the system. New entrants to the sector may compete for any project to expand the system through the bidding process, so that capacity will be added at the lowest possible cost. Yet this remains an issue because so far, as the Argentina and U.K. cases show, incentives to expand capacity through pricing policy mechanisms have not been sufficient.

REGULATION AND PRICING

In the generation segment the trend is to leave the pricing to market forces, with only general regulatory oversight of the working of the pool and of bilateral long-term contracts with major users. Free entry into that segment and coherent, well-enforced antitrust legislation then ought to suffice to guarantee competitive behavior. Regulation of the transmission segment should focus on average cost pricing and access terms and pricing, and providing incentives to efficiently expand the network, if needed. In distribution, the trend is toward price-cap regulation, eventually providing customers with a choice of supplier, and allowing for price flexibility by distributors. Price rigidities limit the potential for better service derived from greater competition, and discourage distribution companies from actively seeking the cheapest and/or more reliable source of energy in the wholesale market. The competitive concessioning of both transmission and distribution for the market should be the foundation on which to build efficient operation of those segments.

POOLS

The main task of the pool as an organization of all actors in the industry should be to make transparent rules for the pricing and allocation of generated power. In fact, an efficient pool creates the set of rules of engagement freely agreed to by all members. Conflict of interest among participants (generators pushing for higher prices and users pushing for lower prices, for example) is the mechanism by which fair rules are obtained. Yet governance of pools remains an issue. Regulatory supervision, through formal participation as a pool member or requiring the regulator's approval before a rule becomes effective, also has to be included to protect the public interest. Arrangements by which two or more utilities pool their resources to achieve savings date back to the 1960s. These pools, which were also used to minimize generation costs by utility trading among utilities, became the basis of the market in most restructuring processes. Going from a mechanism for cost savings through marginal trading (usually including a rule to allocate these savings) to a market in which all energy is traded among freely acting participants is a major step in the organization of the sector.

Pooling as a solution to competition over power transmission systems has by now been tried in several countries. Chile introduced a competitive power pool in 1978, when its system was still publicly owned. Least-cost dispatch continues to be on the basis of audited costs of power plants, not on continuous price bids by generators. Bidding thus takes place implicitly as costs are reset. The United Kingdom introduced a competitive bulk power market on the basis of half-hourly price bids in 1990. The price is determined by ranking the bids of each generator in the system (the price at which it will generate and the quantity it can generate at that price), and then by taking the highest bid needed to meet expected demand in every half-hour period (see figure 11.1). The U.K. pool is open to all participants in the market (very much as a club) in charge of making the rules (known as a pool and settlement agreement) by which the system is governed. Figure 11.2 illustrates the working of the pool in England and Wales. The regulator has the power to veto any rule that it deems to be against the public interest. Nonetheless, both Chile and the U.K. continue to suffer from high market concentration in the generation segment, and a lack of barriers against vertical integration.

Figure 11.1 The U.K. Pool (England and Wales)

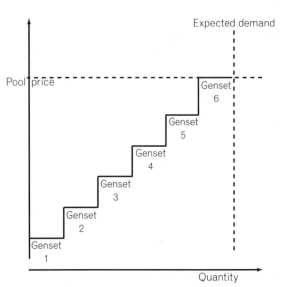

The price in the Pool in England and Wales is determined on the day ahead of operation. The price is determined by ranking the bids (the price at which it will generate and the quantity it can generate at that price) of each generating turbine (genset) in the system. The price is determined by taking the highest price bid needed to meet expected demand in every half-hour period in the day ahead, as shown in the diagram above. The Pool price is therefore determined for every half-hour period on a given day. See Figure 11.2 for sample prices for a full day's cycle in the U.K.

Note that this is a very simplified explanation of the mechanism. In practice, there are other elements to the price, and the bids are complex, nonlinear functions.

The Argentine system introduced in 1992 places strict limits on horizontal and vertical integration, thus effectively creating the conditions for workable competition. However, so far bids are based on audited cost data rather than on price bids by generators. Compañía Administradora del Mercado Mayorista Eléctrico Sociedad Anónima (CAMMESA) is the private Argentine company in charge of administering this wholesale market. Representation on the board is limited to representatives of sectoral, government-created associations of generators, distributors, large users, and transmitters, each holding 20 percent of the shares. The remaining 20 percent is in the hands of the federal government—represented by the Secretary of Energy—who has veto powers over all decisions. CAMMESA is in charge of the physical dispatch and settlements. The rules, however, are made by the Secretary of Energy under the power given by article 35 of the Electricity Act.

All the foregoing systems set transmission prices in an essentially administrative way; that is, they do not allow congestion prices to be established by a market. Norway, on the other hand, is trying to generate prices using the market. Its pool, which was originally limited to large gen-

Figure 11.2 U.K. Pool Prices 1/23/96

Source: Energy Settlements and Information Services Limited, 1/23/96.

erators, was open to all participants by the Electricity Law of 1991. Three markets (one weekly, one daily, and one spot) are operated by the pool, which is also in charge of coordinating the system. These markets have the function of short-term optimization because there is no central dispatch (long-term contracts are for physical energy and therefore determine dispatch). This structure allows generators to minimize costs through trade. These particular arrangements are the outcome of specific situations in each country. The design of the functions and responsibilities of the pool are a cornerstone of the restructuring process that deserves careful analysis.

Results from the introduction of competition are encouraging. In the U.K., productivity of generators has roughly doubled within four years, including for the remaining public nuclear power operator. Productivity in the distribution segment, which is not subject to competition, has also increased, but by only about 10 percent. In Argentina the switch to a private competitive system quickly resolved all of the urgent problems of power shortages and created temporary excess capacity, essentially because the new generating firms efficiently rehabilitated and operated existing plants.

While spot prices are essential to decentralize investment decisions and provide the correct signals for capacity expansion in generators, they can be subject to volatility, making payments and supply obligations unpredictable. To hedge price fluctuations in the spot market, generators and consumers can arrange long-term contracts for power delivery at agreed prices, enhancing efficiency and keeping the pool honest. The workings of long-term contracts are illustrated in box 11.1.

SOME LESSONS FROM POWER SECTOR REFORM IN ENGLAND AND WALES, SCOTLAND, THE U.S., CHILE, AND NORWAY

A study of power sector reforms in eight different power systems—Chile, three pools in the U.S. (FCG, N-EPOOL, and MAPP), Norway, England and Wales, and Scotland and Northern Ireland[2]—identifies alternative approaches to power sector

---

Box 11.1 Long-Term Contracts

In many commodity and financial markets buyers and sellers face a variable spot price. A wide variety of contracts exist to allow players to "hedge" the risk of buying and selling at a variable price. This box explains the basic mechanism in the simplest case.

In a long-term contract, a buyer and seller of a commodity agree to eliminate revenue risks caused by variations in the spot price through fixing a price at which they will contract. There is a variable spot price (SP) and the buyer and the seller decide to fix the price at which they will trade (CP).

In a simple long-term contract a constant quantity (q) is traded.

(1) If SP > CP then the seller pays $q \times (SP - CP)$ to the buyer.
(2) If SP < CP then the buyer pays $q \times (CP - SP)$ to the seller.
(3) If SP = CP then no money changes hands.

If both parties are buying and selling the amount q in the spot market then the financial flows in the financial contract will exactly offset the price variations in the spot market and essentially fix forward the price at which the trade is concluded.

---

reform and draws lessons from the experience to date in reforming power sectors in developing countries. In particular, the report considers alternative approaches to plant dispatch, least-cost expansion, allocation of risk, and transmission pricing (Webb, Carstairs, and Adamson 1996). The main results are as follows.

Dispatch   Dispatch can be based on actual costs, on indexed charges under long-term contracts, or, for larger systems, on competitive bids.

Role of Short-Term
Markets   Close attention is needed to industry structure to make competition in generation effective. The percentage of electricity traded through the spot market affects its short-term liquidity. A more liquid market increases

short-run efficiency and transparency. In systems with vertical integration, such as Scotland and parts of the U.S., typically there is only some limited trade at the margin, and in the absence of a spot market, a pricing mechanism needs to be established. In Chile and England and Wales, 100 percent of electricity is traded through a short-term market.

Contract-Based Dispatch

Northern Ireland provides the only case in which all dispatch is driven by long-term contracts. The four generating plants hold contracts with a central purchasing agency. These are two-part contracts, with capacity payments related to part availability, and energy payments related to the energy produced. The plant is dispatched on the basis of the energy charge.

There is evidence that the energy charge, which is based on a fuel index, has diverged from marginal operating costs. For one plant in Northern Ireland, the plant owner has succeeded in purchasing fuel significantly below the index rate, with consequent supranormal profits. Generators have thus earned high profits, but this has not led to suboptimal dispatch; the Northern Ireland system is small, has a large divergence in marginal operating costs, and the purchaser is obliged to buy only a small share of energy produced by the plant under a "must-take" provision in the contract. However, it is likely that the contract provision which allows for expert reexamination of the fuel indexes used will be called upon.

Cost-Based Dispatch

The N-EPOOL (U.S.) system is dispatched on the basis of actual marginal cost. Procedures were set up to audit and check cost and to calculate the opportunity cost of electricity generated by hydroelectricity.

Many of the cost-based systems are explicitly geared at short-term optimization, and require all pool members to have sufficient capacity to meet their own demand. In other cases, where a cost-based system also provides incentives for investment, there was some evidence that it could encourage "gaming," by which generators seek to increase their overall revenue.

Bid-Based Dispatch

In England and Wales and Norway, generators bid to be dispatched from a pool. For England and Wales the pool covers 100 percent of electricity traded, while for Norway the pool covers around 17 percent. In the England and Wales system generators bid for each half-hour of the following day. The Norwegian system, which is hydro dominated, is more complex. Norwegian generators place bids in a day-ahead market for five periods of each weekday, and for three on weekends. There is also a spot market (the "regulating market") where bids are made for the energy used to balance supply and demand. This too is run on a day-ahead basis.

In both pools there is evidence that generators had enjoyed some success in raising prices above levels that would have been expected in a fully competitive market. In part this appeared to be due to lack of competition in the generation market rather than inherent flaws in market design. In England and Wales, for example, existing thermal generation is split between only two companies. Norway's state-owned generator, Statkraft, appears to have been able to raise pool prices, at least temporarily, from nonfinancially viable levels.[3]

Investment

There are two approaches to investment, a planned approach and a "market-based" approach.

Planned Approach

A planned approach provides an obligation to ensure sufficient capacity through familiar exercises in planning least-cost expansion. Different entities can be made responsible for ensuring sufficient capacity is commissioned. In some U.S. pools this is the responsibility of distribution businesses that have a regional monopoly on supply. In Chile, investment is left to the private sector, but a central body can commission additional capacity—using public funds—if sufficient private investment is not forthcoming.

"Market-Based" System

Chile and England and Wales give incentives to invest through a capacity payment, in addition to the marginal cost-based pool price. Payment of the marginal operating cost of the marginal plant creates a rent for other plants—the difference between their marginal operating cost and their payment—which allows the nonmarginal plant to recoup capacity investments.

Bid-based approaches allow generators (including new entrants) flexibility in building new technologies, which may lower costs over the long term. In England and Wales—as discussed in the next section—generators reduce risks by entering long-term contracts with the regional electricity companies (RECs), which supply electricity to captive customers, and overinvestment may result. The Chilean approach places a cap on capacity payments, but relies on the accuracy of a central planning mechanism to determine new investment. In both approaches, underinvestment has not been the problem that critics feared.

Reserve Margins

A similar distinction can be made on the approach to reserve margins. A planning margin can be adopted and incorporated into the capacity requirements. Alternatively, schemes can attempt to attribute a market value to capacity. Capacity has a high value if it is scarce in relation to demand, so there is a higher probability of load shedding. Both the England and Wales system and the Chile system have developed payment systems that give generators cost signals on both the economic cost of load shedding and the probability of it being shed.

Risk Sharing

Increase in Risk

Investments in generation and transmission require major sunk costs in assets with long lifetimes and low resale values. After vertical separation, generators and distribution companies are exposed to risk on the bulk supply price. Market structures, and in particular a lack of retail competition, mean that the costs of risk reduction can be passed on to consumers. Given this, existing generators and independent power producers (IPPs) have invested against long-term contracts rather than pool-based revenues. There is evidence that this is changing as a greater degree of competition is introduced into electricity retailing. However, significantly, in the U.K. the majority of new investment in generation has been by the RECs diversifying into generation in an attempt to reduce their market exposure.

Role of Contracts

In all of the case studies, generators continued to make their investments on the basis of long-term contracts with distribution companies (which have captive consumers). Where 100 percent of electricity is traded through a pool, these contracts need to be reconciled with the pool pricing system. In England and Wales this is done through the use of a financial hedging contract known as a "contract for differences." This is a purely financial contract by which one or both parties can reduce their exposure to pool price fluctuations.[4]

Impact on Investment

There were no examples in the case studies where generators have made major investments on the basis of forecast spot payments from a pool. In part this may be because none of the case studies have yet introduced full competi-

tion at the retail level. There was evidence emerging from England and Wales of investments on the basis of revenues from the pool rather than long-term contracts. However, no plants have yet been built in England and Wales by independent generators where long-term contracts have not been signed with a REC.[5]

Transmission

Pricing Principles

An efficient tariff for transmission needs to reflect marginal costs—including marginal losses, the costs of transmission constraints, (that is, the cost of running a generation plant out of merit), and the operating and maintenance costs of the transmission wires.

Pricing Practice

Transmission pricing is poorly structured in most of the case studies, and none have transmission tariffs that reflect all the costs. The main cost of poor transmission pricing is poor locational signals for new generation, which would be particularly significant in countries where generation is expanding rapidly.

In the United States transmission charges have historically not been cost reflective. Existing charges have been made on a capacity basis, with lower charges for interruptible transactions. Often transmission charges have been included in the costs of purchased power. In some pools, utilities agreed to share their transmission systems, and have not charged each other for use of their transmission network. New regulation is currently leading to reform of transmission charges in the U.S.

In the England and Wales pool, congestion charges and losses (both energy related) are averaged into an "uplift" payment, which is added to the spot price. These costs are therefore averaged across all customers, which is not cost reflective. Most fixed costs are recovered through a system of zonal charges, which vary by location. These too have been criticized on cost-reflectiveness grounds. Norway and Chile make greater use of locational signals. Norwegian transmission charges include an energy fee based on estimated marginal losses. These are calculated for six regions and three tariff periods. Interestingly, in Chile the reform has gone even further; there the regulated price is set for each node of the network, taking into account the location of electricity generation and marginal losses.

Covering Fixed Costs

In all the countries studied, energy-related transmission charges yielded inadequate revenue. The case studies describe a number of alternative approaches to recovering fixed costs. All of the systems studied use some form of fixed charges (for example, fixed connection charges or capacity-based charges) to generate enough revenue to keep transmission operators financially viable.

A CASE STUDY: ARGENTINA'S POWER SECTOR REFORMS

In 1992 Argentina reorganized its power sector following generally acceptable guidelines and in a way that has met with great success. Transmission and distribution were considered public services and were sold as concessions. The standard contract requires the utilities to provide quality service to all users, maintain equipment, protect the environment, and ensure public safety. Tables 11.2 and 11.3 detail the bidding process, contract terms, and contract requirements for transmission and distribution utilities. Generation was restructured to create a market, so the primary requirement in that area is that generators accept the rules that govern the market. The quality and investment requirements for all three areas appear in table 11.4.

As mentioned earlier, the major institution responsible for Argentina's power sector is CAMMESA, a private company. Its primary responsibilities are to (a) manage the interconnection system, including maximizing safety and quality while minimizing wholesale prices on the hourly or spot market; (b) optimize use of capacity; and (c) supervise the term market and manage the technical implementation of contracts signed on that market. The government has a majority share in CAMMESA, while the four major organizations in the sector (generators, transporters, distributors, and large users) each have 20 percent of the residual. The regulatory institution is the National Entity for the Regulation of Electricity (ENRE), which is financed through fees, fines, and subsidies. ENRE is required to

- Enforce the regulatory framework
- Issue rules and regulations on safety, technical procedures, and service access and quality
- Prevent anticompetitive, monopolistic, discriminatory behavior
- Define the basis for the calculation of tariffs set in contracts
- Publish the general principles to ensure free access to services
- Determine the basis and criteria for the assignment of concessions
- Organize and implement the bidding, adjudication, and signing of contracts
- Organize public hearings
- Monitor respect of property rights, the environment, and public safety

Table 11.2 Transmission and Distribution Concession Contracts in Argentina

Bidding

- Two envelopes, where the first envelope is the technical one that specifies the requirements to be met by bidders and determines who is allowed to present the second envelope. It contains the share of actions to be subscribed by each cobidder; the specification of a single, unified local residence; proof of existence as legal entities; guarantee of $10 million for the offer; and project of implementation plan for contractual obligations.
- The second envelope contains the offer amount in cash and public bonds; bidders had to have assets of at least $300 million, and proven net wealth of no less than $200 million, which had not declined by more than 5 to 10% over the previous year.
- All bids must identify at least one but no more than two experienced operators.
- The economic offer had to be valid for at least 180 days as of the opening of the envelope, and at least $30 million would have to be paid in cash 3 days after selection of the winner; for public bonds the term is 90 days.
- The winner must pay the fees for the lawyers ($1.5 million each for transmission and distribution) and the financial consultants (who are paid 1% of the value of the deal only if there is a deal).

Terms of Contract

- Ninety-five-year concession for exclusivity in a zone, after which new bids will have to be made; proceeds of bid go to the incumbent who is also allowed to bid.
- The term can be extended for a period up to 10 years, to be determined by the regulatory entity (ENRE), which can also modify or suppress zonal exclusivity.
- The term is divided into management periods of 10 years (except for the first, which lasts 15 years).
- At the end of each management period, the ENRE organizes an international bidding to sell majority bundles of stock and sets the tariff regime for the following 5 years; the bidding conditions are similar to the original ones.
- The owner of the majority package—if the price offered by the incumbent is the highest—keeps the property. If he is outbid, the highest bidder has to pay the price bid to the incumbent, and becomes the new majority owner. An independent inspector nominated by ENRE will ensure the proper functioning of the company for one year before the end of the management period, and for the first year of the new management period.
- Failure to deliver obligations results in termination of the contract and fines of more than 20% of yearly income.

Source: Estache, Helou, and Rodriguez-Pardina 1995.

Table 11.3 Transmission and Distribution Contract Requirements in Argentina

Transmission	• Provide service to direct and indirect users • Respect quality norms spelled out in contract • Allow access transport capacity to any agent of the Wholesale Electric Market according to access rules • Invest in and maintain system and connections • Allow free access to installation, including other transporters interconnected • Provide all information and documents to ENRE and CAMESSA as required • Pay for the electricity required for its own consumption • Process on time and conform with request of increases in capacity • Comply with CAMESSA requirements as long as they do not put at risk their installations • Respect the environment • Promote rational use of energy • Guarantee public safety in the way equipment is installed • Ensure that their activities do not damage ecosystems • Promote rational use of energy • Comply with ENRE norms • Do not engage in discriminatory or anticompetitive activities.
Distribution	• Obligation of public service of distribution in the concession zone • Commit to specific quality levels • Respect the rights of users as specified in the contract • Satisfy the total demand for service, including demand for new services • Provide energy for public lighting • Provide electricity at 3x380/220V, 13kV, 2kV, 33kV, 132kV, 220kV, or any as agreed to with ENRE • Make the investment and maintenance required to achieve established quality requirements • Adopt the measures necessary to ensure provision and availability of electricity to meet demand • Increase capacity when needed to provide public service as required by ENRE • Allow third parties undiscriminated access to transport capacity if it does not impede capacity to deliver • Allow large users to rely on their networks in the conditions agreed upon in contract • Guarantee public safety.

Source: Estache, Helou, and Rodriguez-Pardina 1995.

Table 11.4 Quality and Investment Requirements for Argentina's Power Sector

Quality Requirements		
Generation	*Transmission*	*Distribution*
• Technically oriented regulation related to the functioning of the interconnected system • No performance standards to meet.	• Minimum quality standards on 2 aspects: (a) tension, and (b technical service (duration and frequency of outages) • Failures to meet quality standards are penalized through a detailed fine system; the proceeds of these fines go to the users who are victims of the quality gaps.	• Minimum quality standards covering (a) product (tension); (b) technical service (duration and frequency of outages); (c) commercial service (complaints by clients, time to get connection, bill estimates) • For measurement, two steps were defined with different goals: (a) during the first 36 months, measurement of medium tension; (b) as of 37th month, measurement of every user • Failures to meet quality standards are penalized through a detailed fine system; the proceeds go to the users who are victims of the gaps.

Investment Requirements		
Generation	*Transmission*	*Distribution*
• No control of investment by the public sector • Purely competitive regime with free entry and exit.	• No control of investment by the public sector, although investments over US$2 million need ENRE's approval and a public hearing • The concession implies only maintenance and operation of existing facilities plus minimum quality standards and maximum tariffs • The users have to pay for any expansion of the transport system • The abandonment of facilities has to be cleared with ENRE.	• No control of investment by the public sector, although investments over US$2 million need ENRE's approval and a public hearing • Investments are made by concessionaire • Only constraint is based on (a) obligation to meet all demands, (b) minimum quality standards, and (c) maximum tariffs • The abandonment of facilities has to be cleared with ENRE.

Source: Estache, Helou, and Rodriguez-Pardina 1995.

- Take to court relevant issues
- Impose sanctions
- Publish information and advise generators
- Issue an annual report and recommend actions when needed
- Collect information from transporters.

The tariff system, although somewhat complicated by the differing types of regulations that govern each area, holds true to basic regulatory principles. In the wholesale or spot market, generators use a uniform tariff at the point of delivery that is based on the economic costs of the system. All generators charge a single market price determined by the cost of the last unit called upon to generate electricity. The process to determine this price starts with an estimate of the hydroelectric production for the first three years, then in decreasing periods going down to one week, and the resulting generation has to be at minimum costs. The probability of system failure is calculated and the list of generators which will have to operate is established according to their marginal cost (specific consumption and fuel prices). On the basis of these factors, the hourly spot price for the wholesale market is determined by the cost of the fuels of the last unit in operation, after having ranked generators in decreasing order of efficiency. Capacity payments do not enter the spot price; they are made separately at a rate of $10 per megawatt per hour to all available generators. It is an administrated price set by the Secretary of Energy.

The transmission and distribution prices are more straightforward. They have to be designed to provide those transporters and distributors who are performing prudently and economically the opportunity to obtain sufficient revenue to cover reasonable operational costs, and provide a rate of return that is both related to the efficiency and effectiveness of the firm and is similar to an industry average of other risk-oriented activities, or at least comparable nationally and internationally. This implies that the utility must account for reasonable differences in costs existing between the various types of services, considering the form of delivery, the location, and any other relevant characteristic according to the regulatory entity. Finally, with the above constraints in mind, the tariff must guarantee the minimum reasonable cost to users compatible with the reliability of supply. For transporters, the price system[6] is expected to send users economic signals allowing three determinants to drive prices: the energy transported, the connection charge, and the transport capacity. The concessionaire then gets a stable tariff resulting from the expected average of the prices at the connection knots over the following five years. For the distributors, the price system[7] must identify the costs of acquiring electricity from the Mercado Eléctrico Mayorista Argentina (MEM). When large users (those with demand over 100 kilovolts) go directly to the wholesale market, their fee is uniform but has to include the cost of transport. Also as shown in box 11.2, there are effective ways to reduce energy "losses," which obviously impact on the profitability and prices of the distribution companies.

REFORM OF CHILE'S ELECTRICITY SECTOR

The conditions preceding the reforms of Chile's electricity sector include price controls, service rationing, overstaffing, and large deficits in the public electricity utilities.[8] The overall design of the reforms was fitted into a general attempt to deregulate, while maximizing fiscal revenue or minimizing revenue losses characterizing the first wave of privatization. Concentration of the con-

---

Box 11.2 Dealing with Losses in Argentina's Energy Sector

The problems of Edenor, Edesur, and Edelap, the three distribution companies representing 47 percent of Argentina's market, are poor condition, low productivity, and high levels of theft (Estache 1995). During the mid-1990s, for instance, customer "losses" in Edenor and Edesur amounted to 30 and 25 percent, respectively. Yet the companies are only allowed to pass about 11 percent of the losses to the consumers. To cut these losses, Edesur reduced technical and other losses (due, for example, to theft), employment, and overtime. Edesur cut employment from 7,417 in January 1992 to 4,677 in October 1994. Edenor cut employment from 6,368 to 3,759. The amount of overtime allowed was reduced from about forty hours per employee per month to about three to five hours.

Reducing theft was more complex, because doing so involved shantytowns and low-income areas where cutting off power was not viewed as acceptable by the local authorities. The solution was to negotiate a deal with the regional metropolitan area. Edenor and Edesur would place a medium-tension distribution network in those areas and connect only ten or so consumers with low-voltage lines and related transformers. The voltage in these medium-tension lines is too high for an illegal connection. Any illegal use of the low-voltage line will be easy to identify, because the transformer cannot process more than ten users. This places the burden on the entire community to solve the "illegal" problem.

The bills are paid to the concessionaire by the municipality that collects payments from the users. The outcome is obvious. Payment levels in low-income areas have reached 90 percent for Edesur and 50 percent for Edenor.

---

trol of former public companies was also considered an acceptable strategy at the time. Implementation of the reform took place in an environment in which competition was the main goal, but the philosophy of the first wave was still quite present, as will be shown. In fact, the restructuring of the sector was done in two stages. The first stage, between 1974 and 1979, was intended to adjust price to allow the public utilities to achieve self financing and to prepare the groundwork to allow private sector participation. The second stage, between 1979 and

1990, dealt with the main institutional changes discussed below, and with the restructuring of sector generation and transmission, which were separated from distribution. The two existing utilities, Endesa and Chilectra, were decentralized and regionalized. Endesa, the largest company, was divided into fourteen companies: six generation companies (Edelnor [with 240 MW of capacity], Endesa [1,832 MW], Colbún [490 MW], Pehuenche [585 MW], Pilmaiquen [35 MW], and Pullinque [49 MW]); six distribution companies (Emelari, Eliqsa, and Elecda combining 18,000 customers in the north, Esmelat [5,000 customers], Emec [143,000], and Emel [122,000]); and two companies combining generation and distribution (Edelaysen [15,000 customers], and Edelmag [35,000]). Chilectra was divided into three firms: a generating company, Chilgener with 756 MW capacity, and two distribution companies, Chilectra with 1,064,000 clients, and Chilquinta with 322,000 clients.

Privatization per se started in 1986 after introduction in 1982 of the regulatory framework described below. Most divestitures took place between 1986 and 1990—only two generation companies were left to be privatized by 1990, and both have since been privatized. This was done mainly through three mechanisms: sale of the smallest companies through public auctions, awarding the deal to the highest bidder; auction of share packages on the stock market for the largest companies; and sale of small packages of shares in the largest companies (popular capitalism).[9] A major footnote in the description of this restructuring is that Endesa was privatized jointly with its transmission system, which is the largest in the country. The main reason was that the transmission pricing rules had not yet been fully defined and, as shown below, this decision continues to haunt Chile's regulators. Since 1992, Chilean electricity companies have become major players in other privatizations in the region, evidence of the success of this privatization strategy. Chilean electricity companies are present in Argentina, Bolivia, and Peru, and have been actively diversifying their activities into other sectors, as well, such as real estate, water, telecommunications, and cable TV.

The Regulatory Framework

New electricity sector legislation was enacted in Chile in 1982. Its goal is to maximize social welfare by creating conditions in which the energy system can develop and operate efficiently. The law distinguishes three separate segments in the electrical sector: generation, transmission, and distribution. It spells out the main rules for the regulation of these three segments, but also for the allocation of licenses, pricing, investment, quality, and safety. It also makes clear the obligations and rights of all players involved: the service providers as well as the government institutions.

The role of government players. There are three key government institutions. Their creation preceded the actual privatization. The National Energy Commission (NEC) was established in 1978 to develop medium- and long-term guidelines for the sector independently of the potential influence of the large utilities in the sector. The NEC is managed by a board of directors composed of seven ministers, and has an executive secretariat, technical staff, and resources to recruit special advisors as needed. The NEC proposes policies to be implemented through laws, decree, or ministerial resolutions; sets tariffs; and grants licenses to public service distributors for specific areas.

The electricity law also resulted in the creation of an Economic Load Dispatch Center (ELDC) to coordinate the activities of all generating companies; in other words, it is essentially a generators' pool. The ELDC's specific objectives are to achieve the minimum total operating cost for the system as a whole and to ensure equitable market access to all generating companies. Each member of an ELDC is entitled to make direct supply contracts with clients for amounts up to its available firm capacity. Any shortfall has to be purchased from other members at the marginal cost of peak power, equal to the annual cost of increasing by 1 kilowatt installed capacity during peak demand periods.[10] The ELDC plans daily production and computes the instantaneous marginal energy cost by considering the variable costs of generating units currently operating, independently of any existing direct supply contracts. The programming of electricity generation, disregarding supply contracts, gives rise to energy transfers between generators, and these are priced at the systemic instantaneous marginal energy cost.

The last key government actor of the sector is the Superintendency of Electricity and Fuels, created in 1985. It was set up as an administrative branch of the Ministry of Economics. It supervises compliance with the law and regulations and monitors the quality of services. Finally, it deals with users' and suppliers' complaints and prepares the information for the price-setting process carried out by the NEC.

The multiplicity of these institutional actors and their lack of independence may be the most salient feature of these institutional arrangements. The only apparent form of independence in the whole system stems from the role of the antitrust commission. The regional Preventive Commissions (Comisiones Preventivas) and the Resolutive Commission (Comisión Resolutiva) seem to have the required independence, but as explained earlier, may lack the required technical skills to make the most of their independence.

Price regulation. Competition is the norm in generation and in the supply to large users (those requiring more than 2 megawatts of power, and it could be argued that this is too large a number to be able to achieve effective competition). Distribution (to small users) and transmission are considered natural monopolies. The price system consists, thus, of regulated charges for small customers and freely negotiated rates for large customers whose maximum power demand exceeds 2 megawatts. The regulated rates must be within a 10 percent band of the average price of freely negotiated contracts. These contracts represent about 40 percent of total consumption.

The regulated price to final customers has two components: a node price, at which distributors buy energy from generating companies; and a distribution charge. The node price is equal to the sum of the marginal cost of energy, the marginal cost of peak power, and the marginal cost of transmission. It is thus designed to approximate long-run marginal costs. The Ministry of Economics, with technical support from

the NEC, is responsible for calculating node prices. Marginal costs do not fully cover total transmission costs. The law states that the difference is charged to generating firms according to their "area of influence." The law, however, is not explicit as to how to do this, and the charges end up being negotiated between the owner of the grid and the generators. This is a recurrent source of conflict because the owner of the grid is also one of the generators.

The distribution charge is recalculated every four years in a procedure that consists of determining the operating costs of an efficient firm and setting rates to provide a 10 percent real return on the replacement value of assets. These rates are then applied to existing companies to ensure that the industry average return on the replacement value of assets does not exceed 14 percent, or fall below 6 percent. If the actual average industry return falls outside this range, rates are adjusted to the nearest bound. The operating costs of an efficient firm and the replacement value of assets are obtained as a weighted average of estimates made by consultants hired by the industry and by the NEC, respectively, where the weight of the NEC estimate is two-thirds.

Competition and access rules. There are no limits on vertical or horizontal integration. To limit the risks implied by integration, competition to supply large users is allowed. A toll must be paid to the local distribution company, and this is a source of difficulties, as discussed in the next section.

The access rules are different for generation, transmission, and distribution. The law states that the use of property for the generation of electricity requires a concession. This implies that entry is free for thermal generation, while it is not free for hydro and geothermal generation. However, while some firms can operate without a license, most will want to have one since a license provides some exclusive rights. Licenses are obtained through an organized competitive process in which the NEC ranks projects according to costs. Each year it assesses the minimum cost expansion plan for the system and clears the conditions for entry. For transmission, entry is free. For distribution, concessions are needed for systems larger than 1,500 kilowatts. Licenses are granted for an indefinite period, but they can be withdrawn when service quality falls below the legal standard. It is possible for the service areas of two or more operators to overlap to further promote competition in the sector. (See figure 11.3 for the evolution of the price of electricity in Chile.)

Regulatory Pitfalls

Although the regulatory framework assumes competition in generation and supply to large users, there is a problem. Endesa, the dominant firm in the system, together with its affiliates, has 60 percent of installed capacity.[11] It also owns the transmission grid (which it manages through a subsidiary) and has links to 40 percent of the distribution sector through ENERSIS, an investment group that controls Endesa. But the concentration problem is a more generic one. The second generating firm, Chilgener, and the third one, Colbún, own 22 percent and 11 percent of installed capacity, respectively, which gives a Herfindahl Index for the three largest generators of 0.43.

This industry structure, combined with ambiguities in the regulatory framework, increases the risk for new firms that might be considering investing in the generating sector. For instance, the law is not sufficiently explicit about how transmission grid development costs should be allocated between generating companies. While criticism of Chile's transmission pricing policies is well known, and is a major threat to competition in the sector, a review of the behavior of Endesa by Paredes (1995) found no analytical evidence of monopoly pricing. However, some evidence was found of strategic behavior by Endesa in its negotiation of charges. Charges are negotiated between the owner of the grid and the generators, and lack of agreement leads to compulsory arbitration. By delaying its interactions and decisions with other generators, Endesa can favor its own generation companies. An illustration of this problem is provided by the recent attempt to privatize Colbún. Despite the government's efforts to guarantee a successful sale, including retaining the services of the investment bank Kleinwort-Benson, only one of the six firms on the short list made an offer for the company. Unofficially, some of the firms that refrained from making an offer made it known that the reasons were the ownership structure in the sector. While the law establishes a maximum response period, potential bidders know that Endesa will always have an incentive to use the entire period available because it

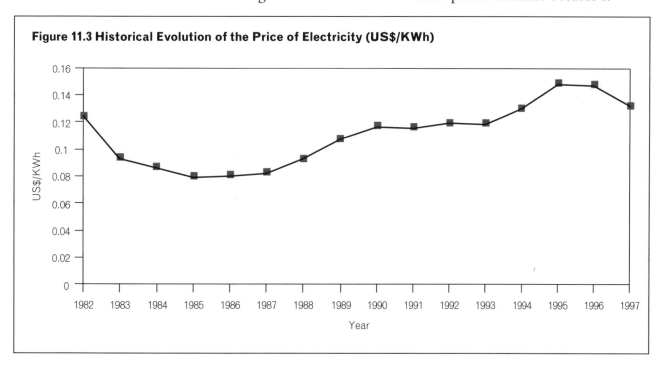

Figure 11.3 Historical Evolution of the Price of Electricity (US$/KWh)

improves the opportunities for business for its own companies.

Even more important, the dominant generating company owns the water rights on the most attractive future projects. Hence, by postponing the development of these projects it can obtain significant rents on its existing capacity. In fact, of the total nonconsuming water rights that have already been appropriated, only 13 percent are being used.[12] Endesa holds 60 percent of allocated nonconsuming water rights, of which it has developed 13 percent. Most of these rights belonged to Endesa prior to its privatization, when it was the only major hydroelectric generator, and it is safe to assume that they represent the most profitable investment opportunities. Moreover, Endesa also applied for additional nonconsuming water rights that would have given it 80 percent of all water rights in the country. However, the Preventive Commission has advised the agency in charge of the rights to refuse such requests unless they were requested for a specific project.

The import of natural gas from Argentina has already lowered entry barriers in the generating sector. Although gas transport has natural monopoly characteristics, ex ante competition between two consortia willing to build a pipeline to transport gas from Argentina, and anti-price-discrimination clauses drafted into the regulatory framework, have brought transport prices down to a competitive level.[13] In fact, to obtain financing, the consortia needed to have contracts signed with large customers, and this led to open competition for customers. The combined-cycle gas turbine electricity power plants that will be built close to demand centers, in conjunction with Colbún's decision to build a transmission line between its generating units and the main demand node, will diminish the impact of the transmission monopoly. Although a number of future power projects will involve combined-cycle gas turbines, and more stringent environmental rules will have to be satisfied in the construction of dams, hydroelectricity is still the most attractive option.

There are also problems in supplying unregulated customers located in the franchise areas of distribution firms, which in 1995 represented 23 percent of all sales to unregulated customers. Indeed, when a generator gains a free-price customer from a distribution firm, it has to negotiate with the latter a toll for using its electricity cables, in which the absence of agreement leads to arbitration. There is enough uncertainty in this procedure for some generating firms to desist in their attempt to supply such clients directly, because it is difficult for a firm to participate in the process of bidding to supply potential customers unless it knows how much it will have to pay in transmission costs. In addition, the distributors are generating firms' main customers, so taking clients from them is bound to be costly. For instance, a claim by Colbún against Chilectra brought before the antitrust agencies in September 1996 focused on this aspect. The lack of competition in supplying unregulated customers is also relevant for regulated customers, because the regulated node price has to be adjusted within a 10 percent band centered on the average of unregulated prices.

There are also significant problems in establishing electricity distribution value added. The fact that the costs of the simulated efficient firm are calculated as a weighted average of studies carried out by the NEC and the firms themselves, gives rise to obvious incentives for each party to bias the estimates. In the 1992 price-setting process, discrepancies in estimating distribution costs and the replacement value of assets in some cases exceeded 50 percent. A better solution would be for an arbitrator to decide which study, in his or her judgment, best reflects the costs of a model firm.

The Resolutive Commission was asked by the National Economic Prosecutor to rule on the vertical disintegration of the group of firms controlled by Enersis. In a June 1997 resolution the commission ruled against compulsory disintegration, but nevertheless issued a series of instructions in recognition of market imperfections in the electricity sector. First, it asked the government to introduce legal amendments to disambiguate the mechanisms for determining transmission and distribution charges. Second, it instructed distributors to, in the future, put their energy requirements out to tender among all generating firms to avoid suspicion of distribution companies favoring related generators, and with the aim of reducing costs to final consumers. Third, the commission resolved that, within a "prudent" time, the Endesa transmission subsidiary (TRANSELEC) should become a joint stock company operating exclusively in electricity transmission, thereby opening the company up for parties other than Enersis to participate in ownership. (See box 11.3 on the privatization of Endesa).

Interactions Between Sectoral Performance and Regulation

A series of situations has been identified which could affect the level of competition in electricity generation, and it is important to see how these situations have influenced sectoral performance. The sector has two anchor prices: the node price calculated by the National Energy Commission (NEC), and the spot price calculated by the Economic Load Dispatch Center (ELDC). Both institutions have incentives to make correct calculations. If the ELDC were to calculate the spot price incorrectly, this would affect generating firms which are net sellers of energy to the ELDC, and they could therefore exercise their power of veto, because decisions have to be unanimous within the ELDC, with any divergence arbitrated by the NEC. The mean node price in the period between the start of the ELDC-SIC system in May 1986, and September 1996, was 11.5 percent above the instantaneous marginal cost calculated by the ELDC. The reason is that ELDC's model is more exact than NEC's, which among other things shows that regulated prices are generally higher than necessary.

Despite the two anchor prices, barriers to entry in generation, due to the ownership structure of the sector and to regulatory ambiguities, might lead to high rates of return. In 1995 the mean return on capital among generating firms in the SIC was 14.1 percent. Given that these firms have other investments, the ratio between operating results and assets (fixed plus current) has also been calculated, giving an average prof-

---

Box 11.3 Privatizing an Electricity Monopoly: Chile's Endesa

The notion that generation, transmission, and distribution functions should be undertaken separately contests the current privatized structure of Endesa. Chile faced limited options for the privatization structure that could be applied to Endesa. The country's geography requires that most transmission lines be shared among generators, so a structure characterized by several completely vertically integrated firms, each serving well-defined territories, was not possible in Chile.

Two aspects related to the current structure of the market might eventually restrain the possibility of competition in the electric industry. First, Endesa, the main industry generator, was privatized with an important share in the generation market and most water rights. Chilean law states that to be granted a concession on water rights, the interested party must submit a development project to the firm holding the water rights. Since Endesa holds the water rights and therefore has a relatively low cost structure for development, it could delay the project or use the rights as an entry deterrent. Second, Endesa became a monopolist from the outset, because it was privatized with 100 percent of the transmission in the Interconnected Transmission System (ITS).

The second point is particularly significant because the distance between the hydrological plants and consumption centers makes transmission costs important in Chile. For example, while the proportion of transmission costs to the total cost of electricity in Spain and England is 4 percent and 7 percent, respectively, in Chile it is 25 percent. A main concern is that Endesa, in its capacity as sole owner of the transmission system, can either increase transmission costs for its generation competitors or give privileged access to its subsidiaries, hence limiting competition.

Source: Paredes 1994.

---

itability of 9.5 percent. This information would not seem to point to the existence of monopoly rents in the sector. However, this could change in the future.

There are problems in the regulation of electricity distribution companies. In 1995 the average rate of return for the industry as a whole was 30 percent, while average operating profits as a percentage of assets (fixed and current) were 20 percent. This is a high figure, especially considering that it is an underestimate because not all current assets are related to the main business. Such rates of profitability are far above those being earned by generating companies, which are subject to a greater degree of uncertainty because they do not have a secure market and they face periods of drought.[14]

Comparison with Argentina and the U.K.

Approaches to reform differ depending on a country's industry structure and regulatory framework. Some countries, including Argentina, Colombia, Norway, Peru, and the U.K., have opted for a sector with mostly separate generation, transmission, and distribution functions, allowing private ownership of these functions. These countries seek to establish a highly competitive generating subsector through the use of contracts between generators and consumers or distributors to establish market prices for electricity at the bulk level. Price regulation is reserved for open access transmission and distribution grids and for retail tariffs for "captive" consumers. Other countries, such as Costa Rica, Jamaica, and the United States, have so far opted for limited competition in generation. Independent power producers supply bulk power to a monopoly grid owner through a competitive bidding or contract process.

In Argentina there are thirty-five generating firms belonging to eight independent groups. The Herfindahl Index for the three largest firms is 0.15, which results in a highly competitive market, where large customers pay up to 30 percent less for electricity than their Chilean counterparts.[15] The price difference is partly explained by the location of gas fields in this country, but the situation should tend to become more equal as the pipeline bringing gas from Argentina comes on stream. In Argentina there is an independent body responsible for administering the sector (CAMMESA), owned jointly by the government and the associations of generators, distributors, transmission firms, and large-scale users.

Although the Argentine and Chilean price systems are similar in various ways, the Chilean system generators are paid the instantaneous marginal cost on regulated sales to distributors. Because distributors pay the seasonal price, equivalent to the node price in Chile, a stabilization fund has been set up to manage surpluses or deficits generated from revenues earned from sales to distributors and the instantaneous marginal cost payments made to generating firms. Differences produced during the season between the spot price and the seasonal price, calculated ex ante, have to be compensated in the following period through the price charged.

Another difference between the Argentine and Chilean price systems is that in the Argentine system distribution franchises, and the transmission concession, are granted for ninety-five years, divided into ten-year management periods (except for the first period which lasts fifteen years). At the start of each period, ENRE, the Argentine regulating entity, sets the tariff regime and calls for competitive bidding for the majority of the firm's shares. If the current holder submits the highest price, it retains ownership. Otherwise, the investor offering the highest bid obtains the concession and pays the current owner the asking price. This mechanism of periodic competition for the franchise is designed to give the incumbent incentives to maintain assets and invest when appropriate to do so.

A third difference between the Argentine and Chilean price systems is institutional. Argentina has a single sector-specific regulator managed by a commission of experts for transmission and distribution under federal responsibility.[16] This entails fewer coordination problems and also increases the accountability for decisions taken or not taken. The funding and staffing of the agency also provide some guarantee of independence, which may be of some relevance to the next wave of regulatory reforms in Chile.

In the United Kingdom, on the other hand, there are three main generating firms. At the beginning of 1996 the two main firms together held 45 percent of installed capacity.[17] The third firm, a thermonuclear plant, had more than 20 percent of capacity, which resulted in a Herfindahl Index for the three largest firms of less than 0.1. In the U.K., the big generating companies are not allowed to participate in either the transmission or distribution segments, while distribution firms can self-generate up to 15 percent of their sales. Transmission was initially left in the hands of the twelve regional distribution companies, which subsequently decided to hive off this segment of the business. (See box 11.4 for a brief history of electricity generation in the U.K.)

The rate system operating in the U.K. differs from the Chilean system in that the spot price (or "pool" price) is determined on the basis of the price offers made by firms per generation unit on a half-hourly basis, and these do not necessarily correspond to the variable costs of the generating plants. In addition, a large share of transactions is carried out at the spot price. The least maximum demand needed to be considered an unregulated customer is 100 kilowatts, and this regime will be extended to all customers in 1998. Several second-tier electricity suppliers

compete with the distribution companies for the provision of unregulated customers. These suppliers buy energy at the spot price from generators, pay transmission and distribution firms the respective tariffs, and then sell the energy at an unregulated price to final consumers. There is a price-cap system for transmission and distribution tolls.

The regulatory institutional arrangements in the U.K. are closer to the Argentine approach than to the Chilean approach. The main difference is that rather than being managed by a commission, the agency is managed by a single regulator. This is now being questioned in the U.K., where many are arguing in favor of a commission, as in the U.S. and Argentina.

In summary, the Argentine and U.K. systems are far less concentrated than the Chilean system, and, unlike the Chilean system, are not vertically integrated. Similarly, the spot price plays a greater

Box 11.4 Electricity Generation in the United Kingdom

The U.K. government's decision to create an effective duopoly in electricity generation resulted from a botched attempt to privatize the state's nuclear generation assets. At first, these were to be vested in the larger of the two companies, National Power, with a smaller company, PowerGen, to ensure that the larger company had sufficient market power to take on the liabilities associated with nuclear generation. At the last minute, however, the City, London's equivalent of Wall Street, balked at the open-ended liabilities involved in the sale of the nuclear assets, which forced the government to split the sector into three—two fossil fuel generators, one with approximately two-thirds of the fossil fuel plant and one with one-third of the market, and the nuclear assets in a state-owned nuclear company. Imports of power came from France and Scotland through interconnectors.

The substantial market power of the two fossil fuel generators created concerns from the outset of the market, and the regulator was constantly monitoring the market and producing reports concluding that market power was being exercised by the two dominant players. A series of negotiations led to a deal announced in February 1994 in which the generators would agree to sell or otherwise divest 6,000 megawatts (4,000 from National Power and 2,000 from PowerGen) of plant, and that they would voluntarily restrict their

bidding in the pool to meet a particular price target, in return for not being referred to the Monopolies and Mergers Commission (MMC). The voluntary price cap was due to be in place for two years, by which time the divestiture was to be completed.

New entrants, the forced divestiture of 6,000 megawatts of the two generators' plants, closure of redundant capacity, and the split-up and sale of the nuclear plant, means that there are substantially greater competitive pressures on the two dominant players than there were at the time of privatization. Indeed, the second of the two companies, PowerGen, is now smaller than Nuclear Electric (now called British Energy), and one of the regional electric companies, Eastern, will soon have substantial generating capacity both through purchases of the divested plant and from their own generation capacity. The structure is now likely to resemble an oligopoly, with four roughly equal-sized competitors and a number of fringe players.

The issues have moved on, however. National Power and PowerGen bid for two of the largest distributors in the country, and it is likely that the MMC will allow them to merge, despite the concerns of the electricity regulator. Vertical integration will now be the dominant issue in the market, with the three largest operators having both generation and distribution components.

role in Argentina and the U.K. than in Chile. In addition, in these countries the lowest maximum power demand to be considered an unregulated customer is less (1 megawatt in Argentina), and it is less difficult for generators to gain access to unregulated customers located in distributor franchise areas. Finally, both Argentina and the U.K. have managed to have a simpler institutional arrangement to ensure the regulation of the sector. While both have their problems, they have the advantage over the Chilean approach of having a smaller number of players and, hence, increased accountability for decisions.

Outstanding Challenges for Chile's Electricity Sector

One of the lessons from these experiences for Chile is that more needs to be done to ensure competition in the electricity sector. For example, to be considered an unregulated customer, companies or any other user must demand a certain level of power. One way to increase competition would be to substantially reduce the required power demand needed to be considered unregulated—to 100 kilowatts, for example. That would allow more power supply users to fall into the unregulated category and, thus, increase the potential for competition. A solution like that would considerably diminish the role of the state because, while the authority would still retain responsibility for setting transmission and distribution rates, it would play more of an intermediary role between trading firms and transmission and distribution companies. This increased competition would also provide better opportunities for overlapping concessions in electricity distribution to meet their purpose.[18]

A revision of the overall regulatory framework should also look into the interests of consumers. The regulators should be granted jurisdiction to set tariffs to ensure that consumers can share in the efficiency gains. This would require transmission and distribution tariffs to be based on more transparent, incentive-based formulas. The issues of pricing and terms of access and interconnection remain. The current structure favors the incumbent integrated firm and thus

does not facilitate competition. These approaches and the provision of equal access would in turn further promote competition, since this is the agenda for the next wave of privatization.

As for transmission, the lessons from the international experience are less promising. Argentine restructuring did separate transmission from generation and distribution, but its pricing rules are not as efficient as one would want, and fail to achieve dynamic efficiency. The main challenge for Chile is to decide whether it is worth going one more step in the direction of restructuring and keeping dispatch and transmission joint. The strengthening of the institutional capability to monitor behavior is at best a backup strategy. It is clear that the first, best strategy, which would involve restructuring Endesa, would be much more politically challenging.

REDEFINED ROLE OF GOVERNMENT

As a result of the sector changes, the trend in the new role of government is toward reduced and indirect participation, rather than the prior role of active intervention in the sector. In particular, the key issues pertain to

1. Policymaking: (a) establish sector development targets; (b) define (through legislation) the roles and jurisdictions of sector regulatory and oversight agencies; (c) manage public resources and issue rights of way or concessions according to legally established criteria and procedures; (d) formulate national electrification and subsidy programs; and (e) enact national environmental rules, standards, and enforcement provisions.
2. Planning functions, which may: (a) remain centralized; (b) be performed as an indicative or nonmandatory exercise; and (c) be totally left to market forces. In this scenario, the central dispatch entity, in which the government may or may not be active, normally continues to coordinate (*not* plan) generating capacity additions with grid-operating requirements. Distribution enterprises are usu-

ally required by law or through their concession contract to meet service demands within the concession area, although the means of achieving this requirement are left to the enterprise's management.

3. Establishing independent regulatory and oversight agencies by law to define, implement, and oversee: (a) entry and exit rules for sector participants and concessionaires; (b) equitable and transparent operating rules and pricing procedures, including access to the network; and (c) prevention of or correcting monopolistic practices in competitive market areas.

4. The state's commercial participation as an enterprise owner: (a) as before, though corporatization or internal restructuring of the enterprise might be pursued to adapt to the sector's new structure, operating rules, and/or competition for markets; and (b) often as the interconnection enterprise in a reformed sector to ensure fair and equal access to the grid.

5. Financial promoter or enabler for sector investments: (a) undertaking legal reforms of banking, investment, and monetary rules to open investment areas to more private domestic and foreign sector participants; (b) promoting domestic capital market expansion (through popular capitalism); (c) extending government guarantees where adequate legal/regulatory framework is lacking; and (d) taking an equity or other active investment role in new projects to attract or secure other financial sources for hydro, nuclear, or other targeted (types of) projects.

PENDING ISSUES

Despite the significant advances secured in the power sector, there are a number of issues that are still in need of attention. While great progress has been made in ownership and structure reform, regulatory reform has lagged behind

considerably. While appropriate legislation on regulation has often been enacted, the creation of the regulatory agency and the implementation of an appropriate pattern of enforcement still remain issues in many developing countries. The administrative capacity of those agencies is limited and their autonomy questionable. Most sector reforms have been too concerned with ownership changes and have failed to perform necessary structural or regulatory changes. It has been a common presumption that the power market functions like a tradable good market and has ignored the interconnection requirements and impossibility of storage. Several decisions have been based on the desire to facilitate the sale of existing assets, to the detriment of long-term sustainability. Nevertheless, in most countries, there has been vertical separation of generation, transmission, and distribution.

Governments tend to assume that all regulation can be handled through asset sales agreements, concession contracts, or detailed laws with little flexibility. This style ignores the 100 years or so of experience in the U.S., which indicates that the best regulatory procedure is to have strong, independent, regulatory commissions overseeing the sector and ensuring that all of the regulatory goals are met.

The power sector, in contrast to telecommunications, is not characterized by rapid technological change—normally only allowing capital recovery in a period roughly equal to the useful life of the assets (twenty to thirty years; more for hydropower)—and can be competitive, at most, in the generation segment of the sector and for the largest customers. As a result, consumer protection for prices and quality, and competition protection against collusion or other anticompetitive behavior, have generally taken a back seat to the protection that is offered to investors. The relative lack of attention to regulatory matters has resulted in unintended vertical reintegration, constraints on new entrants and, generally, moves toward the establishment of private monopolies. It has also resulted in an unclear demarcation between the policy functions of government and its regulatory functions. Finally, it has also led, in some cases, to a separation of the sector regulatory functions among several agencies, with the consequent lack of coordination or duplications.

Capture issues, by either government or operators, remain. There is still excessive politically motivated government interference in the regulatory process, directly or indirectly. The relevant ministries in many countries still retain inappropriate regulatory duties. In addition, very few countries have established clear and efficient principles for access (to the network) terms and pricing, a key element for a well-functioning decentralized power sector. The common principle of uniform pricing imposed on distributors is also a concern. It does not allow the distribution operators to respond to the competitive pressures of bilateral contracts of large users with generating companies, with the end result of diminished market share resulting in higher tariffs for the small users, since the fixed costs now must be spread across a smaller base. A weakness of the new structures is the limited incentives for investment in necessary network expansion. Finally, two other issues that remain unsatisfactorily addressed are the treatment of past unprofitable investments, sometimes forced; and the rules and timetable for the integration or access across different countries' networks.

Overall, in the power sector, the main lesson of privatization and regulatory reform could be summarized in three words: unbundling, decentralization, and competitiveness.

In creating a structural framework for the power sector, one of the major tensions is facilitating competition without sacrificing engineering efficiencies. Indeed, there is a need for structural reforms; there is also a need for deregulation, but it should be remembered that the objective of increased competition should ultimately be the provision of improved service to the public at decreased but efficient prices. Consequently, particular emphasis should be placed on a flexible structure that will allow for the development of multiple pools, for niche marketing, for alternative financial instruments, and for greater ease of entry by many different kinds of players. Only the basic issues should be regulated.

In that vein, countries should focus their regulations on access. Monopoly franchises need to be eliminated. Access to customers and public networks needs to be increased. And as the sector decentralizes, increased attention should be paid to instruments of interconnection of networks (here the technical aspects are more important than the economic) and the interconnection of players.

Other lessons that have emerged include the following:

- Decentralization works—not only in operations, but decentralized investments can work too (for example, Argentina, Chile, Peru, and the United Kingdom).
- Competition is important on both the supply side (as in Argentina, Chile, Norway, and the United Kingdom) and on the demand side (as in Chile, New Zealand, and Norway).
- There are economies of scale in transmission; however, as of yet no one has managed to create a system which organizes transmission optimally.
- Unbundling seems to be the consensus approach (Malaysia and many countries of the European Union are exceptions). Vertical disintegration can work (although it poses regulatory difficulties in both distribution and transmission); however, it is not enough. There is also a need to separate networks from the retail end (as in Bolivia, New Zealand, Norway, and Peru). In addition, interconnection of networks at both high and low voltage is important.
- New instruments need to be developed for both operations and financing. The system must not be too rigid. In restructuring the sector, success depends on working with the initial endowments and sector structure. Particular care should be taken in developing incentives for network expansion.
- It is essential to limit regulatory discretion. Credibility relies on decisions being made "above board." New Zealand, with its light regulatory approach or regulation by threat, proves an exception to this, but it is not an example other countries should try to follow.

NOTES

1. The remaining Latin American and Caribbean countries do not appear to be considering major sectoral changes, although several, for example, Barbados, Dominica, St. Lucia, and other Caribbean countries, are reviewing measures that would improve their regulatory regime or modify their rate procedures.

2. To obtain a copy of this study, including the system case studies, call (202)473-3613.

3. Statkraft announced a policy of not supplying below IINORE/kWh, and punishing "deviators" by momentarily flooding the market and pushing the market price down to zero.

4. By hedging actual pool revenues with a contract for differences (CfDs), generators assure themselves of a revenue stream to pay for the fixed costs of financing and maintaining the plant. Distributors, who buy electricity from the pool, use CfDs to minimize the risks that the price paid for electricity from the pool does not exceed the resale price.

5. The two major thermal generators have built new plants, but they possess a portfolio of contracts and other plants which allows them to hedge risks effectively.

6. This price system uses $RPI - X$ where X is set to zero initially, and with semiannual indexation to the U.S. price index, where the index used is 67 percent PPI and 33 percent CPI. Tariffs are set in U.S. dollars.

7. This price system uses $RPI - X + Y$. This represents the maximum price with total pass-through of the costs of energy in the wholesale market (Y), and indexation to the U.S. price index (X), where X is set to zero, initially. The index used is 67 percent PPI and 33 percent CPI, and the tariffs are set in U.S. dollars.

8. This section is adapted from Bitran, Estache, Guasch, and Serra 1998.

9. Privatization was also conducted through a very specific approach which involved giving shares as a way of returning the financial deposits users had to make per kilowatt of connected power.

10. The firm capacity of each producer is the maximum power which its generating units can contribute in the peak period of the system with a reliability exceeding 95 percent.

11. In 1995, the SIC system had an installed capacity of 4,084 megawatts, while the interconnected system in the north of the country (SNG) had an installed capacity of 1,120 megawatts.

12. The holder of a nonconsuming exploitation right has to restore the water to its natural course after use. Nonconsuming rights are mainly used for hydroelectric generation.

13. A recent ruling by the Preventive Commission in response to a query by the Superintendent of Electricity and Fuels put forward various conditions for awarding franchises for gas transport. These include (a) franchises should be awarded only to firms specializing exclusively in this activity, with no links to final customers, mainly electricity companies; (b) franchises should not be exclusive; and (c) gas transport should be subject to an open access requirement; that is, the services should be provided under nondiscriminatory conditions, and information on supply and conditions should be publicized.

14. Of course, the outcome also depends on elasticities.

15. This considers together the generating plants in which Enersis participates. The same is done for generating plants in which Chilgener participates. By considering grouped firms, concentration is overestimated because although Chilgener and Endesa participate in ownership of more than one plant, they do so with different partners and percentages.

16. Although Argentina has problems stemming from decentralization of the responsibility for regulation of distribution services, this aspect is not relevant to the debate in Chile at this time.

17. However, this percentage underestimates the real market power of the firms because 80 percent of the time the spot price corresponds to the supply price of a power plant belonging to one of these firms!

18. As Paredes (1995) suggests, if overall competition rules are not effective in the sector, overlapping concession areas impede taking advantage of economies of scale rather contribute to promoting competition.

12

NEW FRONTIERS IN REGULATION IN THE COMMUNICATIONS SECTOR: MANAGING AND REGULATING THE SPECTRUM

THE INCREASED DEMAND for wireless telephones, coupled with the increased demand for other wireless communications solutions (wireless Internet and local access networks [LANs], terrestrial and satellite television, to name a few), has resulted in a revolutionary increase in the demand for overall spectrum usage. This demand requires technological and regulatory solutions.

On the technological side, major innovations have increased the efficiency of spectrum bands currently in use, and have allowed bands which were hitherto unusable to be switched

from low-value uses (for example, outside broadcast relays) to high-value uses (for example, wireless local access). As usual, however, regulatory changes follow technology and demand changes by a substantial lag. The increased technological flexibility has exposed the ossified structure of spectrum regulation, requiring regulatory changes if ever-increasing welfare losses are to be prevented. Equipment that before could be used only in a particular band, now can be used relatively efficiently in various bands, while innovation is bringing communications solutions in bands hitherto either unused or used for other purposes. Thus, the traditional model of awarding a license to operate a given service in a given band is fast becoming a barrier to innovation as new technology allows the use of that band for

an alternative, and probably more lucrative, use. These technological shifts have revealed a large latent consumer demand for wireless applications, which increased as wireless solutions gained acceptance.

Regulators throughout the world have responded predictably to this increased demand, using spectrum (as any other resource controlled by government) to maximize political support. The increased demand has increased the political value of spectrum. Thus, regulators have been busy adjusting band plans, reallocating license holders onto alternative bands; auctioning cellular, PCS, WCS, DBS, MDS, and other licenses while protecting incumbents, especially broadcasters; and in general attempting to handle this technological revolution through administrative means.

The outcome, while predictable from a political economy perspective, has generated large rents for incumbents, both wireless and wireline operators; restrained competition in the global telecommunications market; and maintained the regulatory machine in place; while at the same time bending enough to accommodate some of the increased demands. Most developing countries are beginning to address the issue of how to allocate, manage, and regulate the spectrum. This chapter presents the problems with the historical administration of the spectrum, presents a normative theory on how to manage and regulate spectrum efficiently, and concludes with case studies of Guatemala and New Zealand.

ADMINISTRATIVE SPECTRUM ALLOCATION: KEEPING THE POLITICAL RENTS FLOWING

Telecommunications regulators have kept the political rents from spectrum allocation flowing by restricting access to the spectrum and by limiting the type of uses allowed for each specific spectrum band.

There are good reasons to restrict access. Without some access restrictions operators would be interfering with each other, as was the case during the "free for all" period in the early 1900s.[1] But as Hazlett (1990) discusses, limiting interference does not require traditional command-and-control regulation. A much simpler method, which we discuss in more detail below, is to create a fully fledged spectrum property right, granting the spectrum holder the right to use a particular band in any way in a particular geographic area, subject to limits on outputs, such as signal-to-noise ratios.[2] Once these three features of a title are specified, interference can be handled through tort law.

Regulators, however, have restricted access in more subtle ways. In most nations, regulators have been reluctant to allow trading of spectrum titles, both within and across usage. In the U.S. telecommunication law, for example, there are specific provisions against "trafficking" and stockpiling (Shelanski and Huber 1997). Although difficult to enforce, limits on resale imply that oper-

ators with better capabilities to operate a business will not have easy access. Similarly, only recently, and only for very specific applications, has the FCC allowed the partitioning of spectrum bands and its sublease and resale to third parties. Without allowing titleholders to partition their titles in either the time, geographic, or frequency dimensions, the ability to extract better use of the spectrum is limited.[3]

There are, however, no good reasons for imposing usage restrictions on specific bands. Regulators and some equipment manufacturers defend these restrictions also on "interference" grounds, spouting the common refrain that "without usage limitations, the potential for interference is too large, requiring complex monitoring, etc. etc."[4] This, however, as Hazlett (1990) made quite clear, is a vacuous statement. As long as individuals or entities may be sued and fined for trespassing on another's spectrum rights, spectrum users will have incentives to respect the rights of their spectrum neighbors. The bald reality is that limiting usage provides regulators, or the politicians controlling them, with large political rents to distribute as they see fit. This, and not interference, seems to be the main reason for the long life of access restrictions.

Consider, for example, the case of a Mexican wireless operator, Iusacell, which obtained a radio dispatch license for Mexico City in the 1950s.[5] Eventually (with the growth of cellular telephony) this wireless application lost its financial appeal, and service declined. With an investment by Bell Atlantic of US$1 billion, Iusacell renewed its interest in operating the radio license but with a different use, this time to provide fixed wireless local access services. Because the license did not allow it to change uses, Iusacell requested a license modification. Although Iusacell claims that the government had promised it would be allowed to operate the new service with the existing license, the regulatory agency never granted the necessary license modification, and as a consequence this spectrum has remained essentially unused.

Why would a regulator prevent a minor change that would surely seem to promote consumer welfare?[6] Both reasons are tied to the large rents involved. Refusing the modification would protect the rents of the incumbent wireline operator, Telmex, and allow extraction of the substantial windfall gains accruing to the licensee from the modification. The extraction of these rents can take various forms. Since the licensee is willing to pay for the license modification, payments may take the form of direct monetary transfers to the treasury, political contributions, or a combination.[7] Reportedly, this license modification will now take place only after the auction of approximately 300 MHz of communications spectrum in the 450-MHz, 1900-MHz, and 3.4–3.6-GHz bands, and it will require Iusacell to make a payment proportionate to the per-population prices realized for similar spectrum in this auction.

The interference argument as a way to limit access to the spectrum and to limit usage changes, then, is nonsensical. Instead, political economy considerations explain why restrictions on spectrum use are almost ubiquitous regulatory forms: Their purpose is to redistribute rents. Rent distribution, however, is conflicting with technological change and with the explosion in demand for spectrum.

This conflict, however, is not the first time technological change and regulatory procedures have crashed head on. Usually, regulators win, at least for a long while. Consider the introduction of cellular services. Cellular technology was developed by the Bell Labs in the 1950s, but it took until 1968–70 for the FCC to authorize cellular service and "pry 110 loose MHz of upper UHF TV from the broadcasters."[8] In 1981, the FCC created the class of commercial cellular radio telephone service, designating 50 MHz of spectrum in the 800-MHz frequency band for two competing cellular systems in each market (25 MHz for each system). The FCC, however, decided to use the process of comparative hearings for the first thirty markets, whenever there was more than one applicant (and there were many such cases). The FCC moved to lotteries for the remaining markets, but even then, it was not until 1984 that operation began for most major markets. By then, however, the AMPS standard put in place by the FCC was becoming obsolete[9]

(Calhoun 1992, p. 580). The hearings and lotteries dragged out slowly, with the FCC doling out first metropolitan licenses, and only then rural ones, delaying the building of many rural systems until 1990–92.

On the other hand, in the Nordic countries cellular technology was introduced earlier, with Sweden and Norway beginning service in 1981, and Denmark and Finland in 1982. As a consequence of both the earlier introduction of cellular service (a head start of three to eleven years, depending on how one characterizes the FCC's gradual release of licenses) and the relatively higher prices of landline services, penetration today in the Nordic countries stands at roughly twice that of the U.S., as shown in table 12.1.

Regulators, however, have been adjusting to these massive technological changes. In the United States, the FCC has been modifying its procedures in response to substantial pressure from both wireless operators, who take their cases to the courts, and most often win, and to some extent from Congress. Wireless operators have been pressuring the FCC to relax its rules concerning license resale, band fragmentation, and usage changes. Often prompted by judicial reversals, the FCC has slowly been bending its ways. For example, it allowed Nextel to provide a wireless digital service over frequencies that were originally licensed for radio dispatch services. It has also allowed Direct Broadcast Satel-

Table 12.1 Comparison of Cellular Penetration Rates in Selected Countries

Country	Start Year	Penetration (1/1/97) (%)
Norway	1981	28.6
Sweden	1981	27.8
United States	1984	16.8
United Kingdom	1985	11.7
Italy	1985	11.2
Western Europe*		9.2
Germany	1985	7.1
France	1985	4.3

*This population-weighted average also includes all other Western European countries (including Austria, former East Germany, Switzerland, and principalities).
Source: Data from Donaldson, Lufkin, Jenrette 1997, pp.15 and 60.

lite (DBS) licensees substantial flexibility to fragment and lease their spectrum rights. Similarly, it has granted PCS licensees substantial flexibility in their choice of technologies.[10] A major shift in FCC frequency assignment procedures has been the policy of auctioning spectrum licenses. The congressional mandate to auction spectrum was introduced in the budget bill of 1993. It was, however, not the first such mandate; spectrum auctions had been used earlier in Australia and New Zealand. Auctions now have proliferated throughout the world.

Although pundits and scholars alike have attached much importance to the shift toward auctions, it is unclear whether auctions by themselves are such an important regulatory change. Auctions are clearly superior to the previous ways of assigning spectrum licenses, whether by lotteries or by administrative hearings, in that some of the transaction costs associated with transferring the licenses to those that can best use them are reduced, particularly if the FCC restricts the transfers of licenses. On the other hand, auctioning service licenses, like auctioning licenses for cellular services, does not change the nature of the FCC spectrum allocation: It still restricts access and usage changes. Although the licensee will probably be the operator with the highest *current* valuation for the object, the licensee will still be restricted in its ability to change services, to fragment the spectrum, and in general to adapt to future technical and market conditions. Thus, auctions by themselves do not facilitate the regulatory adaptation to technology. What is needed is a more drastic change in the regulatory approach, which has been implemented by certain countries, in particular Guatemala and New Zealand. We discuss their approach and experiences below.

THE WELFARE COST OF ADMINISTRATIVE ASSIGNMENT OF SPECTRUM

Assigning spectrum through administrative procedures generates welfare costs in various forms. First, it grants rents, which will tend to be dissipated through lobbying and other economic and political actions. Second, assigning frequencies to particular uses distorts technological change, because equipment producers will concentrate on developing equipment for particular uses in those bands, independently of whether that is the most efficient way to use the spectrum. The endogeneity of equipment innovation to regulatory specifications implies that we currently have a stock of equipment which is more inflexible in its use across frequency bands than would have been the case if the market determined the service or use for which each frequency band would be used. Equipment rigidity, however, creates further rents across spectrum bands, which in turn translate into social costs. These rents can be assessed by looking at the different valuations across spectrum bands. For example, consider two frequency bands for which there is equipment that allows them to provide similar services. This is the case for frequencies in the 470–820-MHz range, which are currently reserved for UHF television (but which often lay totally unused). These bands could also be used to provide cellular services. Kwerel and Williams (1992) have estimated that reallocating just 6 megahertz from TV to cellular use would have increased consumer surplus by at least US$600 million (in 1991 prices) from 1992 to the year 2000. Essentially, Kwerel and Williams assess the fact that while, around 1992, a megahertz for UHF TV could be purchased for US$6 million, a megahertz for cellular services fetched from US$70 to $160 million. This difference in valuation for spectrum that could be used for a higher value purpose means that there is a large social cost associated with administrative spectrum assignment.[11]

THE BASIC BUILDING BLOCKS FOR A PROPERTY RIGHTS APPROACH TO SPECTRUM ALLOCATION

The idea of a property rights approach to spectrum allocation is not new. The first to suggest a property rights approach in print was Leo Herzel in his 1951 article on the regulation of color television.[12] Professor Herzel's ideas did not fare well; nor did Ronald Coase's writings and speeches on the subject, which were heavily influenced by Herzel's pioneer work.[13] Indeed, it took thirty-seven years for these ideas to take root in legislation. The first legislation that introduced the idea of a property right approach to spectrum use was the 1989 Radio Communications Act of New Zealand. This legislation introduced, for the first time in history, the concept of tradable rights as a substitute for administrative licensing schemes (Crandall 1997). Seven years later El Salvador and Guatemala introduced legislation pushing further the idea of tradable rights.[14] Unlike in New Zealand, in both El Salvador and Guatemala all spectrum not already assigned to broadcasters became subject to licensing under tradable permits without usage restrictions.

To understand whether these regulatory changes are revolutionary, it is important to discuss the basic building blocks that would permit the development of a market for tradable permits in spectrum without usage restrictions.

There are three basic building blocks for the creation of a working market in tradable spectrum permits:

1. Right to sell, fragment, or lease; in other words, right to property
2. Right to use over right to provide a service
3. Handling of interference problems; in other words, prevention of trespassing.

We discuss these building blocks seriatim.

Right to Property

The question is, the right to property over what? The traditional administrative assignment of spectrum rights consisted of specifying the use to which the spectrum would be put,[15] the frequency band, time of broadcasting, power, location of the transmitting facility and, if appropriate, its directionality and location of the receiving antenna. This right could be construed as property if it were allowed to be sold at will.[16] A property right approach to the spectrum would grant the right to transmit over a particular frequency band, over a particular geographic area.

The right to transmit goes hand in hand with the right to receive free of interference.[17]

The right to transmit at a particular frequency band over a particular geographic area, however, is not enough to assure flexibility and innovation. For spectrum use to be transferred to the highest use value, it is necessary that this right be transferable and fragmentable. To be fully transferable and fragmentable, the right cannot be specified in terms of service, but rather in terms of usage or outputs.

Right to Use over Right to Provide Service

To some extent the right to use rather than to provide a particular service is the most drastic departure from the standard administrative spectrum allocation process. As discussed earlier, only recently, and only for very specified spectrum bands, has the FCC provided service flexibility to licensees.[18] Thus, although the FCC has moved to some extent toward a right-of-use doctrine, the move has been haphazard, hesitant, and ad hoc. This right, though, is essential for new technologies to be introduced rapidly.

The Handling of Interference

As discussed above, however, the laws of physics do not allow for an easy definition of the boundaries of the right to transmit. This is particularly problematic for two of the three dimensions of the right: the geographic area and the spectrum band.

Under a property rights approach as that outlined by De Vany and others (1969), spectrum users should care about outputs—in this case, the signal strength in their defined coverage area. But even regulating signal strength directly may be an unwarranted intrusion in individual economic liberty; why not apply the famous maxim "your liberty ends where my nose begins" to the domain of spectrum rights? What is needed is a clear set of rules that defines an individual's right to private "enjoyment" of his or her spectrum, allowing action by others which interferes with such enjoyment to be punishable through tort law.

The important characteristic of a broadcast signal is the received signal-to-noise ratio (SNR) because, as determined by Shannon's Law, the information content of a radio signal (to common users, its quality) is a logarithmic function of the received signal-to-noise ratio. As the signal progressively weakens relative to surrounding noise, degradation accelerates. What is needed, then, is SNR protection, and this is what the FCC tries to do in its engineering function. When a request for a new transmitter license comes in, the FCC plugs into its engineering models data on all the surrounding transmitters, plus the new one, and terrain data, and attempts to compute whether existing licensees' SNR will be adversely affected, and whether sufficiently good SNR can be afforded to the petitioner.

Under a pure property rights approach, this detailed engineering by regulators could be rendered unnecessary by simply distributing the SNR rights, and letting the spectrum holders figure out to what uses their spectrum may be put without infringing on their neighbor's rights. In a sense, the basic limits on a right holder are the rights of the other right holders. Each right holder's right to transmit free of interference limits what the other right holders can do. But the concept "free of interference" is also not well defined, and will naturally depend on the application that a particular right holder is making of its spectrum right. A right holder that uses its spectrum for a very low-power application will receive interference from multiple sources. Thus, to avoid being interfered with, and to avoid interfering with others, the right to transmit over a particular geographic area, time, and spectrum band also has to be limited by a set of minimal technical configurations. Unfortunately, some residual regulatory engineering will be required, because the SNR right is relative and not absolute. A user might experience a poor SNR, but it could be because she is using insufficient transmission power, and not due to malfeasance (that is, interference) from her neighbors.

The right, therefore, needs to be framed in terms of a specific enforcement effort made by the user.[19] A practical means to do so is to specify a reference signal strength, which is measured in practice by the field strength. Provided that the right holder is maintaining her minimum field strength, she enjoys a right to the minimum acceptable SNR. These two parameters, in turn, determine the maximum strength of the background noise.

A further requirement is necessary, however, because noise from multiple sources is cumulative, and it would be difficult to ascribe to a particular source the effect on quality degradation. This noise externality would rapidly escalate power levels, as users try to drown out background noise with ever-increasing transmitter power. The chain of events is very similar to a crowded cocktail party, where very soon everybody has to shout to make themselves heard over the din. The spectrum property right needs, therefore, to specify a maximum signal strength. Again, we should regulate outputs, not inputs. Instead of the detailed FCC-type regulation of antenna heights and transmitter power, it is simpler to specify (a) a maximum field strength at the boundary of the coverage area (to protect geographically adjacent users of the same frequency from cochannel interference), and (b) maximum levels of out-of-band emissions (to protect users of adjacent frequency bands in the same area from adjacent channel interference).

This framework also gives us a natural definition of a coverage area, which could be specified in terms of certain field strength.[20] But nowhere has it been said what the "natural" SNR should be for a particular frequency band at a particular time of day in a particular geographic location. Thus, some amount of engineering is required by the regulator when crafting the original rights, simply to ensure that the set of original rights is not conflicting, and that the defined rights are actually useful (power levels could be set too low, just as zoning restrictions can sometimes kill commercial development). But that is as much as needs to be specified. A right holder would retain the individual determination as to whether to maintain the minimum field strength (and thus enjoy the minimum SNR protection), and whether to do this through many small transmitters, or one large one.[21] With these two technical configurations, we can then define "injurious interference." Injurious, or prejudicial, interference is the one that violates the right holder's right to transmit and receive free of interference, given the technical characteristics of its right.

This discussion, then, shows that if a particular right holder is transmitting in a geographic area and in a spectrum band with no "neighbors," whether in the spectrum dial or in the geographic area, it can substantially increase its power without creating injurious interference. Thus, there is no need to set power limits, as done in the standard administrative process. If, however, a new right holder shows up next door, then the original right holder will have to adjust its transmission to avoid interfering with its new neighbor.

Although most countries have set maximum power levels for each transmitting antenna, interference is the rule of the day in most developing nations. The obvious reason is lack of enforcement of transmission rights. Thus, to have a well-functioning market for transmission rights, a method to enforce such rights must be developed. Effective judiciaries, clear liability, and appropriate penalties would be enough. Indeed, injurious or prejudicial interference is a tort, and the U.S. Supreme Court recognized it as such more than fifty years ago, using no more than common law.[22] Thus, in the same way that companies sue each other for patent violation, stealing industrial secrets, and breach of contract, or individuals sue each other for injuries arising from car accidents, companies could sue each other for prejudicial interference, and obtain compensation for damages.

It could be said that in the same way that suing for car injuries does not stop uninsured motorists from driving and imposing damage on others, the threat of legal action for prejudicial interference would not deter pirate transmissions. While valid, this concern does not take into account that pirate transmissions are difficult to avoid even under today's administrative assignment procedure. Furthermore, in a property right environment, right holders could collect damages from the violator of its right. Thus, unlike today, right holders would have an

extra incentive to find and prosecute those broadcasters that interfere with their transmission rights.

In environments in which courts are not very effective, alternative methods of resolving prejudicial interference could be designed. Guatemala and El Salvador developed an administrative procedure to resolve such interference. Their solution is to use private companies to provide evidence on prejudicial interference. With such evidence, right holders may request from the spectrum agency that the prejudicial interference be eliminated. A trial-type process ensues in which the presumed violator has to either show that it is not violating the plaintiff's right, or pay a prespecified fine. The original burden of proof is on the plaintiff, who has to show not only the existence of prejudicial interference, but also its source.[23]

The International Experience with the Introduction of Spectrum Property Rights

The New Zealand Experience

New Zealand's 1989 Radiocommunications Act set up the first experiment with spectrum property rights.[24] The Act authorized the Ministry of Commerce to introduce tradable rights as a substitute for the traditional administrative assignment process. This scheme has been called the "spectrum-management" approach. In this approach spectrum segments are sold to spectrum managers, who in turn resell or rent to third parties the right to use their spectrum.

Since the passage of the 1989 Act, New Zealand has moved relatively slowly toward a property rights approach. On the one hand, it has sold only a small amount of the spectrum to private individuals under the spectrum-management approach, using mostly simultaneous second- (and later, first-) price auctions. Most spectrum, however, is still administered under the old administrative process.

Although successful in transferring the administration of segments of the broadcasting spectrum to the private sector, there have been substantial problems with this effort. First, so far spectrum managers have failed to do much management, with few transactions taking place. Crandall (1997) reports that the MDS management rights lie almost completely fallow,[25] although their holders paid approximately $800,000 for the rights.

Second, the auction mechanism used by the Ministry of Commerce created substantial political concerns, because there were big differences in prices for similar objects. In some instances, bidders paid less than half their winning bid, while in other instances bidders entered very high bids accompanied by lower bids to assure winning the auction, but with lower bids so that their final price would not be that high.[26] Consequently, there was a substantial amount of strategic defaulting, whereby a winning bidder defaults so that the property is transferred to its own lower bid, which in turn pays the bid below it. There were also complaints of collusion (Crandall 1997), and others obtained properties for zero price.[27]

Overall, most of the criticism of the New Zealand effort has been centered on its auction system, and the fact that it raised substantially less than was expected and, seemingly, less than what the U.S. raised for similar bands. But, as Crandall (1997) shows, once corrected for population and band differences, the differences in average prices between U.S. and New Zealand auctions may reflect the higher per capita income of the U.S.

The reasons for the lack of substantial private reassignment of the spectrum are unclear. On the one hand, the spectrum management approach may have been applied in the wrong bands. It could well be the case that the bands for which spectrum management would work best are those where the standard administrative assignment would be most difficult, like in point-to-point uses. It is unclear whether, in the cellular or MDS segments, selling large spectrum segments creates potential competition problems. Indeed, given the smallness of the New Zealand market, a policy that tends to concentrate spectrum in a few hands may not be the most desirable policy. It is in this respect that the Guatemala experience may be more instructive.

The Guatemala Experience

In 1996 the Guatemala National Assembly passed a revolutionary General Telecommunications Act. The 1996 Act completely deregulated the telecommunications market. It allowed free entry into all segments of the service, required operators to grant access to a limited set of essential resources (basically, origination and termination services) based on private negotiations to be arbitrated by the regulatory agency under very specific and narrowly specified guidelines,[28] and introduced a property rights approach to spectrum use. Spectrum rights would be granted in fully transferable and fragmentable frequency usage titles (TUFs for Títulos de Uso de Frecuencias). The TUFs have no "service" limitation, but do have technical limitations to protect against prejudicial interference.

The basic building block of Guatemala's approach to the spectrum is that all spectrum not currently assigned to the government, to radio and TV stations, to other license holders, or defined as "free," can be requested by any person.[29] Following a request, the regulatory agency must determine whether the request infringes on any other person's rights, and if the agency decides it does not, a period of protest opens up during which other interested parties may object to the granting of a right. The objection may be for two reasons: First, it may be the case that such person already has a right which would be violated by the request, and second, that person may also want a portion of the requested spectrum. In the former case, if the protest is substantiated, the request is not granted. In the latter case, the regulator must start an auction procedure. The law states that if fragmentation would promote competition, the regulator is mandated to auction the desired spectrum in a fragmented fashion. The law also mandates that in this case, the auction be of a simultaneous, ascending multiple-round format.

Since the law went into effect in January 1997, the regulatory agency has received more than 7,000 requests for spectrum use rights. Although the law specifies a very fast process, with approximately four months being the supposed maximum time it may take from request to auction, in fact the law does not penalize the agency for delays. Consequently, the auction process has been a little more drawn out.

The Specialized Mobile Radio Auction

The first auction started on June 4, 1997 and lasted for two weeks.[30] The auction was for 20.8 MHz of nationwide spectrum in the 800-MHz range, which is used in the region for "trunking" or specialized mobile radio (SMR).[31] Initially, there were eleven bidders—ten companies and one individual. Of the ten companies, one was the national telecommunications company, GUATEL. The bidders deposited payments that allowed them to bid initially for more than 60 MHz. The 20.8 MHz of spectrum was fragmented in pairs of outbound and inbound bands, and also in two types of bands, seven band pairs of 1-MHz each, and twelve band pairs of 200-kHz each. The 1-MHz bands were contiguous, as were the 200-kHz bands. The auction ended after two weeks of intense bidding, with total payments of almost US$3 million (17.2 million Quetzals). Seven out of the initial eleven bidders won at least one lot.

It is interesting to compare this result to the auction results in the U.S. The population of Guatemala is approximately 11 million people; its average per capita income is just US$3,000. Thus, on a megahertz per population (MHz/POP) basis, the Guatemala auction resulted in a value of approximately US$0.012. A similar auction in the U.S. resulted in US$0.245 per MHz/POP[32] (see table 12.2).

Although the spectrum bands auctioned are not directly comparable due to variations in equipment standards,[33] we find the comparison indicative of the importance of the property rights approach. Adjusting roughly for the very large differences in personal income, the realized price per MHz/POP in the U.S. was just over twice that in Guatemala. This premium can be understood as resulting from a number of factors: the higher fragmentation of the U.S. auction (blocks were much narrower); the relative scarcity of SMR spectrum in the U.S. (Guatemala auctioned over six times as much *effective* spectrum); the higher proportion of the U.S. population employed in the finance, insurance, and retail trades (FIRE);[34] and environmental factors such as the greater monetary, political, and regulatory stability of the U.S.

In fact, these factors in favor of the U.S. must have been counterbalanced by some of the unique Guatemalan positives. Guatemala's higher population density (approximately three times that of the U.S.) must have helped,[35] as well as its lack of wireline penetration. But we believe that by far the most important factor that managed to put the Guatemalan auctions in the same ballpark as the U.S. was the unique property rights that were for sale.

Winners also knew that they could resell airtime on their ESMR systems to any group of users, or resell their licenses, in whole or in part (by frequency, geographic area, or time of day), to other potential operators, for uses not yet invented. In fact, although the prior use of these frequencies in Guatemala was exclusively for non-interconnected SMR, at least one of the winners of the 1-MHz bands declared its intention

Table 12.2 Comparison of Specialized Mobile Radio Auction Results in the U.S. and Guatemala

Country	$GDP/head	Population (millions)	MHz/POP Auctioned* (millions)	Auction Proceeds (US$ MM)	SMR price (¢/MHz-POP)
United States	27,607	266	830.7	204	24.6
Guatemala	3,080	11.3	235.0	2.8	1.2
Ratio	9x				20.5x
U.S. premium					2.3x

*The U.S. data is adjusted for incumbency according to the FCC's published estimates.

to deploy fixed wireless applications, while others were announcing their intention to deploy advanced ESMR systems to grab a slice of the large cellular market.[36]

The FM Auctions

On August 4, 1997 Guatemala started a second round of auctions in three stages, each two weeks apart. In total, thirty-three FM regional and city-range radio stations were auctioned, with some in the nation's capital. A total of thirty-seven bidders registered, with nineteen bidders winning various radio holdings. A total of US$3 million was obtained.

It is interesting to compare these numbers with those derived from New Zealand's massive radio station auctions. New Zealand, with a per capita income three times as high as that of Guatemala, obtained just slightly more than US$6 million for more than the 300 AM and FM stations, or the equivalent of less than $18,000 per station (Crandall 1987, pp. 12–13). Guatemala obtained approximately US$60,000 per station. These two values are difficult to compare because the Guatemalan stations were all FM, while the New Zealand stations were a mixture of AM and FM. Furthermore, it is not clear whether the extra value obtained in Guatemala reflects that the regulator created artificial radio scarcity, or that it reflects the usage flexibility associated with the Guatemalan TUFs.[37]

The Guatemalan experience is interesting because it is the first experiment implementing a property rights approach to spectrum use. Although it started only recently, it has already proved feasible. The private sector has been willing to bid what are large amounts for Guatemala, even though the scheme to protect against interference is novel and has not yet been tested. Furthermore, participation in the auctions has been nothing short of widespread. The eleven participants at the SMR auctions, and the thirty-seven participants at the radio station auctions, show the value of spectrum fragmentation, particularly in what may be relatively thin markets. This, indeed, may have been the basic strategic failure in New Zealand.

CONCLUSION

The pressure unleashed by technological and demand forces on spectrum regulators is mounting, forcing them to abandon, albeit ever so slowly, the detailed regulation they so favor. In its PCS auctions, the FCC implicitly granted, what seems to many, enormous use flexibility to licensees, allowing any terrestrial use other than broadcasting. It even allowed licensees to choose the transmission standards (unlike Europe, which mandates GSM). In the WCS auction the FCC even abandoned buildout requirements. Under pressure from the likely mass default in the C-block auction, the FCC might allow even more latitude as a means of allowing the licensees to generate more revenue and thus avoid default (De Vany 1996). Although these developments push the regulatory agenda toward property rights, they remain quite distant from what we perceive as the ultimate reform needed to adjust the sector to the current and future technological onslaught—fully fledged property rights in spectrum. Two pioneering free-marketing countries have taken the lead, and we should view these as ambitious experiments. The New Zealand experiment has been slow to bear fruit, for reasons outside the scope of this publication. The Guatemalan experiment is proceeding in earnest, on track to become the most ambitious spectrum privatization ever. There is the potential for the experiences in these countries in the next five to ten years to point to the substantial welfare gains associated with such an approach, and if there is any value to advertising, perhaps to increase the pressure for regulators from other countries to follow their bold path.

NOTES

1. For a good discussion of the period, see Hazlett 1990, pp.133–175.

2. As De Vany and others (1969, pp. 145–162) pointed out, the first step in defining property rights is defining the rights in terms of outputs rather than inputs. For example, current FCC authorizations specify antenna height and directionality, maximum effective radiated power, and many others items, all inputs. The output is the strength of the broadcast signal in the licensee's coverage area and in neigh-

boring areas. An interference problem arises when licensee A's signal in area B is so strong relative to licensee B's own signal, that the signal-to-noise ratio experienced by B's receivers is unacceptable. Thus, interference provisions are better specified in terms of outputs.

3. The FCC has allowed television and radio broadcasters to perform subcarrier transactions, allowing them to carry paid-for information, such as elevator music or data transmission, in the spare space in their signal not used by the main signal (the vertical blanking interval for TV and the subcarrier for both TV and FM radio). Use of the subcarrier was first permitted in 1955, and largely deregulated in 1983. (See Minoli 1991, pp. 256–266.) The FCC has also allowed partitioning of rural cellular licenses among consortia of rural wireline incumbents, and allowed cellular operators to choose their own digital air interfaces (rather than forcing the use of a nationwide standard, such as GSM in Europe). (See Calhoun 1991, pp. 100–114.)

4. See, for example, Comments of National Association of Broadcasters, FCC Docket MM 93–132, p. 73.

5. *Ibid.*

6. The regulator in this case would have had merely to strike out the requirement that users be mobile and that users broadcast with a minimum power of 10 watts. Note that this was not a maximum power requirement and therefore it was not an issue of interference protection.

7. As it turned out, the head of Iusacell fell from grace with the administration; thus, political contributions were out of the question.

8. Calhoun (1992, p. 580) points out that the FCC fashioned SMR and other allocations, as well as cellular, from this single concession from the broadcasters.

9. The AMPS standard used essentially the same technique as conventional analog FM radio in mono.

10. For a discussion of the FCC's movement toward more flexibility, see Shelanski and Huber 1997.

11. Similarly, the large differential in the market value between UHF and VHF licenses can be attributed to artificial scarcity created by the FCC.

12. See also his assessment of how he reached his conclusions in Leo Herzel, 1997, "My 1951 Color Television Article," *Journal of Law and Economics.*

13. See, in particular, Ronald Coase, 1959, "The Federal Communications Commission," *Journal of Law & Economics,* II, pp. 1–40.

14. The authors helped design the reforms of the telecommunication sectors and draft the Telecommunications Laws passed in 1996 by the legislatures of both countries.

15. Traditionally there has been a sharp distinction between broadcasting and communications. The introduction of broadcasting technologies for communications (that

is, cellular, PCS, etc.) has made a mockery of this regulatory difference.

16. The right would, under some conditions, have very little value in alternative use. For example, a right to a point-to-point transmission over a certain frequency from the headquarters of a particular company to one of its branches would have very little value in alternative uses, because a buyer of that right interested in using it for an alternative use would also have to obtain the right to retransmit from the two end-points to the two end-points the buyer is interested in. Under other conditions, it could have a large value, particularly if the permits involve broadcasting types of services, like radio, TV, satellite, or mobile telephony licenses of any sort.

17. The right should also imply a right to prevent undesired reception. (See Shelanski and Huber 1997.)

18. The FCC, for example, reclassified (with congressional authorization) SMR licenses as Commercial Mobile Radio Service (CMRS) licenses, permitting dynamic sharing and interconnection to the PSTN of dispatch radio channels. Other countries have followed in increasing flexibility. For example, in granting PCS licenses, Chile (and the U.S.) has left to the discretion of the licensee the decision of what technology and what type of service to provide over those spectrum bands.

19. In the same way that individuals should use precautionary measures to avoid being hit by a car.

20. This approach is already used by the FCC and other agencies, requiring TV and radio stations to file charts showing their signal's field-strength contours.

21. Changes to these technical restrictions could be adopted as long as "neighboring" spectrum holders do not object.

22. See *Tribune Co. v. Oak Leaves Broadcasting Station,* a 1926 Cook County, Illinois, Circuit Court decision. See, also, Hazlett 1990, for a discussion of this issue, and in general of the evolution of U.S. regulation of the spectrum.

23. To make this process work, all transmission devices have to be registered with the spectrum agency so that presumed violators can be identified.

24. See Crandall 1997 for a discussion of this experience.

25. There have been only minor uses for non-video transmission (Crandall 1997, p.22).

26. It is not clear that this was a rational strategy, but nevertheless it was used.

27. This was the case of a college student who entered a bid for a TV station. Since no one else bid, he was granted the license for zero price, as should have been the case. (See Crandall 1997.)

28. Under pressure to privatize the national incumbent operator, in late 1997 the Guatemalan legislature

amended the General Telecommunications Act. The amendments have the potential to substantially limit competition in international telecommunications services, and to make interconnection negotiations more difficult to resolve. These reforms did not change the spectrum allocation policy.

29. For obvious political reasons, radio and TV stations were grandfathered, being granted rights of use of their spectrum bands. Other private concession holders would not be able to renew their concession upon expiration.

30. The authors participated in the design of this particular auction. The auction was carried out with LAMP®, software developed by the Law & Economics Consulting Group, Inc.

31. SMR is a terrestrial mobile communications system originally designed to operate in a "dispatch" mode, allowing two-way communications between a group of mobile and/or fixed users, such as taxicabs or security guards. The users agree on a given frequency channel, and they can all listen in and take turns using that channel for transmission. Each end-user or group of users is allowed the use of only one channel, so that if the end-user's assigned channel is already in use, the user must wait until the channel is available to transmit. With "trunked" or "enhanced" SMR (ESMR), microprocessors in the handsets scan multiple frequency channels and automatically search for an open one, allowing more users to be served at any one time. The system is also interconnected to the PSTN, permitting ESMR users to dial PSTN users, and to dial other end users on the ESMR system, instead of broadcasting to all users in the group. While ESMRs are currently mostly used for cellular-like voice communications, digital systems are also being developed for data, facsimile, two-way acknowledgment paging and inventory tracking, credit card authorization, automatic vehicle location, fleet management, inventory tracking, remote database access, and voicemail services.

32. The FCC's SMR auction consisted of twenty ten-channel blocks (10 x 2 x 12.5 kHz = 250 kHz per block) in the 900 MHz band in each major trading area. The auction lasted 168 rounds, closing in April 1996. Notably, incumbent licensees in the band retained the right to operate under their existing licenses, and the right to

cochannel and adjacent channel interference protection. The new licensees were awarded the right to authorize expansion of existing systems. The FCC published as part of the bidders' package its estimates of the extent of incumbency for each block and MTA, while disclaiming any responsibility for the accuracy of this information, cautioning bidders to do their own research. The FCC estimated that on average only three of the nominal 5 MHz were usable.

33. SMR commonly operates in either the 800-MHz or 900-MHz band. Systems in the 800-MHz band use two paired 25-kHz channels, while 900-MHz band systems use two paired 12.5-kHz channels. Because of the different sizes of the channel bandwidths between the 800-MHz and 900-MHz systems, traditional SMR equipment is band-specific and incompatible with the other. The narrower channel bandwidths in the 900-MHz band also tend to result in better spectrum use.

34. Cardilli and others (1997) show that the value of SMR spectrum in the U.S. auctions bears a strong positive relation to the proportion of the labor force employed in the FIRE sectors, extending Moreton and Spiller's (1995) analysis of the impact of FIRE employment on, among other things, PCS license valuations. (See Moreton and Spiller 1995 and 1997.)

35. Cardilli and others (1997) also show that the value of SMR spectrum in the U.S. was strongly related to the population density of the license area.

36. While cellular represents one in seven Guatemalan access lines, there is currently only one operator providing only analog (AMP) service.

37. FM stations can be quite valuable because FM subcarrier techniques can allow substantial one-way audio or data transmission, such as paging, news, stock prices, sports scores, elevator music, second-language programming, and so forth. Of the 200 kHz available in a standard FM radio slot, over 40 kHz are unused by standard FM transmission and are available for data transmission, permitting a data stream of 100 kb/s or more, depending on the subcarrier technique used (Minoli 1991). Of course, the Guatemalan property rights approach would allow a right holder to use the entire 200-kHz slot for data transmission if he or she so wished.

13 PRIVATIZING AND REGULATING THE TRANSPORTATION SECTOR: PORTS, RAILROADS, TOLL ROADS, AND AIRPORTS

THE IMPACT OF TRANSPORTATION-related costs on the final cost of products is considerable in Latin American and Caribbean countries. Reducing those costs through sector reforms, regulation, and deregulation can have a major impact on productivity, competitiveness, and growth. Often the products experiencing the greatest impact are exported goods, with significant consequences for the export-led growth strategy pursued by most Latin American and Caribbean countries. In recent years there has been a wide variety of attempts to privatize and regulate the transportation sector, with an equally wide variety of

results. The issues of port, airport, and railroad reform, and toll road policies, are discussed here to provide an overview of reform options and to determine regulatory needs and the appropriate steps to ensure efficient private sector participation.

PORTS

Ports play a more extensive economic role today than ever before. More than 90 percent of trade goes through ports. Unprecedented developments in transport and freight-handling technologies, and changes in shipping practices, have substantially reconfigured transport networks. In the past ports were merely a location where cargo passed between land and sea. Then they became industrial and commercial service cen-

ters. Ports now serve as a dynamic node in the international production and distribution network, and are essential for the success of the export-led development strategy chosen by many countries. Port operations are key to securing an effective multimodal transport system and trade activities, and to improving the competitiveness of export products.

Port management is evolving from being a passive provider of facilities and services to being an active participant in international trade. Port managers act as decisionmakers in the transport chain and manage logistical activities and the flow of goods. Such an evolution is needed to promote trade and transport activities, which in turn generate new revenue-making and value-adding businesses. Experience shows that this transformation is easier said than done, and public sector responsibility in making this happen is paramount. Today it is widely accepted that ports must be cost-effective organizations equipped to deal efficiently with customer needs. This often means that the organization and management of port operations and cargo-handling services must be streamlined to attract potential port users, whose sole interest is to obtain reliable service at low cost.

Public/private partnerships to finance port investments and manage port facilities have been commonplace for many years. Hong Kong's private sector has financed and operated all the related infrastructure under long-term leases; Japan has leased fully developed berths to ocean carriers that equip and manage them to meet their own needs. The United Kingdom has a fully privatized port system. Hong Kong, Japan, and the United Kingdom have expanded private sector involvement in port financing and management to cover more local ports and a variety of maritime transport-related services, improving productivity. Singapore has fully public ports; the Netherlands, Italy, and Spain have public ownership of land and basic infrastructure, but private operation through leasing and concessions. The main issues considered in the reform process are the forms of private sector participation, financing, competition and regulation, labor, trade logistics, access, and administrative and legal arrangements.

Port Reform in Latin America

Latin American countries are now transferring to the private sector functions and services originally performed by the public sector. The process is difficult, because in many cases, the state's traditional role as a provider of infrastructure that functions without the profit motive has restricted the development of a port market. But severe budget constraints and the demand of rapidly growing industrial sectors for adequate port infrastructure and efficient services are pressuring governments to accept the notion of public/private partnerships in financing ports. Increasingly, private sector parties are also managing port assets and providing port services under contractual arrangements with responsible public entities.

The effects of poorly managed ports on trade performance in Latin America have become obvious and are ominous. The implicit tariff induced by inefficient port operations in Latin American and Caribbean countries ranges from 5 to 25 percent. Inefficiencies and high port operating costs are posing serious obstacles to the export-led growth strategies of most countries in the region. For example, a low estimate of net export earnings forgone in Brazil due to inefficient port operations exceeded $1 billion in 1994. Estimated lost earnings for Colombia in 1994 exceeded $200 million. Santos, Latin America's largest port, has become so congested that in 1994 it was barely able to increase cargo tonnage from its 1993 level of 430,000 TEUs (twenty-foot equivalent units), and average waiting time increased from four days to two weeks. Such pervasive inefficiencies are in striking contrast to the performance of privately run terminals in ports such as Hong Kong and Kobe. This and the success of partial reforms in some Latin American countries have gradually induced many governments to reconsider the organization and management of their national port systems. The seriousness of the problem and the existence of relatively easy solutions are behind the current push for port reform in Latin America and the Caribbean.

Most countries in the region are in the process of reforming their port systems and are considering private sector participation options. Argentina, Chile, Colombia, Ecuador, Guatemala, and Uruguay have been leading the way. Port operations have been privatized or concessioned (at least partially) in those five countries within the last four years. Brazil, Honduras, Jamaica, Mexico, Nicaragua, Peru, Trinidad and Tobago, St. Vincent, and Venezuela are in the process of implementing or have begun to consider options for port reform and private sector participation. Most of the remaining countries in the region are eager to expand private sector participation but are uncertain how to handle labor issues, legislative changes, regulatory needs, the new role of port authorities, and the mode of private sector participation.

Even Chile, which has enjoyed the most efficient ports in Latin America for the past ten years, is under pressure. Since 1981 Emporchi, Chile's state-owned port organization, has lived off productivity improvements generated by labor deregulation. This newfound efficiency was a disincentive to investing in port infrastructure and helped to block the full application of the privatization law originally devised to run parallel to labor reform. The problem for Chile's port system now is that infrastructure investment has not kept pace with the traffic that has grown as a result of Chile's buoyant economy. To avoid a logjam, Chile is expanding its concessions program to provide major investment financing.

Besides the desire to reduce demands on the public sector investment budget by eliminating the need to build new port facilities, purchase cargo-handling equipment, and reduce expenditure on port labor, national governments have several important motivations for port privatization and restructuring programs. They wish to take action against expensive and inefficient port operations that constrain foreign trade, and recognize that inefficiencies could divert cargo to neighboring countries. Furthermore, they seek to introduce port operations to the efficiency and know-how of the private sector, thereby improving the prospects of foreign trade. It is important that privatization be pursued for the right reasons. Because a port is not an end in itself, but rather a catalyst for trade, the objective of privatization must be to expand trade.

While appreciating the potential for improving port performance through private sector involvement, governments in many countries have been hesitant to divest national port assets to third (particularly foreign) parties. Central port administrations and labor unions have successfully wielded their political influence in order to preserve their privileges, and governments are reluctant to face the labor problems that will undoubtedly accompany reform. Other obstacles to privatization include a lack of adequate enabling legislation, a lack of confidence in and mistrust of the private sector, and a perceived loss of control to foreign operators.

The character of the privatization process depends to a large extent on a port's ownership and operating structure. In a *landlord port*, port management provides the infrastructure, whereas private companies own the superstructure and employ stevedoring labor. In a *tool port*, management provides the infrastructure and superstructure, whereas private companies employ stevedoring labor. In a *service port*, port management provides (almost) all services, including labor. Overall, most ports in the process of privatization or considering privatization are either tool ports or service ports. Landlord ports are already characterized by a clear division of responsibilities between public port authorities and private enterprises.

The road to whole or partial port privatization has many pitfalls, and certain conditions are necessary for successful port privatization. First, the transformation of a port system requires a great degree of political strength and decisive leadership. Governments must take measures to minimize the negative social and political costs of privatization associated with reductions in labor. These measures involve rousing public support for the transformation by publicizing the high costs of the public sector operations and the economic consequences of this lack of efficiency. Second, significant financial resources are needed to compensate port labor in accord with the labor code and collective bargaining agreements. Finally, a fair tendering process and accurate valuation are essential prerequisites to successful privatization. The salient lessons to be learned from the port reform and regulation process are described below.

A New Mandate for Public Sector Intervention in Ports

Ports form part of a broader transportation network linking transport modes and trade markets, and are a strategic asset of the state. An efficient port management strategy combines private flexibility with public responsibility. Public and private partners provide each other with the services they are best placed to deliver: an efficient and clear regulatory environment and a basic set of well-connected infrastructure networks for the public sector, and a cost-effective transport system for the private sector. There is no valid economic argument for government involvement in most port operations. However, under any port reform scheme, there is a role for the port authority or administration, albeit much reduced and more specific than the current one, mostly in matters of administration, logistics, regulation, externalities, customs, safety, and the environment. The port authority should be an autonomous and decentralized institution.

Public sector intervention in the ports sector can contribute to an efficient port management strategy by

- Ensuring appropriate safety conditions in port and navigation activities and monitoring compliance with environmental protection policy
- Fostering common development policies between ports and cities, helping to set up common planning committees on land development issues, and assisting in designing port relocation operations
- Creating a regulatory and legal environment that encourages private sector participation by ensuring fair competition and effectively monitoring new public/private partnerships without interfering in the commercial sphere
- Undertaking the revision and streamlining of national trade procedures, including customs clearance and documentation and communication standards
- Providing only very selective financing for those essential components of basic infrastructure that are unlikely to have access to private or alternative sources of financing and paving the way for the private sector to cover consequential operational investments
- Sharing some of the noncommercial risks, or appropriately compensating the private operator, particularly when the financial rate of return is below the normal level
- Bearing the political and regulatory risks.

Ports are on the frontier of public and private interest. Efforts to balance these interests are being made in Latin America, where the major economic objective is to use scarce resources efficiently, and the institutional objective is to establish a competitive environment without the development of monopolies. The test of the privatization schemes being witnessed the world over will be whether they preserve such a balance of interests.

Privatization creates a legal relationship between the private operator and the public authority. For this new partnership to achieve the economic and institutional objectives listed above, more privatization must mean better public administration. In addition to its landlord management function, the port authority has to be a warden of the public interest. This requires, above all, development of explicit policies regarding public/private partnerships in national ports, and strong institutional arrangements to oversee the performance of private parties involved in managing port assets and providing port services.

Ports ought to be viewed not in isolation, but as a crucial link in the multimodal transport chain, and port reforms are essential to lowering the cost of traded goods. To increase value added and reduce costs, the complementarities among and physical linkages between transport modes need to be developed.

Ports are an economic good and as such should be ruled by opportunity costs and cost-benefit criteria. This realization might lead to the obsolescence or downsizing of a number of small- and medium-size ports in the region, and to increased competition.

Dramatic improvements can be secured quickly and with little additional investment by improving management and incentives, both characteristics of private sector involvement. For example, as a result of its concession policy, rates in Argentina are down an average of 46 percent on products exported to the United States and Europe. Likewise, as a result of Colombia's concession policy, tariffs have been reduced by 52 percent and productivity has increased by more than 60 percent at the leading ports of Barranquilla, Buenaventura, Cartagena, and Santa Marta. Loading and unloading time has been reduced by more than half. The results in Uruguay are also spectacular. As a consequence of the privatization of port operations, productivity increased by more than 300 percent, effective tariffs decreased by 100 percent, and output increased by 100 percent within eighteen months of establishing the new regime. The concessioning of the terminals of the port of Buenos Aires to private operators has brought fierce competition among terminals, bringing fees down by more than 70 percent and inducing the bankruptcy of one terminal (a consequence of excess capacity). Partial reforms in the port of Guayaquil, Ecuador, transferring and opening operations to private third parties, has increased productivity by more than 50 percent, reduced costs by 60 percent, and increased volume by 50 percent. All this has been accomplished with little investment and in less than one year.

The direct and indirect (forgone earnings) costs of the status quo are not sustainable and are likely to get worse as competition from reformed countries increases, implying further losses of trade, traffic, and chances to secure hub opportunities. Private sector participation in port operations is key to securing efficiency gains. Although full transferability of experiences is unlikely, the success of a wide variety of countries that have privatized operations and concessioned terminals indicates the feasibility and validity of reform and suggests its wide adaptability to most environments. The salient and consensus mode of port reform has been the privatization of port operations and the concessioning of terminals, under autonomous decentralized port administrations. That mode of private sector participation can capture most of the efficiency gains of full privatization (land sales). Full privatization, advocated by some private sector groups, tends to generate more political resistance and controversy, and the added benefits are not significantly higher than those secured by privatization of operations and concessions, when properly designed; thus the saliency of privatization and concessions.

The labor issue, while delicate, can be managed and should not be thought of as an insurmountable obstacle to reform. The success of

Argentina, Mexico, Spain, Trinidad and Tobago, the United Kingdom, and Uruguay, where labor resistance was very strong and labor reductions averaged 60 percent, bears witness to this point. The design of generous (twelve-to-eighteen-months' earnings) labor rationalization programs, including reemployment and training opportunities, is crucial to the success of the program.

Prior to considering private sector participation in port operations, countries should have in place antitrust legislation and an effective enforcement agency. Tariff regulation may not be necessary in large ports with several multiuse terminals, or where nearby ports have adequate road linkages, because competition tends to eliminate monopoly rents. The operators' actions should be overseen by the country's antitrust agency and should clearly comply with antitrust legislation. However, regulation is necessary for small ports (one terminal) without nearby competition.

When concessioning multiple terminals in the same port, a sequential auction (one terminal at a time) is best to secure efficiency and higher revenues. The constraint of having no more than one terminal per operator should usually be imposed, and transfer of concessions should be allowed. The design of the concession is a key determinant of the efficiency level of port operations.

Financing of infrastructure, by and large, should be left to the private sector. Government intervention or facilitation should be guided by the extent of external effects not captured by private investors or operators. Private sector participation, in the short run, might lead to excessive investment and excess capacity. However, the consequences should not be too severe; they are part of the necessary restructuring of ports in Latin America and the Caribbean, and the efficiency gains outweigh the potential costs. Moreover adequate strategic thinking can minimize the levels of overinvestment. While most countries in Latin America and the Caribbean are thinking of creating hub ports, not every country, or port, can be a regional hub. Geographic location, early entry, and efficient operations are the key determinants. Strategic planning and rapid reforms are thus crucial to avoid potentially wasteful investment and to preempt potential competitors. Improved use of technology to manage logistics and operations can also produce significant efficiency gains and lower costs. Complementary reforms to improve trade logistics, insurance frameworks, and customs operations are crucial to reduce costs and to improve export competitiveness.

There was concern over the increasing concentration and degree of monopoly power in the (private) British ports. If this is indeed a serious concern, it should be viewed as a flaw not of the full privatization model, but rather of the antitrust regime, which in the United Kingdom allows any port group to hold up to 25 percent of total port market share. This concern can be easily addressed by limiting cross-concession ownership to less threatening levels.

There are a number of very effective ways to reduce cross-border and transferability risks. They include debt service reserve funds, currency exchange agreements, currency reserve accounts, and currency hedges. Guarantees from the World Bank, the Multilateral Investment Guarantee Agency, the U.S. Export-Import Bank, and the Overseas Private Investment Corporation can be an effective way to reduce political and regulatory risks. Commercial risk can be mitigated through structuring the operator fee as a percentage of revenue, permitting structuring elements such as dual amortization, subordinating distributions to sponsors and sponsor-affiliated fees, obtaining third-party credit support, using take or paying off-take contracts, securing alternate or interruptible users of service, and requiring minimum performance guarantees from the operator. Limited remedies risk can be mitigated through pledging sponsor-owned securities of the entity that owns the project; enabling the transfer of contract rights, assets, cash flow, permits, mortgages, and other collateral agreements; and using indemnities, bond insurance, cure rights, and mandatory equity contributions. Construction and technology risks can be mitigated through business interruption insurance, property and liability insurance, lump-sum date-certain construction contracts, liquidated damages, performance bonds, guarantees or warranties, construction and main-tenance reserves, and independent engineer review of construction.

There are also significant policy and operational implications. Most countries have been concerned with export-growth issues in Latin America and the Caribbean and, as a result, a number of export-promotion projects are under way. Although these projects have value added, they can also induce some distortions, and the benefits tend not to be sustainable. A better approach, if not a complementary one, is to increase the volume of exports by lowering export costs through the reform of port operations, and to increase private sector participation. Such measures not only increase efficiency, produce immediate value added, and increase trade volumes (witness the cases of Argentina, Colombia, Guatemala, and Uruguay), but have long-lasting effects.

RAILWAYS

The predicament of state-owned railways all over the world has led many countries to explore alternatives to the traditional way of running the sector. Countries such as Argentina, Brazil, Chile, New Zealand, and the United Kingdom have opted for concessions or partial or full privatization; others, such as Germany, Japan, Spain, and Sweden, have opted for disintegration of the once-monolithic structure. Some changes are more radical than others, and there is an element of experimentation in all of them. Yet the spirit of all of them is decentralization and disintegration, with increased private sector participation. Our approach follows that spirit, pushing the reforms one step further and offering additional alternatives for consideration.

The production and distribution of railroad services entail a number of stages and much coordination. The traditional railroad company is vertically integrated. Its operations cover a wide range of activities, from the management of large repair shops to the provision, marketing, and scheduling of multiple logistical services. When considering variations on the status quo, the fundamental consideration is whether a common, centralized, and single management or control system is necessary for the efficient provision of railroad services and, by implication, whether several units with autonomous management and control could provide services as efficiently as or more efficiently than a single unit.

Traditionally, state railway firms (or managers) have not been granted residual rights. Consequently, they have had few incentives to operate efficiently. In addition, they have operated as monopolies (although facing intermodal competition). Both factors—competition and claims to residual rights (incentives)—need to be present to improve efficiency. Competition without incentives will accomplish little, because no benefits will accrue to the individual units, and incentives without competition will likely lead to inefficient monopoly rents. As of now, both factors are absent, particularly incentives, in the railroad sector in most Latin American and Caribbean countries. Clearly, some competition is provided by alternative transport modes. However, intermodal competition cannot quite completely replace railway competition because the cost structures of each mode are significantly different. Successful restructuring of any railway company should ensure the presence of both factors. Perhaps the most striking precedent of the potential gains that can be reaped from restructuring state-owned railway companies is provided by British Railways, whose annual growth rate of labor productivity jumped from 0.8 to 3.9 percent during the 1980s (Molyneux and Thompson 1987). This growth was achieved by restructuring into five separate business sectors that cut costs, reduced inefficiencies, and responded with innovative solutions to customers' changing preferences.[1]

The presence of fixed and sunk costs limit the degree of effective competition in the railway sector. Infrastructure, tracks, and stations are needed before the service can be provided. It is obviously inefficient to duplicate the infrastructure; therefore, natural monopoly cost conditions characterize the provision of the physical network. Moreover, those costs are largely sunk, because there is little alternative use of that capital. However, effective competition can be induced in other activities without losing economies of scale. For example, the previous arguments need not apply to the provision of services, which is where restructuring to elicit competition can be most fruitful. For that purpose it is often appropriate to separate the control of infrastructure and coordination of services from the control of rolling stock, wagons, and engines, and the actual provision of services. Vertical separation of these activities should be seriously considered, as should the provision, on fair terms, of equal access to the railway infrastructure by actual and potential operators of services. Competition could be induced not only by separating these types of units vertically, but also by breaking them into more than one unit, even if that were to bring the loss of some economies of scale. Moreover, the restructuring options and private sector access, prescribed to promote interline competition, would be distinctly less onerous than maximum-rate regulation, which mandates burdensome and unwieldy evidence on "stand-alone costs" over large portions of the rail system to determine reasonable rates.

Further, issues of potential market foreclosure should be considered. The possibility of foreclosures arises in a number of related policy issues: end-to-end mergers, joint rates, route cancellations, and access to rail facilities and reciprocal switching. For example, geographical breakups of the company give rise to complementary products. If any segment (track) of the railroad is left as a monopoly, potential foreclosures might exist. Reciprocal switching agreements allow traffic originating on a rival carrier's tracks to be switched to another carrier in the area. Then the issue is whether the monopolist should be free to negotiate with a competitor the transfer price to be paid for the rights, or whether a regulatory agency should prevent foreclosures of the access or should more generally regulate a "fair transfer price."[2] Empirical evidence indicates that the absence of interline competition causes a substantial decline in social welfare, borne by shippers and consumers (Kleit 1989; Grimm, Winston, and Evans 1992). A horizontal breakup diminishes the possibility of market foreclosures. Yet the extent of monopoly power is limited by the existence of substitute services, such as the trucking sector.

Structural breakups and private sector access to infrastructure and the provision of services can further reap the benefits of deregulation of the sector, which often accompanies restructuring of the enterprise. Deregulatory gains come not necessarily from a general lowering of prices, but rather from the elimination of an inefficient rate structure; from improvements in railroad operating efficiency, delivery time, and reliability of service; and from the reduction of excess capacity and unproductive services.

In addition, railroads often provide some services below cost, which requires the establishment of contractual agreements not only with customers, other business units, and external customers, but also with local municipalities, provinces, and the federal government. Contractual arrangements would eliminate the current, often hidden, pattern of subsidies. Those contracts should be based on the quality of service, internal prices, or market prices when applicable, and they should avoid any form of direct cross-subsidization. They should cover the costs of operations. If government entities are not willing or able to contract for the services at cost, the services should be discontinued. An analysis of the financial viability of such suboperation should precede any restructuring analysis. Box 13.1 illustrates the case for Argentina.

Finally, the restructuring process in railways should follow the same general analytical guidelines as described in chapter 10. (The separation of fixed facilities from operations has also been discussed in Moyer and Thompson [1990] as a technique for railway restructuring).

National Railway Company

Most national railway companies are troubled state enterprises. Their obvious problems include financial distress, excess employment, costs of wages and benefits, and technical and managerial inefficiencies in many divisions. This analysis of restructuring and privatization concentrates primarily on organizational issues involving horizontal and vertical grouping within the enterprise for private sector participation. A description of the current situation is presented below, followed by a potential organizational and operational restructuring along the lines described above.

Resources

The basic activities of a national railway company can be described as the loading and unloading of trains; assembly of trains; operating of terminals; operating of stations and shops for the maintenance of rolling beds and rolling stock; construction of new beds and acquisition of rolling stock; coordination and scheduling of traffic, freight, and passenger transport; and marketing of those services.

A description of the stock of resources controlled by a medium-to-large national railway

---

Box 13.1 Summary of Findings of Study on Financial Viability of Railway Services, Argentina

Status	Services
Commercially viable	All freight services Buenos Aires–Mar del Plata intercity service: Concessions were granted

Commercially nonviable and not expendable	All other intercity services:
	    Responsibility returned to provinces
	    Some have been discontinued
	    Some have had concessions issued

Commercially nonviable, but socially essential	Metropolitan commuter rail and subway: Concessions issued supported by government subsidies

company (for example, the Mexican Railway Company) is presented in table 13.1. However, the numbers are often misleading. Fewer resources are in operational condition. For example, out of 1,400 passenger wagons, only 560 are in service (40 percent), 242 are awaiting some type of service, 92 are waiting to be disposed of, and the rest are being evaluated to see if they should be disposed of. The average age of the wagons is sixteen years. Out of 1,600 engines, only 995 are operational (55 percent), and 200 are irreparable. The average age of the engines is fifteen years. In addition, out of an existing network of, say, 26,000 kilometers of rolling beds, 96 percent of the freight traffic takes place in a network that is often less than half of the existing network.

Usually the company is a freight-oriented railway company with a significant role in the country's freight transport system. In contrast, its contribution to the passenger transport market is minimal. This is reflected not only in the stock of freight wagons relative to passenger wagons, but also in the following statistics. For example, the national railway company moves 51 million tons yearly, about 14 percent of the market, or 36,500 million ton-kilometers, with an average trip of 717 kilometers (in addition, the freight service tends to be heavily concentrated; often less than ten products account for more than two-thirds of the total tons transported). In the passenger market, the railway company moves about 18 million passengers a year, or about 2 percent of the market, and 5,600 million passenger-kilometers, with an average trip per passenger of 322 kilometers. While the potential to increase the share of the passenger market is questionable, the potential to increase the freight market is usually significant under more efficient operations. For example, in the United States the railway system accounts for nearly one-third of the volume of freight moved.

Last but not least, a highly valuable resource is the rights-of-way, which are essential to operation and which generate additional rents when marketed to outside parties (utility companies). Those rights provide for continuous links between urban centers, and are very attractive to telecommunications, natural gas, and oil companies. For example, rents are derived from use of railways' rights-of-way for fiber-optic cables.

Cost Structure

For a company with fully integrated operations, the aggregate distribution of costs is typically as follows:

- *Input allocation of costs.* Labor, 67 percent; capital inputs, 21 percent; depreciation, 2 percent; services and others, 10 percent.
- *Activity allocation of costs.* Freight services, 78 percent; passenger services, 15 percent; others, 7 percent.
- *Fixed- and variable-cost allocation.* Fixed costs (maintenance and depreciation, management, debt service, pension liabilities, and services), 75 percent; variable costs (labor for operations, operations en route, loading, and unloading; fuel and energy; use of rolling stock, stations, and rolling beds; coordination of use and scheduling of service; sales and marketing; and maintenance), 25 percent.

Costs and revenues are as follows. For freight operations, thirty-six products generate revenues larger than variable costs, four break even, and fourteen generate deficits. That takes into account the recent 23 percent increase in railway freight tariffs. On average, variable costs exceed average revenue by 10 percent. That statistic, coupled with the breakdown of fixed and variable costs, best describes the financial situation of a typical national railway company. To some extent, the numbers are affected by the sys-

Table 13.1 Resources of a Medium-to-Large National Railway Company

Resources	Quantity
Rolling beds (kilometers)	26,000
Stations	700
Main terminals and warehouses	25
Maintenance shops	30
Rolling stock	
Engines	1,600
Freight wagons	47,000
Passenger and express wagons	1,400
Labor force	55,000

tem of accounting and the labor contract, which is a fixed cost.

Moreover, passenger service as of now represents 20 percent of operating costs and contributes 5 percent of total revenues. The high level of subsidies and inefficiency is reflected in the fact that revenue from passenger service accounts for only 17 percent of the company's total costs. In contrast, revenue from freight operations accounts for 88 percent of the total.

Productivity

Productivity of the typical national railway company is 0.82 ton-kilometers per wagon per year, while the average productivity of railroad enterprises, particularly in industrialized countries, is more like 3.4 ton-kilometers per wagon per year. For example, in the United States the average productivity among the top sixteen railway enterprises is more than 2 million ton-kilometers per wagon per year (Ochoa and Asociados 1990). A large component of that differential is due to differences in speed. While the average speed for the national railway company is 22 kilometers per hour, the comparison railroads travel at an average speed of 75 kilometers per hour. National companies are slower because they use single-track beds, experience delays in loading and unloading (70 percent), have a high percentage of wagons returning empty (42 percent), have smaller loads per wagon (8.5 percent), and have less operational equipment (18 percent). Only 60 percent of national railway company locomotives are available for use at any one time, compared to 90 percent for the average U.S. railway company.[3]

Likewise, there is a significant freight-cost differential between the national railway company and the average U.S. railway company. Measured in terms of dollars per ton-kilometer, that unit cost for a national railway company is more than 20 percent of the average unit cost for a U.S. railway, despite high unit labor and fuel costs in the United States. Additionally, while labor costs as a percentage of input costs are 67 percent for the national railway company, they are 32 percent for the average U.S. railroad.

National railway companies have low productivity and high inefficiency for two reasons: structural (external) and organizational (internal). Among the external factors are poor infrastructure and outdated technology. Among the internal factors are excess labor, inadequate organizational structure, and lack of an effective incentive system. The last two affect particularly the quality and marketing of services and hamper the potential growth of demand. By any standard, national railway companies are overstaffed. Despite efforts to rationalize labor in recent years, through voluntary retirement and attrition programs, national railway companies are still significantly overstaffed. As of now, they have about 55,000 employees, plus between 10,000 and 12,000 temporary workers who fill in during the occasional absence of permanent workers. Moreover, they have the financial liability of about 40,000 pensioners, which represents 15 percent of labor costs and 11 percent of operating costs. Fuel consumption is 50 percent higher than the consumption of U.S. companies per unit of transport or freight.

The recent deregulation of truck tariffs and the extensive privatization of former parastatals in countries with national railway companies have adversely affected the demand for their services. More than 50 percent of the demand came from those enterprises that often were forced to use the national company's services. Those clients, in the process of becoming private themselves, are becoming more sensitive to costs, which has encouraged them to seek alternative, apparently more reliable and cost-effective sources of transport. National railway companies lost about $70 million, which does not include direct budgeted transfers from the government. Recently, their revenues in real terms have declined by 10.7 percent, and their costs in real terms have increased by 12 percent.

Economies of Scale and Integration

Most of the cost involved in maintaining a rolling bed unit is fixed. Because of the significant economies of scale existing in the track and coordination units, no gains are derived from breaking that segment of the national railway company's operations into various units. At best, some geographical subdivision could be considered if size is perceived to be a problem.

However, no economies of scope or scale would be lost by separating the maintenance and repair of engines and wagons from the rest of the enterprise. They are very distinct and technical operations which have little in common with the rest of operations.

Rolling stock operations, passengers, and freight display some economies of scale, but those economies are not excessive and are likely to be exhausted at a relatively low level of operation. Most of them are embedded in the concept of the unit train, but technology and safety impose limits on the length of the train. Variable costs are roughly constant, if the unit of measurement is taken to be the unit train. A constant returns to scale technology is a good approximation of those types of operations. Fixed costs are essentially management costs plus the costs of capital, and they account for roughly 30 percent of the total costs of the operation. Breaking that segment of the enterprise into several similar units able to perform the same operations would not lower efficiency because of economies of scale, but it would provide a competitive environment. The benefits of competition would be lower costs of operations, higher productivity, better quality and reliability of service, and perhaps less need to regulate tariff structures. To achieve these benefits, incentives would have to be linked to relative performance, allowing each unit to retain a share of the residual rights. Likewise, because labor is a major component of operating costs, to achieve cost efficiency and improve the quality of the service, the units should have discretion to contract and sever labor, including determining bonuses and other appropriate compensations that are tied to performance.

Marketing, for both passengers and freight, displays some economies of scale that are probably larger than those connected with running the trains, but are not terribly large. Establishing geographically dispersed offices entails fixed costs that will need to be duplicated if passenger and freight services are divided into several units. Given the large volume of merchandise moved, particularly freight, it would be fair to approximate the technology as a constant returns to scale, particularly for the relevant range of operations. Freight is perhaps the least developed and most important segment of operations and is where the largest returns can be obtained. Particularly in industrialized countries, the railroad sector moves more than one-third of all goods, while national railway companies have only 14 percent of the transport market. Because of that, there is significant potential for growth. The aggressiveness of marketing agents seeking to increase market share, which is usually associated with competitive markets, could well be the vehicle to generate that growth. Nevertheless, growth in itself is not necessarily desirable, particularly if it occurs in products where variable costs exceed revenues. As of now, the average variable cost exceeds the average revenue by 10 percent. Given almost constant returns to scale technology, growth of that service would lead to a larger deficit. The emphasis should be on reducing costs and increasing productivity for those products where variable costs exceed revenues. For products where revenues exceed variable costs, the combination of growth, reduced costs, and increased productivity should be sought.

Significant economies of scale are possible in scheduling, coordination of operations, and infrastructure (tracks, terminals, and stations). Moreover, there are no advantages and numerous disadvantages in breaking these segments into several similar units, and they should remain whole and centralized. Whether they should remain in government hands is a different issue. Although the government could retain the property rights or ownership, a concession to a private entity should be considered.

The arguments just presented focus on the issue of economies of scale gained or lost if horizontal disintegration were to take place at the various stages of operations. However, another aspect needs to be considered: whether economies of scale exist in the vertical integration of its operations and, if they do, to what extent. The three broad categories that determine the extent of vertical integration are technological economies, transactional economies, and market imperfections. A preliminary examination of the operations of national railway companies indicates that no significant technological economies are gained across stages of production, nor do market imperfections justify the vertical integration of their operations. Transactional economies might be lost in a vertical disintegration, but even those losses are not likely to be significant and can be mitigated by the use of transfer prices. Some economies of scope might be lost because of management, but once again the losses are likely to be small and to be more than compensated for by the efficiency gains that potentially can be reaped by the vertical restructuring process.

Fringe and Intermodal Competition

In freight service, the relevant competition is provided by the trucking sector, which has steadily been gaining transport market share. During the last two decades freight transport has been growing at an average annual rate of 4 percent. During the same period, the market share of railways has decreased from 21 to 14 percent, while the share of trucking has increased from 73 to 79 percent. Rate structure and the quality and reliability of service are the major causes of this shift. Deregulation of the autotransport sector, as expected, has affected the demand for freight service provided by national railway companies. The ratios of freight to autotransport range from 123 percent to 85 percent for the twelve most significant (in terms of volume) products (automobiles are an outlier with a ratio of 58.2 percent). Allowing companies the flexibility to negotiate tariffs would enable national railway companies to respond to the increased competition from the autotransport industry.

In passenger services, the relevant competition is provided by public bus services. The changes in this sector have been quite dramatic. During the last two decades the average annual growth rate has been 7.5 percent. In that period the demand for railway services fell by half, and

as of now its market share is about 1 percent. (If services provided within urban settings are excluded, the share increases to 3 percent.) In contrast, the demand for public bus service has grown fivefold, and its market share is 99 percent. That has been the trend, although fares for all railway services are substantially below bus fares for the corresponding service, with the exception of sleeping wagons, where the price is significantly higher. For first- and second-class services, railway fares are 51 and 25 percent, respectively, of bus fares. For special first-class service, the fare is identical to the bus fare (similar service), and for sleeping wagons, the fare is 67 percent more than the closest equivalent bus fare. The apparent reason for the dominance of bus over railway transport is, foremost, time, followed by scheduling and possibly service. Railway service time between two points tends to be on average twice as long as bus service time.

The decrease in passengers and freight has produced a decrease, in real terms, in revenues of 28 and 35 percent, respectively, in the last two years of operation, relative to the highest revenues.

Incentives

The incentive structure designed to induce and reward effective performance is usually set forth through a contract plan. While historically incentives were determined largely by output targets and incompletely defined financial measures (targets), some improvements have been made in the most recent plans. In these, targets have often been replaced with a complex system of weighted performance measures. For example, 40 percent of the evaluation grade is based on deficit control, 20 percent on generation of freight traffic and total use of locomotives, 15 percent each on rehabilitation of rolling stock and fixed facilities, and 10 percent on studies of human resources and structural change in the railway institution.

Although the incentive structure set forth in recent contract plans represents an improvement over the previous incentive structure, it is still deficient. The performance objectives often contain irrelevant, conflicting, and potentially perverse incentives. For example, there are tradeoffs in the weighted performance index between increasing ton-kilometer and deficit control. Increasing freight traffic can increase the deficit. Likewise there are tradeoffs between track maintenance and increased traffic, and between rehabilitation and deficit reduction. The tradeoffs (to management) are based on the weights of the performance measures, and those weights do not necessarily provide the correct signals for, or reflect, marginal social value. Some of the performance measures currently used are not relevant or are redundant, like those regarding the availability of locomotives, which, in any case, will show up indirectly in the deficit measure. These are internal measures that are factored into the cost structure of the enterprise, and the decision to use them or not for setting its own incentives (for the relevant units) should be left to management. As Galenson and Thompson (1991) have stated, the current performance measures guarantee continuing government interference in matters that should be left entirely to the discretion of railway management. Finally, the incentive structure of the contract plan is valid for only one year, and a new one has to be reconvened for the year after. That is too short a time span for anything other than inefficient myopic actions.

Performance measures should be based on clear and relatively simple financial variables (targets) and should cover an extended period to allow efficiency of investment and capital planning to take effect. Compensation, based on those measures, should be designed for the enterprise as a whole. The setting of internal incentives and the decisions on how to divide the compensation across layers and units of the enterprise should be left entirely to the discretion of management.

Government Role

Given the characteristics of the railroad sector, the government has a key role to play in the restructuring process because national railway companies are owned by the state and because a number of services deemed desirable are not financially viable. In almost all countries railway services are subsidized by the government. As of now, direct transfers from the government to the national railway company range between 0.1 and 0.5 percent of gross national product.[4] There are a number of acceptable justifications for the subsidization of railway services, including their social desirability in sparsely populated areas and the reduction of congestion on motorways, but the subsidies ought to be transparent, and the operating company should not be forced to bear the losses. Government involvement is also needed because some of the economically desirable restructuring might be politically damaging because the indebtedness and liabilities of the enterprise affect the quasi-fiscal deficit.

In particular, the issues to be negotiated are

- Establishment of a politically feasible schedule to rationalize excess labor (perceived to be more than one-third of the current labor force)
- Deregulation of tariffs and discretion to abandon services with negative net social costs and benefits
- Government assumption of current pension obligations, prior to concession/privatization
- Contracting for (socially desirable) below-cost services
- Investment for modernization of fixed facilities, equipment, and control systems
- Criteria and sources of financing and the private sector's role
- Financial rescheduling of existing debt
- Privatization or concession of most operations
- Setting up of an independent regulatory agency with jurisdiction over the pricing of noncompetitive aspects of railroad operations, access to network terms, and resolution of disputes between private agents and government agents, and with jurisdiction over access rights and new capital investment rules.

Options for Restructuring

The main objectives to be sought through the restructuring process are increased efficiency (through the reduction of costs and better use of the existing resources), increased productivity, financially viable growth (particularly in the freight service category), and generation of private sector participation in selected areas. Broadly stated, the mechanisms and options through which these objectives can be accomplished are selective horizontal and vertical segmentation of the enterprise, implementation of unit-specific compensation or incentive schemes, and the opening to the private sector of access (wholly or partially) to railway operations. We divide the recommendations into two categories, one for short-term and the other for long-term restructuring. Obviously, the latter is more encompassing and therefore requires a longer time span for implementation, while the former can be started right away with little disruption of ongoing activities.

The short-term recommendations are as follows:

- *Labor.* Labor should be rationalized at a rate politically and socially acceptable, with a target reduction of at least one-third of the labor force by the end of the program, through attrition, voluntary (with incentives) retirement, and a freeze on new hiring. As of now, labor costs exceed two-thirds of operating costs, making financial viability of the enterprise nearly impossible. Pensions, which cover an average of 40,000 pensioners, and liabilities account for 15 percent of labor costs and 11 percent of operating costs and should be transferred to the federal budget.[5]
- *Operations.* Financial and operational autonomy should be granted to maintenance units being concessioned or sold to private operators. Efficiency would improve by reducing slack, and costs would be reduced by decreasing the number of units, by automating the signalization of rolling beds, by modernizing accounting procedures, by computerizing operations and inventory, and by closing down ineffective services in the areas of passengers, express mail, stations, and maintenance units (shops).
- *Private sector participation.* Facilitating the participation of the private sector can range

from the subcontracting of concessionaire services (food, janitorial, medical, and so forth), maintenance services, or services such as running sheds purchased or leased from the national railway company, to full (segmented) privatization of railway operations. In addition, railway assets should be able to be used for nonrail business, allowing private sector entities access (at a price) to the infrastructure and services, both for their own use and for the provision of services to third parties. The private sector should be allowed to construct and operate new terminals, both specific or multiproduct, and to concession and divest repair shops. A number of existing cases of those types of private sector participation are presented in Galenson and Thompson (1991).

- *Organizational structure and incentives.* Reforms include identifying profit centers and decentralizing decisionmaking, granting autonomy, and implementing incentive schemes or compensation (residual rights), preferably related to performance. Comparisons could be established across units or, if necessary and appropriate, across units outside the organization performing comparable activities. Measurable and objective performance criteria should be established for each type of unit. In particular, unit managers should be allowed to retain a fraction of the gains from improved productivity that is not directly linked with the acquisition of new technology, rather than have compensation determined as a percentage of current wages, as is now the case. Specifically, compensation to the operations units, in the form of commissions and similar modes, should be strongly linked to the volume of sales. The freight operations and the various modes of passenger services should be converted into distinct business units, as should the maintenance of rolling beds.
- *Investment priorities.* Capital investment priorities should be directed toward communications, signaling, and management information systems, which will significantly improve the use of existing capacity. New

extensions of tracks could be concessioned to the private sector through competitive bidding, based either on lowest costs or on lowest toll track per unit of service. The latter option clearly has fewer implications for the government budget.

- *Autonomous decisionmaking.* The national railway company needs to be able to make decisions autonomously, relative to the government, or at least to improve the coordination of objectives and decisions, particularly on the choice of standards and investment planning (construction of new routes).

- *Contracting.* Given that most of the passenger services now provided (at subsidized prices) by national railway companies are not financially viable and are undertaken with a social objective more than an economic one, it is imperative to increase transparency by implementing contracts between the affected parties—municipal, provincial, or federal entities, and the preferably private railway company—so the financial burden is explicit. Those entities should assess how much the service is worth to them (how much they are willing to pay for it). If that amount covers the costs of providing the service, then the company should provide it, if no alternative use of those resources generates higher value. Otherwise, the service should be discontinued. (Other activities might generate greater benefits both for the company and for society as a whole, if the same resources were to be used there.) The idea is that the national railway company should be run as an autonomous, financially viable service company that is open to any contractual relation with any party desiring its services.

- *Clear rules of the game.* In the short run and perhaps in the long run as well, private and public operators or entities will coexist. That in itself is bound to create suspicions of unfair use of control or of favorable treatment of state-owned operators, and that can reduce private sector interest. Therefore, to entice private sector participation, the

rules guiding operations, rights, and transactions should be as clear as possible. This is quite important because large sunk costs have to be borne by private participants. The rules and criteria for changing them, and the procedures for resolving disputes and for determining private participation, should be transparent. For example, the following questions need to be addressed: How will nonmarket prices or fees be determined? How will scheduling conflicts be resolved? Will the company have priority? How will a level playing field be guaranteed for all participants? What restrictions will be placed on operations and on entry and exit procedures? How will decisions regarding new routes and their financing be made? How will labor disputes affecting private operators be handled? Without clear rules, both efficiency and private sector participation will be hindered.

- *Creation of an autonomous regulatory agency.* The often common structure of the national railway company remaining both the provider of services, some under exclusive control, and the regulator, is untenable. With private sector participation there is an extensive and competitive interaction between the national railway company and private firms, with the railway company having leverage or monopoly power in some transactions, and further control through scheduling, the provision of access equipment crews, and other complementary services. That conflict of interest might undermine efficiency. Thus, a regulatory agency should be established independent of the national railway company and should be given jurisdiction over tariffs for noncompetitive segments, scheduling, logistics, connecting and access fees, the granting of licenses, concessions, new investments, operating fees for private sector unit trains, and resolution of conflicts (prior to the court system). They should also have jurisdiction over repair and maintenance shops. High setup costs, economies of scale, and geographical separations confer some degree of monopoly power on the operators and concessionaires of those services. The issue is whether the quasi-monopolist should be free to negotiate with a customer or competitor the transfer prices for trackage rights (as in the United States), or repair maintenance fees, or whether the regulatory agency should prevent market foreclosures and should more generally regulate a "fair transfer price" and maintenance and repair services fees. The answer clearly depends on the degree of contestability of the operation. Moreover, the national railway company should be empowered to regulate safety standards, mechanical inspection, professional competence, and the working hours of drivers.

A long-term perspective suggests that the national railway company should be divided into three types of autonomous companies: one for scheduling, rolling beds, terminals, and stations; one for rolling stock and maintenance; and one for operations, freight, and passengers. Moreover, several subcompanies of each type, except the first, should be formed, and concessions or sale and access should be granted to private operators so that a competitive culture can develop.

Clearly, the extent of private participation might render the existence of the equivalent state-owned subcompanies unnecessary. A description of the types of companies follows; the structure is depicted in figure 13.1.

A single company should be in charge of scheduling (rights-of-way), rolling beds, terminals, and stations. The extent of fixed and sunk costs of this activity provides for natural monopoly cost conditions, which warrant the existence of a single entity with control and responsibility for those operations, albeit subject to regulation. However, this company should contain three units or profit centers: one for maintenance and new construction of rolling beds, another for the scheduling and coordination of traffic, and a third for the operation of terminals and stations. User charges for scheduling, access to rolling beds, and use of terminals and stations should be levied on the operating units or private entities when applicable. In the event of congestion, differential pricing (related to time) should be used to determine both access and scheduling fees. This single company could be government-owned and operated or, preferably, the operations could be concessioned to the private sector.

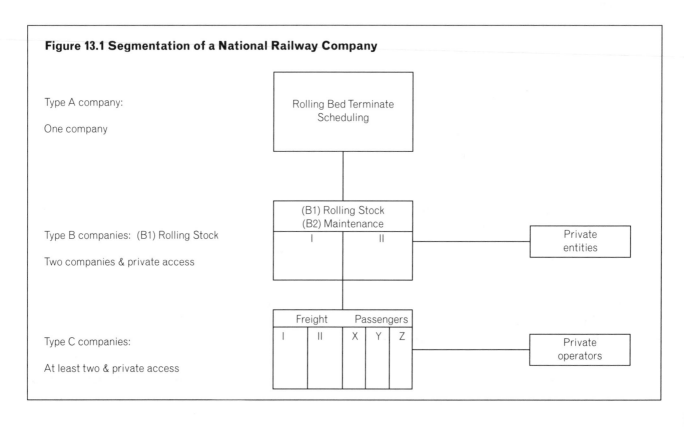

Figure 13.1 Segmentation of a National Railway Company

Type A company:

One company

Rolling Bed Terminate Scheduling

Type B companies: (B1) Rolling Stock

Two companies & private access

(B1) Rolling Stock
(B2) Maintenance

I | II

Private entities

Type C companies:

At least two & private access

Freight | Passengers

I | II | X | Y | Z

Private operators

A number of rolling stock companies could split the property rights of traction and both passenger and freight wagons. With a stock of 1,600 engines, 47,000 freight wagons, and 1,400 passenger wagons, few economies of scale would be lost by partitioning the freight segment into at least two subcompanies, and much would be gained by having increased competition for the pricing and use or placement of equipment. The effect should be to provide better service and increase productivity by reducing idle time, increasing load factors, and lowering turnaround time. Private operators should be allowed access to provide both their own service and service to third parties.

Maintenance should be privatized or subcontracted to private parties. In the event that it is not, it should be tied to the rolling stock companies.

Because service operations are sufficiently distinct, a number of subcompanies (or units by type of service) could be established and offered to the private sector. In particular, freight and passenger operations should be separated, and passenger operations should be separated further into companies serving freight and passengers: at least two (private) subcompanies should carry freight and engage in similar operations, and several companies should carry passengers and be subdivided into provincial, long-distance, and commuter (suburban) service.

Given the relatively low volume of passengers per route, there should be little advantage to having more than one company provide passenger service. The lost economies of scale might easily outweigh any gains from increased competition. On that basis, only different units or profit centers should be created for different types of passenger service. However, it would be appropriate to consider forming more than one unit for freight operations and to extend access to the private sector.

The operations companies are of particular importance, because it is in their area of jurisdiction where significant gains, cost reductions, increased productivity, and growth are possible. In turn they will provide added incentives for improvements in the running of rolling stock

and maintenance companies. Freight and some intercity services have the potential to be profitable, and a significant untapped market exists for both types of services. Establishing the right set of incentives is critical. Marketing the service is their main activity, and compensation should be determined by volume of sales and by relative performance.

Separating rights-of-way and scheduling from operations would give outside parties greater access to the network, which would enhance the likelihood of intramodal competition. Access to the railway infrastructure should be provided at a fair price to potential operators or individual customers wishing to provide their own service.[6] Giving potential private operators access to railway infrastructure would deter cross-subsidization among types of service, which is generally an undesirable feature of a multiproduct pricing system. If cross-subsidization were to exist, profitable entry could occur in the service that is priced above cost. In addition, the suggested separation would improve financial accountability and clarify the cost structure of the units separated. When separated, operations units would be charged variable costs for the use of rolling beds and the costs of scheduling. That would make comparisons between and within modes of performance much easier and would enhance competition in the transport sector.

An advantage of long-term restructuring is that it separates the (essential) monopoly part of national railway company operations from the rest. That separation is desirable because it facilitates the future privatization of parts of the operation. The operations company could remain in government hands, and the rest of the network could be privatized. Moreover, separating rolling beds (rights-of-way) from operations could create opportunities for competitive operations on common track. That competitive argument is behind the Swedish railway restructuring and behind the European Community proposal to require all European railways to separate their railway operations from their rights-of-way functions.

The proposed vertical and horizontal disintegration and the granting of private sector access should be considered as ways to promote competition and capture efficiency gains in the railway sector.

In summary, horizontal and vertical separations could constitute a valid technique for enterprise restructuring, and as such deserve careful consideration. However, if the costs of these separations prove to be excessive, other restructuring tools are at hand.

Current Rail Franchising Agreements

Although there is still vigorous debate about whether contracting out has improved the quality of service, there is little doubt that it has significantly reduced the cost of providing services, primarily due to reduced labor costs. Franchising has generally been adopted as a means of introducing competition and private sector capital into subsidized rail services. The experience of rail franchising in Argentina (Buenos Aires freight and intercity), Sweden, the United Kingdom, and the United States (Boston and Los Angeles) gives some guidance on the franchising arrangements that are likely to be attractive to potential bidders and on possible problems. Although not all of these cases have been fully implemented, the design process is well under way: local transport authorities in Sweden opened the operation of local passenger services to bidding from both private sector firms and the state-owned company. The first contract was awarded to a private sector firm, which has since won additional contracts in competition with the state-owned company.

In the United States, suburban rail services in Boston have been franchised since 1989, and Los Angeles will soon accept bids for commuter service franchises. The Manchester franchise in the United Kingdom began operating in 1992. The Argentine government intends to issue franchise contracts for virtually the entire rail system, including suburban and metro services in Buenos Aires, intercity passenger services, and an extensive network of freight services. There is much to be gained from having a rolling program of franchise awards. It allows mistakes in the design and award of franchises

to be rectified and gives time to build up a pool of potential bidders. The franchiser will need to survey bidders' views in advance and to promote the franchises, particularly if it hopes to attract bids from foreign companies. At least twelve months are needed to move from the request for bids to the award and signing of the final contract.

Evidence on franchise performance is limited. Of the cases mentioned above, only the franchises in Boston, Manchester, and Sweden have been operating for some time. In those cases, franchisees negotiated significant changes in labor contracts, compared with previous or other industry arrangements, reducing the labor force, allowing greater flexibility in the use of labor, and, in Boston, lowering the rates of pay. In Sweden the process of franchising services previously operated by the state-owned railway has had beneficial effects on the rest of the organization. The threat of increased competition has caused the state-owned railway, as a whole, to become more efficient. A striking feature of these examples is the sheer diversity of franchise arrangements observed. The contracts have been written for anywhere from one year (in Sweden) to thirty years (in Argentina). Moreover, in Sweden the typical contract covers only the operation and maintenance of trains, while in Argentina contracts include infrastructure and all rolling stock of traction equipment. Argentina also requires franchise companies to undertake major investments.

In conclusion, both analysis and experience indicate that a key characteristic of franchises is the length of the contract. Short-term contracts maximize the opportunity for competition for the market, which is a primary objective of any franchising process. Long-term franchises, however, make it easier for a wider range of responsibilities to be transferred to the company and offer stronger inducements than do short-term contracts for innovative reorganization. If franchising is to improve the railway industry, the agency in control must create conditions that encourage competition for franchises while giving companies both the motive and opportunity to invest in and improve the service.

ROADS

Many developing countries are experimenting with private toll roads, mostly for fiscal reasons, although most developed nations with mature and broad network coverage, such as the U.S., Canada, Australia, and Northern Europe, continue to rely primarily on tax revenues to finance road maintenance and new construction. As a result of fiscal pressures to maintain macroeconomic stability and the clear priority to invest in the social sector, developing countries have opted for toll financing and private concessions, in their dire need to expand the highway network. However, since many of these countries started building expressways only in the late 1980s and 1990s, there is not a large body of evidence to examine. This section will consider the main issues on road financing, operation, and regulation, and the specifics of the Mexico program,[7] which presents a relatively advanced example and the more general challenges of constructing a successful private toll road system. The other country in Latin America that has been involved in private toll road development has been Argentina, although its involvement has been mostly restricted to new access roads and rings around the Greater Buenos Aires area. The objectives of those two cases contrast. While Mexico was seeking a significant expansion of its road network, Argentina's objective was the reconstruction and maintenance of existing roads. The experiences are reported in this chapter.

The incentives and challenges related to privatizing roadways do not differ greatly from those for privatizing highly durable assets, but some of the issues are quite distinct and most extreme. First, the level of required investment is most significant; most of it qualifies as sunk costs and is long term. The assets are long lived—around twenty to thirty years—and given the standard cash flows (with competitive toll road fees), require a similar number of years to amortize the investment. Financial markets in most developing countries do not provide long-term capital. Efficient pricing, based on marginal costs, does not allow for coverage of the fixed costs; in a first-best context it should reflect marginal congestion costs. It could be as low as zero in times of excess capacity, and at whatever level is necessary to clear the market in times of excess demand congestion. Finally, there are significant externalities in the construction and operation of a highway, which in principle are not captured by the road operator. Arguments in favor of private provision of highways include relieving the government of large investment requirements, increased efficiency of the service, and increased (private) capital investment entering the economy. Opponents of privatization point to insufficient network coverage if cross-subsidies are not allowed, to inefficient pricing, and to potential abuses by the provider if given free rein in setting toll levels.

Besides lowering expenditures of the central government, attracting investment (particularly foreign) clearly would have extremely beneficial effects for any developing economy. Private domestic capital markets in developing countries offer few long-term investments, especially when there is a history of inflation or political instability. Access to international capital markets may be even more limited. Detractors, however, argue that the total pool of savings for the country cannot increase unless the laws allow international investors to participate.

If that is the case, success in tapping new capital markets will be directly related to the government's willingness and ability to provide investors with reasonable security. Both domestic and foreign investors will want guarantees about the rate of future toll increases, and assurances that the government will not unilaterally alter the terms of the franchise agreement. Foreign investors are likely to seek greater assurances because of exchange rate risk, and because their political risks are greater or, at least, more difficult to assess. The more limited the government assurances, therefore, the more limited the pool of investors. In Mexico, for example, the government agreed to a specific toll formula, but uncertainty about other related government policies, and constraints on their participation, limited those interested in the initial road privatizations to domestic entrepreneurs.

Another area of concern is whether a private provider will maintain all aspects of the service as it was when controlled by the government. Transportation planners and economists have long debated the wisdom of financing roads with tolls rather than taxes. One concern is whether toll receipts can or should cover costs, since often as a result of externalities or equity concerns, the social returns considerably exceed private returns. In countries or network areas with low traffic levels, franchisees will have to charge high tolls that may, in turn, lower the number of users. Obviously the criterion to guide the desirability of new highways is whether the social benefits exceed the social costs (and even then, opportunity cost of capital issues would dictate the course of action). If so, and given that low traffic volumes are a particular problem in developing countries, some type of cross-subsidization may be necessary. With toll-financed roads, some areas will not be profitable. If the provider cannot price in such a way as to compensate for low-traffic roads, the quality of service will decrease, particularly toward the end of the concession period. Although this problem is not limited to the privatization question, it increases the opposition to privatization and further complicates the role of government in setting acceptable rates.

Additionally, political pressures for a standardized level of service, such as uniform toll rates over a broad geographic area, can further complicate attempts to privatize highways. Governments may prefer a standardized network as a way of politically or socially integrating a nation. A standardized network can also be helpful in achieving a more uniform pattern of regional economic development, and it can be argued that disruptions are less likely to occur if different parts of a highway system use the same weight and dimension restrictions. However, standardization also reduces the ability of capital to adapt to differing needs, thereby creating use inefficiencies. As a result, networks that require standardized tolls or other similar policies are difficult to privatize, and will attract fewer interested bidders.

The final objection to privatizing roads is the regulatory requirements on the government itself. Although the government will have removed itself from day-to-day operations, it still must oversee the pricing and service provision choices. One unfortunate outcome is that public officials yield to popular pressures and set unrealistically low toll rates. This gap would lead to service inadequacies and shortages. The reverse unfortunate outcome is that public officials are captured by the very firms they regulate, and set tolls well above costs. Striking a balance between protecting the public and providing investors an opportunity to earn adequate rates of return may well be the most challenging aspect of the entire process.

POTHOLES ON THE PATH TO PRIVATIZING ROADS: MEXICO'S PRIVATE TOLL ROAD PROGRAM

Mexico has shifted between toll and tax financing of highways several times as public sector resources have waxed and waned. The country began building its high-performance road system as publicly owned toll roads in the 1950s. Beginning in 1963 a government-owned toll road company built almost 1,000 kilometers of toll roads. Those roads are mostly operated by the federal toll road authority, Caminos y Puentes Federales de Ingresso y Servicios Conexos (CAPUFE), which is an agency of the Ministry of Communications and Transportation. The public toll roads are concentrated around Mexico City, where traffic volume is generally highest. In the early 1970s, however, Mexico shifted to tax financing for new expressways, fueled by the pro public sector regimes of Presidents Luis Echeverria Alvarez (1970–76) and José Lopez Portillo (1976–82). By the mid-1980s, almost 3,000 kilometers of untolled four-lane divided highways had been opened to supplement CAPUFE's 1,000-kilometer toll network.

The rapid expansion of the public sector, combined with the collapse of oil prices in the early 1980s, adversely affected the Mexican economy, which led to another dramatic reversal of government polices. With the Mexican economy experiencing negative growth rates in 1982–83, government budget deficits grew to as much as 16 percent of GDP, and the financing of those deficits helped stimulate severe inflation. In response, President Miguel de la Madrid (1982–88) initiated a program to cut the size of the public sector, which his successor, President Carlos Salinas de Gortari (1988–94), expanded and accelerated. Privatization played a key role in the two presidents' strategies to reduce the government's budget deficit, largely through sale or liquidation of money-losing state enterprises.

Highways did not become a focus of the privatization program until the late 1980s. President de la Madrid raised tolls on the CAPUFE network beginning in 1982, but he hoped to use the proceeds to cover the government's budget deficit rather than to expand the system. The recession also cut traffic growth rates and made road investments a less pressing priority. The need for road improvements became more apparent as the economy began to show signs of recovery, and in 1986 the de la Madrid government asked the national development bank, BANOBRAS, to study the possibility that new toll roads could be built as private concessions. BANOBRAS was optimistic, but recommended an experimental program to test the feasibility. Accordingly, two road concessions totaling 215 kilometers were granted at the end of the de la Madrid administration, with BANOBRAS serving as the concessionaire and financing 50 percent of the project costs, contractors financing 25 percent, and state governments financing the remaining 25 percent.

In February 1986 President Salinas announced a dramatic new program to build 4,000 kilometers of new toll roads and seven new international toll bridges as private concessions before the end of his administration in 1994. The projected cost was almost US$5 billion, which tripled the rate of new highway investment over that of the preceding few years. Accelerated road construction was viewed as an important part of President Salinas' effort to revive the Mexican economy. Road building would stimulate the economy by putting Mexico's construction industry back to work, and high-quality infrastructure was deemed critical to Mexico's long-term prospects. Private toll roads seemed the only choice, since the government was trying to cut the public deficit and was in

the midst of difficult renegotiations of the enormous foreign debt left over from the public expansions of the 1970s.

Under the new program, the Ministry of Communications and Transportation would select the roads to be offered for concessions and specify the initial toll rates. Toll increases were to keep pace with the consumer price index. Bidders would be supplied with preliminary designs, cost estimates, and traffic projections prepared by the ministry. The concession would be awarded to the bidder that offered the shortest concession period, which could in no case exceed twenty years. The new program would rely primarily on private concessionaires and financing, unlike the pilot projects of the previous administration. The concessions were to be awarded to consortia of construction companies and banks. The construction companies were expected to put up 25 to 30 percent of the cost in the form of "sweat equity" by discounting their construction bills by an agreed-on percentage. The banks would finance the remaining 70 to 75 percent. To guard against conflicts of interest, each concession would create a special independent "trust" to review the contractor's bills, disburse the bank financing, and distribute the toll proceeds to the investors.

The government would guarantee its traffic and cost estimates in part. If traffic were less than the ministry forecast, the concessionaire could request an extension of the term of the concession. The concessionaire was responsible for the first 15 percent of any construction cost overruns; overruns in excess of 15 percent and any overruns caused by government-imposed delays or design modifications were grounds for requests for concession extensions. Direct public assistance for the concessionaires was to be kept to a minimum, except that the ministry would assemble the required right-of-way and lease it to the concessionaire for a nominal charge.

The ill-advised emphasis on short concessions was driven largely by the need to attract private capital. Financing long-term debt was nearly impossible in the Mexican domestic capital market during the 1980s, given the virulent inflation at the time; even five-year instruments were rare and could be sold only by the largest and most secure companies. The banks involved in the consortia preferred shorter concessions because they were reluctant to tie up their own funds for long periods. The contractors were also anxious to recover their sweat equity quickly, especially since some of it would be in the form of deferred depreciation on their equipment.

Mexican government officials wanted to ensure that the process of concession bidding was competitive and fair, and thus favored making awards on only one criterion, such as the concession duration. Under the new program, competing proposals would differ only in the duration of the concession, since all bidders would be required to accept the ministry's route and toll rates. Competition along one dimension would make the process transparent to all, and less subject to charges of manipulation or fraud. The private concessionaires included most of the major construction companies and banks in Mexico. Mexico's three largest construction companies were awarded nine of the twenty-nine new concessions signed by the Salinas administration from 1989–91, smaller construction companies were awarded fourteen concessions, and state governments received six (which were not awarded competitively).

Mexico's pace of new toll road construction was extraordinary. However, from an economic efficiency standpoint the program was a disaster. The efficiency problems started with the choice of a minimum concession period as the criterion on which to assign concessions. The basic problem of this approach is that it induces the bidder to propose a fast amortization for an asset which has a much longer life. This criterion, coupled with the ample and predictable opportunities to renegotiate, led to highly inefficient allocations (allegedly there was one bid of eighteen months for a new 60-kilometer highway!). Most of the earlier winning bids were in the six-to-ten-year range, well below the normal life of a well-maintained road. It is inconceivable to expect that the investment in a new highway can be amortized in such a short period. The fast amortization period, in turn, tends to justify charging the maximum tolls permitted. This, in turn, leads to

toll road underutilization, a significant welfare loss. A related problem was that the maximum tolls set by the ministry were too high to induce the minimum amount of traffic the ministry guaranteed. Due to minimum traffic guarantees and the risk of concession cancellation (if traffic exceeded guaranteed traffic), total traffic over the concession period was fixed at the time the concession was awarded (equal to minimum daily traffic guaranteed times the number of days of the concession). Since total traffic is thus given, revenue maximization is achieved by setting the price at its maximum allowed level (accounting for the nonlinear increase over time of maintenance and financial costs).

In addition, a major problem was inaccurate cost and traffic projections by the Ministry of Communications and Transportation. While government officials reported that the costs of most projects were within 15 percent of the estimate, a number of dramatic underestimates occurred. The combination of those inaccuracies and the government guarantees was lethal, leading to highly perverse operators' incentives, and opening the door to capture and highly favorable (to operators) renegotiation opportunities. The Mexican government and the concessionaires blame the poor cost projections largely on the speed with which the concessions were awarded. The designs for the roads were often incomplete when the concessions were put out to bid. Sometimes the federal government or local communities pressed for modifications in the route after the concessions were awarded. Indeed, incomplete plans were somewhat advantageous in that they allowed the concessionaires more freedom to suggest changes in alignment or design when they encountered unexpected problems.

The errors in the traffic projections were blamed not just on the pace of the program but also on the high toll rates for the new concessions. In 1988, before the concession program started, CAPUFE tolls averaged only slightly over US$0.02 per vehicle-kilometer. The toll rates on the new concessions averaged US$0.20 per vehicle-kilometer in 1991, and much higher for trucks. Mexican highway planners had little experience with such high tolls and were sometimes surprised by the amount of traffic diverted to parallel untolled roads. Occupancy rates, not surprisingly, were extremely low—in the 20 to 40 percent range on most toll roads.

Inaccurate cost and traffic projections also encouraged the opportunity to renegotiate concession terms in the event of overruns. Concessionaires might have been more inclined to overlook forecast inaccuracies when the concessions were being awarded because they understood that the concession terms might be renegotiated eventually to reflect more realistic cost and traffic figures. Moreover, some banks and other observers feared that the contractors had strong incentives to pad their construction bills to reduce the real equity they contributed. Obviously, bill padding and the opportunity for renegotiation, common features in most concessions, could undermine the competitive procurement process, particularly the possibility of securing the lowest cost or most efficient contractor.

As a consequence of these problems, toll roads were underused: the ratio of observed traffic to guaranteed traffic was nearly 50 percent; and the tolls were exceedingly high—around US$0.20 per kilometer (between five and ten times higher than comparable tolls in the U.S.). This arrangement was highly inefficient since traffic along the fastest and safest road (the toll road) was kept to a minimum, while traffic in the parallel toll-free road was excessive and congested. That implies, on average, higher congestion and faster deterioration of the toll-free road, maintenance of which is a responsibility of the government. The problem of underuse has been particularly acute in the case of trucks. The projected proportion of truck traffic was on average four times higher than the actual truck traffic. In the end, most of the concessions were renegotiated, with more favorable terms granted to the operators. Ironically, among those terms was extension of the concession agreements, which had been the criterion used to grant the concession.

Another factor that limited the effectiveness of the privatization program was that the government increased its financial contribution to the system. The government awarded the most profitable concessions first, in keeping with its desire to limit public assistance. As the network expanded, profitability declined, and Mexico was forced to gradually increase the direct government aid it offered for concessions. The primary source of the government aid has been surpluses generated by the existing CAPUFE toll roads. Thus, Mexico in effect began to subsidize the more recent private concessions using CAPUFE surpluses.

In the spring of 1990 the Ministry of Communications and Transportation began to solicit bids for concessions that included government promises to pay a fixed share of the estimated construction costs. The government announced that its share of construction costs would never exceed 25 percent of total concessionary toll road investments, but that limit was soon reached. The concessions awarded through July 1990 were financed 29 percent by contractor equity, 61 percent by banks, 5 percent by the federal government, and 5 percent by state governments. By early 1992, however, the contractor and bank shares had declined to 28 percent and 49 percent, respectively, while government's share, most of which was federal, had increased to 23 percent. The government announced its intention to alter the form of public support for new concessions in early 1992. Future government contributions toward construction costs would be treated as equity investments instead of grants; they would thus earn the same returns as the sweat-equity investments of the contractors, instead of no returns at all. The maximum government share would also increase to 40 percent as compared with 30 percent for the contractor and 30 percent debt.

Perhaps one of the few positive aspects of Mexico's aggressive private road program is the way it forced the Mexican capital markets and the government to devise new financial instruments to tap additional sources of funds, albeit not very efficiently. The Mexican banks were collaborative, possibly because they were still nationalized when the concession program began, and may have been pressured by the government to participate. Initially, most banks financed their share of construction costs through normal construction or commercial loans, drawing on the banks' existing pool of savers. Later, many banks began to refinance their contribution by issuing medium-term infrastructure bonds on the domestic bond market. Toll road revenues are not sufficient security to back most of these bonds, however, so they have been guaranteed by the bank. As roads have opened and developed a reliable traffic base, however, a few banks have begun to successfully sell certificates of participation that carry a fixed interest rate (over inflation), and are secured only by a claim against the toll road revenues and not guaranteed by the bank.

The right criterion to assign concession should have been the lowest toll (with the possibility of adjusting it for inflation), with the length of the concession being fixed in the twenty-to-thirty-year range to match the life of the asset. Apart from specific penalties, the granting of an option of first refusal to the operating concessionaire at renewal time should be considered to provide incentives for the proper level of road maintenance. Alternatively and ideally, consideration should be given to awarding what would be in effect a permanent concession, where the tools would be fixed for an initial period of, say, five to ten years (except for inflation), and after that revised for a subsequent period through a process similar to price-cap regulation. An alternative criterion is to select and fix efficient tolls and concession terms and adjudicate the toll road to the minimum lump-sum subsidy required to construct and operate the road. Interested bidders would submit as bids the subsidy they would need. With competitive behavior for the market, a second-best allocation would be obtained. The advantage of the latter option is that it allows for compensating the private operator for the externalities of the project, and partially captures, if necessary, the differential between the social and private benefit, while allowing for efficient pricing. Under neither scheme should the government guarantee levels of traffic.

The Mexican government also wants to attract foreign capital because of concern that further toll-road investments might increase domestic interest rates and displace useful private domestic investment. But it has been difficult to convince foreigners to invest in *new* toll roads, since under the revised Mexican concession system there is no assurance that the government will make investors whole in the event of a cost overrun or traffic shortfall. Mexican investors, who understand the system, appear more willing to assume these risks than are foreigners. Mexico's private concessionaires are trying to refinance some of their older concessions on foreign capital markets. Even though these roads have been opened for only a few years, not many have attracted sufficient traffic to satisfy foreign investors.

The main beneficiaries of the program have been the construction companies. Certainly the highway stock has significantly increased, but it is not clear, from a social standpoint, that a number of those highways should have been built. One lesson the Mexican experience teaches very clearly is the trade-off between the long-term efficiency and short-term government benefits of privatization. The financial difficulties of the public sector forced the government to move quickly in its attempt to enlarge the road system. Although that aspect of the process was successful, the lack of forethought damaged the long-term prospects of private toll roads in the country and cost the government a significant amount of money in unanticipated subsidies and compensations. As usual, the government must find a balance between the needs of the public, those of the company that will provide the service, and its own ability to continue supervision of the sector.

A CASE STUDY OF TRANSPORT PRIVATIZATION AND REGULATION: ARGENTINA

Argentina has taken steps to privatize railways, roads, and ports. Law 23696 (reform of the state) addressed privatization of railways[8] and toll roads, and law 24093 dealt exclusively with ports. The port law is the only one that explicitly states the objectives of the reforms, but the implicit goals are very similar. They are to

- Reduce costs (for ports this means self-financing, while for railroads this means reducing subsidies)
- Promote competition
- Decentralize.

Additionally, the port law reformed the role of the National Authority in an attempt to grant management greater autonomy. The reorganization of all three sectors required horizontal disintegration (separation in the case of roads), with ports and roads being divided more or less geographically, and rail lines divided either by type of service or geographically. Unlike in the case of roadway concessions in Mexico, the privatization contracts are quite long, ranging from ten years (with the option for an equal extension) for metropolitan railways, to thirty years for freight lines. Port concessions vary from eighteen to twenty-five years, and the road concession is also over twenty years. The contract will be terminated in all cases if the concessionaire so chooses or goes bankrupt, if the service is ended, or when the term ends. Moreover, port and road agreements cease if both parties agree, if the facilities are destroyed, or if the concessionaire fails to comply with the terms.

Table 13.2 provides more specific information on the bidding process, the contracts, the regulating entities, and the postprivatization rules for the three transport sectors in Argentina. Unlike the Mexican case, the bidding criterion for the Buenos Aires access roads was the basic toll indexed to the U.S. consumer price index. The government did not provide any guarantee of minimum traffic level or any other guarantee. The concessionaire derives revenue from tolls and from commercial exploitation of service areas as authorized by the regulator. The impact has been considerable. Under the intercity highway concessions, road use more than quadrupled between 1991 and 1996—raising toll revenues from almost US$60 million in 1991 to US$258 in 1996. The maintenance of the intercity highway system, including the concessioned portions, has improved significantly. The share of paved roads in bad condition declined from about 30

percent in 1989 to 25 percent in 1993, and was expected to fall to 10 percent by 1997. Maintenance of the concessioned network is no longer a major drain on government budgets—though government subsidies increased from US$23 million in 1991 to more than US$65 million in 1996, in part because of the government's reluctance to allow toll increases. On the negative side, investment is behind schedule because renegotiations reduced the concessionaires' potential returns. Still unclear, however, is the efficiency of construction and maintenance. There is no information yet on whether the private sector is maintaining the roads at lower cost than the public sector did, or whether it is doing better for the same cost.

Three main lessons emerge from this experience. First, it is critical to have simple and transparent bidding criteria. Second, the rules for renegotiating contracts should be spelled out as early and clearly as possible. They should recognize the importance to the concessionaire of ensuring that renegotiation does not alter its financial return when the problems that led to renegotiation are beyond its control and are government induced. Third, institution building must be taken seriously. Poor coordination among various agencies with jurisdiction over different components of the concession led to poor planning and inefficient decisions (Estache and Carbajo 1996). (See box 13.2 for Santiago's approach to deregulating bus transport.)

Table 13.2 Argentina's Transport Privatization and Regulation

Characteristic	Railways + Subways	Ports	Roads
Concession			
Bidding	• For freight, 2 envelopes; envelope 1 combined technical and financial qualifications; envelope 2 contained weighted selection criteria (experience, staff, business and investment plan, fees to government and rent for use of rolling stock, access pricing, number of former staff to hire, share of Argentine interests); bidders were graded on scale of 1 to 10 for each of the seven criteria, and the highest grade (accounting for weights) won • For metropolitan passengers, three envelopes: 1 covers the technical and operating experience of the bidders; 2A contains a detailed business and operating plan for the specific line; 2B contains the financial proposal for the line, including the subsidy requirement. The award was based on the lowest subsidy (measured as the first ten-year present value of annual subsidies required to operate the line and undertake investment plans, net of the annual flow of fees to be paid to government)	• 2 envelopes: 1 contains technical qualifications and a business plan of bidders (including investment plan and timing, organization, costs, financing options); 2 contains a bid amount for the specific terminal being bid for the minimum fee guaranteed to the government and was linked to expected traffic; the winner is the one with the highest guaranteed bid accounting for the bidder's preference in view of the fact that one bidder is not allowed to get more than one terminal	• 4 envelopes: 1 contains the main requirements, balance sheet information, and statement of experience; 2 contains qualification after prequalified firms are selected by the privatization commission based on additional details on the technical qualification of the company and the nomination of a representative; to get to next stage, qualified bidders had to pay $25,000; then envelope 3 bidder provides a copy of the final version of the contract proposed, and a bank guarantee of the financial strength of the bidder; 4: the specific offer for the toll; the winner is the one with the lowest toll; in case of equality, bidders have four hours to present new offer; if still equal, winner is chosen by lottery
Term	• For metropolitan railway, ten years (twenty years for the subway) with extensions of the same duration in an unspecified form to be agreed on by all parts • For freight, thirty years plus optional ten-year extension	• Concession term varies for the various terminals between eighteen years (terminal 5), twenty-four years (terminals 4 and 5), and twenty-five years (terminals 1, 2, and 3)	• For the west access road, the term of the concession contract is twenty-two years and eight months
Causes of termination	• End of term • Decision of concessionaire • Bankruptcy of concessionaire • End of the service	• End of term • Decision of concessionaire • Bankruptcy of concessionaire • End of the service • Mutual agreement • Destruction of facilities • Compliance failure by concessionaire	• End of term • Decision of concessionaire • Bankruptcy of concessionaire • End of the service • Mutual agreement • Destruction of facilities • Failure of concessionaire to comply
Contract requirements	• Deliver public service of transport by rail of passengers exclusively on the lines for which the concessionaire has responsibility for commercial operation of trains	• The concessionaire has exclusivity over all loading and unloading services in the terminal during the concession period including: reception, expedition, manipulation and stocking, control and	• The concession is a public service, implying that the concessionaire cannot interrupt the service and cannot discriminate among users as long as they comply with norms

Table 13.2 continued...

Characteristic	Railways + Subways	Ports	Roads
Concession	• The public service nature implies that the concession-aire is required to deliver the service without interruption throughout the contract period and must give up any action that would interfere with the service • The concession also includes: * Maintenance of all assets allocated to the service * Implementation of the investment program speci-fied in the contract, * The option of using com-mercially all spaces in sta-tions and on equipment for advertisement • The contract cannot be transferred	recording of all merchandise loaded and unloaded • Mooring and unmooring • Use of equipment • The concessionaire guaran-tees the service to anyone who demands it as needed and will have to allow the unloading, monitoring, or recording crews contracted specifically by boat owners as third party or cosigners for service delivery	• The necessary steps required to allow the fluidity of the traffic flow at any time have to be taken by the con-cessionaire at no extra cost to users • Users must be informed and rerouted properly by the concessionaire in case of problems due to the state of the road, and this must be done in the shortest way pos-sible for the users • Respect and ensure the enforcement of traffic laws
Regulation			
Tariffs	• Definition of a basic tariff based on a price table linking the fare to the distance for a single trip in a single class • The concessionaire is free to set the prices for multiple trips • There is a toll depending on the number of kilometers covered and that must be paid by FA, FEMESA, and other concessionaires for the use of rails on land concessioned	• The tariffs must be public, just, and reasonable, and must be set in such a way that the revenue of the con-cessionaires does not exceed what is required for the nor-mal, efficient exploitation of the terminal, with a return matching the investments made • The tariffs are defined in the bidding documents • In case of gross mis-matches between needs and supply, the Port secretary can reset tariff as needed within the limits of the rules spelled out in the contract; these changes cannot be used to penalize the conces-sionaire for past profits or to compensate them	• The original terms of the contracts stated that the concessionaire's revenue would come from a toll levied on users; the state defined a uniform tariff per kilometer and per type of vehicle for all corridors; this tariff is indexed to domestic prices • The recovery of the tariff starts as soon as the rehabili-tation and improvement work spelled out in the contract have been concluded • There is no guarantee of volume of traffic or any other type of public guarantee • The concessionaires are paying a fee to the govern-ment (set in the bidding doc-uments) during the entire concession period • A renegotiation of the con-tract reduced the basic tariff from $2.3 to $1 for every 100 kilometers, suppressed the fee due to the government, and introduced a subsidy to the concessionaires of $57 million for the whole network

Table 13.2 continued...

Characteristic	Railways + Subways	Ports	Roads
Concession			
Type of regulation	• Cost plus • There is a trigger rule based on a structure of cost agreed upon • The changes in cost over time are compensated through increased tariff or through subsidies, as the government prefers • Tariff varies with quality according to preset rules and indicators	• Undefined • The Port Administration Authority can change tariff according to rule spelled out above • There is no specific trigger mechanism for changes in the contract or any other type of rule for tariff changes	• Maximum price • Set in real terms

Quality requirements	• Explicit minimum levels of quality requirements
	• Improvements in quality linked to increases in tariffs
	• Quality indicators include
	  *Number of trains sent
	  * Service frequency
	  * Service delivered
	  *Timeliness
	  * Quality of escalators (for subways)
		• No specific requirements	• Quality control on maintenance
			• Indicators include
			  * Roughness
			  * Rutting
			  * Cracking
			  * Raveling
			  * Friction
			  * Shoulders
			  * Lighting systems
			  * Signaling
			  * Parking facilities
			• Quality control for customer service
			  * Limit on waiting time at the toll booth (2 minutes)
			  * Maximum number of cars in line (15)

Investment requirements	• Explicit investment program including estimate of investment costs
	• Demand for changes in the investment program can be initiated by both parties to the contract
	• Investment requirements in trains for service group 3 represents 10% of the total; subways represent 90%
	• As counterpart to the investment requirements, the concessionaire will receive payments by the government according to a preset chronogram
		• Explicit investment requirements in 3 stages classified according to degree of urgency: the terms associated are 1, 2, and 5 years respectively
		• The modalities and terms are specified in the contracts
		• The Port Authority contributes a set amount to the financing of these investments
			• 3 types of investment requirements
			  * Stage 1: Investment to be made before collecting any toll
			  * Stage 2: Investment to be made after toll is collected
			  * Stage 3: Investment required as a result of traffic levels higher than those anticipated in the bidding documents

Functions and obligations of regulatory entities	• Controlling the execution of the contractual obligations of the concessionaire • Set basic tariffs, approve their change, and recognize the rights of the concessionaire to increase these tariffs when the quality of service is improved	• Advise the Executive Power on the operation of the ports • Control the execution of the port reform law • Ensure that the beneficiaries of port responsibilities execute their commitments in terms of construction, rehabilitation, and operation	• Monitor technical commitments of the contracts • Evaluate projects proposed to address structural and specific problems in the system • Monitor tariff and concessionaire revenue • Organize auditing and ensure respect of accounting rules

Table 13.2 continued...

Characteristic	Railways + Subways	Ports	Roads
Concession			
	• Approve the services to be delivered by the concessionaire • Monitor execution of service commitment, of their commercialization, of the investment program, and of the maintenance commitments • Control the respect of safety and operational norms • Certify the progress in works and investment programs, and confirm their satisfactory conclusion by formally receiving the goods to be returned to the state during or at the end of the contract • Demand information and organize inspection and auditing • Impose the required penalties through the National Railways Regulation Commission • Contribute to the resolution of controversies between state and concessionaires or between concessionaires (unless specified otherwise in the contract) • Receive and manage complaints by the public • Make the payments to the concessionaire as agreed to in the contract • Collect the fees due by the concessionaire • Do anything else that the entity sees fit to ensure the execution of its responsibilities	• Suspend responsibilities if compliance failures until commitments are met • Promote the modernization and competitiveness of each port in the country • Stimulate and ease private investment in the operation and administration of ports • Provide technical assistance to the provinces and municipalities at their request • Suggest to the executive power general policies on ports and waterways • Assign responsibilities on dredging the access of each port when conflict over responsibilities arise • Enforce national decisions • Coordinate the various entities involved in supervision and control of ports to avoid overlapping • Apply sanctions as needed • Set the term for amortization of investment requirements defined in the law • Define procedures for implementation of agreements between various parts relating to ports	• Receive user complaints through mail, phone, and field surveys • Make an inventory of all accidents to identify problems in networks • Control excess loads for need of additional payments due to additional damage on road • Advise the administrator of DNV on all matters relating to concessions • Organize a recording system for all transactions • Produce a monthly report on respect of contracts and spell out adjustment needs

Source: Prepared by Estache, Helou, and Rodriguez-Pardina.

AIRPORTS: ISSUES, OPTIONS, AND CASE STUDIES

Aviation infrastructure is a combination of commercial and noncommercial operations. Increasingly, it is viewed as a center of commercial business activity, as opposed to a public commodity managed and operated by bureaucrats.[9] Aviation infrastructure encompasses all aspects of air traffic control; a range of facilities and services for the airline industry in the transfer of passengers and goods; and disparate commercial activities including duty-free shopping, hotels, catering, restaurants, car parking, and rental activities. In spite of strong foundations in these areas in Latin America and the Caribbean (LAC), the aviation infrastructure is faced with new challenges in addressing issues of aviation safety and environmental concerns, modernizing, and selectively expanding its facilities in response to growth in air-traffic volume.

These challenges have arisen largely because (a) policymakers have not recognized the need to support development of aviation infrastructure compared to other modes of transport; (b) there has been limited public investment, which has been allocated to other higher-priority sectors, especially during and following the debt crisis; (c) the liberalization of economies has increased demand for better aviation services; and (d) there is a lack of trained personnel to manage operations within a global and commercial framework. Closing the gaps will require more money, better management, and an integrated sector policy framework, plus suitable harmonization of local, national, and international regulatory frameworks. If that occurs, LAC's aviation infrastructure will be better able to contribute to economic development and become more fully integrated into the global marketplace.

The air transport sector will require large capital investments over the next fifteen years—by one estimate, US$250 billion to US$350 billion (International Civil Aviation Organization 1992)—to modernize aircraft fleets; improve airport infrastructure; introduce more sophisticated air navigation systems; and meet the demand of new markets in China, Eastern Europe, the countries of the former Soviet Union, and Southeast Asia and Latin America. These large investments, together with a redefined role for the state, are transforming the air transport sector.

Based on preliminary information, investments in LAC are estimated to be in excess of $6 billion to $7 billion (from public and private sources). Major investments are planned in Argentina, Brazil, Ecuador, Mexico, and Peru, with only Brazil and Mexico considering completely new (greenfield) infrastructures. In contrast, the East Asia and Pacific region has invested or plans to invest over $50 billion in greenfield aviation infrastructure facilities, while at the same time upgrading and maintaining its existing stock. In the East Asia region, aviation infrastructure is an integral part of the transport sector, gearing up to promote the export of goods and services; is managed as a profitable business venture with limited government intervention (though generally government owned); and is a growing and rapidly expanding marketplace. Military involvement in many aspects of its operations has limited the full exploitation of commercial sources of revenues. While average income from airport concessions in Asia is about $8 to $10 per passenger, in LAC it is about $2 to $4 per passenger. There are significant opportunities to price airside and landside charges more aggressively. Aviation infrastructure in LAC generally has made a limited contribution to national and regional economic development compared to other industrialized and developing countries. The level of direct and indirect employment resulting from airport activities is low, especially outside major metropolitan areas; in fact, aviation activities are a drain on the national economy, and capital markets have not been deepened from airport operations because of government restrictions.

Traditionally, the air transport sector—airlines, airports, and air navigation services—has been in state hands. Aviation infrastructure and services have been owned and operated by federal governments (with strong military ties) serving jointly and independently the needs of military, commercial, and individual private operators. For example, in Argentina there are about sixty airports owned and operated by the Air Force for military and/or commercial use, and in addition, there are about 600 general services airports (aerodromes) owned and operated by the private sector.

Argentina is not unique in this form of aviation structure. Brazil, Chile, Colombia, Ecuador, Mexico, and Peru also have extensive aviation networks, with varying degrees of military involvement. This network, though justifiable in many cases, has generally not made the same level of contribution to economic development compared to those in other industrialized and developing countries. Furthermore, the national aviation infrastructure system in many of these countries is a financial drain on the national economy. Within this network, only a few large airports (those serving major capital cities) are marginally profitable, while almost all others receive fiscal transfers for capital and operating expenditures. Aviation infrastructure and services traditionally have been plagued by a series of problems that are responsible for poor performance and low productivity. The most important reason contributing to poor performance is the strong domination by the public sector. This structure has encouraged reliance on public financing, permitted monopoly practices in many aspects of airport operations and services, limited management practices in commercializing operations, and not provided appropriate incentives to promote safe and environmentally sound conditions.

This structure, coupled with declining levels of public support, is placing aviation infrastructure in jeopardy. As a result, facilities and services are not well positioned to (a) serve the growing demand of users—airlines, passengers, cargo operators, exporters, and importers—which are confronted with the need to lower transport costs to remain internationally competitive; (b) meet future growth projections in passenger and cargo traffic; and (c) overcome issues of air safety and environmental concerns. Large geographical distances, limited dedicated cargo centers close to facilities that produce perishable goods, and major administrative bottlenecks have resulted in LAC's transport costs being higher than those of other export-oriented countries. Estimates are that air passenger and cargo traffic will grow between 4 to 6 percent per year through 2003. Those growth projections do not take into consideration the effects of the North America Free Trade Agreement (NAFTA), the Uruguay Round of the General Agreement on Tariff and Trade (GATT), and the World Trade Organization (WTO), which will lead to increased regional trade. The region's air cargo infrastructure facilities are not capable of efficiently handling current levels of traffic, and the situation is expected to deteriorate further in light of growth projections. A few of the large, specialized air cargo carriers are building single-user, state-of-the-art cargo facilities, but they are insufficient to meet the more expansive air cargo requirements.

Consistent with the global trend in other infrastructure sectors, in air transport the state's role is shifting from owner to regulator and policymaker, and operational, investment, and management responsibilities are moving to the private sector. The government's role as economic regulator is particularly important in light of the fact that some airport services are inherently natural monopolies.

The airport business is becoming increasingly multifaceted, extending into real estate, commercial, and other ventures. These activities are of two main types: provision of airside, or aeronautical, services (runways, taxiways, aprons, terminals)—services that by their nature are still considered monopolistic within each airport; and provision of landside services (passenger and aircraft services, food and beverage concessions, duty-free shopping, parking, hotels), where a wider variety of suppliers is possible. The current trend in airport economics is to rely on commercial operations to contribute an increasing share to airport revenues,[10] resulting in less dependence on increases in airside charges. In industrial economies, airside charges are falling in real terms, leading to higher traffic levels and greater airport revenues.[11]

PRIVATE SECTOR OPTIONS

The private sector became involved in the transport sector only recently, beginning with airlines. By the end of 1995, 70 percent of airlines were privately owned, directly or indirectly. Private sector participation in the airport subsector is just starting, with only two successful cases of complete privatization of airport infrastructure:

the U.K. government's privatization of the British Airports Authority (BAA) in 1987, and of the Belfast International Airport (BIA) in 1994. By the beginning of 1995, however, some form of private sector participation was being implemented or was under consideration in fifty-four countries.

Private sector participation in air navigation is at an early stage. Several countries, including Germany, New Zealand, and Switzerland, corporatized their air navigation services through the creation of corporations with independent financial and legal status, as a step toward eventual privatization through public offerings (Juan 1996). And in March 1996, the government of Canada announced its intention to sell the country's air navigation system for Can$1.5 billion to a not-for-profit-corporate entity whose board of directors will include private sector representatives appointed by the federal government and end users.

Private sector participation in airports through ownership, management, or new investment programs can take many forms, including outright sale of shares or assets, concessions, and long-term leases (see table 13.3). Historically, the private sector has managed most of the landside concessions, but governments are now increasingly seeking to involve the private sector in the provision of airside services as well.

The three most important objectives of increasing private sector participation (though not articulated explicitly by governments) have been to (a) improve efficiency, (b) increase fiscal revenue by selling profitable concessions and improving infrastructure through privately financed investments, and (c) reduce the role of the military. Privatization schemes have started to flourish throughout LAC, with some countries being more aggressive than others.

Although there have been only a limited number of privatization transactions, two options seem to be the most suitable for transferring airport activities to the private sector: (a) build operate-transfer (BOT) schemes (a project finance mechanism generally used in developing countries, where the priority is new investment to upgrade and expand facilities), and (b) corporati-

Table 13.3 Options for Private Sector Participation in Airports

	Option 1	Option 2	Option 3
Allocation of responsibilities			
Ownership	State	State	Private sector
Investment	State	Private sector	Private sector
Management and operation	Private sector	Private sector	Private sector
Common strategies for private participation	Service concession Contracting out Management contracts Multiple concessions	Build-operate-transfer schemes Long-term leases Master concessions	Wraparound additions Trade sales Build-own-operate schemes Strategic buyouts (management-employee buyouts) Capital markets
Recent cases	Aéroports du Cameroon Pittsburgh International Airport, United States Kai Tak Airport, Hong Kong	Athens International Airport Lester B. Pearson Airport, Canada La Chinita Airport, Venezuela Palma de Mallorca, Spain	British Airports Authority Sangster International Airport, Jamaica Belfast International Airport

Note: The options include alternatives for selected airside activities, selected landside activities, and all airport activities.

zation followed by full or partial divestiture (generally used in industrial countries, where the priority is to obtain privatization revenues and improve efficiency) (see table 13.4). Developing countries trying to promote private sector participation in airports could choose a combination of the two options, beginning with a BOT scheme that gives way to corporatization with full or partial divestiture. The following are some examples of completed private sector participation in LAC.

- *Airport service concessions* and other airport services (cleaning, building maintenance, etc.) are operated by the private sector under specific and varied agreements among countries and airport locations. In 1989, Argentina concessioned its bonded warehouses, ground-handling services, duty-free shops, car parking, and catering to the private sector under a long-term concession agreement. Generally, governments have not negotiated favorable terms as compared to other countries for similar concession services. For example, national aviation fuel companies generally do not pay concession fees to the airport authority in LAC; in other regions oil companies pay from 3 to 6 percent of revenues. Duty-free concession shops in LAC generally have fixed-term concession rates compared with sliding scales used in other countries. Limited knowledge of and expertise in the design of concession

Table 13.4 Considerations Under Various Airport Privatization Options for Developing Economies

Option	Considerations
Build-operate-transfer (or variants, such as build-own-operate and build-own-operate-transfer)	• Facilitates relatively large new investments • Maintains government ownership (transfer at a later date limits political conflict) • Requires relatively complex procedures and an array of technical and financial specifications • Lack of ownership rights could make raising capital funds more difficult and costly for private sector investors
Full or partial divestiture through a public offering, capital markets, a trade sale, or a combination	• Generates fiscal revenues • Full divestiture limits state intervention • Public offering requires track record of profits and audited financial statements • Public offering requires developed capital markets (rare in developing economies)

contracts and varied approaches have resulted in lower revenues for many aviation authorities, thereby increasing subsidies.

- *Build-operate-transfer (BOT)* allows governments to award a concession or franchise to a private firm or consortia to invest in and build specific segments of the airport infrastructure in return for obtaining a revenue stream from the airport operations for a designated period (generally ranging from ten to fifty years). More than seventeen countries worldwide have adopted this approach, although only two are in use in the LAC region. These BOTs have been used primarily to finance runways or terminal facilities rather than to fundamentally change the incentive structure of airport operations. In 1994 *Colombia* completed the construction of a much-needed second runway at Bogotá Airport using a BOT modality. This is the only example in LAC of using a BOT mechanism for the expansion of a runway. The second example of the BOT mechanism is in airport terminal facilities. For example, in *Mexico,* the Mexico City international passenger terminal building is operated by a private firm that has invested about $150 million in upgrading and maintaining the terminal building. The private firm will use its resources to build works on Aeropuertos y Servicios Auxiliares (ASA) land or installations in exchange for commercial use over a fixed number of years. At the end of the term, the assets and rights of use will revert to ASA. This mechanism helps to achieve financial objectives (substitutes public resources with private funds), but is generally a more expensive form of financing highly cumbersome and complex legal arrangements between the parties, and does not provide appropriate incentives for changing the management culture.
- *Fixed-base operators (FBOs)* traditionally have been used in smaller facilities geared primarily to corporate users and high-income customers. Luxurious facilities have been built by the private sector in *Mexico's* Toluca and San José del Cabo airports. These facili-

ties normally include on-site customs and immigration services, dedicated hangers for guest aircraft, full-service restaurants and gourmet catering, on-site conference facilities, and passenger lounges. Even though these services are generally provided for the high-end users, the trend to convert terminal buildings to provide nontraditional airport services has made this mechanism more available. Other LAC airports have not fully exploited this mechanism, which offers opportunities to further increase commercial sources of revenue.

- *Individual airport concessions (IACs)* are being used more actively among LAC countries. In 1996, *Colombia* transferred to the private sector, under long-term concession arrangements, the management of Cartagena and Barranquilla Airports. In the first half of 1997, another four airports will be transferred under similar arrangements. In 1996, *Bolivia* concessioned to the private sector three major airports (La Paz, Cochabamba, and Santa Cruz), representing 85 percent of national air traffic). IACs are being increasingly used by many countries. However, issues of cross-subsidies among airports, and restructuring of nonviable airports, policy, and regulatory frameworks have not been systematically addressed as an integral part of the individual privatization process.

With a few exceptions—for example, Punta Cana Airport in the *Dominican Republic,* and more recently the airport in Punta del Este, *Uruguay* (both examples of privately owned airports)— private sector involvement in selected activities has been undertaken with the specific intent of not changing the ownership structure and "management culture." Furthermore, these privatizations (a) were not undertaken with the objective of achieving a broader set of reform initiatives (such as reducing fiscal deficits, increasing competition, improving services, and establishing regulatory standards for monopolistic practices); (b) were not executed within the context of the national aviation system; and (c) were not accompanied by policy and regulatory reforms, systematically integrated with reforms in other intermodal transport strategies. Moreover, privatization modalities have actually limited governmental options in achieving fundamental sector reforms. This is particularly noteworthy because many LAC countries have undertaken wide-ranging, complex, and innovative privatizations in utilities and other transport sectors. Generally, governments in many countries have not fully exploited the potential and contributions their air transport can make to economic development. It is doubtful that minor tinkering with ownership changes will be able to systematically address the many challenges facing aviation infrastructure.

The following case studies of Colombia, Jamaica, Canada, and Northern Ireland illustrate some of the issues and approaches in the sector.

Colombia: Innovative Financing

At the end of 1993, the government of Colombia corporatized its Civil Aviation Authority (CAA), separating airport operations from air navigation activities. At the same time, it undertook the development of a second runway at El Dorado International Airport in Bogotá, using a BOT scheme for construction and maintenance of the new runway and maintenance of the existing runway. In May 1995, the government awarded the BOT concession, stipulating investments of US$97 million to the consortium of Ogden, Dragados, and Conconcreto. The concessionaire's investment and operating costs, financing expenses, and profits will be covered by the landing fee revenues, which the CAA will cede during the twenty-year concession. Once bidders fulfilled the technical requirements, bids were evaluated on the basis of the net present value of the minimum landing fee revenue the bidder would require throughout the concession period (landing fees multiplied by estimated traffic volume) and the weighted average landing fee in U.S. dollars. The government has guaranteed a minimum level of revenues (floor pricing), in a rare case of a government's accepting commercial risk. If the landing fee structure or traffic volume, or both, cannot support the required revenue stream, the government would compensate

the concessionaire from a trust fund equivalent to 30 percent of the annual landing fee revenue. The El Dorado transaction demonstrates the flexibility of BOT schemes and is becoming a model for private sector participation in developing such airside airport infrastructure as runways, taxiways, and aprons.

Jamaica: Wraparound Mechanism

In an effort to expand airport facilities to accommodate tourist flow, the Jamaican government established three premises to govern airport privatization and expansion: (a) upgrades would be funded primarily by the private sector, (b) airport operations would be transferred to the private sector, and (c) the government would not provide guarantees.

Sangster International Airport (SIA) in Montego Bay, the program's core case, will be expanded through the construction by SIA Ltd., a new company created by the government, of a new passenger terminal under a build-own-operate (BOO) scheme. Through a forty-nine-year lease arrangement, Airports Authority of Jamaica (AAJ) will transfer to SIA Ltd. the operation of the existing passenger terminals and the remaining landside facilities. The government will grant a management contract to SIA Ltd. for the operation of the airside services now provided by AAJ. Thus, the new expansion, the existing terminal, and the airside facilities will all be under one management, SIA Ltd.

The financial capital structure for SIA Ltd. calls for funds to be raised in domestic, regional, and international markets. At least 70 percent of the entity's shares will be held by the private sector, and up to 30 percent will be held by the government. The government plans to sell shares on a phased basis to maximize the gains on its investment.

Canada: Joint Ownership Structure

Toronto's Lester B. Pearson Airport is a rare case both of joint public/private ownership of facilities on shared premises and of competitive provision of airport infrastructure services. Terminals one and two are owned and operated by Transport Canada, the government transport authority, and terminal three, operating since 1991, is owned by the Terminal Three Limited Partnership (TTLP). Terminal three is operated under a management contract by Lockheed Air Terminal of Canada Inc. (LATC), and it was developed under a build-own-operate-transfer (BOOT) arrangement that includes a sixty-year renewable land lease contract. The development cost for the terminal, which has capacity for 10 million to 12 million passengers, was about Can$570 million.

Transport Canada coordinates activities between Lester B. Pearson Airport's privately and publicly owned terminals. It also provides air navigation services, owns all runways and taxiways, and receives all revenues from landing fees, passenger fees, airline fuel taxes, and ticket taxes. LATC controls the landside activities for terminal three, which begin when aircraft switch from general to terminal three tower control. While airside charges for terminals one and two are purely on a cost-recovery basis, terminal three generates revenues through airline rents and charges (aircraft taxiing and parking, and terminal fees), concessions, and parking to cover not only higher operating costs and capital costs, but also profits.[12] The market is segmented: The average per passenger airside charges at terminal three are twice as high as those at terminals one and two, and the more prestigious international carriers tend to use terminal three, while lower-cost regional or local carriers use the others.

Northern Ireland: Public Security Concerns

The privatization of Belfast International Airport (BIA), one of the two cases of full airport divestiture, illustrates the complexity of dealing with national security matters in a geopolitically sensitive context, and the government's creativity and determination in coming up with viable solutions. The winning bid came from a management and employee buyout team (MEBO Co.), which purchased the Northern Ireland Airports Limited (NIAL) public corporation, entrusted with operating BIA, for about US$72 million. The airport contract was awarded to MEBO Co. in July 1994,

and all the share capital in NIAL was transferred to MEBO Co., except for a golden share of £1. The Department of the Environment for Northern Ireland (DOE) retains ownership of the golden share, which allows it to exercise power in instances related to matters of security and the public interest. In addition, under leasehold control over the 99-year lease agreement between NIAL and the DOE, the DOE and the Ministry of Defense are authorized to enter airport land if NIAL fails to honor its obligation to provide facilities and access to the Ministry of Defense.

Since privatization, passenger traffic through the airport has increased by 17 percent, cargo freight by 17 percent, and turnover by 13 percent—no doubt helped by the cease-fire accord in Northern Ireland.

NOTES

1. To a large extent those gains can be attributed to the widespread use of performance-related incentives for management of the enterprise, greater competitive pressures, and the creation of specialized regulatory agencies with jurisdiction over price controls and the promotion of competition. The five separate profit centers were freight (unsubsidized and unregulated), intercity passenger (unsubsidized and unregulated), provincial commuter and light-density services (regulated and subsidized), London and Southwest commuter services (regulated and subsidized), and parcels (unregulated and unsubsidized), and other corporate activities, such as real estate development.

2. The foreclosure issue in railways has an empirical base as described in Baumol 1975, Grimm and Harris 1983, and Tye 1986. It also appeared, prior to 1984, in the telephone industry in the United States. The long-distance competitors of AT&T, an integrated firm, had to be connected to AT&T's local network. The issue was to determine the transfer price charged to AT&T competitors for access to the network.

3. The average locomotive availability ratio in Latin America is roughly 60 percent, with the actual values ranging from 30 percent in Colombia to 83 percent in Brazil. The values are between 80 and 90 percent for European railways, with the exception of Greece; between 70 and 80 percent for Asian railways; and between 40 and 50 percent for African railways.

4. For example, the subsidies for the Italian, German, French, and U.K. railways are $4.3 billion, $3.5 billion, $3.25 billion, and $605 million, respectively. The idea is to induce the railways to operate as efficiently as possible given the financial constraints. Some are doing better than

others: railways in the U.K. travel 49 percent more kilometers per employee than the West European average, with one-sixth of the public subsidy (*The Economist,* August 3, 1991).

5. Labor redundancy has been and is a chronic problem in railways. Successful restructuring has consistently entailed drastic reductions in the labor force. For example, since 1980, railway companies in France, Japan, New Zealand, Spain, the U.K., and the U.S. have reduced their labor forces between 30 and 60 percent.

6. British Railways provides a good example. Two private companies, Foster Yeoman (a quarrying company that runs its own freight trains) and the Royal Scotsman (which operates deluxe tourist trains), have proven that competitors can run on the same track as British Railways and provide real benefits (*The Economist*, August 3, 1991). Other precedents exist: Japan already has a private railway and has broken its state network into regional companies (with the idea of ultimately privatizing them), Sweden has allowed new entrants access to its nationalized service to compete on local routes, and Holland is considering privatization.

7. Information on the Mexican program is from Gómez-Ibañez and Meyer 1993.

8. Decree 2740 (memorandum of understanding for railway restructuring), Decree 1143/91 (regulatory framework), and Resolution 1456/91 from the Ministry of Economy and Public Works, also apply to railroads and subways.

9. This section is adapted from Juan 1996, and Kapur 1997.

10. At a March 1995 airport conference in East Asia, an official of the International Civil Aviation Organization commented that "airports today could be viewed as large shopping malls with aircraft access gates instead of street exits."

11. *The Economist*, in an article titled "Why Heathrow Is Hell" (August 26, 1995), argued that, theoretically, it is perfectly possible for increasing commercial revenues to obviate the need for aeronautical charges, which, in turn, could saturate an airport's operating capacity.

12. Because of the relative age of its terminals, Transport Canada does not include capital costs in the calculation of airside charges.

11

CREATING THE DETAIL
ENGINEERING OF REGULATION:
COMPETITION POLICIES

IN MANY UTILITY SECTORS technological changes have shattered the idea that a vertically integrated monopoly is the efficient mode of organization. For example, technological developments in electricity transmission have made economies of scale in generation trivial in almost any market situation. Similarly, while there may be a need to coordinate dispatch, it is unclear to what extent the distribution transmission network should also be owned by a single operator. Indeed, several countries are implementing regulatory systems that do not grant exclusive rights to distribution companies. For example, Chile's twenty-one distribution

companies do not have exclusive territories. Telecommunications firms in Brazil and Chile have not been granted exclusive operating rights. New Zealand's regulation of utilities includes neither exclusive rights nor price regulation. Finally, although distribution companies in the United Kingdom have exclusive rights, those rights will be abolished by the end of the 1990s. Similarly, in the transport sector, with the possible exception of certain aspects of railroads, few arguments support de jure vertical integration and a minor presence of natural monopoly activities. The sector is highly contestable. Thus, the arguments for extensive regulation bear little credibility, while the arguments for competition policies are increasingly more powerful.

It is by now well accepted in the telecommunications industry that long-distance service is not a natural monopoly. At least fifty companies provide long-distance services in the United States. Furthermore, even the idea that the local exchange is a natural monopoly has been challenged both by empirical work and by the entry of competitive access providers.[1] The choice of technologies for the provision of local telephone service is now broader than ever. There are several wireless options: analog and digital cellular radio, digital cordless telephony (for example, Digital European Cordless telecommunications), proprietary (noncellular) wireless local loop systems such as Ionica (being installed in Finland), and mobile satellite. There are also fiber-optic cable television options and hybrid solutions.[2] As a result, in the United States local telephone markets are being opened to competition, while current local providers, the Bell companies, are being allowed into the long-distance market as long as their own market is open to competition. The central issue regarding deregulation is the point at which local markets should be deemed competitive. Is it when the local companies have done what is required to allow competition to exist, or when each customer has a genuine choice of service provider? Not surprisingly, the Bell companies have argued for the first condition, while the long-distance companies have argued for the second. The compromise appears to be requiring the Bell companies to face a local competitor that offers service through its own facilities—rather than simply buying and then reselling it—before entering the long-distance market. This is known as "fair facilities-based competition."

As a result of this ever-increasing competition, antitrust agencies are playing a growing role in overseeing the performance of the utilities sector. In New Zealand, the Antitrust Commerce Commission takes action in response to complaints by industry participants, competitors, and utility users. Under its minimalist approach to regulation, the commission, together with the courts, comprises the sole government mechanism for regulating utilities. In Canada, Mexico, the United Kingdom, and the United States, the institutions charged with applying general competition policy are not involved in utility regulation on a day-to-day basis, but they do have extensive powers that are highly relevant to the regulation of utilities. In the United Kingdom the head of the regulatory agency might refer matters to the Monopoly and Mergers Commission, which has far-reaching powers to correct anticompetitive abuses. The possibility of that referral can convince companies to comply with the directives of the regulatory agency (this clearly occurred during the 1992 negotiations on price regulation between British Telecom and Oftel). In the United States, the antitrust division of the Department of Justice provides input to district court decisions concerning competitive market behavior or requests to lift restrictions.

That agency was also instrumental in breaking the AT&T-Bell monopoly in the telecommunications sector.

Thus, competition policy is becoming a potentially key instrument in the regulation of utilities (and also in the regulation of trade policies; see Guasch and Rajapatirana 1994). A number of Latin American countries (Brazil, Chile, Colombia, Jamaica, Mexico, Peru, and Venezuela) have enacted comprehensive antitrust legislation. Argentina's lower chamber of congress has approved a new competition law, but it has yet to be considered by the senate. Bolivia, Costa Rica, El Salvador, Panama, Paraguay, and Trinidad and Tobago are in the process of drafting new laws governing competition policy. Enforcement, while still deficient, is gradually improving and complementing regulation. (See Guasch 1994 for a description and evaluation of competition policies in Latin America.) Competition policies should be seen as a complement to, and in some cases or sectors a substitute for, regulation. And in a number of countries, such as Mexico, the competition agency has been given direct jurisdiction to oversee the utilities sector, to intervene in the event of anticompetitive behavior, and to rule on merger activities. However, although less and less so, there still remain some activities in which competition is unlikely to arise. First, the high sunk investments in distribution (whether of telecommunications or electricity) will provide a credible advantage to the incumbent operator of the distribution network. Entry will therefore occur mostly on the fringes or in segments characterized by relatively small economies of scale.[3] Consequently, access to the distribution network will have to be regulated. Second, in small economies such as most Caribbean and Central American countries, single operators might not exhaust economies of scale, and that will make competition implausible and require comprehensive regulation.

To summarize, although competition policy has become a potentially useful regulatory instrument in several utility sectors, not every country will be able to use it to the same degree, and enforcement of competition policies still remains an issue in most Latin American countries.[4] Because mixing competition and regulation in utility sectors may require substantial regulatory flexibility, countries needing specific rules to restrain administrative discretion may find that promoting competition in some segments creates important contractual problems that deter private sector investment. (See chapter 12 for further discussion of competition policies and their presence and experience in Latin America and the Caribbean.)

COMPETITION POLICIES AS COMPLEMENTS TO REGULATION

The term competition policy encompasses the area commonly known as antitrust or antimonopoly law and practice, and various microindustrial policies affecting markets. Competition laws strive to deter and prevent abuses of market power, dominance, exclusionary practices, and the reaching of agreements among competitors. The laws aim to promote and protect competition and economic efficiency, not to protect the competitors. In the context of preventing abuses of dominant agents and exclusionary practices, properly enforced competition policy can be an appropriate complement to regulatory policies. Moreover, in sectors where deregulation rather than regulation should be the norm, such as transport, services, and other nontradables, and in network-based sectors, competition policies have a major role in fostering a competitive environment.

Antitrust legislation should complement regulation and liberal trade and investment policies by ensuring competitive conduct by incumbents not only in domestic markets for nontraded goods and services, but also for traded products, where distribution services enter as inputs. Although in most countries recent comprehensive trade liberalization and domestic deregulation measures, financial sector reforms, and the removal of price controls and of some public barriers to entry provide the foundations for a healthy competitive environment, they cannot be considered as a complete substitute for an effective antitrust policy. There are a large number of nontraded goods and services, either because they are inherently nontradables (domestic distribution services) or because they have very high transportation costs (fresh vegetables and fruits, fresh dairy products, and some bulky items such as metal ores and cement).

The objective of antitrust legislation should be to deter anticompetitive practices. By focusing on this objective, and excluding other potentially conflicting and questionable populist objectives, such as preventing the development of large enterprises and ensuring "fairness" in the marketplace, an antitrust law could become an effective tool for promoting competition, efficiency, and good business practices and ethics.

In many developing countries, where severe public resource constraints will continue to limit legal and administrative capabilities for some time, it is particularly important to ensure that the antitrust law is transparent, defined clearly (leaving little room for interpretation or discretion by the implementing agency), and relatively easy to enforce. It should also create a level playing field for all participants, focus on actions that clearly and significantly harm competition and consumers, and strike a balance between overburdening (increasing transaction costs) and being too general and vague (having no impact; for further details and discussion see Kovacic 1992).

Competition policy is executed through the legal system and works through its proper and predictable enforcement/deterrence effects. Competition laws essentially address two areas: the conduct of business and the structure of economic markets. Issues of performance are embedded directly or indirectly in these two areas. In the event of transgressions, producers are subject to criminal and civil prosecution, fines, or injunctions.

Conduct Policies

Competition policy prohibits conduct that unfairly diminishes trade, reduces competition, or abuses a market-dominant position. The laws are intended to counter

- *Horizontal restraints*, which are unilateral or collective actions that weaken or restrain competition among firms in the same market. Examples are the fixing of prices or bids (competitors explicitly cooperate to set prices or to prearrange the outcome of auctions); conscious parallelism (tacit agreement on setting prices; it may occur in competitive markets and in oligopolistic ones, so it is considered to be only a symptom of non-competitive behavior); output restraints; market division (suppliers that self-allocate customers among themselves); exclusionary practices; exchange of commercially sensitive information; predation; and restraints on entry.

- *Vertical restraints*, which are provisions in contracts between suppliers and their distributors (and retailers). Vertical restraints may be used to support noncompetitive conduct by competing suppliers, the exercise of market power by distributors, or the segmentation of markets on a geographic basis to practice geographic price discrimination. Examples are exclusive dealing (suppliers that disallow the purchase of competitors' products); refusal to deal; resale price mechanism (suppliers that condition sale to distributors on establishing the distributors' price); territorial restraint (selling in a limited region to support price discrimination); price discrimination; premium offers; tie-ins; and full-line forcing (suppliers that require distributors to carry all the supplier's products).

- *Enforcement standards*, which are set by the legal system and the judiciary. Laws are necessary but not sufficient to achieve the objectives of competition policy. Enforcement depends on the attributes of the legal system and the judiciary, and on how credibly and reliably the laws are upheld.

Structural Policies

Structural policies are the fastest growing means of pursuing antitrust aims. Competition laws influence market structure by affecting transactions between firms (contractual or ownership relationships among suppliers or competitors)—usually mergers, takeovers, joint ventures, and

asset transfers. Structural policies aim to prevent transactions that would reduce the independence of competing suppliers (vertical integration) and increase concentration in the market (horizontal integration). They include

- *Merger control regulation*, which selectively prohibits mergers that would substantially increase concentration in the market or restrain trade among suppliers

- *Premerger notification*, which allows authorities to review proposed mergers prior to execution, thereby making merger control administration more efficient

- *Enforcement and remedial measures under merger control*, which promote competition by breaking up a supplier into smaller independent units, thus preventing the negative increased concentration effects of the merger. Remedial measures such as divestiture and demonopolization are necessary because transactions involving multiproduct firms lead to concerns about competition that affect only a few products. Remedies can effectively replace regulatory supervision of economic conduct with market discipline in some contexts.

Performance Policies

The state compensates for lack of competition by dictating prices or output. Although available, administrative pricing by the antitrust authority is rarely used, because it counters the fundamental premise that markets are more efficient at determining prices and outputs. The standard policy is to regulate various modes and, usually, to apply that regulation only to sectors that display significant natural monopoly characteristics but are also subject to laws governing competition policies. This is the case for most utility sectors, which are subject to government regulation.

While some business practices, such as price fixing, are clearly anticompetitive, others, such as price discrimination, exclusive dealing, or resale price maintenance, often depend on the context. Accordingly, two distinct legal criteria should be and often are used to address those differences among practices. One is the "per se" criterion, where an action is disallowed and punished independent of the intent and consequences. The other is the "rule of reason" criterion, where an action in itself is not disallowed and is punished only if the intent or the consequences are found to be damaging or anticompetitive.[5] While the rule of reason criterion appears to be fairer and more conceptually appealing, it has drawbacks. It significantly increases the cost of litigation and weakens the deterrence effect, which is the fundamental objective of legislation. Therefore, the tradeoffs should be considered. Indeed, when administrative and enforcement capabilities are severely limited, it is highly desirable initially to have a lean antitrust law that focuses mostly on anticompetitive practices that could be treated under the per se criterion: mainly the horizontal restraint cases and those vertical restraint cases that are clearly anticompetitive.[6] After the implementing authorities gain experience and resource constraints ease, the antitrust law could be amended to cover more complex cases of anticompetitive conduct that need to be treated under the rule of reason criterion.

Price agreements, quota agreements, and conspiracies should be judged as illegal per se, notwithstanding the fact that situations or types of agreements can be found that can enhance efficiency. One of them was the subject of *Arizona v. Maricopa County* (1982) in the United States, whereby the setting of maximum prices for medical procedures by physician groups helped insurers reduce uncertainty about potential claims, thereby creating a productive efficiency, presumably of benefit to insurance purchasers. That price agreements can yield efficiency is also shown in emerging conflicts over franchise-type operations. However, the rarity of those situations, coupled with the severe consequences of most agreements and the ease and deterrent effects of litigating per se cases, warrants the per se treatment of agreements. This is not an insignificant point. There are many incidences of all forms of agreements in most economies. Examples have been common in sectors such as cement, financial services and professional activities, fisheries, poultry, and transport. Provisions in law specifically addressing tacit

agreements and conscious parallelism are missing. Although they are important because of their economic consequences, and because of their frequent presence in many environments, they are difficult to prove and thus to prosecute successfully. Therefore they should not be emphasized.

Market power depends on the relative size and structure of the market (the number of competitors, ease of entry, extent of contestability, trade barriers, and availability of present or potential substitutes). Market power exists, in principle, in most utility firms, which often operate as monopolies. Dominance is based on the absolute size of the producing firm, its links to inputs and other output-producing industries, and its influence on and by the international market. Again, dominance is potentially present in utility firms. At issue is how to quantify a dominant position. The standard procedure is to associate it with market share. How to measure it and how to interpret it are the core questions in all cases concerning abuse of monopoly power or of dominant position. After all, it is not unusual in certain environments that a firm with a 20 percent market share can effectively dominate the market. Moreover, the definition and measurement of market share can be a blurry undertaking, depending on how the market is defined. It is of the utmost importance that guidelines be provided for assessing market share and relevant range, particularly for issues related to dominant firms and mergers. Geographic demarcations, sources and destinations of supply and demand, and closeness of substitutes are all factors to be considered when defining the relevant market. The legislation is often mute in that area, but it should not be.

There are two steps to analysis of the relevant market. First, it is necessary to determine which products or services are good substitutes for the goods of firms being investigated. Good substitutes need not be identical products; a significant number of consumers may also consider them to be reasonable alternatives. Second, it is important to consider how easily new firms might enter the market. If one or more of the firms producing in the market raises price, restricts output, or reduces quality, it might become profitable for new firms to enter. If there are no important effective barriers and the lag-entry is not too long, customers cannot be harmed by such actions.

Often in the legislation in many countries, the clause regarding what constitutes an abuse of dominant position outlaws pricing the same good higher in domestic than in international markets. The clause is inappropriate, particularly if there are no protections, barriers to entering the sector, or natural monopoly conditions, and should be removed. One can envision a whole set of circumstances where that pricing policy is efficient. It is perfectly acceptable to have different profit margins in different markets. The margins are triggered by different demand elasticities. However, if there are barriers to entry or protection, the policy should generally be to remove them.

Mergers

Market concentration ought to influence, but not dominate, antitrust decisions. Moreover, although the line can become blurred, there should be a distinction between concentration arrived at through internal growth and concentration arrived at through merger or protection. While mergers could be the desirable result of superior performance and know-how, and a reward for competitive practices, protection need not be so. The critical issue is whether a merger is more like internal growth or more like a price agreement.

The case for merger enforcement is simple. It is largely futile to conduct an anti-price-fixing policy if companies that would conspire to fix prices can readily evade the law by merging to form a quasi monopoly. Similarly, it is generally far easier to avoid abuses of dominant position through a merger policy that discourages the formation of dominant firms than through an ex post effort to regulate their behavior. The antitrust legislation should address merger issues. In particular, the commission should issue non-binding guidelines about what types of mergers are likely to raise concerns and to be closely scrutinized or denied. Such guidelines would reduce administrative and litigation costs and

would deter clear-cut cases, reduce transaction costs, and thus enhance efficiency. In addition, care should be exercised to watch out for controlling interests. It is often the case that while two firms in the same or related market can be legally independent, a major shareholder(s) of one of them has a "controlling" interest in the other. In these cases, for the purpose of evaluating market power or dominant position, the two firms ought to be considered as one.

Legislation in developing countries often does not address this situation, and it should. A merger law and a premerger notification procedure can be designed to accommodate the particular characteristics of the country (such as the existence of relatively small firms and potential economies of scale). For example, the premerger notification standards can be set so that only a relatively small number of very large mergers must be reported, and so that mergers are considered that enhance consumer welfare by creating firms of efficient size. Clearly, particular emphasis needs to be placed on the nontradable and quasi-nontradable sectors, such as perishable goods and goods with a low ratio of price to volume (paints and beverages), because the competition from foreign enterprises in those sectors will be very limited.

Although vertical mergers remain controversial, they should also be considered in the notification procedures. Vertical mergers can produce significant efficiency benefits, reducing transaction and coordination costs and capturing economies of scope and x efficiency. However, they also can foreclose markets, increase the cost of entry, shift market power to other markets, and increase the probability of collusion. In particular, they can be a significant barrier to entry for domestic and foreign producers, and they can delay the impact of opening the economy.

The most damaging situations tend to occur when producing firms control or are integrated with distribution firms. Some evidence of the adverse effect of that type of vertical integration comes from Chile, where the difference between the retail price of consumption goods and the port price of goods, inclusive of tariffs, hovers in the 33-to-139-percent range. That large price differential hints at failures or market foreclosure at the distribution level. Similar price differences exist in Venezuela for products such as fish, cheese, sugar, refrigerators, and automobiles. The experience of Nabisco in the early 1990s in Colombia provides further evidence. Domestic producers, Nabisco's competitors, controlled the distributional channels and foreclosed the market to Nabisco, which then entered joint ventures with local producers and practiced parallel pricing, robbing the country of lower prices and the benefits of opening the economy in that sector.

The standard structure of most Latin American and Caribbean countries is highly concentrated, with relatively large companies and small country markets. The sector level concentration indexes at the C4 level—the sum of the market shares of the four largest companies—often exceed 75 percent, and often those numbers are secured even at the C2 level. For example, in Colombia, as of 1988, almost 70 percent of industrial output was produced under severely and increasingly concentrated oligopolistic structures. While in 1968, 49 percent of intermediate goods industries were highly concentrated, in 1984, 78 percent were highly concentrated. In the capital goods industry, the share of highly concentrated industries rose from 24 to 85 percent. Of course, within the world market those companies are relatively small. Table 14.1 shows aggregate concentration levels for various Latin American countries. These high levels of concentration are not the result of superior efficiency, but rather of past government policies that emphasized quantita-

tive restrictions, quotas, price controls, barriers to entry, vertical integration, high external tariffs, imperfect capital markets, and highly concentrated financial resources.

In many industrialized countries, mergers are discouraged if they raise the concentration index beyond a certain level. For example, that level is a Herfindhal index between 1,000 and 1,800. In Germany, dominance is presumed if the C1 index is 33 percent, if the C3 is 50 percent, or if the C5 is 67 percent. In England, if the joint market share of the merged firms is higher than 25 percent, the merger is investigated. These standards appear too strict for developing countries, whose predicament and conditions are significantly different from those of industrialized countries, and warrant a more flexible approach. Yet the merger developments need to be closely monitored, keeping the described competitive standards present.

Restrictive Practices

Most legislation in Latin American and Caribbean countries does not adequately cover restrictive practices; such practices are covered only insofar as they are part of agreements among producers or address the abuse of dominant position or price discrimination. However, restrictions such as franchise arrangements, vertical restraints, and market foreclosure are not explicitly covered. Some of them are anticompetitive and of common usage and can be covered under the per se rule, and legislation should explicitly cover them. However, in some situations that type of arrangement would warrant exclusive dealing and tied sales (for example, to guarantee quality) as a result of the existence of economic externalities. Consequently, restrictions, particularly those emanating from franchise agreements, should be judged under the rule of reason criterion, and their inclusion in the legislation could be deferred to a future date.

Resale price maintenance, a restrictive practice, is rarely addressed in legislation. The practice of resale price maintenance can be defended based on efficiency gains, such as for products that need to establish an upscale and quality

Table 14.1 Market Concentration Indexes in Latin America
(percentages)

Country	Year	C4
Argentina	1984	43
Brazil	1980	51
Colombia	1984	62
Chile	1980	50
Mexico	1972	73
Peru	1991	69
Venezuela	1991	64

Source: Various estimations.

image and for products that require labor-intensive training of potential customers. In principle the rule of reason criterion to judge that practice would be appropriate. But again, to facilitate litigation and because those favorable occasions are few and the unfavorable occasions can significantly lessen competition, we would advocate for a per se rule instead. The efficiency loss of that choice is small relative to the gains derived from a stronger deterrence effect and from reduced transaction costs.

Predatory pricing practices are controversial and difficult to prove. The important and "obvious" cases can often be treated under the clause covering abuses of dominant positions (small firms rarely have the incentives and resources to engage in predatory pricing). The main reason is that it is very difficult to distinguish anticompetitive from competitive price cuts. Indeed, an important reason for relying on competition is the inability to know what prices should be in its absence.

Unequal Treatment of Agents

Care should be exercised when drafting legislation addressing unequal treatment of seemingly identical agents. Often such legislation states that unequal treatment by suppliers of all their dealers or customers is unlawful. The rule should have exclusions or be subject to interpretation because unequal treatment is often warranted from an efficiency standpoint. The exclusions are based on compensating conditions. That is, dealers and customers with dissimilar conditions face unequal treatment by the supplier in a compensating manner. An economic interpretation is required that is broader than what is stated through the exclusions of compensation. Other differential situations, such as heterogeneity of agents, risk factors, and different markets, also warrant unequal treatment. Consequently, action should be treated under the rule of reason criterion. The key element is the provision of equal terms to similar dealers in similar situations. In that case, heterogeneity would come from self-selection, which is not only acceptable but also desirable.

Barriers to Entry and Professional Activities

Agreements and practices in professional activities that restrict entry, and coordinating practices, should be disallowed. Current legislation is mute on this subject. A case in point is the notary profession in Latin America. Because almost all documents need to be notarized, a question has been posed about the shortage of notaries in Peru. Apparently, there are just forty notaries in Lima, which is clearly not sufficient by any standard and results in unwarranted delays of business transactions, high costs (monopoly rents), and wasteful rent-seeking activities. A professional association is apparently preventing the increase in the number of notaries. That is unwarranted, and an effort should be made to free the entry of qualified individuals into the profession, or into any other profession, for that matter.

Consumer Protection Act

Consumer protection laws should focus on fraud, standards, health, and safety, all areas which are related to deficiencies in consumer information and power. As such, these issues are not directly related to competition. However, poorly designed and vague consumer protection laws could run the risk of inhibiting competition and efficiency-enhancing initiatives, and could become a vehicle for restricting import competition.

Sanctions

The main objective of enacting competition law is to deter anticompetitive behavior, and for any competition law to have a deterrent effect, sanctions must be significant. Often in Latin American and Caribbean countries the level of sanctions is not sufficient to have that effect. Raising the sanctions to very high levels poses the possibility of deterring legitimate activities. A more sensible approach is to make the sanctions a multiple of the unlawful profits earned as a result of the unlawful activity (in the United States the Criminal Fines Improvement Act of 1987 provides that a court may impose a larger alternative—the specified maximum fine—equal to twice the gain or loss caused by the crime). The extent of the losses to customers and related firms as a result of the unlawful behavior of a firm should be considered, because those losses are often greater than the gains secured by the violating firm.

Civil Remedies

Antitrust legislation should provide for civil remedies and class action suits. Private parties should be able to file suits against parties for violations of antitrust legislation and be able to seek compensation for damages and losses. Otherwise, because it generally has limited human resources, the agency in charge will not be able to investigate and litigate properly the usual flow of cases without undue delays, and might be forced to prosecute only select cases. This could lead to wasteful rent-seeking activities and harm the deterrence effect of the act. In addition, if firms know the rights of competitors and customers in litigation and in policing behavior, this can also act as a deterrent. The threat of class action suits, which usually reward five times the amount of damages, increases the deterrence effect of the legislation. Although this policy can lead to abuses and excessive litigation, the tradeoffs are favorable enough to warrant provision of civil remedies. For that purpose, legislation should allow private parties to act as plaintiffs.

Judicial Competence

Enacting antitrust legislation is a step toward creating an environment that facilitates competition. To be effective and deter unwarranted actions, the laws have to be credibly and predictably enforced. As pointed out earlier, the burden of enforcement could be eased by limiting the focus of the law mainly to anticompetitive conduct that can be treated initially under the per se criterion. However, as the law is amended to cover more complex cases of anticompetitive conduct, particularly cases to be evaluated under the rule of reason criterion, effective enforcement will require further specialization and training. To that effect, it would be appropriate to select special-

ized courts, judges, or pseudo-judges (professionals trained in law and economics) to handle antitrust cases.

On a related matter, it is also worth stressing that the antitrust law could serve its purpose better if it were to focus mainly on conduct related to nontraded goods and services markets. Most recent comprehensive trade liberalization measures will expose domestic producers of traded goods to effective import competition.

There is much still to be accomplished in Latin America with respect to competition policies. As of 1996 only seven countries in Latin America and the Caribbean had enacted comprehensive antitrust legislation—Brazil, Chile, Colombia, Jamaica, Mexico, Peru, and Venezuela—and most of this legislation was enacted only within the last four years. Argentina, Ecuador, El Salvador, and Paraguay are in the midst of enacting legislation. Therefore, there is little record to evaluate. Yet, some positive results of competition policies in Latin America are already apparent. In Venezuela competition policies have had a significant impact in breaking and deterring existing price agreements among competitors. In Chile a main focus has been the successful breaking of vertical restraints, while Mexico has focused on merger policy and on breaking collusive practices. Peru has successfully facilitated entry and exit in economic activity and deterred distributional restraints and misleading informational practices. Common issues in all these countries are scarcity of resources, little experience in enforcing the legislation, and questionable focus of their operations (Guasch 1994). There is a strong emphasis on consumer protection cases that, while relevant, have much less impact on welfare than price fixing, abuses of dominant positions, and exclusionary practices.

STRUCTURAL INTERVENTIONS

Structural constraints are concerned primarily with preventing practices that could work against competition, because antitrust legislation has (in the recent past) largely driven the process of telecommunications deregulation. However, in theory at least, the problem of assuring suitable quality of service in price-regulated activities could also require some form of structural constraint. Quality of service has been a serious issue in the past because of the uneasy cooperation among local carriers, other network operators, and regulatory authorities. If, for example, adequate quality of service in the telecommunications sector is interpreted to include universal access to integrated services digital network (ISDN) services, largely deregulated firms might be reluctant to provide such expensive facilities. If regulated prices are low, profit maximization in the absence of regulatory pressures might provide incentives to not make such services universally available. However, the predisposition of telephone company management in favor of high technology (witness the high levels of interest in ISDN and intelligent network features) might mitigate the tendencies of narrow profit-oriented calculation. This might not apply to electricity transmission networks.

Potentially anticompetitive behavior is more likely to be a problem than service quality, but that potential is no greater than in other industries. If price controls are focused predominantly on price rather than on profit, then there would be no incentives for partially regulated firms to attempt to cross-subsidize unregulated activities. Therefore, the problem of cross-subsidy is essentially one of establishing appropriate (relative) pricing rules. Residual issues of competitive policy are related to various kinds of potential discrimination by local carriers. In a completely deregulated environment, these could take the form of outright discrimination, charging different prices for the same services to different groups (for example, in private line charges for local versus interexchange access), or the form of indirect discrimination, such as product bundling of services or forward integration into selected markets coupled with lower-than-normal service charges to downstream subsidiaries.

One solution is to impose open network architecture requirements on local carriers and network operators following deregulation. This would require equal access to network information, specifications, and facilities by all potential network users including local carrier subsidiaries;

equal prices charged to all customers for the same services; and pricing of services on an unbundled basis. A major concern giving rise to open network architecture is the problem of possible price discrimination for enhanced services. Past regulatory history indicates that administrative rules are problematic. For example, the rules must specify what services are to be encompassed. In the United States, although open network architecture is not yet fully developed, incentives could exist for carriers to create services with technical characteristics different from those defined as subject to open network architecture rules in order to offer discriminatory prices. Without any open network architecture rules, however, traditional antitrust penalties should make it attractive for competitors of the local exchange carriers to police price discrimination themselves.

COMPETITION BOUNDARIES

A similar problem arises with the determination of competition boundaries. Because of the potential to shift competition boundaries for opportunistic reasons, such as moving a previously competitive segment into the regulation area or vice versa, some countries may have to be quite explicit about the products that are subject to competition and those that are not. The United Kingdom has partially solved this problem by specifying in the company's license whether its products are subject to regulation, and changing this boundary requires an amendment to the license. Similarly, Colombia's deregulation of value-added services is based on a law, and attempts to regulate the prices of value-added services would require changing the law, which may not be a trivial undertaking (Colombia also deregulated private entry to networks, including international networks). The objective is to secure efficiency gains, preferably through competition. The relationship between efficiency and competition is of course a two-way street, with greater competition spurring greater efficiency. In a study of productivity changes in erstwhile public corporations in the United Kingdom, Haskel and Szymanski (1993) have shown that each 1 percent loss of market share led, on average, across different industries, to a 0.5 percent increase in productivity.[7]

NOTES

1. While some blame the entry of competitive access providers on cream skimming, such providers have entered even in states where regulators have allowed the local operator total price flexibility in competitive markets (for example, Illinois). Thus, if the local exchange company is a natural monopoly, such entry would naturally be deterred. (See Shin and Ying 1992.) The claim that technology allowed competitors to enter while the local network was a natural monopoly would not be credible if the local operator had full price flexibility (Baumol, Panzar, and Willig 1982). Similarly, the claim that competitive access providers are successful because of high access charges is inadequate, because in states with price flexibility local exchange carriers can provide the same services without collecting access charges. However, at last count five companies were providing competitive access in the Chicago area, even though Illinois Bell had total price flexibility in that market segment.

2. Even in relatively small markets such as Sri Lanka, local network competition can be beneficial. Sri Lanka has four cellular operators and some of the lowest prices for cellular telephone service in the world. In 1994 the number of telephone lines in the country increased by about 47,000. Of these, 30,000 were conventional lines provided by state-owned Sri Lanka Telecom, a record increase. The remaining 17,000 lines came from the provision of cellular service. The cellular operators demonstrated the transition of cellular service from a small, specialized, premium part of the market to a substitute for conventional service (Smith 1995).

3. Entry in telecommunications will usually occur in the long-distance market, in private networks, or in cellular and other mobile telephony, rather than in the basic local loop. Yet the existence of cable television provides an opportunity to create, almost overnight, an alternative local loop supplier with much smaller sunk investments than a totally new entrant.

4. In 1986 the Competition Policies Commission in Brazil (CADE) saw its authority significantly weakened by the minister of justice's acceptance of an appeal of a CADE final determination. Although the legality of the decision is open to question, it reflects a backlash against the perceived aggressive enforcement of the existing law. Old-line industrialists have complained that the current law inhibits the potential for mergers that may be desirable in order to provide Brazilian industry with necessary resources and help domestic markets compete internationally.

5. Various kinds of business conduct might weaken or restrain competition, but could also enhance efficiency. These types of conduct present difficult antitrust cases and are usually treated under the rule of reason criterion, which explicitly recognizes that certain types of conduct could have positive effects on efficiency, thus offsetting any harm to competition.

6. Business conduct that may weaken or restrain competition among firms in a given market is generally classified as a *horizontal restraint*. Important horizontal restraints include price fixing, parallel pricing, output restraint, division of market, exclusionary practices, exchange of information, predatory pricing, and restraints on entry. Practices that may affect competition through arrangements and agreements in vertically linked relationships (such as between manufacturer and distributor) are referred to as *vertical restraints*. Examples include exclusive dealings, refusal to deal, resale price maintenance, territorial restraint, price discrimination, premium offers, and tied sales. For further details see Boner and Krueger 1991.

7. Further evidence of the impact of a lack of competitive pressures on prices and costs (and thus welfare) is given by Nippon Telegraph and Telephone Corp., the world's largest publicly owned company, with a full monopoly in the domestic market. Telephone calls between different regions of Japan are often so expensive that it is cheaper to use an overseas telephone carrier and route calls through the West Coast of the United States.

COMPETITION POLICY AS A COMPLEMENT TO REGULATORY POLICY: COMPETITION EXPERIENCE IN LATIN AMERICA

BRAZIL, CHILE, COLOMBIA, Jamaica, Mexico, Peru, and Venezuela have enacted competition legislation in recent years as part of their economic reforms. There has been an effort to liberalize prices and interest rates, reduce tariff barriers, privatize state-owned companies, break monopolies, and deregulate economic activities. This chapter compares laws, institutional enforcement, and jurisprudence in Chile, Colombia, Mexico, Peru, and Venezuela. Brazil's experience with competition policy is too new to evaluate, and little is on record about Jamaica's experience. Other countries in the region, such as Argentina, Bolivia, Ecuador, El Salvador, Guatemala, Paraguay, and Trinidad and Tobago, are in the midst of considering competition legislation.

COMPETITION LAW

In Chile competition law was substantially modified in 1973 (D.L. 211/1973 modifying law 13.305/1959). Reflecting the views of the new political regime, the legislation was drafted in a liberal economic spirit. There is a separate consumer protection law (enforced by the National Council for the Consumer) and an intellectual property law (enforced by a specialized department in the Ministry of Economy).

The 1973 law is not clear on what actions constitute illegal conduct per se (illegal regardless of consequences), or illegal conduct under the rule of reason (illegal depending on the consequences). Under the law, all conduct appears to be dealt with under the rule of reason criterion; the law describes unlawful anticompetitive conduct as any attempt to hinder free competition.[1]

Under the law, anticompetitive conduct is classified as follows, with no distinction made between the per se and rule of reason criteria:

- Horizontal agreements (involving transactions between two or more agents at the same level of the productive process): horizontal price agreements, the creation of share territories or market zones, fixing of quotas, boycotts, unfair propaganda, and exchange of information

- Vertical agreements (involving transactions between two or more agents at different levels of the productive process): exclusive distribution, fixing of resale prices, vertical integration, and discrimination
- Abuse of dominant power: monopoly power, patents, price discrimination, barriers to entry, and dumping and predatory pricing
- Coordination through the ownership of equity
- Depredation through delays in the judicial process
- Restriction on nonmembers undertaking a specific activity
- Legal barriers such as ministerial resolutions.

In Chile mergers are controlled only ex post if they restrict free competition.

In Venezuela competition law was enacted in 1992 in the context of adopting economic policies for a market economy. These economic policies have been backed by a series of laws: the consumer protection law enforced by the Institute of Defense and Education of the Consumer (Law 4403 of March 24, 1992), the antidumping law (Law 4441 of June 18, 1992), the intellectual property law (enforced by the courts), and the competition law (Law 34,880 of January 13, 1992). The competition law covers all unlawful practices that are intended, or are likely, to restrain or bias free competition. The law does not distinguish between the per se criterion and the rule of reason criterion. Horizontal agreements and vertical restraints are prohibited under the law unless it can be proven that they generate major economic efficiency (all practices seem to fall under the per se rule unless they are specifically exempted).

In Mexico a new economic competition law was enacted in December 1992. The law confirms the economic policies of the past decade that support a market economy, and establishes a framework for promoting the competitive process and economic efficiency. Reduction of monopoly power, and thus a positive redistributive effect, is expected to result, but is not an explicit objective of the law. There is a separate intellectual property law (and a newly established

institute for its enforcement), and a separate consumer protection law (enforced by the Consumer Protection Agency under the Ministry of Commerce). The law distinguishes between two categories of anticompetitive conduct: (a) absolute conduct, such as cartels, price fixing, client segmentation, establishment of exclusive spheres of influence, and manipulation of public bids; and (b) relative conduct, also known as vertical agreements. The law treats absolute conduct under the per se rule and treats relative conduct under the rule of conduct. Moreover, merger guidelines aim to ensure the legality of a merger before it goes through. To define the relevant market in which the activity takes place, the law considers the characteristics of the product and the geographic and temporal market.

In Colombia a decree was enacted in 1992 modifying a 1959 competition law. Under the competition law, anticompetitive acts and agreements constitute unfair conduct and are treated under the per se rule. There is a separate consumer protection law and intellectual property law, enforced by the Superintendency of Industry and Commerce.

In Peru competition legislation was enacted in 1991–92 (Law 701/91 addresses monopolies, restrictive agreements, and practices; Law 716/91 addresses consumer protection issues; and Law 26122/92 addresses unfair competition). The laws are deemed to provide for a competitive private sector. Law 701/91 and Law 96 prohibit acts that constitute abuse of dominant power in the market or that limit or distort free competition. The laws offer some examples of abuse of dominant power but do not associate that abuse with market share, and the provisions do not provide any guidelines on this issue (such as how to measure abuse of dominant power). The laws prohibit restrictive practices (such as price fixing and price and quota agreements) under the per se rule, but do not address structural antitrust issues, such as mergers and interlocking directorships.

Argentina was one of the first countries to enact antitrust legislation (1919), although that law has rarely been enforced, and no agency was created to enforce it. The original law was modified in 1980 (Law 22,262) to define what constitutes anticompetitive and unlawful activity, and to create the Commission for the Defense of Competition under the Secretary of Domestic Commerce to supervise compliance with and enforcement of the law. In 1994 congress passed a new encompassing law that addresses the deficiencies of the 1980 law, which were[2] (a) its enforcement authority (the Commission for the Defense of Competition) lacked the resources and political independence to enforce the law, (b) the penalties were not sufficient to deter unlawful activity, (c) there was no mechanism with which to control anticompetitive activity, and (d) no effective private remedies were available to consumers and businesses that were injured by monopoly conduct.

INSTITUTIONAL ENFORCEMENT (OPERATIONAL STRUCTURE)

In Chile competition law is enforced through the Preventive Commission and the Resolutive Commission (both administrative antitrust commissions) and ultimately the supreme court (judicial system). The Resolutive Commission is the appeals forum for the Preventive Commission's decisions, and the first-instance forum for some cases.[3]

A claim may be filed with the national economic prosecutor by the national economic prosecutor ex officio, the Ministry of Economy, affected companies (competitors), clients or agents vertically related to the accused party, and other individuals such as managers or syndicates. The national economic prosecutor is responsible for investigating and prosecuting the case.

In Venezuela the competition law established the Superintendency for the Promotion and Protection of Competition. The superintendency is responsible for enforcing the competition law. It receives complaints (filed by the superintendency ex officio or by any affected or potentially affected individual), investigates the charges, and prosecutes the case. It may also render advisory opinions to the parties interested in undertaking a commercial activity (which runs the risk of being anticompetitive). Its decisions may be appealed to the administrative tribunal within forty-five calendar days of their issuance. Any damaged third

party may claim indemnities before the courts (the statute of limitations is six months).

The superintendency may fine violators up to 10 percent of the annual revenues ("turnover") of the infringing party (revenues are determined using the previous year's resolution). The fines can be increased up to 20 percent and, when violations are recurring, up to 40 percent. The amount of the fine takes into account the extent to which trade was actually restricted, the size of the market, the market share involved, the duration of the restriction, and recurring violations, if any. In case of refusal to comply, an additional fine of approximately $12,000 is imposed, to be successively increased by 50 percent of the original amount in cases of persistent noncompliance. Any violation of the law, when not expressly provided for, is punished with a fine of up to $375. The superintendency belongs administratively to the Ministry of Development and is functionally autonomous. Its budget comes from the executive, and it operates with a staff of about twenty people.

Mexico created the Federal Commission of Competition to induce compliance and enforce competition law. The commission's Department of Investigations is responsible for investigating and prosecuting anticompetitive practices.[4] There is no criterion deriving from the law that would make it easier to decide which cases should be prosecuted; investigation and prosecution are based on what looks objectively suspicious.[5] The commissioners are responsible for resolving cases at the first instance. In addition, the commission may comment on the policies of the federal public administration when they stifle competition issues.

The commission, which has 130 employees, belongs administratively to the Secretary of Commerce and Industrial Development, but enjoys functional autonomy. Its budget comes from the executive. There are five commissioners, appointed by the federal executive, with a ten-year mandate. A proceeding is initiated by the commission acting ex officio, or at the petition of an interested party. According to the law, in the case of absolute practices, any individual—whether an aggrieved party or not—may file a claim. In the case of relative practices, however, only the aggrieved party may file a claim. Similarly, in the case of mergers, the law allows only individuals directly related to the merger to sue. Mexicans argue that the monopoly problems deriving from mergers are eminently public; therefore, private litigation is not relevant and could only be harmful to the merging businesses' profitability. In all cases the law mandates strict confidentiality of all information provided to the commission. The commission's decisions can be appealed to the same commission through the "reconsideration proceeding." If the case is still contested, the parties have recourse to the judicial system.

The following sanctions can be imposed:

- For absolute conduct, sanctions include criminal remedies according to the provisions of the penal code, high fines corresponding to up to 375,000 times the minimum wage in the federal district, and, in very serious cases, fines equal to 10 percent of the assets or sales of the company
- For relative conduct, remedies are conceptually different. Punitive remedies are not so efficient because it is important to correct directly the relative conduct of the economic agents. The penalties include prohibition to operate in certain markets and to undertake certain activities. Fines are only part of the remedy.
- For mergers, criminal penalties and fines are not imposed in an attempt to avoid concentration. According to the law, activities aiming at concentration are suspended or declared void. In addition, monetary sanctions can be imposed up to 225,000 times the amount of the minimum wage in the federal district. Monetary sanctions are also imposed (up to 100,000 times the amount of the minimum salary in the federal district) when there is an intent to avoid the proceedings established under the law. Finally, in order to enforce the provisions related to notifications prior to a merger, the operations cannot be registered at the commercial registry until the commission has reached a decision.

In Colombia the operational structure resembles the one in Venezuela. The Superintendency of Competition, functioning under the Superintendency of Industry and Commerce, enforces the law. It files complaints (as can any consumer), investigates, prosecutes, and serves as a first-instance administrative court. A case can be appealed from the superintendency to the administrative court.

In Peru Decree Law 25868 (issued on November 24, 1992) created the Institute for the Defense of Competition and Intellectual Property (INDECOPI) to oversee compliance with and enforcement of the competition law. INDECOPI is responsible for implementing and enforcing the law intended to establish a competitive market environment and to protect consumer welfare. It combines a broad range of promarket regulatory reforms in an autonomous agency, and serves as a registry for intellectual property rights and an administrative court of first and second instance. Its creation represents a significant change in the institutional infrastructure because it shifts some enforcement and resolution of commercial disputes away from the judicial system. INDECOPI responds to the Ministry of Industry but operates as an autonomous body. Its several commissions enforce the provisions of their respective laws. They also act as administrative courts of first instance, with the power to enforce the law through administrative sanctions.[6] INDECOPI's Tribunal for Free Competition and Intellectual Property functions as an administrative court of second instance for all INDECOPI's commissions and offices. Further appeals go to the supreme court. The creation of INDECOPI established a watchdog for competition and free markets, and brought under its umbrella a number of previously dispersed offices that had little visibility.

JURISPRUDENCE

In Chile, the commissions have concentrated on four areas of unfair conduct: price discrimination, fixing of resale prices, exclusive distribution agreements, and horizontal price agreements. According to the jurisprudence of the commissions, horizontal price agreements rarely have been declared unfair. To the contrary (and quite surprisingly), vertical restraints have been declared unfair far more often, despite criticism that Chilean regulators have not punished vertical agreements adequately or consistently. This, according to Chileans, is not because vertical restraints are more harmful to the consumer, but rather because horizontal agreements receive little treatment in general and because incriminating evidence is difficult to obtain.

Unfair conduct largely concerns differentiating discount prices according to the buyer or distributor. There has been a consistent pattern of sanctioning this practice (at least up to 1988). Differentiating most sale conditions according to the client is treated as monopoly discrimination. The only legitimate conditions are considered to be discounts in the process of commercialization according to the payment and volume of sales. In that case, discounts have to be offered to all who wish to buy according to reasonable, objective, and generally applicable guidelines.

The Preventive Commission dealt with nineteen cases of price discrimination between 1974 and 1993. Some of the cases involved companies seeking consultation prior to engaging in an activity. Four companies were found guilty of price discrimination, and one was awarded a fine (146.24 UF; 1 unidad de fomento equals US$25). During 1976–93, sixteen claims were submitted to the Resolutive Commission. Among them, five were appealed to the supreme court (and only one defendant was acquitted). The other cases were decided by the Resolutive Commission. In all cases fines between 8.03 UF and 873.77 UF were levied.

In Chile there has been consistent objection to the use of resale price fixing as part of monopoly power. When adjudicating a case of resale price fixing, Chilean regulators have so far balanced the commercial relationship between the producer, which imposes the resale price, and the distributor, which implements the fixed price. If the distributor is an agent or a consigned seller for the producer, then fixing the resale price is permitted. In that case, the distributor is linked directly to and acts on behalf of the producer (vertical integration).

On the contrary, when the producer sells goods to the distributor (they are not in a master/agent relationship), resale price fixing is banned. Chilean regulators argue that the distributor cannot be limited (by the producer) in its activity after the purchase-sale agreement. Arguments such as the producer's imposition of quality requirements on the distributor, the existence of a notorious trademark, or the existence of special services provided by the distributor have been rejected.

Between 1974 and 1992 the Preventive Commission dealt with ten cases of resale price fixing. Two out of ten companies were found guilty of fixing prices for the concessionaires. Out of six companies seeking consultations, five obtained a negative judgment; these were companies seeking to suggest prices to their dealers in order to facilitate fiscal calculations. Between 1975 and 1992 the Resolutive Commission decided eighteen cases. Ten companies were found guilty of imposing resale prices on distributors. The companies were awarded fines ranging from 17.33UF to 837.94 UF. Only one company was found to be fixing resale prices legitimately in order to comply with copyright requirements.

The Chilean commissions have looked suspiciously at exclusive distribution contracts as probable collusive price agreements. In that respect they have banned distributors from being the exclusive distributor for potentially competing companies.

To determine the legality of a contract of exclusive distribution, the commissions have focused on the relationship between the producer and the distributor. If the distributor acts on behalf of the producer (as an agent), the exclusivity is deemed fair and legal: The distributor does not risk concentrating a significant part of the distribution of the same article. On the contrary, the commissions have sanctioned companies that do not have an agent relationship (a commercial mandate) with the distributor; in that case, the distributor acts on the company's behalf as a sole and exclusive buyer, eliminating the plurality of demand and acting contrary to competition principles.

Between 1974 and 1993 the Preventive Commission dealt with forty cases of exclusive distribution. Thirteen companies were seeking consultation as to the legality of a contract. The majority of the consultations concluded that the contract was legal, provided that the distributor did not concentrate the total or a significant part of the production of the same good that is produced by other companies. One claim was filed by a competitor and one by a minority distributor, accusing the producer of assigning the rights of exclusive distribution to a company that was also producing the same good. In both cases the defendants were acquitted because the commission did not find the exclusive distribution to constitute an abuse of dominant power. Between 1975 and 1992, the Resolutive Commission decided twelve cases on exclusive distribution, two of which were appealed to the supreme court. The supreme court found the defendant guilty of imposing conditions on his distributor, such as the right to sell only its products and territorial restrictions, and imposed a fine of 128.54 UF.

In Chile, price agreements are usually banned as anticompetitive when the producers can form an authentic monopoly, with prices higher than the competitive price. Given the lack of a per se prohibition in the law, Chilean regulators have been inclined to ban price agreements as unfair trade practices. Such cases are difficult to prosecute, and only a few cases have been presented. To determine the existence of a price agreement, price surveys are conducted. If uniform prices are discovered, a price agreement is presumed to exist.

Between 1974 and 1992 the Preventive Commission dealt with three cases of price agreements. Two of the accused companies were found guilty of agreeing to raise their prices. During the same period, the Resolutive Commission dealt with thirty-one cases, five of which were appealed to the supreme court. The supreme court sanctioned the defendant in three instances, awarding fines ranging from 10.06 UF to 1,263,238 UF.

In Venezuela, between 1992 and 1993, the Superintendency for the Promotion and Protection of Competition prosecuted nine claims (78

percent corresponding to the commercial sector and services, and 22 percent corresponding to the industrial sector), and initiated, ex officio, four proceedings. The cases involved price agreements between cement competitors (the superintendency found the companies liable for anticompetitive conduct and levied a fine of $70,000), and between medical companies (the companies were found liable and a fine was levied corresponding to 3 percent of their sales); price fixing (the accused municipality was found not liable for fixing public transportation prices); exclusive distribution contracts; and boycotts (inducing a refusal to deal).

The superintendency is also consulted by interested parties, public organizations, and private enterprises about technical aspects of the law. Between 1991 and 1993 the superintendency conducted sixteen consultations and investigations. In an important consultation, the superintendency concluded that the fixing of telecommunications tariffs constituted a barrier to competition; only natural monopolies and public services could be subject to fixed prices.

In the area of mergers and acquisitions, six companies sought authorization as to the proposed merger. Among them, three were authorized to go ahead and only one was denied authorization because it would result in undue economic concentration in the paint market. This case was appealed, and there was much debate about whether the decision should fall under the superintendency's jurisdiction and, thus, whether it would be binding.

In Mexico, the commission has investigated several cases of absolute and relative conduct, evaluated a considerable number of mergers, elaborated guidelines for the privatization of infrastructure, and conducted various studies in different economic sectors. In its first year of operation, the commission focused on three areas: mergers between two or more economic agents, investigations ex oficio on possible monopoly practices, and claims by individuals of possible monopoly practices. Among those areas, the first was the most heavily investigated and prosecuted because of the law, which requires companies to notify the commission of most mergers and acquisitions before they go through;[7] because of the long time period required to complete an investigation ex officio; and because of the relative ignorance of the public as to their rights in respect of mergers and acquisitions. The commission also has jurisdiction over mergers and acquisitions that have an impact on the national territory, although the definition of the relevant market may sometimes extend to a foreign territory.

From June 1993 to 1996, the commission received fifty-two notifications of mergers and acquisitions. Among them, forty-five have already been processed: thirty-seven in industry, four in telecommunications, and eleven in finance. Thirty-nine of the cases were found not to be monopolistic. In the remaining cases, the commission either disallowed the merger or demanded compliance with some conditions in order to eliminate the risks of unfair competition. The average time period for determining the legality of the notifications was twenty-seven days (article 21 of the law gives the commission up to forty-five days in which to examine a merger).

On receipt of a merger notification, the commission reviews all information submitted, asks for more information as needed, and decides whether it is necessary to inform the parties not to finalize the agreement. The commission only renders preventive resolutions; that is, if a company has already completed a merger found to be anticompetitive, the parties are responsible for the full cost of divesting the agreement. The commission then examines whether the activity constitutes a corporate restructuring, which means that it takes place for operative reasons. If the activity is not judged to be a corporate restructuring, then the commission will try to evaluate the effects of the merger. According to the law, the criteria for evaluating a merger or concentration are tailored according to the particularities of each case. However, in all cases, the relevant market has to be defined. This entails considering the characteristics (price and quality) of similar products and services, and their geographic position and the possibilities of access to them.

In its first year of operation the commission initiated sixteen investigations in different eco-nomic sectors. Among them, fifteen already have been concluded. In seven cases there was no violation of the federal law of free competition. Where a violation was found, fines were awarded for a total of MXN$2,453,000. Two of the commission's decisions were appealed before the commission (through the reconsideration proceeding).

The commission received twenty-two claims of monopoly practices from individuals. Of the seventeen that have been processed, sixteen were rejected for failing to meet minimum requirements. One of the commission's main objectives is to educate the public about their rights. In that respect the commission has elaborated guidelines for the public regarding the initiation of proceedings for unfair competition practices.

In Colombia twenty-five investigations were initiated in 1993–94. Among them, three cases were prosecuted. The investigation process takes an average period of six months. The fines are awarded in the form of injunctions and monetary fines ranging from 300 up to 2,000 times the minimum monthly salary in Colombia.

In Peru, INDECOPI has focused on disseminating the principles of free competition and its own role, on delegating its authorities to regional institutions, and on investigating and adjudicating cases. All of INDECOPI's commissions have been very active in receiving complaints, investigating ex officio, and deciding cases. The following information about the activities of the various commissions comes from the monthly INDECOPI bulletin.

- *Commissions for the Simplification of Entry and Exit from the Market.* Under their supervision (Law 26116 of December 28, 1992 for business restructuring), the assembly of creditors of two companies approved business restructuring plans, and one of them (a textile company) completed the restructuring process in only three months.

- *Commission for the Supervision of Technical Standards, Metrology, and Nontariff Barriers.* In July 1993, the commission established a new system of metrology control, based on the presumption of truth, freedom to contract, and ex post control. In January 1994 it

294 MANAGING THE REGULATORY PROCESS

authorized the establishment of agencies for quality certification.

- *Commission for the Restraint of Unfair Competition and Advertising.* Since July 1993, the commission adjudicated various unfair competition cases and levied fines ranging from 5 Unidad Imposition Total (UIT) (against a company for deceptive and misleading advertising, a first-instance decision), to 25 UIT (against a company for using similar trademarks that risk confusing the public, a first-instance decision. The UIT is an index that accounts for inflation). In its first month of operation (July 1993), the commission initiated, ex officio, nine actions for deceptive advertising. So far, fines ranging from 0.5 UIT to 2 UIT have been levied, in addition to injunctions.

- *Commission for Free Competition.* The commission concluded investigations on, among other things, price fixing by public transporters and price fixing in the wheat (bread) market. It found that the price fixing amounted to a restrictive practice and ruled for an injunction. In addition, the commission brought a criminal action for abuse of economic power.

- *Commission for Dumping and Subsidies Control.* Since July 1993 the commission has investigated more than twenty-five dumping claims. Among them, it investigated the import of dairy products from Canada, the European Union, and New Zealand, and the import of backing bricks. In the latter case, the commission applied countervailing duties of 11.68 percent.

- *Commission for Consumer Protection.* This commission has received, investigated, and adjudicated the most complaints. Its efforts have consumed a large share of INDECOPI's resources, with high opportunity costs and relatively low welfare impact. It has been very active in helping consumers understand and protect their rights.

Finally, there is an issue of focus in most of the agencies dealing with competition policies in Latin America and the Caribbean. These are obviously incipient institutions, which have little conceptual and practical experience and, as to be expected, have yet to determine what competition policy should be and how best to execute it. Therefore, competition policy agencies in Latin America and the Caribbean should focus in their early stages on fairly clear cases of anticompetitive practices that have significant economic impact, rather than on ambiguous cases that are potentially controversial or have little welfare impact but consume many resources, such as consumer protection cases. This is necessary to avoid damaging the agency's credibility and long-term effectiveness. The vagueness of some of the laws that the agencies enforce underscores the importance of developing that focus. In doing so the agencies could then become an effective complement to the enforcement of competition and regulatory policies.

UTILITY REGULATION AND ANTITRUST REFORM COMPLEMENTARITIES: THE CASE OF CHILE

Reform of the utility sector in Chile started early in the Pinochet period. It was undertaken in the shadow of the antimonopoly statutes that were passed in December 1973 as one of the first acts of the Pinochet regime (Decree Law 211, hereafter D.L. 211). Although prior to passage of D.L. 211, antitrust statutes were on Chile's books, they were inoperative and ineffective, as in most of Latin America. (For a discussion of Chile's antitrust statutes in a comparative perspective see López Echeverría 1986). D.L. 211 made three important changes that became crucial determinants of the evolution of the utility sector: (a) It deemed criminal all anticompetitive actions (articles 1 and 2), (b) it prohibited the granting of a monopoly license to a nongovernmental entity in any area of the economy (article 4, which specifies that only through specific legislation can a particular activity be reserved for government entities), and (c) it created a complex institutional framework for resolving antimonopoly claims of both the private sector and the government. The third feature was crucial to implementing the first two. Indeed, in the utility sector, companies both new and old used D.L. 211 to attempt to enter into de facto closed markets. As the telecommunications case will show, D.L. 211 provided a measure of regulatory flexibility that would not have existed otherwise. Its prohibition of exclusive monopoly rights implies that unless expressly stated by sectoral laws, there are no exclusive service territories, nor exclusive areas of operation. Thus, from 1973 on, there was free entry into all areas of economic activity, including the utility sector. Furthermore, private investors were able to use the mechanisms stipulated in D.L. 211 to force themselves in and to trigger regulatory changes that limit the power of the incumbent firms.

In the utility sector the reforms started with the creation in 1977 and 1978 of specialized regulatory agencies for the electricity and telecommunications sectors. Box 15.1 provides the milestones in the utility reform process. The reforms involve both a change in the regulatory framework and the restructuring and eventual privatization of public companies.

D.L. 211 created four entities: the Office of the National Economic Attorney General, the regional preventive commissions, the Central Preventive Commission, and the Resolutive Commission. These institutions were designed to limit the ability of the government and legislators to influence the outcome of antitrust cases. Three features are important here: (a) the decentralized appointment process (including random appointees), (b) the rotation of membership in the commissions so that no easy quid pro quo could develop between politicians and commissioners, and (c) the design of a complex decisionmaking process.

Let us first focus on the appointment procedures. The national economic attorney general is appointed, as is the comptroller general, for an indefinite term by the president and cannot be removed except by a process instituted by the comptroller general. Each regional preventive commission is chaired by the regional economic secretary and is composed of three other members, one appointed by the governor of the region, one appointed by the regional development council, and one appointed by the presi-

dents of the neighborhood committees. The Central Preventive Commission is composed of five members. The chair is a representative of the Ministry of Economics, and the other members are a representative of the finance minister, two university professors (a lawyer and an economist) appointed by the Council of University Rectors, and a representative of the neighborhood committees of the metropolitan area. The Resolutive Commission is composed of five members. It is chaired by a supreme court justice (appointed by the court itself), and the other members are appointed in the following manner: the ministers of economics and finance each appoint one, and a law school dean and an economics department chair are randomly selected from a list of law schools and economics departments. Membership in all antitrust commissions is for two years.

The appointment process, then, limits the ability of the government to dictate antitrust policy. In particular, although the government has two representatives in the Resolutive Commission, the other three are appointed in an essentially random fashion. Similarly, the preventive commissions have a heavily regional flavor, with the government controlling less than half the appointments. The process for appointing members of the antitrust commissions is consistent with the intent of creating independent entities.

Another important feature that strengthens the independence of the antitrust authorities from the central government is their formal interaction and the potential for subsequent appeals. First, the national economic attorney general is in charge of investigating violations of the antitrust statutes. He or she can investigate on their own or at the request of a preventive commission. He or she can request that the preventive and resolutive commissions take actions under their responsibilities. The national economic attorney general can appear before the Resolutive Commission to argue for or against a decision by the regional preventive commissions, and can appear before the supreme court to argue for or against a resolution by the Resolutive Commission. The regional preventive commissions are in charge of resolving antitrust issues in their regions, while the central Preventive

Box 15.1 Milestones in Chile's Utility Sector Reform

1973
D.L. 211: Antimonopolies statute: Creation of antitrust authorities

1977
Law 1.762: Creation of Subsecretary of Telecommunications (Subtel)

1978
Law 2.224: Creation of the National Energy Commission

1979
Antitrust Commission: Opening of the telecommunications equipment market to competition

1981
Beginning of privatization of electricity distribution assets

1982
D.F.L. 1: Regulatory framework for the electricity sector
Law 18.168: General telecommunications law

1985
Ministerial decree: Organization of Central Dispatch Center
Beginning of privatization of electricity generation plants

1987
D.F.L. 1: Reform of telecommunications law, introducing price-setting framework
Privatization of Chilmetro (largest distribution company)
Privatization of Chilquinta
Privatization of Chilgener (second-largest electricity generator)

1988
D.F.L. 70: Price-setting framework for water companies
Privatization of CTC (the main local telephone company)

1989
Privatization of Entel (the main long-distance company)
Privatization of Endesa (the main generator)
CTC and other local exchange companies request long-distance licenses
Antitrust Commission: Participation of telecommunications companies allowed in both local and long-distance services, requiring the introduction of a multi-carrier system

1990
Supreme Court: The Antitrust Commission ordered to reconsider its 1989 decision on local and long-distance service

1991
Ministerial decree: Regulatory framework for granting water company licenses

1992
Antitrust Commission: Prohibition of partial joint ownership of CTC and Entel

1993
Antitrust Commission: Prior decision upheld that allows telecommunications companies to provide both local exchange and long-distance services based on a multicarrier system
Supreme Court: The Antitrust Commission's 1992 blocking of partial joint ownership of CTC and Entel upheld

1994
Law 3A: Introduction of the multicarrier system for long-distance telecommunications

Commission deals with issues that arise in the metropolitan area or that involve more than one region.

Any person, including the government or the national economic attorney general, may file a complaint in front of a preventive commission, which then undertakes an investigation and issues an order. In the utility sector, following a determination that there is no free competition, the commission may require the Ministry of the Economy to impose regulations on the supply of a particular good or service. All decisions of the Preventive Commissions can be appealed to the Resolutive Commission, the decisions of which cannot be appealed, except when they impose monetary penalties, require the modification of the statute of a corporation, or block a person from belonging to a particular association. In those cases the decision of the Resolutive Commission can be appealed to the supreme court.

If D.L. 211 had stopped with article 4, it would not be that different from the previous antitrust statutes, although article 4 would have raised substantial problems for utility operators whose licenses would have lost their exclusivity. Articles 1 through 4 define anticompetitive behavior and determine that there can be exclusive monopolies or licenses. What makes them so important was the creation of a complex system of checks and balances concerning competition issues. This process has been used several times by both the government and the private sector and has had a significant influence on efforts to open the telecommunications sector to competition.

INSTITUTIONAL DESIGN: PERU'S INSTITUTE FOR THE DEFENSE OF COMPETITION AND INTELLECTUAL PROPERTY

Our institutional analysis of Peru's INDECOPI has four parts. First, we analyze the four major components that can significantly determine the success of any institution: autonomy, accountability, managerial freedom, and incentive structure. Second, we identify the elements of institutional design that can facilitate achieving high levels of those four major components. Third, we identify the factors of function, transaction costs, and jurisdictional design that enhance the effectiveness of the institution, *provided* that a high degree of autonomy, accountability, managerial freedom, and incentive structure is present. Fourth, we analyze the reasons behind the shortcomings of INDECOPI's performance to date, providing recommendations for improvements.

Components of Success

INDECOPI seeks to enforce competition policy law; propose legislative revisions; play an advisory role in related government policies and actions; coordinate with relevant agencies; disseminate information about the law; and provide guidelines about standards for competitive behavior, particularly in areas where the law is vague or subject to misinterpretation or where firms appear to be misinformed. INDECOPI's main efforts have been directed toward developing its institutional image and promoting a free-market economy.

In principle INDECOPI is supposed to be an autonomous institution; in fact, the funding structure and budget constraints are the major obstacles to bona fide autonomy. Any reasonable and desirable expansion of INDECOPI's operations would require additional government transfer of funds that are now discretionary. This discretion obviously limits INDECOPI's autonomy and makes political interference effective, because there is a credible threat that the government will cut budget allocations. INDECOPI's capacity to generate adequate levels of resources is very limited. The allocation of government funds should be set by law and should be determined as a percentage of GDP or of the total government budget. This would create the potential for real autonomy.

The internal structure and personnel contracts are, in principle, designed to strengthen the accountability of each person to his or her supervisor. Professionals do not have job security, and each person is accountable to his or her immediate supervisor. All are accountable to the president of INDECOPI, whose five-year term is renewable by Peru's president and who is directly accountable to him and, indirectly, to the country. The media can exert political pressure on Peru's president to seek the resignation of INDECOPI's president or to not renew his or her appointment. Nevertheless, formal channels exist to evaluate the performance of INDECOPI. The Office of Institutions and Organizations of the State is the formal supervisory entity for the use of funds and functions. In addition, the office of INDECOPI's president undertakes regular internal audits. Furthermore, informal channels, such as the media and private sector, increase INDECOPI's accountability. INDECOPI's activities are highly visible, affecting the day-to-day activities of consumers. Evaluation and criticism of INDECOPI by the media, and the responses of consumers and their political impact, also increase the degree of accountability.

INDECOPI has more managerial freedom than the average state institution, but that freedom is still limited and incomplete. For example, although managers have discretion in filling vacancies, they cannot increase the number of vacancies and have to request written authorization from the minister to increase the salary for a given job classification.

The incentive structure is above average by the standards of public institutions. First, salaries are above the mean for the civil service (although below private sector salaries). Second, loss of employment is a possibility. Third, most jobs are perceived to be a stepping stone (given a record of good performance) to better appointments, mainly in the private sector. INDECOPI's work provides employees with high exposure and invaluable experience. Most professionals do not expect to develop their career path within INDECOPI.

Innovative and Desirable Institutional Design Features

INDECOPI is a relatively new institution. It incorporated the old office of trademarks and copyrights, and no constituency existed to oppose the new mandate; the appointed decisionmaking executives and professionals had no links with the old institution. The average age of its professionals is thirty-four, which means the staff is not tainted by the old bureaucracy or political mode. Nearly half of its professionals come from the private sector and have no political record or political experience. They are technocrats, with no apparent political agenda.

The decisions both on personnel matters and on the selection and resolution of cases are all made by committee and not by any specific individual. This reduces rent seeking and the opportunities to exercise undue influence.

The institutional design of INDECOPI is quite innovative and appealing. It contains an appropriate amount of checks and balances to minimize patronage, arbitrariness, and rent-seeking opportunities. There are three main groups of decisionmakers. The consultative board (consejo consultivo) is composed of four private sector representatives and five public sector representatives, who are nominated by sectors and ministries. This consultative board is responsible for proposing short lists to the board of directors, the board of commissioners, office chiefs, and members of the tribunal. The board of directors is composed of the president of INDECOPI and two

other directors, one nominated by the ministry of economy and one by the ministry of industry. The board of directors selects commissioners and office chiefs from a list submitted by the consultative board and recommends members of the tribunal to the president of the republic. The board determines budget allocations and main strategic policy design, provides a long-term vision and direction for the agency, and approves hiring and labor reductions. The commissions, which are responsible for selecting and deciding cases following the recommendations of the technical secretariat, are composed of four to six members, mostly professionals in the private sector who participate four to eight hours a week, with an expected regular turnover. The commissions also propose the hiring and firing of the technical secretaries.

This decisionmaking structure is characterized by a fair amount of checks and balances in the policies governing the selection and firing of personnel, and in the policies governing the focus, activities, and performance of the institution.

Factors of Function, Transaction Costs, and Jurisdictional Design

A most attractive feature of INDECOPI is that a special appeals court (tribunal) is located within the institution that is staffed by specially appointed judges completely separate from and with no links to the judicial system proper. This court handles any first appeal of the commission's decisions. Given the unreliability, delays, and tradition of the judicial system and the economic complexity of the cases presented, this feature is essential to securing any degree of effectiveness. Any further appeal goes directly to the supreme court.

An issue that often diminishes the effectiveness of an institution is the existence of jurisdictions that overlap or are fragmented among different institutions. Turf wars, coordination problems, and conflicting objectives and approaches among institutions are often the causes of failure. Those problems have been successfully addressed in Peru because INDECOPI integrates all jurisdictional and related responsibilities regarding competition policy issues. INDE-COPI handles not only antitrust and consumer protection issues, but also all trade-related competition issues, such as antidumping and countervailing duties, and intellectual property rights. This level of integration is highly desirable and most innovative. No other country in the world has adopted such an integrated approach. Nevertheless, overlapping jurisdictions with various ministries, such as health and agriculture, and on issues of public services and problems of coordination with regulatory institutions, still exist and need to be worked out.

INDECOPI's Performance Shortcomings

INDECOPI's performance has been mixed. Although some advances have been made in deterring anticompetitive behavior, particularly in the area of consumer protection, performance has fallen short in more important areas, such as antitrust. The reasons are varied and include

- *Lack of political support.* The government does not appear to have given INDECOPI high priority. The government apparently thought INDECOPI could at least placate fears induced by the opening of its economy, yet it did not have a clear idea of how active it wanted INDECOPI to be. The result has been an apparent lack of political support, evidenced by budget shortcomings.
- *Inadequate staffing.* INDECOPI's skill mix is not appropriate to its objectives. It has an excessive number of lawyers (67 percent) relative to economists (10 percent), although subsequent hiring has improved the mix. It needs to bring parity to those numbers. A large part of its work consists of conducting and presenting economic analysis of cases, which its staff is unable to do convincingly.
- *Inadequate budget.* INDECOPI's assigned resources are a major obstacle to securing the stated institutional objectives. Its total 1995 budget was I/.10.7 million (about US$4 million), with a staff of 118 and up to 126 approved positions. Nearly 90 percent of its funding is financed by its own revenues. The registration of brands, copy-

rights, trademarks, and patents accounts for 65 percent of its own revenues, and filing fees for cases and services account for another 10 percent. The government provides 11 percent of its total budget, and that amount cannot be used for wages or salaries. Given its mandate, the budget is woefully inadequate. In addition, it is not proper or efficient to cross-subsidize registration and other fees to antitrust operations. As a result, fees are the highest in the region. Moreover, there is an efficiency limit on how high those fees can be set.

- *Mistaken priorities.* INDECOPI's major focus has been on consumer protection and related cases, to which it allocates more than 10 percent of its budget and human resources. In contrast, it allocates only 2.7 percent of its budget to mainstream antitrust cases (the Tribunal of Free Competition has a staff of only three persons and only one computer with a hard drive). INDECOPI's main priorities have been building its institutional image and preaching the benefits of a free-market economy. INDECOPI spends more on building its institutional image, 2.8 percent, than on deciding antitrust cases, which should be the main focus of its activities.
- *Lack of skills.* Aside from the scarcity of economists and excess of lawyers, the training and experience of these professionals is very limited, particularly in the technical secretariats. Most are barely out of law school and have little or no background in law and economics, not to mention industrial organization. The hiring of some senior experienced economists well versed in industrial organization is critical for INDE-COPI's future. This should be complemented with a program of internships of no less than one month, such as those of the federal trade commissions or antitrust agencies in the United States, Canada, Chile, and Spain.
- *Inadequate salaries.* To avoid excessive turnover of its young professionals and to attract senior professionals, INDECOPI should have the flexibility to assign salaries, in a discriminatory fashion, that are at least 80

percent of comparable private sector salaries. As of now, INDECOPI salaries are on average 70 percent of comparable private sector salaries.

- *Limited deterrence power.* INDECOPI's limited budget and manpower, particularly in handling antitrust cases (D.L. 701), lower the probabilities of detection and investigation; its limited capacity for sound economic analysis lowers the probability of successful litigation; and the relatively low maximum fine of I/.50 (about $40,000) renders INDECOPI's deterrence impact, particularly for antitrust violations, nearly nil, although the 1996 amendments substantially raised the maximum fine.

- *Limited internal flexibility.* There are two problems with the design of the competencies of the commissions and technical secretariats and with their operational functioning vis-à-vis each other. The first problem can be linked to the existing law, because the concept was to have one commission for each piece of legislation. Those several pieces of legislation show considerable overlap. Three commissions and technical secretariats—unfair competition, publicity, and consumer protection—should merge. The conceptual issues—misinformation, misrepresentation, or fraud—are the same in the three commissions, and merging them would save resources and increase efficiency. The second issue concerns interactions across commissions, and resource flexibility. The current design does not allow interaction, communication, or discussion across commissions and technical secretariats, even when the issues and economic analysis have a lot in common. In addition, and just as important, assigning a fixed budget to each commission does not allow resources to be adjusted in light of the number and relevance of cases during the fiscal year.

- *Other issues.* First, issues of jurisdiction need to be resolved. For example, because other institutions have been given, within their by-laws, explicit jurisdiction over food-related and public service cases, INDECOPI

cannot address those cases even when a competition law may have been violated. Second, INDECOPI operates essentially only in Lima. Cases that occur elsewhere in the country cannot be handled, independent of their welfare impact, because INDECOPI does not have the resources or infrastructure to do so. Third, the commissions, except the one handling free competition, lack the power to issue cease and desist orders, an instrument essential to their mandates.

NOTES

1. The law defines the basic elements of anticompetitive conduct. As regards production, anticompetitive conduct includes share of quotas and reduction or paralysis of production. As regards commerce or distribution, it includes share of quotas and assignment of market zones and zones of exclusive distribution of the same product by different producers. As regards the price of goods and services, it includes price agreements and other conduct not specifically mentioned in the law that may eliminate, restrict, or obstruct competition. The criteria for determining such conduct are similar to those used for conduct explicitly classified as unfair under the law, and as interpreted by the national economic prosecutor.

2. See Economists Incorporated 1992, which makes specific recommendations for the new competition law to be enacted. These recommendations are reflected in the draft law awaiting approval by the congress.

3. There are no guidelines as to when the Preventive Commission or the Resolutive Commission is the competent first-instance forum.

4. The commission has four departments: legal, economic investigation, investigations, and mergers and acquisitions.

5. This concern is common in all countries examined. The goal of their competition policy is to deter and prosecute the activity that deters competition. However, the choice of cases to be prosecuted is not easy. One has to take into account the risk of deterring behavior that is not harmful to consumers.

6. Seven commissions cover various aspects of the protection of competition and consumer rights: free competition, dumping and subsidies control, consumer protection, advertising, unfair competition, technical standards and nontariff barriers, and entry and exit barriers. They each consist of four members, usually economists and lawyers.

7. According to the law, mergers and acquisitions that exceed the limits established in the law must be reported to the commission before they go through.

16

CONCLUSION: THE CHALLENGE OF REGULATION

DURING THE DECADE of the 1990s there has been an extraordinary flurry of regulatory activity in most countries, but particularly in developing countries, and especially in the utilities sector. This has occurred mostly as a result of privatizations in the utilities sector; an increased awareness of the need for and benefits of such regulation; and the recognition of the need both to address domestic concerns about monopolistic abuses by private (and mostly foreign) operators, and to restrict government opportunistic behavior that would hamper foreign interest and investment in the sector. The challenge is considerable, not only because the

establishment and operation of an effective regulatory system is a complex undertaking and requires a learning process, but also because of the lack of a regulatory tradition and track record, scarcity of expertise, and weak formal and informal norms protecting private rights, all so prevalent in developing countries. Moreover, the difficulty of establishing an effective regulatory regime is exacerbated by conflicting objectives, such as ensuring sector competition; high revenues from concession/privatization for fiscal reasons; ambitious investment demands; rapid expansion of basic services; distributional factors in the pricing of the services; and the reluctance of most governments to relinquish control of the sector. Governments tempted to use regulation to advance short-term political goals, with inap-

propriate regard for efficiency or implications for investors, and information asymmetries in costs and performance that favor the operators, make the regulatory system vulnerable to capture, thus diminishing credibility and overall welfare. Information and commitment problems can undermine the efforts of even the most well-intentioned regulators.

Consequently, it is not surprising that the development of the required and appropriate regulatory institutions has been slower than desired, and has generated criticism, as illustrated here. While the regulatory initiatives and activities have been many and varied, the results have been mixed, although improving. While there still remains much work to be done in this area both procedurally and substantively, the significant achievements on the regulatory front in most developing countries must be lauded, particularly given the complexities just described. Many developing countries have enacted adequate regulatory laws, deregulated operations that should not have been regulated, established regulatory agencies, and so on. Most reassuring is that the awareness of the need to establish, and benefits of establishing, an effective regulatory regime appears to be increasing, as is the commitment to the process.

The consensus, supported by theory and practice, is that while technological innovations are making feasible the use of competition in many segments of the utilities sector, direct regulation of aspects of these industries continues to be necessary. The general principle is to regulate those segments of the market that display natural monopoly characteristics in order to curtail abuses of monopoly power, and especially to protect consumers, given the lack of competitive alternatives of service, and to ensure access (fair price and quality of service) by would-be competitors to essential facilities often controlled by incumbent companies. At the same time, recognizing that technology and new entrants are eroding market power, governments should help this process along—fostering greater competition, passing antitrust legislation, providing regulatory credibility, and implementing large-scale deregulation in order to help potential market players exploit the technological opportunities. The trend toward liberalization, driven by technological innovation, is unquestionable, yet regulatory needs remain.[1]

Carefully designed regulatory policies and appropriate selection of regulatory instruments and regimes can increase a country's limited powers of commitment and the effectiveness of regulation, promoting private investors' confidence about the stability of the regulatory framework, and limiting the opportunities for regulatory capture from government, industry, or consumers, bringing about needed investment, efficient provision, and increased competitiveness of productive users, thus impacting growth positively. Formal and binding rules need to be specified precisely if they are to provide a credible

anchor for a regulatory system. The mechanisms for rulemaking (law or legally binding contracts) need to be reasonably resilient to pressures for change. And there need to be institutions which credibly enforce both the specific restraints and the restraints on system changes. The overall benefits should be well understood, and they can be significant. For example, aside from increased efficiency, the accompanying expansion of coverage has very positive effects on productivity opportunities, and on the quality of life of individuals with lower incomes who previously were usually excluded from service or were offered very poor quality service. Consequently, the overall impact on welfare and income distribution is considerable.

There are many lessons both from theory and from the brief experience of regulation which should be most useful for the work ahead, either in fine-tuning or creating new initiatives, or for countries still in the midst or only at the beginning of their regulatory experience. What follows is a summary of the salient lessons.

SALIENT LESSONS FOR REGULATORY DESIGN

In the design of basic and detailed regulatory frameworks, institutions and country endowments matter, but so do other factors. In a broad sense the requirements for successful regulation are

1. Regulatory credibility
2. Clear rules for and limits to government and regulator discretion
3. Minimal opportunities for renegotiation
4. Maximum use of competition wherever feasible
5. An incentive-based regulatory framework
6. Appropriate antitrust legislation, well-trained and well-compensated professionals, and effective enforcement.

At the regulatory design detail level (structure, pricing, and service rules, and agency design), several principles should be kept in mind. The standard elements that are often subject to regulation vary from country to country and from sector to sector; however, the four main instruments are (a) price(s), (b) quantity or coverage, (c) number of firms by subactivity, and (d) degree of vertical integration. Other instruments less frequently used include product quality, timeliness of service, and investment. Often, the lack of use of some potential instruments of regulation, such as quality, has to do with severe informational problems and the high cost of monitoring and enforcement. The regulatory functions and the regulated elements depend by and large on the country's regulatory philosophy, endowments, country and sector characteristics, and the extent of competition allowed. For example, New Zealand has virtually no regulatory control of the prices charged to end users, and the U.S. Federal Communications Commission often chooses not to impose technical standards.

While there are tradeoffs in regulatory design, and a country should evaluate them carefully when choosing what to regulate and how, there are salient choices and principles for effective regulatory design, and for reducing the opportunities for regulatory capture in the utilities sectors. They are

1. *Regulation is a Game.* It is a problem of conflict and interactive strategies. Regulation is not a decision theory problem.

2. *Extent of Regulation.* Regulation may be less necessary than is believed. The tradeoffs between regulation and its absence should be carefully assessed; reliance on market-induced competition, narrow and broad, should always be favored over regulation, and when regulation is necessary and appropriate, its form and extent may matter greatly.

3. *Credibility of Regulatory Framework.* For regulation to be effective it has to be credible. Credibility means belief that the rules and framework will not change, opportunities for and success of renegotiation are minimal, and that enforcement will take place. Credibility is secured by embedding the regulatory framework in the most irreversible legal instrument a country can produce. For some countries it is a law, for others a contract. Signals that enforcement will take place are the structure, staffing, and

budget of the regulatory agency and its reputation through performance.

4. *Regulation Should Fit the Country's Institutional Endowments.* The basic and detail engineering of a country's regulatory system have to be tailored to suit the country's institutional endowments. The main criterion is to take the institutional character of the country into account. If the regulatory framework does not fit the institutional and administrative endowments of the country, it will never be credible, successful, or sustainable.

5. *Independence of Regulatory Agency.* The regulatory framework should be lean, detached from the government and from the provision of the service, have its own budget by law or through adequate industry/consumer levies, and should not be under the discretion of the executive branch of government. There are five necessary conditions for regulatory institutions to be effective: (a) managerial freedom (exempting the agency from civil service salary rules that make it difficult to attract and retain well-qualified staff); (b) political and budgetary autonomy (freedom from political and interest-group influence; establishing restrictions on arbitrary removal); (c) accountability (the duty of an agent or employee to respond; that is, to fulfill his or her responsibilities to principal or employer); (d) checks and balances (to limit the power of single individuals within the institution, establishing periodic external audits, and scrutiny of agency's budget and decisions); and (e) incentives (mechanisms to reward financially good performance and punish arbitrary or inadequate performance). Regulatory agencies must operate within a statutory framework that stipulates a preference for competition and market-like regulatory practices, and they must be subject to a variety of substantive constraints and procedural requirements to ensure the integrity, independence, transparency, and accountability of the regulatory process. Among those requirements are affording all interested parties an opportunity to be heard on major policy issues; stipulating deadlines for reaching decisions, and the obligation to supply reasoned justifications for decisions; and establishing due process.

6. *Role of Ministry vs. Agency.* A common reason for inadequate performance of regulatory agencies is the lack of clear demarcation of responsibilities between the agency and the ministry. Clear demarcations have to be clarified and harmonized at the outset. The ministry should retain responsibility for broad sector policy, such as public investment, privatization, sector restructuring, taxation, subsidies, intergovernmental relations, and maintenance of the legislative framework and, arguably, the granting of licenses. The regulatory agency should have responsibility for elaborating detailed standards, administering tariff adjustment rules, monitoring compliance with norms and service quality standards and investments, gathering cost and performance indicators of both the regulated firm and of comparable firms elsewhere, and facilitating the settlement of disputes. In addition, the agency should play a major role in an advisory capacity to the ministry on policy and sector structure.

7. *Favor Single Intersectoral Regulatory Agencies in Small Countries and at Provincial Levels.* In small countries and at the provincial level, where administrative and human resource capabilities are often weak, a single intersectoral regulatory agency should be favored over sector-specific regulatory agencies. Most of the issues cut across sectors, and pooling of resources enhances the learning process. It also reduces the risk of capture by government or industry and facilitates consistency of approaches across sectors.

8. *Regulation Should be Complemented with Antitrust Laws and Proper Enforcement.* Since a number of segments of the utility sectors are and should be open to competition, and function largely unregulated, it is imperative to capture the benefits of competition so that firms do not engage in anticompetitive practices. To deter such practices it is essential to enact modern antitrust laws and to ensure their proper enforcement through proper jurisdiction over the competitive segments of the utility sectors, or at least through an advisory role. Both the antitrust and the regulatory agencies should establish a close collaboration, exploiting complementary expertise. For example, a member of the antitrust agency can be made a member of the utility

agency (as in Australia), or the agencies can make formal submissions to proceedings conducted by the other, or the antitrust agency can determine whether the conditions for effective competition are sufficiently absent to warrant price regulation (as in Mexico), or can act as an appeals body from the utility regulator (as in the U.K.).

ON DISCRETION AND RENEGOTIATION ISSUES

9. *Limited Regulatory Discretion.* Regulation is an ongoing task, fine-tuning and adapting decisions as events unfold. On efficiency grounds this argues for a fair amount of flexibility to be granted to the regulatory agency, with the clear and publicly known principles to be followed in making decisions, so that other parties (particularly providers) can assess the decisions' economic impact on their operations and plan and act accordingly. However, in practice there are often two problems with that framework. One is that the implicit commitment to stick to those principles is not credible and is often violated, with the changes affecting the economic returns of the operator. The other is that the implicit high level of discretion embedded in that framework is vulnerable to influence and capture by interest groups. In general, the regulatory framework should be predictable and have little discretion. Countries should remember, however, that while the need for legal certainty is crucial to creating a competitive environment (overcoming investor hesitancy), too much legal rigidity will impede adaptability. In principle, with the rapid development of technology and managerial techniques, regulatory systems should be able to keep up with changes. However, there are risks, and thus a significant trade-off is involved. The system needs to be adaptable but should not involve too much regulatory discretion. At the expense of some potential efficiency losses, rigidity provides investors with clear rules and reduces capture and rent-seeking opportunities. This is a balancing act that all countries will have to work out over time. It is advisable that for the initial period, when most of the learning by all parties involved takes place, there should be a fairly rigid

structure with little or no discretion by the regulator. Subsequently, at the beginning of review periods, some flexibility can be introduced. Periodic reviews, at five years intervals, are advisable.

10. *Specification of Contingencies that Trigger Regulatory Adjustments.* The regulatory framework should specify the salient contingencies that would trigger adjustments in the regulatory pricing terms, and the conditions and terms for renegotiation and remedies should be clearly specified in the contractual terms. The relationship between the regulator and the regulated industry is best thought of in contractual terms, and like all contracts, the relationship should be clearly specified and should minimize the ability of either party to resort to discretionary or arbitrary actions.

11. *Limit and Deter Opportunities for Renegotiation.* Given the incentives to renegotiate, and the inability to contractually cover all contingencies, financial incentives to penalize frivolous attempts to renegotiate should be built into the license. Whenever technically feasible, overlapping concessions and split concessions should be made to reduce the renegotiation leverage and "hold-up" threats.

12. *Introduce Compulsory Arbitration Mechanisms, Preferably Final Offer when Feasible, for Dispute Settlement.* A compulsory arbitration mechanism and appellate body, preferably with technical expertise and internationally based, should be established to handle disputes. When feasible, use final-offer arbitration schemes. To preserve independence, the ministries should not be involved in the appeals process. The antitrust agency could act as an appellate body (such as in the U.K.), as could an ad hoc tribunal led by the supreme court and comprised of reputable professionals (as in Chile). The appeals process should focus on alleged errors of fact or law, including failure to follow a required process, and the appellate body or tribunal should not be permitted to reconsider the merits of the decision and substitute their own judgment.

ON STRUCTURAL ISSUES

13. *Concession/Privatization Design is Key to an Efficient Sector and Regulatory Performance.* Most performance and regulatory problems can be traced to faulty concession or privatization design. The norm should be careful screening to determine the pool of qualified potential operators, followed by transparent and single criterion competitive bidding for the rights to provide the concession or to purchase the firm. The length of the concession period should be no shorter than the productive life of the physical assets existing or to be acquired; but when feasible, interim periodic competitive rebids for the rights to operate the concession—with rights of first refusal granted to the incumbent operator—should be considered. End-of-concession incentives should also be built into the concession contract. The granting of guarantees on regulatory (unilateral changes) risks, force majeure events, currency convertibility, and repatriation of profits should be provided either through the market, international institutions, or the government. However, guarantees on commercial risks should be avoided.

14. *Unbundling the Sector Prior to Privatization Facilitates Efficiency Gains.* Unbundling the sector prior to privatization by breaking up the company geographically or by activity (long-distance, local exchange, value-added services in telecommunications; generation, transmission, distribution and supply in electricity) induces sector competitiveness much faster than otherwise and results in higher efficiency gains. Unbundling in Chile (activity partition) and Argentina (geographical partition) are examples.

15. *Exclusivity Rights, in Principle, Should Not Be Granted.* Exclusivity rights might be considered only under very limited situations where coordination costs are extremely high. There is little conceptual support for granting exclusivity rights. If the activity does possess natural monopoly characteristics, it has de facto exclusive rights. Then the granting of exclusivity rights de jure is not necessary. And if the activity does not possess natural monopoly characteristics, there is no justification for granting a legal monopoly through exclusivity rights. Only in situations with significant coordination problems or transaction costs (or significant nonhedgeable risks), such as central dispatches or logistics, should granting exclu-

sivity rights be considered. It is also often argued that exclusive rights are needed to successfully address the rebalancing-of-rates issue. This, again, is a misconception, as the case of El Salvador illustrates. Another argument often used to justify exclusivity rights is (universal) service obligations, with implicit or explicit subsidies to certain groups or areas. Again, this is a weak argument. This a relative prices issue, and rather than institutionalizing cross-subsidies (as is often the case), it is better handled with either specific transfers to the operating company or, preferably, with transfers directly to the targeted consumers through vouchers or income tax credits. This ought to eliminate the need for cross-subsidization and "cream-skimming" opportunities by potential entrants. While any potential investors prefer exclusivity rights, the absence of exclusivity rights does not deter their participation. The examples are multiple.[2]

ON DETAIL REGULATION

16. *Incentive Price-Cap Regulation Tends to Lead to Higher Efficiency Relative to Rate-of-Return Regulation.* Price-cap regulation tends to induce much better performance than rate-of-return regulation, despite its potential ratchet effect. The rate-of-return regulation approach resolves the problem of utilities earning monopoly profits, but results in the regulated firm overinvesting in its capital stock, and reducing incentives to efficient cost cutting. Both lead to higher (than feasible and efficient) prices for final users. However, regulators' attempts to tackle this problem have led to legal battles with firms over whether new investments can be justified in terms of meeting demand. Litigation has made cost-of-capital regulation very expensive. Price-cap regulation reduces those problems. Until sufficient competition develops, direct-price regulation would be best. Prices should be linked to a general index of inflation for a period without price changes (about five years) to produce incentives to improve efficiency. That is, the profits from increased profitability should not be removed instantly by price reductions. The price controls should apply to a basket of tariffs in which man-

agement would be free—with some constraints—to alter relative prices. That means the operator could incorporate new information about costs or markets without involving the regulator. However, the regulator ought to have responsibility to prevent undue discrimination in tariffs. Countries that have switched from rate-of-return to price-cap regulation have seen increased efficiency gains. However, care should be exercised in setting the initial prices.

17. *"Yardstick" Regulation Should be a Component of Detail Regulation Whenever Feasible.* The use of benchmark comparisons with similar firms or with a "model" firm (as in Chile), providing standards for "reasonable" cost and performance indicators, can and should be an essential component of regulatory evaluations inasmuch as it reduces subjectivity of evaluations, provides incentives for efficiency, and lessens considerably the cost of regulatory oversight and data (costs) gathering from the firm with its associated incentive problems.

18. *Strong Regulatory Emphasis on the Network, Access Prices, and Quality of Service.* The key to opening markets lies in the terms on which new entrants have access to the existing network. In that vein, states should focus their regulations on the local exchange and on access to it. Although the introduction of local competition can reduce regulation of the final product, separating the network from the retail segment can pose problems. Countries ought to manage competition and cooperation. The absence of regulation of interconnection to the network can bring long delays (as has been the case in the telecommunications sectors in Chile, Mexico, New Zealand, and the United Kingdom). Countries ought to simplify the process of interconnection—develop simplified guidelines as in Australia—and bring in an arbiter quickly upon negotiation failure, as in Mexico. The basic issue is how should the underlying cost of the network (mostly capital, and usually already paid for by taxpayers) be allocated? Access to customers and public networks needs to be increased, and as the sector decentralizes, increased attention should be paid to instruments of interconnection of networks (here the technical aspects are more

important than the economic) and the interconnection of players. The power of the incumbent network operator to fight off potential entrants is significant and needs to be restrained if new entry is to occur.[3] The salient choice for access pricing is global price caps, when feasible, that incorporate access pricing and final goods pricing. On efficiency grounds, they dominate cost-based or efficient component pricing rules for interconnection rates in network structures. A distant second best is efficient component pricing.

19. *Cross-Subsidization Should be Avoided.* Cross-subsidization leads to efficiency distortions, and even more relevant, provides arguments for exclusive rights, thus preventing or delaying entry and competition. Equity and universal service issues should be addressed through income transfers (either to the operator or to the targeted groups). The examples of Chile and Colombia illustrate the feasibility of such schemes.

20. *Rebalancing Tariffs.* The use of competition in non-natural monopoly segments obviously requires substantial price rebalancing, particularly in the telecommunications sector. Indeed, in telecommunications the non-natural monopoly segment turned out to be the one most used by businesses, and consequently the one whose pricing was most distorted. Likewise, the prices of local calls are usually heavily subsidized at the expense of interurban and international calls. Similarly, prior to the transfer of operations to the private sector, prices for water and electricity are often regressive and do not reflect marginal costs. Introducing competition ought to bring down the prices, requiring substantial rebalancing of prices and, in the telecommunications sector in particular, increasing local exchange prices. Rebalancing yields significant economic welfare benefits and removes an important impediment to the development of local competition. The issue is how fast the rebalancing process should be, since it has important economic and political impacts. The window of opportunity presented at the time of privatization ought to be used to make significant price adjustments. The faster full rebalancing is achieved, the faster competition will be developed. As long as some prices differ from marginal costs, protection and exclusivity rights have to be provided at the expense of competition and the benefits it can produce. Likewise, as competition develops, the provider ought to be given the discretion to adjust prices (downward) to respond to competitive pressures.

21. *Price Discrimination Should Be Allowed.* The provider should be granted flexibility to vary prices across users and times of services, all within the broad price-cap regime, to respond to competitive pressures and capacity constraints. This is particularly appropriate for distribution companies in the energy sectors when faced with competition from independent generators contracting directly with large users. In addition, price discrimination based on differential costs of services and demand elasticities should also be allowed. The latter is most relevant to assign all unattributable fixed and common costs of the utility among its services. Those fixed costs should be recovered by mark-ups above marginal costs inversely related to the elasticity of demand for that service (Ramsey pricing).

22. *Information on Costs, Training, and Networks of Regulators.* Finally, a recommendation on information. Many regulatory problems derive from the limited information that is available to regulators and from their limited expertise on the subject. Firms have private information about technology, costs, and demand, so can manipulate to their advantage access to information by regulators. To limit the impact of that problem, it is imperative from the start to develop procedures for gathering relevant information, and that a core of the agency staff receives extensive training in regulatory matters. To facilitate both information gathering and training, it is important to avidly pursue linkages and close collaboration among regulators sharing problems, initiatives, and successful practices. That would also facilitate the process of benchmarking, a most effective means for regulatory oversight. A salient procedure to secure those linkages is the establishment of a network of regulators, both by electronic means and by periodic meetings.

These lessons, when properly adapted to each country's own environment, can significantly increase the likelihood of effective regulation. While the challenges are significant, so are the efforts that developing countries are making to face them. This is a learning process, and while mistakes have been and will be made, the trend is clear. Regulation is here to stay and is gradually improving. As all parties involved increase their awareness and understanding of the issues, balancing constituencies are being formed. They will strengthen the system of informed checks and balances and enhance the credibility of the system and the effective and transparent management of the regulatory process, limiting the opportunities for arbitrary decisions and capture—elements which, ultimately, are the major determinants of a successful regulatory regime.

NOTES

1. For example, in the telecommunications sector the European Parliament endorsed a directive requiring its members to (a) open their telecommunications market to competition in the provision of public voice telephony services; (b) eliminate monopoly control of the telecommunications infrastructure; (c) establish no limitations on the number of licenses issued; (d) allow alternative networks already open to competition—owned by utilities such as rail, electricity, and water—to be used to carry telecommunications services, such as data transmissions, services for closed user groups, and value-added network services; (e) introduce full competition in the mobile and personal communications sector (mobile operators cannot be subject to licensing restrictions in the provision of services and can construct their own infrastructure, use alternative networks, or interconnect with other networks); (f) make interconnection obligatory and require safeguards to ensure cost-oriented interconnecting pricing; and (g) prohibit cross-subsidization of services to avoid barriers to market entry. Likewise, the 1996 U.S. telecommunications law eliminates restrictions preventing the long-distance and regional Bell telephone companies from entering each other's markets. However, before the local Bells can compete in the long-distance market, they must demonstrate to the FCC that they face competition from companies which use the Bell's own facilities, rather than from those that merely resell bulk-bought space on Bell lines. And the FCC must also establish the rules under which new service will interact with the existing Bell infrastructure.

2. In New Zealand, Telecom NZ was successfully privatized in a policy environment of open entry in all market segments, a case similar to Chile in the long-distance market. In the Philippines, foreign investors such as NYNEX, Cable & Wireless, and Telstra have entered the market as competitors or partners of competitors. In Mexico a large domestic cellular operator with support from Bell Atlantic has proposed installing a fixed wireless network to serve 1.5 million customers. In southern India, US West has proposed a telecom build-own-operate scheme and has not asked for an exclusive franchise. Other examples show that investors have accepted competition in Australia, Chile, Malaysia, Sweden, the United Kingdom, and the United States, and in the cellular market of almost every country.

3. For example, as of 1996 Mexico's Telmex (after termination of its legal monopoly on long distance) tried to exercise its power by charging a (relatively high) connection fee to its network of US$.147 per minute by maintaining for its own use the dialing codes which customers recognize as being the codes for long-distance connections, and by failing to agree with competitors on the terms and conditions under which they will sign contacts with their own customers. Competitors, whether they be America's MCI, Britain's Mercury, or Japan's IDC, often owe their existence to government-imposed constraints on the incumbents. Chile's approach to fair regulation of access terms has been one of the more successful. On privatizing Entel, the local monopoly, in 1989, Chile immediately introduced competition in long-distance and international traffic from Telex, and in 1994 it opened the market completely. A scheme allowing customers to select their carrier by simply dialing a three- or four-digit company code, and then the number required (made possible by an almost 100 percent digital network) every time they make a call has attracted two Baby Bells and five Chilean operating companies and produced significant price competition, driving down the cost of international tariffs to the lowest in Latin America. As a result, as of 1996, a peak-time three-minute call to the U.S. was US$1.65, compared to US$5 in Mexico and US$6 in Argentina.

BIBLIOGRAPHY

Ackerman, Bruce A., and William T. Hassler. 1981. *Clean Coal/Dirty Air: Or How the Clean Air Act Became a Multibillion-Dollar Bail-Out for High-Sulfur Coal Producers and What Should Be Done About It*. New Haven, CT: Yale University Press.

Airfare Management Unit. 1996. The American Express European Airfare Index, Paris.

____. 1995. The American Express European Airfare Index, Paris.

Alexander, I., and Antonio Estache. 1977. "A Back-of-the-Envelope Approach to Assess the Cost of Capital for Network Regulators." World Bank, Washington, D.C., December.

Alexander, I., C. Mayer, and H. Weeds. 1996. "Regulatory Structure and Risk in Infrastructure Firms: An International Comparison." Policy Research Working Paper 1698. World Bank, Washington, D.C.

Anderson, Robert, Alan Carlin, Al McGartland, and Jennifer Weinberger. 1995. "Cost Savings from the Use of Market Incentives for Pollution Control." Draft for submission in the forthcoming book on Market-Based Approaches to Environmental Policy. Chicago: University of Illinois Press.

Argentina, Government of. 1993. "Concession Contract." Buenos Aires.

Armstrong, Mark, and Chris Doyle. 1995. "Access Pricing, Entry and the Baumol-Willig Rule." *University of Southampton Discussion Paper in Economics and Econometrics*: 9422, September 1994, p. 34.

Arrow, Kenneth J. 1974. *The Limits of Organization*. New York: Norton.

Arrow, Kenneth J., Maureen L. Cropper, George C. Eads, Robert W. Hahn, Lester B. Lave, Roger G. Noll, Paul R. Portney, Milton Russell, Richard Schmalensee, V. Kerry Smith, and Robert N. Stavins. 1996. *Benefit-Cost Analysis in Environmental, Health, and Safety Regulation: A Statement of Principles*. Washington, D.C.: AEI Press.

Baron, David P. 1988. "Design of Regulatory Mechanisms and Institutions." In Richard Schmalensee and Robert D. Willig, Eds., *Handbook of Industrial Organization*. Amsterdam, NY: North-Holland.

____. 1987. "Procurement Contracting: Efficiency, Renegotiation and Performance Evaluation." *Information Economics & Policy* 3 (2): 109–142.

Barzel, Yoram. 1989. *Economic Analysis of Property Rights*. Cambridge, U.K.: Cambridge University Press.

Baumol, William J. 1975. "Payment by Performance in Rail Passenger Transportation: An Innovation in Amtrak's Operations." *Bell Journal of Economics* 6 (1): 281–98.

____. 1982. "Measurement Cost and the Organization of Markets." *Journal of Law and Economics* 9: 27–48.

Baumol, William J., and J. Gregory Sidak. 1994. *Toward Competition in Local Telephony*. Cambridge, MA: MIT Press.

Baumol, William J., John C. Panzar, and Robert D. Willig. 1982. *Contestable Markets and the Theory of Industry Structure*. New York: Harcourt Brace Jovanovich.

Baysan, Tercan, and J. Luis Guasch. 1993. *Peru: Establishing a Competitive Market Environment*. Washington, D.C.: World Bank.

Beardsley, Scott, and Michael Patsalos-Fox. 1995. "Getting Telecoms Privatization Right." *McKinsey Quarterly* 1.

Berstein, D. 1996. "Electricity Policy in Chile from 1980 Onwards: Analysis and Results." Economic Development Institute. World Bank, Washington, D.C.

Bhattacharya, Sudipto, and J. Luis Guasch. 1988. "Heterogeneity, Tournaments, & Hierarchies." *Journal of Political Economy* 96 (4): 867–881.

Bitran, Eduardo, Antonio Estache, J. Luis Guasch, and Pablo Serra. 1998. *Privatizing and Regulating Chile's Utilities: Successes, Failures, and Outstanding Challenges*. Economic Development Institute. World Bank, Washington, D.C.

Bitran, Eduardo, and F. Saez. 1994. "Privatization and Regulation in Chile." The Brookings Institution, Washington, D.C.

Bitran, Eduardo, and P. Serra. 1994. "Regulatory Issues in the Privatization of Public Utilities: The Chilean Experience." *Quarterly Review of Economics and Finance* 34.

Bitran, Eduardo, and Ricardo Paredes. 1995. "The Chilean Regulatory Experience." Mimeo.

Boner, Roger Alan, and Reinald Krueger. 1991. *The Basics of Antitrust Policy: A Review of Ten Nations and the European Communities*. Technical Paper 160. Washington, D.C.: World Bank.

Braeutigam, Ronald R., and John C. Panzar. 1989. "Diversification Incentives Under Price Based and Cost Based Regulation." *Rand Journal of Economics* 20 (3): 373–391.

____. 1993. "Effects of the Change from Rate-of-Return to Price-Cap Regulation." *American Economic Review* 83 (2): 191–98.

Braeutigam, Ronald R., and Roger G. Noll. 1984. "The Regulation of Surface Freight Transportation: The Welfare Effects Revisited." *Review of Economics and Statistics* 56 (February): 80–87.

Business Week. 1989. March 27.

Cabral, Luis, and Michael H. Riordan. 1989. "Incentives for Cost Reduction under Price Cap Regulation." *Journal of Regulatory Economics* 1 (2): 93–102.

Calhoun, George. 1991. *Digital Cellular Radio*. Norwood, MA: Artech House, pp. 100–114.

____. 1992. *Wireless Access and the Local Telephone Network*. Norwood, MA: Artech House, p. 580.

Calvert, Robert. 1992. "A Rational Choice Theory of Social Institutions: Cooperation, Coordination, and Commitment." Rochester, NY: University of Rochester.

Cardilli, Carlo, Stuart Jack, Daniel Vincent, Gerry Wall, and Leonard Waverman. 1997. "Assessment of Market Values of Canadian Cellular, PCS and ESMR Licenses." Report to Industry Canada #U4200-6-0008. Ottawa, Canada, February.

Carlton, D. W. 1983. "The Need for Coordination among Firms, with Special Reference to Network Industries." *University of Chicago Law Review* 50: 446–65.

Caves, Douglas W., Laurits R. Christensen, and Joseph A. Swanson. 1981. "Productivity Growth, Scale Economics and Capacity Utilization in US Railroads, 1955–1974." *American Economic Review* 71 (5): 994–1002.

____. 1981. "The High Cost of Regulating U.S. Railroads." *Regulation* 41–46, January/February.

Caves, Douglas W., Laurits R. Christensen, Michael W. Tretheway, and Robert J. Windle. 1985. "The Effect of New Entry on Productivity Growth in the U.S. Airline Industry." *Logistics and Transportation Review* 21 (4): 299–335.

____. 1987. "An Assessment of the Efficiency Effects of U.S. Airline Deregulation via an International Comparison." In Elizabeth E. Bailey, Ed., *Public Regulation: New Perspectives on Institutions and Policies*. Cambridge, MA: MIT Press.

Chisari, Omar, Antonio Estache, and Carlos Romero. 1997a. "Winners and Losers from Utilities Privatization and Deregulation: Lessons from a General Equilibrium Model of Argentina." World Bank, Washington, D.C.

____. 1997b. "The Distribution of Gains from Utility Privatization and Regulation in Argentina." In *The Private Sector in Infrastructure*. World Bank, Washington, D.C., 41–44.

Christiansen, G. B., and R. H. Haveman. 1981. "Public Regulations and the Slowdown in Productivity Growth." *American Economic Review* 71 (5): 320–25.

Coase, Ronald H. 1959. "The Federal Communications Commission." *Journal of Law & Economics* 2: 1-40.

____. 1960. "The Nature of Social Cost." *Journal of Law and Economics* 3 (2): 1–44.

____. 1988. "R. H. Coase Lectures." *Journal of Law, Economics, and Organization* 4 (1): 3–8.

Consulting Services Group. 1995. The American Express Domestic Airfare Index, New York.

____. 1996. The American Express Domestic Airfare Index, New York.

Cox, G. 1987. *The Efficient Secret*. New York: Cambridge University Press.

Crandall, Robert W. 1988. "What Ever Happened to Deregulation?" In *Assessing the Reagan Years*, David Boaz, Ed. Cato Institute, Washington, D.C.

____. 1997. "New Zealand Spectrum Policy: A Model for the United States?" *Journal of Law & Economics*.

Crew, M. A., and P. R. Kleindorfer. 1985. "Governance Costs of Rate-of-Return Regulation." *Journal of Institutional and Theoretical Economics* 141: 104–23.

Crónica. 1995. June 25, p. 37. (Guatemala)

____. 1995. "Hubo Mano de Mano." September 29. (Guatemala)

____. 1995. "Otra Mano Peluda." September 29, p. 19. (Guatemala)

De Vany, Arthur. 1996. "Implementing a Market-Based Spectrum Policy." *Journal of Law & Economics* 12: 51–63.

De Vany, Arthur, R. D. Eckert, C. T. Meyers, D. J. O'Hara, and R. C. Scott. 1969. "A Property System for Market Allocation of the Electromagnetic Spectrum: A Legal-Economic-Engineering Study. *Stanford Law Review* 3: 145–162.

Denison, Edward F. 1979. *Accounting for Slower Economic Growth: The United States in the 1970's*. The Brookings Institution, Washington, D.C.

Djian, Jean Pierre. 1994. "Concession Contract for Water and Wastewater Services in Buenos Aires." Paper presented at the 1994 conference Private Sector Provision of Public Services, French Ministry of Public Works, Paris.

Dnes, Antony W. 1991. "Franchising, Natural Monopoly, and Privatization." In Cento Veljanovski, Ed., *Regulators and the Market: An Assessment of the Growth of Regulation in the U.K.* London: Institute of Economic Affairs.

Donaldson, Lufkin, Jenrette. 1997. *The Wireless Communications Industry*. Spring, pp.15 and 60.

Dornberger, Simon, Shirley Meadowcroft, and David Thompson. 1986. "Competitive Tendering and Efficiency: The Case of Refuse Collection." *Fiscal Studies* 7: 69–87.

Duetsch, Larry L. 1993. *Industry Studies*. Englewood Cliffs, NJ: Prentice Hall.

Economides, Nicholas, and Lawrence J. White. 1995. "Access and Interconnection Pricing: How Efficient is the Efficient Component Pricing Rule?" *Working Paper Series*. Leonard N. Stern School of Business, Department of Economics. No. EC-95-04: 1–26.

Economists Incorporated. 1992. *Report of the Advisory Team on Competition Policy and Consumer Protection in Argentina*. August. Washington, D.C.

Edison Electric Institute. 1995. *The Impact of Deregulation: An Overview across Five Industries*. Washington, D.C.

El Mercurio. 1994. "New Competition in the Market for Telecommunication." January 10. (Chile)

_____. 1995. January 13, p. B20.

Electricity Association Services Ltd. 1995. "International Electricity Prices." Issue 23, London.

Esfahani, H. S. 1993. "Regulations, Institutions, and Economic Performance: The Political Economy of the Philippines' Telecommunications Sector." World Bank, Washington, D.C.

Eskridge, W. N., Jr. 1991. "Overriding Supreme Court Statutory Interpretation Decisions." *Yale Law Journal* 101 (2): 331–455.

Estache, Antonio. 1995. "How to Set Up a Regulatory Agency in a Province." World Bank, LA1CO, Washington, D.C.

_____. 1997. "Multimodal Transport Sector Reform and Issues in Brazil." World Bank Report. Washington, D.C.

Estache, Antonio, F. Helou, and M. Rodriguez-Pardina. 1995. "A Portable Version of Electricity Regulation in Argentina." Latin America and the Caribbean, Country Department I. World Bank, Washington, D.C.

_____. 1996. "Argentina, Reforming Provincial Utilities: Issues, Challenges, and Best Practice." Report 15063-AR. World Bank, Washington, D.C.

Estache, Antonio, and José Carbajo. 1996. "Designing Toll Road Concessions–Lessons from Argentina." *Viewpoint*, Note No. 99, PSD, December. World Bank, Washington, D.C.

Estache, Antonio, and Martin Rodriguez-Pardina. 1997. "Regulating Water Concessions Lessons from the Buenos Aires Concession." *The Private Sector in Infrastructure: Strategy, Regulation and Risk.* World Bank, September Washington, D.C.

_____. 1997. "Regulatory Lessons from Argentina's Power Concessions." *The Private Sector in Infrastructure: Strategy, Regulation and Risk.* World Bank Group, September. Washington, D.C.

_____. 1997. "The Real Possibility of Competitive Generation Markets in Hydro Systems—The Case of Brazil." *The Private Sector in Infrastructure: Strategy, Regulation and Risk.* World Bank, September. Washington, D.C.

Estache, A., F. Helou, M. Rodriguez-Pardina. 1995. "A Portable Version of Privatization and Regulation." World Bank Latin American and Caribbean Country Department I. Washington, D.C.

Evans, David S., Ed. 1983. *Breaking up Bell: Essays on Industrial Organization and Regulation.* Amsterdam: North-Holland and Elsevier Science Publishing Co.

Face, Howard K. 1988. "The First Case Study in Telecommunications Social Contracts." *Public Utilities Fortnightly* 121 (9) April 28.

Fama, Eugene F. 1980. "Agency Problems and the Theory of the Firm." *Journal of Political Economy* 88 (2): 288–307.

Far Eastern Economic Review. 1989. August 17.

FCC Docket MM 93-132. Comments of the National Association of Broadcasters.

Ferejohn, John, and C. I. Shipan. 1990. "Congressional Influence on Bureaucracy." *Journal of Law, Economics, and Organization* 6 (1): 1–20.

Financial Times. 1995. "Power in Latin America." July, p. 23.

Fiorina, Morris. 1983. "Legislative Choice of Regulatory Forums: Legal Process or Administrative Process?" *Public Choice.*

Foote, William Fulbright. 1997. "Mexican Turnpikes Take a Heavy Toll." *Wall Street Journal,* April 4.

Frances, Antonio. 1993. *Alo Venezuela: Apertura y Privatización de las Telecomunicaciones.* Caracas: Conatel, Ediciones IESA.

Frankema, Mark W., and Paul A. Pautler. 1984. "An Economic Analysis of Taxicab Regulations." Bureau of Economics Staff Report. Bureau of Economics, U.S. Federal Trade Commission, Washington, D.C., May.

Freeman, A. Myrick. 1990. "Water Pollution Policy." In *Public Policies for Environmental Protection*, Paul R. Portney, Ed. Resources for the Future, Washington, D.C.

Friedman, Milton. 1995. "Getting Back to Real Growth." *Wall Street Journal,* A14, August 1.

Fundacion de Investigaciones Economicas Latinoamericanas. 1991. *Regulatory Costs in Argentina.* Buenos Aires, Argentina.

Galal, Ahmed. 1994. "Regulation and Commitment in the Development of Telecommunication in Chile." *Policy Research Working Paper 1294.* Policy Research Department. World Bank, Washington, D.C.

Galal, Ahmed, Leroy P. Jones, Panjak Tandoon, and Ingo Vogelsang. 1994. *Welfare Consequences of Selling Public Enterprises: An Empirical Analysis.* World Bank, Washington, D.C.

Galenson, Alice, and Louis S. Thompson. 1991. "The Evolution of the World Bank's Railway Lending." *World Bank Discussion Papers 269.* Washington D.C.

Gallardo, Joselito S., Bikki K. Randhawa, and Orlando J. Sacay. 1997. "Microfinance as a Regular Commercial Banking Product." *Viewpoint*, Note No. 131, November. World Bank, Washington, D.C.

Gardner, Bruce L. 1987. *Protection of U.S. Agriculture: Why, How, and Who Loses?* University of Maryland Department of Agricultural & Resource Economics Working Paper No. 87–15.

Geanakoplos, John, and Paul Milgrom. 1985. "Theory of Hierarchies Based on Limited Managerial Attention."

Cowles Foundation for Research Economics, Discussion Paper 75: 1–55. New Haven, CT: Yale University.

Gely, R. M., and Pablo T. Spiller. 1990. "A Rational Choice Theory of Supreme Court Statutory Decisions, with Applications to the State Farm and Grove City Cases." *Journal of Law, Economics, and Organization* 6 (2): 263–30.

General Telecommunications Law of 1982. (Chile)

Gilbert, Richard J. 1996. *International Comparisons of Electricity Regulation.* Cambridge University Press.

Gilbert, Richard J., and Edward P. Kahn, Eds. 1996. *International Comparisons of Electricity Regulation.* New York: Cambridge University Press.

Gillick, David. 1992. "Telecommunications Policies and Regulatory Structures: New Issues and Trends." *Telecommunications Policy* 16 (9): 726–31.

Glynn, D. R. 1992. "The Mechanisms of Price Control." *Utilities Policy* 2 (4): 90–99.

Goldberg, Victor. 1976. "Regulation and Administered Contracts." *Bell Journal of Economics* 7 (2): 426–448.

Gómez-Ibáñez, José A., and John R. Meyer. 1993. *Going Private: The International Experience with Transport Privatization.* Washington, D.C.: The Brookings Institution.

Good, David H., Lars-Hendrich Röller, and Robin C. Sickles. 1993. "U.S. Airline Deregulation: Implications for European Transport." *Economic Journal* 103 (July): 1028–1041.

Graham, Daniel, and Robert C. Marshall. 1987. "Collusive Bidder Behavior at Single Object Second Price and English Auctions." *Journal of Political Economy* 95: 1217–39.

Graham, Daniel, Robert C. Marshall, and Jean-François Richard. 1990. "Differential Payments within a Bidder Coalition and the Shapley Value." *American Economic Review* 80: 493–510.

Green, Richard. 1997a. "Has Price Cap Regulation of U.K. Utilities Been a Success?" *Viewpoint*, Note No. 132, November. World Bank, Washington, D.C.

____. 1997b. "Utility Regulation—A Critical Path for Revising Price Controls." *Viewpoint*, Note No. 133, November. World Bank, Washington, D.C.

Grimm, Curtis M., Clifford Winston, and Carol A. Evans. 1992. "Foreclosure of Railroad Markets: A Test of Chicago Leverage Theory." *Journal of Law and Economics* 35 (2): 295–310.

Grimm, Curtis M., and Robert G. Harris. 1983. "Vertical Foreclosure in the Rail Freight Industry: Economic Analysis and Policy Prescriptions." *ICC Practitioners Journal* 50: 508–531.

____. 1988. "A Qualitative Choice Analysis of Rail Routings: Implications for Vertical Foreclosure and Competition Policy." *Logistics and Transportation Review* 24 (1): 49–67.

Grossman, Sanford J., and Oliver D. Hart. 1983. "Implicit Contracts Under Asymmetric Information." *Quarterly Journal of Economics* 98 (1): 123–56.

____. 1986. "Costs and Benefits of Ownership: A Theory of Vertical and Lateral Integration." *Journal of Political Economy* 94 (8): 691–719.

Guasch, J. Luis. 1994. "Competition Policies in Latin America." World Bank, LATAD, Washington, D.C.

____. 1995. "Issues in Infrastructure Concession Design and Financing." In Ravi Ramamurti, Ed., *Infrastructure Reforms in Latin America.* Baltimore, MD: Johns Hopkins University Press.

____. 1996. "Lessons for Port Reforms." In J. L. Guasch and Leandre Amargos, Eds., *New Port Policies in Latin America and Caribbean.* Barcelona, Spain: New Press.

____. 1997. "Labor Reform and Job Creation: The Unfinished Agenda in Latin American and Caribbean Countries." *Directions in Development.* World Bank, Washington, D.C.

Guasch, J. Luis, and Charles Blitzer. 1993. "State-Owned Monopolies: Horizontal and Vertical Restructuring and Private Sector Access Issues." Latin America and the Caribbean Technical Department Regional Studies Program. Regional Study 22. World Bank, Washington, D.C.

Guasch, J. Luis, and Robert G. Marshall. 1993. "Competitive Provision of Goods and Services to Government by Private Sector in Developing Countries." Latin America and the Caribbean Regional Study. Latin America and the Caribbean Division. World Bank, Washington, D.C.

____. 1994. "Competitive Provision of Goods and Services to Government by Private Sector in Developing Countries." World Bank Technical Report. Latin America and the Caribbean Division. World Bank, Washington, D.C.

Guasch, J. Luis, and Robert Hahn. 1996. "The Costs and Benefits of Regulation: The Roots of Regulatory Failure." World Bank, LATAD, Washington D.C.

____. 1998. "The Costs and Benefits of Regulation: Implications for Developing Countries." *The World Bank Research Observer.* World Bank, Washington, D.C.

Guasch, J. Luis, and Sarath Rajapatirana. 1994. "The Interface of Trade, Investment, and Competition Policies: Issues and Challenges for Latin America." Policy Research Working Paper 1393. December. The World Bank, Washington, D.C.

Guasch, J. Luis, and Sudipto Bhattacharya. 1988. "Heterogeneity, Tournaments, and Hierarchies." *Journal of Political Economy*, August.

Guasch, J. Luis, and Thomas Glaessner. 1993. "Using Auctions to Allocate and Price Long-Term Credit." *World Bank Research Observer* 8 (2): 169–94.

Hachette, D. 1994. "Comment on Bitran and Saez." The Brookings Institution, Washington, D.C.

Hachette, D., and R. Luders. 1993. *Privatization in Chile.* International Center for Economic Growth, San Francisco.

Hahn, Robert W. 1996. "Regulatory Reform: What do the Government's Numbers Tell Us?" In Robert W. Hahn, Ed., *Risks, Costs, and Lives Saved: Getting Better Results from Regulation.* New York: Oxford University Press and AEI Press.

Hahn, Robert W., and John Hird. 1991. "The Costs and Benefits of Regulation: Review and Synthesis." *Yale Journal on Regulation* 8: 233–278.

Hamilton, James T., and Christopher H. Schroeder. 1994. "Strategic Regulators and the Choice of Rulemaking Procedures: The Selection of Formal vs. Informal Rules in Regulating Hazardous Waste." *Law and Contemporary Society* 57 (2): 111–60.

Hansen, Robert G. 1988. "Auctions with Endogenous Quantity." *Rand Journal of Economics* 19: 44–58.

Hart, Oliver, and Jean Tirole. 1990. "Vertical Integration and Market Foreclosures." *Brookings Papers on Economic Activity* 548: 1–102. Cambridge, MA: Massachusetts Institute of Technology, Department of Economics.

Hartman, Raymond S., and David Wheeler. 1995. "Incentive Regulation: Market-Based Pollution Control for the Real World?" In Claudio R. Frischtak, Ed., *Regulatory Policies and Reform: A Comparative Perspective.* Pre-publication Edition, Private Sector Development Department. World Bank, Washington, D.C.

Haskel, Jonathan, and Stefan Szymanski. 1993. "The Effects of Privatization, Restructuring, and Competition on Productivity Growth in U.K. Public Corporations." Working Paper. Economics Department, Queen Mary and Westfield College.

Hausman, Jerry, and Timothy Tardiff. 1996. "Valuation and Regulation of New Services in Telecommunications." MIT Discussion Paper. Cambridge, MA: MIT.

Hazilla, Michael, and Raymond J. Kopp. 1990. "The Social Cost of Environmental Quality Regulations: A General Equilibrium Analysis." *Journal of Political Economy* 98 (4): 853–73.

Hazlett, Thomas W. 1990. "The Rationality of U.S. Regulation of the Broadcast Spectrum." *Journal of Law & Economics* 33.

_____. 1994. "Spectrum Auctions–Only a First Step." *Wall Street Journal,* December 20.

Hazlett, Thomas W., and Robert J. Michaels. 1993. "The Cost of Rent-Seeking: Evidence from Cellular Telephone License Lotteries." *Southern Economic Journal* 59 (3): 425–35.

Hendricks, Kenneth, and Robert H. Porter. 1988. "An Empirical Study of an Auction with Asymmetric Information." *American Economic Review* 78: 865–83.

Herzel, Leo. 1951. "'Public Interest' and the Market in Color Television Regulation." *University of Chicago Law Review* 18: 802–16.

_____. 1997. "My 1951 Color Television Article." *Journal of Law and Economics* 20: 61-70.

Hill, Alice E., and Manuel A. Abdalla. 1993. "Regulation, Institutions, and Commitment: Privatization and Regulation in Argentine Telecommunications Sector." World Bank, Latin America and the Caribbean Department, Washington, D.C.

Hirshleifer, Jack, and John Riley. 1992. *The Analytics of Uncertainty and Information.* Cambridge, U.K.: Cambridge University Press.

Holmstrom, Bengt R., and Jean Tirole. 1987. "Theory of the Firm." Massachusetts Institute of Technology. Working Paper 456: 1–117. Cambridge, MA: MIT.

Hopkins, Thomas D. 1992. *Costs of Regulation: Filling the Gaps.* Report prepared for Regulatory Information Service Center, Washington, D.C.

_____. 1994. "Estimates of the Cost of Regulation." Rochester Institute of Technology.

Huber, Peter W., and John Thorne. 1997. "Economic Licensing Reform." In Robert W. Hahn, Ed., *Reviving Regulatory Reform.* New York: Cambridge University Press and AEI Press, forthcoming.

Hufbauer, Gary C., Diane T. Berliner, and Kimberlie A. Elliot. 1986. *Trade Protection in the United States: 31 Case Studies.* Institute for International Economics, Washington, D.C.

Idelovitch, Emanuel. 1994. "The Transition from Public to Private Operation: The Buenos Aires Water Sector Case." World Bank, LATAD, Washington, D.C.

Industry Commission. 1995. "The Growth and Revenue Implications of Hilmer and Related Reforms." A Report by the Industry Commission to the Council of Australian Governments, Belconnen ACT, March.

International Civil Aviation Organization. 1992. "Investment Requirements for Airport and Route Facility Infrastructure to the Year 2010." ICAO Circular 236-AT/95.

International Telecommunication Union. 1993. *The Changing Role of Government in an Era of Deregulation: Briefing Report, Options for Regulatory Processes and Procedures in Telecommunications.* ITU Regulatory Colloquium 1, Geneva.

Jacquemin, Alexis, and Margaret Slade. 1986. "Cartels, Collusion, and Horizontal Merger." *Discussion Paper* 86 (5): 1–124. University of British Columbia, Department of Economics.

Jantscher, Gerald R. 1975. *Bread Upon the Waters: Federal Aid to the Maritime Industries 52.* The Brooking Institution, Washington, D.C.

Jarrell, Gregg A. 1984. "Change at the Exchange: The Causes and Effects of Deregulation." *Journal of Law and Economics* 27 (October): 273–312.

Jorgenson, Dale W., and Peter J. Wilcoxen. 1992. "Environmental Regulation and U.S. Economic Growth." *Rand Journal of Economics* 21: 314–40.

Joskow, Paul L. 1972. "The Determination of the Allowed Rate of Return in a Formal Regulatory Proceeding." *Bell Journal of Economics and Management Science* 3 (2): 632-44.

____. 1973. "Pricing Decisions of Regulated Firms: A Behavioral Approach." *Bell Journal of Economics and Management Science* 4 (1): 118–40.

____. 1974. "Inflation and Environmental Concern: Structural Change in the Process of Public Utility Price Regulation." *Journal of Law and Economics* 17 (2): 291–328.

Joskow, Paul L., and R. G. Noll. 1981. "Regulation in Theory and Practice: An Overview." In G. Fromm, Ed., *Studies in Public Regulation*. Cambridge, MA: MIT Press.

____. 1990. *Markets for Power*. Cambridge, MA: MIT Press.

Joskow, Paul L., and Richard Schmalensee. 1986. "Incentive Regulation for Electric Utilities." *Yale Journal of Regulation* 4 (1): 1–50.

Juan, Ellis J. 1996. "Privatizing Airports: Options and Case Studies." Viewpoint Note No. 82, PSD. World Bank, Washington, D.C., June.

Kahn, Alfred. 1991. *The Economics of Regulation: Principles and Institutions*. Cambridge, MA: MIT Press.

Kahn, Alfred E., and William E. Taylor. 1994. "The Pricing of Inputs Sold to Competitors: A Comment." *Yale Journal on Regulation* 11 (1): 225–40.

Kapur, Anil. 1997. "Private Sector Participation in Aviation Infrastructure in LAC: An Assessment." World Bank Report, Washington, D.C.

Katz, Michael L. 1989. "Vertical Contractual Relations." In Richard Schamlensee and Robert D. Willig, Eds., *Handbook of Industrial Organization, Volume 1*. Handbooks in Economics, No. 10. Amsterdam, Oxford, and Tokyo; North-Holland; distributed in the U.S. by Elsevier Science, New York, pp. 655–721.

Katz, Michael L., and Carl Shapiro. 1991. "Systems Competition and Network Effects." *Journal of Economic Perspectives* 8 (2): 93–115.

Kerf, Michel, David R. Gray, Timothy Irwin, Celine Levesque, and Robert R. Taylor. 1998. "Concessions for Infrastructure, A Guide to Their Design and Award." World Bank Technical Paper No. 399. Washington, D.C.

Kessides, Ioannis, and Robert Willig. 1995. "Restructuring Regulation of the Railroad Industry." In C. Frischtak, Ed., *Regulatory Policies and Reform: A Comparative Perspective*. Private Sector Development Department. World Bank, Washington, D.C.

Klein, Michael. 1996. "Competition in Network Industries." Policy Research Working Paper 1591. April. World Bank, Washington, D.C.

Kleit, Andrew N. 1989. "An Analysis of Vertical Relationships Among Railroads: Why Competitive Access Should Not Be An Antitrust Concern." *Federal Trade Commission Bureau of Economics Working Paper* 176. October, p. 25.

Koedijk, Kees, and Jeroen Kremers. 1996. "Market Opening, Regulation and Growth in Europe." *Economic Policy: A European Forum* 10 (23): 445–467.

Kovacic, W. E. 1992. "Competition Policy, Economic Development, and the Transition to Free Markets in the Third World: The Case of Zimbabwe." *Antitrust Law Journal* 61 (1).

Kwerel, Evan R., and John R. Williams. 1992. "Changing Channels: Voluntary Reallocation of UHF Television Spectrum." Office of Plans & Policies Working Paper Series. Washington D.C.: Federal Communications Commission.

La Nación. 1990. International Edition. March 19. (Argentina)

____. 1990. International Edition. October 29. (Argentina)

____. 1991. June 26. (Argentina)

Laffont, Jean-Jacques, and Jean Tirole. 1993. *A Theory of Incentives in Procurement and Regulation*. Cambridge, MA: MIT Press.

____. 1994. "Access Pricing and Competition." *European Economic Review* 38 (9): 1673–1710.

Lazear, Edward P., and Sherwin Rosen. 1980. "Rank-Order Tournaments as Optimum Labor Contracts." *Journal of Political Economy* 89 (5): 841–864.

Lee, Dwight R., and Richard B. McKenzie. 1991. *Quicksilver Capital: How the Rapid Movement of Wealth has Changed the World*. New York: Free Press.

Levmore, S. N. 1992. "Bicameralism: When are Two Decisions Better Than One?" *International Review of Law and Economics* 12 (2): 145–168.

Levy, Brian, and Pablo T. Spiller. 1993. "Regulation, Institutions, and Commitment in Telecommunications: A Comparative Analysis of Five Country Studies." In Michael Bruno and Boris Pleskovic, Eds., *Proceedings of the World Bank Annual Conference on Development Economics 1993*. World Bank, Washington, D.C.

Lewis, Tracy R. 1996. "Protecting the Environment When Costs and Benefits are Privately Known." *Rand Journal of Economics* 27 (4): 819–847.

Liebowitz, S. J., and Stephen E. Margolis. 1994. "Network Externality: An Uncommon Tragedy." *Journal of Economic Perspectives* 8 (2): 133–150.

Lipschitz, Leslie, Jeroen Kremers, Thomas Mayer, and Donogh McDonal. 1989. "The Federal Republic of Germany: Adjustment in a Surplus Country," Occasional paper, No. 64. International Monetary Fund, Washington, D.C.

Litan, Robert, and William Nordhaus. 1983. *Reforming Federal Regulation.* New Haven, CT: Yale University Press.

Littlechild, Steven C. 1983. "The Structure of Telephone Tariffs." *International Journal of Industrial Organization* 1 (4): 365–377.

Loeb, Martin, and Wesley Magat. 1969. "A Decentralized Method for Utility Regulation." *Journal of Law and Economics* 12 (2).

Loury, Glenn C. 1983. "Efficiency and Equity Impacts of Deregulation." In Robert H. Haveman and Julius Margolis, Eds., *Public Expenditure and Public Policy Analysis.* Boston, MA: Houghton Mifflin.

Lyon, T. P. 1992. "Regulation with 20-20 Hindsight: Heads I Win, Tails You Lose." *Rand Journal of Economics* 22 (4): 481–595.

MacAvoy, Paul. 1977. *Federal Milk Marketing Orders and Price Supports.* American Enterprise Institute, Washington, D.C.

_____. 1992. *Industry Regulation and the Performance of the American Economy.* New York: W. W. Norton & Co.

Macey, J. T. 1992. "Organization Design and Political Control of Administrative Agencies." *Journal of Law Economics and Organization* 8 (1): 93–110.

Mailath, George, and Peter Zemsky. 1991. "Collusion in Second Price Auctions with Heterogeneous Bidders." *Games and Economic Behavior* 3: 467–86.

Marshall, Robert, Michael Meurer, and Jean-François Richard. 1990. "Curbing Agency Problems in the Procurement Process by Protest Oversight." *Rand Journal of Economics.*

_____. 1991. "The Private Attorney General Meets Public Contract Law: Procurement Oversight by Protest." *Hofstra Law Review* Fall: 1–71.

_____. 1992. "Litigation Settlement and Collusion." *Quarterly Journal of Economics* 109 (2): 211–239.

Martínez, Gabriel, and Guillermo Farber. 1994. *Desregulación económica (1989–1993): Una visión de la modernización de México.* Mexico: Fondo de Cultura Económica.

Mathios, A. S., and R. T. Rogers. 1987. "The Impact of Alternative Forms of State Regulation of AT&T on Direct Dial, Long-Distance Telephone Rates." *Rand Journal of Economics* 20 (3).

McAfee, R. Preston, and John McMillan. 1987. "Auctions and Bidding." *Journal of Economic Literature* 25: 708–47.

_____. 1988. *Incentives in Government Contracting.* Toronto: University of Toronto Press.

_____. 1990. "Bidding Rings." *American Economic Review* 82: 579–99.

McCubbins, Mathew D. 1991. "Party Politics, Divided Government, and Budget Deficits." In Samuel Kernell, Ed., *Parallel Politics: Economic Policymaking in the United States and Japan.* Tokyo: Japan Center for International Exchange; Washington, D.C.: The Brookings Institution, pp. 83–118.

_____. 1995. "Utility Regulation, Economic Development, and Political Stability: The Contrasting Cases of Argentina and Chile." Working paper No. 160. University of Maryland Center for Institutional Reform and the Informal Sector.

McCubbins, Mathew D., Roger G. Noll, and Barry R. Weingast. 1987. "Administrative Procedures as Instruments of Political Control." *Journal of Law, Economics and Organization* 3 (2): 243–77.

_____. 1990. "Positive and Normative Models of Procedural Rights: An Integrative Approach to Administrative Procedures." *Journal of Law, Economics and Organization* 6 (10): 307–32.

McMullen, B. Starr, and Linda R. Stanley. 1988. "The Impact of Deregulation on the Production Structure of the Motor Carrier Industry." *Economic Inquiry* 26 (April): 299–316.

Mihlar, Fazil. 1996. "Regulatory Overkill: The Costs of Regulation in Canada." Fraser Institute, Vancouver, British Columbia, Canada.

Milgrom. 1986. "Quasirents, Influence and Organization Form." *Cowles Discussion Paper Series* No. 797: 1-41. Yale University.

Minoli, Daniel. 1991. *Telecommunications Technology Handbook.* Norwood, MA: Artech House, pp. 256–266.

Mitchell, Bridger M., and Ingo Vogelsang. 1991. *Telecommunications Pricing: Theory and Practice.* A Rand Research Study. New York and Melbourne: Cambridge University Press.

_____. 1995. "Expanded Competitiveness and Regulatory Safeguards in Local Telecommunications Markets." *Managerial and Decision Economics* 16 (4): 451–67.

Molyneux, Richard, and David Thompson. 1987. "Nationalised Industry Performance: Still Third-Rate?" *Fiscal Studies (U.K.)* 8 (2): 48–82.

Montenegro, Armando. 1995. "Economic Reforms in Colombia: Regulation and Deregulation, 1990–94." Economic Development Institute, World Bank, Washington, D.C.

Moreton, Patrick S., and Pablo T. Spiller. 1995. "What's in the Air: Synergies and their Impact on the FCC's Broadband PCS License Auctions." Working paper presented at the conference, The Law and Economics of Property Rights to Radio Spectrum, July.

_____. 1997. "Multi-license Bidding Strategies in the FCC Broadland PCS Spectrum Auction." University of California, Berkeley, Working Paper.

Morrall, John F. 1986. "A Review of the Record." *Regulation* 10: 25–34, November-December. Updated by the author.

Morrison, Steven, and Clifford Winston. 1986. *The Economic Effects of Airline Deregulation.* The Brookings Institution, Washington, D.C.

_____. 1989. "Enhancing the Performance of the Deregulated Air Transportation System." *Brookings Papers on Economic Activity: Microeconomics,* 61–123.

_____. 1994. "The Evolution of the Airline Industry." Boston: Northeastern University, August.

_____. 1995. *The Evolution of the Airline Industry.* The Brookings Institution, Washington, D.C.

Morton, Colleen, Ed. 1997. *Trade and Investment Growth in Latin America and the Caribbean.* Westview Press.

Moyer, Neil E., and Louis S. Thompson. 1990. "Options for Reshaping the Railway." Policy Research Working Paper 926. World Bank, Washington, D.C.

Muñoz, O. 1993. *Despues de la Privatizacion: Haciael Estado Regulador.* O. Muñoz, Ed. CIEPLAN, Santiago.

Nalebuff, Barry, and Joseph E. Stiglitz. 1983. "Prices and Incentives: Toward a General Theory of Compensation and Competition." *Bell Journal of Economics* 14 (1): 21–43.

National Economic Research Associates. 1993. "Regulatory Costs: Topic 12."

Navarro, Peter. 1996. "Electric Utilities: The Argument for Radical Deregulation." *Harvard Business Review* 74 (1) January–February: II 2–25.

New York Times. 1989. September 24.

New Zealand Ministry of Commerce. 1995. "Regulation of Access to Vertically Integrated Natural Monopolies." Discussion paper. August. Wellington, N.Z.: Ministry of Commerce.

Newberry, David M. 1995. "A Template for Power Reform." *Viewpoint,* Note No. 54, September. World Bank, Washington, D.C.

_____. 1997. "Pool Reform and Competition in Electricity." Department of Applied Economics, University of Cambridge. *DAE Working Papers Amalgamated Series,* No. 9734. Cambridge, England.

Nigeria Manufacturers Association. 1996. "The Impact of Custom Processes in Nigeria." The Nigeria Manufacturers Association Reports.

Noll, Roger. 1997. "The Economics and Politics of the Slowdown in Regulatory Reform." In Robert W. Hahn, Ed. *Reviving Regulatory Reform.* New York: Cambridge University Press and AEI Press, forthcoming.

North, Douglass C. 1981. *Structure and Change in Economic History.*

_____. 1990. *Institutions, Institutional Change, and Economic Performance.* Cambridge, U.K.: Cambridge University Press.

North, Douglass C., and Barry R. Weingast. 1989. "Constitutions and Commitment: The Evolution of Institutions Governing Public Choice in Seventeenth-Century England." *Journal of Economic History* 49 (4): 803–32.

North, Douglass C., and R. P. Thomas. 1973. *The Rise of the Western World: A New Economic History.* Cambridge, U.K.: Cambridge University Press.

Ochoa, F., and S. C. Asociados. 1990. *Evalución de los Sistemas de Costos e Integración de un Modelo Sistematizado de Tarifas.* Vols. I, II, III, and IV, November. Mexico.

OECD (Organization for Economic Cooperation and Development). 1995. "Control and Management of Government Regulation." PUMA (95) 9, Paris.

_____. 1996. "Regulatory Reform: A Country Study of Australia." PUMA/REG (96) 1, Paris.

_____. 1997a. "Regulatory Reform." Report. Paris.

_____. 1997b. "The Economy-Wide Effects of Regulatory Reform." *The OECD Report on Regulatory Reform, Volume II: Thematic Studies.* Paris, Chapter 1, 21–190.

_____. 1997c. *Communications Outlook.* Paris.

_____. 1998. *Communications Outlook 1997.* Paris.

Oftel (Office of Telecommunications). 1988. "The Regulation of British Telecom's Prices: A Consultative Document." London, U.K. January.

Ordover, Janusz A., Garth Saloner, and Steven C. Salop. 1990. "Equilibrium Vertical Foreclosure." *American Economic Review* 80 (3): 127–142.

Paredes, Ricardo D. 1993. "Privatización y Regulación: Lecciones de la Experiencia Chilena." In O. Muñoz, Ed., *Despues de la Privatización: Haciael Estado Regulador.* CIEPLAN, Santiago.

_____. 1994. "Privatization and Regulation in a Less Developed Economy: The Chilean Case." Santiago: Universidad de Chile.

_____. 1995. "Evaluating the Cost of Bad Regulation in Newly Privatized Sector: The Chilean Case." *Revista de Analisis Economico* 10 (2): 89–112.

_____. 1996. "Competition Policies in an Economy without Market Tradition." Economic Development Institute. World Bank, Washington, D.C.

Peltzman, Sam. 1973. "An Evaluation of Consumer Protection Legislation: The 1962 Drug Amendments." *Journal of Political Economics,* 81 (5): 1049–1071.

Petrazzini, B. 1995. "Telephone Privatization in a Hurry: Argentina." In Ravi Ramamurti, Ed., *Privatizing Monopolies.* Baltimore, MD: The Johns Hopkins University Press.

Portney, Paul R. 1990. "Air Pollution Policy." In Paul R. Portney, Ed., *Public Policies for Environmental Protection.* Resources for the Future, Washington, D.C.

Posner, Richard A. 1975. "The Social Costs of Monopoly and Regulation." *Journal of Political Economy* 83: 807–27.

____. 1976. *The Robinson-Patman Act: Federal Regulation of Price Differences.* Washington, D.C.: American Enterprise Institute for Public Policy Research.

President's Commission on Privatization. 1988. "Privatization: Toward More Effective Government." Report on the President's Commission on Privatization, Washington, D.C., March.

Quian, Y. 1990. "Hierarchy, Loss of Control and a Theory of State-ownership in Socialist Economies." Stanford University.

Ramajo, Germán. 1992. "Telecommunications in Chile: The True and False Dilemmas." Presented at the conference, Telecommunication in Chile: Vertical Integration, Free Competition. Santiago, Chile, June.

Ramsey, Frank. 1927. "A Contribution to the Theory of Taxation." *Economic Journal* (March).

Ramseyer, Mark. 1994. "The Puzzling (In)Dependence of Courts: A Comparative Approach." *Journal of Legal Studies* 4: 721–48.

Resolution 151. July 18, 1983. (Chile)

Resolution 389. 1993. Resolutive Commission. April 16. (Chile)

Riordan, M. H. 1992. "Relevance of the New Regulatory Economics for Telecommunications." World Bank, Washington, D.C.

Roberts, R. Blaine, G. S. Maddala, and Gregory Enholm. 1978. "Determinants of the Requested Rate of Return and the Rate of Return Granted in a Formal Regulatory Process." *Bell Journal of Economics* 9 (2): 611–21.

Robinson, James C. 1995. "The Impact of Environmental and Occupational Health Regulation on Productivity Growth in U.S. Manufacturing." *Yale Journal on Regulation* 12: 387–434.

Rohlfs, Jeffrey, Charles L. Jackson, and Tracey E. Kelly. 1991. "Estimate of the Loss to the United States Caused by the FCC's Delay in Licensing Cellular Telecommunications." NERA Discussion paper, Washington, D.C., November.

Rucker, Randall R., and Walter N. Thurman. 1990. "The Economic Effects of Supply Controls: The Simple Analysis of the U.S. Peanut Program." *Journal of Law and Economics* 33 (1): 483–515.

Salinger, Michael A. 1988. "Vertical Mergers and Market Foreclosure." *Quarterly Journal of Economics* 103 (2): 345–56.

Salzberg, Eli M. 1991. "The Delegation of Legislative Powers to the Courts and the Independence of the Judiciary."

Scherer Industrial Organization, J. Shepsle, and B. R. Weingast. 1981. "Structure-Induced Equilibrium and Legislative-Choice." *Public Choice* 37: 503–19.

Schmalensee, Richard. 1979. *The Control of Natural Monopoly.* Lexington, IL: D. C. Heath and Co.

Schwartz, Bernard. 1984. *American Administrative Law,* 2d ed. London: Sir Isaac Pitman & Sons, Ltd.

Schwartz, Eli P., Pablo T. Spiller, and Santiago Urbiztondo. 1994. "A Positive Theory of Legislative Intent." *Law and Contemporary Problems* 57 (1–2): 51–74.

Secretaria De Comercio Y Fomento Industrial. 1996. "Economic Deregulation in Mexico." December.

Serra, P. 1995. "La Politica de Competencia en Chile." *Revista de Analisis Economico* 10 (2): 63–88.

Shelanski, Howard, and Peter Huber. 1997. "The Attributes and Administrative Creation of Property Rights in Spectrum." *Journal of Law Economics and Organization.*

Shepherd, Geoffrey. 1995. "On the Design of Institutions." World Bank, Washington, D.C.

Shepsle, J., and B. R. Weingast. 1987a. "The Institutional Foundations of Committee Power." *American Political Science Review* 81 (1): 85–105.

____. 1987b. "Institutionalizing Majority Rule: A Social Theory with Policy Implications." *AEA Papers and Proceedings* 100: 367–71.

____. 1989. "Penultimate Power: Conference Committees and the Legislative Process." Hoover Institution Working Paper P-89-7. Stanford, CA: Hoover Institution, Stanford University.

Shimpo, Seiji, and Fumihira Nishizake. 1997. "Measuring the Effects of Regulatory Reform in Japan: A Review." Discussion Paper No. 74: 1–26. Economic Research Institute, Economic Planning Agency.

Shin, R. T., and J. S. Ying. 1992. "Unnatural Monopolies in Local Telephone." *Rand Journal of Economics* 23 (4): 171–83.

Shugart, M. S., and J. M. Carey. 1992. *Presidents and Assemblies.* New York: Cambridge University Press.

Smith, Peter. 1995. "End of the Line for the Local Loop Monopoly?" Viewpoint 63. World Bank, Washington, D.C.

Smith, Warrick. 1994. "Funding the Regulatory Agencies." World Bank, PSD, Washington, D.C.

Spiller, Pablo T. 1985. "On Vertical Mergers." *Journal of Law and Economics* 1 (2): 285–312.

____. 1990a. "Governmental Institutions and Regulatory Policy: A Rational Choice Analysis of Telecommunications Deregulation." University of Illinois, Department of Economics.

____. 1990b. "Politicians, Interest Groups and Regulators: A Multiple Principals Agency Theory of Regulation, (or Let Them be Bribed)." *Journal of Law and Economics* 33 (1): 65–101.

_____. 1992. "Agency Discretion under Judicial Review." *Formal Theory of Politics II: Mathematical Modelling in Political Science* 16 (8/9): 185–200. Mathematical and Computer Modelling.

_____. 1993. "Institutions and Regulatory Commitment in Utilities' Privatization." *Industrial and Corporate Change.*

_____. 1995. "A Positive Political Theory of Regulatory Instruments: Contracts, Administrative Law or Regulatory Specificity." USC Law Review, forthcoming.

Spiller, Pablo, and Carlo G. Cardilli. "The Frontier of Telecommunications Deregulation: Small Countries Leading the Pack. *Journal of Economic Perspectives* 11 (4): 127–138.

Spiller, Pablo T., and Cezley I. Sampson. 1993b. "Regulation, Institutions, and Commitment: The Jamaican Telecommunications Sector." World Bank, PRD, Washington, D.C.

Spiller, Pablo T., and E. Tiller. 1994. "Invitations to Override: Congressional Reversals of Supreme Court Decisions." *International Review of Law & Economics*, forthcoming.

Spiller, Pablo T., and Ingo Vogelsang. 1993. "Notes on Public Utility Regulation in the UK: 1850–1950." University of Illinois.

_____. 1994. "Regulation, Institutions, and Commitment: The British Telecommunications Sector." World Bank, PRD, Washington, D.C.

Spiller, Pablo T., and Luis Viana. 1992. "How Not to Do It: Electricity Regulation in Argentina, Brazil, Chile, and Uruguay." University of California, Berkeley, Department of Economics.

Spiller, Pablo T., and R. M. Gely. 1990. "A Rational Choice Theory of Supreme Court Statutory Decisions with Applications to the State Farm and Grove City Cases." *Journal of Law, Economics, and Organization* 6 (2): 263–300.

Stigler, George J. 1971a. *The Organization of Industry.* Chicago: University of Chicago Press.

_____. 1971b. "The Theory of Economic Regulation." *Bell Journal of Economics* 2: 3–21.

Sweeney, George. 1981. "Adoption of Cost-Saving Innovations by a Regulated Firm." *American Economic Review* 71 (June): 437–47.

Tandon, Panjak. 1992. "Teléfonos de México." Paper presented at the conference Welfare Consequences of Selling Public Enterprises: Case Studies from Chile, Malaysia, Mexico, and the United Kingdom. World Bank, Washington, D.C., June.

Taylor, William E., and Lester D. Taylor. 1993. "Postdivestiture Long-Distance Competition in the United States." *American Economic Review* 83 (May): 185–90.

Telefónica de Argentina. 1991. *Prospectus.* Buenos Aires. December.

Tengs, Tammy O., and John D. Graham. 1996. "The Opportunity Costs of Haphazard Social Investments in Life-Saving." In Robert W. Hahn, Ed., *Risks, Costs, and Lives Saved: Getting Better Results from Regulation.* New York: Oxford University Press and AEI Press.

The Economist. 1989. October 14.

_____. 1993. June 12.

_____. 1993. September 4.

_____. 1995. "Why Heathrow is Hell." August 26.

_____. 1996. August 24.

The Gleaner. 1971. June 9. (Jamaica)

The News. 1995. November 8, p. 28. (Mexico)

Thieblot, A. J. 1975. "The Davis-Bacon Act." Labor Relations & Public Policy Series, Report No. 10, Industrial Research Unit, The Wharton School, University of Pennsylvania.

Thompson, L. 1992. "Restructuring the Railway Sector: Issues and Options." Mimeo. World Bank, Washington, D.C.

Thompson, Louis S., and Karim-Jacques Budin. 1997. "Global Trends to Railways Concessions Delivering Positive Results," Viewpoint 134, December. World Bank, Washington, D.C.

Tirole, Jean. 1986. "Procurement and Renegotiation." *Journal of Political Economy* 94 (4): 235–59.

_____. 1988. *The Theory of Industrial Organization.* Cambridge, MA: MIT Press.

Tribune Co. v. Oak Leaves Broadcasting Station. 1926. Cook County, Illinois, Circuit Court decision.

Tye, William B. 1986. "Stand-Alone Costs as an Indicator of Market Dominance and Rate Reasonableness Under the Staggers Rail Act." *International Journal of Transport Economics* 13 (1): 21–40.

_____. 1987. *Encouraging Competition Among Competitors: The Case of Motor Carrier Deregulation and Collective Ratemaking.* New York: Quorum Books.

_____. 1990. *The Theory of Contestable Markets: Applications to Regulatory and Antitrust Problems in the Rail Industry.* New York: Greenwood Press.

University of California, Berkeley. 1997. "Multi-License Bidding Strategies in the FCC Broadband PCS Spectrum Auction. Working paper, January.

Van Bergeijk, Peter A., and Robert C. Haffner. 1995. *Privatization, Deregulation and the Macroeconomy.* Cheltenham, U.K.: Elgar, distributed by Ashgate, Brookfield, VT.

Viscusi, W. Kip. 1983. *Risk by Choice: Regulating Health and Safety in the Work Place.* Cambridge, MA: Harvard University Press.

Viscusi, W. Kip, John M. Vernon, and Joseph E. Harrington, Jr. 1995. *Economics of Regulation and Antitrust.* Cambridge, MA: MIT Press.

Wall Street Journal. 1991. "Special Report: Telecommunications." Section R, October 4.

____. 1995. "For Retailers, Red Tape is Worse Abroad."

____. 1995. "Power Plays: California's Struggle Shows How Hard it is to Deregulate Utilities." November 12.

Webb, Michael, Jamie Carstairs, and Seabron Adamson. 1996. "Power Sector Reforms: Some Lessons from England and Wales, Chile, U.S., Norway, Scotland and Northern Ireland." *London Economics Report.*

Weidenbaum, Murray, and Robert DeFina. 1978. *The Cost of Federal Regulation of Economic Activity.* American Enterprise Institute Reprint No. 88, Washington, D.C.

Weingast, Barry R. 1984. "The Congressional-Bureaucratic System: A Principal Agent Perspective." *Public Choice* 147–92.

____. 1995. "Economic Role of Political Institutions." *Journal of Law, Economics, and Organization* 11 (1): 1–31.

Weingast, Barry R., and M. Moran. 1983. "Bureaucratic Discretion or Congressional Control: Regulatory Policy Making by the Federal Trade Commission." *Journal of Political Economy* 91 (10): 765–800.

Wenders, John T. 1987. *The Economics of Telecommunications: Theory and Policy.* Cambridge, MA: Ballinger.

White, Lawrence J. 1991. *The S&L Debacle: Public Policy Lessons for Bank and Thrift Regulation.* New York: Oxford University Press.

____. 1997. "U.S. Public Policy Toward Network Industries." In Robert W. Hahn, Ed., *Reviving Regulatory Reform.* New York: Cambridge University Press and AEI Press.

Williamson, Oliver E. 1975. *Markets and Hierarchies: Analysis and Antitrust Implications.* New York: Free Press.

____. 1976. "Franchise Bidding for Natural Monopolies: In General and with Respect to CATV." *Bell Journal of Economics* 7 (1): 73–104.

____. 1979. "Transaction-Cost Economics: The Governance of Contractual Relations." *Journal of Law and Economics* 22 (1): 3–61.

____. 1981. "The Vertical Integration of Production: Market Failure Considerations." *The American Economic Review* 59 (May): 112–23.

____. 1985. *The Economic Institutions of Capitalism.* New York: Free Press.

____. 1988. "The Logic of Economic Organization." *Journal of Law, Economics, and Organization* 4 (1): 65–93.

Willig, Robert D., and William J. Baumol. 1987. "Using Competition as a Guide." *Regulation* 1: 28–35.

Winston, Clifford. 1985. "Conceptual Developments in the Economics of Transportation: An Interpretive Survey." *Journal of Economic Literature* 23 (1): 57–94.

____. 1993. "Economic Deregulation: Days of Reckoning for Microeconomists." *Journal of Economic Literature* 31 (September): 1263–89.

____. 1996. "U.S. Industry Adjustment to Economic Deregulation." Paper presented at AEI conference, Regulatory Reform: Making Costs Count, Washington, D.C., December.

Winston, Clifford, Thomas M. Corsi, Curtis M. Grimm, and Carol Evans. 1990. *The Economic Effects of Surface Freight Deregulation.* Washington, D.C.: The Brookings Institution.

World Bank. 1974. "Current Economic Position and Prospects of Jamaica." LA3CO, February. Washington, D.C.

____. 1985. *Bureaucrats in Business.* Washington, D.C.

____. 1993. *World Development Report 1993.* New York: Oxford University Press.

____. 1994. *World Development Report 1994.* New York: Oxford University Press.

____. 1996. "Towards a New Role for the State in the Provision of Public Service in Uruguay." Report No. 16154. Latin America and the Caribbean Regional Study. Washington, D.C.

____. 1997. "Uruguay: Towards a New Role for the State in Uruguay's Utilities." Report No. 16154-UY. Infrastructure Division Country Department I; Latin America and the Caribbean Region. June 16. Washington, D.C.

____. 1997. *World Development Report 1997.* New York: Oxford University Press.

____. 1998. "Regulatory Institutions for Utilities & Competition: International Experience." Private Sector Development Department. Washington, D.C.